MAZDA TRUCKS
1994-98 REPAIR MANUAL

CHILTON'S

Covers all U.S. and Canadian models of Mazda B2300, B2500, B3000, B4000, MPV and Navajo

by **Matthew E. Frederick,** A.S.E., S.A.E.

CHILTON *Automotive Books*

PUBLISHED BY **HAYNES NORTH AMERICA, Inc.**

Manufactured in USA
© 1999 Haynes North America, Inc.
ISBN 0-8019-9097-1
Library of Congress Catalog Card No. 98-74836
1234567890 9876543210

Haynes Publishing Group
Sparkford Nr Yeovil
Somerset BA22 7JJ England

Haynes North America, Inc
861 Lawrence Drive
Newbury Park
California 91320 USA

ABCDE
FGHIJ
KLMNO
PQR

Contents

Contents

DRIVE TRAIN   7

SUSPENSION AND STEERING   8

BRAKES   9

BODY AND TRIM   10

GLOSSARY

MASTER INDEX

SAFETY NOTICE

Proper service and repair procedures are vital to the safe, reliable operation of all motor vehicles, as well as the personal safety of those performing repairs. This manual outlines procedures for servicing and repairing vehicles using safe, effective methods. The procedures contain many NOTES, CAUTIONS and WARNINGS which should be followed, along with standard procedures to eliminate the possibility of personal injury or improper service which could damage the vehicle or compromise its safety.

It is important to note that repair procedures and techniques, tools and parts for servicing motor vehicles, as well as the skill and experience of the individual performing the work vary widely. It is not possible to anticipate all of the conceivable ways or conditions under which vehicles may be serviced, or to provide cautions as to all possible hazards that may result. Standard and accepted safety precautions and equipment should be used when handling toxic or flammable fluids, and safety goggles or other protection should be used during cutting, grinding, chiseling, prying, or any other process that can cause material removal or projectiles.

Some procedures require the use of tools specially designed for a specific purpose. Before substituting another tool or procedure, you must be completely satisfied that neither your personal safety, nor the performance of the vehicle will be endangered.

Although information in this manual is based on industry sources and is complete as possible at the time of publication, the possibility exists that some car manufacturers made later changes which could not be included here. While striving for total accuracy, the authors or publishers cannot assume responsibility for any errors, changes or omissions that may occur in the compilation of this data.

PART NUMBERS

Part numbers listed in this reference are not recommendations by Haynes North America, Inc. for any product brand name. They are references that can be used with interchange manuals and aftermarket supplier catalogs to locate each brand supplier's discrete part number.

SPECIAL TOOLS

Special tools are recommended by the vehicle manufacturer to perform their specific job. Use has been kept to a minimum, but where absolutely necessary, they are referred to in the text by the part number of the tool manufacturer. These tools can be purchased, under the appropriate part number, from your local dealer or regional distributor, or an equivalent tool can be purchased locally from a tool supplier or parts outlet. Before substituting any tool for the one recommended, read the SAFETY NOTICE at the top of this page.

ACKNOWLEDGMENTS

The publisher expresses appreciation to Mazda Corp. for their generous assistance.

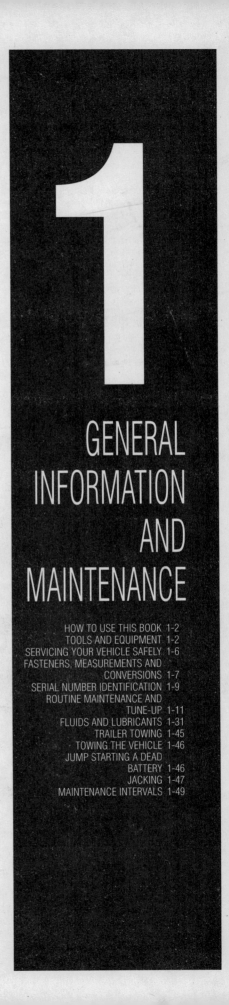

1

GENERAL
INFORMATION
AND
MAINTENANCE

HOW TO USE THIS BOOK

Chilton's Total Car Care manual for the Mazda B Series Pick-up Truck, Navajo and MPV is intended to help you learn more about the inner workings of your vehicle while saving you money on its upkeep and operation.

The beginning of the book will likely be referred to the most, since that is where you will find information for maintenance and tune-up. The other sections deal with the more complex systems of your vehicle. Systems (from engine through brakes) are covered to the extent that the average do-it-yourselfer can attempt. This book will not explain such things as rebuilding a differential because the expertise required and the special tools necessary make this uneconomical. It will, however, give you detailed instructions to help you change your own brake pads and shoes, replace spark plugs, and perform many more jobs that can save you money and help avoid expensive problems.

A secondary purpose of this book is a reference for owners who want to understand their vehicle and/or their mechanics better.

Where to Begin

Before removing any bolts, read through the entire procedure. This will give you the overall view of what tools and supplies will be required. So read ahead and plan ahead. Each operation should be approached logically and all procedures thoroughly understood before attempting any work.

If repair of a component is not considered practical, we tell you how to remove the part and then how to install the new or rebuilt replacement. In this way, you at least save labor costs.

Avoiding Trouble

Many procedures in this book require you to "label and disconnect . . ." a group of lines, hoses or wires. Don't be think you can remember where everything goes—you won't. If you hook up vacuum or fuel lines incorrectly, the vehicle may run poorly, if at all. If you hook up electrical wiring incorrectly, you may instantly learn a very expensive lesson.

You don't need to know the proper name for each hose or line. A piece of masking tape on the hose and a piece on its fitting will allow you to assign your own label. As long as you remember your own code, the lines can be reconnected by matching your tags. Remember that tape will dissolve in gasoline or solvents; if a part is to be washed or cleaned, use another method of identification. A permanent felt-tipped marker or a metal scribe can be very handy for marking metal parts. Remove any tape or paper labels after assembly.

Maintenance or Repair?

Maintenance includes routine inspections, adjustments, and replacement of parts which show signs of normal wear. Maintenance compensates for wear or deterioration. Repair implies that something has broken or is not working. A need for a repair is often caused by lack of maintenance. for example: draining and refilling automatic transmission fluid is maintenance recommended at specific intervals. Failure to do this can shorten the life of the transmission/transaxle, requiring very expensive repairs. While no maintenance program can prevent items from eventually breaking or wearing out, a general rule is true: MAINTENANCE IS CHEAPER THAN REPAIR.

Two basic mechanic's rules should be mentioned here. First, whenever the left side of the vehicle or engine is referred to, it means the driver's side. Conversely, the right side of the vehicle means the passenger's side. Second, screws and bolts are removed by turning counterclockwise, and tightened by turning clockwise unless specifically noted.

Safety is always the most important rule. Constantly be aware of the dangers involved in working on an automobile and take the proper precautions. Please refer to the information in this section regarding SERVICING YOUR VEHICLE SAFELY and the SAFETY NOTICE on the acknowledgment page.

Avoiding the Most Common Mistakes

Pay attention to the instructions provided. There are 3 common mistakes in mechanical work:

1. Incorrect order of assembly, disassembly or adjustment. When taking something apart or putting it together, performing steps in the wrong order usually just costs you extra time; however, it CAN break something. Read the entire procedure before beginning. Perform everything in the order in which the instructions say you should, even if you can't see a reason for it. When you're taking apart something that is very intricate, you might want to draw a picture of how it looks when assembled in order to make sure you get everything back in its proper position. When making adjustments, perform them in the proper order. One adjustment possibly will affect another.

2. Overtorquing (or undertorquing). While it is more common for overtorquing to cause damage, undertorquing may allow a fastener to vibrate loose causing serious damage. Especially when dealing with aluminum parts, pay attention to torque specifications and utilize a torque wrench in assembly. If a torque figure is not available, remember that if you are using the right tool to perform the job, you will probably not have to strain yourself to get a fastener tight enough. The pitch of most threads is so slight that the tension you put on the wrench will be multiplied many times in actual force on what you are tightening.

There are many commercial products available for ensuring that fasteners won't come loose, even if they are not torqued just right (a very common brand is Loctite®). If you're worried about getting something together tight enough to hold, but loose enough to avoid mechanical damage during assembly, one of these products might offer substantial insurance. Before choosing a threadlocking compound, read the label on the package and make sure the product is compatible with the materials, fluids, etc. involved.

3. Crossthreading. This occurs when a part such as a bolt is screwed into a nut or casting at the wrong angle and forced. Crossthreading is more likely to occur if access is difficult. It helps to clean and lubricate fasteners, then to start threading the bolt, spark plug, etc. with your fingers. If you encounter resistance, unscrew the part and start over again at a different angle until it can be inserted and turned several times without much effort. Keep in mind that many parts have tapered threads, so that gentle turning will automatically bring the part you're threading to the proper angle. Don't put a wrench on the part until it's been tightened a couple of turns by hand. If you suddenly encounter resistance, and the part has not seated fully, don't force it. Pull it back out to make sure it's clean and threading properly.

Be sure to take your time and be patient, and always plan ahead. Allow yourself ample time to perform repairs and maintenance.

TOOLS AND EQUIPMENT

◆ **See Figures 1 thru 15**

Without the proper tools and equipment it is impossible to properly service your vehicle. It would be virtually impossible to catalog every tool that you would need to perform all of the operations in this book. It would be unwise for the amateur to rush out and buy an expensive set of tools on the theory that he/she may need one or more of them at some time.

The best approach is to proceed slowly, gathering a good quality set of those tools that are used most frequently. Don't be misled by the low cost of bargain tools. It is far better to spend a little more for better quality. Forged wrenches, 6 or 12-point sockets and fine tooth ratchets are by far preferable to their less expensive counterparts. As any good mechanic can tell you, there are few worse experiences than trying to work on a vehicle with bad tools. Your monetary savings will be far outweighed by frustration and mangled knuckles.

Begin accumulating those tools that are used most frequently: those associated with routine maintenance and tune-up. In addition to the normal assortment of screwdrivers and pliers, you should have the following tools:

• Wrenches/sockets and combination open end/box end wrenches in sizes from 1/8–3/4 in. or 3–19mm, as well as a 13/16 in. or 5/8 in. spark plug socket (depending on plug type).

➡**If possible, buy various length socket drive extensions. Universal-joint and wobble extensions can be extremely useful, but be careful when using them, as they can change the amount of torque applied to the socket.**

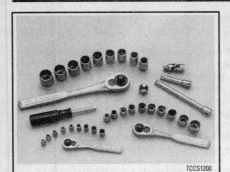

TCCS1200

Fig. 1 All but the most basic procedures will require an assortment of ratchets and sockets

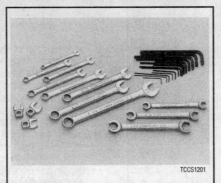

TCCS1201

Fig. 2 In addition to ratchets, a good set of wrenches and hex keys will be necessary

TCCS1202

Fig. 3 A hydraulic floor jack and a set of jackstands are essential for lifting and supporting the vehicle

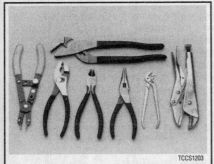

TCCS1203

Fig. 4 An assortment of pliers, grippers and cutters will be handy for old rusted parts and stripped bolt heads

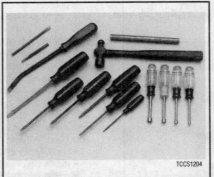

TCCS1204

Fig. 5 Various drivers, chisels and prybars are great tools to have in your toolbox

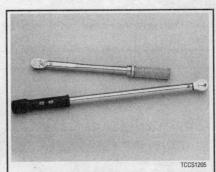

TCCS1205

Fig. 6 Many repairs will require the use of a torque wrench to assure the components are properly fastened

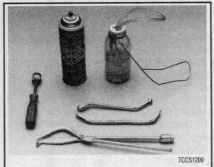

TCCS1209

Fig. 7 Although not always necessary, using specialized brake tools will save time

TCCS1210

Fig. 8 A few inexpensive lubrication tools will make maintenance easier

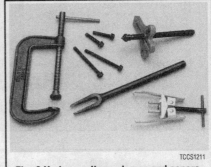

TCCS1211

Fig. 9 Various pullers, clamps and separator tools are needed for many larger, more complicated repairs

TCCS1212

Fig. 10 A variety of tools and gauges should be used for spark plug gapping and installation

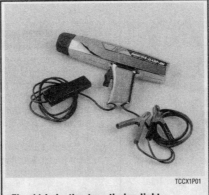

TCCX1P01

Fig. 11 Inductive type timing light

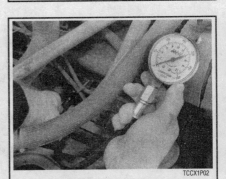

TCCX1P02

Fig. 12 A screw-in type compression gauge is recommended for compression testing

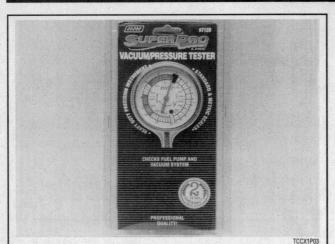

Fig. 13 A vacuum/pressure tester is necessary for many testing procedures

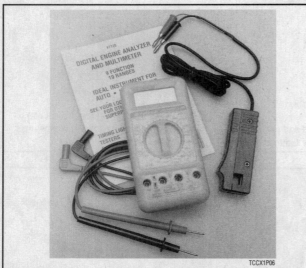

Fig. 14 Most modern automotive multimeters incorporate many helpful features

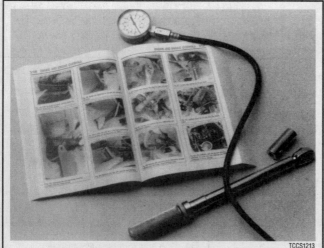

Fig. 15 Proper information is vital, so always have a Chilton Total Car Care manual handy

- Jackstands for support.
- Oil filter wrench.
- Spout or funnel for pouring fluids.
- Grease gun for chassis lubrication (unless your vehicle is not equipped with any grease fittings)
- Hydrometer for checking the battery (unless equipped with a sealed, maintenance-free battery).
- A container for draining oil and other fluids.
- Rags for wiping up the inevitable mess.

In addition to the above items there are several others that are not absolutely necessary, but handy to have around. These include an equivalent oil absorbent gravel, like cat litter, and the usual supply of lubricants, antifreeze and fluids. This is a basic list for routine maintenance, but only your personal needs and desire can accurately determine your list of tools.

After performing a few projects on the vehicle, you'll be amazed at the other tools and non-tools on your workbench. Some useful household items are: a large turkey baster or siphon, empty coffee cans and ice trays (to store parts), a ball of twine, electrical tape for wiring, small rolls of colored tape for tagging lines or hoses, markers and pens, a note pad, golf tees (for plugging vacuum lines), metal coat hangers or a roll of mechanic's wire (to hold things out of the way), dental pick or similar long, pointed probe, a strong magnet, and a small mirror (to see into recesses and under manifolds).

A more advanced set of tools, suitable for tune-up work, can be drawn up easily. While the tools are slightly more sophisticated, they need not be outrageously expensive. There are several inexpensive tach/dwell meters on the market that are every bit as good for the average mechanic as a professional model. Just be sure that it goes to a least 1200–1500 rpm on the tach scale and that it works on 4, 6 and 8-cylinder engines. The key to these purchases is to make them with an eye towards adaptability and wide range. A basic list of tune-up tools could include:

- Tach/dwell meter.
- Spark plug wrench and gapping tool.
- Feeler gauges for valve adjustment.
- Timing light.

The choice of a timing light should be made carefully. A light which works on the DC current supplied by the vehicle's battery is the best choice; it should have a xenon tube for brightness. On any vehicle with an electronic ignition system, a timing light with an inductive pickup that clamps around the No. 1 spark plug cable is preferred.

In addition to these basic tools, there are several other tools and gauges you may find useful. These include:

- Compression gauge. The screw-in type is slower to use, but eliminates the possibility of a faulty reading due to escaping pressure.
- Manifold vacuum gauge.
- 12V test light.
- A combination volt/ohmmeter
- Induction Ammeter. This is used for determining whether or not there is current in a wire. These are handy for use if a wire is broken somewhere in a wiring harness.

As a final note, you will probably find a torque wrench necessary for all but the most basic work. The beam type models are perfectly adequate, although the newer click types (breakaway) are easier to use. The click type torque wrenches tend to be more expensive. Also keep in mind that all types of torque wrenches should be periodically checked and/or recalibrated. You will have to decide for yourself which better fits your pocketbook, and purpose.

Special Tools

Normally, the use of special factory tools is avoided for repair procedures, since these are not readily available for the do-it-yourself mechanic. When it is possible to perform the job with more commonly available tools, it will be pointed out, but occasionally, a special tool was designed to perform a specific function and should be used. Before substituting another tool, you should be convinced that neither your safety nor the performance of the vehicle will be compromised.

Special tools can usually be purchased from an automotive parts store or from your dealer. In some cases special tools may be available directly from the tool manufacturer.

DIAGNOSTIC TEST EQUIPMENT

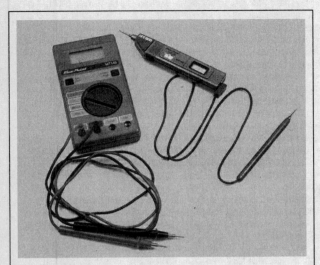

Digital multimeters come in a variety of styles and are a "must-have" for any serious home mechanic. Digital multimeters measure voltage (volts), resistance (ohms) and sometimes current (amperes). These versatile tools are used for checking all types of electrical or electronic components

Modern vehicles equipped with computer-controlled fuel, emission and ignition systems require modern electronic tools to diagnose problems. Many of these tools are designed solely for the professional mechanic and are too costly and difficult to use for the average do-it-yourselfer. However, various automotive aftermarket companies have introduced products that address the needs of the average home mechanic, providing sophisticated information at affordable cost. Consult your local auto parts store to determine what is available for your vehicle.

Trouble code tools allow the home mechanic to extract the "fault code" number from an on-board computer that has sensed a problem (usually indicated by a Check Engine light). Armed with this code, the home mechanic can focus attention on a suspect system or component

Sensor testers perform specific checks on many of the sensors and actuators used on today's computer-controlled vehicles. These testers can check sensors both on or off the vehicle, as well as test the accompanying electrical circuits

Hand-held scanners represent the most sophisticated of all do-it-yourself diagnostic tools. These tools do more than just access computer codes like the code readers above; they provide the user with an actual interface into the vehicle's computer. Comprehensive data on specific makes and models will come with the tool, either built-in or as a separate cartridge

SERVICING YOUR VEHICLE SAFELY

⬧ **See Figures 16, 17 and 18**

It is virtually impossible to anticipate all of the hazards involved with automotive maintenance and service, but care and common sense will prevent most accidents.

The rules of safety for mechanics range from "don't smoke around gasoline," to "use the proper tool(s) for the job." The trick to avoiding injuries is to develop safe work habits and to take every possible precaution.

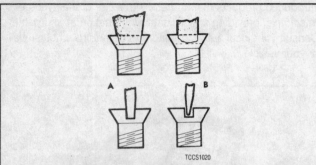

Fig. 16 Screwdrivers should be kept in good condition to prevent injury or damage which could result if the blade slips from the screw

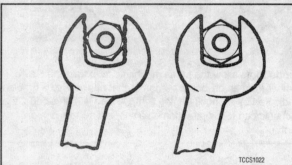

Fig. 17 Using the correct size wrench will help prevent the possibility of rounding off a nut

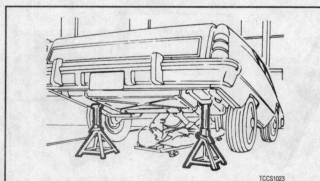

Fig. 18 NEVER work under a vehicle unless it is supported using safety stands (jackstands)

Do's

• Do keep a fire extinguisher and first aid kit handy.
• Do wear safety glasses or goggles when cutting, drilling, grinding or prying, even if you have 20–20 vision. If you wear glasses for the sake of vision, wear safety goggles over your regular glasses.

• Do shield your eyes whenever you work around the battery. Batteries contain sulfuric acid. In case of contact with, flush the area with water or a mixture of water and baking soda, then seek immediate medical attention.
• Do use safety stands (jackstands) for any undervehicle service. Jacks are for raising vehicles; jackstands are for making sure the vehicle stays raised until you want it to come down.
• Do use adequate ventilation when working with any chemicals or hazardous materials. Like carbon monoxide, the asbestos dust resulting from some brake lining wear can be hazardous in sufficient quantities.
• Do disconnect the negative battery cable when working on the electrical system. The secondary ignition system contains EXTREMELY HIGH VOLTAGE. In some cases it can even exceed 50,000 volts.
• Do follow manufacturer's directions whenever working with potentially hazardous materials. Most chemicals and fluids are poisonous.
• Do properly maintain your tools. Loose hammerheads, mushroomed punches and chisels, frayed or poorly grounded electrical cords, excessively worn screwdrivers, spread wrenches (open end), cracked sockets, slipping ratchets, or faulty droplight sockets can cause accidents.
• Likewise, keep your tools clean; a greasy wrench can slip off a bolt head, ruining the bolt and often harming your knuckles in the process.
• Do use the proper size and type of tool for the job at hand. Do select a wrench or socket that fits the nut or bolt. The wrench or socket should sit straight, not cocked.
• Do, when possible, pull on a wrench handle rather than push on it, and adjust your stance to prevent a fall.
• Do be sure that adjustable wrenches are tightly closed on the nut or bolt and pulled so that the force is on the side of the fixed jaw.
• Do strike squarely with a hammer; avoid glancing blows.
• Do set the parking brake and block the drive wheels if the work requires a running engine.

Don'ts

• Don't run the engine in a garage or anywhere else without proper ventilation—EVER! Carbon monoxide is poisonous; it takes a long time to leave the human body and you can build up a deadly supply of it in your system by simply breathing in a little at a time. You may not realize you are slowly poisoning yourself. Always use power vents, windows, fans and/or open the garage door.
• Don't work around moving parts while wearing loose clothing. Short sleeves are much safer than long, loose sleeves. Hard-toed shoes with neoprene soles protect your toes and give a better grip on slippery surfaces. Watches and jewelry is not safe working around a vehicle. Long hair should be tied back under a hat or cap.
• Don't use pockets for toolboxes. A fall or bump can drive a screwdriver deep into your body. Even a rag hanging from your back pocket can wrap around a spinning shaft or fan.
• Don't smoke when working around gasoline, cleaning solvent or other flammable material.
• Don't smoke when working around the battery. When the battery is being charged, it gives off explosive hydrogen gas.
• Don't use gasoline to wash your hands; there are excellent soaps available. Gasoline contains dangerous additives which can enter the body through a cut or through your pores. Gasoline also removes all the natural oils from the skin so that bone dry hands will suck up oil and grease.
• Don't service the air conditioning system unless you are equipped with the necessary tools and training. When liquid or compressed gas refrigerant is released to atmospheric pressure it will absorb heat from whatever it contacts. This will chill or freeze anything it touches.
• Don't use screwdrivers for anything other than driving screws! A screwdriver used as an prying tool can snap when you least expect it, causing injuries. At the very least, you'll ruin a good screwdriver.
• Don't use an emergency jack (that little ratchet, scissors, or pantograph jack supplied with the vehicle) for anything other than changing a flat! These jacks are only intended for emergency use out on the road; they are NOT designed as a maintenance tool. If you are serious about maintaining your vehicle yourself, invest in a hydraulic floor jack of at least a 1½ ton capacity, and at least two sturdy jackstands.

FASTENERS, MEASUREMENTS AND CONVERSIONS

Bolts, Nuts and Other Threaded Retainers

▶ See Figures 19 and 20

Although there are a great variety of fasteners found in the modern car or truck, the most commonly used retainer is the threaded fastener (nuts, bolts, screws, studs, etc.). Most threaded retainers may be reused, provided that they are not damaged in use or during the repair. Some retainers (such as stretch bolts or torque prevailing nuts) are designed to deform when tightened or in use and should not be reinstalled.

Whenever possible, we will note any special retainers which should be replaced during a procedure. But you should always inspect the condition of a retainer when it is removed and replace any that show signs of damage. Check all threads for rust or corrosion which can increase the torque necessary to achieve the desired clamp load for which that fastener was originally selected. Additionally, be sure that the driver surface of the fastener has not been compromised by rounding or other damage. In some cases a driver surface may become only partially rounded, allowing the driver to catch in only one direction. In many of these occurrences, a fastener may be installed and tightened, but the driver would not be able to grip and loosen the fastener again.

If you must replace a fastener, whether due to design or damage, you must ALWAYS be sure to use the proper replacement. In all cases, a retainer of the same design, material and strength should be used. Markings on the heads of most bolts will help determine the proper strength of the fastener. The same material, thread and pitch must be selected to assure proper installation and safe operation of the vehicle afterwards.

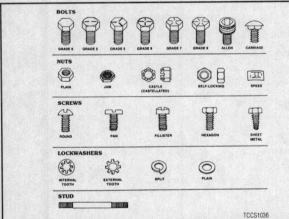

Fig. 19 There are many different types of threaded retainers found on vehicles

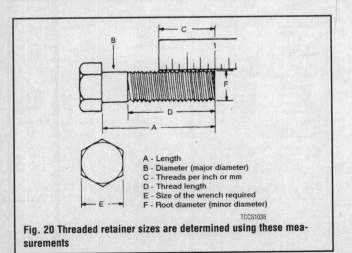

A - Length
B - Diameter (major diameter)
C - Threads per inch or mm
D - Thread length
E - Size of the wrench required
F - Root diameter (minor diameter)

Fig. 20 Threaded retainer sizes are determined using these measurements

Thread gauges are available to help measure a bolt or stud's thread. Most automotive and hardware stores keep gauges available to help you select the proper size. In a pinch, you can use another nut or bolt for a thread gauge. If the bolt you are replacing is not too badly damaged, you can select a match by finding another bolt which will thread in its place. If you find a nut which threads properly onto the damaged bolt, then use that nut to help select the replacement bolt.

❋❋ WARNING

Be aware that when you find a bolt with damaged threads, you may also find the nut or drilled hole it was threaded into has also been damaged. If this is the case, you may have to drill and tap the hole, replace the nut or otherwise repair the threads. NEVER try to force a replacement bolt to fit into the damaged threads.

Torque

Torque is defined as the measurement of resistance to turning or rotating. It tends to twist a body about an axis of rotation. A common example of this would be tightening a threaded retainer such as a nut, bolt or screw. Measuring torque is one of the most common ways to help assure that a threaded retainer has been properly fastened.

When tightening a threaded fastener, torque is applied in three distinct areas, the head, the bearing surface and the clamp load. About 50 percent of the measured torque is used in overcoming bearing friction. This is the friction between the bearing surface of the bolt head, screw head or nut face and the base material or washer (the surface on which the fastener is rotating). Approximately 40 percent of the applied torque is used in overcoming thread friction. This leaves only about 10 percent of the applied torque to develop a useful clamp load (the force which holds a joint together). This means that friction can account for as much as 90 percent of the applied torque on a fastener.

TORQUE WRENCHES

▶ See Figure 21

In most applications, a torque wrench can be used to assure proper installation of a fastener. Torque wrenches come in various designs and most automotive supply stores will carry a variety to suit your needs. A torque wrench should be used any time we supply a specific torque value for a fastener. Again, the general rule of "if you are using the right tool for the job, you should not have to strain to tighten a fastener" applies here.

Beam Type

The beam type torque wrench is one of the most popular types. It consists of a pointer attached to the head that runs the length of the flexible beam (shaft) to a scale located near the handle. As the wrench is pulled, the beam bends and the pointer indicates the torque using the scale.

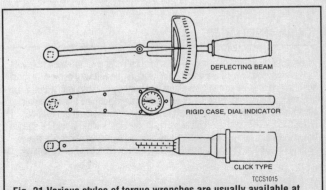

Fig. 21 Various styles of torque wrenches are usually available at your local automotive supply store

Click (Breakaway) Type

Another popular design of torque wrench is the click type. To use the click type wrench you pre-adjust it to a torque setting. Once the torque is reached, the wrench has a reflex signaling feature that causes a momentary breakaway of the torque wrench body, sending an impulse to the operator's hand.

Pivot Head Type

▶ See Figure 22

Some torque wrenches (usually of the click type) may be equipped with a pivot head which can allow it to be used in areas of limited access. BUT, it must be used properly. To hold a pivot head wrench, grasp the handle lightly, and as you pull on the handle, it should be floated on the pivot point. If the handle comes in contact with the yoke extension during the process of pulling, there is a very good chance the torque readings will be inaccurate because this could alter the wrench loading point. The design of the handle is usually such as to make it inconvenient to deliberately misuse the wrench.

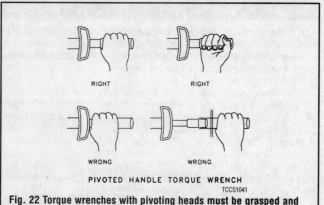

RIGHT   RIGHT

WRONG   WRONG

PIVOTED HANDLE TORQUE WRENCH

TCCS1041

Fig. 22 Torque wrenches with pivoting heads must be grasped and used properly to prevent an incorrect reading

➡ It should be mentioned that the use of any U-joint, wobble or extension will have an effect on the torque readings, no matter what type of wrench you are using. For the most accurate readings, install the socket directly on the wrench driver. If necessary, straight extensions (which hold a socket directly under the wrench driver) will have the least effect on the torque reading. Avoid any extension that alters the length of the wrench from the handle to the head/driving point (such as a crow's foot). U-joint or wobble extensions can greatly affect the readings; avoid their use at all times.

Rigid Case (Direct Reading)

A rigid case or direct reading torque wrench is equipped with a dial indicator to show torque values. One advantage of these wrenches is that they can be held at any position on the wrench without affecting accuracy. These wrenches are often preferred because they tend to be compact, easy to read and have a great degree of accuracy.

TORQUE ANGLE METERS

Because the frictional characteristics of each fastener or threaded hole will vary, clamp loads which are based strictly on torque will vary as well. In most applications, this variance is not significant enough to cause worry. But, in certain applications, a manufacturer's engineers may determine that more precise clamp loads are necessary (such is the case with many aluminum cylinder heads). In these cases, a torque angle method of installation would be specified. When installing fasteners which are torque angle tightened, a predetermined seating torque and standard torque wrench are usually used first to remove any

compliance from the joint. The fastener is then tightened the specified additional portion of a turn measured in degrees. A torque angle gauge (mechanical protractor) is used for these applications.

Standard and Metric Measurements

▶ See Figure 23

Throughout this manual, specifications are given to help you determine the condition of various components on your vehicle, or to assist you in their installation. Some of the most common measurements include length (in. or cm/mm), torque (ft. lbs., inch lbs. or Nm) and pressure (psi, in. Hg, kPa or mm Hg). In most cases, we strive to provide the proper measurement as determined by the manufacturer's engineers.

Though, in some cases, that value may not be conveniently measured with what is available in your toolbox. Luckily, many of the measuring devices which are available today will have two scales so the Standard or Metric measurements may easily be taken. If any of the various measuring tools which are available to you do not contain the same scale as listed in the specifications, use the accompanying conversion factors to determine the proper value.

The conversion factor chart is used by taking the given specification and multiplying it by the necessary conversion factor. For instance, looking at the first line, if you have a measurement in inches such as "free-play should be 2 in." but your ruler reads only in millimeters, multiply 2 in. by the conversion factor of 25.4 to get the metric equivalent of 50.8mm. Likewise, if the specification was given only in a Metric measurement, for example in Newton Meters (Nm), then look at the center column first. If the measurement is 100 Nm, multiply it by the conversion factor of 0.738 to get 73.8 ft. lbs.

CONVERSION FACTORS

LENGTH–DISTANCE

Inches (in.)	x 25.4	= Millimeters (mm)	x .0394	= Inches
Feet (ft.)	x .305	= Meters (m)	x 3.281	= Feet
Miles	x 1.609	= Kilometers (km)	x .0621	= Miles

VOLUME

Cubic Inches (in3)	x 16.387	= Cubic Centimeters	x .061	= in3
IMP Pints (IMP pt.)	x .568	= Liters (L)	x 1.76	= IMP pt.
IMP Quarts (IMP qt.)	x 1.137	= Liters (L)	x .88	= IMP qt.
IMP Gallons (IMP gal.)	x 4.546	= Liters (L)	x .22	= IMP gal.
IMP Quarts (IMP qt.)	x 1.201	= US Quarts (US qt.)	x .833	= IMP qt.
IMP Gallons (IMP gal.)	x 1.201	= US Gallons (US gal.)	x .833	= IMP gal.
Fl. Ounces	x 29.573	= Milliliters	x .034	= Ounces
US Pints (US pt.)	x .473	= Liters (L)	x 2.113	= Pints
US Quarts (US qt.)	x .946	= Liters (L)	x 1.057	= Quarts
US Gallons (US gal.)	x 3.785	= Liters (L)	x .264	= Gallons

MASS–WEIGHT

Ounces (oz.)	x 28.35	= Grams (g)	x .035	= Ounces
Pounds (lb.)	x .454	= Kilograms (kg)	x 2.205	= Pounds

PRESSURE

Pounds Per Sq. In. (psi)	x 6.895	= Kilopascals (kPa)	x .145	= psi
Inches of Mercury (Hg)	x .4912	= psi	x 2.036	= Hg
Inches of Mercury (Hg)	x 3.377	= Kilopascals (kPa)	x .2961	= Hg
Inches of Water (H₂O)	x .07355	= Inches of Mercury	x 13.783	= H₂O
Inches of Water (H₂O)	x .03613	= psi	x 27.684	= H₂O
Inches of Water (H₂O)	x .248	= Kilopascals (kPa)	x 4.026	= H₂O

TORQUE

Pounds–Force Inches (in-lb)	x .113	= Newton Meters (N·m)	x 8.85	= in-lb
Pounds–Force Feet (ft-lb)	x 1.356	= Newton Meters (N·m)	x .738	= ft-lb

VELOCITY

Miles Per Hour (MPH)	x 1.609	= Kilometers Per Hour (KPH)	x .621	= MPH

POWER

Horsepower (Hp)	x .745	= Kilowatts	x 1.34	= Horsepower

FUEL CONSUMPTION*

Miles Per Gallon IMP (MPG)	x .354	= Kilometers Per Liter (Km/L)	
Kilometers Per Liter (Km/L)	x 2.352	= IMP MPG	
Miles Per Gallon US (MPG)	x .425	= Kilometers Per Liter (Km/L)	
Kilometers Per Liter (Km/L)	x 2.352	= US MPG	

*It is common to covert from miles per gallon (mpg) to liters/100 kilometers (1/100 km), where mpg (IMP) x 1/100 km = 282 and mpg (US) x 1/100 km = 235.

TEMPERATURE

Degree Fahrenheit (°F) = (°C x 1.8) + 32

Degree Celsius (°C) = (°F – 32) x .56

TCCS1044

Fig. 23 Standard and metric conversion factors chart

SERIAL NUMBER IDENTIFICATION

Vehicle Identification Number (VIN)

▶ **See Figures 24 and 25**

A 17 digit combination of numbers and letters forms the vehicle identification number (VIN).

The VIN is stamped on a metal tab that is riveted to the instrument panel close to the windshield. The VIN plate is visible by looking through the windshield on the driver's side.

On MPV models, the VIN is also stamped on the firewall directly behind the engine.

By looking at the 17 digit VIN number, a variety of information about the vehicle can be determined.

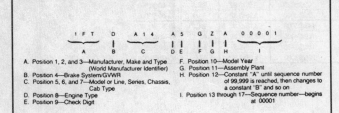

A. Position 1, 2, and 3—Manufacturer, Make and Type (World Manufacturer Identifier)
B. Position 4—Brake System/GVWR
C. Position 5, 6, and 7—Model or Line, Series, Chassis, Cab Type
D. Position 8—Engine Type
E. Position 9—Check Digit
F. Position 10—Model Year
G. Position 11—Assembly Plant
H. Position 12—Constant "A" until sequence number of 99,999 is reached, then changes to a constant "B" and so on
I. Position 13 through 17—Sequence number—begins at 00001

85551016

Fig. 24 A sample breakdown of the VIN number

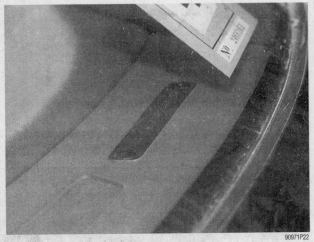

90971P22

Fig. 25 Location of the VIN code plate on the front edge of the driver side dashboard underneath the windshield

- The first 3 digits represent the manufacturer, make and type of vehicle (world manufacturer identifier).
- The 4th digit identifies the gross vehicle weight rating (GVWR Class) and brake system. For incomplete vehicles, the 4th digit determines the brake system only. All brake systems are hydraulic.
- The 5th, 6th and 7th digits identify model or series, chassis and body type.
- The 8th digit identifies the engine.
- The 9th digit is a check digit.
- The 10th digit identifies the model year.
- The 11th digit identifies the assembly plant.
- Digits 12–17 make up the production sequence number.

Engine

B SERIES PICK-UP & NAVAJO

The engine identification code is a letter located in the eighth digit of the Vehicle Identification Number stamped on a metal tab that is riveted to the instrument panel close to the windshield. Specific engine data is located on a label attached to the timing cover.

MPV

The engine number is located on a machined pad extending from the cylinder block just below the distributor.

ENGINE IDENTIFICATION

Year	Model	Engine Displacement Liters (cc)	Engine Series (ID/VIN)	Fuel System	No. of Cylinders	Engine Type
1994	B Series Pick-up	2.3 (2298)	A	MFI	4	SOHC
		3.0 (2968)	U	MFI	6	OHV
		4.0 (4016)	X	MFI	6	OHV
	MPV	2.6 (2606)	G6	MFI	4	SOHC
		3.0 (2954)	JE	MFI	6	SOHC
	Navajo	4.0 (4016)	X	MFI	6	OHV
1995	B Series Pick-up	2.3 (2298)	A	MFI	4	SOHC
		3.0 (2968)	U	MFI	6	OHV
		4.0 (4016)	X	MFI	6	OHV
	MPV	2.6 (2606)	G6	MFI	4	SOHC
		3.0 (2954)	JE	MFI	6	SOHC
1996	B Series Pick-up	2.3 (2298)	A	MFI	4	SOHC
		3.0 (2968)	U	MFI	6	OHV
		4.0 (4016)	X	MFI	6	OHV
	MPV	3.0 (2954)	JE	MFI	6	SOHC
1997	B Series Pick-up	2.3 (2298)	A	MFI	4	SOHC
		3.0 (2968)	U	MFI	6	OHV
		4.0 (4016)	X	MFI	6	OHV
	MPV	3.0 (2954)	JE	MFI	6	SOHC
1998	B Series Pick-up	2.5 (2500)	C	MFI	4	SOHC
		3.0 (2968)	U	MFI	6	OHV
		4.0 (4016)	X	MFI	6	OHV
	MPV	3.0 (2954)	JE	MFI	6	SOHC

MFI: Multi-port Fuel Injection

90971C02

VEHICLE IDENTIFICATION CHART

Engine Code						Model Year	
Code	Liters	Cu. In. (cc)	Cyl.	Fuel Sys.	Eng. Mfg.	Code	Year
A	2.3	140 (2298)	4	MFI	Ford	R	1994
C	2.5	152 (2500)	4	MFI	Ford	S	1995
G6	2.6	159 (2606)	4	MFI	Mazda	T	1996
JE	3.0	180 (2954)	6	MFI	Mazda	V	1997
U	3.0	182 (2968)	6	MFI	Ford	W	1998
X	4.0	245 (4016)	6	MFI	Ford		

MFI: Multi-port Fuel Injection

90971C01

GENERAL ENGINE SPECIFICATIONS

Year	Engine ID/VIN	Engine Displacement Liters (cc)	Fuel System Type	Net Horsepower @ rpm	Net Torque @ rpm (ft. lbs.)	Bore x Stroke (in.)	Compression Ratio	Oil Pressure (lbs. @ rpm)
1994	A	2.3 (2298)	MFI	100@4600	133@2600	3.78x3.13	9.2:1	40–60@2000
	G6	2.6 (2606)	MFI	121@4600	149@3500	3.62x3.86	8.4:1	44–58@3000
	JE	3.0 (2954)	MFI	155@5000	169@4000	3.54x3.05	8.5:1	53–75@3000
	U	3.0 (2968)	MFI	140@4800	160@3000	3.50x3.14	9.3:1	40–60@2500
	X	4.0 (4016)	MFI	①	②	3.95x3.32	9.1:1	40–60@2000
1995	A	2.3 (2298)	MFI	112@4800	135@2400	3.78x3.13	9.2:1	40–60@2000
	G6	2.6 (2606)	MFI	121@4600	149@3500	3.62x3.86	8.4:1	44–58@3000
	JE	3.0 (2954)	MFI	155@5000	169@4000	3.54x3.05	8.5:1	53–75@3000
	U	3.0 (2968)	MFI	147@5000	162@3250	3.50x3.14	9.2:1	40–60@2500
	X	4.0 (4016)	MFI	160@4200	220@3000	3.95x3.32	9.1:1	40–60@2000
1996	A	2.3 (2298)	MFI	112@4800	135@2400	3.78x3.13	9.1:1	40–60@2000
	JE	3.0 (2954)	MFI	155@5000	169@4000	3.54x3.05	8.5:1	53–75@3000
	U	3.0 (2968)	MFI	147@5000	162@3250	3.95x3.32	9.2:1	40–60@2500
	X	4.0 (4016)	MFI	160@4200	220@3000	3.95x3.32	9.1:1	40–60@2000
1997	A	2.3 (2298)	MFI	112@4800	135@2400	3.78x3.13	9.1:1	40–60@2000
	JE	3.0 (2954)	MFI	155@5000	169@4000	3.54x3.05	8.5:1	53–75@3000
	U	3.0 (2968)	MFI	147@5000	162@3250	3.95x3.32	9.2:1	40–60@2500
	X	4.0 (4016)	MFI	160@4200	220@3000	3.95x3.32	9.1:1	40–60@2000
1998	C	2.5 (2500)	MFI	119@5000	146@3000	3.78x3.40	9.4:1	40–60@2000
	JE	3.0 (2954)	MFI	155@5000	169@4000	3.54x3.05	8.5:1	53–75@3000
	U	3.0 (2968)	MFI	150@5000	185@3750	3.95x3.32	9.1:1	40–60@2500
	X	4.0 (4016)	MFI	160@4200	225@3000	3.95x3.32	9.0:1	40–60@2000

① B Series Truck: 160@4000
   Navajo: 160@4500
② B Series Truck w/manual transmission: 225@2500
   B Series Truck w/automatic transmission: 220@2800
   Navajo w/manual transmission: 220@2500
   Navajo w/automatic transmission: 220@2200

90971C03

Transmission

▶ See Figure 26

On manual transmissions, the identification number is located on a plate attached to the main transmission case. On the plate you find the assigned part number, serial number and bar code used for inventory purposes. On B Series truck and Navajo automatic transmissions, the identification number is stamped on a plate that hangs from the lower left extension housing bolt. On MPV automatic transmissions, the identification number is stamped on a plate that is bolted to the side of the transmission.

The tag identifies when the transmission was built, it's code letter and model number.

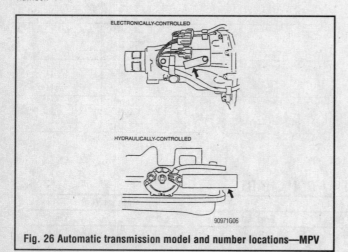
Fig. 26 Automatic transmission model and number locations—MPV

Drive Axle

FRONT

▶ See Figure 27

The identification number is stamped on a plate on the differential housing.

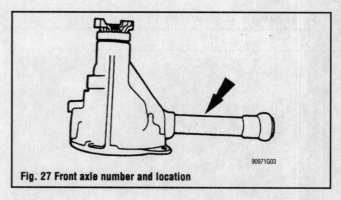
Fig. 27 Front axle number and location

REAR

▶ See Figure 28

The rear axle identification code is stamped on a metal tag hanging from one of the axle cover–to–carrier bolts in the cover bolt circle.

Transfer Case

All vehicles can be equipped with a mechanical or electronic shift transfer case. The identification number is stamped on a plate on the side of the case.

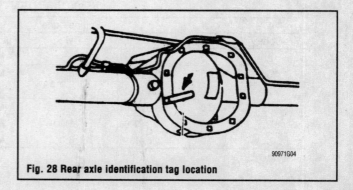
Fig. 28 Rear axle identification tag location

UNDERHOOD MAINTENANCE COMPONENT LOCATIONS—EXCEPT MPV

1. Air cleaner housing (conical style)
2. Coolant overflow tank
3. Washer fluid tank
4. Heater hoses
5. Upper radiator hose
6. Engine oil fill cap
7. Spark plug wires
8. Transmission fluid level dipstick
9. Engine oil level dipstick
10. Brake fluid reservoir
11. Power steering reservoir and dipstick
12. Battery
13. Radiator cap
14. Vehicle systems warning labels
15. Serpentine belt routing label
16. Emission and tune-up label
17. Engine air intake hose

UNDERHOOD COMPONENT LOCATIONS—MPV

1. Vehicle Identification Number (VIN) (stamped into the firewall)
2. EVAP canister
3. Brake master cylinder
4. Automatic transmission fluid dipstick
5. Engine oil dipstick
6. Distributor cap and rotor
7. Windshield washer fluid reservoir
8. Battery
9. Power steering pump
10. Engine oil fill cap
11. Air filter housing
12. Coolant recovery tank

90971P07

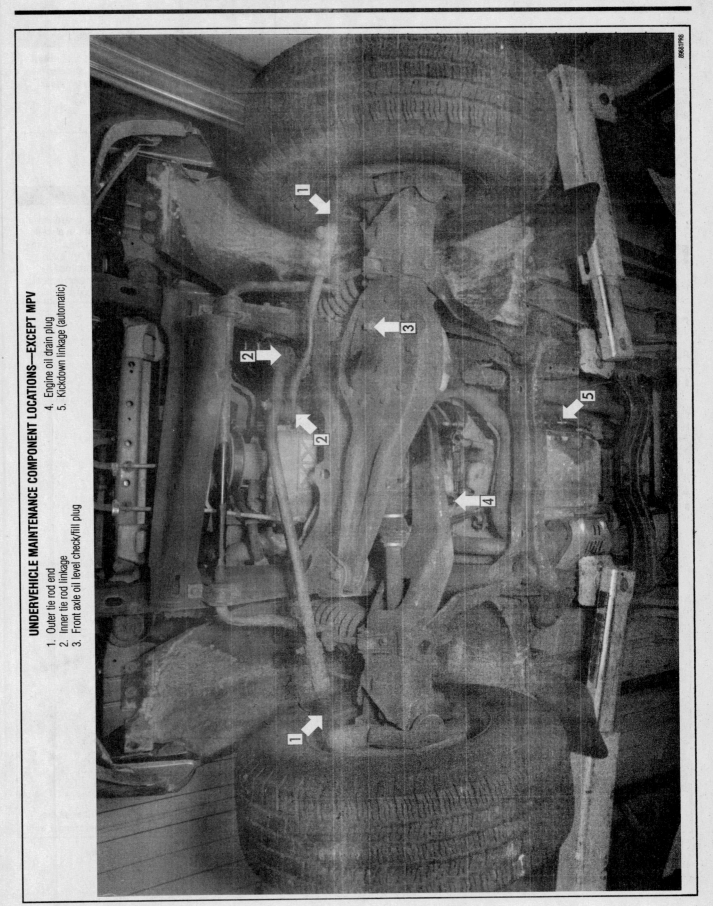

UNDERVEHICLE MAINTENANCE COMPONENT LOCATIONS—EXCEPT MPV

1. Outer tie rod end
2. Inner tie rod linkage
3. Front axle oil level check/fill plug
4. Engine oil drain plug
5. Kickdown linkage (automatic)

89661P8

Proper maintenance and tune-up is the key to long and trouble-free vehicle life, and the work can yield its own rewards. Studies have shown that a properly tuned and maintained vehicle can achieve better gas mileage than an out-of-tune vehicle. As a conscientious owner and driver, set aside a Saturday morning, say once a month, to check or replace items which could cause major problems later. Keep your own personal log to jot down which services you performed, how much the parts cost you, the date, and the exact odometer reading at the time. Keep all receipts for such items as engine oil and filters, so that they may be referred to in case of related problems or to determine operating expenses. As a do-it-yourselfer, these receipts are the only proof you have that the required maintenance was performed. In the event of a warranty problem, these receipts will be invaluable.

The literature provided with your vehicle when it was originally delivered includes the factory recommended maintenance schedule. If you no longer have this literature, replacement copies are usually available from the dealer. A maintenance schedule is provided later in this section, in case you do not have the factory literature.

Air Cleaner (Element)

The air cleaner is a paper element type. The paper cartridge should be replaced every 30,000 miles, under normal conditions. Under dusty or severe conditions, the filter should be inspected frequently and changed as necessary.

➡**Check the air filter more often if the vehicle is operated under severe dusty conditions and replace it as necessary.**

REMOVAL & INSTALLATION

▶ **See Figures 29 and 30**

The B Series Pick-up, Navajo and MPV vehicles use the square panel air cleaner housing. The square panel type retains the housing cover by bolts or, on later models, snap clips.
1. Loosen the clamp that secures the intake hose assembly to the air cleaner.
2. If necessary, unplug the MAF (Mass Air Flow) and/or IAT (Intake Air Temperature) sensor electrical connector from the air cleaner housing.

➡**Some air cleaner assemblies will have enough "give" in the air inlet pipe and sensor wiring harnesses to allow filter replacement without removing or disconnecting these items.**

3. Disconnect the hose and inlet tube from the air cleaner.
4. Remove the screws or snap clips attaching the air cleaner cover.
5. Seperate the lid from the housing base.
6. Remove the air filter.
7. Installation is the reverse of removal. Don't overtighten the hose clamps! A torque of 12–15 inch lbs. is sufficient.

Fuel Filter

➡**On MPV models, the fuel filter is located on the right fender well just below the battery. On B Series Pick-up and Navajo models, the fuel filter is located on the right rear frame member, near the fuel tank.**

REMOVAL & INSTALLATION

MPV Models

▶ **See Figure 31**

✴ CAUTION

Observe all applicable safety precautions when working around fuel. Whenever servicing the fuel system, always work in a well ventilated area. Do not allow fuel spray or vapors to come in contact with a spark or open flame. Keep a dry chemical fire extinguisher near the work area. Always keep fuel in a container specifically designed for fuel storage; also, always properly seal fuel containers to avoid the possibility of fire or explosion.

1. Relieve the pressure from the fuel system.
2. Disconnect the battery negative cable.
3. Slide the fuel line clamps back off the connections on the filter. Then, slowly pull one connection off just until fuel begins to seep out. Place a small plastic container or stuff a couple of rags under the filter to absorb any excess fuel.
4. Pull both fuel hoses off the connectors. Remove the filter from the clamp. On some models, it will be necessary to unbolt the fuel filter from the mounting bracket.
To install:
5. Place the new filter in the clamp or attach to the bracket if so equipped.
6. Connect the hoses to the filter connections and secure the hoses with the clamps.
7. Connect the negative battery cable.
8. Start the engine and check the fuel filter connections for leaks.

B Series Pick-up and Navajo Models

▶ **See Figure 32**

➡**The inline reservoir type fuel filter should last the life of the vehicle under normal driving conditions. If the filter does need to be replaced, proceed as follows:**

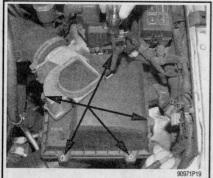

Fig. 29 Loosen the 5 air cleaner housing cover retaining bolts

Fig. 30 While holding the air cleaner housing cover up, remove the filter element out of the housing

Fig. 31 Location of the fuel filter on the right side engine compartment fender well

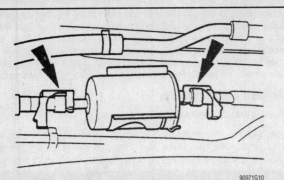

Fig. 32 Remove the "hairpin" clip retainers to access the fuel line fittings

❋❋ CAUTION

If the fuel filter is being serviced with the rear of the vehicle higher than the front, or if the tank is pressurized, fuel leakage or siphoning from the tank fuel lines could occur. to prevent this condition, maintain the vehicle front end at or above the level of the rear of vehicle. also, relieve tank pressure by loosening the fuel fill cap. cap should be tightened after pressure is relieved.

1. Shut the engine off. Depressurize the fuel system.
2. Raise and support the vehicle safely.
3. Detach the fuel lines from both ends of the fuel filter by disengaging both push connect fittings. Install new retainer clips in each push connect fitting.
4. Note which way the **flow** direction arrow points on the old filter.
5. Remove the filter from the bracket by loosening the filter retaining clamp enough to allow the filter to pass through.

➡**The flow direction arrow should be positioned as installed in the bracket to ensure proper flow of fuel through the replacement filter.**

6. Install the filter in the bracket, ensuring proper direction of flow as noted by arrow. Tighten clamp to 15–25 inch lbs.
7. Install the push connect fittings at both ends of the filter.
8. Lower the vehicle.
9. Start the engine and check for leaks.

PCV Valve

REMOVAL & INSTALLATION

▶ **See Figures 33 and 34**

Remove the PCV valve by simply disconnecting the vacuum hose from the valve, then pulling the valve from the rocker cover grommet.

Evaporative Canister

▶ **See Figure 35**

The fuel evaporative emission control canister should be inspected for damage or leaks at the hose fittings. Repair or replace any old or cracked hoses. Replace the canister if it is damaged in any way. The evaporatve canister can be found in the following locations:
- 1994–95 MPV—right side rear of the engine compartment
- 1996–98 MPV—underneath the right side of the vehicle near toward the front
- 1994–97 B Series Pick-up and Navajo—left side radiator support, under the hood.
- 1998 B Series Pick-up—left side inner frame rail underneath the vehicle

SERVICING

The evaporative and emission components are designed and tested to exceed 120,000 mi. (193,116km) or 10 years of vehicle use. No maintenance or service should be required, except in the case of damage or malfunction. If either condition should exist, simply replace that component.

Battery

PRECAUTIONS

Always use caution when working on or near the battery. Never allow a tool to bridge the gap between the negative and positive battery terminals. Also, be careful not to allow a tool to provide a ground between the positive cable/terminal and any metal component on the vehicle. Either of these conditions will cause a short circuit, leading to sparks and possible personal injury.

Do not smoke or all open flames/sparks near a battery; the gases contained in the battery are very explosive and, if ignited, could cause severe injury or death.

All batteries, regardless of type, should be carefully secured by a battery hold-down device. If not, the terminals or casing may crack from stress during vehicle operation. A battery which is not secured may allow acid to leak, making it discharge faster. The acid can also eat away at components under the hood.

Always inspect the battery case for cracks, leakage and corrosion. A white corrosive substance on the battery case or on nearby components would indicate a leaking or cracked battery. If the battery is cracked, it should be replaced immediately.

GENERAL MAINTENANCE

Always keep the battery cables and terminals free of corrosion. Check and clean these components about once a year.

Keep the top of the battery clean, as a film of dirt can help discharge a battery that is not used for long periods. A solution of baking soda and water may be used for cleaning, but be careful to flush this off with clear water. DO NOT let any of the solution into the filler holes. Baking soda neutralizes battery acid and will de-activate a battery cell.

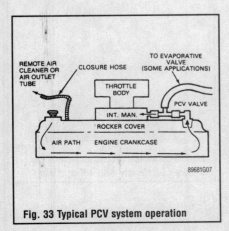

Fig. 33 Typical PCV system operation

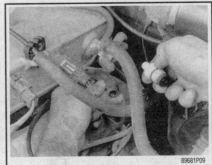

Fig. 34 Remove the PCV valve from between the hose and the valve cover grommet

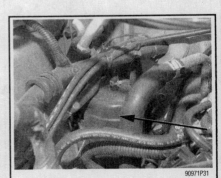

Fig. 35 Location of the evaporative canister near the firewall on the right side fender well—1994–95 MPV shown

Batteries in vehicles which are not operated on a regular basis can fall victim to parasitic loads (small current drains which are constantly drawing current from the battery). Normal parasitic loads may drain a battery on a vehicle that is in storage and not used for 6–8 weeks. Vehicles that have additional accessories such as a phone or an alarm system may discharge a battery sooner. If the vehicle is to be stored for longer periods in a secure area and the alarm system is not necessary, the negative battery cable should be disconnected to protect the battery.

Remember that constantly deep cycling a battery (completely discharging and recharging it) will shorten battery life.

BATTERY FLUID

▶ **See Figure 36**

Check the battery electrolyte level at least once a month, or more often in hot weather or during periods of extended vehicle operation. On non-sealed batteries, the level can be checked either through the case (if translucent) or by removing the cell caps. The electrolyte level in each cell should be kept filled to the split ring inside each cell, or the line marked on the outside of the case.

If the level is low, add only distilled water through the opening until the level is correct. Each cell must be checked and filled individually. Distilled water should be used, because the chemicals and minerals found in most drinking water are harmful to the battery and could significantly shorten its life.

If water is added in freezing weather, the vehicle should be driven several miles to allow the water to mix with the electrolyte. Otherwise, the battery could freeze.

Although some maintenance-free batteries have removable cell caps, the electrolyte condition and level on all sealed maintenance-free batteries must be checked using the built-in hydrometer "eye." The exact type of eye will vary. But, most battery manufacturers, apply a sticker to the battery itself explaining the readings.

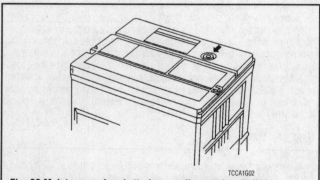

TCCA1G02

Fig. 36 Maintenance-free batteries usually contain a built-in hydrometer to check fluid level

➡**Although the readings from built-in hydrometers will vary, a green eye usually indicates a properly charged battery with sufficient fluid level. A dark eye is normally an indicator of a battery with sufficient fluid, but which is low in charge. A light or yellow eye usually indicates that electrolyte has dropped below the necessary level. In this last case, sealed batteries with an insufficient electrolyte must usually be discarded.**

Checking the Specific Gravity

▶ **See Figures 37, 38 and 39**

A hydrometer is required to check the specific gravity on all batteries that are not maintenance-free. On batteries that are maintenance-free, the specific gravity is checked by observing the built-in hydrometer "eye" on the top of the battery case.

❊❊ CAUTION

Battery electrolyte contains sulfuric acid. If you should splash any on your skin or in your eyes, flush the affected area with plenty of clear water. If it lands in your eyes, get medical help immediately.

The fluid (sulfuric acid solution) contained in the battery cells will tell you many things about the condition of the battery. Because the cell plates must be kept submerged below the fluid level in order to operate, the fluid level is extremely important. And, because the specific gravity of the acid is an indication of electrical charge, testing the fluid can be an aid in determining if the battery must be replaced. A battery in a vehicle with a properly operating charging system should require little maintenance, but careful, periodic inspection should reveal problems before they leave you stranded.

At least once a year, check the specific gravity of the battery. It should be between 1.20 and 1.26 on the gravity scale. Most auto stores carry a variety of inexpensive battery hydrometers. These can be used on any non-sealed battery to test the specific gravity in each cell.

The battery testing hydrometer has a squeeze bulb at one end and a nozzle at the other. Battery electrolyte is sucked into the hydrometer until the float is lifted from its seat. The specific gravity is then read by noting the position of the float. If gravity is low in one or more cells, the battery should be slowly charged and checked again to see if the gravity has come up. Generally, if after charging, the specific gravity between any two cells varies more than 50 points (0.50), the battery should be replaced, as it can no longer produce sufficient voltage to guarantee proper operation.

CABLES

▶ **See Figures 40, 41, 42 and 43**

Once a year (or as necessary), the battery terminals and the cable clamps should be cleaned. Loosen the clamps and remove the cables, negative cable first. On top post batteries, the use of a puller specially made for this purpose is recommended. These are inexpensive and available in most parts stores. Side terminal battery cables are secured with a small bolt.

TCCA1P07

Fig. 37 On non-sealed batteries, the fluid level can be checked by removing the cell caps

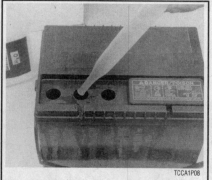

TCCA1P08

Fig. 38 If the fluid level is low, add only distilled water until the level is correct

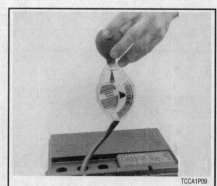

TCCA1P09

Fig. 39 Check the specific gravity of the battery's electrolyte with a hydrometer

Clean the cable clamps and the battery terminal with a wire brush, until all corrosion, grease, etc., is removed and the metal is shiny. It is especially important to clean the inside of the clamp thoroughly (an old knife is useful here), since a small deposit of oxidation there will prevent a sound connection and inhibit starting or charging. Special tools are available for cleaning these parts, one type for conventional top post batteries and another type for side terminal batteries. It is also a good idea to apply some dielectric grease to the terminal, as this will aid in the prevention of corrosion.

After the clamps and terminals are clean, reinstall the cables, negative cable last; DO NOT hammer the clamps onto battery posts. Tighten the clamps securely, but do not distort them. Give the clamps and terminals a thin external coating of grease after installation, to retard corrosion.

Check the cables at the same time that the terminals are cleaned. If the cable insulation is cracked or broken, or if the ends are frayed, the cable should be replaced with a new cable of the same length and gauge.

CHARGING

✳✳ CAUTION

The chemical reaction which takes place in all batteries generates explosive hydrogen gas. A spark can cause the battery to explode and splash acid. To avoid personal injury, be sure there is proper ventilation and take appropriate fire safety precautions when working with or near a battery.

A battery should be charged at a slow rate to keep the plates inside from getting too hot. However, if some maintenance-free batteries are allowed to discharge until they are almost "dead," they may have to be charged at a high rate to bring them back to "life." Always follow the charger manufacturer's instructions on charging the battery.

REPLACEMENT

When it becomes necessary to replace the battery, select one with an amperage rating equal to or greater than the battery originally installed. Deterioration and just plain aging of the battery cables, starter motor, and associated wires makes the battery's job harder in successive years. This makes it prudent to install a new battery with a greater capacity than the old.

Belts

INSPECTION

♦ See Figures 44, 45, 46, 47 and 48

Inspect the belts for signs of glazing or cracking. A glazed belt will be perfectly smooth from slippage, while a good belt will have a slight texture of fabric visible. Cracks will usually start at the inner edge of the belt and run outward. All worn or damaged drive belts should be replaced immediately. It is best to replace all drive belts at one time, as a preventive maintenance measure, during this service operation.

ADJUSTMENT

♦ See Figure 49

Belt tension can be checked by pressing on the belt at the center point of its longest straight run. The belt should give about 1/4–1/2 in. If the belt is loose, it will slip. If the belt is too tight it will damage bearings in the driven unit. Those units being driven, such as the alternator, power steering pump or compressor, have a bolt which when loosened allows the unit to move for belt adjustment. Sometimes it is necessary to loosen the pivot bolt also, to make the adjustment.

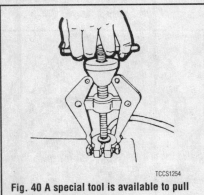

Fig. 40 A special tool is available to pull the clamp from the post

Fig. 41 The underside of this special battery tool has a wire brush to clean post terminals

Fig. 42 Place the tool over the battery posts and twist to clean until the metal is shiny

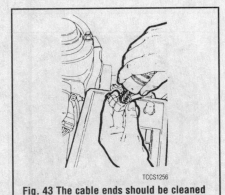

Fig. 43 The cable ends should be cleaned as well

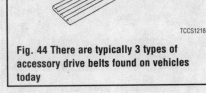

Fig. 44 There are typically 3 types of accessory drive belts found on vehicles today

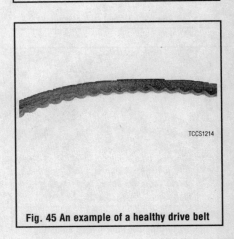

Fig. 45 An example of a healthy drive belt

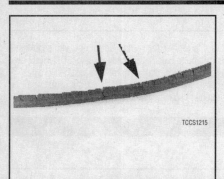

Fig. 46 Deep cracks in this belt will cause flex, building up heat that will eventually lead to belt failure

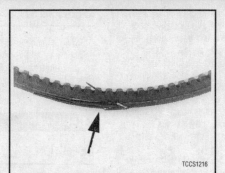

Fig. 47 The cover of this belt is worn, exposing the critical reinforcing cords to excessive wear

Fig. 48 Installing too wide a belt can result in serious belt wear and/or breakage

REMOVAL & INSTALLATION

Non-Serpentine (MPV)

▶ See Figure 50

POWER STEERING PUMP BELT

▶ See Figures 51, 52 and 53

1. Turn the ignition **OFF** and remove the key. Allow the engine to cool.
2. Loosen the idler pulley locknut to release the drive belt tension.
3. Remove the power steering belt.

To install:

4. Install the power steering belt and make sure it is correctly seated on the pulleys.
5. Adjust the power steering belt tension/deflection by turning the adjusting bolt. A new belt should deflect 0.26–0.28 in. (6.6–7.2mm) and a used belt should deflect 0.28–0.31 in. (7–8mm).
6. Tighten the idler pulley locknut to 27–38 ft. lbs. (37–52 Nm).
7. Run the engine for 5 minutes and then recheck the belt deflection.

ALTERNATOR BELT

▶ See Figures 54, 55, 56 and 57

1. Turn the ignition **OFF** and remove the key. Allow the engine to cool.
2. Remove the power steering pump belt and A/C compressor belt, if necessary.
3. Loosen the alternator upper bracket adjusting bolt.
4. Loosen the lower through-bolt.
5. Remove the alternator belt.

To install:

6. Install the alternator belt and make sure it is correctly seated on the pulleys.

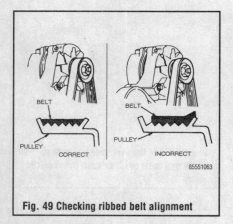

Fig. 49 Checking ribbed belt alignment

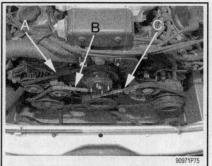

Fig. 50 (A) Alternator belt, (B) Power steering pump belt, (C) A/C compressor belt—MPV with 3.0L engine shown

Fig. 51 Using a boxwrench, loosen the power steering pump belt idler pulley lockbolt

Fig. 52 Loosen the power steering pump belt by turning the idler pulley adjusting bolt

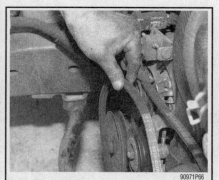

Fig. 53 Remove the power steering pump belt

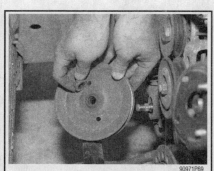

Fig. 54 To access the alternator pivot bolt, you must first remove the power steering pump pulley

Fig. 55 Loosen the alternator pivot bolt located just below the alternator assembly

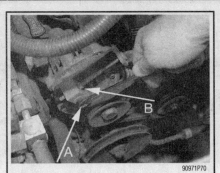

Fig. 56 Loosen the alternator adjuster lockbolt (A), then turn the adjustment nut (B) to loosen the slack on the belt . . .

Fig. 57 . . . then remove the alternator belt

7. Turn the adjusting bolt to adjust the belt deflection. New belts should deflect 0.39–0.47 in. (10–12mm). Used belts should deflect 0.43–0.51 in. (11–13mm).

8. Once the correct deflection has been reached, tighten the upper bracket lock bolt to 14–19 ft. lbs. (19–25 Nm).

9. Tighten the lower through-bolt to 28–38 ft. lbs. (38–51 Nm).

10. Install and tension the power steering pump belt and A/C compressor belt, if necessary.

11. Run the engine for 5 minutes and then recheck the belt deflection.

A/C COMPRESSOR BELT

♦ See Figures 58, 59 and 60

1. Turn the ignition **OFF** and remove the key. Allow the engine to cool.

2. Remove the power steering pump belt and alternator belt, if necessary.

3. Loosen the tensioner bracket adjusting bolt and tensioner pulley center locknut to release the drive belt tension.

4. Remove the A/C belt.

To install:

5. Install the A/C belt, and make sure it is correctly seated on the pulleys.

6. Adjust the A/C belt tension/deflection by turning the tensioner bracket adjusting bolt. A new belt should deflect 0.33–0.39 in. (8.5–10mm), and a used belt should deflect 0.39–0.45 in. (10–11.5mm).

7. Tighten the tensioner pulley center locknut to 27–38 ft. lbs. (37–52 Nm).

8. Install and tension the alternator belt, if necessary, and the power steering pump belt.

9. Run the engine for 5 minutes and then recheck the belt deflection.

Serpentine (Navajo and B Series Pick-up)

♦ See Figures 61, 62, 63 and 64

All Navajo and B Series Pick-up engines utilize one wide-ribbed V-belt to drive the engine accessories such as the water pump, alternator, air conditioner compressor, air pump, etc. Because this belt uses a spring loaded tensioner for adjustment, belt replacement tends to be somewhat easier than on engines where accessories are pivoted and bolted in place for tension adjustment, such as the MPV. Basically, all belt replacement involves is to pivot the tensioner to loosen the belt, then slide the belt off of the pulleys. The two most important points are to pay CLOSE attention to the proper belt routing (since serpentine belts tend to be "snaked" all different ways through the pulleys) and to make sure the V-ribs are properly seated in all the pulleys.

Although belt routing diagrams have been included in this section, the first places you should check for proper belt routing are the labels in your engine compartment. These should include a belt routing diagram which may reflect changes made during a production run.

1. Disconnect the negative battery cable for safety. This will help assure that no one mistakenly cranks the engine over with your hands between the pulleys.

➡Take a good look at the installed belt and make a note of the routing. Before removing the belt, make sure the routing matches that of the belt routing label or one of the diagrams in this book. If for some reason a diagram does not match (you may not have the original engine or it may have been modified,) carefully note the changes on a piece of paper.

2. For tensioners equipped with a ½ inch square hole, insert the drive end of a large breaker bar into the hole. Use the breaker bar to pivot the tensioner away

Fig. 58 Loosen the A/C compressor belt idler pulley lockbolt using an open end wrench

Fig. 59 Loosen the A/C compressor belt idler pulley adjusting bolt just enough to be able to remove the belt

Fig. 60 Remove the A/C compressor belt

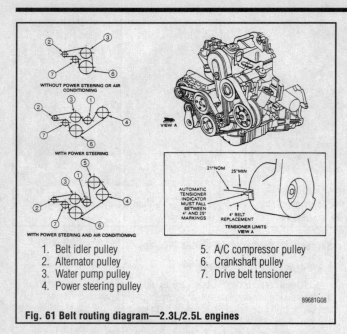

1. Belt idler pulley
2. Alternator pulley
3. Water pump pulley
4. Power steering pulley
5. A/C compressor pulley
6. Crankshaft pulley
7. Drive belt tensioner

Fig. 61 Belt routing diagram—2.3L/2.5L engines

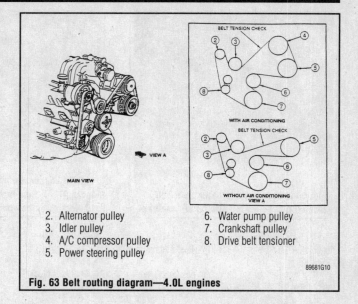

2. Alternator pulley
3. Idler pulley
4. A/C compressor pulley
5. Power steering pulley
6. Water pump pulley
7. Crankshaft pulley
8. Drive belt tensioner

Fig. 63 Belt routing diagram—4.0L engines

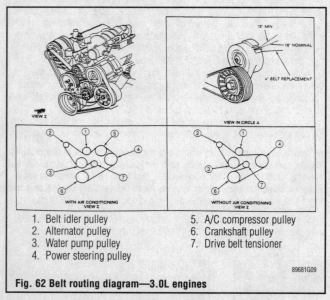

1. Belt idler pulley
2. Alternator pulley
3. Water pump pulley
4. Power steering pulley
5. A/C compressor pulley
6. Crankshaft pulley
7. Drive belt tensioner

Fig. 62 Belt routing diagram—3.0L engines

Fig. 64 Once the tension is relieved, slip the belt off the pulley then slowly release the tensioner

from the drive belt. For tensioners not equipped with this hole, use the proper-sized socket and breaker bar (or a large handled wrench) on the tensioner idler pulley center bolt to pivot the tensioner away from the belt. This will loosen the belt sufficiently that it can be pulled off of one or more of the pulleys. It is usually easiest to carefully pull the belt out from underneath the tensioner pulley itself.

3. Once the belt is off one of the pulleys, gently pivot the tensioner back into position. DO NOT allow the tensioner to snap back, as this could damage the tensioners internal parts.

4. Now finish removing the belt from the other pulleys and remove it from the engine.

To install:

5. While referring to the proper routing diagram (which you identified earlier), begin to route the belt over the pulleys, leaving whichever pulley you first released it from for last.

6. Once the belt is mostly in place, carefully pivot the tensioner and position the belt over the final pulley. As you begin to allow the tensioner back into contact with the belt, run your hand around the pulleys and make sure the belt is properly seated in the ribs. If not, release the tension and seat the belt.

7. Once the belt is installed, take another look at all the pulleys to double check your installation.

8. Connect the negative battery cable, then start and run the engine to check belt operation.

9. Once the engine has reached normal operating temperature, turn the ignition **OFF** and check that the belt tensioner arrow is within the proper adjustment range.

Timing Belts

SERVICING

➡ **Only the 2.3L B Series Pick-up and 3.0L MPV engines use a rubber timing belt. All other engines use a timing chain, and no periodic inspection is required.**

The 2.3L B Series Pick-up and 3.0L MPV engines utilizes a timing belt to drive the camshaft from the crankshaft's turning motion and to maintain proper valve timing. Some manufacturer's schedule periodic timing belt replacement to assure optimum engine performance, to make sure the motorist is never stranded should the belt break (as the engine will stop instantly) and for some (manufacturer's with interference motors) to prevent the possibility of severe internal engine damage should the belt break.

Although these engines are not listed as interference motors (a motor whose valves might contact the pistons if the camshaft was rotated separately from the crankshaft) the first 2 reasons for periodic replacement still apply. Mazda does not publish a replacement interval for this motor, but most belt manufacturers recommend intervals anywhere from 45,000 miles (72,500 km) to 90,000 miles (145,000 km). You will have to decide for yourself if the peace of mind offered by a new belt is worth it on higher mileage engines.

But whether or not you decide to replace it, you would be wise to check it periodically to make sure it has not become damaged or worn. Generally speaking, a severely damaged belt will show as engine performance would drop dramatically, but a damaged belt (which could give out suddenly) may not give as much warning. In general, any time the engine timing cover(s) is(are) removed you should inspect the belt for premature parting, severe cracks or missing teeth. Also, an access plug is provided in the upper portion of the timing cover so that camshaft timing can be checked without cover removal. If timing is found to be off, cover removal and further belt inspection or replacement is necessary.

Hoses

INSPECTION

▶ See Figures 65, 66, 67 and 68

Upper and lower radiator hoses along with the heater hoses should be checked for deterioration, leaks and loose hose clamps at least every 15,000 miles (24,000 km). It is also wise to check the hoses periodically in early spring and at the beginning of the fall or winter when you are performing other maintenance. A quick visual inspection could discover a weakened hose which might have left you stranded if it had remained unrepaired.

Whenever you are checking the hoses, make sure the engine and cooling system are cold. Visually inspect for cracking, rotting or collapsed hoses, and replace as necessary. Run your hand along the length of the hose. If a weak or swollen spot is noted when squeezing the hose wall, the hose should be replaced.

REMOVAL & INSTALLATION

▶ See Figures 69 and 70

✳✳ CAUTION

Never remove the pressure cap while the engine is running, or personal injury from scalding hot coolant or steam may result. If possible, wait until the engine has cooled to remove the pressure cap. If this is not possible, wrap a thick cloth around the pressure cap and turn it slowly to the stop. Step back while the pressure is released from the cooling system. When you are sure all the pressure has been released, use the cloth to turn and remove the cap.

1. Remove the radiator pressure cap.
2. Position a clean container under the radiator and/or engine draincock or plug, then open the drain and allow the cooling system to drain to an appropriate level. For some upper hoses, only a little coolant must be drained. To remove hoses positioned lower on the engine, such as a lower radiator hose, the entire cooling system must be emptied.
3. Loosen the hose clamps at each end of the hose requiring replacement. Clamps are usually either of the spring tension type (which require pliers to squeeze the tabs and loosen) or of the screw tension type (which require screw or hex drivers to loosen). Pull the clamps back on the hose away from the connection.
4. Twist, pull and slide the hose off the fitting, taking care not to damage the neck of the component from which the hose is being removed.

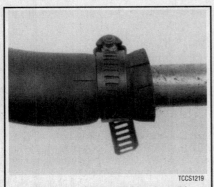

Fig. 65 The cracks developing along this hose are a result of age-related hardening

TCCS1219

Fig. 66 A hose clamp that is too tight can cause older hoses to separate and tear on either side of the clamp

TCCS1220

Fig. 67 A soft spongy hose (identifiable by the swollen section) will eventually burst and should be replaced

TCCS1221

Fig. 68 Hoses are likely to deteriorate from the inside if the cooling system is not periodically flushed

TCCS1222

Fig. 69 Squeeze the spring clamp with pliers and slide it away from hose fitting

89681P12

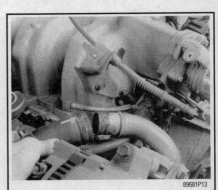

Fig. 70 Twist and pull the hose from the fitting to remove it.

89681P13

→If the hose is stuck at the connection, do not try to insert a screwdriver or other sharp tool under the hose end in an effort to free it, as the connection and/or hose may become damaged. Heater connections especially may be easily damaged by such a procedure. If the hose is to be replaced, use a single-edged razor blade to make a slice along the portion of the hose which is stuck on the connection, perpendicular to the end of the hose. Do not cut deep so as to prevent damaging the connection. The hose can then be peeled from the connection and discarded.

5. Clean both hose mounting connections. Inspect the condition of the hose clamps and replace them, if necessary.

To install:

6. Dip the ends of the new hose into clean engine coolant to ease installation.

7. Slide the clamps over the replacement hose, then slide the hose ends over the connections into position.

8. Position and secure the clamps at least ¼ in. (6.35mm) from the ends of the hose. Make sure they are located beyond the raised bead of the connector.

9. Close the radiator or engine drains and properly refill the cooling system with the clean drained engine coolant or a suitable mixture of ethylene glycol coolant and water.

10. If available, install a pressure tester and check for leaks. If a pressure tester is not available, run the engine until normal operating temperature is reached (allowing the system to naturally pressurize), then check for leaks.

✷✷ CAUTION

If you are checking for leaks with the system at normal operating temperature, BE EXTREMELY CAREFUL not to touch any moving or hot engine parts. Once temperature has been reached, shut the engine OFF, and check for leaks around the hose fittings and connections which were removed earlier.

CV-Boots

INSPECTION

◆ **See Figures 71 and 72**

The MPV and 1998 B Series Pick-up 4-wheel drive models use an Independent Front Suspension (IFS) drive axle which utilizes Constant Velocity (CV) joint equipped axle half-shafts. All other 4-wheel drive front axles are equipped with U-joints, which do not use a rubber boot to protect the joint and retain the grease.

The CV (Constant Velocity) boots should be checked for damage each time the oil is changed and any other time the vehicle is raised for service. These boots keep water, grime, dirt and other damaging matter from entering the CV-joints. Any of these could cause early CV-joint failure which can be expensive to repair. Heavy grease thrown around the inside of the front wheel(s) and on the brake caliper/drum can be an indication of a torn boot. Thoroughly check the boots for missing clamps and tears. If the boot is damaged, it should be replaced immediately. Please refer to Section 7 for procedures.

Spark Plugs

A typical spark plug consists of a metal shell surrounding a ceramic insulator. A metal electrode extends downward through the center of the insulator and protrudes a small distance. Located at the end of the plug and attached to the side of the outer metal shell is the side electrode. The side electrode bends in at a 90⁻ angle so that its tip is just past and parallel to the tip of the center electrode. The distance between these two electrodes (measured in thousandths of an inch or hundredths of a millimeter) is called the spark plug gap.

The spark plug does not produce a spark but instead provides a gap across which the current can arc. The coil produces anywhere from 20,000 to 50,000 volts (depending on the type and application) which travels through the wires to the spark plugs. The current passes along the center electrode and jumps the gap to the side electrode, and in doing so, ignites the air/fuel mixture in the combustion chamber.

SPARK PLUG HEAT RANGE

◆ **See Figure 73**

Spark plug heat range is the ability of the plug to dissipate heat. The longer the insulator (or the farther it extends into the engine), the hotter the plug will operate; the shorter the insulator (the closer the electrode is to the block's cooling passages) the cooler it will operate. A plug that absorbs little heat and remains too cool will quickly accumulate deposits of oil and carbon since it is not hot enough to burn them off. This leads to plug fouling and consequently to misfiring. A plug that absorbs too much heat will have no deposits but, due to the excessive heat, the electrodes will burn away quickly and might possibly lead to preignition or other ignition problems. Preignition takes place when plug tips get so hot that they glow sufficiently to ignite the air/fuel mixture before the actual spark occurs. This early ignition will usually cause a pinging during low speeds and heavy loads.

The general rule of thumb for choosing the correct heat range when picking a spark plug is: if most of your driving is long distance, high speed travel, use a colder plug; if most of your driving is stop and go, use a hotter plug. Original equipment plugs are generally a good compromise between the 2 styles and most people never have the need to change their plugs from the factory-recommended heat range.

REMOVAL & INSTALLATION

◆ **See Figures 74, 75 and 76**

→**Mazda recommends replacing standard spark plugs every 30,000 miles (48,000km) and platinum plugs every 60,000 miles (96,000km).**

A set of spark plugs usually requires replacement after about 20,000–30,000 miles (32,000–48,000km), depending on your style of driving. In normal operation plug gap increases about 0.001 in. (0.025mm) for every 2500 miles (4000km). As the gap increases, the plug's voltage requirement also increases. It requires a greater voltage to jump the wider gap and about two to three times as much voltage to fire the plug at high speeds than at idle. The improved air/fuel ratio control of modern fuel injection combined with the higher voltage output of modern ignition systems will often allow an engine to run significantly

Fig. 71 CV-boots must be inspected periodically for damage

TCCS1011

Fig. 72 A torn boot should be replaced immediately

TCCS1010

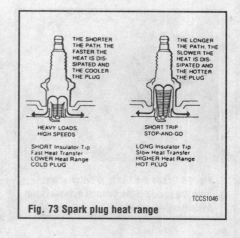

THE SHORTER THE PATH, THE FASTER THE HEAT IS DISSIPATED AND THE COOLER THE PLUG

THE LONGER THE PATH, THE SLOWER THE HEAT IS DISSIPATED AND THE HOTTER THE PLUG

HEAVY LOADS, HIGH SPEEDS

SHORT TRIP STOP-AND-GO

SHORT Insulator Tip
Fast Heat Transfer
LOWER Heat Range
COLD PLUG

LONG Insulator Tip
Slow Heat Transfer
HIGHER Heat Range
HOT PLUG

TCCS1046

Fig. 73 Spark plug heat range

Fig. 74 Remove the spark plug wire boot from the spark plug

Fig. 75 Using a spark plug socket, an extension and a ratchet, unscrew the spark plug from the cylinder head . . .

Fig. 76 . . . then pull the socket and spark plug straight out from the cylinder head

longer on a set of standard spark plugs, but keep in mind that efficiency will drop as the gap widens (along with fuel economy and power).

When you're removing spark plugs, work on one at a time. Don't start by removing the plug wires all at once, because, unless you number them, they may become mixed up. Take a minute before you begin and number the wires with tape. Also, an anti-seize compound should be used before installing the plugs into the cylinder head.

1. Disconnect the negative battery cable, and if the vehicle has been run recently, allow the engine to thoroughly cool.

2. Carefully twist the spark plug wire boot to loosen it, then pull upward and remove the boot from the plug. Be sure to pull on the boot and not on the wire, otherwise the connector located inside the boot may become separated.

3. Using compressed air, blow any water or debris from the spark plug well to assure that no harmful contaminants are allowed to enter the combustion chamber when the spark plug is removed. If compressed air is not available, use a rag or a brush to clean the area.

➡Remove the spark plugs when the engine is cold, if possible, to prevent damage to the threads. If removal of the plugs is difficult, apply a few drops of penetrating oil or silicone spray to the area around the base of the plug, and allow it a few minutes to work.

4. Using a spark plug socket that is equipped with a rubber insert to properly hold the plug, turn the spark plug counterclockwise to loosen and remove the spark plug from the bore.

✳✳ WARNING

Be sure not to use a flexible extension on the socket. Use of a flexible extension may allow a shear force to be applied to the plug. A shear force could break the plug off in the cylinder head, leading to costly and frustrating repairs.

To install:

5. Inspect the spark plug boot for tears or damage. If a damaged boot is found, the spark plug wire must be replaced.

6. Using a wire feeler gauge, check and adjust the spark plug gap. When using a gauge, the proper size should pass between the electrodes with a slight drag. The next larger size should not be able to pass while the next smaller size should pass freely.

➡Coat the spark plug threads with an anti-seize compound before installing it into the cylinder head.

7. Carefully thread the plug into the bore by hand. If resistance is felt before the plug is almost completely threaded, back the plug out and begin threading again. In small, hard to reach areas, an old spark plug wire and boot could be used as a threading tool. The boot will hold the plug while you twist the end of the wire and the wire is supple enough to twist before it would allow the plug to crossthread.

✳✳ WARNING

Do not use the spark plug socket to thread the plugs. Always carefully thread the plug by hand or using an old plug wire to prevent the possibility of crossthreading and damaging the cylinder head bore.

8. Carefully tighten the spark plug. If the plug you are installing is equipped with a crush washer, seat the plug, then tighten about ¼ turn to crush the washer. If you are installing a tapered seat plug, tighten the plug to specifications provided by the vehicle or plug manufacturer.

9. Apply a small amount of silicone dielectric compound to the end of the spark plug lead or inside the spark plug boot to prevent sticking, then install the boot to the spark plug and push until it clicks into place. The click may be felt or heard, then gently pull back on the boot to assure proper contact.

INSPECTION & GAPPING

◆ **See Figures 77, 78, 79 and 80**

Check the plugs for deposits and wear. If they are not going to be replaced, clean the plugs thoroughly. Remember that any kind of deposit will decrease the efficiency of the plug. Plugs can be cleaned on a spark plug cleaning machine, which can sometimes be found in service stations, or you can do an acceptable

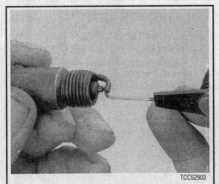

Fig. 77 Checking the spark plug gap with a feeler gauge

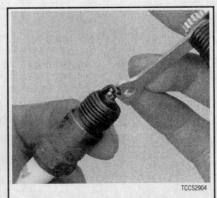

Fig. 78 Adjusting the spark plug gap

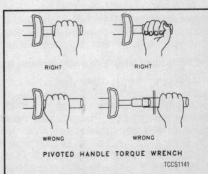

RIGHT   RIGHT

WRONG   WRONG

PIVOTED HANDLE TORQUE WRENCH

Fig. 79 If the standard plug is in good condition, the electrode may be filed flat—WARNING: do not file platinum plugs

A **normally worn** spark plug should have light tan or gray deposits on the firing tip.

A **carbon fouled** plug, identified by soft, sooty, black deposits, may indicate an improperly tuned vehicle. Check the air cleaner, ignition components and engine control system.

This spark plug has been **left in the engine too long**, as evidenced by the extreme gap- Plugs with such an extreme gap can cause misfiring and stumbling accompanied by a noticeable lack of power.

An **oil fouled** spark plug indicates an engine with worn poston rings and/or bad valve seals allowing excessive oil to enter the chamber.

A **physically damaged** spark plug may be evidence of severe detonation in that cylinder. Watch that cylinder carefully between services, as a continued detonation will not only damage the plug, but could also damage the engine.

A **bridged or almost bridged** spark plug, identified by a build-up between the electrodes caused by excessive carbon or oil build-up on the plug.

TCCA1P40

Fig. 80 Inspect the spark plug to determine engine running conditions

job of cleaning with a stiff brush. If the plugs are cleaned, the electrodes must be filed flat. Use an ignition points file, not an emery board or the like, which will leave deposits. The electrodes must be filed perfectly flat with sharp edges; rounded edges reduce the spark plug voltage by as much as 50%.

Check spark plug gap before installation. The ground electrode (the L-shaped one connected to the body of the plug) must be parallel to the center electrode and the specified size wire gauge (please refer to the Tune-Up Specifications chart for details) must pass between the electrodes with a slight drag.

➡**NEVER adjust the gap on a used platinum type spark plug.**

Always check the gap on new plugs as they are not always set correctly at the factory. Do not use a flat feeler gauge when measuring the gap on a used plug, because the reading may be inaccurate. A round-wire type gapping tool is the best way to check the gap. The correct gauge should pass through the electrode gap with a slight drag. If you're in doubt, try one size smaller and one larger. The smaller gauge should go through easily, while the larger one shouldn't go through at all. Wire gapping tools usually have a bending tool attached. Use that to adjust the side electrode until the proper distance is obtained. Absolutely never attempt to bend the center electrode. Also, be careful not to bend the side electrode too far or too often as it may weaken and break off within the engine, requiring removal of the cylinder head to retrieve it.

Spark Plug Wires

TESTING

▶ **See Figure 81**

➡Only test one spark plug wire at a time. When the check is complete return the plug wire to its original location. If the wire is defective and more wires are to be checked, mark the wire as such, return it to its original location, then inspect the other wires. Once all of the wires are checked, replace the defective wires one at a time. This will avoid any mix-ups.

1. Visually inspect the spark plug wires for burns, cuts or breaks in the insulation. Check the spark plug boots and the nipples on the coil. Replace any damaged wiring.

2. Inspect the spark plug wires to insure that they are firmly seated on the coil pack.

3. Disconnect the spark plug wire thought to be defective at the spark plug.

4. Using an ohmmeter, measure the resistance between the coil terminal and the spark plug terminal.

Fig. 81 Checking individual plug wire resistance with a digital ohmmeter

➡ **Never, under any circumstances, measure resistance by puncturing the spark plug wire.**

5. If the measured resistance is less than 7000 ohms per foot of wire, the wire is good. If the measured resistance is greater than 7000 ohms per foot, the wire is defective and should be replaced.

REMOVAL & INSTALLATION

▶ **See Figures 82 and 83**

When removing spark plug wires, use great care. Grasp and twist the insulator back and forth on the spark plug to free the insulator. Do not pull on the

Fig. 82 Note that the spark plug wires and distributor cap are numbered for correct wiring placement at the factory (C refers to ignition coil wire)

wire directly as it may become separated from the connector inside the insulator.

To install:

➡ **Whenever a high tension wire is removed for any reason form a spark plug, coil or distributor terminal housing, silicone grease must be applied to the boot before it is reconnected. Using a small clean tool, coat the entire interior surface of the boot with silicone grease or an equivalent.**

1. Install each wire in or on the proper terminal of the coil pack or distributor cap. Be sure the terminal connector inside the insulator is fully seated. The No. 1 terminal is identified on the cap.
2. Remove wire separators from old wire set and install them on new set in approximately same position.
3. Connect wires to proper spark plugs. Be certain all wires are fully seated on terminals.

Distributor Cap and Rotor

➡ **2.6L, 3.0L MPV and 1994 B Series Pick-up engines use a distributor equipped ignition system. All other models use a distributorless ignition.**

REMOVAL & INSTALLATION

Distributor Cap

▶ **See Figures 84 and 85**

1. As a precaution, label all of the spark plug wires with their perspective cylinder number.
2. Loosen the cap hold-down screws.
3. Remove the cap by lifting straight up to prevent damage to the rotor blade and spring.

➡ **If the plug wires do not have enough slack to allow cap removal, confirm that they are properly labeled and remove them from the cap.**

4. Installation is the reverse of the removal procedure. Note the position of the square alignment locator, or keyway, and tighten the hold-down screws.

Distributor Rotor

▶ **See Figure 86**

1. Remove the distributor cap.
2. Pull straight up on the rotor to disengage it from the shaft and armature.
3. Installation is the reverse of the removal procedure. Align the locating boss on the rotor with the hole on the armature, or the flat on the shaft, then insure that it is fully seated on the shaft.

Fig. 83 Be sure to number all the spark plug wires to the correct terminal on the distributor cap before disconnecting them

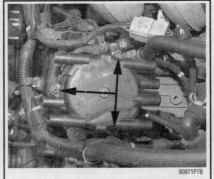

Fig. 84 Loosen the three distributor cap retaining screws . . .

Fig. 85 . . . then remove the cap from the distributor

Fig. 86 After removing the distributor cap, pull the rotor straight up and off of the distributor shaft

INSPECTION

Distributor Cap

▶ **See Figure 87**

1. Wash the inside and outside surfaces of the cap with soap and water then dry it with compressed air.
2. Inspect the cap for cracks, broken or worn carbon button, or carbon tracks. Also inspect the cap terminals for dirt and corrosion.
3. Replace the cap if any of the above conditions are observed.

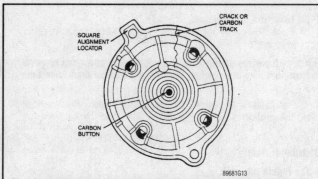

Fig. 87 Inspection points for the distributor cap—note the square alignment locator which limits the cap to one installation position

Distributor Rotor

▶ **See Figure 88**

1. Wash the rotor with soap and water then dry with it compressed air.
2. Inspect the rotor for cracks, carbon tracks, burns or damage to the blade or spring.
3. Replace the rotor if any of the above conditions are observed.

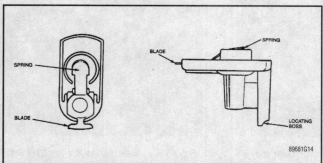

Fig. 88 Inspection points for the distributor rotor—note that some rotors have a locating boss which fits in the armature

Ignition Timing

➡ **No periodic checking or adjustment of the ignition timing is necessary for any of the vehicles covered by this manual. However, the distributor ignition system used by 1994 B Series Pick-ups with 3.0L engines and all MPV models can be adjusted, should the distributor be removed and installed or otherwise disturbed.**

GENERAL INFORMATION

Ignition timing is the measurement, in degrees of crankshaft rotation, of the point at which the spark plugs fire in each of the cylinders. It is measured in degrees before or after Top Dead Center (TDC) of the compression stroke.

Because it takes a fraction of a second for the spark plug to ignite the mixture in the cylinder, the spark plug must fire a little before the piston reaches TDC. Otherwise, the mixture will not be completely ignited as the piston passes TDC and the full power of the explosion will not be used by the engine.

The timing measurement is given in degrees of crankshaft rotation before the piston reaches TDC (BTDC). If the setting for the ignition timing is 5° BTDC, the spark plug must fire 5° before each piston reaches TDC. This only holds true, however, when the engine is at idle speed.

As the engine speed increases, the pistons go faster. The spark plugs have to ignite the fuel even sooner if it is to be completely ignited when the piston reaches TDC. On all engines covered by this manual, spark timing changes are accomplished electronically by the engine and ignition control computers.

If the ignition is set too far advanced (BTDC), the ignition and expansion of the fuel in the cylinder will occur too soon and tend to force the piston down while it is still traveling up. This causes engine ping. If the ignition spark is set too far retarded, after TDC (ATDC), the piston will have already passed TDC and started on its way down when the fuel is ignited. This will cause the piston to be forced down for only a portion of its travel. This will result in poor engine performance and lack of power.

Timing marks consisting of 0 marks or scales can be found on the rim of the crankshaft pulley and the timing cover. The mark(s) on the pulley correspond(s) to the position of the piston in the number 1 cylinder. A stroboscopic (dynamic) timing light is used, which is hooked into the circuit of the No. 1 cylinder spark plug. Every time the spark plug fires, the timing light flashes. By aiming the timing light at the timing marks while the engine is running, the exact position of the piston within the cylinder can be easily read since the stroboscopic flash makes the pulley appear to be standing still. Proper timing is indicated when the mark and scale are in proper alignment.

Because these vehicles utilize high voltage, electronic ignition systems, only a timing light with an inductive pickup should be used. This pickup simply clamps onto the No. 1 spark plug wire, eliminating the adapter. It is not susceptible to cross-firing or false triggering, which may occur with a conventional light, due to the greater voltages produced by electronic ignition.

INSPECTION & ADJUSTMENT

1994 B Series Pick-up With 3.0L Engine

▶ **See Figure 89**

➡ **Always refer to the Vehicle Emission Information Label in the engine compartment to verify the timing adjustment procedure.**

1. Place automatic transmission in **PARK** or manual transmission in **NEUTRAL**. The air conditioning and heater controls and all accessories should be in the **OFF** position.
2. Connect an inductive timing light and tachometer to the engine, according to the manufacturer's instructions.
3. Disconnect the single wire in-line spout connector or remove the shorting bar from the double wire spout connector.
4. Start the engine and bring to normal operating temperature.

➡ **To set timing correctly, a remote starter should not be used. Use the ignition key only to start the vehicle. Disconnecting the start wire at the starter relay will cause the TFI module to revert to start mode timing after the vehicle is started. Reconnecting the start wire after the vehicle is running will not correct the timing.**

5. Check the idle speed, and adjust if needed.

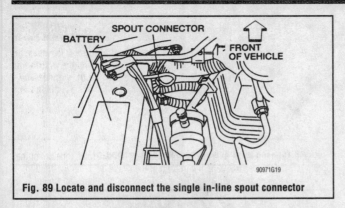

Fig. 89 Locate and disconnect the single in-line spout connector

6. Check the initial timing by aiming the timing light at the timing marks and pointer. Refer to the underhood emission label for specifications.

7. If the marks do not align, shut off the engine and loosen the distributor hold-down bolt. Start the engine, aim the timing light and turn the distributor until the timing marks align. Shut off the engine and tighten the distributor hold-down bolt.

8. Reconnect the single wire in-line spout connector or reinstall the shorting bar on the double wire spout connector. Check the timing advance to verify the distributor is advancing beyond the initial setting.

9. Remove the timing light and tachometer.

MPV Model With 2.6L Engine

◆ See Figures 90 and 91

1. Apply the parking brake and place the gearshift lever in **P**.

2. Start the engine and bring to normal operating temperature. Make sure all electrical loads and the A/C switch are **OFF**.

3. Connect a timing light and connect a tachometer to the **IG** terminal of the diagnostic connector.

4. Connect a jumper wire between the **TEN** and **GND** terminals of the diagnostic connector.

5. Check the idle speed and adjust, if necessary. The idle speed should be 780–820 rpm.

6. Aim the timing light at the timing scale on the timing belt cover and the timing mark on the crankshaft pulley. The timing should be 4–6 degrees BTDC.

7. If the timing is not as specified, loosen the distributor mounting bolt and turn the distributor to adjust. After adjustment, tighten the bolt to 19 ft. lbs. (25 Nm) and recheck the timing.

8. Remove the jumper wire and all test equipment.

MPV Model With 3.0L Engine

1994–95

◆ See Figures 90 and 91

1. Apply the parking brake and place the gearshift lever in **P**.

2. Start the engine and bring to normal operating temperature. Make sure all electrical loads and the A/C switch are **OFF**.

3. Connect a timing light and connect a tachometer to the **IG** terminal of the diagnostic connector.

4. Connect a jumper wire between the **TEN** and **GND** terminals of the diagnostic connector.

5. Check the idle speed and adjust, if necessary. The idle speed should be 780–820 rpm.

6. Aim the timing light at the timing scale on the timing belt cover and the timing mark on the crankshaft pulley. The timing should be 4–6 degrees BTDC.

7. If the timing is not as specified, loosen the distributor mounting bolt and turn the distributor to adjust. After adjustment, tighten the bolt to 19 ft. lbs. (25 Nm) and recheck the timing.

8. Remove the jumper wire and all test equipment.

1996–98

◆ See Figures 91 and 92

1. Apply the parking brake and place the gearshift lever in **P**.

2. Start the engine and bring to normal operating temperature. Make sure all electrical loads and the A/C switch are **OFF**.

3. Connect a timing light to the high-tension lead No. 1.

4. Connect the SST 49 B019 9A0 (system selector) to the data link connector.

5. Set the switch A to position No. 1 and set the test switch to SELF TEST. Verify that the idle speed is within specifications. If not, adjust it. Specification is 500–900 rpm.

6. Verify that the timing mark (yellow) is within the specification. Specification is BTDC 10–12°.

7. If not as specified, loosen the distributor lock bolts and turn the distributor to make the adjustment.

8. Tighten the distributor lock bolts to 14–18 ft. lbs. (19–25 Nm).

9. Disconnect the SST (system selector) and verify that the timing mark (yellow) is within specification. Specification is ATDC 2–BTDC 34°.

10. Stop the engine and disconnect the timing light.

Valve Lash

No periodic valve lash adjustments are necessary on these engines. All the engines utilize hydraulic valvetrains to automatically maintain proper valve lash.

Idle Speed and Mixture Adjustments

NAVAJO & B SERIES PICK-UP MODELS

The engines covered by this manual utilize sophisticated multi-port fuel injection systems in which an engine control computer utilizes information from various sensors to control idle speed and air fuel mixtures. No periodic adjustments are either necessary or possible on these systems. If a problem is suspected, please refer to Sections 4 and 5 of this manual for more information on electronic engine controls and fuel injection.

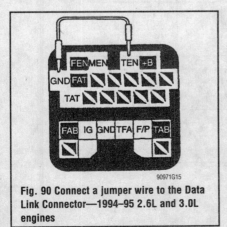

Fig. 90 Connect a jumper wire to the Data Link Connector—1994–95 2.6L and 3.0L engines

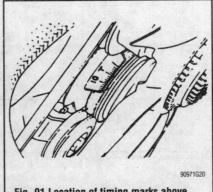

Fig. 91 Location of timing marks above the crankshaft pulley

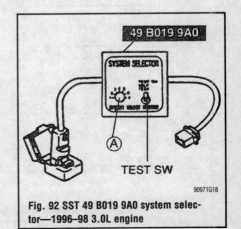

Fig. 92 SST 49 B019 9A0 system selector—1996–98 3.0L engine

MPV MODELS

The air/fuel mixture is computer controlled according to the needs of the engine and is not adjustable. If the air/fuel mixture is too lean or too rich, other problems with the engine and/or engine control system exist. The following adjustment applies only to the idle speed.

1994–95

♦ **See Figures 90, 93 and 94**

1. Apply the parking brake. Place the shift lever in **P**.
2. Start the engine and bring to normal operating temperature. Make sure all accessories are **OFF**.
3. Connect a tachometer to the engine according to the manufacturer's instructions.
4. Check the idle speed and adjust, if necessary; it should be 750–790 rpm for 2.6L engines or 780–820 rpm for 3.0L engines.
5. Connect a jumper wire between the **TEN** terminal and the **GND** terminal of the data link connector.
6. Adjust the idle speed by turning the air adjusting screw.
7. Remove the jumper wire.
8. Remove all test equipment.

1996–98

♦ **See Figures 92 and 93**

1. Apply the parking brake and place the gearshift lever in **P**.
2. Start the engine and bring to normal operating temperature. Make sure all electrical loads and the A/C switch are **OFF**.
3. Connect a tachometer to the engine according to the manufacturer's instructions.
4. Connect the SST 49 B019 9A0 (system selector) to the data link connector.
5. Set the switch A to position No. 1 and set the test switch to SELF TEST. Verify that the idle speed is within 760–800 rpm.
6. Adjust the idle speed by turning the air adjusting screw.
7. Remove all test equipment.

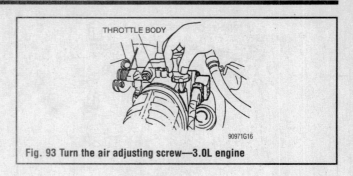

Fig. 93 Turn the air adjusting screw—3.0L engine

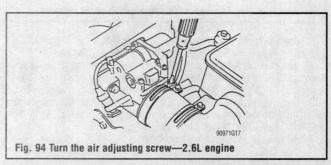

Fig. 94 Turn the air adjusting screw—2.6L engine

Windshield Wipers

ELEMENT (REFILL) CARE & REPLACEMENT

♦ **See Figures 95, 96 and 97**

For maximum effectiveness and longest element life, the windshield and wiper blades should be kept clean. Dirt, tree sap, road tar and so on will cause

TUNE-UP SPECIFICATIONS

Year	Engine ID/VIN	Engine Displacement Liters (cc)	Spark Plugs Gap (in.)	Ignition Timing (deg.) MT	Ignition Timing (deg.) AT	Fuel Pump (psi)	Idle Speed (rpm) MT	Idle Speed (rpm) AT	Valve Clearance In.	Valve Clearance Ex.
1994	A	2.3 (2298)	0.044	8-12B	8-12B	35-45	525-575	525-575	HYD	HYD
	G6	2.6 (2606)	0.041	—	4-6B	30-37	—	750-790	HYD	HYD
	JE	3.0 (2954)	0.041	—	10-12B	30-37	—	780-820	HYD	HYD
	U	3.0 (2968)	0.044	8-12B	8-12B	35-45	①	①	HYD	HYD
	X	4.0 (4016)	0.054	8-12B	8-12B	35-45	①	①	HYD	HYD
1995	A	2.3 (2298)	0.044	8-12B	8-12B	35-45	①	①	HYD	HYD
	G6	2.6 (2606)	0.041	—	4-6B	30-36	—	750-790	HYD	HYD
	JE	3.0 (2954)	0.041	—	10-12B	30-36	—	780-820	HYD	HYD
	U	3.0 (2968)	0.044	8-12B	8-12B	35-40	①	①	HYD	HYD
	X	4.0 (4016)	0.054	8-12B	8-12B	35-40	①	①	HYD	HYD
1996	A	2.3 (2298)	0.044	8-12B	8-12B	35-40	①	①	HYD	HYD
	JE	3.0 (2954)	0.041	—	10-12B	30-36	—	760-800	HYD	HYD
	U	3.0 (2968)	0.044	8-12B	8-12B	35-40	①	①	HYD	HYD
	X	4.0 (4016)	0.054	8-12B	8-12B	35-40	①	①	HYD	HYD
1997	A	2.3 (2298)	0.044	8-12B	8-12B	35-40	①	①	HYD	HYD
	JE	3.0 (2954)	0.041	—	10-12B	31-38	—	①	HYD	HYD
	U	3.0 (2968)	0.044	8-12B	8-12B	35-40	①	①	HYD	HYD
	X	4.0 (4016)	0.054	8-12B	8-12B	35-40	①	①	HYD	HYD
1998	C	2.5 (2500)	0.044	10B	10B	56-72	①	①	HYD	HYD
	JE	3.0 (2954)	0.041	—	10-12B	31-38	—	①	HYD	HYD
	U	3.0 (2968)	0.044	10B	10B	56-72	①	①	HYD	HYD
	X	4.0 (4016)	0.054	NA	NA	56-72	①	①	HYD	HYD

NOTE: The Vehicle Emission Control Information (VECI) label often reflects specification changes made during production.
The label must be used if they differ from those in this chart

B - Before top dead center
HYD - Hydraulic
① Idle speed is electronically controlled and cannot be adjusted
NA- Not Available

90971C04

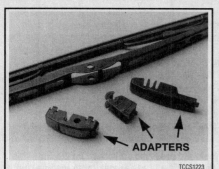

Fig. 95 Most aftermarket blades are available with multiple adapters to fit different vehicles

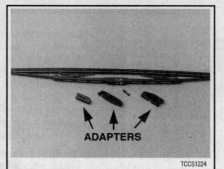

Fig. 96 Choose a blade which will fit your vehicle, and that will be readily available next time you need blades

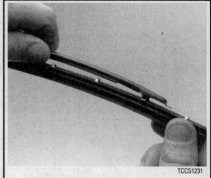

Fig. 97 When installed, be certain the blade is fully inserted into the backing

streaking, smearing and blade deterioration if left on the glass. It is advisable to wash the windshield carefully with a commercial glass cleaner at least once a month. Wipe off the rubber blades with the wet rag afterwards. Do not attempt to move wipers across the windshield by hand; damage to the motor and drive mechanism will result.

To inspect and/or replace the wiper blade elements, place the wiper switch in the **LOW** speed position and the ignition switch in the **ACC** position. When the wiper blades are approximately vertical on the windshield, turn the ignition switch to **OFF**.

Examine the wiper blade elements. If they are found to be cracked, broken or torn, they should be replaced immediately. Replacement intervals will vary with usage, although ozone deterioration usually limits element life to about one year. If the wiper pattern is smeared or streaked, or if the blade chatters across the glass, the elements should be replaced. It is easiest and most sensible to replace the elements in pairs.

If your vehicle is equipped with aftermarket blades, there are several different types of refills and your vehicle might have any kind. Aftermarket blades and arms rarely use the exact same type blade or refill as the original equipment.

Regardless of the type of refill used, be sure to follow the part manufacturer's instructions closely. Make sure that all of the frame jaws are engaged as the refill is pushed into place and locked. If the metal blade holder and frame are allowed to touch the glass during wiper operation, the glass will be scratched.

Tires and Wheels

Common sense and good driving habits will afford maximum tire life. Make sure that you don't overload the vehicle or run with incorrect pressure in the tires. Either of these will increase tread wear. Fast starts, sudden stops and sharp cornering are hard on tires and will shorten their useful life span.

➡**For optimum tire life, keep the tires properly inflated, rotate them often and have the wheel alignment checked periodically.**

Inspect your tires frequently. Be especially careful to watch for bubbles in the tread or sidewall, deep cuts or underinflation. Replace any tires with bubbles in the sidewall. If cuts are so deep that they penetrate to the cords, discard the tire. Any cut in the sidewall of a radial tire renders it unsafe. Also look for uneven tread wear patterns that may indicate the front end is out of alignment or that the tires are out of balance.

TIRE ROTATION

▶ **See Figure 98**

Tires must be rotated periodically to equalize wear patterns that vary with a tire's position on the vehicle. Tires will also wear in an uneven way as the front steering/suspension system wears to the point where the alignment should be reset.

Rotating the tires will ensure maximum life for the tires as a set, so you will not have to discard a tire early due to wear on only part of the tread. Regular rotation is required to equalize wear.

When rotating "unidirectional tires," make sure that they always roll in the same direction. This means that a tire used on the left side of the vehicle must not be switched to the right side and vice-versa. Such tires should only be

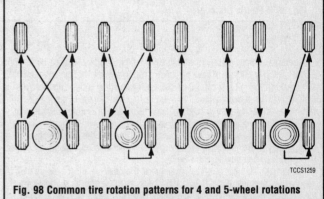

Fig. 98 Common tire rotation patterns for 4 and 5-wheel rotations

rotated front-to-rear or rear-to-front, while always remaining on the same side of the vehicle. These tires are marked on the sidewall as to the direction of rotation; observe the marks when reinstalling the tire(s).

Some styled or "mag" wheels may have different offsets front to rear. In these cases, the rear wheels must not be used up front and vice-versa. Furthermore, if these wheels are equipped with unidirectional tires, they cannot be rotated unless the tire is remounted for the proper direction of rotation.

➡**The compact or space-saver spare is strictly for emergency use. It must never be included in the tire rotation or placed on the vehicle for everyday use.**

TIRE DESIGN

▶ **See Figure 99**

For maximum satisfaction, tires should be used in sets of four. Mixing of different brands or types (radial, bias-belted, fiberglass belted) should be avoided. In most cases, the vehicle manufacturer has designated a type of tire on which the vehicle will perform best. Your first choice when replacing tires should be to use the same type of tire that the manufacturer recommends.

When radial tires are used, tire sizes and wheel diameters should be selected to maintain ground clearance and tire load capacity equivalent to the original specified tire. Radial tires should always be used in sets of four.

※※ CAUTION

Radial tires should never be used on only the front axle.

When selecting tires, pay attention to the original size as marked on the tire. Most tires are described using an industry size code sometimes referred to as P-Metric. This allows the exact identification of the tire specifications, regardless of the manufacturer. If selecting a different tire size or brand, remember to check the installed tire for any sign of interference with the body or suspension while the vehicle is stopping, turning sharply or heavily loaded.

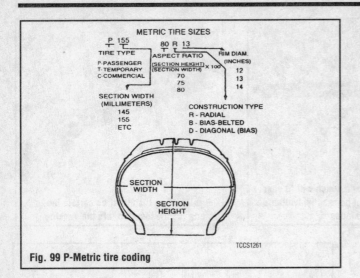

Fig. 99 P-Metric tire coding

Snow Tires

Good radial tires can produce a big advantage in slippery weather, but in snow, a street radial tire does not have sufficient tread to provide traction and control. The small grooves of a street tire quickly pack with snow and the tire behaves like a billiard ball on a marble floor. The more open, chunky tread of a snow tire will self-clean as the tire turns, providing much better grip on snowy surfaces.

To satisfy municipalities requiring snow tires during weather emergencies, most snow tires carry either an M + S designation after the tire size stamped on the sidewall, or the designation "all-season." In general, no change in tire size is necessary when buying snow tires.

Most manufacturers strongly recommend the use of 4 snow tires on their vehicles for reasons of stability. If snow tires are fitted only to the drive wheels, the opposite end of the vehicle may become very unstable when braking or turning on slippery surfaces. This instability can lead to unpleasant endings if the driver can't counteract the slide in time.

Note that snow tires, whether 2 or 4, will affect vehicle handling in all non-snow situations. The stiffer, heavier snow tires will noticeably change the turning and braking characteristics of the vehicle. Once the snow tires are installed, you must re-learn the behavior of the vehicle and drive accordingly.

➡ Consider buying extra wheels on which to mount the snow tires. Once done, the "snow wheels" can be installed and removed as needed. This eliminates the potential damage to tires or wheels from seasonal removal and installation. Even if your vehicle has styled wheels, see if inexpensive steel wheels are available. Although the look of the vehicle will change, the expensive wheels will be protected from salt, curb hits and pothole damage.

TIRE STORAGE

If they are mounted on wheels, store the tires at proper inflation pressure. All tires should be kept in a cool, dry place. If they are stored in the garage or basement, do not let them stand on a concrete floor; set them on strips of wood, a mat or a large stack of newspaper. Keeping them away from direct moisture is of paramount importance. Tires should not be stored upright, but in a flat position.

INFLATION & INSPECTION

◗ **See Figures 100 thru 105**

The importance of proper tire inflation cannot be overemphasized. A tire employs air as part of its structure. It is designed around the supporting strength of the air at a specified pressure. For this reason, improper inflation drastically reduces the tire's ability to perform as intended. A tire will lose some air in day-to-day use; having to add a few pounds of air periodically is not necessarily a sign of a leaking tire.

Two items should be a permanent fixture in every glove compartment: an accurate tire pressure gauge and a tread depth gauge. Check the tire pressure (including the spare) regularly with a pocket type gauge. Too often, the gauge

on the end of the air hose at your corner garage is not accurate because it suffers too much abuse. Always check tire pressure when the tires are cold, as pressure increases with temperature. If you must move the vehicle to check the tire inflation, do not drive more than a mile before checking. A cold tire is generally one that has not been driven for more than three hours.

A plate or sticker is normally provided somewhere in the vehicle (door post, hood, tailgate or trunk lid) which shows the proper pressure for the tires. Never counteract excessive pressure build-up by bleeding off air pressure (letting some air out). This will cause the tire to run hotter and wear quicker.

✳✳ CAUTION

Never exceed the maximum tire pressure embossed on the tire! This is the pressure to be used when the tire is at maximum loading, but it is rarely the correct pressure for everyday driving. Consult the owner's manual or the tire pressure sticker for the correct tire pressure.

Once you've maintained the correct tire pressures for several weeks, you'll be familiar with the vehicle's braking and handling personality. Slight adjustments in tire pressures can fine-tune these characteristics, but never change the cold pressure specification by more than 2 psi. A slightly softer tire pressure will give a softer ride but also yield lower fuel mileage. A slightly harder tire will give crisper dry road handling but can cause skidding on wet surfaces. Unless you're fully attuned to the vehicle, stick to the recommended inflation pressures.

All automotive tires have built-in tread wear indicator bars that show up as ½ in. (13mm) wide smooth bands across the tire when 1/16 in. (1.5mm) of tread remains. The appearance of tread wear indicators means that the tires should be replaced. In fact, many states have laws prohibiting the use of tires with less than this amount of tread.

You can check your own tread depth with an inexpensive gauge or by using a Lincoln head penny. Slip the Lincoln penny (with Lincoln's head upside-down) into several tread grooves. If you can see the top of Lincoln's head in 2 adjacent grooves, the tire has less than 1/16 in. (1.5mm) tread left and should be replaced. You can measure snow tires in the same manner by using the "tails" side of the Lincoln penny. If you can see the top of the Lincoln memorial, it's time to replace the snow tire(s).

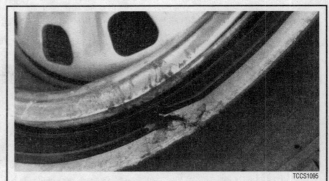

Fig. 100 Tires with deep cuts, or cuts which bulge, should be replaced immediately

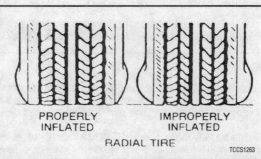

Fig. 101 Radial tires have a characteristic sidewall bulge; don't try to measure pressure by looking at the tire. Use a quality air pressure gauge

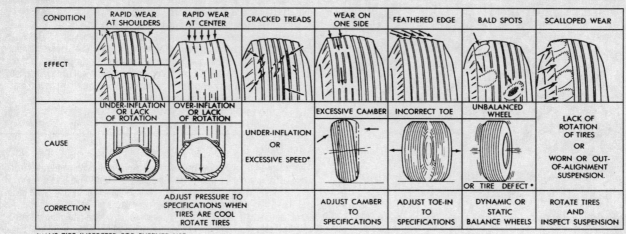

CONDITION	RAPID WEAR AT SHOULDERS	RAPID WEAR AT CENTER	CRACKED TREADS	WEAR ON ONE SIDE	FEATHERED EDGE	BALD SPOTS	SCALLOPED WEAR
EFFECT							
CAUSE	UNDER-INFLATION OR LACK OF ROTATION	OVER-INFLATION OR LACK OF ROTATION	UNDER-INFLATION OR EXCESSIVE SPEED*	EXCESSIVE CAMBER	INCORRECT TOE	UNBALANCED WHEEL OR TIRE DEFECT *	LACK OF ROTATION OF TIRES OR WORN OR OUT-OF-ALIGNMENT SUSPENSION.
CORRECTION		ADJUST PRESSURE TO SPECIFICATIONS WHEN TIRES ARE COOL ROTATE TIRES		ADJUST CAMBER TO SPECIFICATIONS	ADJUST TOE-IN TO SPECIFICATIONS	DYNAMIC OR STATIC BALANCE WHEELS	ROTATE TIRES AND INSPECT SUSPENSION

*HAVE TIRE INSPECTED FOR FURTHER USE.

TCCS1267

Fig. 102 Common tire wear patterns and causes

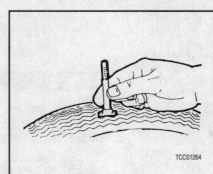

Fig. 103 Tread wear indicators will appear when the tire is worn

TCCS1265

Fig. 104 Accurate tread depth indicators are inexpensive and handy

TCCS1264

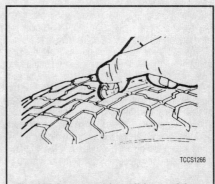

Fig. 105 A penny works well for a quick check of tread depth

TCCS1266

FLUIDS AND LUBRICANTS

Fluid Disposal

Used fluids such as engine oil, transmission fluid, antifreeze and brake fluid are hazardous wastes and must be disposed of properly. Before draining any fluids, consult with the local authorities; in many areas, waste oil, etc. is being accepted as part of recycling programs. A number of service stations and auto parts stores are also accepting waste fluids for recycling.

Be sure of the recycling center's policies before draining any fluids, as many will not accept different fluids that have been mixed together, such as oil and antifreeze.

Oil and Fuel Recommendations

ENGINE OIL

♦ **See Figures 106 and 107**

The recommended oil viscosities for sustained temperatures ranging from below 0°F (–20°C) to above 32°F (0°C) are listed in this section. They are broken down into multi–viscosity and single viscosities. Multi–viscosity oils are recommended because of their wider range of acceptable temperatures and driving conditions.

➡**Mazda recommends that SAE 5W–30 viscosity engine oil should be used for all climate conditions, however, SAE 10W–30 is acceptable for vehicles operated in moderate to hot climates.**

When adding oil to the crankcase or changing the oil or filter, it is important that oil of an equal quality to original equipment be used in your truck. The use of inferior oils may void the warranty, damage your engine, or both.

The SAE (Society of Automotive Engineers) grade number of oil indicates the viscosity of the oil (its ability to lubricate at a given temperature). The lower the SAE number, the lighter the oil; the lower the viscosity, the easier it is to crank the engine in cold weather but the less the oil will lubricate and protect the engine in high temperatures. This number is marked on every oil container.

Oil viscosities should be chosen from those oils recommended for the lowest anticipated temperatures during the oil change interval. Due to the need for an oil that embodies both good lubrication at high temperatures and easy cranking in cold weather, multigrade oils have been developed. Basically, a multigrade oil is thinner at low temperatures and thicker at high temperatures. For example, a 10W–40 oil (the W stands for winter) exhibits the characteristics

Temperature Range for SAE Viscosity Numbers									
Temperature °F	–20	0	20	40	60	80	100	120	
(°C)	–30	–20	–10	0	10	20	30	40	50
Engine oil		5W-30							
					10W-30				

90971G07

Fig. 106 Engine oil viscosity chart

Fig. 107 Look for the API oil identification label when choosing your engine oil

of a 10 weight (SAE 10) oil when the truck is first started and the oil is cold. Its lighter weight allows it to travel to the lubricating surfaces quicker and offer less resistance to starter motor cranking than, say, a straight 30 weight (SAE 30) oil. But after the engine reaches operating temperature, the 10W–40 oil begins acting like straight 40 weight (SAE 40) oil, its heavier weight providing greater lubrication with less chance of foaming than a straight 30 weight oil.

The API (American Petroleum Institute) designations, also found on the oil container, indicates the classification of engine oil used under certain given operating conditions. Only oils designated for use Service SG heavy duty detergent should be used in your truck. Oils of the SG type perform may functions inside the engine besides their basic lubrication. Through a balanced system of metallic detergents and polymeric dispersants, the oil prevents high and low temperature deposits and also keeps sludge and dirt particles in suspension. Acids, particularly sulfuric acid, as well as other by–products of engine combustion are neutralized by the oil. If these acids are allowed to concentrate, they can cause corrosion and rapid wear of the internal engine parts.

✳✳ CAUTION

Non–detergent motor oils or straight mineral oils should not be used in your Ford gasoline engine.

Synthetic Oil

There are many excellent synthetic and fuel–efficient oils currently available that can provide better gas mileage, longer service life, and in some cases better engine protection. These benefits do not come without a few hitches, however; the main one being the price of synthetic oils, which is three or four times the price per quart of conventional oil.

Synthetic oil is not for every truck and every type of driving, so you should consider your engine's condition and your type of driving. Also, check your truck's warranty conditions regarding the use of synthetic oils.

High mileage engines are the wrong candidates for synthetic oil. Older engines with wear have a problem with synthetics: they "use" (consume during operation) more oil as they age. Slippery synthetic oils get past these worn parts easily. If your engine is "using" conventional oil, it will use synthetics much faster. Also, if your truck is leaking oil past old seals you'll have a much greater leak problem with synthetics.

FUEL

▶ **See Figure 108**

All of these vehicles must use lead–free gasoline. It is recommended that these vehicles avoid the use of premium grade gasoline. This is due to the engine control system being calibrated towards the use of regular grade gasoline. The use of premium grades may actually cause driveability problems. Also, Mazda advises against the use of gasoline with an octane rating lower than 87 which can cause persistant and heavy knocking, and may cause internal engine damage.

OPERATION IN FOREIGN COUNTRIES

If you plan to drive your vehicle outside the United States or Canada, there is a possibility that fuels will be too low in anti–knock quality and could produce engine damage. It is wise to consult with local authorities upon arrival in a foreign country to determine the best fuels available.

Engine

OIL LEVEL CHECK

▶ **See Figures 109, 110 and 111**

Check the engine oil level every time you fill the gas tank. The oil level should be above the **ADD** or **L** (LOW) mark and not above the **FULL** or **F** mark on the dipstick. Make sure that the dipstick is inserted into the crankcase as far as possible and that the vehicle is resting on level ground. Also, allow a few minutes after turning off the engine for the oil to drain into the pan or an inaccurate reading will result.

1. Open the hood and remove the engine oil dipstick.
2. Wipe the dipstick with a clean, lint–free rag and reinsert it. Be sure to insert it all the way.
3. Pull out the dipstick and note the oil level. It should be between the **FULL** or **F** mark and the **ADD** or **L** (LOW) mark.
4. If the level is below the lower mark, install the dipstick and add fresh oil to bring the level within the proper range. Do not overfill.
5. Recheck the oil level and close the hood.

➡ **Use a multi–grade oil with API classification SG or better.**

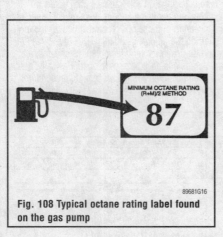

Fig. 108 Typical octane rating label found on the gas pump

Fig. 109 The oil level dipstick is located on the right side of the engine—MPV

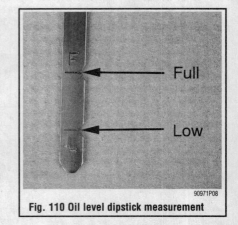

Fig. 110 Oil level dipstick measurement

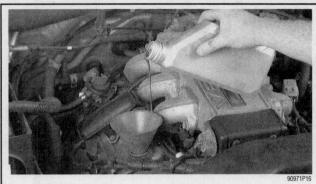

Fig. 111 Pour the engine oil, using a funnel, through the oil fill hole located on the right side valve cover—MPV

OIL & FILTER CHANGE

▶ See Figures 112 thru 120

➡The engine oil and oil filter should be changed at the recommended intervals on the Maintenance Chart. Though some manufacturer's have at times recommended changing the filter only at every other oil change, we recommend that you always change the filter with the oil. The benefit of fresh oil is quickly lost if the old filter is clogged and unable to do its job. Also, leaving the old filter in place leaves a significant amount of dirty oil in the system.

The oil should be changed more frequently if the vehicle is being operated in a very dusty area. Before draining the oil, make sure that the engine is at operating temperature. Hot oil will hold more impurities in suspension and will flow better, allowing the removal of more oil and dirt.

➡It is usually a good idea to place your ignition key in the box or bag with the bottles of fresh engine oil. In this way it will be VERY HARD to forget to refill the engine crankcase before you go to start the engine.

1. Raise and support the vehicle safely on jackstands. Make sure the oil drain plug is at the lowest point on the oil pan. If not, you may have to raise the vehicle slightly higher on one jackstand (side) than the other.

2. Before you crawl under the car, take a look at where you will be working and gather all the necessary tools: such as a few wrenches or a strip of sockets, the drain pan, a clean rag, and, if the oil filter is more accessible from underneath the vehicle, you will also want to grab a bottle of oil, the new filter and a filter wrench at this time.

❋❋ CAUTION

The EPA warns that prolonged contact with used engine oil may cause a number of skin disorders, including cancer! You should make every effort to minimize your exposure to used engine oil. Protective gloves should be worn when changing the oil. Wash your hands and any other exposed skin areas as soon as possible after exposure to used engine oil. Soap and water, or waterless hand cleaner should be used.

3. Position the drain pan beneath the oil pan drain plug. Keep in mind that the fast flowing oil, which will spill out as you pull the plug from the pan, will flow with enough force that it could miss the pan. Position the drain pan accordingly and be ready to move the pan more directly beneath the plug as the oil flow lessens to a trickle.

4. Loosen the drain plug with a wrench (or socket and driver), then carefully unscrew the plug with your fingers. Use a rag to shield your fingers from the heat. Push in on the plug as you unscrew it so you can feel when all of the screw threads are out of the hole (and so you will keep the oil from seeping past the threads until you are ready to remove the plug). You can then remove the plug quickly to avoid having hot oil run down your arm. This will also help assure that you have the plug in your hand, not in the bottom of a pan of hot oil.

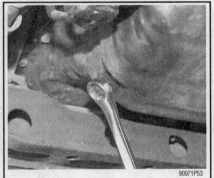

Fig. 112 Using a box wrench, loosen the oil pan drain plug

Fig. 113 Unscrew the plug by hand. Keep an inward pressure on the plug as you unscrew it, so the oil won't escape until you pull the plug away to drain the oil

Fig. 114 Clean up the oil pan drain plug and always replace the crush washer

Fig. 115 An oil filter can be removed with a variety of tools. One tool that is good to use is the filter wrench . . .

Fig. 116 . . . another good tool is an end cap filter wrench used along with a ratchet and extension

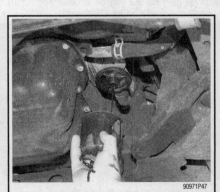

Fig. 117 Remove the oil filter. Be careful not to spill the oil out of it

Fig. 118 Be sure to clean the gasket mounting surface of any dirt before installing a new oil filter

Fig. 119 Before installing a new oil filter, lightly coat the rubber gasket with clean engine oil

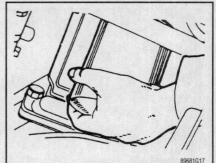

Fig. 120 Always install the new filter by hand (an oil filter wrench will usually lead to overtightening)

☀☀ CAUTION

Be careful of the oil; when at operating temperature, it is hot enough to cause a severe burn.

5. Allow the oil to drain until nothing but a few drops come out of the drain hole. Check the drain plug to make sure the threads and sealing surface are not damaged. Install a new gasket onto the drain plug. Carefully thread the plug into position and tighten it with a torque wrench to 15–20 ft. lbs. (20–27 Nm) for the B Series Pick-up and Navajo models or 22–30 ft. lbs. (30–41 Nm) for the MPV models. If a torque wrench is not available, snug the drain plug and give a slight additional turn. You don't want the plug to fall out (as you would quickly become stranded), but the pan threads are EASILY stripped from overtightening (and this can be time consuming and/or costly to fix).

6. The oil filter is located on the bottom passenger side of the 2.6L and 4.0L engines and on the driver side of all other engines; position the drain pan beneath it. To remove the filter, you may need an oil filter wrench since the filter may have been fitted too tightly and/or the heat from the engine may have made it even tighter. A filter wrench can be obtained at any auto parts store and is well-worth the investment. Loosen the filter with the filter wrench. With a rag wrapped around the filter, unscrew the filter from the boss on the side of the engine. Be careful of hot oil that will run down the side of the filter. Make sure that your drain pan is under the filter before you start to remove it from the engine. Should some of the hot oil happen to get on you, there will be a place to dump the filter in a hurry and the filter will usually spill a good bit of dirty oil as it is removed.

7. Wipe the base of the mounting boss with a clean, dry cloth. When you install the new filter, smear a small amount of fresh oil on the gasket with your finger, just enough to coat the entire contact surface. When you tighten the filter, rotate it about a half-turn after it contacts the mounting boss (or follow any instructions which are provided on the filter or parts box).

☀☀ WARNING

Never operate the engine without engine oil, otherwise SEVERE engine damage will be the result.

8. Remove the jackstands and carefully lower the vehicle, then IMMEDIATELY refill the engine crankcase with the proper amount of oil. DO NOT WAIT TO DO THIS because if you forget and someone tries to start the car, severe engine damage will occur.

9. Refill the engine crankcase slowly, checking the level often. You may notice that it usually takes less than the amount of oil listed in the capacity chart to refill the crankcase. But, that is only until the engine is run and the oil filter is filled with oil. To make sure the proper level is obtained, run the engine to normal operating temperature. While the engine is warming, look under the vehicle for any oil leaks, and if found, shut the engine **OFF** immediately, then fix the leak. Shut the engine **OFF**, allow the oil to drain back into the oil pan, and recheck the level. Top off the oil at this time to the fill mark.

➡If the vehicle is not resting on level ground, the oil level reading on the dipstick may be slightly off. Be sure to check the level only when the car is sitting level.

10. Drain your used oil in a suitable container for recycling and clean-up your tools, as you will be needing them again in a few thousand more miles (kilometers).

Manual Transmission

FLUID RECOMMENDATION

The lubricant in the transmission should be checked and changed periodically, except when the vehicle has been operated in deep water and water has entered the transmission. When this happens, change the lubricant in the transmission as soon as possible. Use ATF DEXRON-II, M-III or MERCON in the Mazda M5OD transmission.

LEVEL CHECK

The fluid level should be checked every six months or 60,000 miles (96,000 km), whichever comes first.

1. Park the truck on a level surface, turn the engine **OFF**, FIRMLY apply the parking brake and block the drive wheels.

➡Ground clearance may make access to the transmission filler plug impossible without raising and supporting the vehicle, BUT, if this is done, the truck MUST be supported at four corners and level. If only the front or rear is supported, an improper fluid level will be indicated. If you are going to place the truck on four jackstands, this might be the perfect opportunity to rotate the tires as well.

2. Remove the filler plug from the side of the transmission case using a ⅜ in. drive ratchet and extension. The fluid level should be even with the bottom of the filler hole.

3. If additional fluid is necessary, add it through the filler hole using a siphon pump or squeeze bottle.

4. When you are finished, carefully install the filler plug, but DO NOT overtighten it and damage the housing.

DRAIN & REFILL

Under normal conditions, the manufacturer feels that manual transmission fluid should not need to be changed. However, if the truck is driven in deep water (as high as the transmission casing) it is a good idea to replace the fluid. Little harm can come from a fluid change when you have just purchased a used vehicle, especially since the condition of the transmission fluid is usually not known.

If the fluid is to be drained, it is a good idea to warm the fluid first so it will flow better. This can be accomplished by 15–20 miles of highway driving. Fluid when warmed to normal operating temperature will flow faster, drain more completely and remove more contaminants from the housing.

1. Drive the vehicle to assure the fluid is at normal operating temperature.

2. Raise and support the vehicle securely on jackstands. Remember that the vehicle must be supported level (usually at four points) so the proper amount of fluid can be added.

3. Place a drain pan under the transmission housing, below the drain plug. Remember that the fluid will likely flow with some force at first (arcing outward from the transmission), and will not just drip straight downward into the pan. Position the drain pan accordingly and move it more directly beneath the drain plug as the flow slows to a trickle.

➡To insure that the fill plug is not frozen or rusted in place, remove it from the transmission BEFORE removing the drain plug. It would be unfortunate to drain all of your transmission fluid and then realize that the fill plug is stripped or frozen in place.

4. Remove the fill plug, then the drain plug and washer, allowing the transmission fluid to drain out.

➡The transmission drain plug may have a square receiver which is designed to accept a ⅜ in. driver such as a ratchet or extension.

5. Once the transmission has drained sufficiently, install the drain plug, with a new washer, until secure. Tighten the drain plug to 30–42 ft. lbs. (40–58 Nm).

6. Fill the transmission with the specified amount and type of oil through the hole until the level reaches the bottom of the hole.

7. Install the filler plug, with a new washer, once you are finished.

8. Remove the jackstands and carefully lower the vehicle.

Automatic Transmission

FLUID RECOMMENDATION

Refer to the dipstick or vehicle owner's manual to confirm Automatic Transmission Fluid (ATF) specifications. These vehicles utilize the following types of ATF:

- Navajo: Mercon ATF
- 1994 B Series Pick-up and all MPV: Dexron II or M-III
- 1995–96 B Series Pick-up: Mercon or M-III
- 1997–98 B Series Pick-up: Mercon

DO NOT use improper fluids such as gear oil. Use of improper fluids could lead to leaks or transmission damage.

LEVEL CHECK

◆ See Figures 121, 122 and 123

It is very important to maintain the proper fluid level in an automatic transmission. If the level is either too high or too low, poor shifting operation and internal damage are likely to occur. For this reason, a regular check of the fluid level is essential.

Although it is best to check fluid at normal operating temperature, it can be checked overnight cold, if the ambient temperatures are 50–95°F (21–35°C). If so, on B Series Pick-up and Navajo models, refer to the dots on the transmission dipstick instead of the cross-hatched area and level marking lines.

1. Drive the vehicle for 20–30 minutes, allowing the transmission to reach operating temperature.

➡If the car is driven at extended highway speeds, is driven in city traffic in hot weather or is being used to pull a trailer, fluid temperatures will likely exceed normal operating and checking ranges. In these circumstances, give the fluid time to cool (about 30 minutes) before checking the level.

2. Park the car on a level surface, apply the parking brake and leave the engine idling. Make sure the parking brake is FIRMLY ENGAGED. Shift the transmission and engage each gear, then place the selector in **P** (PARK).

3. Open the hood and locate the transmission dipstick. Wipe away any dirt in the area of the dipstick to prevent it from falling into the filler tube. Withdraw the dipstick, wipe it with a clean, lint-free rag and reinsert it until it fully seats.

4. Withdraw the dipstick and hold it horizontally while noting the fluid level. It should be between the upper (FULL) and the lower (ADD) marks, or notches (MPV).

5. If the level is below the lower mark, use a funnel and add fluid in small quantities through the dipstick filler neck. Keep the engine running while adding fluid and check the level after each small amount. DO NOT overfill as this could lead to foaming and transmission damage or seal leaks.

➡Since the transmission fluid is added through the dipstick tube, if you check the fluid too soon after adding fluid an incorrect reading may occur. After adding fluid, wait a few minutes to allow it to fully drain into the transmission.

DRAIN, PAN/FILTER SERVICE & REFILL

◆ See Figures 124 thru 132

Under normal service (moderate highway driving excluding excessive hot or cold conditions), the manufacturer feels that automatic transmission fluid should not need periodic changing. However, if a major service is performed to the transmission, or if the transmission fluid becomes burnt or discolored through severe usage (most vehicles fall in this category) the fluid should be changed to prevent transmission damage. A preventive maintenance change is therefore recommended for most vehicles at least every 42,000 miles (70,000 km) on B Series Pick-ups and Navajo models or 60,000 miles (96,000 km) on MPV models.

➡Although not a required service, transmission fluid changing can help assure a trouble-free transmission. Likewise, changing the transmission filter at this time is also added insurance.

1. Raise the car and support it securely on jackstands.

➡The torque converters on some transmissions are equipped with drain plugs. Because it may take some time to drain the fluid from the converter, you may wish to follow that procedure at this time, then come back to the pan and filter removal.

2. Place a large drain pan under the transmission.

3. Remove the pan bolts, except for one mounting bolt at each corner. Carefully break the gasket seal allowing most of the fluid to drain over the edge of the pan.

Fig. 121 Automatic transmission fluid level dipstick is located on the right side of the engine in the rear of the compartment—MPV

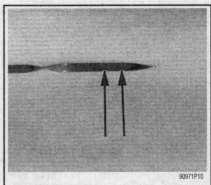

Fig. 122 The fluid level should be between the two arrows

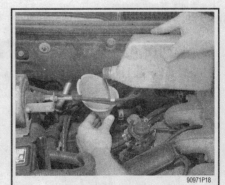

Fig. 123 Use a funnel (to avoid spills) and add the required type and amount of ATF

Fig. 124 Using a 10mm socket, remove the pan bolts except for one mounting bolt at each corner

Fig. 125 After removing the rear corner pan bolts, carefully lower the pan by hand

Fig. 126 Lower the pan

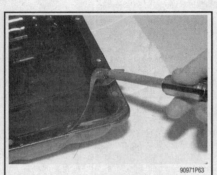

Fig. 127 Once the pan is removed, discard the old gasket and insure that the mating surfaces are clean

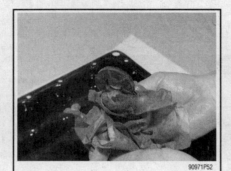

Fig. 128 Remove the magnet from the bottom of the transmission oil pan and clean it

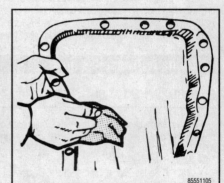

Fig. 129 Clean the pan thoroughly with a safe solvent and allow it to air dry

Fig. 130 Remove the filter mounting bolts using a 10mm socket

Fig. 131 Remove the transmission filter from the trans valve body. Be sure that the O-ring seal also comes out with the filter

Fig. 132 Install a new pan gasket

✷✷ CAUTION

DO NOT force the pan while breaking the gasket seal. DO NOT allow the pan flange to become bent or otherwise damaged.

4. When fluid has drained to the level of the pan flange, remove the pan bolts and carefully lower the pan doing your best to drain the rest of the fluid into the drain pan.

5. Clean the transmission oil pan thoroughly using a safe solvent, then allow it to air dry. DO NOT use a cloth to dry the pan which might leave behind bits of lint. Discard the old pan gasket.

6. If necessary, remove the Automatic Transmission Fluid (ATF) filter mounting retainers, then remove the filter by pulling it down and off of the valve body. Make sure any gaskets or seals are removed with the old filter. The transmission usually has one round seal and a rectangular gasket.

7. Install the new oil filter screen making sure all gaskets or seals are in place, then secure using the retaining screws, if applicable.

8. Place a new gasket on the fluid pan, then install the pan to the transmission. Tighten the pan mounting bolts in a crisscross pattern to 71–119 inch lbs. (8–13 Nm) on B Series Pick-ups/Navajo models and 113–115 inch lbs. (12–13 Nm) on MPV models.

9. Add 4 quarts (6 quarts if the torque converter was drained) of fluid to the transmission through the filler tube.

10. Remove the jackstands and carefully lower the vehicle.

11. Start the engine and move the gear selector through all gears in the shift pattern. Allow the engine to reach normal operating temperature.

12. Check the transmission fluid level. Add fluid, as necessary, to obtain the correct level.

Transfer Case

FLUID RECOMMENDATION

These vehicles utilize the following fluids when adding or refilling the transfer case:
- Navajo: Mercon automatic transmission fluid
- MPV: API service GL-4/GL-5, SAE 75 W-90 or 80 W-90
- 1994–96 B Series Pick-up: Dexron II or M-III automatic transmission fluid
- 1997–98 B Series Pick-up: Mercon or M-III automatic transmission fluid

LEVEL CHECK

▶ See Figures 133, 134, 135, 136 and 137

1. Position the vehicle on level ground.
2. On B Series Pick-up and Navajo models, remove the transfer case fill plug (the upper plug) located on the rear of the transfer case. On MPV models, remove the oil level plug located on the rear of the transfer case between the drain and fill plugs. The fluid level should be up to that hole.
3. If lubricant doesn't run out when the plug is removed, add lubricant until it does run out.
4. For B Series Pick-up and Navajo models, apply sealant to the threads of the filler plug and install. For MPV models, install the level plug and new washer. Tighten the filler or level plug to 14–18 ft. lbs. (19–25 Nm).

DRAIN & REFILL

▶ See Figures 133, 134 and 138

The manufacturer recommends that the transfer case fluid should be changed every 60,000 miles (96,000km). However, if the vehicle is driven in deep water (as high as the transfer case housing) it is a good idea to replace the fluid. Little harm can come from a fluid change when you have just purchased a used vehicle, especially since the condition of the transfer case fluid is usually not known.

If the fluid is to be drained, it is a good idea to warm the fluid first so it will flow better. This can be accomplished by 15–20 miles of highway driving. Fluid when warmed to normal operating temperature will flow faster, drain more completely and remove more contaminants from the housing.

1. Drive the vehicle to assure the fluid is at normal operating temperature.
2. Raise and support the vehicle securely on jackstands. Remember that the vehicle must be supported level (usually at four points) so the proper amount of fluid can be added.
3. Place a drain pan under the transfer case housing, below the drain plug. Remember that the fluid will likely flow with some force at first (arcing outward from the transmission), and will not just drip straight downward into the pan. Position the drain pan accordingly and move it more directly beneath the drain plug as the flow slows to a trickle.

➡ To insure that the fill plug is not frozen or rusted in place, remove it from the transfer case BEFORE removing the drain plug. It would be unfortunate to drain all of your transfer case fluid and then realize that the fill plug is stripped or frozen in place.

4. Remove the fill plug, the level plug (MPV models), then the drain plug and allow the transfer case fluid to drain out.

➡ On B Series Pick-up and Navajo models, the transfer case drain plug is usually a square receiver which is designed to accept a ⅜ in. driver such as a ratchet or extension.

5. Once the transfer case has drained sufficiently, install the drain plug. For B Series Pick-up and Navajo models, apply sealant to the threads of the drain plug, then install. For MPV models, install the drain plug and new washer. Tighten the drain plug to 14–22 ft. lbs. (19–30 Nm) on B Series Pick-up/Navajo and 29–43 ft. lbs. (40–58 Nm) on MPV models.
6. Fill the transfer case to the proper level with the required fluid.
7. For B Series Pick-up and Navajo models, apply sealant to the threads of the filler plug and install. For MPV models, install the level and filler plugs

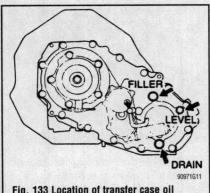

Fig. 133 Location of transfer case oil filler, level and drain plugs—MPV

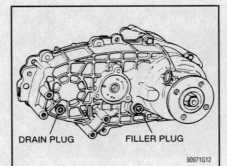

Fig. 134 Location of transfer case oil filler and drain plugs—B Series Pick-up and Navajo

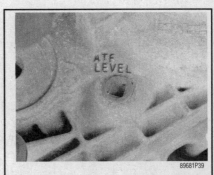

Fig. 135 The transfer case fill/level check plug is the upper most plug, located on the rear of the case

Fig. 136 Remove the plug using a ⅜ in. drive ratchet

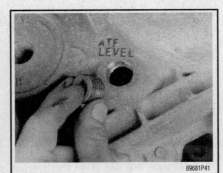

Fig. 137 Once the plug is removed, fluid should trickle out of the hole. If not, add Mercon ATF fluid until it does

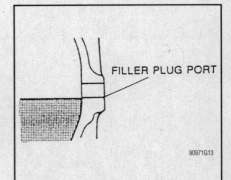

Fig. 138 Verify that the oil level is near the filler or level plug port

along with new washers. Tighten the filler plug (B Series Pick-up/Navajo) or level plug (MPV) to 14–18 ft. lbs. (19–25 Nm). Tighten the filler plug (MPV) to 29–43 ft. lbs. (40–58 Nm).

8. Remove the jackstands and carefully lower the vehicle.

Front and Rear Drive Axle

FLUID RECOMMENDATION

Use hypoid gear lubricant API Service GL-5 SAE 80W or 90W. On Navajo models with four wheel drive, the front axle requires 75W gear lubricant.

➡ If the differential is a Traction-Lok limited-slip unit, be sure to use 4 oz. of Friction Modifier, or equivalent special limited-slip additive with the lubricant.

LEVEL CHECK

▶ See Figures 139 thru 144

The fluid level in the drive axles should be checked at each oil change. The axle (or differential) housing does not have a dipstick to check fluid level. Instead, a filler plug is located on the differential housing (also referred to as a "pumpkin"), at a level just barely above the level to which fluid should fill the housing. To check the fluid level:

1. Make sure the transmission is in **P** (A/T) or in gear on a manual, then FIRMLY set the parking brake and block the drive wheels.

2. Check under the vehicle to see if there is sufficient clearance for you to access the filler plug on the side of the differential housing. If not you will have to raise and support the vehicle using jackstands at four points to make sure it is completely level. Failure to support the vehicle level will prevent from properly checking or filling the drive axle fluid.

3. Thoroughly clean the area surrounding the fill plug. This will prevent any dirt from entering the housing and contaminating the gear oil.

4. Remove the fill plug and make sure that the gear oil is up to the bottom of the fill hole. If a slight amount of lubricant does not drip out of the hole when the plug is removed, additional lubricant should be added. Use hypoid gear lubricant SAE 80, SAE 90 or SAE 75 (on Navajo 4WD front axles only).

➡ If the differential is a Traction-Lok limited-slip unit, be sure to use 4 oz. of Friction Modifier, or equivalent special limited-slip additive with the lubricant.

5. Once you are finished, install the fill plug, then (if raised) remove the jackstands and lower the vehicle.

DRAIN & REFILL

Drain and refill the drive axle housings every 100,000 miles (160,000 km) on B Series Pickup/Navajo models, 60,000 miles (96,000 km) on MPV models, or any time the vehicle is driven in high water (up to the axle). Although some fluid can be removed using a suction gun, the best method is to remove the axle housing cover (if equipped) to ensure that all of any present contaminants are removed. As with any fluid change, the oil should be at normal operating temperature to assure the best flow and removal of fluid/contaminants.

➡ If there is no housing cover or drain plug, you will need to use a suction gun through the fill hole to remove the fluid.

Drive Axle Equipped with a Housing Cover

▶ See Figures 145, 146, 147, 148 and 149

1. Drive the vehicle until the lubricant reaches normal operating temperature.

2. If necessary for access, raise and support the vehicle safely using jackstands, but be sure that the vehicle is level so you can properly refill the axle when you are finished.

➡ If a suction gun is used to drain the fluid, remove the fill plug and insert the suction tube into the fill hole until it rests at the lowest most point inside the housing. Operate the suction gun as per the manufactur-

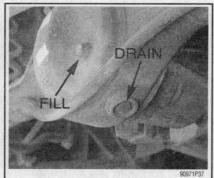

Fig. 139 Location of the drain and fill plugs on the rear differential case

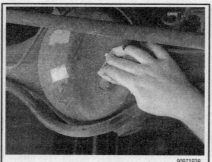

Fig. 140 Wipe the area clean around the differential oil fill plug before opening to prevent any dirt from entering

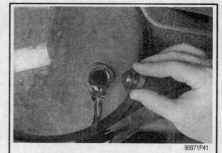

Fig. 141 After loosening the differential oil fill plug using a 24 mm box wrench, remove the plug and allow any excess fluid to drain into a container

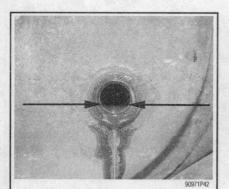

Fig. 142 After removing the fill plug, look inside the hole and inspect the fluid level

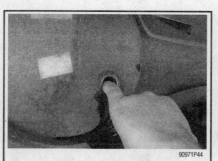

Fig. 143 If the fluid level is not visible, stick your finger into the hole and check to see if the level reaches the bottom of the filler hole

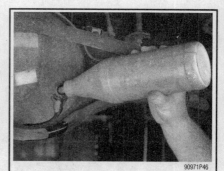

Fig. 144 Fill the differential housing with the correct amount and type of gear oil until fluid starts to trickle out

Fig. 145 Remove the fill plug, then clean the area around the axle housing cover to prevent dirt from entering it

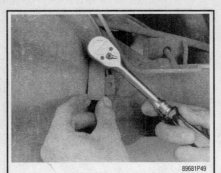

Fig. 146 Loosen and remove all but two of the cover retaining bolts. Don't lose the axle identification tag

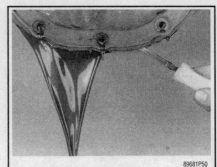

Fig. 147 With the remaining bolts loose, carefully pry out on the cover (to break the seal) and allow the fluid to drain

Fig. 148 Once most of the fluid has drained, remove the remaining bolts and pull the cover from the housing

Fig. 149 Remove any old gasket material from the sealing surfaces then clean them of any residual oil

ers directions. When the fluid is completely removed, skip to the differential filling procedure.

3. Use a wire brush to clean the area around the differential. This will help prevent dirt from contaminating the differential housing while the cover is removed.

4. Position a drain pan under the drive axle.

5. Loosen and remove all but 2 of the housing cover's upper or side retaining bolts. The remaining 2 bolts should then be loosened to within a few turns of complete removal. Use a small prytool to carefully break the gasket seal at the base of the cover and allow the lubricant to drain. Be VERY careful not to force or damage the cover and gasket mating surface.

6. Once most of the fluid has drained, remove the final retaining bolts and separate the cover from the housing.

To fill the differential:

7. Carefully clean the gasket mating surfaces of the cover and axle housing of any remaining gasket or sealer. A putty knife is a good tool to use for this. You may want to cover the differential gears using a rag or piece of plastic to prevent contaminating them with dirt or pieces of the old gasket.

8. Install the housing cover using a new gasket and sealant. Tighten the retaining bolts using a crisscross pattern.

➡**Make sure the vehicle is level before attempting to add fluid to the drive axle, otherwise an incorrect fluid level will result.**

9. Refill the drive axle housing using the proper grade and quantity of lubricant. Install the filler plug, operate the vehicle and check for any leaks.

Drive Axle Equipped with a Drain Plug

▶ **See Figures 150 thru 155**

1. Drive the vehicle until the lubricant reaches normal operating temperature.

2. If necessary for access, raise and support the vehicle safely using jackstands, but be sure that the vehicle is level so you can properly refill the axle when you are finished.

3. Use a wire brush to clean the area around the drain and fill plugs. This will help prevent dirt from contaminating the differential housing while the plugs are removed.

4. Position a drain pan under the drive axle.

5. Remove the fill plug and washer first, then the drain plug and washer second. Wipe the plugs clean.

6. Once most of the fluid has drained, install the drain plug with a new washer. Tighten the drain plug to 29–39 ft. lbs. (40–53 Nm).

Fig. 150 Be careful not to lose the fill plug washer, however, inspect the condition of the washer and replace it if necessary

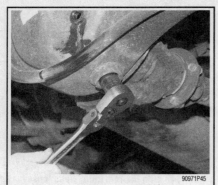

Fig. 151 Using a 24 mm socket, loosen the drain plug

Fig. 152 Remove the differential drain plug and allow the fluid to drain in an approved container

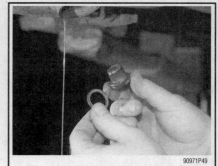

Fig. 153 Be careful not to lose the differential drain plug washer, inspect and replace if necessary

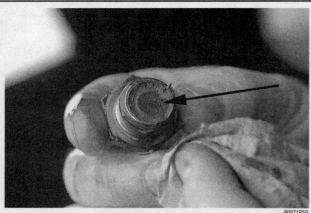

Fig. 154 Most differential drain plugs have a small magnet in the center to catch any small metallic fragments in the fluid

Fig. 155 Always inspect the air vent tube or cap (located on the top of the differential housing) for obstructions and clean if necessary

To fill the differential:

→Make sure the vehicle is level before attempting to add fluid to the drive axle, otherwise an incorrect fluid level will result.

7. Refill the drive axle housing using the proper grade and quantity of lubricant. Install the fill plug with a new washer. Tighten the fill plug to 29–39 ft. lbs. (40–53 Nm).

8. Lower the vehicle.

9. Operate the vehicle and check for any leaks.

Cooling System

♦ See Figure 156

✳ CAUTION

Never remove the radiator cap under any conditions while the engine is running! Failure to follow these instructions could result in damage to the cooling system and/or personal injury. To avoid having scalding hot coolant or steam blow out of the radiator, use extreme care when removing the radiator cap from a hot radiator. Wait until the engine has cooled, then wrap a thick cloth around the radiator cap and turn it slowly to the first stop. Step back while the pressure is released from the cooling system. When you are sure the pressure has been released, press down on the radiator cap (with the cloth still in position), turn and remove the cap.

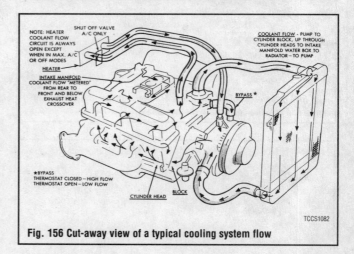

Fig. 156 Cut-away view of a typical cooling system flow

FLUID RECOMMENDATIONS

The recommended coolant for all vehicles covered by this manual is a 50/50 mixture of ethylene glycol antifreeze and water for year-round use. Choose an aluminum compatible, good quality antifreeze with water pump lubricants, rust inhibitors and other corrosion inhibitors along with acid neutralizers.

INSPECTION

♦ See Figures 157, 158, 159 and 160

Any time you have the hood open, glance at the coolant recovery tank to make sure it is properly filled. Top off the cooling system using the recovery tank and its markings as a guideline. If you top off the system, make a note of it to check again soon. A coolant level that consistently drops is usually a sign of

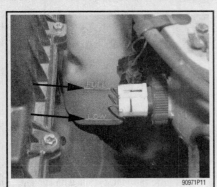

Fig. 157 Coolant overflow tank full and low level measurements

Fig. 158 Pull the cap and suction tube out of the coolant overflow tank to top off the cooling system

Fig. 159 Fill the engine coolant overflow tank to the FULL line

a small, hard to detect leak, though in the worst case it could be a sign of an internal engine leak (blown head gasket/cracked block? . . . check the engine oil for coolant contamination). In most cases, you will be able to trace the leak to a loose fitting or damaged hose (and you might solve a problem before it leaves you stranded). Evaporating ethylene glycol antifreeze will leave small, white (salt like) deposits, which can be helpful in tracing a leak.

At least annually or every 15,000 miles (24,000 km), all hoses, fittings and cooling system connections should be inspected for damage, wear or leaks. Hose clamps should be checked for tightness, and soft or cracked hoses should be replaced. Damp spots, or accumulations of rust or dye near hoses or fittings indicate possible leakage. These must be corrected before filling the system with fresh coolant. The pressure cap should be examined for signs of deterioration and aging. The fan belt and/or other drive belt(s) should be inspected and adjusted to the proper tension. Refer to the information on drive belts found earlier in this section. Finally, if everything looks good, obtain an antifreeze/coolant testing hydrometer in order to check the freeze and boil-over protection capabilities of the coolant currently in your engine. Old or improperly mixed coolant should be replaced.

❈❈ CAUTION

When draining coolant, keep in mind that cats and dogs are attracted to ethylene glycol antifreeze, and are likely to drink any that is left in an uncovered container or in puddles on the ground. This will prove fatal in sufficient quantity. Always drain coolant into a sealable container. Coolant may be reused unless it is contaminated or several years old.

At least once every 3 years or 36,000 miles (48,000 km), the engine cooling system should be inspected, flushed and refilled with fresh coolant. If the coolant is left in the system too long, it loses its ability to prevent rust and corrosion. If the coolant has too much water, it won't protect against freezing.

If you experience problems with your cooling system, such as overheating or boiling-over, check the simple before expecting the complicated. Make sure the system can fully pressurize (are all the connections tight/is the radiator cap on properly, is the cap seal intact?). Ideally, a pressure tester should be connected to the radiator opening and the system should be pressurized and inspected for

leaks. If no obvious problems are found, use a hydrometer antifreeze/coolant tester (available at most automotive supply stores) to check the condition and concentration of the antifreeze in your cooling system. Excessively old coolant or the wrong proportions of water and coolant will hurt the coolant's boiling and freezing points.

Check the Radiator Cap

▶ See Figure 161

While you are checking the coolant level, check the radiator cap for a worn or cracked gasket. If the cap doesn't seal properly, fluid will be lost and the engine will overheat. Worn caps should be replaced with new ones.

Clean Radiator of Debris

▶ See Figure 162

Periodically, clean any debris—leaves, paper, insects, etc.— from the radiator fins. Pick the large pieces off by hand. The smaller pieces can be washed away with water pressure from a hose.

Carefully straighten any bent radiator fins with a pair of needle-nosed pliers. Be careful; the fins are very soft. Don't wiggle the fins back and forth too much. Straighten them once and try not to move them again.

DRAINING, FLUSHING & REFILLING

▶ See Figures 163, 164, 165 and 166

❈❈ CAUTION

When draining coolant, keep in mind that cats and dogs are attracted to ethylene glycol antifreeze, and are likely to drink any that is left in an uncovered container or in puddles on the ground. This will prove fatal in sufficient quantity. Always drain coolant into a sealable container. Coolant may be reused unless it is contaminated or several years old.

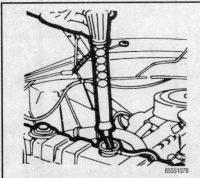

Fig. 160 Checking antifreeze protection with an inexpensive tester

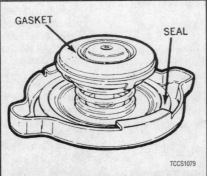

Fig. 161 Be sure the rubber gasket on the radiator cap has a tight seal

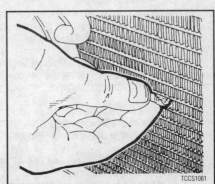

Fig. 162 Periodically remove all debris from the radiator fins

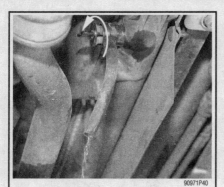

Fig. 163 Use the radiator draincock to drain the engine coolant

Fig. 164 Pour coolant into the radiator until it reaches just below the filler neck

Fig. 165 To refill the system with coolant, remove the radiator cap. NEVER remove the cap if the system is HOT

Fig. 166 The system should be pressure checked whenever leakage is suspected and can't be seen

A complete drain and refill of the cooling system at least every 30,000 miles (48,000 km) or 3 years will remove the accumulated rust, scale and other deposits. The recommended coolant for most late model vehicles is a 50/50 mixture of ethylene glycol and water for year-round use. Choose a good quality antifreeze with water pump lubricants, rust inhibitors and other corrosion inhibitors along with acid neutralizers.

➡Before opening the radiator petcock, spray it with some penetrating lubricant.

1. Drain the existing antifreeze and coolant. Open the radiator and engine drains (petcocks) or disconnect the bottom radiator hose at the radiator outlet. The engine block drain plugs can also be temporarily removed to drain coolant, but they are often hard to get at and it is not really necessary for this procedure.

2. Close the petcock or reconnect the hose (and install any block drain plugs which may have been removed), then fill the system with water.

3. Add a can of quality radiator flush.

4. Idle the engine until the upper radiator hose gets hot.

5. Drain the system again.

6. Repeat this process until the drained water is clear and free of scale.

7. Close all petcocks and connect any loose hoses.

8. If equipped with a coolant recovery system, flush the reservoir with water and leave empty.

9. Determine the capacity of the coolant system, then properly refill the cooling system with a 50/50 mixture of fresh coolant and water, as follows:

   a. Fill the radiator with coolant until it reaches the radiator filler neck seat.

   b. Start the engine and allow it to idle until the thermostat opens (the upper radiator hose will become hot).

   c. Turn the engine OFF and refill the radiator until the coolant level is at the filler neck seat.

   d. Fill the engine coolant overflow tank with coolant to the FULL HOT mark, then install the radiator cap.

10. If available, install a pressure tester and check for leaks. If a pressure tester is not available, run the engine until normal operating temperature is reached (allowing the system to naturally pressurize), then check for leaks.

✳✳ CAUTION

If you are checking for leaks with the system at normal operating temperature, BE EXTREMELY CAREFUL not to touch any moving or hot engine parts. Once the temperature has been reached, shut the engine OFF, and check for leaks around the hose fittings and connections which were removed earlier.

11. Check the level of protection with an antifreeze/coolant hydrometer.

Brake Master Cylinder

FLUID RECOMMENDATIONS

✳✳ WARNING

BRAKE FLUID EATS PAINT. Take great care not to splash or spill brake fluid on painted surfaces. Should you spill a small amount on the car's finish, don't panic, just flush the area with plenty of water.

When adding fluid to the system ONLY use fresh DOT 3 brake fluid from a sealed container. DOT 3 brake fluid will absorb moisture when it is exposed to the atmosphere, which will lower its boiling point. A container that has been opened once, closed and placed on a shelf will allow enough moisture to enter over time to contaminate the fluid within. If your brake fluid is contaminated with water, you could boil the brake fluid under hard braking and loose all/some of the brake system. Don't take the risk, buy fresh brake fluid whenever you must add to the system.

LEVEL CHECK

◆ See Figures 167, 168, 169 and 170

Brake fluid level and condition is a safety related item and it should be checked ANY TIME the hood is opened. Your vehicle should not use brake fluid rapidly (unless there is a leak in the system), but the level should drop slowly in relation to brake pad wear.

The master cylinder reservoir is located under the hood, on the left side firewall. All vehicles covered by this manual should be equipped with a see-through plastic reservoir. This makes checking the level easy and helps reduce the risk of fluid contamination (since you don't have to expose the fluid by opening the cap to check the level). Fluid should be kept near the FULL line or between the MIN and MAX lines, depending on how the reservoir is marked.

If it becomes necessary to add fluid to the system, take a moment to clean the area around the cap and reservoir. Use a clean rag to wipe away dust and dirt which could enter the reservoir after the cover is removed. If the level of the brake fluid is less than half the volume of the reservoir (and the brake pads are not approaching a replacement point), it is advised that you check the brake system for leaks. Leaks in the hydraulic system often occur at the wheel cylinders.

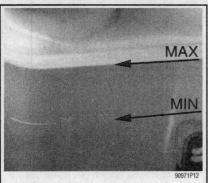

Fig. 167 Level of brake fluid as measured on the reservoir

Fig. 168 Be sure to clean the brake fluid reservoir cap and surrounding area before opening it

Fig. 169 Remove the brake fluid reservoir cap . . .

Fig. 170 . . . then top off or fill the brake fluid reservoir

Clutch Master Cylinder

FLUID RECOMMENDATIONS

The hydraulic clutch control system consists of a fluid reservoir, a master cylinder, a slave cylinder and connecting tubing. It uses heavy duty brake fluid meeting DOT 3 specification.

LEVEL CHECK

▶ See Figure 171

The clutch master cylinder reservoir is located under the hood, on the left side firewall. The fluid in the reservoir will slowly decrease or drop as the clutch wears. As long as the fluid level is visible at or near the line on the reservoir body, it is not necessary to "top-off" the fluid level. However, add fluid if it is necessary.

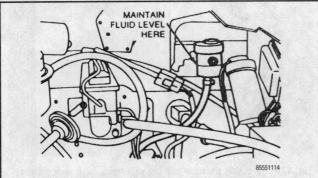

Fig. 171 Clutch master cylinder reservoir location

➡Before removing the clutch master cylinder reservoir cap, make sure the vehicle is resting on level ground and clean all dirt away from the top of the reservoir.

Power Steering Pump Reservoir

FLUID RECOMMENDATIONS

MPV Models

All MPV models use either DEXRON II Automatic Transmission Fluid (ATF) or M-III ATF. Ensure that the fluid added is new and clean.

Navajo Models

All Navajo models use either Type F Automatic Transmission Fluid (ATF) or DEXRON II ATF. Ensure that the fluid is new and clean.

B Series Pick-up Models

1994–97 MODELS

1994–97 models use either Type F Automatic Transmission Fluid (ATF) or DEXRON II ATF. Ensure that the fluid is new and clean.

1998 MODELS

1998 models use either Mercon® IV Automatic Transmission Fluid (ATF) or M-III ATF. Ensure that the fluid is new and clean.

LEVEL CHECK

▶ See Figures 172, 173 and 174

The level of the power steering fluid should be checked in the reservoir periodically, at least once a year on the B Series Pick-up and Navajo models or at every oil change on MPV models. Fluid is checked using the dipstick attached to the reservoir cap. It is recommended that you check the fluid at normal operating temperature (HOT) on B Series Pick-up/Navajo models and after the engine has cooled on MPV models.

❊❊ WARNING

Extensive driving with a low power steering fluid level can damage the power steering pump.

1. On B Series Pick-up and Navajo models, perform the following:
   a. Warm the fluid to normal operating temperature by driving for at least one mile, or start the engine and allow it to idle for five minutes.
   b. With the engine idling, turn the steering wheel back-and-forth several times from lock-to-lock, then center the wheels and shut the engine **OFF**.
2. Locate the power steering pump reservoir, then remove the cap/dipstick and note the level as indicated by the markings (FULL HOT/FULL COLD—B Series Pick-up and Navajo or FULL/LOW—MPV). To be sure of your reading, put the cap back in position, remove it again and double check the level.

Fig. 172 Power steering fluid level dipstick location in the lower right side of the engine compartment—MPV

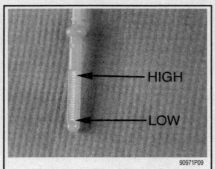

Fig. 173 Power steering fluid level should measure between the HIGH and LOW markings on the dipstick

Fig. 174 Place a long-nosed funnel into the filler tube and add the correct amount of fluid—MPV

3. If the level is below the indicator markings, add fluid to bring it up to the proper level (a funnel is usually very helpful). If you are checking the level after running the engine or driving, make sure you add enough fluid to bring it to the FULL or FULL HOT range, but like most automotive fluids, DO NOT overfill.

4. When you are finished, install the dipstick and be sure it is secure.

Manual Steering Gear

The steering gear is filled with steering gear grease at the factory. Changing of this lubricant should not be performed and the housing should not be drained.

Chassis Greasing

Chassis greasing should be performed every 7,500 miles (12,000 km) for most vehicles. Greasing can be performed with a commercial pressurized grease gun or at home by using a hand-operated grease gun. Wipe the grease fittings clean before greasing in order to prevent the possibility of forcing any dirt into the component.

Check the steering, driveshaft and front suspension components for grease fittings. There are far less grease points on the modern automotive chassis than there were on trucks of yesteryear.

A water resistant long life grease that meets Mazda's specification should be used for all chassis greasing applications.

Body Lubrication

Whenever you take care of chassis greasing it is also advised that you walk around the vehicle and give attention to a number of other surfaces which require a variety of lubrication/protection.

HOOD/DOOR LATCH & HINGES

Wipe clean any exposed surfaces of the door hatches and hinges, hood latch and auxiliary catch. Then, treat the surfaces using an NLGI No. 2 Lithium based, or equivalent, multi-purpose grease.

LOCK CYLINDERS

Should be treated with a non-freezing lubricant during cold weather. Consult your local parts supplier for equivalent lubricants.

DOOR WEATHERSTRIPPING

Spray the door weatherstripping using a silicone lubricant to help pressure the rubber.

TAILGATE

Spray a silicone lubricant on all of the pivot and friction surfaces to eliminate any squeaks or binds. Work the tailgate to distribute the lubricant.

BODY DRAIN HOLES

Be sure that the drain holes in the doors and rocker panels are cleared of obstruction. A small screwdriver can be used to clear them of any debris.

Wheel Bearings

➥This procedure only covers the repacking (or greasing) of the wheel bearings for the B Series Pick-up and Navajo models. The MPV comes equipped with integral hub/bearing assemblies and therefore, no service, other than replacement, is possible. For the removal procedures see the appropriate section for your vehicle. For 4 wheel drive vehicles, see Section 7. For 2 wheel drive vehicles, see Section 8.

REPACKING

◆ See Figures 175 and 176

It is recommended that the front wheel bearings be cleaned, inspected and repacked every 30,000 miles (48,000km) and as soon as possible if the front hubs have been submerged in water.

➥Sodium based grease is not compatible with lithium based grease. Be careful not to mix the two types. The best way to prevent this is to completely clean all of the old grease from the hub assembly before installing any new grease.

Before handling the bearings there are a few things that you should remember to do and try to avoid.

DO the following:
- Remove all outside dirt from the housing before exposing the bearing.
- Treat a used bearing as gently as you would a new one.
- Work with clean tools in clean surroundings.
- Use clean, dry canvas gloves, or at least clean, dry hands.
- Clean solvents and flushing fluids are a must.

Fig. 175 Thoroughly pack the bearing with fresh, high temperature wheel-bearing grease before installation

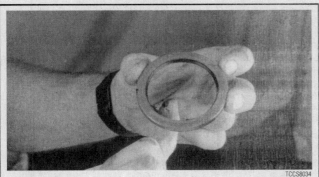

Fig. 176 Apply a thin coat of fresh grease to the new bearing grease seal before installing it into the hub

- Use clean paper when laying out the bearings to dry.
- Protect disassembled bearings from rust and dirt. Cover them up.
- Use clean rags to wipe bearings.
- Keep the bearings in oil–proof paper when they are to be stored or are not in use.
- Clean the inside of the housing before replacing the bearing.

Do NOT do the following:

- Don't work in dirty surroundings.
- Don't use dirty, chipped, or damaged tools.
- Try not to work on wooden work benches, or use wooden mallets.
- Don't handle bearings with dirty or moist hands.
- Do not use gasoline for cleaning; use a safe solvent.
- Do not spin–dry bearings with compressed air. They will be damaged.
- Do not spin unclean bearings.
- Avoid using cotton waste or dirty clothes to wipe bearings.
- Try not to scratch or nick bearing surfaces.
- Do not allow the bearing to come in contact with dirt or rust at any time.

➡**4WD vehicles should refer to Section 7 for bearing removal. 2WD vehicles should refer to Section 8 for bearing removal.**

1. Remove the bearing assemblies from the hub.

➡**Do not spin the bearings with compressed air while drying them.**

2. Clean the inner and outer bearings with solvent. Thoroughly clean the hub, bearing cups and spindle. Remove any traces of the old grease. Dry all of the components with a soft, lint-free cloth.

3. Inspect the cups for scratches, pits, excessive wear, and other damage. If found, replace them.

   a. The cups are removed from the hub by driving them out with a drift pin. They are installed in the same manner.

4. If it is determined that the cups are in satisfactory condition and are to remain in the hub, inspect the bearings in the same manner. Replace the bearings if necessary.

➡**When replacing either the bearing or the cup, both parts should be replaced as a unit.**

5. Cover the spindle with a clean cloth, and brush all loose dirt from the dust shield. Carefully remove the cloth to prevent dirt from falling from it.

6. Pack the inside of the hub with wheel bearing grease. Add grease to the hub until the grease is flush with the inside diameter of the bearing cup.

7. Pack the bearing assembly with wheel bearing grease. A bearing packer is desirable for this operation. If a packer is not available, place a large portion of grease into the palm of your hand and sliding the edge of the roller cage through the grease with your other hand, work as much grease in between the rollers as possible.

➡**As an alternate method, place a large portion of grease, and the bearing to be packed, into a sealable heavy plastic bag. Squeeze the bag to force the grease into the bearing. This may reduce the mess usually associated with bearing repacking.**

8. Position the inner bearing cone and roller assembly in the inner cup. Apply a light film of grease to the lips of a new grease seal and install the seal into the hub.

9. Carefully position the hub and rotor assembly onto the spindle. Be careful not to damage the grease seal.

10. Place the outer bearing into position on the spindle and into the bearing cup. Install the adjusting nut finger tight.

11. Adjust the wheel bearings.

12. Install any remaining components which were removed.

TRAILER TOWING

◗ **See Figure 177**

General Recommendations

Your vehicle was primarily designed to carry passengers and cargo. It is important to remember that towing a trailer will place additional loads on your vehicles engine, drivetrain, steering, braking and other systems. However, if you decide to tow a trailer, using the prior equipment is a must.

Local laws may require specific equipment such as trailer brakes or fender mounted mirrors. Check your local laws.

Trailer Weight

The weight of the trailer is the most important factor. A good weight-to-horsepower ratio is about 35:1, 35 lbs. of Gross Combined Weight (GCW) for every horsepower your engine develops. Multiply the engine's rated horsepower by 35 and subtract the weight of the vehicle passengers and luggage. The number remaining is the approximate ideal maximum weight you should tow, although a numerically higher axle ratio can help compensate for heavier weight.

Hitch (Tongue) Weight

Calculate the hitch weight in order to select a proper hitch. The weight of the hitch is usually 9–11% of the trailer gross weight and should be measured with the trailer loaded. Hitches fall into various categories: those that mount on the frame and rear bumper, the bolt-on type, or the weld-on distribution type used for larger trailers. Axle mounted or clamp-on bumper hitches should never be used.

Check the gross weight rating of your trailer. Tongue weight is usually figured as 10% of gross trailer weight. Therefore, a trailer with a maximum gross weight of 2000 lbs. will have a maximum tongue weight of 200 lbs. Class I trailers fall into this category. Class II trailers are those with a gross weight rating of 2000–3000 lbs., while Class III trailers fall into the 3500–6000 lbs. category. Class IV trailers are those over 6000 lbs. and are for use with fifth wheel trucks, only.

When you've determined the hitch that you'll need, follow the manufacturer's

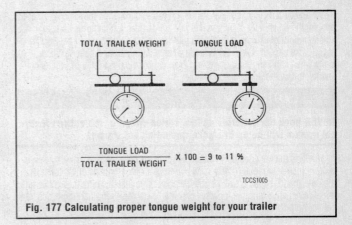

Fig. 177 Calculating proper tongue weight for your trailer

installation instructions, exactly, especially when it comes to fastener torques. The hitch will subjected to a lot of stress and good hitches come with hardened bolts. Never substitute an inferior bolt for a hardened bolt.

Oil Cooler

Aftermarket engine oil coolers are helpful for prolonging engine oil life and reducing overall engine temperatures. Both of these factors increase engine life. While not absolutely necessary in towing Class I and some Class II trailers, they are recommended for heavier Class II and all Class III towing. Engine oil cooler systems usually consist of an adapter, screwed on in place of the oil filter, a remote filter mounting and a multi-tube, finned heat exchanger, which is mounted in front of the radiator or air conditioning condenser.

TRANSMISSION

An automatic transmission is usually recommended for trailer towing. Modern automatics have proven reliable and, of course, easy to operate, in trailer towing. The increased load of a trailer, however, causes an increase in the temperature of the automatic transmission fluid. Heat is the worst enemy of an automatic transmission. As the temperature of the fluid increases, the life of the fluid decreases.

It is essential, therefore, that you install an automatic transmission cooler.

TOWING THE VEHICLE

▶ See Figure 178

➡Mazda recommends that a flat bed tow service be utilized. If a flat bed tow truck is not available, tow the vehicle with the rear wheels lifted, front hubs unlocked (4WD models) and the steering wheel locked in the straight ahead position using a clamping device designed for towing. DO NOT lock the steering wheel using only the ignition key activated steering lock, as damage to the steering column can occur.

Your vehicle can be towed forward with the driveshaft connected as long as you do not exceed 50 miles in distance and 35 MPH in speed. The transmission must always be placed in the N (neutral) position. Severe damage to the transmission can occur if these limits are exceeded. However, if the vehicle must be towed faster than 35 MPH and/or further than 50 miles, disconnect and support the driveshaft. With the driveshaft disconnected, do not exceed 55 MPH. If your vehicle has to be towed backward and is a 4WD model, unlock the front axle driving hubs, to prevent the front differential from rotating and place the transfer case in neutral. Also clamp the steering wheel on all models, in the straight ahead position with a clamping device designed for towing service.

JUMP STARTING A DEAD BATTERY

▶ See Figure 179

Whenever a vehicle is jump started, precautions must be followed in order to prevent the possibility of personal injury. Remember that batteries contain a small amount of explosive hydrogen gas which is a by-product of battery charging. Sparks should always be avoided when working around batteries, especially when attaching jumper cables. To minimize the possibility of accidental sparks, follow the procedure carefully.

✳ CAUTION

NEVER hook the batteries up in a series circuit or the entire electrical system will go up in smoke, including the starter!

Hooking the batteries up in parallel circuit increases battery cranking power without increasing total battery voltage output. Output remains at 12 volts. On the other hand, hooking two 12 volt batteries up in a series circuit (positive terminal to negative terminal, positive terminal to negative terminal) increases total battery output to 24 volts (12 volts plus 12 volts).

The cooler, which consists of a multi-tube, finned heat exchanger, is usually installed in front of the radiator or air conditioning compressor, and hooked in-line with the transmission cooler tank inlet line. Follow the cooler manufacturer's installation instructions.

Select a cooler of at least adequate capacity, based upon the combined gross weights of the vehicle and trailer.

Cooler manufacturers recommend that you use an aftermarket cooler in addition to, and not instead of, the present cooling tank in your radiator. If you do want to use it in place of the radiator cooling tank, get a cooler at least two sizes larger than normally necessary.

➡A transmission cooler can, sometimes, cause slow or harsh shifting in the transmission during cold weather, until the fluid has a chance to come up to normal operating temperature. Some coolers can be purchased with or retrofitted with a temperature bypass valve which will allow fluid flow through the cooler only when the fluid has reached above a certain operating temperature.

Handling A Trailer

Towing a trailer with ease and safety requires a certain amount of experience. It's a good idea to learn the feel of a trailer by practicing turning, stopping and backing in an open area such as an empty parking lot.

✳ WARNING

Do not attach chains to the bumpers or bracketing. All attachments should be made to structural members.

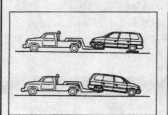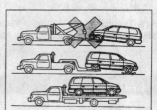

90971G08

Fig. 178 Proper towing configurations

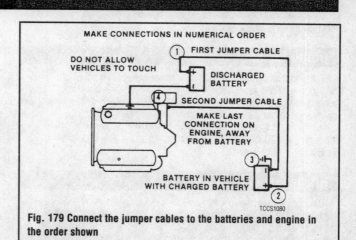

MAKE CONNECTIONS IN NUMERICAL ORDER

DO NOT ALLOW VEHICLES TO TOUCH

① FIRST JUMPER CABLE

DISCHARGED BATTERY

SECOND JUMPER CABLE

MAKE LAST CONNECTION ON ENGINE, AWAY FROM BATTERY

③

② BATTERY IN VEHICLE WITH CHARGED BATTERY

TCCS1080

Fig. 179 Connect the jumper cables to the batteries and engine in the order shown

Jump Starting Precautions

• Be sure that both batteries are of the same voltage. Vehicles covered by this manual and most vehicles on the road today utilize a 12 volt charging system.

• Be sure that both batteries are of the same polarity (have the same terminal, in most cases NEGATIVE grounded).

• Be sure that the vehicles are not touching or a short could occur.

• On serviceable batteries, be sure the vent cap holes are not obstructed.

• Do not smoke or allow sparks anywhere near the batteries.

• In cold weather, make sure the battery electrolyte is not frozen. This can occur more readily in a battery that has been in a state of discharge.

• Do not allow electrolyte to contact your skin or clothing.

Jump Starting Procedure

1. Make sure that the voltages of the 2 batteries are the same. Most batteries and charging systems are of the 12 volt variety.

2. Pull the jumping vehicle (with the good battery) into a position so the jumper cables can reach the dead battery and that vehicle's engine. Make sure that the vehicles do NOT touch.

3. Place the transmissions/transaxles of both vehicles in **Neutral** (MT) or **P** (AT), as applicable, then firmly set their parking brakes.

➡**If necessary for safety reasons, the hazard lights on both vehicles may be operated throughout the entire procedure without significantly increasing the difficulty of jumping the dead battery.**

4. Turn all lights and accessories OFF on both vehicles. Make sure the ignition switches on both vehicles are turned to the **OFF** position.

5. Cover the battery cell caps with a rag, but do not cover the terminals.

6. Make sure the terminals on both batteries are clean and free of corrosion or proper electrical connection will be impeded. If necessary, clean the battery terminals before proceeding.

7. Identify the positive (+) and negative (–) terminals on both batteries.

8. Connect the first jumper cable to the positive (+) terminal of the dead battery, then connect the other end of that cable to the positive (+) terminal of the booster (good) battery.

9. Connect one end of the other jumper cable to the negative (–) terminal on the booster battery and the final cable clamp to an engine bolt head, alternator bracket or other solid, metallic point on the engine with the dead battery. Try to pick a ground on the engine that is positioned away from the battery in order to minimize the possibility of the 2 clamps touching should one loosen during the procedure. DO NOT connect this clamp to the negative (–) terminal of the bad battery.

✳✳ CAUTION

Be very careful to keep the jumper cables away from moving parts (cooling fan, belts, etc.) on both engines.

10. Check to make sure that the cables are routed away from any moving parts, then start the donor vehicle's engine. Run the engine at moderate speed for several minutes to allow the dead battery a chance to receive some initial charge.

11. With the donor vehicle's engine still running slightly above idle, try to start the vehicle with the dead battery. Crank the engine for no more than 10 seconds at a time and let the starter cool for at least 20 seconds between tries. If the vehicle does not start in 3 tries, it is likely that something else is also wrong or that the battery needs additional time to charge.

12. Once the vehicle is started, allow it to run at idle for a few seconds to make sure that it is operating properly.

13. Turn ON the headlights, heater blower and, if equipped, the rear defroster of both vehicles in order to reduce the severity of voltage spikes and subsequent risk of damage to the vehicles' electrical systems when the cables are disconnected. This step is especially important to any vehicle equipped with computer control modules.

14. Carefully disconnect the cables in the reverse order of connection. Start with the negative cable that is attached to the engine ground, then the negative cable on the donor battery. Disconnect the positive cable from the donor battery and finally, disconnect the positive cable from the formerly dead battery. Be careful when disconnecting the cables from the positive terminals not to allow the alligator clips to touch any metal on either vehicle or a short and sparks will occur.

JACKING

▶ **See Figures 180, 181, 182, and 183**

It is very important to be careful about running the engine, on vehicles equipped with limited slip differentials, while the vehicle is up on a jack. This is because if the drive train is engaged, power is transmitted to the wheel with the best traction and the vehicle will drive off the jack, resulting in possible damage or injury.

➡**To raise your Mazda with the jack supplied, refer to the accompanying illustrations. Do not lift the vehicle by the front bumper.**

Jack the vehicle from under the differential/axle, body pinchwelds (MPV only), front lower control arms (1998 B Series Pick-up) or frame/crossmember. Be sure and block the diagonally opposite wheel to prevent the vehicle from moving. Place jackstands under the vehicle at the points illustrated when you are going to work under the vehicle.

✳✳ CAUTION

On models equipped with an under chassis mounted spare tire, remove the tire, wheel or tire carrier from the vehicle before it is placed in a high lift position in order to avoid sudden weight release from the chassis.

When supporting the vehicle on jackstands, position them under the front pinch welds just behind the front wheels (MPV) or the frame rail/bracket close to the front, behind each front wheel (B Series Pick-up and Navajo). The rear

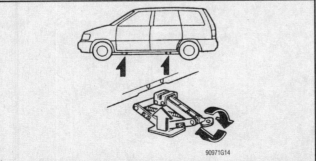

Fig. 180 Jack positioning under the body pinchwelds (MPV)—2WD models; support the vehicle with jackstands placed at the same locations

Fig. 181 Jack positioning under the body pinchwelds (MPV)—4WD models; support the vehicle with jackstands placed at the same locations

Fig. 182 Lift the front by positioning the jack under the lower front shock absorber mount—1994–97 B Series Pick-up and Navajo

Fig. 183 Lift the rear by positioning the jack under the rear spring mount—B Series Pick-up and Navajo

jackstands should be placed under the rear pinch welds just ahead of the rear wheels (MPV), both rear spring shackles (1994–97 B Series Pick-up and Navajo) and rear section of each frame rail (1998 B Series Pick-up). Be careful not to touch the rear shock absorber mounting brackets.

✳✳ CAUTION

The jack supplied with your vehicle was meant for changing tires. It was not meant to support the vehicle while you work under it. Whenever it is necessary to get under the vehicle to perform service operations, be sure that it is adequately supported on jackstands.

MAINTENANCE INTERVALS

Fig. 184 — ENGINE / AIR CLEANER / IGNITION SYSTEM / FUEL SYSTEM / COOLING SYSTEM / CHASSIS AND BODY

Maintenance Interval \ Maintenance Item	Months	6	12	18	24	30	36	42	48
	×1,000 Km	12	24	36	48	60	72	84	96
	×1,000 Miles	7.5	15	22.5	30	37.5	45	52.5	60
ENGINE									
Engine oil		R	R	R	R	R	R	R	R
Oil filter		R	R	R	R	R	R	R	R
Drive belts (tension)									—
Engine timing belt (JE engine, except California)		Replace every 60,000 miles (96,000 km)							
Engine timing belt (JE engine, California)		Inspect at 60,000 miles (96,000 km) and again at 90,000 miles (144,000 km)							
Oxygen sensor		Replace every 105,000 miles (168,000 km)							
PCV valve		Replace every 80,000 miles (128,000 km)							
Hoses and tubes for emission		Replace every 80,000 miles (128,000 km)							—
AIR CLEANER									
Air cleaner element					R				R
IGNITION SYSTEM									
Spark plugs					R				R
Initial ignition timing									I*
FUEL SYSTEM									
Idle speed			—						R*
Fuel filter							—		I*
Fuel lines and hoses		Inspect every 105,000 miles (168,000 km)							
Fuel hoses (California)		Inspect every 105,000 miles (168,000 km)							
COOLING SYSTEM									
Cooling system						—			—
Engine coolant					R				R
CHASSIS AND BODY									
Brake lines, hoses, and connections			—						—
Brake fluid					R				R
Disc brakes			—						

Fig. 184 Regular maintenance interval chart (1 of 2)—MPV

90971G21

Fig. 185 — CHASSIS AND BODY / AIR CONDITIONER SYSTEM (IF EQUIPPED)

Maintenance Interval \ Maintenance Item	Months	6	12	18	24	30	36	42	48
	×1,000 Km	12	24	36	48	60	72	84	96
	×1,000 Miles	7.5	15	22.5	30	37.5	45	52.5	60
CHASSIS AND BODY									
Automatic transmission fluid									R
Steering operation and linkages					I				I
Front suspension ball joints					I				I
Front axle oil (4WD)									R
Rear axle oil									R
Transfer case oil (4WD)					I				R
Drive shaft dust boots (4WD)					I				I
Propeller shaft joints (4WD)			L	L	L	L	L	L	L
Bolts and nuts on chassis and body					I				—
Exhaust system heat shields					I				—
All locks and hinges			L	L	L	L	L	L	L
AIR CONDITIONER SYSTEM (IF EQUIPPED)									
Refrigerant amount							I		—
A/C compressor operation									

Chart symbols:
I : Inspect and repair, clean, or replace if necessary.
R : Replace
L : Lubricate

Remarks:
- After 48 months or 60,000 miles (96,000 km), continue to follow the described maintenance at the recommended intervals.
- This maintenance is required for all states except California. However, we recommend that it also be performed on California vehicles.

Fig. 185 Regular maintenance interval chart (2 of 2)—MPV

90971G22

Maintenance Item / Maintenance Interval	Number of months or miles { km }, whichever comes first											
Months	4	8	12	16	20	24	28	32	36	40	44	48
×1,000 Km	8	16	24	32	40	48	56	64	72	80	88	96
×1,000 Miles	5	10	15	20	25	30	35	40	45	50	55	60
ENGINE												
Engine oil	R	R	R	R	R	R	R	R	R	R	R	R
(Puerto Rico)	Replace every 3,000 miles { 5,000 km } or 3 months											
Oil filter	R	R	R	R	R	R	R	R	R	R	R	R
Drive belts (tension)						I						I
Engine timing belt (JE engine, except California)	Replace every 60,000 miles { 96,000 km }											
Engine timing belt (JE engine, California)	*2 Inspect at 60,000 miles { 96,000 km }, and against 90,000 miles { 144,000 km }											
	Replace every 105,000 miles { 168,000 km }											
Oxygen sensor	Replace every 80,000 miles { 128,000 km }											
PCV valve												I
Hoses and tubes for emission	Replace every 80,000 miles { 128,000 km }											I
AIR CLEANER												
Air cleaner element			I			R			I			R
IGNITION SYSTEM												
Spark plugs			I			R			I			R
Initial ignition timing												I*
FUEL SYSTEM												
Idle speed			I						I			
Fuel filter												R*
Fuel lines and hoses						I						I*
Fuel hoses (California)	Inspect every 105,000 miles { 168,000 km }											
COOLING SYSTEM												
Cooling system						I						I
Engine coolant						R						R
CHASSIS AND BODY												
Brake lines, hoses, and connections						I						I
Brake fluid						R						R
Disc brakes			I			I			I			I

90971G23

Fig. 186 Severe maintenance interval chart (1 of 2)—MPV

Maintenance Item / Maintenance Interval	Number of months or miles { km }, whichever comes first											
Months	4	8	12	16	20	24	28	32	36	40	44	48
×1,000 Km	8	16	24	32	40	48	56	64	72	80	88	96
×1,000 Miles	5	10	15	20	25	30	35	40	45	50	55	60
CHASSIS AND BODY												
Steering operation and linkages						I						I
Front suspension ball joints						I						I
Front axle oil (4WD) Rear axle oil						R						R
Automatic transmission fluid						R						R
Transfer case oil (4WD)						R						R
Drive shaft dust boots (4WD)						I						I
Propeller shaft joints (4WD)			L			L			L			L
Bolts and nuts on chassis and body			I			I			I			I
Exhaust system heat shields						I						I
All locks and hinges	L	L	L	L	L	L	L	L	L	L	L	L
AIR CONDITIONER SYSTEM (IF EQUIPPED)												
Refrigerant amount			I			I			I			I
A/C compressor operation			I			I			I			I

Chart symbols:
I : Inspect and repair, clean, or replace if necessary.
(Inspect, and if necessary replace...Air cleaner element JE engine only)
R : Replace
L : Lubricate

Remarks:
- After 48 months or 60,000 miles { 96,000 km }, continue to follow the described maintenance at the recommended intervals.
- * This maintenance is required for all states except California. However, we recommend that it also be performed on California vehicles.

90971G24

Fig. 197 Severe maintenance interval chart (2 of 2)—MPV

Fig. 189 Severe maintenance interval chart—Navajo and B Series Pick-up

Note
- Follow Schedule 1 except for the following items:

Maintenance Interval	Number of Miles (kilometers) (Thousands)																
Miles	3	6	9	12	15	18	21	24	27	30	33	36	39	42	45	48	51
km	5	10	15	20	25	30	35	40	45	50	55	60	65	70	75	80	85
Maintenance Item																	
Engine																	
Engine oil	Replace every 3,000 miles (4,800 km) or 6 months																
Oil filter	Replace every 3,000 miles (4,800 km) or 6 months																
Ignition system																	
Spark plugs *																	
Chassis and body																	
Automatic transmission shift linkage (cable system fluid)				I/L		I/L		I/L		I/L		I/L		I/L		I/L	
Front wheel bearings					I					I					I		
Disc brake system				I	I	I	I	I	I	I	I	I	I	I	I	I	I
Caliper slide rails				L		L		L		L		L		L		L	
Drum brake linings, lines and hoses				I		I		I		I		I		I		I	
Exhaust system for leaks, damage, looseness				I		I		I		I		I		I		I	
Exhaust system shielding (for trapped material)				I		I		I		I		I		I		I	
Propeller shaft U-joints (if equipped with grease fittings)				L		L		L		L		L		L		L	
Rear propeller shaft double cardan joint centering ball (short bed 4x4)				L		L		L		L		L		L		L	
Front axle RH axle – shaft slip yoke (4x4)				L		L		L		L		L		L		L	
Steering linkage joints (if equipped with grease fittings)				L		L		L		L		L		L		L	
Automatic transmission fluid							R					R					
Change manual transmission fluid										R							
Rotate tires			A		A		A		A		A		A		A		A
Propeller shaft slip yoke (if equipped)				L		L		L		L		L		L		L	
Clutch reservoir fluid level				L		L		L		L		L		L		L	

Chart symbols:

I : Inspect, and if necessary correct, clean or replace
A : Adjust
R : Replace
T : Tighten
L : Lubricate

* : Replace at 96,000 km (60,000 miles)

90971G26

Fig. 188 Regular maintenance interval chart—Navajo and B Series Pick-up

Maintenance Interval	Number of Miles (kilometers) (Thousands)																
Miles	5	10	15	20	25	30	35	40	45	50	55	60	65	70	75	80	85
km	8	16	24	32	40	48	56	64	72	80	88	96	104	112	121	128	136
Maintenance Item																	
Engine																	
Engine oil—every 6 months or	R	R	R	R	R	R	R	R	R	R	R	R	R	R	R	R	R
Oil filter—every 6 months or	R	R	R	R	R	R	R	R	R	R	R	R	R	R	R	R	R
PCV valve												R					
Air cleaner																	
Air cleaner element — every 30 months or						R						R					
Ignition system																	
Spark plugs (2.3L) 8 Spark Plugs	Replace every 100,000 miles																
Spark plugs (3.0L/4.0L)	Replace every 100,000 miles																
Cooling system																	
Engine coolant – Replace initially at 48 months. Thereafter, replace every 36 months or										R					R		
Coolant condition and protection, hoses and clamps – annually – prior to cold weather every 12 months or				I		I		I		I		I		I		I	
Chassis and body																	
Wheel lug nut torque*1	I	I	I	I	I	I	I	I	I	I	I	I	I	I	I	I	I
Rotate tires	A	A	A	A	A	A	A	A	A	A	A	A	A	A	A	A	A
Clutch reservoir fluid level	I/L	I/L	I/L	I/L	I/L	I/L	I/L	I/L	I/L	I/L	I/L	I/L	I/L	I/L	I/L	I/L	I/L
Automatic transmission shift linkage (cable system/fluid)		I		I		I		I		I		I		I		I	
Front wheel bearings					I/L					I/L					I/L		
Disc brake system			I	I	I	I	I	I	I	I	I	I	I	I	I	I	I
Caliper slide rails		L		L		L		L		L		L		L		L	
Drum brake linings, lines and hoses				I		I		I		I		I		I		I	
Exhaust system for leaks, damage, looseness				I		I		I		I		I		I		I	
Manual transmission oil												R					
Exhaust system shielding (for trapped material)				I		I		I		I		I		I		I	
Propeller shaft U-joints (if equipped with grease fittings)	L	L	L	L	L	L	L	L	L	L	L	L	L	L	L	L	L
Parking brake system (for damage and operation)				I		I		I		I		I		I		I	
Rear propeller shaft double cardan joint centering ball (short bed 4x4)		L		L		L		L		L		L		L		L	
Front axle RH axle – shaft slip yoke (4x4)		L		L		L		L		L		L		L		L	
Spindle needle bearing, spindle thrust bearing (4x4)						I/L						I/L					
Hub lock lubrication (4x4)						I/L						I/L					
Transfer case oil (4x4)						R						R					
Steering linkage joints (if equipped with grease fittings)	L	L	L	L	L	L	L	L	L	L	L	L	L	L	L	L	L
Rear axle lubricant*2																	
Accessory drive belts												I					
Propeller shaft slip yoke (if equipped)		L		L		L		L		L		L		L		L	
Transfer case shift lever pivot bolt and control rod connecting pins (4x4)						L						L					
Automatic transmission fluid						R						R					
Fuel filter						R						R					

*1: The wheel lug nuts must be retightened to the proper specifications at 800 km (500 miles) of new vehicle operation, at any wheel change, or at any other time the wheel lug nuts have been loosened.

*2: Replace rear axle lube quantities every 160,000 km (100,000 miles) or if the axles have been submerged in water. Otherwise, the lube should not be checked or changed unless a leak is suspected or repair is required.

Chart symbols:

I : Inspect, and if necessary correct, clean or replace
A : Adjust
R : Replace
T : Tighten
L : Lubricate

90971G25

CAPACITIES

Year	Model	Engine ID/VIN	Engine Displacement Liters (cc)	Engine Oil with Filter (qts.)	Transmission Man. ①	Transmission Auto. ②	Transfer Case (pts.)	Drive Axle Front (pts.)	Drive Axle Rear (pts.)	Fuel Tank (gal.)	Cooling System wo/AC (qts.)	Cooling System w/AC (qts.)
1994	B Series	A	2.3 (2298)	5.0	5.6	9.7 ③	2.5	3.5	5.0	④	6.5	7.2
	Pick-up	U	3.0 (2968)	4.5	5.6	9.7 ③	2.5	3.5	5.0	④	9.5	10.2
		X	4.0 (4016)	5.0	5.6	9.7 ③	2.5	3.5	5.0	④	7.8	8.6
	MPV	G6	2.6 (2606)	5.0	—	7.9	—	—	3.2	19.6	7.6	7.6
		JE	3.0 (2954)	5.0	—	9.1	3.2	3.6	3.2	⑤	10.3	10.3
	Navajo	X	4.0 (4016)	5.0	5.6	9.7 ③	2.5	3.5	5.5	19.3	7.8	8.6
1995	B Series	A	2.3 (2298)	5.0	5.6	9.7 ③	2.5	3.5	5.0	④	6.5	7.2
	Pick-up	U	3.0 (2968)	4.5	5.6	9.7 ③	2.5	3.5	5.0	④	9.5	10.2
		X	4.0 (4016)	5.0	5.6	9.7 ③	2.5	3.5	5.0	④	7.8	8.6
	MPV	G6	2.6 (2606)	5.0	—	7.9	—	—	3.2	19.6	7.6	7.6
		JE	3.0 (2954)	5.0	—	9.1	3.2	3.6	3.2	⑤	10.3	10.3
1996	B Series	A	2.3 (2298)	5.0	5.6	9.7 ③	2.5	3.5	5.0	④	6.5	7.2
	Pick-up	U	3.0 (2968)	4.5	5.6	9.7 ③	2.5	3.5	5.0	④	9.5	10.2
		X	4.0 (4016)	5.0	5.6	9.7 ③	2.5	3.5	5.0	④	7.8	8.6
	MPV	JE	3.0 (2954)	5.0	—	9.1	3.2	3.6	3.2	⑤	10.3	10.3
1997	B Series	A	2.3 (2298)	5.0	5.6	9.7	—	—	5.0	④	6.5	7.2
	Pick-up	U	3.0 (2968)	4.5	5.6	9.7 ③	2.5	3.5	5.0	④	9.5	10.2
		X	4.0 (4016)	5.0	5.6	9.7 ③	2.5	3.5	5.0	④	7.8	8.6
	MPV	JE	3.0 (2954)	5.0	—	9.1	3.2	3.6	3.2	⑤	10.3	10.3
1998	B Series	C	2.5 (2500)	4.5	5.6	9.5	—	—	5.0	④	⑥	⑥
	Pick-up	U	3.0 (2968)	4.5	5.6	9.5 ③	2.5	3.25	5.0	④	⑥	⑥
		X	4.0 (4016)	5.0	5.6	9.5 ③	2.5	3.25	5.0	④	⑥	⑥
	MPV	JE	3.0 (2954)	5.0	—	9.1	3.2	3.6	3.2	⑤	10.3	10.3

① All measurements given are in pints (pts.)

② All meaurements given are in quarts (qts.)

③ Measurement given is for 4x2 vehicles
for 4x4 vehicles, add 0.3 pts.

④ Regular cab/short bed: 16.3
Regular cab/long bed: 19.6
Cab Plus: 20.0

⑤ 19.6 gallon tank on 2wd models
19.8 gallon tank on 4wd models

⑥ 2.5L engine with manual transmission: 10.5
2.5L engine with automatic transmission: 10.2
3.0L engine with manual transmission: 15.2
3.0L engine with automatic transmission: 14.8
4.0L engine with manual transmission: 13.5
4.0L engine with automatic transmission: 13.2

90971C05

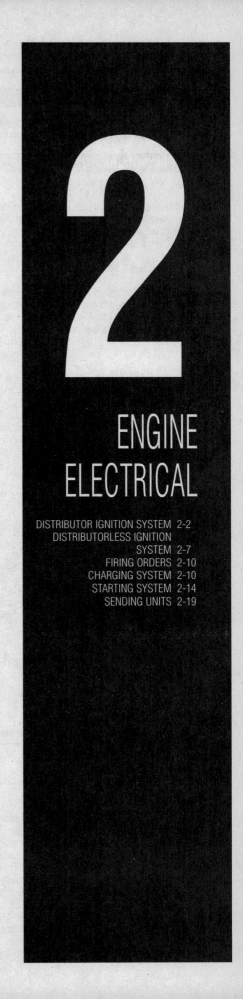

2

ENGINE
ELECTRICAL

DISTRIBUTOR IGNITION SYSTEM

➡️**For information on understanding electricity and troubleshooting electrical circuits, please refer to Section 6 of this manual.**

General Information

▶ **See Figure 1**

Only the 3.0L engine for 1994 B Series Pick-up and all MPV vehicle engines are equipped with the distributor ignition system. The distributor ignition system consists of the following components:

- Ignition Control Module (ICM)
- Distributor
- Camshaft Position (CMP) sensor
- Ignition coil

The distributor ignition system covered in this manual has two distinct configurations. The first configuration is known as the distributor mounted system, because the Ignition Control Module (ICM) is either mounted directly on the distributor housing, or is an integral component of the distributor housing. The second configuration is known as a remote mount system, since the ICM is mounted on top of the left strut tower (MPV) or the radiator support (B Series Pick-up).

The distributor is sealed and houses the CMP. The distributor does not utilize vacuum or centrifugal advance mechanisms; the ignition timing is automatically controlled by the Powertrain Control Module (PCM) and the ICM.

This electronic ignition is a Thick Film Integrated (TFI) ignition system. The TFI module is also known as the Ignition Control Module (ICM) which reports engine position and rpm to the PCM. The PCM then determines the proper spark timing and advance, and returns a reference signal to tell the TFI module to switch the coil, thereby by creating a spark.

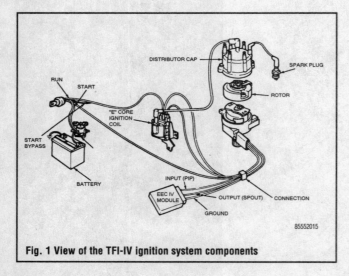

Fig. 1 View of the TFI-IV ignition system components

SYSTEM OPERATION

▶ **See Figures 2 and 3**

The CMP sensor, housed inside the distributor, responds to a rotating metallic shutter mounted on the distributor shaft. This rotating shutter produces a digital Profile Ignition Pick-up (PIP) signal, which is used by the PCM and ICM to provide base timing information, determine engine speed (rpm) and crankshaft position. The distributor shaft rotates at one-half crankshaft speed, therefore the shutter rotates once for every two crankshaft revolutions.

The ICM functions in either one of two modes: push start or Computer Controlled Dwell (CCD). The push start mode allows for increased dwell, or coil on time, when starting the engine. During this mode, the ICM determines when to turn on the ignition coil based on engine speed information. The coil is turned off, thereby firing, whenever a rising edge of a SPark OUTput (SPOUT) signal is received. The SPOUT signal is generated by the PCM, and provides spark tim-

ing information to the ICM. During the push start mode, the SPOUT signal only indicates the timing for coil firing; the falling edge of the SPOUT signal is ignored. Despite the name, the push start mode is also enabled during engine starting with the ignition key.

➡️**Do not attempt to push start a vehicle equipped with an automatic transmission.**

During the CCD mode, both edges of the SPOUT signal are utilized. The leading edge of the SPOUT signal is used by the ICM in the same manner as during the push start mode. The falling edge of the signal is generated to control the timing for turning the ignition coil on (the ICM no longer controls this function as during the push start mode). During the CCD mode, the coil on time, or dwell, is entirely controlled by the PCM through the SPOUT signal.

In the event that the SPOUT signal from the PCM is disrupted, the ICM will use the PIP signal from the CMP to fire the ignition coil, which results in a fixed spark angle and dwell.

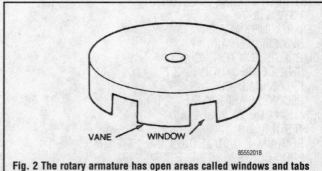

Fig. 2 The rotary armature has open areas called windows and tabs called vanes

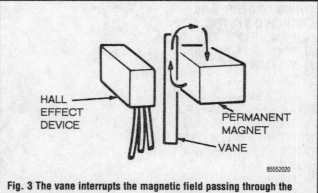

Fig. 3 The vane interrupts the magnetic field passing through the Hall effect device

Diagnosis and Testing

SERVICE PRECAUTIONS

- Always turn the key **OFF** and isolate both ends of a circuit whenever testing for shorts or continuity.
- Never measure voltage or resistance directly at the processor connector.
- Always disconnect solenoids and switches from the harness before measuring for continuity, resistance or energizing by way of a 12-volt source.
- When disconnecting connectors, inspect for damaged or pushed-out pins, corrosion, loose wires, etc. Service if required.

PRELIMINARY CHECKS

1. Visually inspect the engine compartment to ensure that all vacuum lines and spark plug wires are properly routed and securely connected.

2. Examine all wiring harness and connectors for insulation damage, burned, overheated, loose or broken conditions. Ensure that the ICM is securely fastened to the front fender apron.

3. Be certain that the battery is fully charged and that all accessories are OFF during the diagnosis.

TEST PROCEDURES

→Perform the test procedures in the order in which they are presented here.

Ignition Coil Secondary Voltage Test

CRANK MODE

1. Connect a spark tester between the ignition coil wire and a good engine ground.

2. Crank the engine and check for spark at the tester.

3. Turn the ignition switch **OFF.**

4. If no spark occurs, check the following:
   a. Inspect the ignition coil for damage or carbon tracking.
   b. Check that the distributor shaft is rotating when the engine is being cranked.

5. If a spark did occur, check the distributor cap and rotor for damage or carbon tracking. Go to the Ignition Coil Secondary Voltage (Run Mode) Test.

RUN MODE

1. Fully apply the parking brake. Place the gear shift lever in Neutral (manual transmission) or Park (automatic transmission).

2. Disconnect the **S** terminal wire at the starter relay. Attach a remote starter switch.

3. Turn the ignition switch to the**RUN** position.

4. Using the remote starter switch, crank the engine and check for spark.

5. Turn the ignition switch**OFF.**

6. If no spark occurred, the problem lies with the wiring harness. Inspect the wiring harness for short circuits, open circuits and other defects.

7. If a spark did occur, the problem is not in the ignition system.

Spark Timing Advance Test (1994 B Series Pick-up with 3.0L engine)

Spark timing advance is controlled by the engine control module. This procedure checks the capability of the ignition module to receive the spark timing command from the engine control module. The use of a volt/ohmmeter is required.

1. Turn the ignition switch **OFF.**

2. Disconnect the pin-in-line connector (SPOUT connector) near the TFI module.

3. Start the engine and measure the voltage, at idle, from the SPOUT connector to the distributor base. The reading should equal battery voltage.

4. If the result is okay, the problem lies within the EEC-IV system.

5. If the result was not satisfactory, separate the wiring harness connector from the ignition module. Check for damage, corrosion or dirt. Service as necessary.

6. Measure the resistance between terminal No. 5 and the pin-in-line connector. This test is done at the ignition module connector only. The reading should be less than 5 ohms.

7. If the reading is okay, replace the TFI module.

8. If the result was not satisfactory, service the wiring between the pin inline connector and the TFI connector.

Ignition Coil

TESTING

External Mounted Ignition Coil

COIL PRIMARY RESISTANCE TEST

▶ See Figures 4, 5 and 6

1. Turn the ignition switch off, then disconnect the ignition coil connector.

2. Check for dirt, corrosion or damage.

3. Use an ohmmeter to measure the resistance from the positive (+) to negative (−) terminals of the ignition coil. The 2.6L has a pair of positive and negative terminals on each side of the coil.

4. The resistance measurements should read as follows:
- 3.0L engine(B Series Pick-up): 0.3–1.0 ohms at 68°F (20°C)
- 3.0L engine (MPV): 0.72–0.88 ohms at 68°F (20°C)
- 2.6L engine: side 1—0.77–0.95 ohms and side 2—0.9–1.1k ohms at 68°F (20°C

5. If the reading is between these specifications, the ignition coil is OK; continue on to the Ignition Coil Secondary Resistance Test. If the reading is less than or greater than these specifications, replace the ignition coil.

COIL SECONDARY RESISTANCE TEST

▶ See Figures 7 and 8

1. Turn the ignition switch off, then disconnect the ignition coil connector.

2. Use an ohmmeter to measure the resistance between the negative (-) terminal to the high voltage terminal of the ignition coil.

3. The secondary resistance measurements should read as follows:
- 3.0L engine (B Series Pick-up): 6,500–11,500 ohms at 68°F (20°C)
- 3.0L engine (MPV): 10,000–30,000 ohms at 68°F (20°C)
- 2.6L engine: 6,000–30,000 ohms at 68°F (20°C

4. If the reading is between these specifications, the ignition coil is OK. If the reading is less than or greater than these specifications, replace the ignition coil.

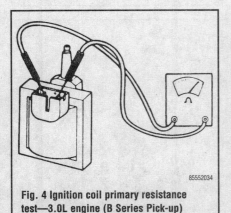

Fig. 4 Ignition coil primary resistance test—3.0L engine (B Series Pick-up)

Fig. 5 Checking the primary ignition coil reesistance—3.0L engine (MPV)

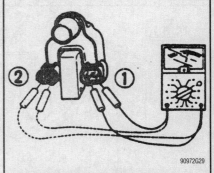

Fig. 6 Ignition coil primary resistance test—2.6L engine

Internal Mounted Ignition Coil

➡The ignition coil is an integral component of the distributor assembly on 1996–98 MPV 3.0L engines. If the ignition coil requires service, the distributor must be replaced.

COIL PRIMARY RESISTANCE TEST

▶ See Figure 9

1. Turn the ignition switch off, then unplug the distributor 3-pin connector.
2. Use an ohmmeter to measure the resistance between terminals A and B on the distributor side.
3. The resistance should measure 0.49–0.74 ohms at 68°F (20°C).
4. If the reading is between these specifications, the ignition coil is OK; continue on to the Ignition Coil Secondary Resistance Test. If the reading is less than or greater than these specifications, replace the distributor assembly.

COIL SECONDARY RESISTANCE TEST

▶ See Figure 10

1. Turn the ignition switch off, then unplug the distributor 3-pin connector.
2. Remove the distributor cap.
3. Use an ohmmeter to measure the resistance between terminal A and the ignition coil tower.
4. The resistance should measure 20–31k ohms at 68°F (20°C).
5. If the reading is between these specifications, the ignition coil is OK. If the reading is less than or greater than these specifications, replace the distributor assembly.

REMOVAL & INSTALLATION

Navajo and B Series Pick-up Models

1. Disconnect the negative battery cable.
2. Label and detach all wiring from the ignition coil.

3. Remove the ignition coil-to-bracket bolts, then remove the ignition coil.
4. If necessary, at this time the radio ignition interference capacitor can be removed from the ignition coil.
To install:
5. If necessary, install the radio interference capacitor onto the ignition coil. Tighten the mounting bolt to 25–35 inch lbs. (2.8–4.0 Nm).
6. Position the ignition coil onto the mounting bracket, then install and tighten the mounting bolts to 25–35 inch lbs. (2.8–4.0 Nm).
7. Attach all wiring to the ignition coil, then connect the negative battery cable.

MPV Models

➡The ignition coil on 1996–98 MPV models is an integral component of the distributor and cannot be serviced separately. If service is required the distributor must be replaced.

1. Disconnect the negative battery cable.
2. Disconnect the distributor lead and wiring harness.
3. Remove the 2 ignition coil mounting bracket bolts.
4. Remove the ignition coil from the vehicle.
5. Install in reverse order.

Ignition Control Module (ICM)

REMOVAL & INSTALLATION

Navajo and B Series Pick-up Models

REMOTE MOUNTED MODULE

▶ See Figure 11

1. Disconnect the negative battery cable.
2. Label and detach all wiring from the ICM.

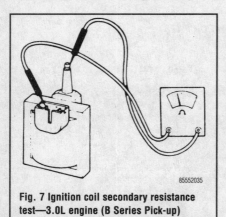

Fig. 7 Ignition coil secondary resistance test—3.0L engine (B Series Pick-up)

85552035

Fig. 8 Checking the ignition coil reesistance—3.0L engine (MPV)

90972P02

90972G30

Fig. 9 Distributor 3-pin connector terminals—1996–98 3.0L engine

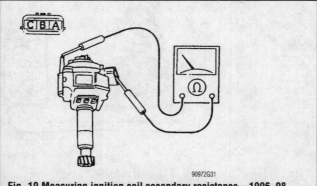

90972G31

Fig. 10 Measuring ignition coil secondary resistance—1996–98 3.0L engine

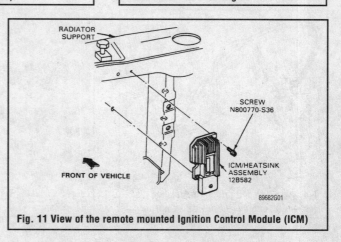

89682G01

Fig. 11 View of the remote mounted Ignition Control Module (ICM)

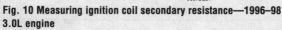

3. Remove the ICM/heatsink-to-fender apron bolts, then remove the ICM/heatsink.

4. If necessary, at this time the ICM can be removed from the heat sink.

To install:

5. Apply an approximately ⅟₃₂ in. (0.80mm) thick layer of silicone dielectric compound (D7AZ-19A331-A or equivalent) to the base plate of the ICM.

6. Install the ICM onto the heat sink. Tighten the mounting bolts to 15–35 inch lbs. (1.7–4.0 Nm).

7. Position the ICM onto the right-hand, front fender apron, then install and tighten the mounting bolts to 90–120 inch lbs. (10–14 Nm).

8. Attach all wiring to the ICM, then connect the negative battery cable.

DISTRIBUTOR MOUNTED MODULE

1. Disconnect the negative battery cable.
2. Remove the distributor assembly from the engine.
3. Place the distributor on the workbench and remove the module retaining screws. Pull the right side of the module down the distributor mounting flange and back up to disengage the module terminal from the connector in the distributor base. The module may be pulled toward the flange and away from the distributor.

➡ **Do not attempt to lift the module from the mounting surface, except as explained above. The pins will break at the distributor module connector.**

To install:

4. Coat the base plate of the TFI ignition module uniformly with ⅟₃₂ inch of silicone dielectric compound WA–10 or equivalent.

5. Position the module on the distributor base mounting flange. Carefully position the module toward the distributor bowl and engage the three connector pins securely.

6. Install the retaining screws. Tighten to 15–35 inch lbs (1.7–4.0 Nm), starting with the upper right screw.

7. Install the distributor into the engine. Install the cap and wires.

8. Reconnect the negative battery cable.

9. Recheck the initial timing. Adjust if necessary.

MPV Models

1994–95

The ignition control module is mounted on the same bracket as the ignition coil and is located on the left side strut tower in the engine compartment.

1. Disconnect the negative battery cable.
2. Disconnect the wiring harness from the ignition control module.
3. Remove the 2 ignition control module mounting fasteners.
4. Remove the ignition control module from the vehicle.
5. Install in reverse order.

1996–98

➡ **The ignition control module on 1996–98 MPV models is an integral component of the distributor and cannot be serviced separately. If ignition control module service is required, the distributor must be replaced.**

Distributor

REMOVAL & INSTALLATION

Navajo and B Series Pick-up Models

▸ **See Figures 12 and 13**

1. Rotate the engine until the No. 1 piston is on Top Dead Center (TDC) of its compression stroke.

2. Disconnect the negative battery cable. Disconnect the vehicle wiring harness connector from the distributor. Before removing the distributor cap, mark the position of the No. 1 wire tower on the cap for reference.

3. Loosen the distributor cap hold-down screws and remove the cap. Matchmark the position of the rotor to the distributor housing. Position the cap and wires out of the way.

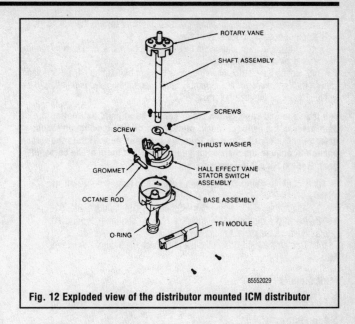

Fig. 12 Exploded view of the distributor mounted ICM distributor

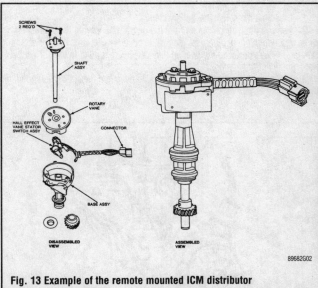

Fig. 13 Example of the remote mounted ICM distributor

4. Scribe a mark in the distributor body and the engine block to indicate the position of the distributor in the engine.

5. Remove the distributor hold-down bolt and clamp.

➡ **Some engines may be equipped with a security-type distributor hold-down bolt. If this is the case, use distributor wrench T82L–12270–A or equivalent, to remove the retaining bolt and clamp.**

6. Remove the distributor assembly from the engine. Be sure not to rotate the engine while the distributor is removed.

To install:

7. Make sure that the engine is still with the No. 1 piston up on TDC of its compression stroke.

➡ **If the engine was disturbed while the distributor was removed, it will be necessary to remove the No. 1 spark plug and rotate the engine clockwise until the No. 1 piston is on the compression stroke. Align the timing pointer with TDC on the crankshaft damper or flywheel, as required.**

8. Check that the O-ring is installed and in good condition on the distributor body.

9. On all vehicles:

a. Rotate the distributor shaft so the rotor points toward the mark on the distributor housing made previously.

b. Rotate the rotor slightly so the leading edge of the vane is centered in the vane switch state assembly.

c. Rotate the distributor in the block to align the leading edge of the vane with the vane switch stator assembly. Make certain the rotor is pointing to the No. 1 mark on the distributor base.

➡If the vane and vane switch stator cannot be aligned by rotating the distributor in the cylinder block, remove the distributor enough to just disengage the distributor gear from the camshaft gear. Rotate the rotor enough to engage the distributor gear on another tooth of the camshaft gear. Repeat Step 9 if necessary.

10. Install the distributor hold-down clamp and bolt(s); tighten them slightly.

11. Attach the vehicle wiring harness connector to the distributor.

12. Install the cap and wires. Install the No. 1 spark plug, if removed.

13. Recheck the initial timing.

14. Tighten the hold-down clamp and recheck the timing. Adjust if necessary.

MPV Models

2.6L ENGINE

♦ **See Figure 14**

1. Disconnect the negative battery cable.

2. Remove the distributor cap from the distributor, leaving the spark plug wires attached. If spark plug wire removal is necessary to remove the distributor cap, tag the wires prior to removal so they can be reinstalled in the correct position.

3. Disconnect the electrical connectors and vacuum hose(s), if equipped, from the distributor.

4. Mark the position of the rotor in relation to the distributor housing and the position of the distributor housing on the cylinder head.

5. Remove the distributor hold-down bolt(s) and remove the distributor.

6. Check the distributor O-ring for cuts or other damage and replace, if necessary.

3.0L ENGINE

♦ **See Figures 15, 16, 17 and 18**

1. Disconnect the negative battery cable.

2. Label and remove the spark plug wires.

3. Turn the crankshaft so the No. 1 cylinder is at TDC of compression.

4. Disconnect the electrical connector from the distributor.

5. Mark the position of the rotor in relation to the distributor housing and the position of the distributor housing on the cylinder head.

6. Remove the distributor hold-down bolt(s), then remove the distributor.

7. Check the distributor O-ring for cuts or other damage and replace, if necessary.

INSTALLATION

Timing Not Disturbed

2.6L ENGINE

1. Lubricate the distributor O-ring with clean engine oil.

2. Install the distributor with the hold-down bolt(s), aligning the marks that were made during removal. Tighten the hold-down bolt(s) to 14–19 ft. lbs. (19–25 Nm).

3. Connect the electrical connectors and vacuum hose(s), if equipped.

4. Install the distributor cap on the distributor. Connect the spark plug wires, if removed.

5. Connect the negative battery cable. Start the engine and check the ignition timing.

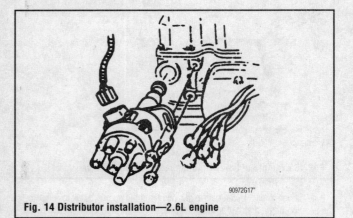

Fig. 14 Distributor installation—2.6L engine

Fig. 15 Disengage the distributor electrical connector

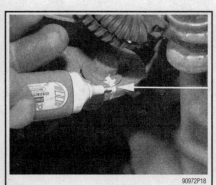

Fig. 16 Be sure to matchmark the positioning of the distributor at the hold-down bolt

Fig. 17 Matchmark the location of the rotor to the distributor assembly

Fig. 18 Remove the distributor assembly from out of the vehicle

3.0L ENGINE

1. Lubricate the distributor O-ring with clean engine oil.
2. On the 1996–98, align the matchmarks on the distributor shaft and the distributor drive gear.
3. Install the distributor with the hold-down bolt, aligning the marks that were made during removal. Tighten the hold-down bolt to 14–18 ft. lbs. (19–25 Nm).
4. Connect the electrical connector.
5. Connect the spark plug wires.
6. Connect the negative battery cable. Start the engine and check the ignition timing.

Timing Disturbed

2.6L ENGINE

1. Disconnect the spark plug wire from the No. 1 cylinder spark plug and remove the spark plug. Make sure the engine is cool enough to touch, place a finger over the spark plug hole.
2. Turn the crankshaft in the normal direction of rotation until compression is felt at the spark plug hole.
3. Align the mark on the crankshaft pulley with the TDC mark on the timing belt cover.
4. Lubricate the distributor O-ring with clean engine oil.
5. Turn the distributor shaft until the rotor points to the No. 1 spark plug tower on the distributor cap and install the distributor. Install the distributor hold-down bolt(s) and align the distributor housing with the mark made on the cylinder head during removal. Snug the bolt(s).
6. Connect the electrical connectors and vacuum hose(s), if equipped.
7. Install the distributor cap on the distributor. Connect the spark plug wires, if removed.
8. Install the spark plug in the No. 1 cylinder and connect the spark plug wire.

9. Connect the negative battery cable. Start the engine and adjust the ignition timing. Tighten the distributor hold-down bolt(s) to 14–19 ft. lbs. (19–25 Nm) after the timing has been set.

3.0L ENGINE

1. Disconnect the spark plug wire from the No. 1 cylinder spark plug and remove the spark plug. After making sure the engine is cool enough to touch, place a finger over the spark plug hole.
2. Turn the crankshaft in the normal direction of rotation until compression is felt at the spark plug hole.
3. On the 1996–98, align the mark on the crankshaft pulley with the TDC mark on the timing belt cover.
4. Lubricate the distributor O-ring with clean engine oil.
5. Align the matchmarks on the distributor shaft and the distributor drive gear.
6. Turn the distributor shaft until the rotor points to the No. 1 spark plug tower on the distributor cap and install the distributor. Install the distributor hold-down bolt(s) and align the distributor housing with the mark made on the cylinder head during removal. Snug the bolt(s).
7. Connect the electrical connector.
8. Connect the spark plug wires.
9. Install the spark plug in the No. 1 cylinder and connect the spark plug wire.
10. Connect the negative battery cable. Start the engine and adjust the ignition timing. Tighten the distributor hold-down bolt to 14–18 ft. lbs. (19–25 Nm) after the timing has been set.

Camshaft Position (CMP) Sensor

For Camshaft Position (CMP) sensor procedures, please refer to Section 4 in this manual.

DISTRIBUTORLESS IGNITION SYSTEM

General Information

The distributorless ignition system used by 1995–98 3.0L, 1994–98 2.3L, 2.5L and 4.0L B Series Pick-up and Navajo engines are referred to as the Electronic Distributorless Ignition System (EDIS). It eliminates the conventional distributor by utilizing multiple ignition coils instead. The EDIS consists of the following components:
- Crankshaft Position (CKP) sensor
- Ignition Control Module (ICM)
- Ignition coil(s)
- The spark angle portion of the Powertrain Control Module (PCM)
- Related wiring

➡**The function of the ICM was incorporated into the PCM beginning with the EEC-V system; otherwise the newer system operates in the same manner.**

SYSTEM OPERATION

The CKP sensor is a variable reluctance sensor, mounted near the crankshaft damper and pulley.

The crankshaft damper has a 36 minus 1 tooth wheel (data wheel) mounted on it. When this wheel rotates the magnetic field (reluctance) of the CKP sensor changes in relationship with the passing of the teeth on the data wheel. This change in the magnetic field is called the CKP signal.

➡**The base ignition timing is set at 10 (plus or minus 2 degrees) degrees Before Top Dead Center (BTDC) and is not adjustable.**

The CKP signal is sent to the PCM, which uses the signal to determine base ignition timing and rpm calculations.

The one missing tooth on the data wheel creates one large space between two of the teeth. The PCM utilizes this large space as a reference to help determine base ignition timing and engine speed (rpm), and to synchronize the ignition coils for the proper spark timing sequence.

All engines, except the 2.3L engine, utilize one ignition coil pack, which contains three separate ignition coils, whereas the 2.3L engine uses two separate ignition coil packs, each of which contains two ignition coils. Each ignition coil fires two spark plugs simultaneously. One of the two plugs being fired is on the compression stroke (this plug uses most of the voltage) and the other plug is on the exhaust stroke (this plug uses very little of the voltage). Since these two plugs are connected in series, the firing voltage of one plug is negative (with respect to ground) and the other plug is positive.

Diagnosis and Testing

SERVICE PRECAUTIONS

- Always turn the ignition key **OFF** and isolate both ends of a circuit whenever testing for shorts or continuity.
- Never measure voltage or resistance directly at the processor connector.
- Always disconnect solenoids and switches from the harness before measuring for continuity, resistance or energizing by way of a 12-volt source.
- When disconnecting connectors, inspect for damaged or pushed-out pins, corrosion, loose wires, etc. Service if required.

PRELIMINARY CHECKS

1. Visually inspect the engine compartment to ensure that all vacuum lines and spark plug wires are properly routed and securely connected.
2. Examine all wiring harnesses and connectors for insulation damage, burned, overheated, loose or broken connections.
3. Be certain that the battery is fully charged and that all accessories are **OFF** during the diagnosis.

SECONDARY SPARK TEST

▶ **See Figure 19**

1. Remove the spark plug from the engine.
2. Connect the spark plug to the high tension lead.
3. Using insulated pliers, hold the high tension lead and spark plug approximately 0.20–0.39 inch (5–10mm) from a good ground.
4. Crank the engine and verify that there is a strong blue spark.

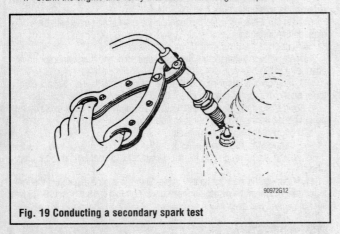

Fig. 19 Conducting a secondary spark test

Ignition Coil Pack(s)

TESTING

Primary and Secondary Circuit Tests

1. Turn the ignition switch **OFF**, disconnect the battery, then detach the wiring harness connector from the ignition coil to be tested.
2. Check for dirt, corrosion or damage on the terminals.

PRIMARY RESISTANCE

▶ **See Figures 20 and 21**

1. Use an ohmmeter to measure the resistance between the following terminals on the ignition coil, and note the resistance:

Except 2.3L/2.5L engine
- B+ to Coil 1
- B+ to Coil 2
- B+ to Coil 3

2.3L/2.5L engine
- B+ to Coil 1
- B+ to Coil 2

or,
- B+ to Coil 3
- B+ to Coil 4

The resistance between all of these terminals should have been between 0.3–1.0 ohms. If the resistance was more or less than this value, the coil should be replaced with a new one.

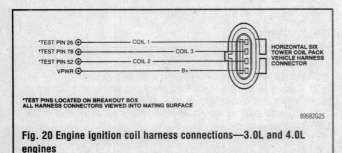

Fig. 20 Engine ignition coil harness connections—3.0L and 4.0L engines

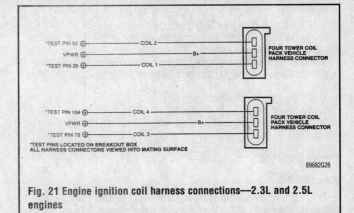

Fig. 21 Engine ignition coil harness connections—2.3L and 2.5L engines

SECONDARY RESISTANCE

▶ **See Figures 20 and 21**

1. Measure, using the ohmmeter, and note the resistance between each corresponding coil terminal and the two spark plug wire towers on the ignition coil. The coil terminals and plug wires towers are grouped as follows:

Except 2.3L/2.5L engines:
- Terminal 3 (coil 1)—spark plugs 1 and 5
- Terminal 2 (coil 3)—spark plugs 2 and 6
- Terminal 1 (coil 2)—spark plugs 3 and 4

2.3L/2.5L engines (right-hand coil pack):
- Terminal 1 (coil 2)—spark plugs 2 and 3
- Terminal 3 (coil 1)—spark plugs 1 and 4

2.3L/2.5L engines (left-hand coil pack):
- Terminal 1 (coil 4)—spark plugs 2 and 3
- Terminal 3 (coil 3)—spark plugs 1 and 4

If the resistance for all of the readings was between 6,500–11,500 ohms, the ignition coils are OK. If any of the readings was less than 6,500 ohms or more than 11,500 ohms, replace the corresponding coil pack.

➡ **On 2.3L/2.5L engines, if one coil pack is found to be defective, the other pack does not need to be replaced.**

REMOVAL & INSTALLATION

▶ **See Figures 22, 23 and 24**

➡ **All engines, except the 2.3L and 2.5L engines, utilize one coil pack containing three separate coils. The 2.3L and 2.5L engines use two coil packs containing two separate coils each.**

1. Disconnect the negative battery cable.
2. Unplug the electrical harness connector from the ignition coil pack.

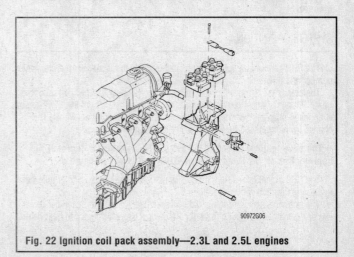

Fig. 22 Ignition coil pack assembly—2.3L and 2.5L engines

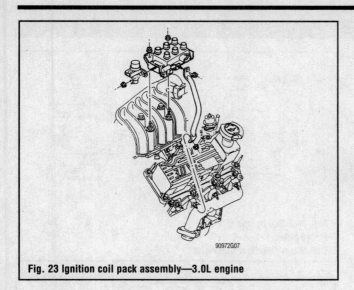

Fig. 23 Ignition coil pack assembly—3.0L engine

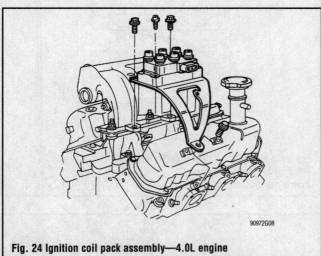

Fig. 24 Ignition coil pack assembly—4.0L engine

3. On the 3.0L engine, loosen the mounting nut and remove the EGR vacuum regulator from the ignition coil.

4. Label and remove the spark plug wires from the ignition coil terminal towers by squeezing the locking tabs to release the coil boot retainers.

5. Remove the coil pack mounting screws and remove the coil pack.

To install:

6. Install the coil pack and the retaining screws. On 2.3L, 2.5L and 4.0L engines, tighten the retaining screws to 44–62 inch lbs. (5–7 Nm). On the 3.0L engine, tighten the retaining screws to 12–14 ft. lbs. (16–20 Nm).

➡Be sure to place some dielectric compound into each spark plug boot prior to installation of the spark plug wire.

7. On the 3.0L engine, install the EGR vacuum regulator to the ignition coil and tighten the mounting nuts to 6–8 ft. lbs. (8–12 Nm).

8. Attach the spark plug wires and electrical harness connector to the coil pack.

9. Connect the negative battery cable.

Ignition Control Module (ICM)

REMOVAL & INSTALLATION

♦ **See Figures 25, 26 and 27**

➡Only 1994 B Series Pick-up and Navajo ignition systems use an external ICM. The 1995–98 B Series Pick-ups have incorporated the ICM into the Power Control Module (PCM).

1. Disconnect the negative battery cable.
2. Detach the wiring harness connector(s) from the ICM.
3. Remove the mounting bolt(s), then remove the ICM.

To install:

4. Apply an even coat of approximately 1/32 inch (0.80mm) of silicone dielectric compound to the mounting surface of the ICM.

5. Place the ICM into the vehicle in proper position and install the mounting bolt(s). Tighten the bolt(s) to 22–31 inch lbs (2.5–3.5 Nm).

6. Attach the wiring harness connector(s) to the ICM.

7. Connect the negative battery cable.

Camshaft Position (CMP) and Crankshaft Position (CKP) Sensors

For procedures on these sensors, please refer to Section 4 in this manual.

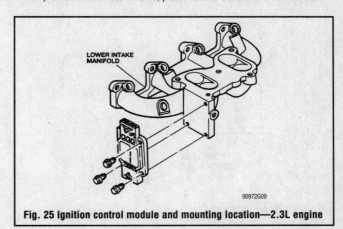

Fig. 25 Ignition control module and mounting location—2.3L engine

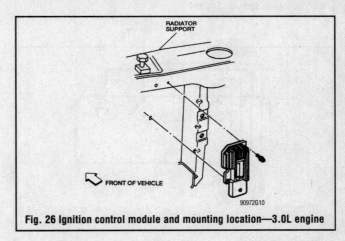

Fig. 26 Ignition control module and mounting location—3.0L engine

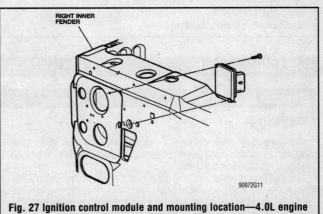

Fig. 27 Ignition control module and mounting location—4.0L engine

FIRING ORDERS

▶ See Figures 28, 29, 30, 31 and 32

➡To avoid confusion, remove and tag the spark plug wires one at a time, for replacement.

If a distributor is not keyed for installation with only one orientation, it could have been removed previously and rewired. The resultant wiring would hold the correct firing order, but could change the relative placement of the plug towers in relation to the engine. For this reason it is imperative that you label all wires before disconnecting any of them. Also, before removal, compare the current wiring with the accompanying illustrations. If the current wiring does not match, make notes in your book to reflect how your engine is wired.

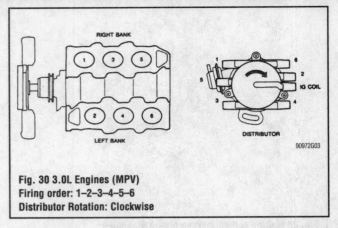

Fig. 30 3.0L Engines (MPV)
Firing order: 1–2–3–4–5–6
Distributor Rotation: Clockwise

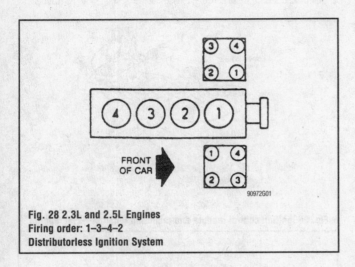

Fig. 28 2.3L and 2.5L Engines
Firing order: 1–3–4–2
Distributorless Ignition System

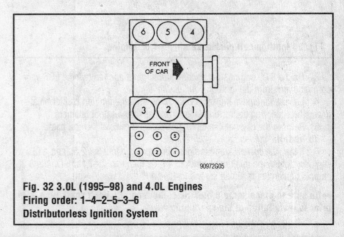

Fig. 31 3.0L Engines (1994 B Series Pick-up)
Firing order: 1–4–2–5–3–6
Distributor Rotation: Clockwise

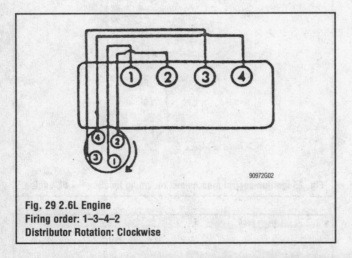

Fig. 29 2.6L Engine
Firing order: 1–3–4–2
Distributor Rotation: Clockwise

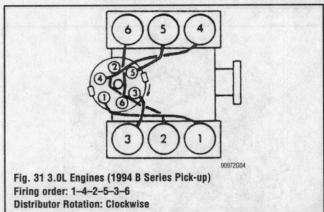

Fig. 32 3.0L (1995–98) and 4.0L Engines
Firing order: 1–4–2–5–3–6
Distributorless Ignition System

CHARGING SYSTEM

General Information

▶ See Figure 33

The charging system is a negative (-) ground system which consists of an alternator, a regulator, a charge indicator, a storage battery, wiring connecting the components, and fuse link wire.

The alternator is belt-driven from the engine. Energy is supplied from the alternator/regulator system to the rotating field through two brushes to two slip-rings. The slip-rings are mounted on the rotor shaft and are connected to the field coil. This energy supplied to the rotating field from the battery is called

excitation current and is used to initially energize the field to begin the generation of electricity. Once the alternator starts to generate electricity, the excitation current comes from its own output rather than the battery.

The alternator produces power in the form of alternating current. The alternating current is rectified by 6 diodes into direct current. The direct current is used to charge the battery and power the rest of the electrical system.

When the ignition key is turned **ON**, current flows from the battery, through the charging system indicator light on the instrument panel, to the voltage regulator, and to the alternator. Since the alternator is not producing any current, the alternator warning light comes on. When the engine is started, the alternator begins to produce current and turns the alternator light off. As the alternator turns and pro-

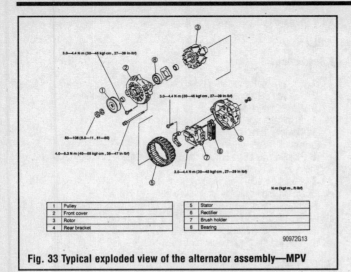

1	Pulley	5	Stator
2	Front cover	6	Rectifier
3	Rotor	7	Brush holder
4	Rear bracket	8	Bearing

90972G13

Fig. 33 Typical exploded view of the alternator assembly—MPV

duces current, the current is divided in two ways: one part to the battery to charge the battery and power the electrical components of the vehicle, and one part is returned to the alternator to enable it to increase its output. In this situation, the alternator is receiving current from the battery and from itself. A voltage regulator is wired into the current supply to the alternator to prevent it from receiving too much current, which, in turn, would cause it to produce too much current. Conversely, if the voltage regulator does not allow the alternator to receive enough current, the battery will not be fully charged and will eventually drain.

The battery is connected to the alternator at all times, whether the ignition key is turned **ON** or not. If the battery were shorted to ground, the alternator would also be shorted. This would damage the alternator. To prevent this, a fuse link is installed in the wiring between the battery and the alternator. If the battery is shorted the fuse link melts, protecting the alternator.

Alternator Precautions

To prevent damage to the alternator and regulator, the following precautions should be taken when working with the electrical system:
- Never reverse the battery connections.
- Booster batteries for starting must be connected properly: positive-to-positive and negative-to-ground.
- Disconnect the battery cables before using a fast charger; the charger has a tendency to force current through the diodes in the opposite direction for which they were designed. This burns out the diodes.
- Never use a fast charger as a booster for starting the vehicle.
- Never disconnect the voltage regulator while the engine is running.
- Avoid long soldering times when replacing diodes or transistors. Prolonged heat is damaging to AC generators.
- Do not use test lamps of more than 12 volts (V) for checking diode continuity.
- Do not short across or ground any of the terminals on the AC generator.
- The polarity of the battery, generator, and regulator must be matched and considered before making any electrical connections within the system.
- Never operate the alternator on an open circuit. make sure that all connections within the circuit are clean and tight.
- Disconnect the battery terminals when performing any service on the electrical system. This will eliminate the possibility of accidental reversal of polarity.
- Disconnect the battery ground cable if arc welding is to be done on any part of the vehicle.

Alternator

TESTING

General Information

There are many possible ways in which the charging system can malfunction. Often the source of a problem is difficult to diagnose, requiring special

equipment and a good deal of experience. This is usually not the case, however, where the charging system fails completely and causes the dash board warning light to come on or the battery to discharge. To troubleshoot a complete system failure, only two pieces of equipment are needed: a test light, to determine that current is reaching a certain point and a current indicator (ammeter), to determine the direction of the current flow and its measurement in amps. This test works under three assumptions:

1. The battery is known to be good and fully charged.
2. The alternator belt is in good condition and adjusted to the proper tension.
3. All connections in the system are clean and tight.

➡ **In order for the current indicator to give a valid reading, the vehicle must be equipped with battery cables which are of the same gauge size and quality as original equipment battery cables.**

Before commencing with the following tests, turn off all electrical components on the vehicle. Make sure the doors of the vehicle are closed. If the vehicle is equipped with a clock, disconnect the clock by removing the lead wire from the rear of the clock.

Battery No-Load Test

1. Ensure that the ignition switch is turned **OFF**.
2. Connect a tachometer to the engine by following the manufacturer's instructions.
3. Using a Digital Volt Ohmmeter (DVOM) measure the voltage across the positive (+) and negative (-) battery terminals. Note the voltage reading for future reference.

Ensure that all electrical components on the vehicle are turned off. Be sure the doors of the vehicle are closed. If the vehicle is equipped with a clock, disconnect the clock by removing the lead wire from the rear of the clock.

4. Start the engine and have an assistant run it at 1500 rpm.
5. Read the voltage across the battery terminals again. The voltage should now be between 14.1–14.7 volts.

   a. If the voltage increase is less than 2.5 volts over the base voltage measured in Step 3, perform the Battery Load test.

   b. If there was no voltage increase, or the voltage increase was greater than 2.5 volts, perform the Alternator Load and No-Load tests.

Battery Load Test

1. With the engine running, turn the air conditioner ON (if equipped) or the blower motor on high speed and the headlights on high beam.
2. Have your assistant increase the engine speed to approximately 2000 rpm.
3. Read the voltage across the battery terminals again.

   a. If the voltage increase is 0.5 volts over the base voltage measured in Battery No-Load test Step 3, the charging system is working properly. If your problem continues, there may be a problem with the battery.

   b. If the voltage does not increase as indicated, perform the Alternator Load and No-Load tests.

Alternator Load Test

✻✻ WARNING

Do NOT use a normal Digital Volt Ohmmeter (DVOM) for this test; your DVOM will be destroyed by the large amounts of amperage from the car's battery. Use a tester designed for charging system analysis, such an Alternator, Regulator, Battery and Starter Motor Tester unit.

1. Switch the tester to the ammeter setting.
2. Attach the positive (+) and negative (-) leads of the tester to the battery terminals.
3. Connect the current probe to the **B+** terminal on the alternator.
4. Start the engine and have an assistant run the engine at 2000 rpm. Adjust the tester load bank to determine the output of the alternator. Alternator output should be within ten percent of the alternator's output rating; if so, continue with the Alternator No-Load test. If the output is not within ten percent of the alternator's output rating, there is a problem in the charging system. Have the system further tested by a Ford qualified automotive technician.

Alternator No-Load Test

1. Using the same tester as in the Alternator Load Test, switch the tester to the voltmeter function.

2. Connect the voltmeter positive (+) lead to the alternator **B+** terminal and the negative (-) lead to a good engine ground.

3. Turn all of the electrical accessories off and shut the doors.

4. While an assistant operates the engine at 2000 rpm, check the alternator output voltage. The voltage should be between 13.0–15.0 volts. If the alternator does not produce voltage within this range there is a problem in the charging system. Have the system further tested by a Mazda qualified automotive technician.

REMOVAL & INSTALLATION

Navajo and B Series Pick-up Models

▶ See Figure 34

1. Disconnect the negative battery cable.
2. Remove the accessory drive belt.
3. Label and disengage all of the wiring connectors from the alternator. To disconnect push-on type terminals, disengage the lock tab and pull straight off.
4. Remove the alternator bolts, then remove the alternator from the engine

To install:

5. Position the alternator on the engine.
6. Install the alternator mounting bolts. Tighten the mounting bolts to 30–40 ft. lbs. (40–55 Nm).
7. Install the accessory drive belt. Ensure that the drive belt is properly installed on the pulleys before starting the engine.
8. Attach all engine wiring harness connectors to the alternator.
9. Connect the negative battery cable.

MPV Models

2.6L ENGINE

▶ See Figure 35

1. Disconnect the negative battery cable.
2. Tag and disconnect the wire and connector from the alternator.
3. Remove the drive belt.
4. Remove the support mounting bolt and nut.
5. Remove the alternator assembly.

To install:

6. Position the alternator assembly against the engine and install the support bolt.
7. Install the adjusting strap mounting bolt.
8. Install and adjust the alternator belt.
9. Tighten the support mounting bolt to 28–38 ft. lbs. (38–51 Nm), and the adjusting bolt to 14–18 ft. lbs. (19–25 Nm).
10. Connect all alternator terminals.
11. Connect the negative battery cable.

3.0L ENGINE

▶ See Figures 36 thru 42

1. Disconnect the negative battery cable. Wait at least 90 seconds before performing any work.
2. Remove the drive belts.
3. Remove the power steering pulley.
4. Remove the mounting and adjusting bolts.
5. After removing the mounting fasteners, pull the alternator unit out just enough to disconnect the wire and connector from the behind.
6. Remove the alternator assembly.

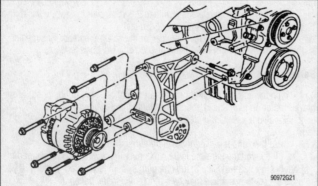

Fig. 34 Alternator installation—2.3L engine, 2.5L engine similar

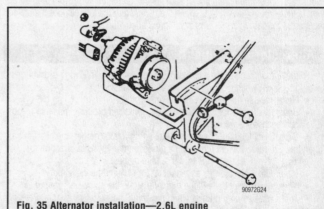

Fig. 35 Alternator installation—2.6L engine

Fig. 36 Remove the top adjuster locking bolt from the alternator . . .

Fig. 37 . . . then loosen and remove the lower alternator pivot bolt

Fig. 38 Pull the alternator out slightly and disconnect the wires behind the alternator

Fig. 39 Remove the alternator unit from the vehicle

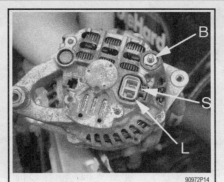
Fig. 40 Alternator wiring terminal identifications

Fig. 41 Mount the alternator in a bench vise with a correct fitting socket and compress the rubber mounting bushing into the bracket hole

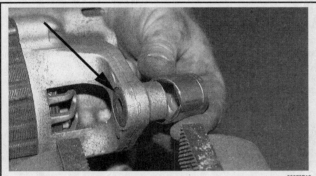
Fig. 42 Check to make sure that the bushing is not damaged and compressed properly

7. Mount the alternator onto a bench vise. Using a correct fitting socket, compress the rubber mounting bushing into the bracket hole. Check to make sure that the bushing is compressed properly and not damaged.

To install:

8. Position the alternator assembly against the engine and install the support bolt.

9. Install the adjusting strap mounting bolt.

10. Install the power steering pulley. Tighten the nut to 29–43 ft. lbs. (40–58 Nm).

11. Install and adjust the drive belts.

12. Tighten the support mounting bolt to 28–38 ft. lbs. (38–51 Nm), and the adjusting bolt to 14–18 ft. lbs. (19–25 Nm).

13. Connect all alternator terminals.

14. Connect the negative battery cable.

Voltage Regulator

REMOVAL & INSTALLATION

B Series Pick-up and Navajo

▶ See Figures 43 and 44

1. Disconnect the negative battery cable.

2. Remove 4 Torx® head screws holding the voltage regulator to the alternator rear housing. Remove the regulator, with the brush and terminal holder attached.

3. Hold the regulator in one hand and pry off the cap covering the **A** terminal screw head with a small prybar.

4. Remove 2 Torx® head screws retaining the regulator to the brush holder. Separate the regulator from the brush holder.

To install:

5. Install the brush holder on the regulator with 2 retaining screws. Tighten the screws to 25–35 inch lbs. (2.8–4.0 Nm).

6. Install the cap on the head of the **A** terminal screw.

7. Depress the brushes into the holder and hold the brushes in position by inserting a standard size paper clip, or equivalent tool, through both the location hole in the regulator and through the holes in the brushes.

8. Install the regulator/brush holder assembly and remove the paper clip. Install the attaching screws and tighten to 20–30 inch lbs. (2.3–3.4 Nm).

9. Connect the negative battery cable.

MPV

The internal voltage regulator used on alternators used with these vehicles is not removable or, in any other way, serviceable. If the voltage regulator is found to be defective, a new alternator must be installed.

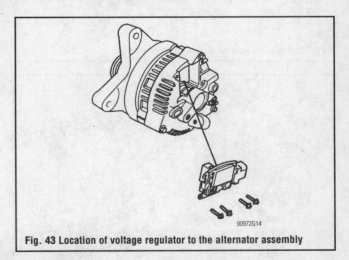
Fig. 43 Location of voltage regulator to the alternator assembly

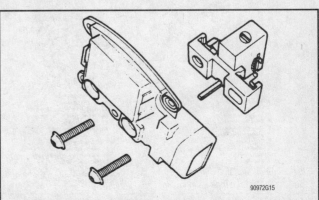
Fig. 44 Separating the brush holder from the voltage regulator

STARTING SYSTEM

General Information

▶ See Figures 45 and 46

The starting system is designed to rotate the engine at a speed fast enough for the engine to start. The starting system is comprised of the following components:

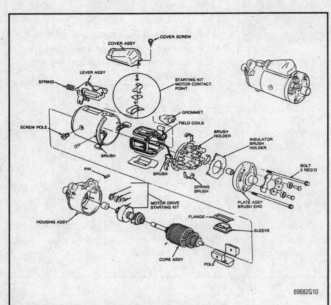

Fig. 45 Exploded view of the coil type starter

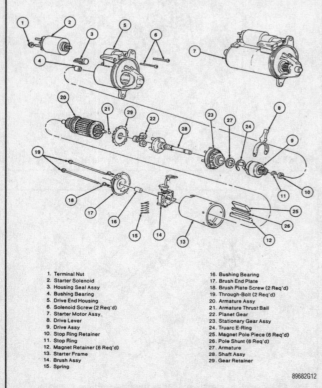

1. Terminal Nut
2. Starter Solenoid
3. Housing Seal Assy
4. Bushing Bearing
5. Drive End Housing
6. Solenoid Screw (2 Req'd)
7. Starter Motor Assy
8. Drive Lever
9. Drive Assy
10. Stop Ring Retainer
11. Stop Ring
12. Magnet Retainer (6 Req'd)
13. Starter Frame
14. Brush Assy
15. Spring
16. Bushing Bearing
17. Brush End Plate
18. Brush Plate Screw (2 Req'd)
19. Through-Bolt (2 Req'd)
20. Armature Assy
21. Armature Thrust Ball
22. Planet Gear
23. Stationary Gear Assy
24. Truarc E-Ring
25. Magnet Pole Piece (6 Req'd)
26. Pole Shunt (6 Req'd)
27. Armature
28. Shaft Assy
29. Gear Retainer

Fig. 46 Exploded view of the permanent magnet type starter

- Permanent magnet gear-reduction starter motor with a solenoid-actuated drive
- Battery
- Remote control starter switch (part of the ignition switch)
- Park/Neutral Position (PNP) or Manual Lever Position (MLP) switch (on 1994 automatic transmission models) or Transmission Range (TR) sensor (on 1995–98 automatic transmission models)
- Clutch Pedal Position (CPP) switch (on manual transmission models)
- Starter relay (Navajo/B Series Pick-up)
- Heavy circuit wiring

Heavy cables, connectors and switches are utilized by the starting system because of the large amount of amperage this system is required to handle while cranking the engine. For premium starter motor function, the resistance in the starting system must be kept to an absolute minimum.

A discharged or faulty battery, loose or corroded connections, or partially broken cables will result in slower-than-normal cranking speeds. The amount of damage evident may even prevent the starter motor from rotating the engine at all.

Vehicles equipped with a manual transmission are equipped with a Clutch Pedal Position (CPP) switch in the starter circuit, which is designed to prevent the starter motor from operating unless the clutch pedal is depressed. Vehicles equipped with automatic transmissions are equipped with either a Park/Neutral Position (PNP) switch, a Manual Lever Position (MLP) switch or a Transmission Range (TR) sensor in the starter circuit. These switches prevent the starter motor from functioning unless the transmission range selector lever is in Neutral (**N**) or Park (**P**).

The starter motor is a 12 volt assembly, which has the starter solenoid mounted on the drive end-housing. The starter solenoid energizes when the relay contacts are closed. When the solenoid energizes, the starter drive engages with the flywheel ring gear, rotating the crankshaft and starting the engine. An overrunning clutch in the starter drive assembly protects the starter motor from excessive speed when the engine starts.

Starter

TESTING

Navajo and B Series Pick-up Models

▶ See Figures 47 and 48

Use the charts to help locate and diagnose starting system problems. Remember that the starter uses large amounts of current during operation, so use all appropriate precautions during testing.

MPV Models

▶ See Figure 49

ON VEHICLE TEST

▶ See Figures 49 and 50

Be sure that the battery is fully charged before starting this test
1. Turn the ignition switch to the **START** position.
2. Verify that the starter motor operates.
3. If the starter motor does not operate, measure the voltage between terminal S and ground, using a voltmeter.
4. If the voltage measures 8V or more, the starter is not working properly.
5. If the voltage measures less than 8V, the wiring harness is the fault.

➡If the magnetic switch is hot, it may not function even though the voltage is standard or greater.

MAGNETIC SWITCH PULL OUT TEST

▶ See Figures 49, 51 and 52

1. Apply battery positive voltage to terminal S and body ground, verify that the pinion is pulled out.
2. On 3.0L engines only, measure the pinion gap while the pinion is pulled out. It should measure 0.02–0.08 inch (0.5–2.0 mm).

System Inspection

CAUTION: When disconnecting the plastic hardshell connector at the solenoid "S" terminal, grasp the plastic connector and pull lead off. DO NOT pull separately on lead wire.

WARNING: WHEN SERVICING STARTER OR PERFORMING OTHER UNDERHOOD WORK IN THE VICINITY OF THE STARTER, BE AWARE THAT THE HEAVY GAUGE BATTERY INPUT LEAD AT THE STARTER SOLENOID IS "ELECTRICALLY HOT" AT ALL TIMES.

A protective cap or boot is provided over this terminal on all carlines and must be replaced after servicing. Be sure to disconnect battery negative cable before servicing starter.

1. Inspect starting system for loose connections.
2. If system does not operate properly, note condition and continue diagnosis using the symptom chart.

WARNING: WHEN WORKING IN AREA OF THE STARTER, BE CAREFUL TO AVOID TOUCHING HOT EXHAUST COMPONENTS.

CONDITION	POSSIBLE SOURCE	ACTION
Starter solenoid does not pull-in and starter does not crank (Audible click may or may not be heard).	• Open fuse. • Low battery. • Inoperative fender apron relay. • Open circuit or high resistance in external feed circuit to starter solenoid. • Inoperative starter.	• Check fuse continuity. • Refer to appropriate battery section in this manual. • Go to Evaluation Procedure 2. • Go to Test A. • Replace starter. See removal and installation procedure.
Unusual starter noise during starter overrun.	• Starter not mounted flush (cocked). • Noise from other components. • Ring gear tooth damage or excessive ring gear runout. • Defective starter.	• Realign starter on transmission bell housing. • Investigate other powertrain accessory noise contributors. • Refer to appropriate engine section in this manual. • Replace starter. See removal and installation procedure.
Starter cranks but engine does not start.	• Problem in fuel system. • Problem in ignition system. • Engine related concern.	• Refer to appropriate fuel system section in this manual. • Refer to appropriate ignition system section in this manual. • Refer to appropriate engine section in this manual.
Starter cranks slowly.	• Low battery. • High resistance or loose connections in starter solenoid battery feed or ground circuit. • Ring gear runout excessive. • Inoperative starter.	• Refer to appropriate battery section in this manual. • Check that all connections are secure. • Refer to appropriate engine section in this manual. • Replace Starter. See removal and installation procedure.
Starter remains engaged and runs with engine.	• Shorted ignition switch. • Battery cable touching solenoid "S" terminal (inoperative or mispositioned cable). • Inoperative starter.	• Refer to appropriate ignition system section in this manual. • Replace or relocate cable and replace starter. • Replace starter. See removal and installation procedure.

Fig. 47 Starter system inspection chart

8982G08

Evaluation Procedure 1

NOTE: Hoist vehicle (if necessary) to access starter solenoid terminals.

CAUTION: Remove plastic safety cap on starter solenoid and disconnect hardshell connector at solenoid "S" terminal.

CHECK STARTER MOTOR — TEST A

TEST STEP	RESULT	ACTION TO TAKE
A1 CHECK FOR VOLTAGE TO STARTER • Key OFF. Transmission in Park or Neutral. • Check for voltage between starter B+ terminal and starter drive housing. • Is voltage OK? (12-12.45V)	Yes ► No ►	GO to A2. CHECK wire connections between battery and starter solenoid and the ground circuit for open or short.
A2 CHECK STARTER MOTOR • Key OFF. Transmission in Park or Neutral. • Connect one end of a jumper wire to the starter B+ terminal and momentarily touch the other end to solenoid "S" terminal. • Does starter crank?	Yes ► No ►	CHECK connections from output of fender apron relay to "S" terminal for open or short. Defective starter. REPLACE starter.

Evaluation Procedure 2

CHECK FENDER APRON RELAY — TEST B

TEST STEP	RESULT	ACTION TO TAKE
B1 CHECK FENDER APRON RELAY • Key in START. Transmission in Park or Neutral. • Is case ground OK?	Yes ► No ►	GO to B2. SERVICE ground. GO to B2.
B2 CHECK VOLTAGE AT FENDER APRON RELAY START TERMINAL • Key in START. Transmission in Park or Neutral. • Check for voltage between fender apron relay start terminal and case ground. • Is voltage OK? (12-12.45 V)	Yes ► No ►	GO to B3. Open circuit or high resistance exists in external circuit wiring or components. Check the following: • All circuit connections including plastic hardshell connector at solenoid "S" terminal to make sure it is not broken or distorted. • Ignition switch. • Neutral switch or manual lever position sensor. • Anti-theft contact.
B3 CHECK OUTPUT TERMINAL VOLTAGE • Key in START. Transmission in Park or Neutral. • Check for voltage at output terminal of fender relay. • Is voltage OK?	Yes ► No ►	REFER to Starter System Diagnosis in this section. Defective fender apron relay. REMOVE and REPLACE relay.

Fig. 48 Starter system evaluation procedure chart

89982G09

3. If not within specifications, adjust with an adjustment washer (drive housing front cover-magnetic switch).

RETURN TEST

▶ See Figure 49

1. Disengage the motor wire from terminal M, and then connect battery power to terminal M and ground the body.
2. Using a small prying tool, pull out the overrunning clutch. Verify that the overrunning clutch returns to its original position when released.

NO-LOAD TEST

▶ See Figures 49 and 53

1. Verify that the battery is fully charged.
2. Connect the battery, starter, ammeter and voltmeter as illustrated.
3. Operate the starter and verify that it turns smoothly.
4. Measure the voltage and current while the starter is operating.
2.6L engine:
- Voltage: 11.5V
- Current (amps): 100 max.
3.0L engine:
- Voltage: 11.0V
- Current (amps): 90 max.
5. If not as specified, replace the starter motor.

REMOVAL & INSTALLATION

Navajo and B Series Pick-up Models

▶ See Figure 54

1. Disconnect the negative battery cable.
2. Raise the front of the vehicle and install jackstands beneath the frame. Firmly apply the parking brake and place blocks in back of the rear wheels.
3. Tag and disconnect the wiring at the starter.

✳✳ WARNING

When detaching the hardshell connector at the S-terminal, grasp the plastic shell to pull it off. Do not pull on the wire itself. Ensure to pull the connector straight off to prevent damage to the connector and S-terminal. If any part of the connector is damaged, replace the damaged component.

---

4. Remove the starter mounting bolts and remove the starter.
To install:
5. Position the starter motor against the engine and install the mounting bolts. Tighten the mounting bolts to 15–19 ft. lbs. (21–27 Nm).
6. Install the starter solenoid connector by pushing it straight on. Ensure that the connector locks in position with a notable click.
Install the starter cable nut to the starter solenoid B-terminal. Tighten the nut to 80–123 inch lbs. (9–14 Nm).
7. Connect any remaining wiring to the starter motor.
8. Lower the front of the vehicle and remove the wheel blocks.
9. Connect the negative battery cable.

MPV Models

2WD

▶ See Figures 55 thru 60

1. Disconnect the negative battery cable. Raise and safely support the vehicle.
2. Remove the starter motor mounting bolts.
3. Pull the starter motor out just far enough to disconnect the electrical connectors from the starter.
4. Remove the starter from the vehicle.
5. After removing the starter, examine the condition of the gear and flywheel teeth.
To install:
6. Place the starter in position, after cleaning the mounting flange surfaces.

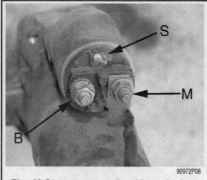

Fig. 49 Starter motor solenoid terminal identifications

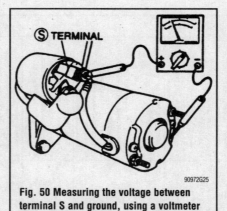

Fig. 50 Measuring the voltage between terminal S and ground, using a voltmeter

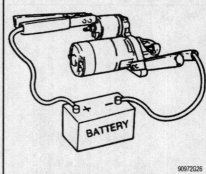

Fig. 51 Apply battery positive voltage to terminal S and body ground

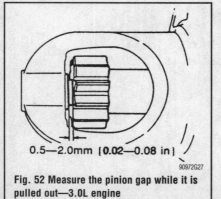

Fig. 52 Measure the pinion gap while it is pulled out—3.0L engine

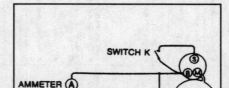
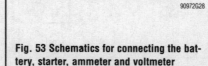

Fig. 53 Schematics for connecting the battery, starter, ammeter and voltmeter

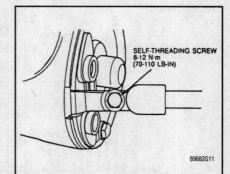

Fig. 54 Some starters use a self-threading bolt to hold the starter cable

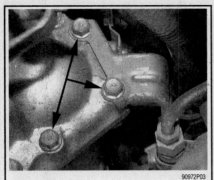

Fig. 55 Remove the three starter motor-to-transmission mounting bolts

Fig. 56 Pull the starter motor out just far enough to access the starter motor wiring connections

Fig. 57 Disconnect the starter motor wiring harness connectors

Fig. 58 Carefully pull the starter motor forward and out from below the vehicle

Fig. 59 After removing the starter motor, inspect the starter motor gear teeth . . .

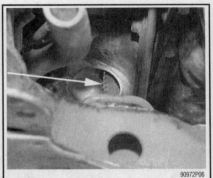

Fig. 60 . . . then inspect the flywheel gear teeth

7. Install and tighten the mounting bolts. Tighten the starter mounting bolts to 27–38 ft. lbs. (37–52 Nm) on 1994–95 vehicles and 24–33 ft. lbs. (32–46 Nm) on 1996–98 vehicles.

8. Connect all wiring connectors. Connect the negative battery cable.

4WD

▶ See Figure 61

1. Disconnect the negative battery cable.
2. Remove the drive belts.
3. Remove the power steering pump pulley.
4. Remove the alternator.
5. Raise and safely support the vehicle. Remove the splash shields.
6. Remove the power steering pump mounting bolts and position the pump aside, without disconnecting the power steering hoses.
7. Remove the automatic transmission cooler line brackets.
8. Mark the position of the driveshaft on the axle flange, and remove the front driveshaft.
9. Remove the wiring harness bracket and the automatic transmission cooler line bracket that is next to the starter.
10. Disconnect the electrical connectors from the starter.
11. Remove the fuel and brake line shield.
12. Remove the starter mounting bolts and remove the starter.

To install:

13. Clean the mounting surface flanges. Place the starter motor into position and install the mounting bolts. Tighten the starter mounting bolts to 28–38 ft. lbs. (38–51 Nm).
14. Install the fuel and brake line shield.
15. Connect the starter motor wiring. Install the wiring harness bracket.
16. Connect the driveshaft.
17. Install the transmission cooler line brackets.
18. Install the power steering pump and the splash shields.
19. Lower the vehicle.
20. Install the alternator.

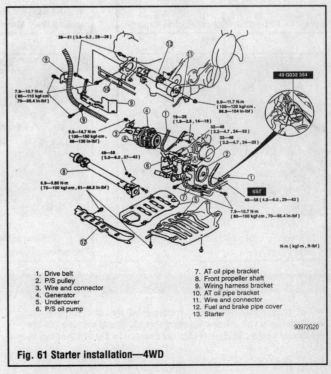

Fig. 61 Starter installation—4WD

1. Drive belt
2. P/S pulley
3. Wire and connector
4. Generator
5. Undercover
6. P/S oil pump
7. AT oil pipe bracket
8. Front propeller shaft
9. Wiring harness bracket
10. AT oil pipe bracket
11. Wire and connector
12. Fuel and brake pipe cover
13. Starter

21. Install the power steering pump pulley.
22. Install and adjust the drive belts.
23. Connect the negative battery cable.

RELAY REPLACEMENT

▶ **See Figures 62 thru 68**

→This procedure only applies to B Series Pick-up models with relay/solenoids that are a separate component of the starter assembly.

1. Disconnect the negative battery cable from the battery.
2. If necessary, remove the power distribution box cover.
3. Disconnect the positive battery cable from the battery terminal.
4. Remove the nut securing the positive battery cable to the relay.
5. Remove the positive cable and any other wiring under that cable.
6. Label and remove the push-on wires from the front of the relay.
7. Remove the nut and disconnect the cable from the starter side of the relay.
8. Remove the relay mounting bolts and remove the relay.

To install:

9. Install the relay and mounting bolts. Tighten the mounting bolts until snug.
10. Attach all wiring to the relay.
11. If equipped, install the power distribution box cover.
12. Connect the positive (+) cable to the battery.
13. Connect the negative (-) cable to the battery.

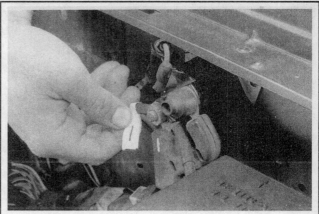

Fig. 62 Label all of the wires on the starter relay before removing them

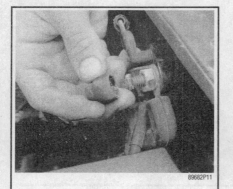

Fig. 63 Also remove any protective caps

Fig. 64 Remove the push-on connectors by pulling them straight off

Fig. 65 Remove the cable securing nuts . . .

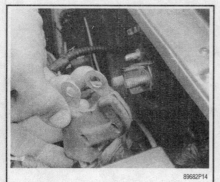

Fig. 66 . . . then remove all of the cables from the relay

Fig. 67 Remove the relay-to-fender apron attaching screws . . .

Fig. 68 . . . then remove the relay from the fender

SENDING UNITS

→This section describes the operating principles of sending units, warning lights and gauges. Sensors that provide information to the Electronic Control Module (ECM) are covered in Section 4 of this manual.

Instrument panels contain a number of indicating devices (gauges and warning lights). These devices are composed of two separate components. One is the sending unit, mounted on the engine or other remote part of the vehicle, and the other is the actual gauge or light in the instrument panel.

Several types of sending units exist, however most can be characterized as being either a pressure type or a resistance type. Pressure type sending units convert liquid pressure into an electrical signal which is sent to the gauge. Resistance type sending units are most often used to measure temperature and use variable resistance to control the current flow back to the indicating device. Both types of sending units are connected in series by a wire to the battery (through the ignition switch). When the ignition is turned **ON**, current flows from the battery through the indicating device and on to the sending unit.

Coolant Temperature Sender

The coolant temperature sender is located in the following positions:
• 2.3L/2.5L engine—left side rear of the engine, below the cylinder head
• 3.0L engine (B Series Pick-up)—top front of the engine, on the intake manifold
• 4.0L engine—top left front of the engine, on the intake manifold
• 2.6L engine—top front of the engine
• 3.0L engine (MPV)—top front of the engine, on the right-hand side of the intake manifold

TESTING

▶ **See Figures 69 and 70**

Before going to the trouble of removing the sender from the engine block and testing it, perform the tests presented in the accompanying chart to ensure that it is the sender malfunctioning, and not another part of the circuit.
1. Remove the coolant temperature sender from the engine block.
2. Attach an ohmmeter to the sender unit as follows:

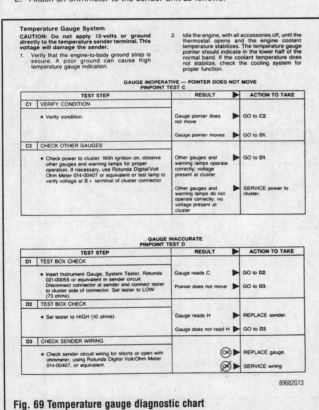

Fig. 69 Temperature gauge diagnostic chart

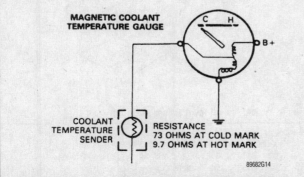

Fig. 70 Temperature gauge and sending unit wiring schematic

a. Attach one lead to the metal body of the sender unit (near the sender unit's threads).
b. Attach the other lead to the sender unit's wiring harness connector terminal.
3. With the leads still attached, place the sender unit in a pot of cold water so that neither of the leads is immersed in the water. The portion of the sender unit which normally makes contact with the engine coolant should be submerged.
4. Measure and note the resistance.
5. Slowly heat the pot up (on the stove) to 190–210° F (88–99° C) and observe the resistance of the sender unit. The resistance should evenly and steadily decrease as the water temperature increases. The resistance should not jump drastically or decrease erratically.
6. If the sender unit did not function as described, replace the sender unit with a new one.

REMOVAL & INSTALLATION

▶ **See Figure 71**

⁑ CAUTION

Ensure that the engine is cold prior to opening the cooling system or removing the sender from the engine. The cooling system on a hot engine is under high pressures, and released hot coolant or steam can cause severe burns.

1. Disconnect the negative battery cable.
2. Remove the radiator cap to relieve any system pressure.
3. Disconnect the wiring at the sender.
4. Remove the coolant temperature sender from the engine.
To install:
5. Coat the threads on the sender with Teflon® tape or electrically conductive sealer, then install the sender. Tighten the sender to 107–143 inch lbs. (12–16 Nm) on Navajo/B Series Pick-up, and 57–82 inch lbs. (6–9 Nm) on MPV.
6. Attach the wiring to the sender and connect the negative battery cable.
7. If necessary, add antifreeze to replace any lost coolant, then install the radiator cap.

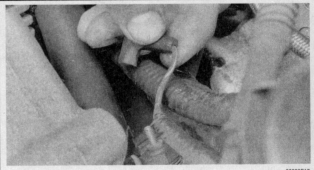

Fig. 71 The sending unit uses a push-on wire connector. To remove, simply pull straight up from the sender

Oil Pressure Sender Switch

➡ Oil pressure senders are used for oil pressure gauges, whereas the oil pressure switches are used for vehicles equipped only with a low oil pressure warning lamp.

The oil pressure senders/switches are located as follows:
• 2.3L/2.5L engines—Left side rear of the engine, in the cylinder head
• 3.0L engine (B Series Pick-up)—Behind the right cylinder head, in the engine block
• 4.0L engine—Left side front of the engine, below the cylinder head in the engine block
• 2.6L engine—Right-hand side of the engine block, above the oil filter
• 3.0L engine (MPV)—Left-hand lower side of the engine, on the oil filter adapter

TESTING

1. To test the oil pressure switch, open the hood and locate the switch.
2. Disconnect the wire from the switch. Attach one end of a jumper wire to the terminal on the end of the wire, then touch the other end of the jumper wire to a good engine ground (any bare metal engine surface). Have an assistant observe the instrument gauge cluster while you do this and tell you if the low oil warning lamp illuminates or not; the low oil warning lamp should illuminate.
   a. If the lamp does not illuminate, skip to Step 3.
   b. If the lamp does illuminate, replace the switch with a new one.
3. Before jumping to any bad conclusions, try a different area for grounding the jumper wire on the engine. If the lamp still does not illuminate, touch the jumper wire end to the negative (-) battery post.
   a. If the lamp illuminates, the problem lies with the engine not being properly grounded.
   b. If the lamp does not illuminate, skip to Step 4.
4. Connect the original wire to the oil pressure switch. While sitting in the vehicle, turn the ignition switch to the **ON** position without actually starting the engine. Observe the other lights on the instrument cluster.
   a. If all of the other lights illuminate when turning the ignition switch **ON**, the oil pressure switch is defective and must be replaced.
   b. If none of the other lights illuminate, there is a problem with power supply to the instrument cluster and gauges.

REMOVAL & INSTALLATION

1. Disconnect the negative battery cable.
2. Disconnect the wiring at the sender/switch.
3. Remove the oil pressure sender/switch from the engine.
To install:
4. Coat the threads with electrically conductive sealer and thread the unit into place. Tighten the sender/switch to 10–13 ft. lbs (13–17 Nm).
5. Attach the wiring to the sender/switch and connect the negative battery cable.

Low Oil Level Sensor

The low oil level sensor is located in the engine oil pan on all Navajo/B Series Pick-up models with the 3.0L and 4.0L engines.

TESTING

♦ See Figures 72 and 73

Use the accompanying diagnostic chart to help pinpoint low oil level sensor malfunctioning.

➡ **The ignition switch should be turned OFF for a minimum of 5 minutes between checks to ensure that the electronic relay, which has a 5 minute timer, has reset.**

REMOVAL & INSTALLATION

♦ See Figure 74

➡ **Always install a new gasket whenever the oil level sensor is removed**

1. Turn the engine **OFF**.
2. Raise the front of the vehicle and install jackstands beneath the frame. Firmly apply the parking brake and place blocks in back of the rear wheels.
3. Drain at least 2 quarts (1.9 liters) of engine oil out of the pan.
4. Disconnect the sensor wiring.
5. Remove the sensor from the oil pan using a 1 in. (26mm) socket or wrench. Discard the old gasket.
To install:
6. Install a new gasket onto the sensor.19

➡ **When installing the new gasket, the flange faces the sensor and the words "panside" should face the oil pan.**

7. Install the sensor and gasket assembly into the oil pan. Tighten the sensor to 13–20 ft. lbs. (17–27 Nm).

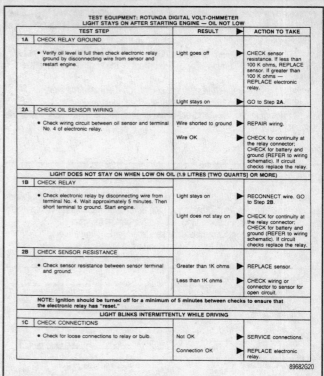

Fig. 72 Low oil level indicator diagnostic chart

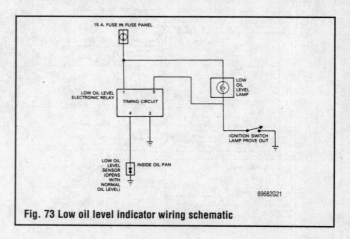

Fig. 73 Low oil level indicator wiring schematic

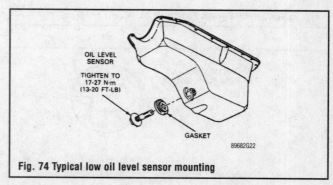

Fig. 74 Typical low oil level sensor mounting

8. Connect the electrical wire to the sensor.
9. Lower the front of the vehicle and remove the wheel blocks.
10. Refill the crankcase to the proper level.
11. Start the engine and check for leaks.

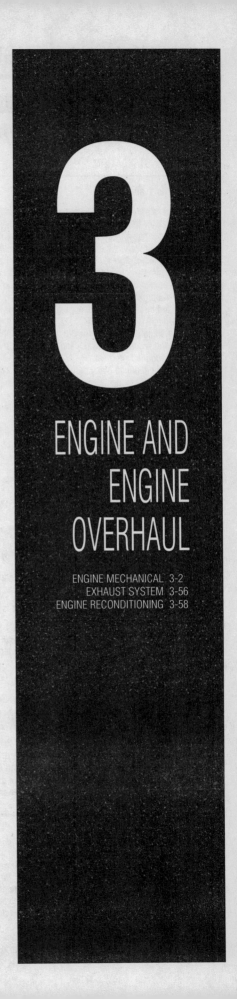

3

ENGINE AND ENGINE OVERHAUL

ENGINE MECHANICAL

Engine

REMOVAL & INSTALLATION

◆ **See Figures 1 and 2**

In the process of removing the engine, you will come across a number of steps which call for the removal of a separate component or system, such as "disconnect the exhaust system" or "remove the radiator." In most instances, a detailed removal procedure can be found elsewhere in this manual.

It is virtually impossible to list each individual wire and hose which must be disconnected, simply because so many different model and engine combinations have been manufactured. Careful observation and common sense are the best possible approaches to any repair procedure.

Removal and installation of the engine can be made easier if you follow these basic points:

• If you have to drain any of the fluids, use a suitable container.
• Always tag any wires or hoses and, if possible, the components they came from before disconnecting them.
• Because there are so many bolts and fasteners involved, store and label the retainers from components separately in muffin pans, jars or coffee cans. This will prevent confusion during installation.
• After unbolting the transmission or transaxle, always make sure it is properly supported.
• If it is necessary to disconnect the air conditioning system, have this service performed by a qualified technician using a recovery/recycling station. If the system does not have to be disconnected, unbolt the compressor and set it aside.
• When unbolting the engine mounts, always make sure the engine is properly supported. When removing the engine, make sure that any lifting devices are properly attached to the engine. It is recommended that if your engine is supplied with lifting hooks, your lifting apparatus be attached to them.
• Lift the engine from its compartment slowly, checking that no hoses, wires or other components are still connected.
• After the engine is clear of the compartment, place it on an engine stand or workbench.
• After the engine has been removed, you can perform a partial or full teardown of the engine using the procedures outlined in this manual.

➥**On vehicles equipped with air conditioning, it is vital to refer to Section 1 prior to performing this procedure.**

1. On models equipped with air conditioning, have the system discharged and evacuated by a MVAC, EPA-certified, automotive technician. Have the A/C compressor removed from the engine.
2. Disconnect the negative battery cable.
3. Remove the hood.
4. Remove the air intake tube and the accessory drive belt(s).

⁂ CAUTION

When draining engine coolant, keep in mind that cats and dogs are attracted to ethylene glycol antifreeze and could drink any that is left in an uncovered container or in puddles on the ground. This will prove fatal in sufficient quantity. Always drain coolant into a sealable container. Coolant should be reused unless it is contaminated or is several years old.

5. Drain the cooling system.
6. Remove the cooling fan, shroud, radiator and all cooling system hoses.
7. On all models, label and detach all engine wiring and vacuum hoses which will interfere with engine removal. Position the wire harness out of the way.
8. On all models, the engine wiring harness is removed with the engine. Only label and detach the harness connectors from components which must be removed. Also unplug the harness at the main bulkhead (firewall), transmission and PCM connections.
9. Unbolt the power steering pump from the engine and position it out of the way. The fluid lines do not have to be disconnected.

10. Detach the accelerator and transmission control cables from the throttle body, and the control cables' mounting bracket from the engine.
11. Release fuel system pressure, then disconnect the fuel supply and return lines from the engine.
12. Remove any remaining mounting brackets and/or drive belt tensioners.
13. Raise the vehicle and safely support it on jackstands.

⁂ CAUTION

The EPA warns that prolonged contact with used engine oil may cause a number of skin disorders, including cancer! You should make every effort to minimize your exposure to used engine oil. Protective gloves should be worn when changing the oil. Wash your hands and any other exposed skin areas as soon as possible after exposure to used engine oil. Soap and water, or waterless hand cleaner should be used.

14. Drain the engine oil and remove the oil filter.
15. Detach the exhaust system from the exhaust manifolds.

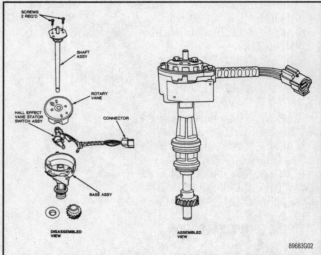

Fig. 1 Engine mounting points for 3.0L engines (B Series Pick-up)

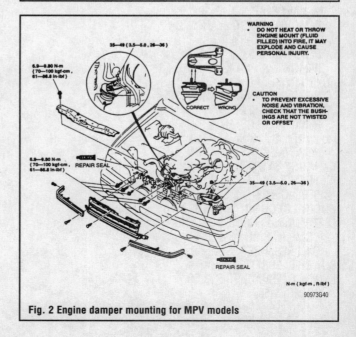

Fig. 2 Engine damper mounting for MPV models

16. Remove the starter motor and starter motor wiring from the engine.
17. Label and detach any under vehicle engine wiring, which will interfere with engine removal.
18. On vehicles equipped with automatic transmissions, matchmark the position of the torque converter to the flywheel. Remove the bolts.
19. Remove all of the engine-to-transmission bolts.

➡All 2.3L, 2.5L, 3.0L (Pick-up) and 4.0L engines use a plate between the engine and the transmission. Some models may have a smaller, removable, flywheel/flexplate

20. If equipped, remove the transmission oil cooler line retainers-to-engine bolts.
21. Remove the front engine support insulator-to-crossmember retaining fasteners.
22. If equipped, remove the engine damper mounting bracket from the engine. The bracket may use two TORX® bolts for the lower mounting points.
23. Partially lower the vehicle and support it with jackstands in the new position.
24. Support the transmission with a floor jack.
25. Using an engine crane or hoist, lift the engine out of the vehicle. Be sure to lift the engine slowly and check often that nothing (such as wires, hoses, etc.) will cause the engine to hang up on the vehicle.
26. At this point, the engine can be installed on an engine stand.
To install:

➡Lightly oil all bolts and stud threads, except those specifying special sealant, prior to installation.

27. Using the hoist or engine crane, slowly and carefully position the engine in the vehicle. Make sure the exhaust manifolds are properly aligned with the exhaust pipes.
28. Align the engine to the transmission and install two engine-to-transmission bolts.

➡Seat the left-hand side, front engine support insulator locating pin prior to the right-hand side, front engine support insulator.

29. Lower the engine onto the front engine support insulators.
30. Detach the engine crane or hoist from the engine.
31. Remove the floor jack from beneath the transmission fluid pan.
32. Tighten the two installed engine-to-transmission bolts, then raise and securely support the vehicle on jackstands.
33. Install and tighten the remaining engine-to-transmission bolts.
34. The remainder of installation is the reverse of the removal procedure. Be sure to tighten the fasteners to the values presented in the torque specification chart.

⁕⁕ WARNING

Do NOT start the engine without first filling it with the proper type and amount of clean engine oil, and installing a new oil filter. Otherwise, severe engine damage will result.

35. Fill the crankcase with the proper type and quantity of engine oil. If necessary, adjust the transmission and/or throttle linkage.
36. Install the air intake duct assembly.
37. Connect the negative battery cable, then fill and bleed the cooling system.
38. Bring the engine to normal operating temperature, then check for leaks.
39. Stop the engine and check all fluid levels.
40. Install the hood, aligning the marks that were made during removal.
41. If equipped, have the A/C system properly leak-tested, evacuated and charged by a MVAC-trained, EPA-certified, automotive technician.

Valve (Rocker Arm) Cover

REMOVAL & INSTALLATION

2.3L Engines
♦ See Figure 3

➡To service the valve cover on the 2.3L engine, the throttle body assembly and EGR supply tube must first be removed. Refer to the necessary service procedures.

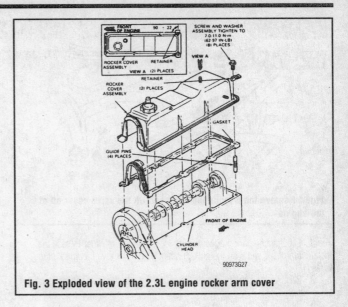
Fig. 3 Exploded view of the 2.3L engine rocker arm cover

1. Disconnect the negative battery cable.
2. Unplug any electrical connections on the air intake hose, then remove the hose.
3. Remove any splash shielding from around the throttle body.
4. Remove the throttle body assembly from the intake manifold.
5. Label and disconnect any electrical connections, including spark plug cables, that will interfere with the removal of the valve cover.
6. If necessary, remove the EGR supply tube.
7. Remove the valve cover retaining bolts and remove the valve cover.

➡A gentle tap with a soft hammer may help to break the seal on the gasket.

⁕⁕ WARNING

Never pry between the valve cover and the cylinder head. Damage to the machined sealing surface, or distortion to the valve cover could occur, resulting in an oil leak.

8. Remove the valve cover gasket from the cover.
To install:
9. Thoroughly clean the gasket mating surfaces on the cover and the cylinder head.
10. Install a new gasket to the valve cover.
11. Place the valve cover onto the cylinder head and install all of the retaining bolts finger-tight.
12. Alternately tighten the bolts to 62–97 inch lbs. (7–11 Nm).
13. If removed, install the EGR supply tube.
14. Install any electrical connections which were removed.
15. Install the throttle body to the intake manifold.
16. Install any splash shielding removed from around the throttle body.
17. Install the air intake hose and attach the wire harness connections which were removed.
18. Reconnect the negative battery cable.
19. Start the engine and check for leaks.

2.5L Engines
♦ See Figure 4

1. Disconnect the negative battery cable.
2. Disengage the wiring connector from the Intake Air Temperature (IAT) sensor.
3. Remove the air cleaner duct assembly.
4. Remove the accelerator control splash shield.
5. Disconnect the accelerator cable.
6. Disconnect the crankcase vent hose from the valve cover.
7. Unplug the wiring harness connectors from the Idle Air Control (IAC) valve and the Throttle Position Sensor (TPS).

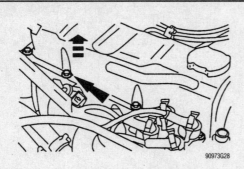

Fig. 4 Remove the 8 mounting bolts and lift the valve cover off of the engine

Fig. 5 Install the cam cover with a new gaskets and seal washers for the bolts

8. Label each spark plug wire prior to its removal in order to ease the installation of the wires on the correct spark plugs. Remove the spark plug wires.

9. Remove the exhaust side spark plug wire retainer from the studs on the valve cover.

10. Remove the throttle body.

11. Remove the vacuum line from the EGR valve and intake.

12. Remove the valve cover mounting bolts.

13. Remove the valve cover. Remove and discard gasket.

To install:

14. Clean all gasket material from the cylinder heads and rocker arm cover gasket surfaces.

15. Install a new gasket on the valve cover.

16. Install the valve cover and mounting bolts. Tighten the mounting bolts to 80–115 inch lbs. (9–13 Nm).

17. Connect the vacuum line to the EGR valve and intake.

18. Install the throttle body.

19. Install the exhaust side spark plug wire retainer onto the valve cover studs.

20. Connect the spark plug wires.

21. Plug in the wiring harness connectors to the IAC valve and TPS.

22. Connect the crankcase vent hose to the valve cover.

23. Connect the accelerator cable.

24. Install the accelerator control splash shield.

25. Install the air cleaner duct assembly.

26. Attach the wiring connector to the IAT sensor.

27. Connect the negative battery cable. Start the engine and check for oil leaks.

2.6L Engine

1. Disconnect the battery ground cable.

2. Disconnect the accelerator cable.

3. Remove the air intake pipe and resonance chamber.

4. Tag and disconnect any wires and hoses in the way.

5. Unbolt and remove the cover.

6. Thoroughly clean all mating surfaces of old gasket material and/or sealer. The cover may use a gasket or RTV gasket sealer. If a gasket is used, coat the new gasket with sealer and position it on the head. If RTV material is used, squeeze a ⅛ inch bead on the head sealing surface.

7. Install the rocker cover. Torque the bolts to 52—78 inch lbs. (6–9 Nm).

3.0L Engine (MPV)

▶ See Figure 5

1. Disconnect the air bypass valve cable.

2. Loosen the clamps and remove the air intake crossover.

3. Disconnect the PCV valve at the cover.

4. Remove the retaining bolts and remove the cam cover.

5. To install the cover, first supply new gaskets and seal washers for the bolts.

6. Tighten the bolts in several stages, going back and forth across the cover to 30–40 inch lbs. (3.5–4.5 Nm).

7. Once all the associated components are installed, start the engine and allow it to reach normal operating temperature. Check for oil leaks.

3.0L Engine (1994–97 B Series Pick-up)

▶ See Figure 6

➡ The valve covers installed on the 3.0L engine incorporate integral (built in) gaskets which should last the life of the vehicle. Replacement gaskets are available if required.

1. Disconnect the negative battery cable.

2. Remove the air cleaner/inlet duct hose assembly.

3. Remove the throttle body assembly.

4. Label and disconnect any vacuum lines that are in the way.

5. Remove the ignition coil pack, if equipped.

6. Remove the upper intake manifold.

7. If removing the right valve cover, perform the following steps:
   a. Disconnect the alternator wiring harness.
   b. Disconnect the closure hose from the valve cover.
   c. Disengage the engine harness connectors from the valve cover.
   d. Remove the fuel injector harness stand-offs from the inboard valve cover studs and move them out of the way.
   e. Disconnect the PCV hose from the oil fill adapter.

8. If removing the left valve cover, perform the following steps:
   a. Remove the PCV valve.
   b. Remove the fuel injector harness stand-offs from the inboard valve cover studs and move them out of the way.

9. Tag and remove the spark plug wires.

10. Remove the spark plug wire separator assembly from the valve cover mounting studs and move them out of the way.

11. Remove the valve cover mounting fasteners.

12. Carefully slide a sharp, thin bladed knife between the cylinder head-to-cover mounting surface and the valve cover gasket at the two RTV junctions. Cut only the RTV sealer and avoid cutting the integral valve cover gasket.

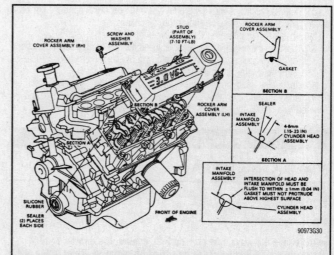

Fig. 6 Rocker arm cover installation on 1994–97 3.0L engines

13. Remove the valve cover(s). It will probably be necessary to tap the cover loose with a plastic or rubber mallet. Make sure that the RTV sealer does not pull the gasket from the valve cover.

To install:

14. Apply a bead of sealer at the cylinder head-to-intake manifold rail step (two places per rail).

➡️When positioning the valve cover to the cylinder head, lower the cover straight down over the holes. Once the cover comes in contact with the RTV sealer, any adjustment for mounting bolt alignment can roll the gasket from the valve cover channel, resulting in leaks.

15. Install the valve cover onto the cylinder head in correct position, then install the mounting bolts. Tighten the mounting bolts to 7–10 ft. lbs. (10–14 Nm).
16. Install the spark plug wire separator assembly onto the valve cover mounting studs.
17. Connect the spark plug wires.
18. If installing the left valve cover, perform the following steps:
    a. Install the fuel injector harness stand-offs onto the inboard valve cover studs.
    b. Install the PCV valve.
19. If installing the right valve cover, perform the following steps:
    a. Connect the PCV hose to the oil fill adapter.
    b. Install the fuel injector harness stand-offs onto the inboard valve cover studs.
    c. Install the engine harness connectors onto the valve cover.
    d. Connect the closure hose to the valve cover.
    e. Connect the alternator wiring harness.
20. Install the upper intake manifold.
21. Install the ignition coil pack, if equipped.
22. Connect any disengaged vacuum lines.
23. Install the throttle body assembly.
24. Install the air cleaner/inlet duct hose assembly.
25. Disconnect the negative battery cable.

3.0L Engine (1998 B Series Pick-up)

▶ **See Figure 7**

➡️Failure to install new valve cover gaskets and valve cover reinforcement pieces will result in oil leaks.

1. Disconnect the negative battery cable.
2. If removing the right valve cover, perform the following steps:
    a. Disconnect the engine control sensor wiring from the ignition coil.
    b. Disconnect and label the right side spark plug wires.
    c. Disconnect the Intake Air Temperature (IAT) and Mass Air Flow (MAF) sensor wiring harnesses. Position the wiring harnesses aside.
    d. Disconnect any vacuum lines.
    e. Remove the ignition coil mounting bracket.
    f. Disconnect the crankcase ventilation tube.
3. If removing the left valve cover, perform the following steps:
    a. Remove the upper intake manifold.
    b. Disconnect and label the left side spark plug wires.
4. Remove the valve cover mounting fasteners.

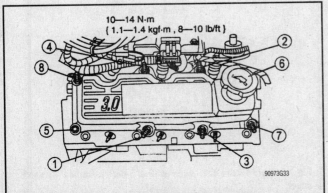

Fig. 7 Valve cover mounting fastener tightening sequence

5. Remove the valve cover(s). It will probably be necessary to tap the cover loose with a plastic or rubber mallet.
6. Remove the valve cover gasket(s) if necessary.

To install:

7. Clean all gasket material from the cover and head.
8. Before installing the new gasket(s), apply a 0.16–0.23 inch (4–6mm) bead of silicone sealant to the seam between the lower intake manifold and cylinder head.
9. Install the new gasket(s).
10. Install the valve cover onto the cylinder head in correct position, then install the mounting fasteners. Tighten the mounting fasteners in correct sequence to 8–10 ft. lbs. (10–14 Nm).
11. If installing the left valve cover, perform the following steps:
    a. Connect the left side spark plug wires.
    b. Install the upper intake manifold.
12. If installing the right valve cover, perform the following steps:
    a. Connect the crankcase ventilation tube.
    b. Install the ignition coil mounting bracket.
    c. Connect any vacuum lines.
    d. Connect the IAT and MAF sensor wiring harnesses.
    e. Connect the right side spark plug wires.
    f. Connect the engine control sensor wiring to the ignition coil.
13. Connect the negative battery cable.

4.0L Engine (Navajo and 1994–97 B Series Pick-up)

▶ **See Figures 8 thru 14**

➡️Failure to install new valve cover gaskets and valve cover reinforcement pieces will result in oil leaks.

1. Disconnect the negative battery cable.
2. Remove the accelerator cable shield.
3. Remove the air inlet duct hose.
4. If equipped, remove the A/C pipe bolt from the upper intake manifold.
5. Tag and remove the spark plug wires.
6. If removing the right valve cover, perform the following steps:
    a. Remove the alternator.
    b. Remove the ignition coil pack.
    c. Move the any wiring harnesses out of the way.
    d. Disconnect the oil filler neck vacuum hose.
    e. Remove the right wiring harness by pulling up on the clip.
7. If removing the left valve cover, perform the following steps:
    a. Remove the upper intake manifold.
    b. If equipped, disengage the A/C compressor clutch connector.
    c. If equipped, remove the A/C compressor mounting bolts and position the compressor off to the side.
    d. Disconnect the power brake vacuum hose.
    e. Disconnect and tag the hoses connected to the vacuum tee.
    f. Remove the PCV valve.
    g. Remove the left wiring harness by pulling up on the clip.
    h. Remove the fuel hose clip bolt and position the hoses to gain access to the upper cover bolts.
8. Remove the valve cover mounting bolts and reinforcement plates.
9. Remove the valve cover(s). It will probably be necessary to tap the cover loose with a plastic or rubber mallet.
10. Remove the valve cover gaskets.

To install:

11. Clean all gasket material from the cover and head.
12. Before installing the new gasket(s), apply sealant to the seam between the lower intake manifold and cylinder head and a 0.125 inch (8mm) ball to each bolt hole on the exhaust manifold side of the cylinder head cover.
13. Install the new gasket(s).
14. Install the valve cover onto the cylinder head in correct position, then install the reinforcement plates and mounting bolts. Tighten the mounting bolts to 5–6 ft. lbs. (6–8 Nm).
15. If installing the left valve cover, perform the following steps:
    a. Position the fuel hoses correcctly and install the fuel hose clip bolt.
    b. Install the left wiring harness and push down on the clip.
    c. Install the PCV valve.
    d. Connect the hoses to the vacuum tee.

Fig. 8 To remove the valve cover, first disconnect the crankcase breather vent tube

Fig. 9 Label and unplug any electrical connections . . .

Fig. 10 . . . as well as vacuum fittings which will inhibit valve cover removal

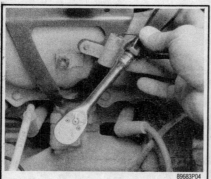

Fig. 11 Remove the coil pack mounting bracket attaching bolts . . .

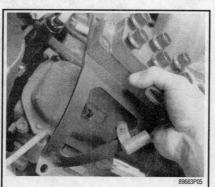

Fig. 12 . . . then remove the coil pack and bracket from the engine

Fig. 13 Remove the valve cover hold-down bolts . . .

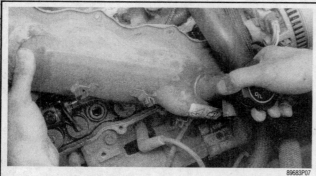

Fig. 14 . . . then remove the cover from the engine. A slight tap with a soft-faced hammer helps to break the seal

4.0L Engine (1998 B Series Pick-up)

▶ See Figures 15 and 16

➡Failure to install new valve cover gaskets and valve cover reinforcement pieces will result in oil leaks.

1. Disconnect the negative battery cable.
2. If removing the right valve cover, perform the following steps:
   a. Remove the air cleaner outlet tube.
   b. Drain the cooling system.
   c. Remove the upper radiator hose.
   d. Disengage the engine control sensor wiring from the Mass Air Flow (MAF) sensor and alternator.
   e. Disconnect the heater water hose.
   f. Disconnect the cruise control actuator cable.
   g. Disconnect the hose from the vacuum reservoir.

e. Connect the power brake vacuum hose.
f. Install the A/C compressor in position onto the mounting bracket, if equipped. Tighten the mounting bolts to 18–23 ft. lbs. (24–30 Nm).
g. Plug in the A/C compressor clutch connector, if equipped.
h. Install the upper intake manifold.
16. If installing the right valve cover, perform the following steps:
   a. Install the right wiring harness and push down on the clip.
   b. Connect the oil filler neck vacuum hose.
   c. Place the wiring harnesses back in position on top of the valve cover.
   d. Install the ignition coil pack.
   e. Install the alternator.
17. Connect the spark plug wires.
18. Install the A/C pipe bolt to the upper intake manifold, if equipped.
19. Install the air inlet duct hose.
20. Install the accelerator cable shield.
21. Connect the negative battery cable.

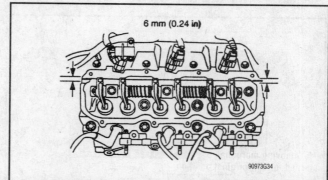

Fig. 15 Apply a bead of silicone sealant before installing the valve cover

6 mm (0.24 in)

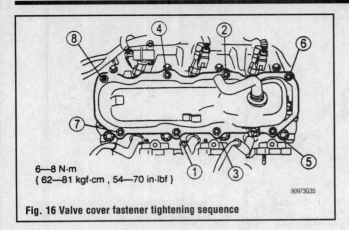

6—8 N·m
{ 62—81 kgf·cm , 54—70 in·lbf }

90973G35

Fig. 16 Valve cover fastener tightening sequence

h. Disconnect and tag the spark plug wires.

3. If removing the left valve cover, perform the following steps:
   a. Remove the upper intake manifold.
   b. Disconnect the vacuum lines from the EGR valve.
   c. Loosen the mounting bolts and remove the EGR valve.
   d. Remove the nut and stud bolt.

4. Remove the valve cover mounting bolts and stud bolt.

5. Remove the valve cover(s). It will probably be necessary to tap the cover loose with a plastic or rubber mallet.

6. Remove the valve cover gaskets.

To install:

7. Clean all gasket material from the cover and head.

8. Before installing the new gasket(s), apply a 0.24 inch (6mm) bead of silicone sealant to the seam between the lower intake manifold and cylinder head.

9. Install the new gasket(s).

10. Install the valve cover onto the cylinder head in correct position, then install the mounting bolts. Tighten the mounting bolts in correct sequence to 54—70 inch lbs. (6—8 Nm).

11. If installing the left valve cover, perform the following steps:
    a. Install the nut and stud bolt, then install the EGR valve.
    b. Connect the vacuum lines to the EGR valve.
    c. Install the upper intake manifold.

12. If installing the right valve cover, perform the following steps:
    a. Connect the spark plug wires.
    b. Connect the hose to the vacuum reservoir.
    c. Connect the cruise control actuator cable.
    d. Connect the heater water hose.
    e. Engage the engine control sensor wiring to the MAF sensor and alternator.
    f. Connect the upper radiator hose.
    g. Install the air cleaner outlet tube.
    h. Refill the cooling system.

13. Connect the negative battery cable.

Rocker Arms/Shafts

REMOVAL & INSTALLATION

2.3L/2.5L Engines (B Series Pick-up)

▶ See Figure 17

➡ **A special tool is required to compress the valve spring.**

1. Remove the valve cover and associated parts as required.

2. Rotate the camshaft so that the base circle of the cam is against the cam follower you intend to remove.

➡ **If removing more than one cam follower, label them so they can be returned to their original position.**

3. Using special tool 49-UN01-135 or equivalent, depress the valve spring, as necessary, and slide the cam follower over the lash adjuster and out from under the camshaft.

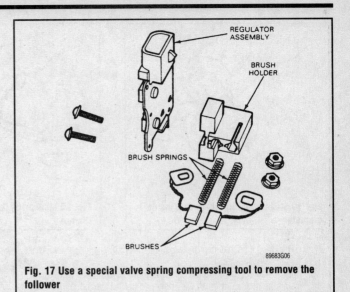

REGULATOR
ASSEMBLY

BRUSH
HOLDER

BRUSH SPRINGS

BRUSHES

89683G06

Fig. 17 Use a special valve spring compressing tool to remove the follower

4. Install the cam follower in the reverse order of removal. Lubricate the followers with SAE 50W engine oil meeting current API specification prior to installing.

2.6L Engine (MPV)

▶ See Figures 18, 19 and 20

1. Disconnect the negative battery cable.

2. Remove the air intake hose.

3. Remove the rocker arm cover.

4. Loosen the rocker arm/shaft assembly mounting bolts in 2–3 steps in the proper sequence. Remove the rocker arm/shaft assembly together with the bolts.

5. If necessary, disassemble the rocker arm/shaft assembly, noting the position of each component to ease reassembly.

6. Check for wear or damage to the contact surfaces of the shafts and rocker arms; replace as necessary.

7. Measure the rocker arm inner diameter, it should be 0.8268–0.8281 in. (21.000–21.033mm). Measure the rocker arm shaft diameter, it should be 0.8252–0.8260 in. (20.959–20.980mm).

8. Subtract the shaft diameter from the rocker arm diameter to get the oil clearance. The oil clearance should be 0.0008–0.0029 in. (0.020–0.074mm) and should not exceed 0.004 in. (0.10mm). Replace parts, as necessary, if the oil clearance is not within specification.

To install:

9. Apply clean engine oil to the rocker arm shafts and rocker arms and assemble the rocker arm/shaft assembly in the reverse order of disassembly, noting the following:
   a. The intake side shaft has twice as many oil holes as the exhaust side shaft.

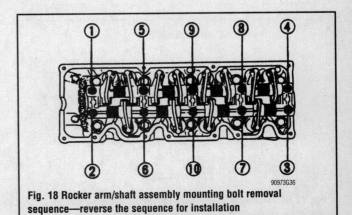

90973G36

Fig. 18 Rocker arm/shaft assembly mounting bolt removal sequence—reverse the sequence for installation

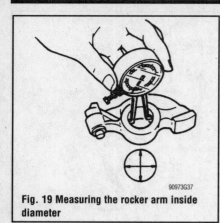

Fig. 19 Measuring the rocker arm inside diameter

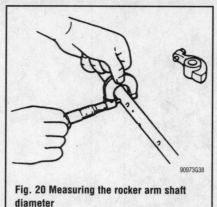

Fig. 20 Measuring the rocker arm shaft diameter

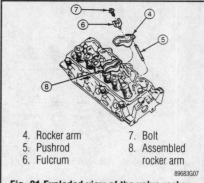

4. Rocker arm	7. Bolt
5. Pushrod	8. Assembled
6. Fulcrum	rocker arm

Fig. 21 Exploded view of the valve rocker arms used on the 3.0L engines

b. The No. 4 camshaft cap has an oil hole from the cylinder head; make sure it is installed correctly.

10. Apply clean engine oil to the camshaft journals and valve stem tips.

11. Install the rocker arm/shaft assembly and tighten the mounting bolts, in sequence, in 2–3 steps to a maximum torque of 14–19 ft. lbs. (19–25 Nm).

12. Coat a new gasket with silicone sealer and install on the rocker arm cover. Apply sealer to the cylinder head in the area of the half circle seals and install the rocker arm cover. Install the mounting bolts and tighten to 52–78 inch lbs. (5.9–8.8 Nm).

13. Install the air intake hose. Connect the negative battery cable, start the engine and check for leaks and proper operation.

3.0L Engines (B Series Pick-up)

▶ **See Figure 21**

1. Remove the rocker arm covers.
2. Remove the single retaining bolt at each rocker arm.
3. The rocker arm and pushrod may then be removed from the engine. Keep all rocker arms and pushrods in order so they may be installed in their original locations.
4. Installation is the reverse of removal. Lubricate the rocker arm assemblies with SAE 50W engine oil. Insure that the fulcrums are properly seated into the cylinder head. Tighten the rocker arm fulcrum bolts to 18–28 ft. lbs. (24–38 Nm).

3.0L Engine (MPV)

▶ **See Figures 19, 20 and 22**

1. Disconnect the negative battery cable.
2. If removing the driver's side rocker arm/shaft assembly, proceed as follows:
   a. Remove the air inlet tube.
   b. Tag and disconnect the necessary electrical connectors and vacuum hoses from the throttle body and intake air pipe.
   c. Disconnect the throttle cable.
   d. Remove the throttle body and intake air pipe.
3. Remove the rocker arm cover.

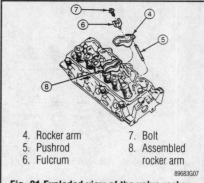

INTAKE SIDE

EXHAUST SIDE

Fig. 22 Rocker arm/shaft assembly mounting bolt removal sequence—reverse the sequence for installation

4. Loosen the rocker arm and shaft assembly mounting bolts in sequence, in 2–3 steps. Remove the assembly with the bolts.

5. If necessary, disassemble the rocker arm/shaft assembly, noting the position of each component to ease reassembly.

6. Remove the valve lifter (Hydraulic Lash Adjuster—HLA) and inspect it. Replace the HLA as necessary.

7. Check for wear or damage to the contact surfaces of the shafts and rocker arms; replace as necessary.

8. Measure the rocker arm inner diameter, it should be 0.7480–0.7493 in. (19.000–19.033mm). Measure the rocker arm shaft diameter, it should be 0.7464–0.7472 in. (18.959–18.980mm).

9. Subtract the shaft diameter from the rocker arm diameter to get the oil clearance. The oil clearance should be 0.0008–0.0029 in. (0.020–0.074mm) and should not exceed 0.004 in. (0.10mm). Replace parts, as necessary, if the oil clearance is not within specification.

To install:

10. To install the HLA, pour engine oil into the rocker arm oil reservoir. Apply engine oil to the HLA, and carefully install the HLA into the rocker arm.

11. Apply clean engine oil to the rocker arm shafts and rocker arms and assemble the rocker arm/shaft assembly. The intake side shaft has twice as many oil holes as the exhaust side shaft.

12. Apply clean engine oil to the camshaft journals and valve stem tips.

13. Install the rocker arm/shaft assembly and tighten the mounting bolts, in sequence, in 2–3 steps to a maximum torque of 14–19 ft. lbs. (19–25 Nm).

➡**Be careful that the rocker arm shaft spring does not get caught between the shaft and mounting boss during installation.**

14. Coat a new gasket with silicone sealant and install on the rocker arm cover. Install the rocker arm cover with new seal washers and tighten the bolts to 30–39 inch lbs. (3.4–4.4 Nm).

15. Install the intake air pipe, throttle body and air intake tube, if removed. Connect the throttle cable and the necessary electrical connectors and vacuum hoses.

16. Connect the negative battery cable, start the engine and check for leaks and proper operation.

4.0L Engine (Navajo and B Series Pick-up)

▶ **See Figures 23, 24 and 25**

1. Remove the valve rocker arm covers.
2. Remove the rocker arm shaft stand attaching bolts by loosening the bolts two turns at a time, in sequence (from the end of shaft to middle shaft).
3. Lift off the rocker arm and shaft assembly. If equipped, remove the oil baffle.

To install:

4. If equipped, loosen the valve lash adjusting screws a few turns. Apply engine oil to the assembly to provide the initial lubrication.

5. If equipped, install the oil baffle.

6. Install rocker arm shaft assembly to the cylinder head and guide adjusting screws on to the pushrods.

7. Install and tighten rocker arm stand attaching bolts to specification, two turns at a time, in sequence (from middle of shaft to the end of shaft).

8. Adjust the valve lash to the cold specified setting. Refer to Section 1 under Valve Lash Adjustment for procedures.

9. Install the valve rocker arm covers.

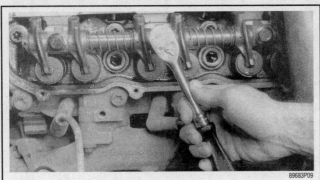

Fig. 23 To remove the rocker shaft, first remove the valve cover, then loosen the shaft retaining bolts . . .

Fig. 24 . . . and remove the assembly from the cylinder head

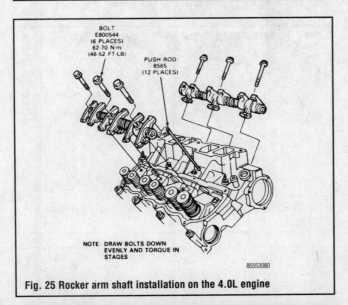

Fig. 25 Rocker arm shaft installation on the 4.0L engine

Thermostat

REMOVAL & INSTALLATION

➡If the replacement thermostat is equipped with a jiggle pin, the pin must be install facing upwards toward the top of the engine (12 o'clock), and should be on the side facing the water outlet. When installing the thermostat gasket, the seal print side should face the cylinder head.

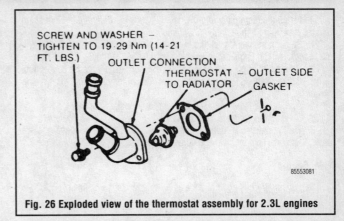

Fig. 26 Exploded view of the thermostat assembly for 2.3L engines

✸✸ CAUTION

When draining the coolant, keep in mind that cats and dogs are attracted by ethylene glycol antifreeze, and are quite likely to drink any that is left in an uncovered container or in puddles on the ground. This will prove fatal in sufficient quantity. Always drain the coolant into a sealable container. Coolant should be reused unless it is contaminated or several years old.

2.3L Engine

▶ See Figure 26

1. Disconnect the negative battery cable.
2. Drain the cooling system below the level of the coolant outlet housing.
3. Disconnect the heater return hose at the thermostat housing.
4. Remove the coolant outlet housing retaining bolts and slide the housing with the hose attached to one side.
5. Remove the thermostat from the outlet.
6. Remove the gasket from the engine block and clean both mating surfaces.

➡It is good practice to check the operation of a new thermostat before it is installed in an engine. Place the thermostat in a pan of boiling water. If it does not open more than ¼ in., do not install it in the engine.

To install:

7. Coat a new gasket with water resistant sealer and position it on the outlet of the engine. The gasket must be in place before the thermostat is installed.
8. Install the thermostat with the bridge (opposite end from the spring) inside the elbow connection and turn it clockwise to lock it in position, with the bridge against the flats cast into the elbow connection.
9. Position the elbow connection onto the mounting surface of the outlet, so that the thermostat flange is resting on the gasket and install the retaining bolts. Tighten the retaining bolts to 14–21 ft. lbs. (20–30 Nm).
10. Connect the heater hose to the thermostat housing.
11. Connect the negative battery cable.
12. Fill the radiator and operate the engine until it reaches operating temperature. Check the coolant level and adjust as necessary.

2.5L Engine

1. Disconnect the negative battery cable.
2. Drain the cooling system.
3. Disconnect the heater return hose at the thermostat housing.
4. Disengage the ECT sensor and engine coolant temperature sender wiring connectors.
5. Disconnect the upper radiator hose from the thermostat housing connection.
6. Loosen the mounting bolts and remove the housing from the cylinder head.
7. Remove the thermostat and gasket from the housing.
8. Clean both thermostat gasket mating surfaces.

To install:

9. Position the thermostat gasket properly onto the housing. The gasket must be in place before the thermostat is installed.

10. Install the thermostat into the housing by first turning and then locking into the recess of the housing.

11. Position the thermostat and housing onto the mating surface of the cylinder head. Install and tighten the retaining bolts to 14–21 ft. lbs. (20–30 Nm).

12. Connect the upper radiator hose to the thermostat housing connection.

13. Connect the ECT sensor and engine coolant temperature sender wiring harnesses.

14. Connect the heater return hose to the thermostat housing.

15. Connect the negative battery cable.

16. Fill the radiator and operate the engine until it reaches operating temperature. Check the coolant level and adjust as necessary.

2.6L Engine

The thermostat housing is at the end of the upper hose, on the cylinder head side, above the alternator.

1. Disconnect the negative battery cable.

2. Drain the cooling system to a point below the housing.

3. Remove the upper hose.

4. Remove the upper nut and lower bolt and remove the housing.

5. Remove the gasket and thermostat. Discard the gasket.

6. Thoroughly clean the mating surfaces of the head and housing.

To install:

7. Position the new thermostat in the head with the jiggle pin on the upper side.

8. Coat the gasket with an adhesive sealer and stick it in place on the head.

9. Install the housing and tighten the nut and bolt to 14–18 ft. lbs. (19–25 Nm).

10. Connect the negative battery cable.

11. Fill the radiator and operate the engine until it reaches operating temperature. Check the coolant level and adjust as necessary.

3.0L Engine (MPV)

♦ See Figures 27, 28, 29, 30 and 31

The thermostat housing is located at the engine end of the lower radiator hose.

1. Disconnect the negative battery cable.

2. Raise and support the front end on jackstands.

3. Drain the cooling system.

4. Remove the lower hose.

5. Unbolt and remove the housing and thermostat.

➡**Some engines have a housing which incorporates an O-ring, eliminating the need for a gasket. On these engines, use no sealer when replacing the housing. On engines which incorporate a gasket, thoroughly clean the mating surfaces and use a new gasket coated with adhesive sealer.**

6. Install a new thermostat in the housing and position the housing on the engine. Some housings are equipped with a location mark on the side, the mark should face the front of the engine when the housing is installed. Tighten the bolts to 14–18 ft. lbs. (19–25 Nm).

7. Install the lower hose.

8. Connect the negative battery cable.

9. Fill the radiator and operate the engine until it reaches operating temperature. Check the coolant level and adjust as necessary.

3.0L Engine (B Series Pick-up)

♦ See Figure 32

1. Disconnect the negative battery cable.

2. Drain the cooling system.

3. Remove the upper radiator hose.

4. Remove the thermostat housing bolts.

5. Remove the housing and thermostat as an assembly.

6. Remove the thermostat from the housing.

To install:

7. Clean all gasket material from the housing and engine.

8. Turn the thermostat clockwise into the housing until the thermostat bridge is perpendicular to the mounting holes.

9. Position the housing on the engine, using a new gasket coated with sealer. Tighten the bolts to 18 ft. lbs. (25 Nm).

Fig. 27 After moving the hose clamp away from the thermostat housing pipe, disconnect the lower radiator hose

Fig. 28 Using a socket, remove the three thermostat housing mounting bolts

Fig. 29 After the mounting bolts are removed, remove the thermostat housing from the engine

Fig. 30 Pull the thermostat down out of the opening in the engine

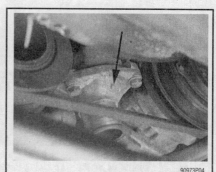

Fig. 31 During assembly, make sure that the notch sticking out of the side of the housing is facing outward

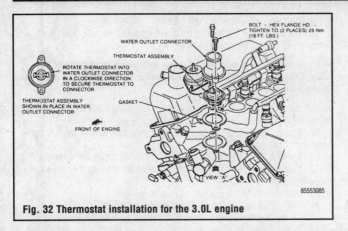

Fig. 32 Thermostat installation for the 3.0L engine

10. Install the hose, fill and bleed the cooling system, connect the negative battery cable and start the engine. Check for leaks.

4.0L Engine

1. Drain the cooling system.
2. Disconnect the negative battery cable.
3. Remove the air cleaner duct assembly.
4. Remove the upper radiator hose.
5. Remove the 3 thermostat housing attaching bolts.
6. Remove the thermostat housing. You may have to tap it loose with a plastic mallet or your hand.
7. Pull the thermostat from the intake manifold.

To install:

> ### ❊ WARNING
>
> **Do not use a sharp metal tool for scraping. Damage to the sealing surfaces could result and cause a leak.**

8. Clean all mating surfaces thoroughly.
9. Make sure that the sealing ring is properly installed on the thermostat rim. Position the thermostat in the housing making sure that the air release valve is in the **up** (12 o'clock) position.
10. Coat the mating surfaces of the housing and engine with an adhesive type sealer. Position the new gasket on the thermostat and place the housing on the engine. Tighten the bolts to specification.

Intake Manifold

The engines covered by this manual utilize an upper and lower intake manifold assembly. If necessary, only the upper intake manifold may be removed by following the intake manifold procedure up to that point. Obviously, installation would also begin at the upper intake steps.

> ### ❊ CAUTION
>
> **When draining the coolant, keep in mind that cats and dogs are attracted by ethylene glycol antifreeze, and are quite likely to drink any that is left in an uncovered container or in puddles on the ground. This will prove fatal in sufficient quantity. Always drain the coolant into a sealable container. Coolant should be reused unless it is contaminated or several years old.**

REMOVAL & INSTALLATION

> ### ❊ WARNING
>
> **Anytime the upper or lower intake manifold has been removed, cover all openings with a rag or a sheet of plastic to prevent dirt and debris from falling into the engine.**

2.3L Engines

♦ See Figures 33 and 34

The intake manifold is a two–piece (upper and lower) aluminum casting. Runner lengths are tuned to optimize engine torque and power output. The manifold provides mounting flanges for the air throttle body assembly, fuel supply manifold, accelerator control bracket and the EGR valve and supply tube. A vacuum fitting is installed to provide vacuum to various engine accessories. Pockets for the fuel injectors are machined to prevent both air and fuel leakage. The following procedure is for the removal of the intake manifold with the fuel charging assembly attached.

1. Make sure the ignition is off, then drain the coolant from the radiator (engine cold).
2. Disconnect the negative battery cable and secure it out of the way.
3. Release the fuel system pressure.
4. Label and unplug any electrical connectors related to the intake manifold assemblies being removed.
5. Tag and disconnect the vacuum lines at the upper intake manifold vacuum tree, at the EGR valve and at the fuel pressure regulator and canister purge line as necessary.
6. Remove the throttle linkage shield and disconnect the throttle linkage and speed control cable (if equipped). Unbolt the accelerator cable from the bracket and position the cable out of the way.
7. Disconnect the air intake hose, air bypass hose and crankcase vent hose.
8. Disconnect the PCV hose from the fitting on the underside of the upper intake manifold.
9. Loosen the clamp on the coolant bypass line at the lower intake manifold and disconnect the hose.
10. Disconnect the EGR tube from the EGR valve by removing the flange nut.
11. Remove the upper intake manifold retaining nuts. Remove the upper intake manifold and throttle body assembly.

➥**If you only need to remove the upper intake manifold, stop at this point. Otherwise, continue with the procedure to also remove the lower intake manifold.**

12. Disengage the push connect fitting at the fuel supply manifold and fuel return lines. Disconnect the fuel return line from the fuel supply manifold.
13. Remove the engine oil dipstick bracket retaining bolt.
14. Unplug the electrical connectors from all four fuel injectors and move the harness aside.
15. Remove the four bottom retaining bolts from the lower manifold. The front two bolts also secure an engine lifting bracket. Once the bolts are removed, remove the lower intake manifold.
16. Clean and inspect the mounting faces of the lower intake manifold and cylinder head. Both surfaces must be clean and flat. If the intake manifold upper or lower section is being replaced, it will be necessary to transfer components from the old to the new part.

To install:

17. To install, first clean and oil the manifold bolt threads. Install a new lower manifold gasket.
18. Position the lower manifold assembly to the head and install the engine lifting bracket. Install the four top manifold retaining bolts finger-tight. Install the four remaining manifold bolts and tighten to 12–15 ft. lbs. (single plug 2.3L engines) or 15–22 ft. lbs. (2.3L twin plug engines), following the sequence illustrated.

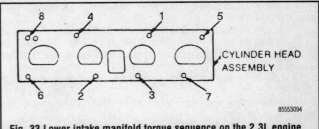

Fig. 33 Lower intake manifold torque sequence on the 2.3L engine

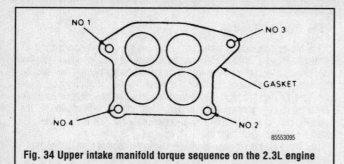

Fig. 34 Upper intake manifold torque sequence on the 2.3L engine

19. Engage the four electrical connectors to the injectors.
20. Install the engine oil dipstick, then connect the fuel return and supply lines to the fuel supply manifold.

➡ **The following procedures are for installing the upper intake manifold.**

21. Make sure the gasket surfaces of the upper and lower intake manifolds are clean. Place a gasket on the lower intake manifold assembly, then place the upper intake manifold in position.
22. Install the retaining bolts and tighten in sequence to 15–22 ft. lbs.
23. Connect the EGR tube to the EGR valve and tighten it to 18 ft. lbs.
24. Connect the coolant bypass line and tighten the clamp. Connect the PCV system hose to the fitting on the underside of the upper intake manifold.
25. If removed, install the vacuum tee on the upper intake manifold. Use Teflon® tape on the threads and tighten to 12–18 ft. lbs. Reconnect the vacuum lines to the tee, the EGR valve and the fuel pressure regulator and canister purge line as necessary.
26. Hold the accelerator cable bracket in position on the upper intake manifold and install the retaining bolt. Tighten the bolt to 10–15 ft. lbs.
27. Install the accelerator cable to the bracket.
28. Position a new gasket on the fuel charging assembly air throttle body mounting flange. Install the air throttle body to the fuel charging assembly. Install two retaining nuts and two bolts and tighten to 15–25 ft. lbs.
29. Connect the accelerator and speed control cable (if equipped), then install the throttle linkage shield.
30. Reconnect any electrical harness plugs which were removed.
31. Connect the air intake hose, air bypass hose and crankcase ventilation hose.
32. Reconnect the negative battery cable. Refill the cooling system to specifications and pressurize the fuel system by turning the ignition switch on and off (without starting the engine) at least six times. Leaving the ignition on for at least five seconds each time.
33. Start the engine and let it idle while checking for fuel, coolant and vacuum leaks. Correct as necessary. Road test the vehicle for proper operation.

2.5L Engine

▶ **See Figures 35 and 36**

1. Make sure the ignition is off, then drain the coolant from the radiator (engine cold).
2. Disconnect battery negative cable.
3. Release the fuel system pressure.
4. Remove the accessory drive belt.
5. Loosen the mounting bolt and remove the oil level dipstick and tube assembly.
6. Label and unplug any electrical connectors related to the intake manifold assemblies being removed.
7. Remove air cleaner air intake duct from throttle body.
8. Remove the throttle control splash shield.
9. Disconnect throttle cable, cruise control cable (if equipped) and bracket assembly.
10. Label and disconnect all vacuum hoses from fittings on upper intake manifold.
11. Disconnect the heater water hose from the intake manifold and the heater line on the vehicle.
12. Disconnect EGR tube at EGR valve and loosen the fitting on the exhaust manifold.
13. Remove the EGR valve.

14. Remove the EVAP emissions tube.
15. Loosen the the 7 mounting bolts and remove the upper intake manifold. Remove and discard the sealing gasket.

➡ **If you only need to remove the upper intake manifold, stop at this point. Otherwise, continue with the procedure to also remove the lower intake manifold.**

16. Remove the A/C compressor from the mounting bracket and move off to the side. Do not disconnect any A/C hoses.
17. Loosen the 3 mounting bolts and one stud, then remove the A/C compressor mounting bracket.
18. Remove the dash panel ground cable from the intake manifold stud.
19. Disengage the wiring harness connector from the retainer on the lower intake manifold.
20. Disconnect the fuel line spring lock coupling.
21. Unplug the fuel injector wiring harness connectors.
22. Loosen the mounting nut and bolt, then remove the engine lifting eye.
23. Remove intake manifold attaching bolts. Note length of manifold attaching bolts during removal so that they may be installed in their original positions. Tap manifold lightly with a plastic mallet to break gasket seal. Lift off manifold.
24. Remove all old gasket material and sealing compound.
To install:
25. Apply sealing compound to the joining surfaces. Place the intake manifold gasket in position.
26. Apply sealing compound to the attaching bolt bosses on the lower intake manifold and position the intake manifold. Follow the tightening sequence and tighten the bolts in 2 stages to the following specifications:
• Stage 1: 45–89 inch lbs. (7–10 Nm)
• Stage 2: 19–28 ft. lbs. (26–38 Nm)
27. Place the engine lifting eye into position on the engine, then install and tighten the mounting nut and bolt.
28. Plug in the fuel injector wiring harness connectors.
29. Connect the fuel line to the fuel rail, engaging the spring lock coupling.
30. Engage the wiring harness connector to the retainer on the lower intake manifold.

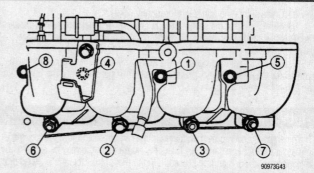

Fig. 35 Lower intake manifold tightening sequence and procedure for the 2.5L engine

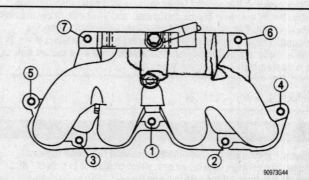

Fig. 36 Upper intake manifold tightening sequence and procedure for the 2.5L engine

31. Attach the dash panel ground cable to the intake manifold stud.

32. Install the A/C compressor mounting bracket and tighten the 3 mounting bolts and one stud.

33. Place the A/C compressor onto the bracket and tighten the mounting fasteners.

➡ **The following procedures are for installing the upper intake manifold.**

34. Mount the upper-to-lower intake manifold sealing gasket and install the upper intake manifold. Follow the tightening sequence and tighten the 7 bolts in 2 stages to the following specifications:
- Stage 1: 45–89 inch lbs. (7–10 Nm)
- Stage 2: 19–28 ft. lbs. (26–38 Nm)

35. Install the EVAP emissions tube.

36. Install the EGR valve. Connect the EGR tube to the EGR valve, then tighten the fitting to the exhaust manifold.

37. Connect the heater water hose to the intake manifold and the heater line on the vehicle. Tighten the hose clamps.

38. Connect all vacuum hoses to the fittings on upper intake manifold.

39. Connect throttle cable, cruise control cable (if equipped) and bracket assembly.

40. Install the throttle control splash shield.

41. Install the air cleaner air intake duct to the throttle body.

42. Plug in any electrical connectors related to the removal of the intake manifold assembly.

43. Install the oil level dipstick/tube assembly and tighten the mounting bolt.

44. Install the accessory drive belt.

45. Connect battery negative cable.

46. Refill and bleed the cooling system.

47. Run engine at fast idle and check for coolant and oil leaks.

2.6L Engines

▶ **See Figure 37**

1. Relieve the fuel system pressure and disconnect the negative battery cable. Drain the cooling system.

2. Disconnect the air intake tube and ventilation hose. Remove the air pipe and resonance chamber.

3. Disconnect the accelerator cable and coolant hoses. Tag and disconnect the electrical connectors to the solenoid valve, throttle sensor and idle switch.

4. Remove the throttle body.

5. Remove the upper intake manifold brackets.

6. Tag and disconnect the vacuum hoses and PCV hose. Tag and disconnect the intake air thermosensor connector and ground wire.

7. Remove the injector harness bracket and remove the upper intake manifold.

8. Tag and disconnect the vacuum hoses from the lower intake manifold. Disconnect the fuel lines.

9. Remove the fuel supply manifold and the injectors. Remove the injector harness and bracket.

10. Remove the pulsation damper and the intake manifold bracket. Remove the attaching nuts and remove the lower intake manifold.

To install:

11. Clean all gasket mating surfaces.

12. Position a new intake manifold-to-cylinder head gasket and install the lower intake manifold. Tighten the nuts to 14–19 ft. lbs. (19–25 Nm).

13. Install the intake manifold bracket and pulsation damper. Install the injector harness and bracket. Tighten the pulsation damper and injector harness bracket bolts to 69–95 inch lbs. (7.8–11.0 Nm).

14. Install the injectors and the fuel supply manifold. Tighten the fuel supply manifold attaching bolts and tighten to 14–19 ft. lbs. (19–25 Nm).

15. Connect the fuel lines. Connect the vacuum hoses to the lower intake manifold.

16. Position a new gasket and install the upper intake manifold. Tighten the attaching bolts/nuts to 14–19 ft. lbs. (19–25 Nm).

17. Install the injector harness bracket. Connect the ground wire and air thermosensor electrical connector. Connect the PCV hose and the vacuum hoses to the upper intake manifold.

18. Install the upper intake manifold brackets.

19. Position a new gasket and install the throttle body. Tighten the mounting nuts to 14–19 ft. lbs. (19–25 Nm).

20. Connect the electrical connectors at the idle switch, throttle sensor and solenoid valve.

21. Connect the coolant hoses and the accelerator cable. Install the air pipe and resonance chamber.

22. Connect the ventilation hose and air intake hose. Connect the negative battery cable.

23. Fill and bleed the cooling system. Run the engine and check for leaks and proper operation.

3.0L Engine (MPV)

1994–95

▶ **See Figures 38 and 39**

✳✳ CAUTION

Fuel injection systems remain under pressure after the engine has been turned OFF. Properly relieve fuel pressure before disconnecting any fuel lines. Failure to do so may result in fire or personal injury. Do not allow fuel spray or fuel vapors to come in contact with a spark or open flame. Keep a dry chemical fire extinguisher nearby. Never store fuel in an open container due to risk of fire or explosion.

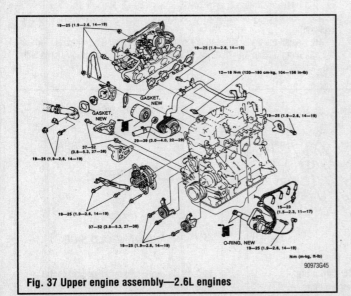

Fig. 37 Upper engine assembly—2.6L engines

90973G45

Fig. 38 Remove the front cover from the dynamic chamber and unplug the electrical connector to the shutter valve actuator before removing the dynamic chamber

90973P47

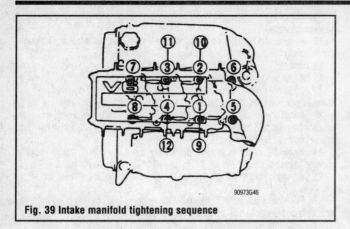

Fig. 39 Intake manifold tightening sequence

1. Relieve the fuel system pressure, and disconnect the negative battery cable. Drain the cooling system.

2. Remove the air intake tube from the throttle body. Disconnect the accelerator cable.

3. Disconnect the throttle sensor connector and the coolant hoses. Remove the throttle body.

4. Tag and disconnect the vacuum hoses. Remove the bypass air control valve and the intake air pipe.

5. Remove the extension manifolds. Remove the dynamic chamber (upper intake plenum) with the shutter valve actuator.

6. Remove the fuel supply manifold and the injectors. Disconnect the coolant hoses.

7. Loosen the lower intake manifold nuts, in sequence, in 2 steps, then remove the lower intake manifold.

To install:

8. Clean all gasket mating surfaces.

9. Position new lower intake manifold gaskets, and install the lower intake manifold.

10. Install the intake manifold washers with the white paint mark upward. Install the nuts and tighten, in sequence, in 2 steps to a maximum torque of 14–19 ft. lbs. (19–25 Nm).

11. Install the injectors and the fuel supply manifold. Tighten the attaching bolts to 14–19 ft. lbs. (19–25 Nm).

12. Connect the coolant hoses.

13. Install a new O-ring on the lower intake manifold and install the upper intake plenum. Apply clean engine oil to new O-rings and install on the extension manifolds. Position new gaskets and install the extension manifolds. Tighten the attaching nuts to 14–19 ft. lbs. (19–25 Nm).

14. Position a new gasket and install the intake air pipe. Install the bypass air control valve. Tighten the attaching bolts/nuts to 14–19 ft. lbs. (19–25 Nm).

15. Position a new gasket and install the throttle body. Tighten the attaching nuts to 14–19 ft. lbs. (19–25 Nm).

16. Connect the coolant and vacuum hoses. Connect the throttle sensor connector and accelerator cable.

17. Adjust the accelerator cable deflection to 0.039–0.118 inch (1–3mm).

18. Connect the air intake tube and the negative battery cable.

19. Fill and bleed the cooling system. Run the engine and check for leaks and proper operation.

1996–98

♦ See Figures 40, 41 and 42

⁂ **CAUTION**

Fuel injection systems remain under pressure after the engine has been turned OFF. Properly relieve fuel pressure before disconnecting any fuel lines. Failure to do so may result in fire or personal injury. Do not allow fuel spray or fuel vapors to come in contact with a spark or open flame. Keep a dry chemical fire extinguisher nearby. Never store fuel in an open container due to risk of fire or explosion.

1. Relieve the fuel system pressure, and disconnect the negative battery cable. Drain the cooling system.

2. Remove the clamps and remove the air intake hose from the throttle body and the MAF sensor.

3. Disconnect the accelerator cable and if equipped, the cruise control cable.

4. Disconnect the throttle position sensor connector.

5. Remove the 2 bolts and the 2 nuts and remove the throttle body unit and gasket.

6. Disconnect the hoses and connector and remove the BAC valve.

7. Remove the VRIS solenoid valve.

8. Remove the PRC solenoid valve No. 1 and the PRC solenoid valve No. 2.

9. Remove the 2 bolts and the 2 nuts and remove the VRIS shutter valve actuator and the gasket.

10. Remove the mounting bolts and the dynamic chamber.

11. Disconnect the fuel delivery pipe from the fuel distributor. Disconnect the fuel injector connectors, remove the mounting nuts and remove the fuel distributor with the injectors.

12. Remove the water hoses from the water outlet and remove the water outlet.

13. Disconnect any water hoses and vacuum hoses from the intake manifold. Remove the mounting nuts, washers, and remove the intake manifold and gaskets.

To install:

➡ Face the bead of the intake manifold gasket toward the intake manifold.

14. Install the intake manifold with 2 new gaskets, the mounting washers and nuts. Hint: install the manifold washers with the white paint marks facing up. Torque the mounting nuts to 14–18 ft. lbs. (19–25 Nm).

15. Reinstall any water hoses and vacuum hoses to the intake manifold and reclamp.

16. Install the water outlet to the intake manifold with a new gasket. Torque the mounting nuts to 14–18 ft. lbs. (19–25 Nm). Reinstall the water hoses with the clamps.

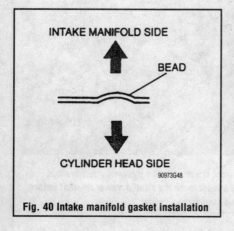

Fig. 40 Intake manifold gasket installation

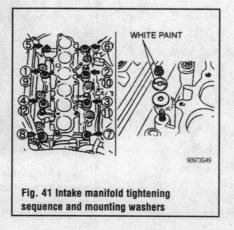

Fig. 41 Intake manifold tightening sequence and mounting washers

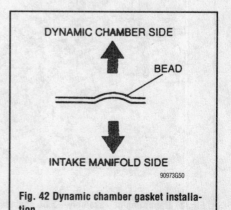

Fig. 42 Dynamic chamber gasket installation

17. Reinstall the fuel delivery pipe with the injectors and torque the mounting nuts to 14–18 ft. lbs. (19–25 Nm). Reconnect the fuel delivery pipe and reconnect the fuel injector connectors.

➡**Face the bead of the dynamic chamber gasket toward the dynamic chamber.**

18. Install the dynamic chamber with a new gasket. Torque the mounting bolts to 70–95.4 inch lbs. (7.9–10.7 Nm).

19. Install the VRIS shutter valve actuator with a new gasket and the 2 nuts and 2 bolts. Torque the bolts and nuts to 70–95.4 inch lbs. (7.9–10.7 Nm).

20. Install the PRC solenoid valve No. 2 and the PRC solenoid valve No. 1.

21. Reinstall the VRIS solenoid and connect the connectors.

22. Install the BAC valve with a new gasket. Torque the 2 mounting bolts and the 2 nuts to 70–95.4 inch lbs. (7.9–10.7 Nm). Reconnect the hoses and connector.

23. Using a new gasket, install the throttle body assembly with the 2 bolts and the 2 nuts. Torque the bolts and nuts to 14–16 ft. lbs. (19–25 Nm).

24. Reconnect the throttle position sensor connector.

25. Reconnect the accelerator cable and if equipped, the cruise control cable.

26. Install the air intake hose to the throttle body assembly and the MAF sensor with the 2 clamps.

27. Refill the cooling system, reconnect the negative battery cable, start the engine and operate until normal temperature, check for coolant leaks, and proper operation.

3.0L Engine (B Series Pick-up)

▶ **See Figures 43, 44 and 45**

➡**The throttle body on 1994–97 B Series Pick-up is cast integral to the upper intake manifold. To remove the upper intake manifold, refer to Section 5 for throttle body removal.**

1. Drain the cooling system (with the engine cold).
2. Disconnect the battery ground cable.
3. Depressurize the fuel system and remove the air intake throttle body (1994–97) or throttle body (1998) as outlined in Section 5.
4. On 1998 B Series Pick-up, remove the upper intake manifold.
5. Disconnect the fuel return and supply lines.
6. Remove the fuel injector wiring harness from the engine.
7. Disconnect the upper radiator hose.
8. Disconnect the water outlet heater hose.
9. If equipped with distributor ignition, disconnect the distributor cap with the spark plug wires attached. Matchmark and remove the distributor assembly.
10. If equipped with distributorless ignition, Label and remove the spark plug wires from the coil pack, then remove the coil pack.
11. Remove the valve covers.
12. Remove the rocker arms and pushrods.
13. Remove the intake manifold attaching bolts and studs (Torx® socket required).
14. Lift the intake manifold off the engine. Use a plastic mallet to tap lightly around the intake manifold to break it loose, if necessary. Do not pry between the manifold and cylinder head with any sharp instrument. The manifold can be removed with the fuel rails and injectors in place.
15. Remove the manifold side gaskets and end seals and discard. If the manifold is being replaced, transfer the fuel injector and fuel rail components to the new manifold on a clean workbench. Clean all gasket mating surfaces.

To install:

16. First lightly oil all attaching bolts and stud threads. The intake manifold, cylinder head and cylinder block mating surfaces should be clean and free of old silicone rubber sealer. Use a suitable solvent to clean these areas.

17. Apply silicone rubber sealer (D6AZ–19562–A or equivalent) to the intersection of the cylinder block assembly and head assembly at four corners as illustrated.

➡**When using silicone rubber sealer, assembly must occur within 15 minutes after sealer application. After this time, the sealer may start to set–up and its sealing effectiveness may be reduced. In high temperature/humidity conditions, the RTV will start to skin over in about 5 minutes.**

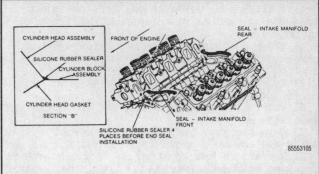

Fig. 43 Silicone sealer and intake end seal application for the 3.0L engine

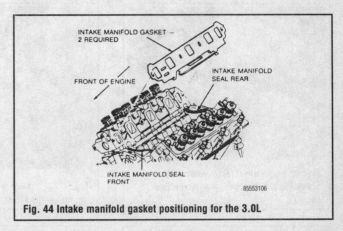

Fig. 44 Intake manifold gasket positioning for the 3.0L

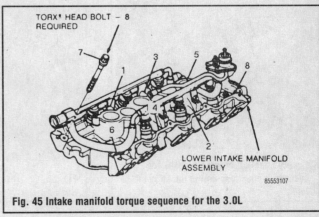

Fig. 45 Intake manifold torque sequence for the 3.0L

18. Install the front intake manifold seal and rear intake manifold seal, then secure them with retaining features.

19. Position the intake manifold gaskets in place and insert the locking tabs over the tabs on the cylinder head gaskets.

20. Apply silicone rubber sealer over the gasket in the same places as in Step 14.

21. Carefully lower the intake manifold into position on the cylinder block and cylinder heads to prevent smearing the silicone sealer and causing gasketing voids.

22. Install the retaining bolts. Tighten in two stages, using the sequence illustrated, first to 11 ft. lbs., then to 18 ft. lbs.

23. If installing a new manifold, install fuel supply rail and injectors. Refer to the necessary service procedures.

24. Install the pushrods and rocker arms. Apply oil to pushrod and fulcrum prior to installation. Rotate the crankshaft to place the lifter on the heel position or base circle of camshaft. Tighten to 8 ft. lbs. to seat fulcrum in cylinder head. Final bolt torque is 24 ft. lbs.

25. Install valve covers, fuel injector harness, throttle body assembly (1994–97) or upper intake manifold and throttle body (1998), hose and electrical connections.

26. If equipped with distributor ignition, install the distributor assembly, using the matchmarks made earlier to insure correct alignment. Install the distributor cap and spark plug wires.

27. If equipped with distributorless ignition, install the coil pack then install the spark plug wires to their original locations.

28. Install coolant hoses. Connect all vacuum lines. Reconnect fuel lines. Install fuel line safety clips.

29. Fill and bleed cooling system. If any engine coolant accidentally spilled into the engine while the intake was off, change engine oil and filter.

30. Install air cleaner hose. Connect battery ground cable. Start engine and check for coolant, oil, fuel and vacuum leaks.

31. If equipped with distributor ignition, verify base initial timing as outlined. Check and adjust engine idle as necessary.

4.0L Engine

▶ See Figures 46 thru 62

The intake manifold is a 4–piece assembly, consisting of the upper intake manifold, the throttle body, the fuel supply manifold, and the lower intake manifold.

1. Disconnect the battery ground cable.
2. Remove the weather shield.
3. Remove the air cleaner intake duct.
4. Disconnect the throttle cable and bracket.
5. Tag and unplug all vacuum lines connected to the manifold.
6. Tag and disconnect all electrical wires attached to the upper manifold assembly.
7. Relieve the fuel system pressure.
8. Tag and remove the spark plug wires.

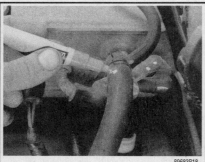

Fig. 46 Begin the intake removal by unbolting the throttle linkage weather shield . . .

Fig. 47 . . . then remove the air intake duct from the throttle body

Fig. 48 Disconnect the throttle linkage, then unbolt and remove the cable bracket

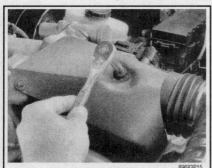

Fig. 49 Label all of the electrical and vacuum connections on the intake manifold . . .

Fig. 50 . . . then disconnect the vacuum lines . . .

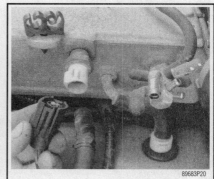

Fig. 51 . . . and the electrical harness plugs

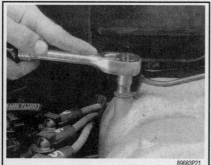

Fig. 52 Also, ensure that any brackets which are bolted to the manifold are unfastened

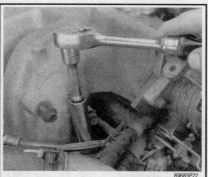

Fig. 53 Remove the upper intake manifold attaching bolts . . .

Fig. 54 . . . then lift the manifold from the engine

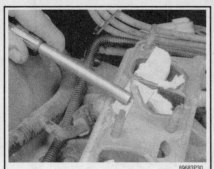

Fig. 55 Stuff rags into the intake runners, then remove the old upper intake gasket; use care when scraping

Fig. 56 Disconnect the fuel supply and return lines from the injector fuel rail

Fig. 57 Label all of the electrical connections on the lower intake manifold . . .

Fig. 58 . . . then disconnect them. Next, remove the valve covers

Fig. 59 Remove the lower intake manifold attaching bolts . . .

Fig. 60 . . . then lift the manifold from the engine

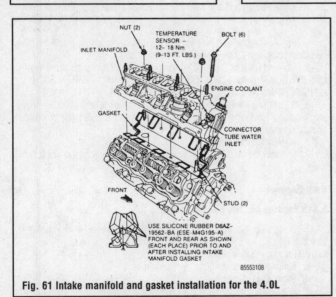

Fig. 61 Intake manifold and gasket installation for the 4.0L

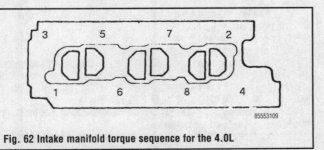

Fig. 62 Intake manifold torque sequence for the 4.0L

9. Remove the EDIS ignition coil and bracket.
10. Remove the 6 attaching nuts and lift off the upper manifold.

➡ If you only need to remove the upper intake manifold, stop at this point. Otherwise, continue with the procedure to also remove the lower intake manifold.

11. Disconnect the fuel supply and return lines from the injector fuel rail.
12. Label and disconnect all of the electrical connections on the lower manifold assembly.
13. Remove the valve covers.
14. Remove the lower intake manifold bolts. Tap the manifold lightly with a plastic mallet and remove it.
15. Clean all surfaces of old gasket material.

To install:
16. Apply RTV silicone gasket material at the junction points of the heads and manifold.

➡ This material will set within 15 minutes, so work quickly!

17. Install new manifold gaskets and again apply the RTV material.
18. Position the manifold and install the nuts hand-tight. Tighten the nuts in 4 stages, using the sequence shown, as follows:
- Stage 1: 22 inch lbs. (3 Nm)
- Stage 2: 88 inch lbs. (10 Nm)
- Stage 3: 115 inch lbs. (13 Nm)
- Stage 4: 11–13 ft. lbs. (14–18 Nm)
19. Once again, apply RTV material to the manifold/head joints.
20. Install the valve covers using new gaskets.

➡ The following procedures are for installing the upper intake manifold.

21. Position a new gasket and install the upper manifold. Tighten the nuts to 15–18 ft. lbs. (20–25 Nm).
22. Install the EDIS coil.
23. Connect the fuel and return lines.
24. Install the throttle body.
25. Connect all wires.

26. Connect all vacuum lines.
27. Connect the throttle linkage.
28. Install the weather shield.
29. Install the air cleaner and duct.
30. Fill and bleed the cooling system.
31. Connect the battery ground.
32. Run the engine and check for leaks.

Exhaust Manifold

REMOVAL & INSTALLATION

✳✳ CAUTION

Allow the engine to cool before attempting to remove the manifolds. Serious injury can result from contact with hot exhaust manifolds.

2.3L Engines

▶ **See Figure 63**

1. Disconnect the negative battery cable.
2. Remove the air cleaner outlet tube.
3. Remove the EGR transducer lines at the tube. Loosen and remove the EGR valve-to-exhaust manifold tube.
4. Disconnect the exhaust pipe from the exhaust manifold.
5. Remove the two nuts securing the lifting bracket/transducer mount, and remove the bracket.
6. Remove the exhaust manifold mounting bolts/nuts and remove the manifold.
7. Install the exhaust manifold in the reverse order. Torque the manifold in sequence in two steps:
   • Step 1: 5–7 ft. lbs. (7–9 Nm)
   • Step 2: 16–23 ft. lbs. (22–31 Nm)

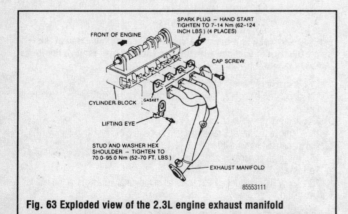

Fig. 63 Exploded view of the 2.3L engine exhaust manifold

2.5L Engines

▶ **See Figure 64**

1. Disconnect the negative battery cable.
2. Unplug the wiring harness connector from the Intake Air Temperature (IAT) sensor.
3. Remove the air cleaner outlet duct.
4. Disconnect and label any vacuum hoses necessary to gain access to the exhaust manifold.
5. Loosen the fitting at the EGR valve and disconnect the fitting at the exhaust manifold.
6. Disconnect the catalytic converter from the exhaust manifold.
7. Loosen the 2 mounting nuts and remove the rear engine lifting eye.
8. Remove the 2 studs and 6 manifold mounting bolts.
9. Lift the manifold from the cylinder head.

10. Clean gasket surfaces on the exhaust manifold and the cylinder head.

To install:

11. Install a new exhaust manifold gasket.
12. Position the exhaust manifold onto the cylinder head. Install and tighten the 2 studs and 6 mounting bolts, in sequence, in 2 stages to the following specifications:
   • Stage 1: 15–16 ft. lbs. (20–23 Nm)
   • Stage 2: 45–59 ft. lbs. (60–80 Nm)
13. Install the rear engine lifting eye and tighten the 2 mounting nuts to 15–22 ft. lbs. (20–30 Nm).
14. Install the catalytic converter to the exhaust manifold and tighten the mounting fasteners.
15. Connect the EGR tube to the exhaust manifold and tighten the fitting. Tighten the EGR tube fitting at the EGR valve.
16. Connect all of the vacuum hoses that were disconnected for the removal procedure.
17. Install the air cleaner outlet duct.
18. Plug in the wiring harness connector to the IAT sensor.
19. Connect the negative battery cable.

3.0L Engine (B Series Pick-up)

1. Disconnect the negative battery cable. Raise and safely support the vehicle as necessary.
2. Remove the spark plugs.
3. If removing the left side exhaust manifold remove the oil level indicator tube retaining nut, rotate the dipstick assembly out of the way. Also, if equipped, loosen the EGR tube flare nut at the valve and remove the tube bolt at the manifold.
4. Remove the manifold to exhaust pipe attaching nuts, then separate the exhaust pipe from the manifold.
5. Remove the exhaust manifold attaching bolts and the manifold.

To install:

6. Clean all gasket mating surfaces.
7. Lightly oil all bolt and stud threads before installation. If a new manifold is being installed, the oxygen sensor will have to be transferred to the new part.
8. Position the exhaust manifold on the cylinder head and install the manifold attaching bolts. Tighten them to 19 ft. lbs. (25 Nm).
9. Connect (replace gasket if so equipped) the exhaust pipe to the manifold, then tighten the attaching nuts to 30 ft. lbs. (41 Nm). TIGHTEN BOTH NUTS IN EQUAL AMOUNTS TO CORRECTLY SEAT INLET PIPE FLANGE.
10. If installing the left side manifold, install the oil tube dipstick assembly (apply sealer to the tube) as necessary. Also reattach the EGR tube and components if removed.
11. Install the spark plugs.
12. Connect the negative battery cable. Start the engine and check for leaks.

4.0L Engine

▶ **See Figures 65, 66, 67, 68 and 69**

1. Disconnect the negative battery cable. Remove the oil level indicator tube bracket.
2. Raise and safely support the vehicle.
3. Remove the exhaust pipe-to-manifold bolts.
4. Lower the vehicle.
5. If removing the left-hand manifold, disconnect the power steering pump hoses.
6. If removing the right-hand manifold, remove the hot air intake shroud which is bolted around the manifold.
7. Unbolt and remove the manifold.
8. Clean and lightly oil all fastener threads.
9. Installation is the reverse of removal. Replace all gaskets if so equipped. Torque the manifold bolts to 19 ft. lbs. (25 Nm); the exhaust pipe nuts to 20 ft. lbs. (27 Nm). TIGHTEN BOTH EXHAUST PIPE RETAINING NUTS IN EQUAL AMOUNTS TO CORRECTLY SEAT INLET PIPE FLANGE.
10. If installing the left-hand manifold, reconnect the power steering pump hoses, then fill and bleed the system.
11. Connect the negative battery cable and run the engine to check for leaks.

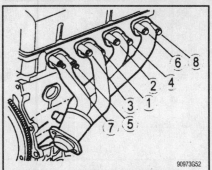

Fig. 64 Exhaust manifold mounting bolt and stud tightening sequence for the 2.5L engine

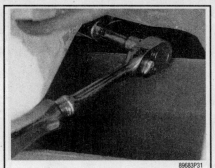

Fig. 65 To remove the exhaust manifold, first remove the exhaust pipe-to-manifold bolts from underneath

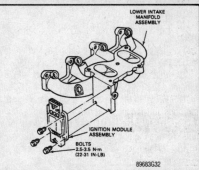

Fig. 66 Unbolt the hot air intake shroud, which wraps around the manifold and covers some of the attaching bolts

Fig. 67 Remove the shroud . . .

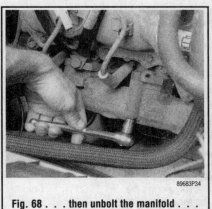

Fig. 68 . . . then unbolt the manifold . . .

Fig. 69 . . . and lift it from the engine

2.6L Engine

▶ See Figure 70

1. Disconnect the negative battery cable.
2. Drain the cooling system.

✳✳ CAUTION

When draining the coolant, always drain the coolant into a sealable container. Coolant should be reused unless it is contaminated or several years old.

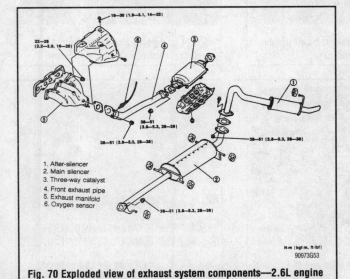

Fig. 70 Exploded view of exhaust system components—2.6L engine

1. After-silencer
2. Main silencer
3. Three-way catalyst
4. Front exhaust pipe
5. Exhaust manifold
6. Oxygen sensor

3. Remove the oil dipstick tube.
4. Remove the coolant bypass pipe.
5. Disconnect the exhaust pipe from the manifold.
6. Remove the heat shield.
7. Unbolt and remove the manifold. Discard the gasket.

To install:

8. Clean all mating surfaces. Place a new gasket and exhaust manifold in position and loosely install the mounting bolts. After all of the manifold bolts and attached components are loosely installed, secure all mounting bolts. Torque the bolts to 16–21 ft. lbs. (22–28 Nm).
9. Install the heat shield and tighten the mounting bolts to 14–22 ft. lbs. (19–30 Nm).
10. Connect the exhaust pipe to the manifold. Torque the bolts to 28–38 ft. lbs. (38–51 Nm).
11. Install the coolant bypass pipe.
12. Install the oil dipstick tube.
13. Fill and bleed the cooling system.
14. Connect the negative battery cable.

3.0L Engine (MPV)

1. Disconnect the negative battery cable. Wait at least 90 seconds before performing any work.
2. Raise and safely support the vehicle.
3. If necessary remove the engine splash shield.
4. Disconnect the oxygen sensor connector.
5. Remove the nuts attaching the 3 way pre-catalytic convertor to the main catalytic convertor and the LH exhaust manifold. Remove the 3 way pre-catalytic convertor and the gaskets.
6. Remove the bolts and the LH and the RH exhaust manifold insulators.
7. Remove the attaching bolts and nuts and the center exhaust pipe insulators.
8. Remove the bolts securing the center exhaust manifold to the LH and RH exhaust manifolds. Remove the center exhaust manifold and the gaskets.
9. Remove the mounting nuts, the LH and the RH exhaust manifolds, and the gaskets.

To install:

10. Before installation make sure all mating surfaces are clean of any gasket material.

11. Install the RH and the LH exhaust manifolds with new gaskets and torque the mounting nuts to 16–20 ft. lbs. (22–36 Nm).

12. Install the center exhaust manifold with 2 new gaskets to the RH and LH exhaust manifolds. Torque the bolts to 14–18 ft. lbs. (19–24 Nm).

13. Reinstall the RH and the LH exhaust manifold insulators with the attaching bolts. Torque the bolts to 14–18 ft. lbs.

14. Install the exhaust insulator to the center exhaust pipe with the bolts and nuts. Torque the bolts and nuts to 14–18 ft. lbs. (19–24 Nm).

15. Install the 3 way pre-catalytic convertor using new gaskets to the LH exhaust manifold and the main catalytic convertor. Torque the nuts to 28–38 ft. lbs. (38–52 Nm).

16. Reconnect the oxygen sensor connector.

17. If necessary, reinstall the engine splash shield.

18. Safely lower the vehicle and reconnect the negative battery cable.

Radiator

REMOVAL & INSTALLATION

▶ **See Figures 71 thru 80**

1. Disconnect the negative battery cable.
2. Drain the cooling system.

✳✳ CAUTION

When draining the coolant, keep in mind that cats and dogs are attracted by ethylene glycol antifreeze, and are quite likely to drink any that is left in an uncovered container or in puddles on the ground. This will prove fatal in sufficient quantity. Always drain the coolant into a sealable container. Coolant should be reused unless it is contaminated or several years old.

3. If necessary, remove the air cleaner duct.

4. Separate the upper and lower hoses from the radiator.

5. Disconnect the coolant reservoir hose from the radiator.

6. On MPV equipped with the 2.6L engine, remove the purge solenoid valve and mounting bracket

7. If equipped with an automatic transmission, disconnect the transmission cooler lines from the bottom of the radiator.

8. Loosen the mounting bolts, then remove the engine fan and radiator shroud from the vehicle.

9. Remove the radiator retaining bolts or the upper supports and lift the radiator from the vehicle.

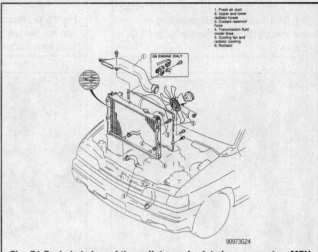

Fig. 71 Exploded view of the radiator and related components—MPV shown, others similar

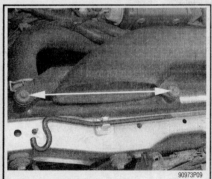

Fig. 72 Remove the two air inlet duct mounting bolts . . .

Fig. 73 . . . then remove the air inlet duct from the engine compartment

Fig. 74 Using pliers or an equivalent tool, disconnect the hose from the radiator

Fig. 75 Disconnect the rubber radiator-to-overflow tank hose at the radiator

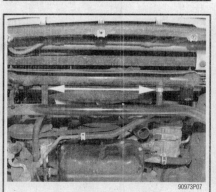

Fig. 76 Disconnect the fluid cooler lines . . .

Fig. 77 . . . then plug the cooler lines and the openings in the radiator

Fig. 78 Remove the left side radiator mounting bolts . . .

Fig. 79 . . . then remove the two right side radiator mounting bolts

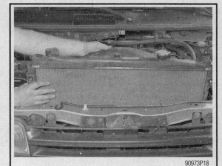
Fig. 80 Lift the radiator and shroud assembly out of the vehicle, with the engine fan in the shroud opening

10. Install the radiator in the reverse order of removal. Fill the cooling system and check for leaks. On automatic transmission equipped vehicles, run the engine until normal operating temperature is reached, then check the transmission fluid level. Correct as needed.

Engine Fan

REMOVAL & INSTALLATION

➡Refer to exploded view illustration before starting this service procedure.

❊❊ WARNING

The following procedures for removing the fan clutch gives the factory recommended loosening and tightening directions for the fan hub nut. However, it has been our experience that certain aftermarket parts manufacturers have changed this to enable use of universal fit parts. We recommend trying the factory direction first, then, if the nut doesn't seem to be moving, reverse the direction. Placing too much load on the water pump snout will break it.

MPV

◆ See Figures 81 and 82

1. Disconnect the negative battery cable.
2. Loosen and remove the drive belts.
3. Remove the bolts that retain the fan shroud to the radiator support. Remove (if there is enough room between the fan blades and radiator) or position the shroud back over the water pump and fan assembly, if necessary to gain working room.
4. Loosen and remove the fan to water pump mounting nuts and remove the fan assembly. Don't lay the fan, if equipped with a fan clutch, on its side. Fluid

Fig. 82 After the fan mounting nuts have been removed, slide the fan assembly forward and place inside the radiator shroud

could be lost and the fan clutch might require replacement. Inspect the condition of the fan blades, if any are cracked or damaged, replace the fan.
5. Install the fan assembly in position on the water pump and pulley. Secure the fan assembly with the mounting nuts. Tighten the nuts to 70–95 inch lbs. (8–11 Nm). Install the shroud and drive belts. Adjust the drive belts to the proper tension.
6. Connect the negative battery cable.

B Series Pick-up and Navajo

2.3L AND 2.5L ENGINES

◆ See Figure 83

➡The 2.3L engine does not use a fan hub nut. It is retained by four bolts which also secure the pump pulley to the water pump.

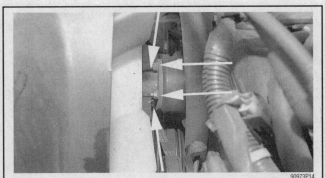
Fig. 81 Remove the four fan assembly-to-water pump pulley mounting nuts

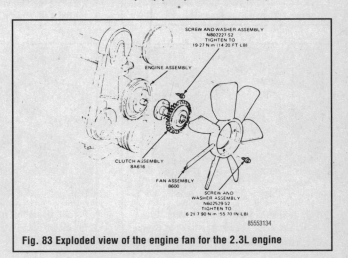
Fig. 83 Exploded view of the engine fan for the 2.3L engine

1. If not equipped with A/C, disconnect the overflow tube from the fan guard, then unbolt and remove the guard.

2. If equipped with A/C, disconnect the overflow tube from the shroud, remove the mounting screws and lift the shroud off the brackets. Place the shroud behind the fan.

3. Remove the 4 clutch/fan assembly-to-pulley screws and remove the clutch/fan assembly. Vehicles equipped with A/C should remove the clutch/fan and shroud together.

4. If necessary, remove the fan-to-clutch bolts to separate the fan from the clutch.

5. Installation is the reverse of removal. Torque the fan-to-clutch screws to 55–70 inch lbs. (6–8 Nm); the fan/clutch assembly-to-pulley bolts to 12–18 ft. lbs. (16–24 Nm).

3.0L ENGINE

▶ See Figure 84

1. If necessary, remove the air cleaner outlet tube.
2. Using Strap Wrench D79L-6731-A and Fan Clutch Nut Wrench T83T-6312-B, or their equivalents, loosen the large nut attaching the clutch to the water pump hub.

➡ **According to the manufacturer, the nut uses LH threads and is loosened clockwise.**

3. Remove the two upper fan shroud retaining bolts. If the overflow hose is routed through the fan shroud, remove it from the shroud.
4. Lift up on the fan shroud to disengage the lower mounting clips.
5. Remove the fan/clutch assembly and the fan shroud together.
6. If necessary, remove the fan-to-clutch bolts to separate the fan from the clutch.
   To install:
7. Installation is the reverse of removal. Torque the fan-to-clutch bolts to 55–70 inch lbs. (6–8 Nm); the hub nut to 30–100 ft. lbs. (41–135 Nm) for 1991–95 models and 34–46 ft. lbs. (46–63 Nm) for 1996–97 models. Don't forget, the nut uses LH threads and is tightened counterclockwise.

4.0L ENGINE

▶ See Figures 85, 86, 87, 88 and 89

1. If necessary, remove the air cleaner outlet tube.

➡ **According to the manufacturer, the nut uses RH threads and is loosened counterclockwise.**

2. Using Fan Clutch Pulley Holder T84T-6312-C and Fan Clutch Nut Wrench T84T-6312-D, or their equivalents, loosen the large nut attaching the clutch to the water pump hub.

➡ **Some models have enough room between the shroud and the engine to remove the fan without unbolting the shroud.**

3. Remove the two upper fan shroud retaining bolts. If the overflow hose is routed through the fan shroud, remove it from the shroud.
4. Lift up on the fan shroud to disengage the lower mounting clips.
5. Remove the fan/clutch assembly and the fan shroud together.
6. If necessary, remove the fan-to-clutch bolts to separate the fan from the clutch.
   To install:
7. Installation is the reverse of removal. Torque the fan-to-clutch bolts to 55–70 inch lbs. (6–8 Nm); the hub nut to 30–100 ft. lbs. (41–135 Nm) for 1991–95 models and 34–46 ft. lbs. (46–63 Nm) for 1996–97 models. Don't forget, the nut uses RH threads and is tightened clockwise.

Water Pump

REMOVAL & INSTALLATION

✳✳ CAUTION

When draining engine coolant, keep in mind that cats and dogs are attracted to ethylene glycol antifreeze and could drink any that is

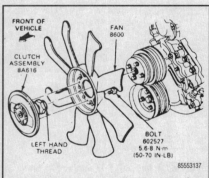

Fig. 84 Exploded view of the engine fan for the 2.9L and 3.0L engines

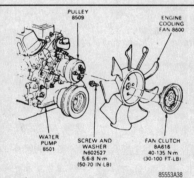

Fig. 85 Exploded view of the engine fan for the 4.0L engine

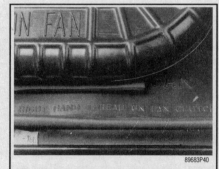

Fig. 86 Before attempting to unfasten the engine fan, check the fan shroud for indications of normal or reverse threads

Fig. 87 Remove the air intake tube. You will need these specialized tools to unfasten the fan clutch nut

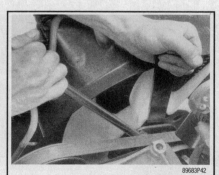

Fig. 88 Using the special tools, loosen the fan clutch nut in the direction indicated on the shroud.

Fig. 89 Remove the fan and clutch assembly from the vehicle

left in an uncovered container or in puddles on the ground. This will prove fatal in sufficient quantity. Always drain coolant into a sealable container. Coolant should be reused unless it is contaminated or is several years old.

B Series Pick-up and Navajo

2.3L ENGINE

▶ **See Figure 90**

1. Disconnect the negative battery cable.
2. Drain the cooling system.
3. Remove the two bolts that retain the fan shroud and position the shroud back over the fan.
4. Remove the four bolts that retain the cooling fan. Remove the fan and shroud.
5. Loosen and remove the accessory drive belt.
6. Remove the water pump pulley.
7. Remove the heater hose at the water pump.
8. Remove the timing belt cover. Remove the lower radiator hose from the water pump.
9. Remove the water pump mounting bolts and the water pump. Clean all gasket mounting surfaces.
10. Install the water pump in the reverse order of removal. Coat the threads of the mounting bolts with sealer before installation.
11. Tighten the water pump-to-engine block mounting bolts to 14–21 ft. lbs. (20–30 Nm).
12. Fill the radiator with the specified amount and type of engine coolant.
13. Connect the negative battery cable.
14. Start the engine and check for leaks, then bleed the cooling system.

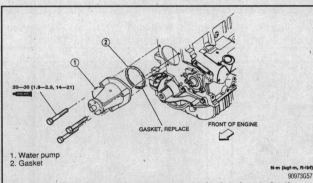

1. Water pump
2. Gasket

20—30 (1.9—2.9, 14—21)

GASKET, REPLACE FRONT OF ENGINE

N-m (kgf·m, ft-lbf)
90973G57

Fig. 90 Exploded view of the water pump and related parts for the 2.3L engine

2.5L ENGINE

▶ **See Figure 91**

1. Disconnect the negative battery cable.
2. Drain the cooling system.
3. Remove the cooling fan and shroud.
4. Remove the accessory drive belt.
5. Raise and safely support the vehicle.
6. Disconnect the lower radiator hose from the water pump.
7. Disconnect the lower heater water hose from the inlet tube.
8. Loosen the screws and remove the inlet tube.
9. Remove the water pump pulley.
10. Remove the timing belt cover.
11. Remove the water pump mounting bolts and the water pump. Clean all gasket mounting surfaces.
To install:
12. Apply grease to three locations on the new water pump, as illustrated.
13. Place the new gasket in position and install the water pump onto the engine. Tighten the water pump mounting bolts to 15–20 ft. lbs. (20–30 Nm).
14. Install the timing belt cover.
15. Install the water pump pulley.

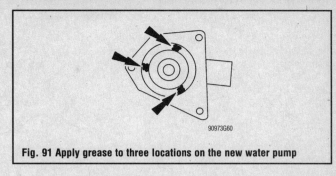

90973G60

Fig. 91 Apply grease to three locations on the new water pump

16. Apply grease to the new O-ring seal, install the inlet tube and tighten the mounting screws.
17. Connect the lower heater water hose to the inlet tube. Tighten the hose clamp.
18. Connect the lower radiator hose to the water pump. Tighten the hose clamp.
19. Lower the vehicle.
20. Install the accessory drive belt.
21. Install the cooling fan and shroud.
22. Fill the radiator with the specified amount and type of engine coolant.
23. Connect the negative battery cable.
24. Start the engine and check for leaks, then bleed the cooling system.

3.0L ENGINE

▶ **See Figure 92**

1. Disconnect the battery ground cable.
2. Drain the cooling system.
3. Remove the engine fan.
4. Loosen the 4 water pump pulley bolts.
5. Remove the accessory drive belts.
6. Remove the water pump pulley.
7. Remove the alternator adjusting arm and throttle body brace.
8. Remove the lower radiator hose.
9. Disconnect the heater hose at the pump.
10. Rotate the belt adjuster out of the way.
11. Remove the water pump attaching bolts. Note their location for installation.
12. Remove the pump and discard the gasket.
13. Thoroughly clean the pump and engine mating surfaces.
To install:
14. Using an adhesive type sealer, position a new gasket on the timing cover.
15. Position the water pump and start the bolts. When all the bolts are started, torque them to specifications. Refer to the necessary illustration.
16. Install the lower hose and connect the radiator hose.
17. Install the pulley and hand-tighten the 4 bolts.
18. Install the alternator adjusting arm and brace.
19. Install the belts and tension them. See Section 1.
20. Tighten the 4 pulley bolts to 19 ft. lbs. (26 Nm).
21. Install the fan.
22. Fill and bleed the cooling system.
23. Connect the battery ground cable. Run the engine and check for leaks.

4.0L ENGINE

▶ **See Figures 93 thru 101**

1. Disconnect the negative battery cable.
2. Drain the cooling system.
3. Remove the fan and fan clutch assembly.

➡ **See the engine fan removal procedure in this section.**

4. Remove the lower radiator hose from the water pump.
5. Loosen the water pump pulley attaching bolts.
6. Loosen the alternator mounting bolts and remove the belt. On vehicles with air conditioning, remove the tensioner pulley, alternator and bracket.
7. Remove the A/C compressor and power steering pump mounting bracket, without disconnecting the lines, and set off to the side.

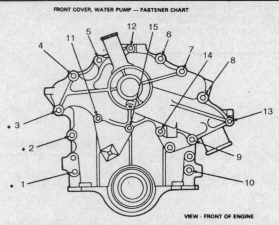

FRONT COVER, WATER PUMP — FASTENER CHART

VIEW - FRONT OF ENGINE

Fastener and Hole No.	Fasteners			
	Part No.	Size	N·m	Ft-Lb
• 1	N804215	M8 x 1.25 x 72.25	25	19
• 2	N804215	M8 x 1.25 x 72.25	25	19
• 3	N606547-S8	M8 x 1.25 x 70.0	25	19
4	N606547-S8	M8 x 1.25 x 70.0	25	19
5	N605909-S8	M8 x 1.25 x 42.0	25	19
6	N804154-S8	M8 x 1.25 x 99.3	25	19
7	N606547-S8	M8 x 1.25 x 70.0	25	19
8	N606547-S8	M8 x 1.25 x 70.0	25	19
9	N606547-S8	M8 x 1.25 x 70.0	25	19
10	N605909-S8	M8 x 1.25 x 42.0	25	19
11	N804168-S8	M6 x 1.0 x 25.0	10	7
12	N804168-S8	M6 x 1.0 x 25.0	10	7
13	N804168-S8	M6 x 1.0 x 25.0	10	7
14	N804168-S8	M6 x 1.0 x 25.0	10	7
15	N804168-S8	M6 x 1.0 x 25.0	10	7

NOTE: •Apply Pipe Sealant with Teflon D8AZ-19554-A (ESG-M4G194-A) Sealer to Fastener Threads

85553152

Fig. 92 3.0L engine water pump and front cover fastener chart

Fig. 93 To service the water pump, first drain the cooling system, then remove the engine fan/clutch . . .

89683P44

Fig. 94 . . . and the fan shroud from the vehicle

89683P45

Fig. 95 Remove the lower radiator hose from the water pump. Position a drain pan underneath to catch any coolant

89683P46

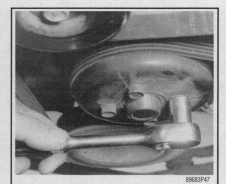

Fig. 96 Loosen the water pump pulley attaching bolts . . .

89683P47

Fig. 97 . . . before removing the accessory drive belt . . .

89683P48

Fig. 98 . . . then with the drive belt out of the way, finish removing the water pump pulley

89683P49

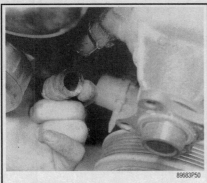

Fig. 99 Remove the heater hose connection at the water pump

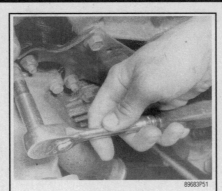

Fig. 100 Remove all of the water pump attaching bolts . . .

Fig. 101 . . . then remove the pump from the engine

8. Remove the water pump pulley.
9. Disconnect the heater hose at the pump.
10. Remove the attaching bolts and remove the water pump.
To install:
11. Clean the mounting surfaces of the pump and front cover thoroughly. Remove all traces of gasket material.
12. Apply adhesive gasket sealer to both sides of a new gasket and place the gasket on the pump.
13. Position the pump on the cover and install the bolts finger–tight. When all bolts are in place, torque them to 72–108 inch lbs. (9–12 Nm).
14. Install the pulley.
15. On vehicles with air conditioning, install the alternator, bracket and tensioner pulley.
16. Install the A/C compressor and power steering pump mounting bracket.
17. Install and adjust the drive belt.
18. Connect the hoses and tighten the clamps.
19. Install the fan and clutch assembly.
20. Fill and bleed the cooling system.
21. Connect the negative battery cable, then start the engine and check for leaks.

MPV Models

2.6L ENGINE

▶ **See Figure 102**

1. Disconnect the battery ground.
2. Drain the cooling system.
3. Remove the accessory drive belts.

Fig. 102 Water pump assembly—2.6L engine

4. Remove the fan and shroud.
5. Remove the water pump pulley.
6. Unbolt and remove the water pump.
7. Thoroughly clean the gasket mounting surfaces.
To install:
8. Using a new gasket coated with sealer, position the water pump on the engine. Tighten the bolts to 14–18 ft. lbs. (19–25 Nm).
9. Install the fan and pulley.
10. Install the drive belts and shroud.
11. Fill the cooling system.
12. Run the engine and check for leaks.

3.0L ENGINE

▶ **See Figures 103, 104 and 105**

1. Position the engine at TDC on the compression stroke.
2. Properly relieve the fuel system pressure.
3. Disconnect the negative battery cable.
4. Remove the air cleaner assembly.
5. Drain the cooling system.
6. Remove the spark plug wires.
7. Remove the fresh air duct assembly.
8. Remove the cooling fan, water pump pulley and radiator cowling.
9. Remove the drive belts.
10. Remove the air conditioning compressor idler pulley. If necessary, remove the compressor and position it to the side without disconnecting the hose lines.
11. Remove the crankshaft pulley and baffle plate.
12. Remove the coolant bypass hose.
13. Remove the upper radiator hose.
14. Remove the timing belt covers.
15. Remove the timing belt. If reusing the belt be sure to mark the direction of rotation.
16. Unbolt and remove the water pump. Discard the gasket.
17. Thoroughly clean the mating surfaces of the pump and engine.
To install:
18. Position the pump and a new gasket, coated with sealer, on the engine. Torque the bolts to 14–18 ft. lbs. (19–25 Nm).
19. Install the timing belt.
20. Install the timing belt cover assembly.
21. Install the upper radiator hose.
22. Install the coolant bypass hose.
23. Install the crankshaft pulley and baffle plate.
24. Install the compressor.
25. Install the air conditioning compressor idler pulley.
26. Install and adjust the drive belts.
27. Install the cooling fan and radiator cowling.
28. Install the fresh air duct assembly.
29. Install the spark plug wires.
30. Fill the cooling system.
31. Install the air cleaner assembly.
32. Connect the negative battery cable.

Fig. 103 Remove the water pump pulley

Fig. 104 Remove the water pump assembly from the engine

Fig. 105 Clean the water pump-to-engine mating surface of all gasket material

Cylinder Head

REMOVAL & INSTALLATION

➡ Before installing the cylinder heads, have them cleaned and professionally checked. If there is a problem, generally, it will not go away by simply installing new gaskets. Cylinder heads can and do warp, which is the major cause of gasket failure. This is usually due to overheating.

※※ CAUTION

When draining the coolant, keep in mind that cats and dogs are attracted by ethylene glycol antifreeze, and are quite likely to drink any that is left in an uncovered container or in puddles on the ground. This will prove fatal in sufficient quantity. Always drain the coolant into a sealable container. Coolant should be reused unless it is contaminated or several years old.

Navajo and B Series Pick-up Models

2.3L ENGINE

▶ See Figure 106

1. Disconnect the negative battery cable.
2. Drain cooling system.
3. Remove air cleaner assembly.
4. Remove the heater hose-to-valve cover retaining screws.
5. Label and remove the spark plug wires.
6. Remove the spark plugs.
7. Label and disconnect all of the upper engine components and alternator wiring harnesses.
8. Disconnect required vacuum hoses.
9. Remove dipstick tube and bracket.
10. Remove the valve cover.
11. Remove intake manifold retaining bolts.
12. Loosen alternator retaining bolts and remove belt from the pulley. Remove mounting bracket retaining bolts to the head.
13. Remove the upper radiator hose from the vehicle.
14. Remove the timing belt cover. For power steering-equipped vehicles, unbolt the power steering pump bracket and position it off to the side.
15. Loosen the timing belt idler retaining bolts. Position idler in the unloaded position and tighten the retaining bolts.
16. Remove the timing belt.
17. Remove four nuts and/or stud bolts retaining heat stove to exhaust manifold.
18. Remove the eight exhaust manifold retaining bolts.
19. Remove the timing belt idler and two bracket bolts.
20. Remove the timing belt idler spring stop from the cylinder head.
21. Disconnect the oil sending unit lead wire.
22. Remove the cylinder head retaining bolts.
23. Remove the cylinder head.

24. Clean the cylinder head, intake manifold and exhaust manifold gasket surfaces.
25. Blow oil out of the cylinder head bolt block hoses.
26. Clean valve cover gasket surface on the head.
27. Check cylinder head for flatness.
To install:
28. Position head gasket on the block.
29. Clean rocker arm cover (cam cover).
30. Install valve cover gasket to the valve cover.
31. Position cylinder head to block.
32. Install cylinder head retaining bolts and tighten, in three steps, in sequence, to the following specifications:
 • Step 1: 52 ft. lbs. (70 Nm)
 • Step 2: 52 ft. lbs. (70 Nm)
 • Step 3: Turn all cylinder head bolts an additional 90–100°
33. Connect oil sending unit lead wires.
34. Install the timing belt idler spring stop to the cylinder head.
35. Position the timing belt idler to the cylinder head, and install its retaining bolts.
36. Install the eight exhaust manifold retaining bolts and/or stud bolts.
37. Install four nuts and/or stud bolts retaining heat stove to exhaust manifold.
38. Install the timing belt.
39. Install the timing belt cover.
40. Install the upper radiator hose and radiator and tighten the retaining clamps.
41. Position the alternator bracket to cylinder head and install its retainers.
42. If removed, position the power steering pump bracket to the engine and install its attaching bolts.

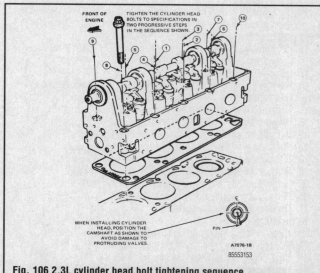

Fig. 106 2.3L cylinder head bolt tightening sequence

43. Install the accessory drive belt.
44. Position the intake manifold to the cylinder head, and install its retaining bolts.
45. Install the valve cover.
46. Install the spark plugs.
47. Install the dipstick tube and bracket.
48. Connect the appropriate vacuum hoses.
49. Connect all of the upper engine components and alternator wiring harnesses.
50. Position and connect the spark plug wires.
51. Install the heater hose-to-valve cover retaining screws.
52. Fill and bleed the cooling system.
53. Install the air cleaner.
54. Connect the negative battery cable.
55. Start the engine and check for leaks.

2.5L ENGINE

◆ See Figure 107

➡ According to the manufacturer, you must use new cylinder head bolts when installing the head.

1. Disconnect the battery ground cable.
2. Relieve the fuel system pressure.
3. Drain the cooling system.
4. Loosen the water pump pulley bolts.
5. Remove the accessory drive belt.
6. Remove the cooling fan assembly.
7. Remove the upper and lower intake manifold.
8. Label and remove the spark plug wires.
9. Remove the spark plugs.
10. Remove the oil level dipstick tube.
11. Remove the EGR valve-to-exhaust manifold tube.
12. Remove the valve cover.
13. Remove the drive belt.
14. Disengage the engine control sensor wiring harness from the A/C compressor.

➡ The official Mazda factory repair information recommends recovering the A/C refrigerant so that the A/C hoses can be disconnected for the purpose of removal of the compressor from the vehicle. However, in order to remove the cylinder head, it may only be necessary to remove the compressor from the mounting bracket and move it off to the side without disconnecting any hoses. If this is the case, no refrigerant recovery is necessary. If the hoses must be disconnected, the refrigerant can only be recovered by a technician certified to do this type of procedure.

15. Remove the A/C compressor from the mounting bracket and position it aside. It may be possible to hold the compressor off to the side without disconnecting any refrigerant hoses. However, if the refrigerant hoses must be disconnected, the A/C system must be evacuated, which requires taking the vehicle to a professional shop for a technician who is certified to perform these procedures using official refrigerant recovery equipment.
16. Remove the A/C compressor mounting bracket with the power steering pump attached and position it out of the way.
17. Remove the alternator.
18. Remove the upper and lower radiator hoses. Remove the heater water hose from the inlet tube on the water pump.
19. Remove the water pump inlet tube.
20. Remove the alternator mounting bracket.
21. Remove the ignition coil packs and mounting bracket.
22. Remove the timing belt cover.
23. Remove the timing belt.
24. Remove the exhaust manifold.
25. Remove and discard the cylinder head mounting bolts.
26. Remove and discard the cylinder head gasket.
27. Check cylinder head for flatness.

To install:
28. Clean the head gasket mating surfaces.
29. Position the new head gasket on the block.
30. Position the cylinder head onto the engine block.
31. Install new cylinder head retaining bolts and tighten, in three steps, in sequence, to the following specifications:

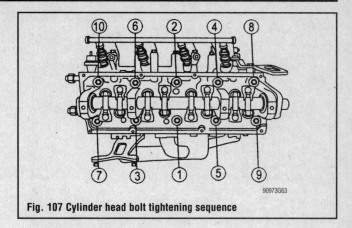

Fig. 107 Cylinder head bolt tightening sequence

- Step 1: 52 ft. lbs. (70 Nm)
- Step 2: 52 ft. lbs. (70 Nm)
- Step 3: Turn all cylinder head bolts an additional 90–100°
32. Install the exhaust manifold.
33. Install the timing belt.
34. Install the timing belt cover.
35. Install the mounting bracket and ignition coil packs.
36. Install the alternator mounting bracket and tighten the mounting bolts.
37. Install the water pump inlet tube. Connect the heater water hose to the inlet tube.
38. Install the upper and lower radiator hoses. Tighten the hose clamps.
39. Install the alternator.
40. Install the A/C compressor mounting bracket and tighten the mounting bolts.
41. Install the A/C compressor to the mounting bracket and tighten the mounting bolts. Connect the refrigerant hoses, if disconnected.
42. Plug in the engine control sensor wiring harness connector to the compressor.
43. Install the drive belt.
44. Install the valve cover.
45. Install the EGR valve-to-exhaust manifold tube.
46. Install the oil level dipstick tube.
47. Install the spark plugs and connect the spark plug wires.
48. Install the lower and upper intake manifold.
49. Install the cooling fan assembly.
50. Install the accessory drive belt.
51. Tighten the water pump pulley bolts.
52. Fill the cooling system bleed the system.
53. Connect the battery ground cable.
54. Operate the engine at fast idle and check for oil, fuel and coolant leaks.
55. If necessary, have the A/C system recharged.

3.0L ENGINE

◆ See Figures 108, 109 and 110

➡ According to the manufacturer, you must use new cylinder head bolts when installing the heads.

1. Drain the cooling system (engine cold) into a clean container and save the coolant for reuse.
2. Disconnect the battery ground cable.
3. Remove the air cleaner.
4. Relieve fuel pressure. Disconnect fuel lines as necessary. Mark vacuum line location and remove lines.
5. Disconnect upper and lower radiator hoses—position out of the way.
6. Label and remove the ignition wires from the spark plugs and locating studs.
7. If equipped, mark the distributor housing to block and note rotor position. Remove the distributor.
8. Remove coil assembly.
9. Remove the throttle body. See Section 5.
10. Remove the accessory drive belt.
11. If the left-hand cylinder head is being removed:

a. Remove the power steering pump and bracket assembly. DO NOT disconnect the hoses. Tie the assembly out of the way.

b. Remove the engine oil dipstick and tube. Rotate or remove tube assembly.

c. Remove the fuel line retaining bracket bolt from the front of cylinder head.

12. If the right-hand head is being removed:

a. Disconnect alternator electrical harnesses.

b. Remove belt tensioner assembly.

c. Remove the alternator and bracket.

d. Remove hose from valve cover to oil fill adapter.

13. Remove the spark plugs.

14. Remove the exhaust manifold(s).

15. Remove the rocker arm covers as previously described.

16. Loosen rocker arm fulcrum retaining bolts enough to allow the rocker arm to be lifted off the pushrod and rotate to one side.

➡️**Regardless of which cylinder head is being removed, the #3 cylinder intake valve pushrod must be removed to allow removal of the intake manifold.**

17. Remove the pushrods, keeping them in order so they may be installed in their original locations.

18. Remove the intake manifold as outlined. Refer to the necessary service procedure.

19. Loosen the cylinder head attaching bolts in reverse of the torque sequence, then remove the bolts and lift off the cylinder head(s). Remove and discard the old cylinder head gasket(s).

To install:

20. Clean the cylinder heads, intake manifold, valve rocker arm cover and cylinder block gasket surfaces of all traces of old gasket material and/or sealer.

21. Lightly oil all bolt and stud bolt threads except those specifying special sealant. Position the new head gasket(s) on the cylinder block, using the dowels for alignment. The dowels should be replaced if damaged.

22. Position the cylinder head(s) on the block and install new attaching bolts. Tighten the head bolts in sequence to 59 ft. lbs. (80 Nm). Back off all bolts one full turn (360 degrees). Retighten the cylinder head bolts in sequence, in two steps to 37 ft. lbs. (50 Nm). Final tighten to 68 ft. lbs. (92 Nm).

23. Install intake manifold as outlined.

24. Dip each pushrod in heavy engine oil then install the pushrods in their original locations.

25. For each valve, rotate the crankshaft until the tappet rests on the heel (base circle) of the camshaft lobe before tightening the fulcrum attaching bolts. Position the rocker arms over the pushrods. Install the fulcrums (tighten to 8 ft. lbs. to seat fulcrum) and then tighten the fulcrum attaching bolts to 24 ft. lbs. (32 Nm). Refer to the necessary illustration for details if necessary.

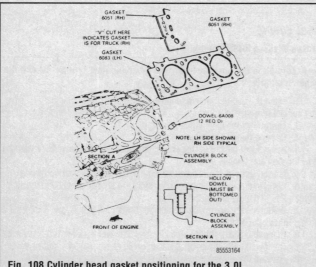

Fig. 108 Cylinder head gasket positioning for the 3.0L

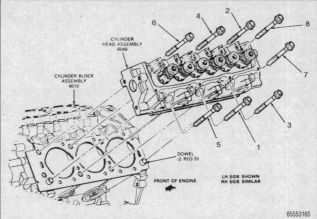

Fig. 109 Cylinder head installation & bolt torque sequence for the 3.0L

The fulcrums must be fully seated in the cylinder head and pushrods must be seated in the rocker arm sockets prior to final tightening.

26. Lubricate all rocker arm assemblies with heavy engine oil. If the original valve train components are being installed, a valve clearance check is not required. If, however, a component has been replaced, the valve clearance should be checked.

27. Install the exhaust manifold(s).

28. Install the dipstick tube and spark plugs.

29. Position the rocker arm cover with a new gasket on the cylinder head and install the retaining bolts. Note the location of the spark plug wire routing clip stud bolts.

30. Install the injector harness.

31. If equipped, install the distributor.

32. Install the ignition coil assembly.

33. Install the spark plug wires.

34. Install the throttle body and new gasket. Refer to the necessary service procedures.

35. If the left hand cylinder head was removed, perform the following:

a. Install the fuel line retaining bracket bolt to the front of cylinder head. Torque to 26 ft. lbs. (35 Nm).

b. Install the engine oil dipstick and tube assembly.

c. Install the power steering pump and bracket assembly.

36. If the right hand cylinder head was removed, perform the following:

a. Install hose from valve cover to oil fill adapter.

b. Install the alternator and bracket.

c. Install belt tensioner assembly.

d. Reconnect alternator electrical harnesses.

37. Install the accessory drive belt.

38. Connect fuel lines. Install fuel line safety clips.

39. Install all radiator hoses. Connect vacuum lines.

40. Drain and change engine oil.

⁂ CAUTION

The EPA warns that prolonged contact with used engine oil may cause a number of skin disorders, including cancer! You should make every effort to minimize your exposure to used engine oil. Protective gloves should be worn when changing the oil. Wash your hands and any other exposed skin areas as soon as possible after exposure to used engine oil. Soap and water, or waterless hand cleaner should be used.

41. Install the air cleaner.

42. Fill and bleed the cooling system.

43. Connect the battery ground cable.

44. Start the engine and check for leaks. If equipped with distributor ignition, verify base ignition timing.

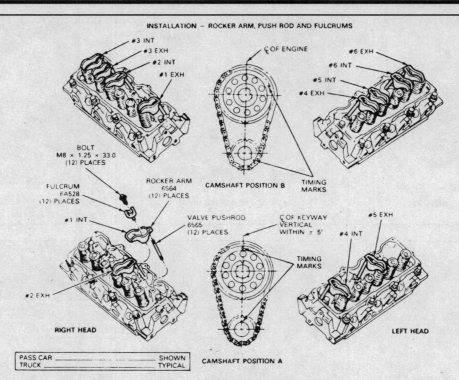

INSTALLATION – ROCKER ARM, PUSH ROD AND FULCRUMS

ASSEMBLY PROCEDURE

1. ROTATE CAMSHAFT TO POSITION "A" AS SHOWN.
2. INSTALL PUSH RODS (6565) (12) PLACES-PUSH RODS MUST BE SEATED PROPERLY ON TAPPET ASSEMBLY
3. INSTALL ROCKER ARMS (6564), FULCRUMS (6A528) AND BOLTS IN LOCATIONS AS SPECIFIED IN CAMSHAFT POSITION "A", TORQUE BOLTS TO 11 N·m AS REQ'D TO SEAT FULCRUMS IN CYLINDER HEAD
4. ROTATE CRANKSHAFT 120° TO POSITION "B"
5. INSTALL ROCKER ARMS (6564), FULCRUMS (6A528), AND BOLTS IN LOCATIONS AS SPECIFIED IN CAMSHAFT POSITION "B", TORQUE BOLTS TO 11 N·m AS REQ'D TO SEAT FULCRUMS IN CYLINDER HEAD

NOTE: FULCRUMS MUST BE FULLY SEATED IN CYLINDER HEADS AND PUSH RODS MUST BE FULLY SEATED IN ROCKER ARM SOCKETS PRIOR TO FINAL TORQUE.

6. APPLY ESE-M2C39-F OIL TO ROCKER ARM ASSEMBLIES.
7. FINAL TORQUE BOLTS TO 32.0 N·m (CAMSHAFT MAY BE IN ANY POSITION).

NOTE: CAMSHAFT POSITIONS "A" AND "B" ARE REQUIRED TO PLACE TAPPET ASSEMBLY ON BASE CIRCLE OF CAMSHAFT LOBE TO CHECK COLLAPSED TAPPET GAP.

FULCRUM AND BOLT MUST BE FULLY SEATED AFTER FINAL TORQUE

4.69-2.15 WITH TAPPET FULLY COLLAPSED ON BASE CIRCLE OF CAM LOBE AFTER ASSEMBLY REF. QUALITY AUDIT ONLY.

CYL. NO.	CAMSHAFT POSITION	
	A	B
	SET GAP OF VALVES NOTED	
1	INT.	EXH.
2	EXH.	INT.
3	NONE	INT.-EXH.
4	INT.	EXH.
5	EXH.	INT.
6	NONE	INT.-EXH.

Fig. 110 Valve rocker arm installation procedure and collapsed lifter gap clearance check for the 3.0L engine

4.0L ENGINE

▶ **See Figures 111 thru 119**

1. Drain the cooling system (engine cold) into a clean container and save the coolant for reuse.
2. Disconnect the battery ground cable.
3. Remove the air cleaner.
4. Remove the rocker arm covers as previously described.
5. Remove the upper and lower intake manifolds as described earlier.
6. If the left cylinder head is being removed:
   a. Remove the accessory drive belt.
   b. Remove the air conditioning compressor.
   c. Remove the power steering pump and bracket assembly. DO NOT disconnect the hoses. Tie the assembly out of the way.
   d. Remove the spark plugs.
7. If the right head is being removed:
   a. Remove the accessory drive belt.
   b. Remove the alternator and bracket.
   c. Remove the ignition coil pack and bracket.
   d. Remove the spark plugs.
8. Remove the exhaust manifold(s).
9. Remove the rocker shaft assembly.
10. Remove the pushrods, keeping them in order so they may be installed in their original locations.
11. Loosen the cylinder head attaching bolts in reverse of the torque sequence, then remove the bolts and discard them. They cannot be re–used.
12. Lift off the cylinder head(s).
13. Remove and discard the old cylinder head gasket(s).

To install:

14. Clean the cylinder heads, intake manifolds, valve rocker arm cover and cylinder block gasket surfaces of all traces of old gasket material and/or sealer. Refer to the following overhaul procedures for cylinder head component removal, valve replacement, resurfacing, etc.

Fig. 111 After removing the intake manifold, loosen the accessory mounting bracket bolts . . .

Fig. 112 . . . then remove the bracket and accessory

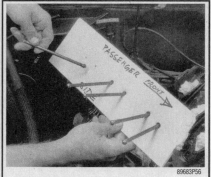

Fig. 113 Remove the rocker shafts and, keeping them in order, the pushrods

Fig. 114 Loosen and remove the cylinder head attaching bolts . . .

Fig. 115 . . . then lift the cylinder head from the engine

Fig. 116 Remove and discard the old cylinder head gasket

Fig. 117 With rags placed in the cylinder bores, scrape the gasket mating surfaces clean

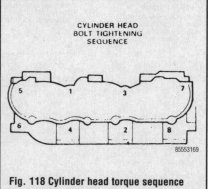

Fig. 118 Cylinder head torque sequence for the 4.0L engine

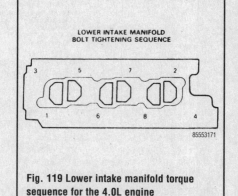

Fig. 119 Lower intake manifold torque sequence for the 4.0L engine

15. Lightly oil all bolt and stud bolt threads except those specifying special sealant. Position the new head gasket(s) on the cylinder block, using the dowels for alignment. The dowels should be replaced if damaged.

➡The cylinder head(s) and intake manifold are torqued alternately and in sequence, to assure a correct fit and gasket crush.

16. Position the cylinder head(s) on the block.
17. Apply a bead of RTV silicone gasket material to the mating joints of the head and block at the 4 corners. Install the intake manifold gasket and again apply the sealer.

➡This sealer sets within 15 minutes, so work quickly!

18. Install the lower intake manifold.
19. Tighten the intake manifold fasteners, in sequence, to 36–72 inch lbs. (4–8 Nm).

✳✳ WARNING

Do not re-use the old head bolts. ALWAYS use new head bolts!

20. Tighten the head bolts, in sequence, to 59 ft. lbs. (80 Nm).
21. Tighten the intake manifold fasteners, in sequence, to 6–11 ft. lbs. (8–15 Nm).
22. Tighten the head bolts, in sequence, an additional 80–85 degrees tighter. 85 degrees is a little less than ¼ turn, ¼ turn would equal 90 degrees.
23. Tighten the intake manifold fasteners, in sequence, to 11–15 ft. lbs. (15–20 Nm); then, in sequence, to 15–18 ft. lbs. (20–24 Nm).
24. Dip each pushrod in heavy engine oil then install the pushrods in their original locations.
25. Install the rocker arm/shaft assembly(ies).

26. Apply another bead of RTV sealer at the 4 corners where the intake manifold and heads meet.
27. Install the valve covers.
28. Install the upper intake manifold. Tighten the nuts to 15–18 ft. lbs. (20–24 Nm).
29. Install the exhaust manifold(s).
30. Install the spark plugs and wires.
31. If the left head was removed, install the power steering pump, compressor and drive belt.
32. If the right head was removed, install the coil pack and bracket, alternator and bracket, and the drive belt.
33. Install the air cleaner.
34. Fill the cooling system.

➡ At this point, it's a good idea to change the engine oil. Coolant contamination of the engine oil often occurs during cylinder head removal.

35. Connect the battery ground cable.
36. Start the engine and check for leaks.

MPV Models

2.6L ENGINE

▶ **See Figures 120 and 121**

1. Properly relieve the fuel system pressure.

✳✳ CAUTION

Never smoke when working around gasoline! Avoid all sources of sparks or ignition. Gasoline vapors are EXTREMELY volatile!

2. Disconnect the negative battery cable.
3. Remove the air cleaner assembly.
4. Drain the coolant.
5. Position the engine at TDC on the compression stroke so all the pulley matchmarks are aligned.
6. Remove the accelerator cable. Remove the air intake pipe and resonance chamber.
7. Remove the accessory drive belts and A/C belt idler.
8. Remove the upper radiator hose.
9. Remove the brake vacuum hose.
10. Remove the spark plug wires.
11. Remove the spark plugs.
12. Remove the oil cooler coolant hose.
13. Remove the canister hose.
14. Remove the fuel lines.
15. Disconnect the oxygen sensor.
16. Remove the solenoid valves.
17. Disconnect the emissions harness.
18. Remove the rocker cover. Check to ensure the engine is set on TDC. The timing mark on the camshaft sprocket should be 90 degrees to the right, parallel to the top of the cylinder head. Make sure the yellow crankshaft pulley timing mark is aligned with the indicator pin.
19. Mark the position of the distributor rotor in relation to the distributor housing, and the distributor housing in relation to the cylinder head. Remove the distributor. Do not rotate the engine after distributor removal.
20. Hold the crankshaft pulley with a suitable tool and remove the distributor drive gear/camshaft pulley retaining bolt and the drive gear. Remove the upper timing cover assembly.
21. Push the timing chain adjuster sleeve in towards the left, and insert a 0.0787 in. (2mm) diameter x 1.77 in. (45mm) long pin into the lever hole to hold it in place.
22. Wire the chain to the pulley and remove the pulley from the camshaft. Do not allow the sprocket and chain to fall down into the engine and cause the chain to become disengaged from the crankshaft sprocket.
23. Remove the intake manifold bracket.
24. Disconnect the exhaust pipe.
25. Remove the 2 front head bolts.
26. Remove the remaining head bolts starting from the rear and working around toward the center of the head.
27. Lift off the head.

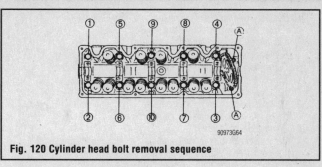

Fig. 120 Cylinder head bolt removal sequence

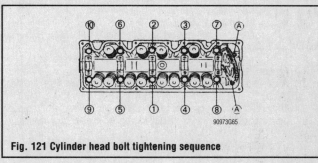

Fig. 121 Cylinder head bolt tightening sequence

28. Discard the head gasket.
29. Thoroughly clean the mating surfaces of the head and block.
30. Check the head and block for flatness with a straightedge.
To install:
31. Apply RTV sealer to the top front of the block.
32. Place a new head gasket on the block.
33. Position the head on the block.
34. Clean the head bolts and apply oil to the threads.
35. Tighten the head bolts, in 2 even steps, to 64 ft. lbs. (87 Nm).
36. Tighten the 2 front bolts, to 17 ft. lbs. (23 Nm).
37. Place the camshaft pulley on the camshaft and tighten the bolt to to 95 inch lbs. (11 Nm); the nut to 87 inch lbs. (10 Nm).
38. Connect the exhaust pipe.
39. Install the intake manifold bracket.
40. Install the upper timing cover assembly.
41. Install the distributor.
42. Install the rocker cover.
43. Connect the emissions harness.
44. Install the solenoid valves.
45. Connect the oxygen sensor.
46. Install the fuel lines.
47. Install the canister hose.
48. Install the oil cooler coolant hose.
49. Install the spark plugs.
50. Install the spark plug wires.
51. Install the brake vacuum hose.
52. Install the upper radiator hose.
53. Install the accessory drive belts.
54. Install the accelerator cable.
55. Fill the cooling system.
56. Install the air cleaner assembly.
57. Connect the negative battery cable.

3.0L ENGINE

▶ **See Figures 122 and 123**

✳✳ CAUTION

Fuel injection systems remain under pressure after the engine has been turned OFF. Properly relieve fuel pressure before disconnecting any fuel lines. Failure to do so may result in fire or personal injury. Do not allow fuel spray or fuel vapors to come in contact with a spark or open flame. Keep a dry chemical fire extinguisher nearby. Never store fuel in an open container due to risk of fire or explosion.

1. Position the engine at TDC on the compression stroke.
2. Properly relieve the fuel system pressure.
3. Disconnect the negative battery cable.
4. Remove the air cleaner assembly.
5. Disconnect the accelerator cable.
6. Drain the cooling system.
7. Remove the spark plug wires.
8. Remove the fresh air duct assembly.
9. Remove the cooling fan and radiator cowling.
10. Remove the drive belts.
11. Remove the air conditioning compressor idler pulley. If necessary, remove the compressor and position it to the side.
12. Remove the crankshaft pulley and baffle plate.
13. Remove the coolant bypass hose.
14. Remove the upper radiator hose.
15. Remove the timing belt cover assembly retaining bolts. Remove the timing belt cover assembly and gasket.
16. Turn the crankshaft to align the mating marks of the pulleys.
17. Remove the upper idler pulley.
18. Remove the timing belt. If reusing the belt be sure to mark the direction of rotation.
19. Disconnect and plug canister, brake vacuum and fuel hoses. If equipped with automatic transmission, disconnect the automatic transmission vacuum hose.
20. Remove the 3-way solenoid valve assembly and disconnect all engine harness connector and grounds.
21. If equipped with automatic transmission, remove the dipstick. Disconnect the required vacuum hoses. Disconnect the accelerator linkage.
22. Remove the distributor and the EGR pipe.
23. Remove the 6 extension manifolds. Remove the O-rings from the extension manifolds and replace with new ones. Remove the intake manifold by loosening the retaining bolts in the proper sequence.
24. Remove the cylinder head cover, gasket and seal washers.
25. Remove the center exhaust pipe insulator and pipe. Disconnect the exhaust manifold retaining bolts. Remove the exhaust manifold with insulator.
26. Remove the seal plate.
27. Remove the cylinder head retaining bolts in the proper sequence in 2 or 3 stages. Remove the cylinder head from the vehicle.
28. Thoroughly clean the cylinder head and cylinder block contact surfaces to remove any dirt or oil. Check the cylinder head for warpage and cracks. The maximum allowable warpage is 0.10mm. Inspect the cylinder head bolts for damaged threads and make sure they are free from grease and dirt. After the bolts are cleaned, measure the length of each bolt and replace out of specifications bolts as required.
    a. Length: Intake—108mm; Exhaust—138mm
    b. Maximum: Intake—109mm; Exhaust—139mm
29. Check the oil control plug projection at the cylinder block. Projection should be 0.53–0.57mm. If correct, apply clean engine oil to a new O-ring and position it on the control plug.

To install:

30. Place the new cylinder head gasket on the left bank with the **L** mark facing up. Place the new cylinder head gasket on the right bank with the **R** mark facing up. Install the cylinder onto the block. Tighten the head bolts in the following manner:
    a. Coat the threads and the seating faces of the head bolts with clean engine oil.
    b. Tighten the bolts in the proper sequence to 14 ft. lbs.(19 Nm).

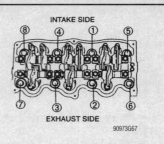

Fig. 123 Cylinder head bolt tightening sequence

    c. Paint a mark on the head of each bolt.
    d. Using this mark as a reference, tighten the bolts in the proper sequence an additional 90 degrees.
    e. Repeat the previous step.
31. Install the seal plate.
32. Install the exhaust manifold with insulator.
33. Connect the exhaust manifold retaining bolts.
34. Install the center exhaust pipe insulator and pipe.
35. Install the cylinder head cover, gasket and seal washers.
36. Install the intake manifold by loosening the retaining bolts in the proper sequence.
37. Install the O-rings from the extension manifolds.
38. Install the 6 extension manifolds.
39. Install the distributor and the EGR pipe.
40. If equipped with automatic transmission, install the dipstick. Connect the required vacuum hoses. Connect the accelerator linkage.
41. Install the 3-way solenoid valve assembly and connect all engine harness connector and grounds.
42. Connect the canister, brake vacuum and fuel hoses. If equipped with automatic transmission, connect the automatic transmission vacuum hose.
43. To install the timing belt, first the automatic tensioner must be loaded. To load the tensioner:
    a. Place a flat washer on the bottom of the tensioner body to prevent damage to the body and position the unit on an arbor press.
    b. Press the rod into the tensioner body. Do not use more than 2000 lbs. (8900 N) of pressure.
    c. Once the rod is fully inserted into the body, insert a suitable L-shaped pin or a small Allen wrench through the body and the rod to hold the rod in place.
    d. Remove the unit from the press and install onto the block and torque the mounting bolt to 14–19 ft. lbs. (19–26 Nm).
    e. Leave the pin in place, it will be removed later.
44. Make sure all the timing marks are aligned properly. With the upper idler pulley removed, hang the timing belt on each pulley in the order.
45. Install the upper idler pulley and torque the mounting bolt to 27–38 ft. lbs. (37–52 Nm).
46. Rotate the crankshaft twice in the normal direction of rotation to align all the timing marks.
47. Make sure all the marks are aligned correctly.
48. Remove the pin from the auto tensioner. Again turn the crankshaft twice in the normal direction of rotation and make sure all the timing marks are aligned properly.
49. Check the timing belt deflection by applying 22 lbs. of force. If the deflection is not 5–7mm, repeat the adjustment procedure.

➡**Excessive belt deflection is caused by auto tensioner failure or an excessively stretched timing belt.**

50. Install the upper idler pulley.
51. Install the timing belt cover assembly and new gasket.
52. Install the upper radiator hose.
53. Install the coolant bypass hose.
54. Install the crankshaft pulley and baffle plate.
55. Install the A/C compressor.
56. Install the air conditioning compressor idler pulley.
57. Install the accessory drive belts.
58. Install the cooling fan and radiator cowling.
59. Install the fresh air duct assembly.

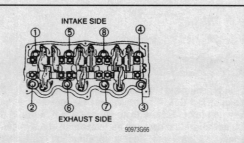

Fig. 122 Cylinder head bolt removal sequence

60. Install the spark plug wires.
61. Connect and adjust the accelerator cable.
62. Fill the cooling system.
63. Install the air cleaner assembly.
64. Connect the negative battery cable.

Oil Pan

REMOVAL & INSTALLATION

2.3L and 2.5L Engines

▶ **See Figures 124 and 125**

1. Disconnect the battery ground cable.
2. Remove the engine assembly from vehicle.

✳✳ CAUTION

Do NOT turn the engine assembly upside down with the oil pan still attached. Sludge and debris in the oil pan will fall into the cylinders, pistons and connecting rods, possibly causing rapid wear. Sludge may also plug the engine oil pickup screen.

3. Mount the engine on a stand with the engine mounted in the upright position.
4. Remove the oil pan mounting bolts.
5. Remove the oil pan from the engine.
6. Remove and discard the oil pan gasket. Thoroughly clean all gasket mating surfaces.

To install:

➡ **Wait no longer than 4 minutes after applying silicone gasket sealant to install the oil pan.**

7. Apply a 0.24 inch (6mm) bead of silicone gasket sealant in six places as illustrated.

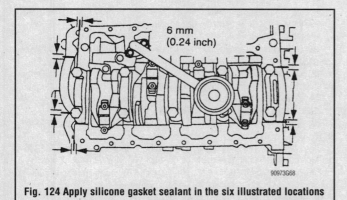

Fig. 124 Apply silicone gasket sealant in the six illustrated locations

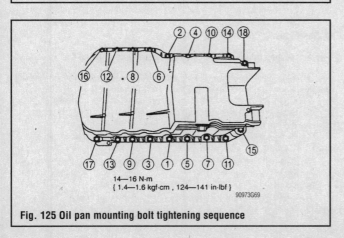

Fig. 125 Oil pan mounting bolt tightening sequence

8. Position and press into place the new oil pan gasket onto the oil pan mounting flange.
9. Using a straight edge, line up the oil pan to the engine block.
10. Install the oil pan mounting bolts. The 2 long bolts are installed in the two rear pan holes (holes 15 and 18 shown in the illustration) near the flywheel.
11. Tighten the oil pan bolts, in sequence, to 124–141 inch lbs. (14–16 Nm).
12. Install the engine assembly into the vehicle.
13. Connect the negative battery cable. Fill the engine with the proper amount and type of engine oil. Add all necessary fluids and be sure that all components are installed/connected correctly.

2.6L Engine

▶ **See Figure 126**

1. Disconnect the negative battery cable.
2. Raise and support the front end on jackstands.
3. Drain the oil.
4. Remove the splash pan.
5. Remove the engine braces.
6. Remove the stabilizer bracket.
7. Unbolt and remove the oil pan.
8. Clean the mounting bolts, oil pan and engine block gasket surfaces thoroughly of any debris and old gasket material.

To install:

9. Apply silicone gasket sealant to the oil pan along the inside of the mounting bolt holes, overlapping the ends.
10. Be sure to install the oil pan to the engine block within 5 minutes after applying the silicone gasket sealant.
11. Install and tighten the oil pan mounting bolts to screws to 70–95 inch lbs. (8–11 Nm).
12. Install all other parts in reverse order of removal.
13. Fill the engine with the correct type and amount of new engine oil.
14. Connect the negative battery cable.
15. Start the engine and check for leaks.
16. After turning off the engine, recheck the oil level.

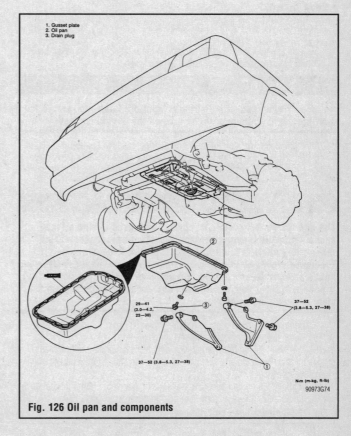

Fig. 126 Oil pan and components

3.0L Engine (MPV)

1. Disconnect the negative battery cable.
2. Raise and safely support the vehicle.
3. On 4WD, attach a suitable engine lifting tool to hold the engine.
4. Drain the oil.
5. Remove the splash shield.
6. On 2WD, remove the 2 engine braces (gusset plates).
7. On 4WD, perform the following procedures:
   a. Remove the fresh-air duct and the cooling fan cowling.
   b. Remove the driver's side engine mount.
   c. Remove the transmission lower mount.
   d. Remove the oil cooler hose and pipe.
   e. Remove the stabilizer brackets.
8. Unbolt and remove the oil pan.

To install:

9. Clean the oil pan and engine block gasket surfaces thoroughly.
10. Install a new pan gasket.
11. Install the oil pan and tighten the bolts to 61–87 inch lbs. (7–10 Nm).
12. On 4WD, perform the following procedures:
   a. Install the stabilizer brackets, then tighten the bolts to 14–18 ft. lbs. (19–25 Nm).
   b. Install the oil cooler hose and pipe.
   c. Install the transmission lower mount. Tighten the mounting bolt to 32–44 ft. lbs. (44–60 Nm), and the nut to 24–33 ft. lbs. (32–46 Nm).
   d. Install the engine mount. Tighten the mounting bolts to 26–36 ft. lbs. (35–49 Nm).
   e. Install the cooling fan cowling and the fresh-air duct.
13. On 2WD, install the engine braces, then tighten the mounting bolts to 28–38 ft. lbs. (38–51 Nm).
14. Install the splash shield and tighten the bolts to 61–87 inch lbs. (7–10 Nm).
15. On 4WD, remove the engine lifting tool.
16. Fill the engine oil, and lower the vehicle.
17. Connect the negative battery cable.

3.0L Engine (B Series Pick-up)

♦ **See Figure 127**

1. Disconnect the negative battery cable.
2. Remove the oil level dipstick.
3. Remove the fan shroud. Leave the fan shroud over the fan assembly.
4. Remove the motor mount nuts from the frame.

> **※ WARNING**
>
> On models equipped with distributor ignition, failure to remove the distributor will damage or break it when the engine is lifted.

5. If equipped, mark and remove the distributor assembly from the engine.
6. Raise and support the vehicle safely. Remove the oil level sensor wire.
7. Drain the engine oil from the crankcase into a suitable container and dispose of it properly.

> **※ CAUTION**
>
> The EPA warns that prolonged contact with used engine oil may cause a number of skin disorders, including cancer! You should make every effort to minimize your exposure to used engine oil. Protective gloves should be worn when changing the oil. Wash your hands and any other exposed skin areas as soon as possible after exposure to used engine oil. Soap and water, or waterless hand cleaner should be used.

8. Remove the starter motor from the engine.
9. Remove the transmission inspection cover.
10. On 1994–97 models, remove the right hand axle I-Beam. The brake caliper must be removed and secured out of the way. Refer to the necessary service procedures.
11. Remove the oil pan attaching bolts, using a suitable lifting device, raise the engine about 2 inches. Remove the oil pan from the engine block.

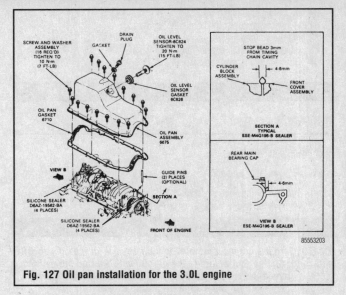

Fig. 127 Oil pan installation for the 3.0L engine

➡ Oil pan fits tightly between the transmission spacer plate and oil pump pickup tube. Use care when removing the oil pan from the engine.

12. Clean all gasket surfaces on the engine and oil pan. Remove all traces of old gasket and/or sealer.

To install:

13. Apply a 0.16–0.23 inch (4–6mm) bead of RTV sealer to the junctions of the rear main bearing cap and block, and the front cover and block. The sealer sets in 15 minutes, so work quickly!
14. Apply adhesive to the gasket mating surfaces and install oil pan gasket.
15. Install the oil pan on the engine block.
16. Tighten the oil pan bolts in 5 steps to the following specifications:
   • Step 1: Tighten the 4 corner oil pan bolts to 7–10 ft. lbs. (10–14 Nm)
   • Step 2: Tighten the remaining bolts to 7–10 ft. lbs. (10–14 Nm)
   • Step 3: Tighten the 4 corner oil pan bolts again to 7–10 ft. lbs. (10–14 Nm)
   • Step 4: Loosen all of the oil pan bolts one full turn
   • Step 5: Tighten all of the oil pan bolts to 7–10 ft. lbs. (10–14 Nm)
17. Install low–oil level sensor connector. Lower engine assembly to original position.
18. On 1994–97 models, install right hand axle I-Beam. Install the brake caliper. Refer to the necessary service procedures.
19. Install transmission inspection cover. Install starter motor.
20. Lower the vehicle and install the fan shroud.
21. Install motor mount retaining nuts. If removed, install distributor assembly.
22. Replace the oil level dipstick. Connect the battery ground. Fill crankcase with the correct amount of new engine oil. Start engine and check for leaks.
23. If equipped with distributor ignition, check the base ignition timing.

4.0L Engine

1994–97

♦ **See Figures 128 and 129**

➡ Review the complete service procedure before starting this repair.

1. Disconnect the negative battery cable. Remove the complete engine assembly from the vehicle. Refer to the necessary service procedures in this section.
2. Mount the engine on a suitable engine stand with oil pan facing up.
3. Remove the oil pan attaching bolts (note location of 2 spacers) and remove the pan from the engine block.
4. Remove the oil pan gasket and crankshaft rear main bearing cap wedge seal.
5. Clean all gasket surfaces on the engine and oil pan. Remove all traces of old gasket and/or sealer.

To install:

6. Install a new crankshaft rear main bearing cap wedge seal. The seal should fit snugly into the sides of the rear main bearing cap.

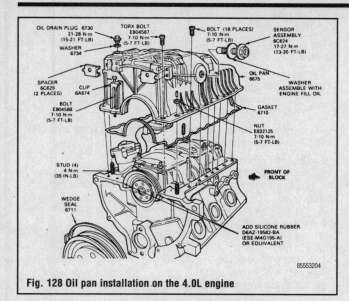

Fig. 128 Oil pan installation on the 4.0L engine

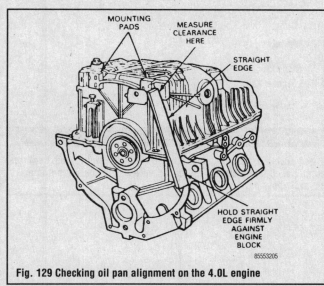

Fig. 129 Checking oil pan alignment on the 4.0L engine

7. Position the oil pan gasket to the engine block and place the oil pan in correct position on the 4 locating studs.

8. Tighten the oil pan retaining bolts EVENLY to 5–7 ft. lbs. (7–10 Nm).

9. The transmission bolts to the engine and oil pan. There are 2 spacers on the rear of the oil pan to allow proper mating of the transmission and oil pan. If these spacers were lost, or the oil pan was replaced, you must determine the proper spacers to install. To do this:

a. With the oil pan installed, place a straightedge across the machined mating surface of the rear of the block, extending over the oil pan–to–transmission mounting surface.

b. Using a feeler gauge, measure the gap between the oil pan mounting pad and the straightedge.

c. Repeat the procedure for the other side.

d. Select the spacers as follows:
- Gap = 0.011–0.020 in.; spacer = 0.010 in.
- Gap = 0.021–0.029 in.; spacer = 0.020 in.
- Gap = 0.030–0.039 in.; spacer = 0.030 in.

➡Failure to use the correct spacers will result in damage to the oil pan and oil leakage.

10. Install the selected spacers to the mounting pads on the rear of the oil pan before bolting the engine and transmission together. Install the engine assembly in the vehicle.

11. Connect the negative battery cable. Start the engine and check for leaks.

1998

▶ **See Figures 130 and 131**

1. Disconnect the negative battery cable.
2. Attach the engine lifting brackets.
3. Remove the 4 motor mount retaining nuts.
4. Raise and safely support the engine assembly with an engine hoist and a three bar engine support.
5. Raise and support the vehicle safely.
6. Remove the starter motor.
7. Drain the engine oil from the crankcase into a suitable container and dispose of it properly.

✳✳ CAUTION

The EPA warns that prolonged contact with used engine oil may cause a number of skin disorders, including cancer! You should make every effort to minimize your exposure to used engine oil. Protective gloves should be worn when changing the oil. Wash your hands and any other exposed skin areas as soon as possible after exposure to used engine oil. Soap and water, or waterless hand cleaner should be used.

8. Remove the oil pan Torx® head bolts.
9. Remove the oil pan attaching nuts and bolts. Remove the oil pan from the engine block.
10. Clean all gasket surfaces on the engine and oil pan. Remove all traces of old gasket and/or sealer.

To install:
11. Apply a 0.24 inch (6mm) bead of RTV sealer to the six places illustrated. The sealer sets in 15 minutes, so work quickly!

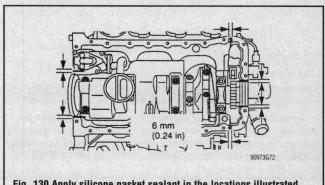

Fig. 130 Apply silicone gasket sealant in the locations illustrated

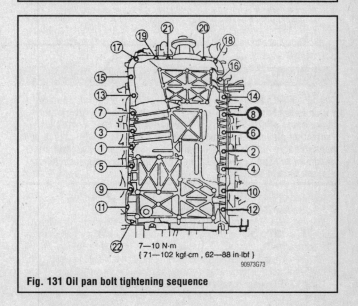

Fig. 131 Oil pan bolt tightening sequence

12. Install the new oil pan gasket.

13. Using a straight edge, line up the oil pan to the engine block.

14. Tighten the oil pan bolts to 7–10 ft. lbs. (10–14 Nm) evenly in the sequence illustrated.

15. Install the starter motor.

16. Lower the vehicle.

17. Using the engine hoist, remove the three bar engine support and lower the engine assembly to original position.

18. Tighten the 4 motor mount retaining nuts and remove the engine lifting brackets.

19. Connect the negative battery cables.

20. Fill crankcase with the correct amount of new engine oil. Start engine and check for leaks.

Oil Pump

REMOVAL & INSTALLATION

Navajo and B Series Pick-up Models

EXCEPT 2.5L AND 1995–97 2.3L ENGINES

♦ See Figure 132

➡The oil pumps are not serviceable. If defective, they must be replaced.

1. Follow the service procedures under Oil Pan Removal and remove the oil pan assembly.

2. Remove the oil pick-up and tube assembly from the pump.

3. Remove the oil pump retainer bolts and remove the oil pump.

To install:

4. Prime the oil pump with clean engine oil by filling either the inlet or outlet port with clean engine oil. Rotate the pump shaft to distribute the oil within the pump body.

5. Install the pump and tighten the mounting bolts to:

- 14–21 ft. lbs. (19–29 Nm) on 1994 2.3L engines
- 30–40 ft. lbs. (40–55 Nm) on 3.0L engines
- 13–15 ft. lbs. (17–21 Nm) on 4.0L engines

✽✽ WARNING

Do not force the oil pump if it does not seat readily. The oil pump driveshaft may be misaligned with the distributor or shaft assembly. If the pump is tightened down with the driveshaft misaligned, damage to the pump could occur. To align, rotate the intermediate driveshaft into a new position.

6. Install the oil pick-up and tube assembly to the pump. If there is a gasket between the pump and the pick-up, use a new gasket when installing.

7. Install the oil pan as previously described.

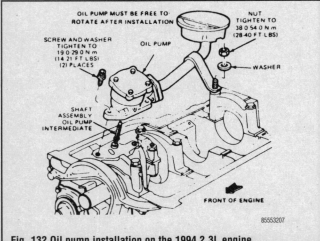

Fig. 132 Oil pump installation on the 1994 2.3L engine

2.5L AND 1995–97 2.3L ENGINES

➡The oil pump is located on the front of the engine and is turned by the timing belt.

1. Disconnect the negative battery cable.

2. Remove the timing belt.

3. Detach the camshaft position sensor (CMP) electrical connector.

4. Remove the oil pump sprocket bolt and sprocket.

➡Use a prybar or drift through one of the holes in the pump sprocket to keep it from turning while loosening the bolt.

5. Unbolt the camshaft position sensor.

6. Remove the four bolts retaining the oil pump to the engine block.

7. Remove the oil pump from the front of the engine and discard the pump-to-block gasket.

8. Inspect the oil pump and O-rings and replace as necessary. Clean all gasket mating surfaces thoroughly.

9. Installation is the reverse of the removal procedure, however note the following:

   a. Prime the oil pump and with 8 ounces (236ml) of new engine oil and lubricate the O-rings with same.

   b. Use a new pump-to-block gasket.

   c. Tighten the oil pump bolts to 89–123 inch lbs. (10–14 Nm), the camshaft position sensor bolts to 45–61 inch lbs. (5–7 Nm) and the oil pump sprocket bolt to 30–40 ft. Lbs. (40–55 Nm).

MPV Models

2.6L ENGINE

♦ See Figure 133

1. Disconnect the battery ground.

2. Drain the cooling system.

✽✽ CAUTION

When draining the coolant, always drain the coolant into a sealable container. Coolant should be reused unless it is contaminated or several years old.

3. Remove the accessory drive belts.

4. Remove the fan and shroud.

5. Remove the water pump pulley.

6. Unbolt and remove the water pump.

7. Remove the crankshaft pulley.

8. Remove the oil pan.

9. Remove the timing chain cover.

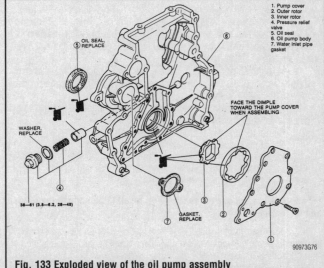

Fig. 133 Exploded view of the oil pump assembly

➡**The pump is built into the cover**

10. Remove the oil pickup tube.
11. Remove the pump cover from the case.
12. Remove the inner and outer rotors.
13. Remove the pressure relief valve.
14. Remove and discard the water inlet pipe gasket.

To install:

15. Install a new water inlet pipe gasket using adhesive sealer.
16. Install the oil pickup tube using a new gasket. Tighten the bolts to 95 inch lbs. (11 Nm).
17. Install the pressure relief valve. Tighten the plug to 28–45 ft. lbs. (38–61 Nm).
18. Install the inner and outer rotors.
19. Install the pump cover.
20. Using new gaskets coated with sealer, install the timing chain cover. Tighten the bolts to 19 ft. lbs.
21. Tighten the oil pickup brace bolt to 95 inch lbs. (11 Nm).
22. Install the oil pan. Tighten the bolts to 95 inch lbs. (11 Nm).
23. Install the crankshaft pulley. Tighten the bolt to 145 ft. lbs. (197 Nm).
24. Install the water pump.
25. Install the water pump pulley.
26. Install the fan and shroud.
27. Install the accessory drive belts.
28. Fill the cooling system.
29. Connect the battery ground.

3.0L ENGINE

1. Disconnect the negative battery cable. Raise and support the vehicle safely.
2. Drain the engine oil and the cooling system.
3. Remove the crankshaft pulley and the timing belt covers.
4. Remove the timing belt, crankshaft sprocket and key.
5. Remove the thermostat and gasket.
6. Remove the oil pan, oil strainer and O-ring.
7. Unbolt and remove the oil pump and gasket.

To install:

8. Press in a new oil seal and coat the seal lip with clean engine oil. Use a new gasket, O-ring and sealant as required. Tighten the oil pump retaining bolts to 14–18 ft. lbs. (19–25 Nm).
9. Install the oil pan and tighten the pan bolts 5–8 ft. lbs. (8–11 Nm).
10. Install the crankshaft sprocket and key.
11. Install the timing belt and covers. Install the crankshaft pulley and tighten the pulley bolt to 116–123 ft. lbs. (157–167 Nm).
12. Install the thermostat and gasket. Tighten the thermostat housing bolts 14–18 ft. lbs. (19–25 Nm).
13. Fill the crankcase to the recommended level with fresh oil. Fill the cooling system.
14. Crank the engine to prime the oil pump.
15. Start the engine and check for leaks.

Crankshaft Damper

REMOVAL & INSTALLATION

▶ **See Figures 134, 135 and 136**

1. Disconnect the negative battery cable.
2. Remove the engine fan/clutch assembly and shroud.
3. Remove the accessory drive belt(s).
4. On those engines with a separate damper and pulley, remove the retaining bolts, then separate the crankshaft damper from the pulley.
5. Remove the pulley-to-crankshaft bolt and washer.
6. If necessary, use a puller tool to remove the damper/pulley from the crankshaft.
7. If equipped, remove the crankshaft key.

To install:

❊❊ WARNING

On MPV models equipped with the 3.0L engine, the crankshaft position sensor rotor is on the rear of the damper/pulley and can be easily damaged.

8. Inspect the front cover seal and replace if necessary.
9. On 3.0L (B Series Pick-up) and 4.0L engines, perform the following:
   a. Coat the rubbing surface of the damper/pulley with clean engine oil.
   b. Apply a small amount of RTV sealant to the damper keyway groove.
   c. On the B Series Pick-up with the 3.0L engine, use a crankshaft damper installation tool to press the damper onto the crankshaft. Install and tighten the retaining bolt to 93–121 ft. lbs. (125–165 Nm).

❊❊ WARNING

Never hammer on the damper to install it.

10. Install the crankshaft pulley. Tighten the crankshaft pulley retaining bolt(s) to the following specifications:
   - 4.0L engine: 30–37 ft. lbs. (40–50 Nm), plus an additional 80–90°
   - 3.0L engine (B Series Pick-up): 39–53 ft. lbs. (53–72 Nm)
   - 3.0L engine (MPV): 116–122 ft. lbs. (157–166 Nm)
   - 2.6L engine: 131–144 ft. lbs. (177–196 Nm)
   - 2.3L and 2.5L engines: 93–121 ft. lbs. (125–165 Nm)
11. Install the accessory drive belt(s).
12. Install the engine fan/clutch assembly and the shroud.
13. Connect the negative battery cable. Run the engine and check for oil leaks.

Fig. 134 Loosen the crankshaft pulley center nut

Fig. 135 Remove the crankshaft pulley retaining bolt

Fig. 136 Remove the crankshaft pulley, keep the small bolt in for installation purposes

Timing Belt Cover

REMOVAL & INSTALLATION

2.3L/2.5L Engines

▶ See Figure 137

1. Disconnect the negative battery cable.
2. Rotate the engine so that No. 1 cylinder is at TDC on the compression stroke. Check that the timing marks are aligned on the camshaft and crankshaft pulleys. An access plug is provided in the cam belt cover so that the camshaft timing can be checked without removal of the cover or any other parts. Set the crankshaft to TDC by aligning the timing mark on the crank pulley with the TDC mark on the belt cover. Look through the access hole in the belt cover to make sure that the timing mark on the cam drive sprocket is lined up with the pointer on the inner belt cover.

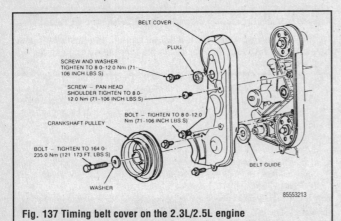

Fig. 137 Timing belt cover on the 2.3L/2.5L engine

➡Always turn the engine in the normal direction of rotation. Backward rotation may cause the timing belt to jump time, due to the arrangement of the belt tensioner.

3. Drain cooling system. Remove the upper radiator hose as necessary. Remove the fan blade and water pump pulley bolts.

❊❊ CAUTION

When draining the coolant, keep in mind that cats and dogs are attracted by ethylene glycol antifreeze, and are quite likely to drink any that is left in an uncovered container or in puddles on the ground. This will prove fatal in sufficient quantity. Always drain the coolant into a sealable container. Coolant should be reused unless it is contaminated or several years old.

4. Loosen the alternator retaining bolts and remove the drive belt from the pulleys. Remove the water pump pulley.
5. Loosen and position the power steering pump mounting bracket and position it aside.
6. Remove the timing belt outer cover retaining bolts and any interlocking tabs and remove the cover.

To install:

7. Install the timing belt cover.
8. Install the water pump pulley and fan blades. Install upper radiator hose if necessary. Refill the cooling system.
9. Position the alternator and drive belts, then adjust and tighten it to specifications.
10. Connect the negative battery cable.

3.0L Engine (MPV)

▶ See Figures 138 thru 143

1. Disconnect the negative battery cable, and drain the cooling system.
2. Drain the engine coolant.
3. Remove the air cleaner duct assembly.

Fig. 138 Remove the A/C compressor belt idler pulley assembly

Fig. 139 Remove the cooling system bypass hose between the upper and lower hoses at the engine

Fig. 140 Disconnect the upper radiator hose at the engine

Fig. 141 Remove the mounting fasteners, then remove the left side timing belt cover

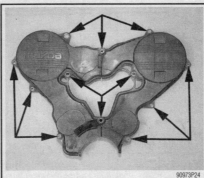

Fig. 142 Note the locations of the timing belt cover mounting fasteners

Fig. 143 Ater removing the mounting fasteners, remove the right side timing belt cover

4. Remove the cooling fan and radiator shroud.
5. Remove the accessory drive belt.
6. Remove the A/C compressor idler pulley.
7. Remove the crankshaft pulley.
8. Remove the coolant bypass and upper radiator hoses.
9. Remove the timing belt covers.

To install:

10. Install the timing belt covers and cover gaskets. Tighten the timing belt cover fasteners to 70–95 inch lbs. (8–11 Nm).
11. Install the coolant bypass and upper radiator hoses. Tighten the hose clamps.
12. Install the crankshaft pulley.
13. Install the A/C compressor idler pulley.
14. Install the accessory drive belt.
15. Install the cooling fan and the radiator shroud.
16. Install the air cleaner duct assembly.
17. Fill and bleed the cooling system.
18. Connect the negative battery cable.
19. Run the engine and check for leaks and proper operation. Check the idle speed and the ignition timing.

Timing Chain Cover and Seal

REMOVAL & INSTALLATION

2.6L Engine

◗ See Figure 144

❊❊ CAUTION

Fuel injection systems remain under pressure after the engine has been turned OFF. Properly relieve fuel pressure before disconnecting any fuel lines. Failure to do so may result in fire or personal injury. Do not allow fuel spray or fuel vapors to come in contact with a spark or open flame. Keep a dry chemical fire extinguisher nearby. Never store fuel in an open container due to risk of fire or explosion.

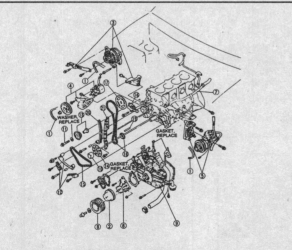

1. Drive belt
2. Water pump pulley
3. Alternator and bracket
4. P/S oil pump and bracket
5. A/C compressor and bracket
6. Water pump
7. Coolant bypass pipe
8. Crankshaft pulley
9. Chain cover
10. Spacer
11. Idler sprocket assembly lock bolt
12. Chain guides
13. Idler sprocket assembly
14. Crankshaft sprocket
15. Balancer chain
16. Chain adjuster
17. Camshaft pulley
18. Timing chain and timing gear
19. Key
20. Chain lever
21. Chain guide

90973G78

Fig. 144 Timing chain and related components

---

1. Relieve the fuel system pressure, and disconnect the negative battery cable.
2. Drain the cooling system and engine oil.
3. Remove the fan shroud and cooling fan.
4. Remove the cylinder head.
5. Remove the oil pan.
6. Remove the drive belts.
7. Remove the water pump pulley.
8. Remove the alternator and bracket.
9. Remove the power steering pump and bracket.
10. Without disconnecting the A/C lines, remove the A/C compressor mounting bolts and remove the A/C compressor. Secure the compressor out of the way. Remove the bolts and the A/C compressor mounting bracket.
11. Remove the water pump.
12. Remove the coolant bypass pipe.
13. Remove the bolt, and by using a suitable puller, remove the crankshaft pulley.
14. Loosen the mounting bolts and remove the timing chain cover.

To install:

15. Install the timing cover with a new gasket Torque the timing cover bolts to 14–19 ft. lbs. (19–25 Nm).
16. Install the crankshaft pulley.
17. Install the coolant bypass pipe.
18. Install the water pump.
19. Install the power steering pump bracket and the power steering pump.
20. Mount the A/C compressor bracket and install the A/C compressor.
21. Mount the alternator bracket and the alternator. Plug in the alternator wiring harness connector.
22. Install the water pump pulley.
23. Install the drive belts and adjust to specifications.
24. Install the oil pan.
25. Install the cylinder head.
26. Install the fan shroud and cooling fan.
27. Fill the crankcase with the proper type and quantity of engine oil. Fill and bleed the cooling system. Run the engine and check for leaks and proper operation.
28. Check the idle speed and ignition timing and adjust, if necessary.

3.0L Engine (B Series Pick-up)

◗ See Figures 145 and 146

➡The A/C system must be discharged to remove the front cover. Have the A/C refrigerant reclaimed by a MVAC certified shop. The front seal can be serviced with the engine in the vehicle. Remove the crankshaft damper, then follow the seal replacement procedure under installation.

1. Disconnect the negative battery cable.
2. Drain the cooling system and crankcase.

❊❊ CAUTION

When draining the coolant, keep in mind that cats and dogs are attracted by ethylene glycol antifreeze, and are quite likely to drink any that is left in an uncovered container or in puddles on the ground. This will prove fatal in sufficient quantity. Always drain the coolant into a sealable container. Coolant should be reused unless it is contaminated or several years old.

3. Remove the cooling fan.
4. Loosen the water pump pulley bolts. Remove the accessory drive belts. Remove the water pump pulley.
5. Remove the alternator adjusting arm and brace assembly. Remove the heated air intake duct from the engine.
6. Remove the upper motor mount retaining nuts. Remove the A/C compressor upper bolts, then remove the front cover front nuts on vehicles with automatic transmission and A/C.
7. Raise the vehicle. Remove the A/C compressor bolts and bracket if so equipped and position the assembly aside.
8. Remove the crankshaft pulley and damper assembly. Remove the oil pan.

➡According to the manufacturer, you must remove the water pump to remove the cover. However, we have found that on some models and/or years the water pump can be left bolted to the cover, thereby reducing some of the labor. Try removing the cover with the water pump attached first.

9. Lower the vehicle. Remove the lower radiator hose. Remove the water pump.

10. If necessary, remove the crankshaft position sensor.

11. Remove the timing cover to cylinder block attaching bolts. Carefully remove the timing cover from the cylinder block.

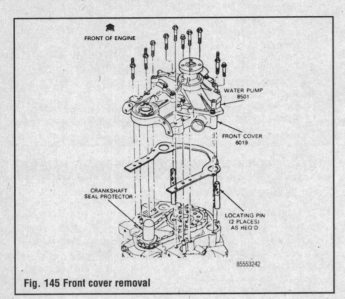

Fig. 145 Front cover removal

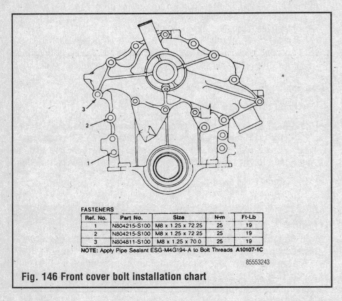

FASTENERS				
Ref. No.	Part No.	Size	N·m	Ft-Lb
1	N804215-S100	M8 x 1.25 x 72.25	25	19
2	N804215-S100	M8 x 1.25 x 72.25	25	19
3	N804811-S100	M8 x 1.25 x 70.0	25	19

NOTE: Apply Pipe Sealant ESG-M4G194-A to Bolt Threads

Fig. 146 Front cover bolt installation chart

12. Inspect the oil seal. If the seal needs replacing, follow the procedures under installation.

To install:

13. Clean timing cover and oil pan sealing surfaces. Clean and inspect all parts. The camshaft retaining bolt has a drilled oil passage for timing chain assembly lubrication. Clean oil passage with solvent. Do not replace with standard bolt.

14. Install timing cover assembly. Install retaining bolts with pipe sealant and tighten to 19 ft. lbs. (25 Nm). Refer to the illustration.

15. If the front seal needs to be replaced, proceed as follows:

   a. Using a front cover seal removal tool, or equivalent, remove the front seal.

   b. Lubricate the engine front cover and oil seal lip inner lip with engine oil.

   c. Using a seal driver/installation tool, install the new seal into the front cover.

16. If necessary, install the crankshaft position sensor.

17. Install oil pan and water pump. Refer to the necessary procedures in this section.

18. Install crankshaft damper and pulley assembly.

19. Install drive belt components. Install drive belts and adjust.

20. Fill crankcase. Refill and bleed cooling system. Connect the negative battery cable. Start engine check for coolant, oil and exhaust leaks.

4.0L Engine

▶ **See Figures 147 thru 153**

➡ **Review the complete service procedure before starting this repair. Refer to the necessary service procedures in this section. The front seal can be serviced with the engine in the vehicle. Remove the crankshaft damper, then follow the seal replacement procedure under installation.**

1. Disconnect the negative battery cable. Remove/lower the oil pan.

2. Drain the cooling system.

✳✳ CAUTION

When draining the coolant, keep in mind that cats and dogs are attracted by ethylene glycol antifreeze, and are quite likely to drink any that is left in an uncovered container or in puddles on the ground. This will prove fatal in sufficient quantity. Always drain the coolant into a sealable container. Coolant should be reused unless it is contaminated or several years old.

3. Remove the engine fan and shroud.

4. Remove the air conditioning compressor and position it out of the way. DO NOT disconnect the refrigerant lines!

5. Remove the power steering pump and position it out of the way. DO NOT disconnect the hoses!

6. Remove the alternator.

7. Remove the water pump.

8. Remove the drive pulley/damper from the crankshaft.

9. Remove the crankshaft timing sensor.

10. Remove the front cover attaching bolts. It may be necessary to tap the cover loose with a plastic mallet.

Fig. 147 To remove the front cover, remove the fan, shroud and unbolt the front cover-to-accessory bracket brace . . .

Fig. 148 . . . then remove the brace. Also remove the damper and any other obstructions to the cover

Fig. 149 Remove the front cover attaching bolts

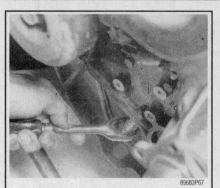

Fig. 150 Don't forget about the oil pan-to-front cover attaching bolts

Fig. 151 Remove the old gaskets and thoroughly clean all of the mating surfaces

Fig. 152 Place the cover on a bench and carefully knock the old seal out of the cover using a hammer and punch

Fig. 153 Use an ordinary seal driver, and seat a new seal into the cover at the same position as the old one

11. Inspect the oil seal. If the seal needs replacing, follow the procedures under installation.

To install:

12. Thoroughly clean all of the gasket and sealing surfaces and remove all traces of the old gaskets, oil, grease and/or dirt. Use new gaskets and apply a thin layer of sealant/adhesive to them.

➡️ If the specialized tools aren't available, the front seal can be replaced using normal hand tools. Before installing the cover, use a punch to carefully knock the old seal out of the cover, and a seal driver to seat the new seal.

13. Install the front cover and attaching bolts. Tighten the bolts to 13–15 ft. lbs. (17–21 Nm). Refer to the illustration.

14. If the front seal needs to be replaced, proceed as follows:
   a. Using a seal removal tool, remove the front seal.
   b. Lubricate the engine front cover and oil seal lip inner lip with engine oil.
   c. Using a seal driver/installation tool, install the new seal into the front cover.

15. Install the crankshaft timing sensor.
16. Install the drive pulley/damper.
17. Install the water pump.
18. Install the fan.
19. Install the alternator.
20. Install the power steering pump.
21. Install the air conditioning compressor.
22. Install the oil pan.
23. Fill the cooling system.
24. Fill the crankcase with the proper grade and amount of engine oil. Connect the negative battery cable. Start the engine and check for leaks, then road-test the vehicle for proper operation.

Timing Belt and Sprockets

2.3L/2.5L Engines

▶ See Figures 154 and 155

1. Disconnect the negative battery cable.
2. Rotate the engine so that No. 1 cylinder is at TDC on the compression stroke. Check that the timing marks are aligned on the camshaft and crankshaft pulleys. An access plug is provided in the cam belt cover so that the camshaft timing can be checked without removal of the cover or any other parts. Set the crankshaft to TDC by aligning the timing mark on the crank pulley with the TDC mark on the belt cover. Look through the access hole in the belt cover to make sure that the timing mark on the cam drive sprocket is lined up with the pointer on the inner belt cover.

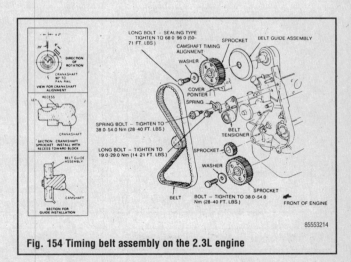

Fig. 154 Timing belt assembly on the 2.3L engine

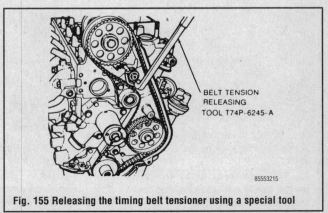

Fig. 155 Releasing the timing belt tensioner using a special tool

➡**Always turn the engine in the normal direction of rotation. Backward rotation may cause the timing belt to jump time, due to the arrangement of the belt tensioner.**

3. Remove the timing belt cover.

4. Loosen the belt tensioner pulley assembly, then position a camshaft belt adjuster tool (T74P–6254–A or equivalent) on the tension spring rollpin and retract the belt tensioner away from the timing belt. Tighten the adjustment bolt to lock the tensioner in the retracted position.

5. Remove the timing belt.

To install:

6. Install the new belt over the crankshaft sprocket and then counterclockwise over the auxiliary and camshaft sprockets, making sure the lugs on the belt properly engage the sprocket teeth on the pulleys. Be careful not to rotate the pulleys when installing the belt.

7. Release the timing belt tensioner pulley, allowing the tensioner to take up the belt slack. If the spring does not have enough tension to move the roller against the belt (belt hangs loose), it might be necessary to manually push the roller against the belt and tighten the bolt.

➡**The spring cannot be used to set belt tension; a wrench must be used on the tensioner assembly.**

8. Rotate the crankshaft two complete turns by hand (in the normal direction of rotation) to remove the slack from the belt, then tighten the tensioner adjustment and pivot bolts to specifications. Refer to the necessary illustrations. Make sure the belt is seated properly on the pulleys and that the timing marks are still in alignment when No. 1 cylinder is again at TDC/compression.

9. Install the crankshaft pulley and belt guide.

10. Install the timing belt cover.

11. Connect the negative battery cable.

12. Start the engine and check the engine performance. Make any necessary adjustments.

3.0L Engine (MPV)

▶ **See Figures 156 thru 170**

1. Disconnect the negative battery cable, and drain the cooling system.

2. Remove the timing belt covers.

3. Remove the upper idler pulley.

4. Turn the crankshaft to align the matching marks on the sprockets. If the timing belt is to be reused, make an arrow on the belt to indicate rotation direction.

5. Remove the timing belt and automatic tensioner.

6. Using SST 49 H012 010 tool or its equivalent, loosen and remove the camshaft sprocket lock bolts. Remove the camshaft sprockets.

7. Using a suitable puller, remove the crankshaft sprocket.

To install:

8. Install the crankshaft sprocket to the crankshaft.

9. Install the camshaft sprockets with the lock bolts and torque the bolts to 52–59 ft. lbs. (71–80 Nm).

10. Set a plane washer at the bottom of the tensioner body to prevent damage to the body plug. Press in the tensioner rod slowly, using a press or a vise.

➡**Do not press the tensioner rod more than 2200 lbs. (9800N).**

11. Insert a pin to hold the tensioner rod in the body. Install the automatic tensioner and tighten the mounting bolts to 14–19 ft. lbs. (19–25 Nm).

12. Install the crankshaft pulley lock bolt and loosely tighten. Check the alignment of the matching marks on the sprockets.

13. With the upper idler pulley removed, install the timing belt, making sure there is no slack between the crankshaft and camshaft sprockets. If the timing belt is being reused, it must be installed in the same direction of rotation.

Fig. 156 Remove the upper idler pulley

Fig. 157 Location of the timing marks on the timing belt cover

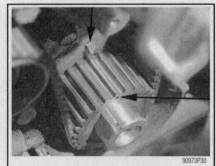

Fig. 158 Before removing the timing belt, line up the timing marks on the crankshaft sprocket and the engine block . . .

Fig. 159 . . . the right side camshaft sprocket and the mark on the cylinder head . . .

Fig. 160 . . . and the left side camshaft sprocket and the cylinder head

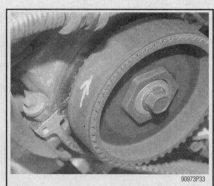

Fig. 161 Mark the direction of rotation on the timing belt if installing the same belt

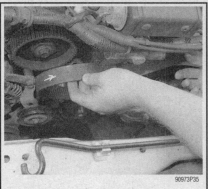

Fig. 162 Rmove the timing belt

Fig. 163 Remove the timing belt tensioner from the front of the engine

Fig. 164 Remove the cranshaft sprocket by pulling straight off of the crankshaft

Fig. 165 After removing the crankshaft sprocket, remove the woodruff key. Be careful not to lose this

Fig. 166 Place the washer on the tensioner allowing the plug on the tensioner to fit through the hole in the washer

Fig. 167 Mount the tensioner assembly and washer in the bench vise as shown

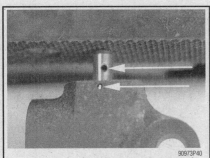

Fig. 168 When compressing the tensioner and plunger, be sure to line up the holes of the plunger to the hole in the tensioner body

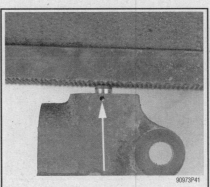

Fig. 169 Once the plunger and tensioner holes are aligned . . .

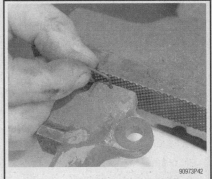

Fig. 170 . . . place a small hex key into the holes to keep the plunger compressed

14. Install the upper idler pulley and tighten the attaching bolt to 27–38 ft. lbs. (37–52 Nm).

15. Turn the crankshaft twice in the direction of rotation and align the matching marks. If the marks do not align, repeat the previous three steps.

16. Remove the pin from the automatic tensioner. Turn the crankshaft twice and align the matching marks. Make sure the marks are aligned.

17. Check the timing belt deflection. The deflection should be 0.20–0.28 in. (5–7mm). Do not apply tension other than that of the automatic tensioner.

18. If the deflection is not correct, repeat the previous three steps.

19. Remove the crankshaft pulley lock bolt.

20. Install the timing belt cover, along with the related components.

21. Reinstall the crankshaft pulley and torque the lock bolt to 116–123 ft. lbs. (37–52 Nm).

22. Fill and bleed the cooling system.

23. Run the engine and check for leaks and proper operation. Check the idle speed and the ignition timing.

Timing Chain and Gears

REMOVAL & INSTALLATION

✳✳ CAUTION

When draining the coolant, keep in mind that cats and dogs are attracted by ethylene glycol antifreeze, and are quite likely to drink any that is left in an uncovered container or in puddles on the ground. This will prove fatal in sufficient quantity. Always drain the coolant into a sealable container. Coolant should be reused unless it is contaminated or several years old.

2.6L Engine

♦ **See Figures 171, 172 and 173**

✳✳ CAUTION

Fuel injection systems remain under pressure after the engine has been turned OFF. Properly relieve fuel pressure before disconnecting any fuel lines. Failure to do so may result in fire or personal injury. Do not allow fuel spray or fuel vapors to come in contact with a spark or open flame. Keep a dry chemical fire extinguisher nearby. Never store fuel in an open container due to risk of fire or explosion.

1. Relieve the fuel system pressure, and disconnect the negative battery cable.
2. Remove the timing chain cover bolts and the cover.
3. Remove the spacer, the idler sprocket assembly lock bolt, the chain guides, and the idler sprocket assembly.
4. Remove the balancer chain.
5. Remove the timing chain adjuster and the timing chain.
6. Remove the lock bolts and remove the crankshaft timing sprocket and the camshaft sprocket.
7. Remove the key and the chain lever and guide.
8. Inspect the chain, sprockets and guides for damage and/or wear.

To install:

9. Install the timing chain guides and tighten to 7–9 ft. lbs. (10–12 Nm).
10. If removed, install the tensioner onto the cylinder block.
11. Align the plated links of the timing chain with the timing marks on the sprockets as the chain and sprockets are assembled. Secure the pulley and chain with wire to prevent misalignment.
12. Hold the chain tensioner head in, then slide the crankshaft sprocket onto the crankshaft and place the camshaft sprocket on the sprocket holder.
13. Install the balancer shaft drive sprocket on the crankshaft. Assemble the balancer shaft sprockets to the balancer shaft chain, making sure the timing marks on the sprockets are aligned with the polished links on the chain.

➥**Be careful not to confuse the right and left sprockets as they are installed in opposite directions.**

14. While holding the assembled sprockets and chain, align the timing mark on the crankshaft sprocket with the chain and install the balancer shaft sprockets. Temporarily tighten the bolts by hand.
15. Install the right and left lower balancer chain guides and tighten the mounting bolts to 69–95 inch lbs. (7.8–11.0 Nm).
16. Install the upper chain guide and loosely tighten the mounting and adjusting bolts. Set the chain guide to the fully downward position.
17. Tighten the idler sprocket assembly lock bolt to 27–38 ft. lbs. (37–52 Nm), and install the spacer.
18. Rotate both balancer shaft sprockets slightly to position the chain slack at the center between the left balancer shaft sprocket and the oil pump sprocket.
19. Adjust the balancer chain tension as follows:
    a. Loosen the upper chain guide adjusting bolt.
    b. Push on the chain guide just above the adjusting slot with a force of approximately 11 lbs. (49N), then pull back the guide 0.126–0.149 inch (3.2–3.8mm). Tighten the bolt to 69–95 inch lbs. (7.8–11.0 Nm). Tighten the guide pivot bolt to the same specification.
    c. The chain slack at the notch in the guide should be 0.12 inch (3mm) when the guide is properly adjusted.
20. Install the timing chain cover with a new gasket.
21. Fill the crankcase with the proper type and quantity of engine oil. Fill and bleed the cooling system. Run the engine and check for leaks and proper operation.
22. Check the idle speed and ignition timing and adjust, if necessary.

3.0L Engine (B Series Pick-up)

♦ **See Figures 174 and 175**

1. Disconnect the negative battery cable.
2. Drain the cooling system and crankcase.
3. Remove the timing chain cover.
4. Rotate crankshaft until No. 1 piston is at TDC and timing marks are aligned in the correct position.

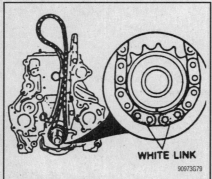

Fig. 171 Crankshaft sprocket chain alignment—2.6L engine

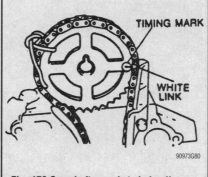

Fig. 172 Camshaft sprocket chain alignment—2.6L engine

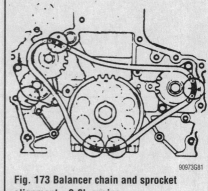

Fig. 173 Balancer chain and sprocket alignment—2.6L engine

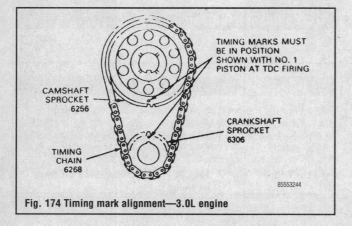

Fig. 174 Timing mark alignment—3.0L engine

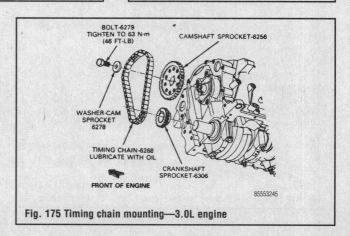

Fig. 175 Timing chain mounting—3.0L engine

5. Remove the camshaft sprocket retaining bolt and washer. Check timing chain deflection for excessive wear.

6. Slide sprockets and timing chain forward and remove as assembly.

To install:

7. Clean timing cover and oil pan sealing surfaces. Clean and inspect all parts. The camshaft retaining bolt has a drilled oil passage for timing chain assembly lubrication. Clean oil passage with solvent. Do not replace with standard bolt.

8. Slide sprockets and timing chain on as assembly with timing marks in the correct location. Install camshaft retaining bolt and washer. Tighten bolt to 46 ft. lbs. (62 Nm). Lubricate the timing chain assembly.

9. Install timing cover assembly. Install retaining bolts with pipe sealant and tighten as outlined.

10. Refill and bleed cooling system. Connect the negative battery cable. Start engine check for coolant, oil and exhaust leaks.

4.0L Engine

▶ **See Figures 176 thru 191**

➡ **Review the complete service procedure before starting this repair. Refer to the necessary service procedures in this section.**

1. Disconnect the negative battery cable.
2. Drain the cooling system.
3. Remove the front cover.
4. Remove the radiator.
5. Rotate the engine by hand until the No.1 cylinder is at TDC compression, and the timing marks are aligned.

6. Remove the lower tensioner bolt and install a holding clip in the bolt hole and the slot on the rubbing block.
Unbolt and remove the tensioner.

7. Remove the camshaft sprocket bolt and sprocket retaining key.

8. Remove the camshaft and crankshaft sprockets with the timing chain.

9. If necessary, remove the chain guide.

To install:

10. Install the timing chain guide. Make sure the pin of the guide is in the hole in the block. Tighten the bolts to 84–96 inch lbs. (9–11 Nm).

11. Align the timing marks on the crankshaft and camshaft sprockets and install the sprockets and chain.

12. Install the camshaft sprocket bolt and sprocket retaining key. Make sure that the timing marks are still aligned.

13. Install the tensioner with the clip in place to keep it retracted.

14. Install the crankshaft key. Make sure the timing marks are still aligned.

15. Make sure the tensioner side of the chain is held inward and the other side is straight and tight.

16. Install the camshaft sprocket bolt and tighten it to 50 ft. lbs. (68 Nm).

17. Remove the tensioner clip.

18. Check camshaft end-play.

19. Install the front cover.

20. Install the radiator.

21. Fill the cooling system.

22. Fill the crankcase to the proper level. Connect the negative battery cable. Start engine check for leaks and roadtest the vehicle for proper operation.

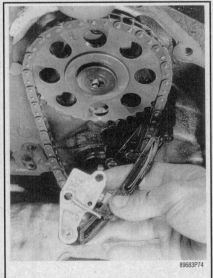

Fig. 176 To remove the timing chain and sprockets, first remove the engine front cover

Fig. 177 Remove the tensioner lower attaching bolt . . .

Fig. 178 . . . and install a holding clip in the bolt hole and the slot on the rubbing block

Fig. 179 Unbolt and remove the tensioner

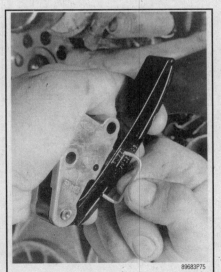

Fig. 180 A close-up view of a homemade holding clip . . .

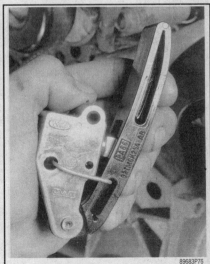

Fig. 181 . . . and its proper positioning on the tensioner

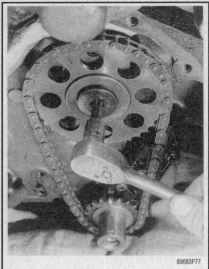

Fig. 182 Loosen the camshaft sprocket bolt . . .

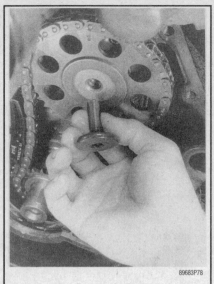

Fig. 183 . . . then remove it

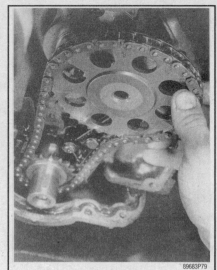

Fig. 184 Remove the camshaft sprocket and chain

Fig. 185 If necessary, unbolt the chain guide attaching bolts . . .

Fig. 186 . . . and remove the guide from the engine

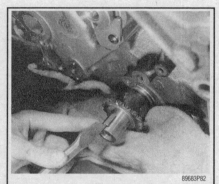

Fig. 187 To remove the crankshaft sprocket, use a chisel to loosen the keyway . . .

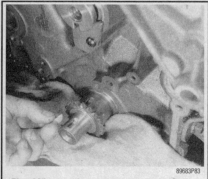

Fig. 188 . . . then remove the keyway from the crankshaft

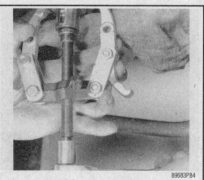

Fig. 189 Using a jawed puller, tighten the center bolt . . .

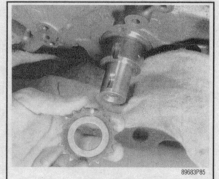

Fig. 190 . . . and pull the crankshaft sprocket from the engine

TIMING CHAIN DEFLECTION

1. Remove the timing chain tensioner.
2. Rotate the crankshaft counterclockwise (as viewed from the front of the engine) to take up the slack on the left hand side of the chain.
3. Mark a reference point on a block approximately at mid–point of the chain. Measure from this point to the chain.
4. Rotate the crankshaft in the opposite direction to take up the slack on the right hand side of the chain. Force the left hand side of the chain out with your fingers and measure the distance between the reference point and the chain. The deflection is the difference between the two measurements.

5. If the deflection measurement exceeds specification, replace the timing chain and sprockets.
6. If the wear on the tensioner face exceeds 1.5mm, replace the tensioner.
7. When installing the crankshaft sprocket, fill the keyway chamfer cavity with EOAZ–19554–AA Threadlock and Sealer or equivalent, flush with the front face of the sprocket.

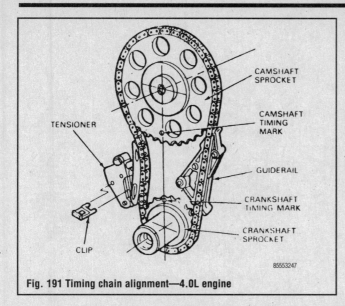

Fig. 191 Timing chain alignment—4.0L engine

Camshafts

REMOVAL & INSTALLATION

> **❈❈ CAUTION**
>
> When draining the coolant, keep in mind that cats and dogs are attracted by ethylene glycol antifreeze, and are quite likely to drink any that is left in an uncovered container or in puddles on the ground. This will prove fatal in sufficient quantity. Always drain the coolant into a sealable container. Coolant should be reused unless it is contaminated or several years old.

2.3L and 2.5L Engines

▶ See Figure 192

➡The following procedure covers camshaft removal and installation with the cylinder head on or off the engine. If the cylinder head has been removed, follow Steps 7–9 then skip to Step 12.

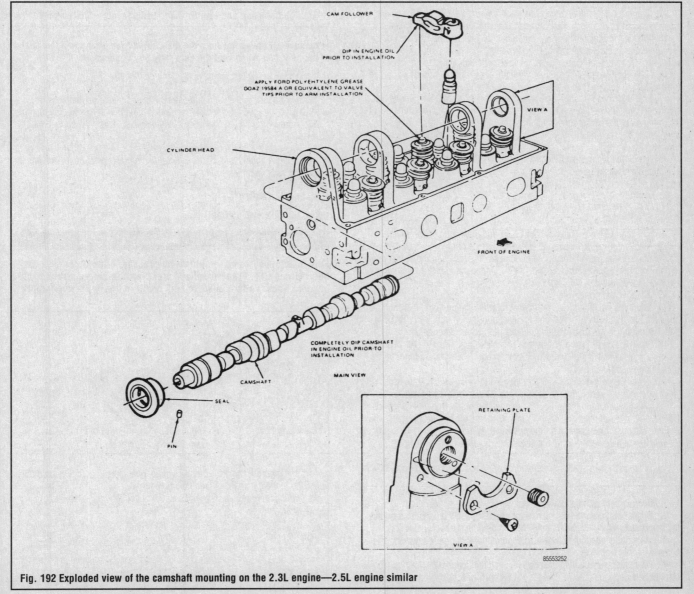

Fig. 192 Exploded view of the camshaft mounting on the 2.3L engine—2.5L engine similar

1. Drain the cooling system. Remove the air cleaner assembly and disconnect the negative battery cable.

2. Remove the spark plug wires from the plugs, disconnect the retainer from the valve cover and position the wires out of the way. Disconnect rubber vacuum lines as necessary.

3. Remove all drive belts. Remove the alternator mounting bracket–to–cylinder head mounting bolts, position bracket and alternator out of the way.

4. Disconnect and remove the upper radiator hose. Disconnect the radiator shroud.

5. Remove the fan blades and water pump pulley and fan shroud. Remove cam belt and valve covers.

6. Align engine timing marks at TDC for No. 1 cylinder. Remove cam drive belt.

7. Remove the rocker arms (camshaft followers).

8. Remove the camshaft drive gear and belt guide using a suitable puller. Remove the front oil seal with a sheet metal screw and slide hammer.

9. Remove the camshaft retainer located on the rear mounting stand by unbolting the two bolts.

10. Jack up the front of the vehicle and support on jackstands. Remove the front motor mount bolts. Disconnect the lower radiator hose from the radiator. Disconnect and plug the automatic transmission cooler lines.

11. Position a piece of wood on a floor jack and raise the engine carefully as far as it will go. Place blocks of wood between the engine mounts and cross-member pedestals.

12. Remove the camshaft by carefully withdrawing toward the front of the engine. Caution should be used to prevent damage to cam bearings, lobes and journals.

13. Check the camshaft journals and lobes for wear. Inspect the cam bearings, if worn (unless the proper bearing installing tool is on hand), the cylinder head must be removed for new bearings to be installed by a machine shop.

14. Camshaft installation is in the reverse order of service removal procedure. Coat the camshaft with a heavy SF (or better) grade oil before sliding it into the cylinder head. Install a new front seal. Apply a coat of sealer or teflon tape to the cam drive gear bolt before installation. After any procedure requiring removal of the rocker arms, each lash adjuster must be fully collapsed after assembly, then released. This must be done before the camshaft is turned.

15. Refill cooling system. Start engine and check for leaks. Road test the vehicle for proper operation.

2.6L Engine

▶ **See Figure 193**

1. Disconnect the negative battery cable, and drain the cooling system.

2. Remove the rocker cover. Check to ensure the engine is set on TDC. The timing mark on the camshaft sprocket should be 90 degrees to the right, parallel to the top of the cylinder head. Make sure the yellow crankshaft pulley timing mark is aligned with the indicator pin.

3. Remove the seal cover.

4. Mark the position of the distributor rotor in relation to the distributor housing, and the distributor housing in relation to the cylinder head. Remove the distributor. Do not rotate the engine after distributor removal.

5. Hold the crankshaft pulley with a suitable tool and remove the distributor drive gear/camshaft pulley retaining bolt and the drive gear. Remove the upper timing cover assembly.

6. Push the timing chain adjuster sleeve in towards the left, and insert a 2mm diameter x 45mm long pin into the lever hole to hold it in place.

7. Wire the chain to the pulley and remove the pulley from the camshaft. Do not allow the sprocket and chain to fall down into the engine and cause the chain to become disengaged from the crankshaft sprocket.

8. Remove the rocker arm/shaft assembly.

9. Remove the camshaft.

10. Inspect the camshaft for wear and/or damage and replace if necessary.

To install:

11. Apply clean engine oil to the camshaft journals, lobes and bearings. Install the camshaft with the dowel pin facing upwards.

12. Install the rocker arm/shaft assembly and tighten the bolts, in sequence, in 2–3 steps to 14–19 ft. lbs. (19–25 Nm). Make sure the rocker arm shaft spring does not get caught between the shaft and mounting boss during installation.

13. Install the camshaft sprocket and tighten the bolt to 37–44 ft. lbs. (50–60 Nm).

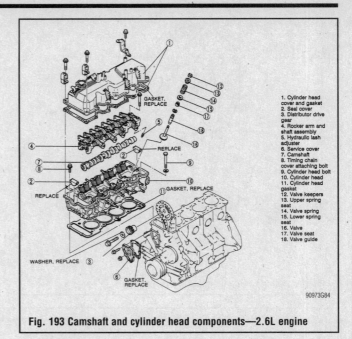

1. Cylinder head cover and gasket
2. Seal cover
3. Distributor drive gear
4. Rocker arm and shaft assembly
5. Hydraulic lash adjuster
6. Service cover
7. Camshaft
8. Timing chain cover attaching bolt
9. Cylinder head bolt
10. Cylinder head
11. Cylinder head gasket
12. Valve keepers
13. Upper spring seat
14. Valve spring
15. Lower spring seat
16. Valve
17. Valve seat
18. Valve guide

Fig. 193 Camshaft and cylinder head components—2.6L engine

➡ **Remove all old sealer from the distributor drive gear and apply sealer to the gear face, then seat the gear fully on the camshaft.**

14. Install the distributor drive gear and distributor.

15. Install the seal cover.

16. Coat a new gasket with silicone sealant and install on the rocker arm cover. Install the cover and tighten the bolts to 53–78 inch lbs. (6–9 Nm).

17. Remove the timing chain adjuster sleeve pin. Install the upper timing chain cover.

18. Connect the negative battery cable. Fill and bleed the cooling system.

19. Run the engine and check for leaks and proper operation. Check the idle speed and ignition timing.

3.0L Engine (MPV)

▶ **See Figures 194 and 195**

✷✷ CAUTION

Fuel injection systems remain under pressure after the engine has been turned OFF. Properly relieve fuel pressure before disconnecting any fuel lines. Failure to do so may result in fire or personal injury.

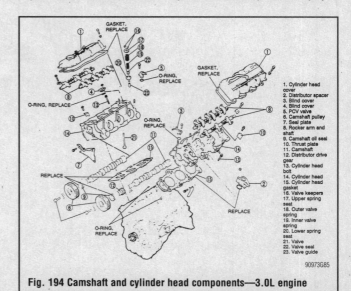

1. Cylinder head cover
2. Distributor spacer
3. Blind cover
4. Blind cover
5. PCV valve
6. Camshaft pulley
7. Seal plate
8. Rocker arm and shaft
9. Camshaft oil seal
10. Thrust plate
11. Camshaft
12. Distributor drive gear
13. Cylinder head bolt
14. Cylinder head
15. Cylinder head gasket
16. Valve keepers
17. Upper spring seat
18. Outer valve spring
19. Inner valve spring
20. Lower spring seat
21. Valve
22. Valve seal
23. Valve guide

Fig. 194 Camshaft and cylinder head components—3.0L engine

Do not allow fuel spray or fuel vapors to come in contact with a spark or open flame. Keep a dry chemical fire extinguisher nearby. Never store fuel in an open container due to risk of fire or explosion.

1. Disconnect the negative battery cable.
2. Drain the cooling system.
3. Relieve the fuel system pressure.
4. Remove the PCV valve and blind cover.
5. Remove the cylinder head.
6. If removing the driver's side camshaft, remove the distributor and the distributor spacer.
7. Remove the camshaft sprocket bolt and sprocket.
8. Remove the seal plate. Pry out the camshaft seal, being careful not to damage the seal housing.
9. Remove the rocker arm/shaft assembly.
10. Remove the thrust plate bolts and remove the thrust plate. Slide the camshaft out of the cylinder head. If removing the driver's side camshaft, remove the distributor drive gear.
11. Inspect the camshaft for wear and/or damage and replace if necessary.

To install:

➡**If installing the driver's side camshaft, remove all old sealer from the distributor drive gear and apply sealer to the gear face, then seat the gear fully on the camshaft.**

12. Apply clean engine oil to the camshaft journals, lobes and bearings. Install the camshaft and the thrust plate. Tighten the thrust plate to 69–95 inch lbs. (7.8–11.0 Nm).
13. Apply clean engine oil to a new camshaft seal lip and press the seal into the cylinder head, using a seal installer.
14. Install the rocker arm/shaft assembly and tighten the bolts, in sequence, in 2–3 steps to 14–19 ft. lbs. (19–25 Nm). Make sure the rocker arm shaft spring does not get caught between the shaft and mounting boss during installation.
15. Install the seal plates and tighten the bolts to 69–95 inch lbs. (7.8–11.0 Nm).
16. Align and install the camshaft sprocket. Tighten the bolt to 52–59 ft. lbs. (71–80 Nm).
17. If installing the driver's side camshaft, apply clean engine oil to a new O-ring and install on the distributor spacer. Install the spacer and tighten the nuts to 69–95 inch lbs. (7.8–11.0 Nm). Install the distributor.
18. Install the cylinder head.
19. Install the blind cover and PCV valve.
20. Connect the negative battery cable.
21. Fill and bleed the cooling system.
22. Run the engine and check for leaks and proper operation. Check the idle speed and ignition timing.

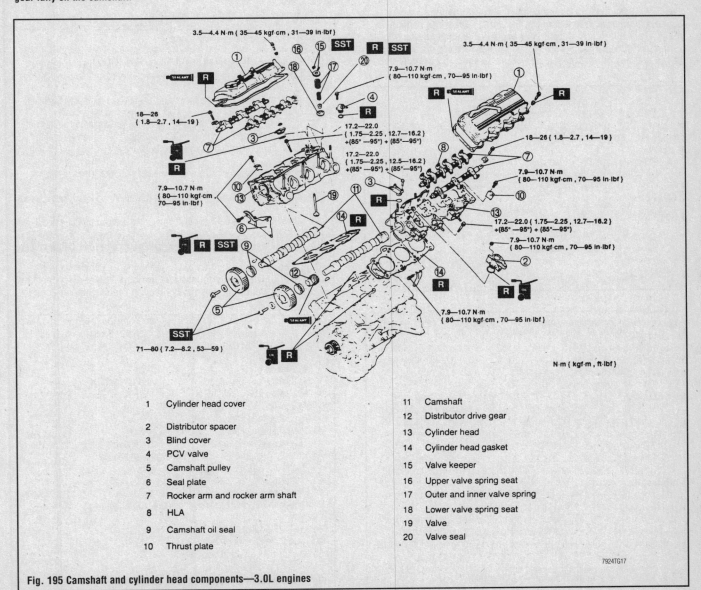

1	Cylinder head cover
2	Distributor spacer
3	Blind cover
4	PCV valve
5	Camshaft pulley
6	Seal plate
7	Rocker arm and rocker arm shaft
8	HLA
9	Camshaft oil seal
10	Thrust plate
11	Camshaft
12	Distributor drive gear
13	Cylinder head
14	Cylinder head gasket
15	Valve keeper
16	Upper valve spring seat
17	Outer and inner valve spring
18	Lower valve spring seat
19	Valve
20	Valve seal

7924TG17

Fig. 195 Camshaft and cylinder head components—3.0L engines

3.0L Engine (B Series Pick-up)

▶ See Figures 196 and 197

1. Disconnect the negative battery cable.
2. Remove the air cleaner hoses.
3. Remove the fan and spacer, and shroud.
4. Drain the cooling system. Remove the radiator.
5. Remove the condenser.
6. Relieve the fuel system pressure.
7. Remove the fuel lines at the fuel supply manifold.
8. Tag and disconnect all vacuum hoses in the way.
9. Tag and disconnect all wires in the way.
10. Remove the engine front cover and water pump.
11. Remove the alternator.
12. Remove the power steering pump and secure it out of the way. DO NOT disconnect the hoses!
13. Remove the air conditioning compressor and secure it out of the way. DO NOT disconnect the hoses!
14. Remove the throttle body.
15. Remove the fuel injection harness.
16. Drain the engine oil into a suitable container and dispose of it properly.

❊❊ CAUTION

The EPA warns that prolonged contact with used engine oil may cause a number of skin disorders, including cancer! You should make every effort to minimize your exposure to used engine oil. Protective gloves should be worn when changing the oil. Wash your hands and any other exposed skin areas as soon as possible after exposure to used engine oil. Soap and water, or waterless hand cleaner should be used.

17. Turn the engine by hand to 0 BTDC of the power stroke on No. 1 cylinder.
18. Disconnect the spark plug wires from the plugs.
19. If equipped, remove the distributor cap with the spark plug wires as an assembly.
20. If equipped, matchmark the rotor, distributor body and engine. Disconnect the distributor wiring harness and remove the distributor.
21. Remove the valve covers.
22. Remove the intake manifold.
23. Loosen the rocker arm bolts enough to pivot the rocker arms out of the way and remove the pushrods. Identify them for installation. They must be installed in their original positions!
24. Remove the valve lifters. Identify them for installation.
25. Remove the crankshaft pulley/damper.
26. Remove the starter.
27. Remove the oil pan.
28. Turn the engine by hand until the timing marks align at TDC of the power stroke on No.1 piston.
29. Check the camshaft end-play. If excessive, you'll have to replace the thrust plate.
30. Remove the camshaft gear attaching bolt and washer, then slide the gear off the camshaft.
31. Remove the camshaft thrust plate.
32. Carefully slide the camshaft out of the engine block, using caution to avoid any damage to the camshaft bearings.

To install:

33. Oil the camshaft journals and cam lobes with heavy SG engine oil (50W). Install the spacer ring with the chamfered side toward the camshaft, then insert the camshaft key.
34. Install the camshaft in the block, using caution to avoid any damage to the camshaft bearings.
35. Install the thrust plate. Tighten the attaching screws to 84 inch lbs.
36. Rotate the camshaft and crankshaft as necessary to align the timing marks. Install the camshaft gear and chain. Tighten the attaching bolt to 46 ft. lbs. (62 Nm).
37. Coat the tappets with 50W engine oil and place them in their original locations.
38. Apply 50W engine oil to both ends of the pushrods. Install the pushrods in their original locations.
39. Pivot the rocker arms into position. Tighten the fulcrum bolts to 8 ft. lbs. (11 Nm).
40. Rotate the engine until both timing marks are at the tops of their sprockets and aligned. Tighten the following fulcrum bolts to 18 ft. lbs. (24 Nm):
   - No.1 intake
   - No.2 exhaust
   - No.4 intake
   - No.5 exhaust
41. Rotate the engine until the camshaft timing mark is at the bottom of the sprocket and the crankshaft timing mark is at the top of the sprocket, and both are aligned. Tighten the following fulcrum bolts to 18 ft. lbs. (24 Nm):
   - No.1 exhaust
   - No.2 intake
   - No.3 intake and exhaust
   - No.4 exhaust
   - No.5 intake
   - No.6 intake and exhaust
42. Now, tighten all the bolts to 24 ft. lbs. (33 Nm).
43. Turn the engine by hand to 0 BTDC of the power stroke on No. 1 cylinder.
44. Install the engine front cover and water pump assembly.
45. Install the oil pan.
46. Install the crankshaft damper/pulley.
47. Install the intake manifold and tighten the mounting bolts to the specifications and in the sequence described under Intake Manifold removal and installation.
48. Install the valve covers.
49. Install the injector harness.
50. If equipped, install the distributor.
51. Install the cap and wires.
52. Install the throttle body.

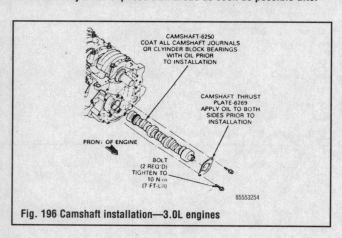

Fig. 196 Camshaft installation—3.0L engines

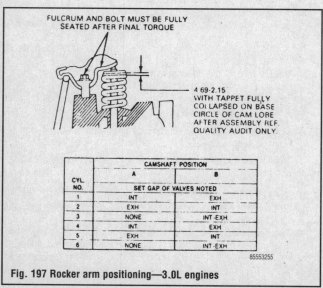

Fig. 197 Rocker arm positioning—3.0L engines

53. Install the alternator.
54. Install the power steering pump.
55. Install the compressor.
56. Connect all wires.
57. Connect all vacuum lines.
58. Install the radiator and condenser.
59. Install the fan and clutch.
60. Install the fuel lines.
61. Install the starter.
62. Refill the cooling system.
63. Replace the oil filter and refill the crankcase with the specified amount of engine oil.
64. Reconnect the battery ground cable.
65. Start the engine and check the ignition timing and idle speed. Adjust if necessary. Run the engine at fast idle and check for coolant, fuel, vacuum or oil leaks.

4.0L Engine

▶ See Figures 198 and 199

1. Disconnect the negative battery cable.
2. Drain the engine oil into a suitable container and dispose of it properly.

✷✷ CAUTION

The EPA warns that prolonged contact with used engine oil may cause a number of skin disorders, including cancer! You should make every effort to minimize your exposure to used engine oil. Protective gloves should be worn when changing the oil. Wash your hands and any other exposed skin areas as soon as possible after exposure to used engine oil. Soap and water, or waterless hand cleaner should be used.

3. Drain the cooling system.
4. Remove the radiator.
5. Remove the condenser.
6. Remove the fan and spacer, and shroud.
7. Remove the air cleaner hoses.
8. Tag and remove the spark plug wires.
9. Remove the EDIS ignition coil and bracket.
10. Remove the crankshaft pulley/damper.
11. Remove the clamp, bolt and oil pump drive from the rear of the block.
12. Remove the alternator.
13. Relieve the fuel system pressure.
14. Remove the fuel lines at the fuel supply manifold.
15. Remove the upper and lower intake manifolds as previously described.
16. Remove the rocker arm covers.
17. Remove the rocker shaft assemblies.
18. Remove the pushrods. Identify them for installation. They must be installed in their original positions!
19. Remove the tappets. Identify them for installation.
20. Remove the oil pan as previously described.
21. Remove the engine front cover and water pump.
22. Place the timing chain tensioner in the retracted position and install the retaining clip.
23. Turn the engine by hand until the timing marks align at TDC of the power stroke on No.1 piston.
24. Check the camshaft end-play. If excessive, you'll have to replace the thrust plate.
25. Remove the camshaft gear attaching bolt and washer, then slide the gear off the camshaft.
26. Remove the camshaft thrust plate.
27. Carefully slide the camshaft out of the engine block, using caution to avoid any damage to the camshaft bearings.

To install:

28. Oil the camshaft journals and cam lobes with a heavy (50W) SG grade (or better) engine oil.
29. Install the camshaft in the block, using caution to avoid any damage to the camshaft bearings.
30. Install the thrust plate. Make sure that it covers the main oil gallery. Tighten the attaching screws to 96 inch lbs. (11 Nm).

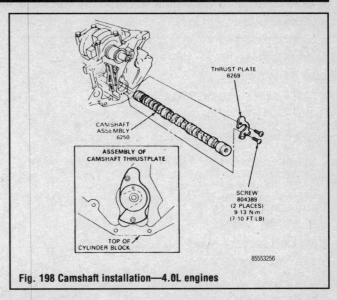

Fig. 198 Camshaft installation—4.0L engines

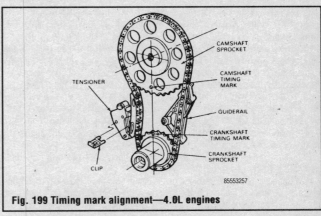

Fig. 199 Timing mark alignment—4.0L engines

31. Rotate the camshaft and crankshaft as necessary to align the timing marks. Install the camshaft gear and chain. Tighten the attaching bolt to 50 ft. lbs. (68 Nm).
32. Remove the clip from the chain tensioner.
33. Install the engine front cover and water pump assembly. Refer to the necessary service procedures in this Section.
34. Install the crankshaft damper/pulley.
35. Install the oil pan.
36. Coat the tappets with 50W engine oil and place them in their original locations.
37. Apply 50W engine oil to both ends of the pushrods. Install the pushrods in their original locations.
38. Install the upper and lower intake manifolds.
39. Install the rocker shaft assemblies.
40. Install the valve covers.
41. Install the fan and clutch.
42. Install the fuel lines.
43. Install the oil pump drive.
44. Install the alternator.
45. Install the EDIS coil and plug wires. Coat the inside of each wire boot with silicone lubricant.
46. Install the radiator and condenser.
47. Refill the cooling system.
48. Replace the oil filter and refill the crankcase with the specified amount of engine oil.
49. Reconnect the battery ground cable.
50. Start the engine and check the ignition timing and idle speed. Adjust if necessary. Run the engine at fast idle and check for coolant, fuel, vacuum or oil leaks.

INSPECTION

Camshaft Lobe Lift

♦ See Figure 200

2.3L, 2.5L, 2.6L AND 3.0L (MPV) ENGINES

Check the lift of each lobe in consecutive order and make a note of the readings. Camshaft assembly specifications are sometimes modified by Mazda after production. Refer to a local reputable machine shop as necessary.

1. Remove the valve cover.
2. Measure the distance between the major (A–A) and minor (B–B) diameters of each cam lobe with a Vernier caliper and record the readings. The difference in the readings on each cam diameter is the lobe lift.
3. If the readings do not meet specifications, replace the camshaft and all rocker arms/cam followers.
4. Install the valve cover.

3.0L (B SERIES PICK-UP) AND 4.0L ENGINES

Check the lift of each lobe in consecutive order and make a note of the reading. Camshaft assembly specifications are sometimes modify by MAZDA after production. Refer to a local reputable machine shop as necessary.

1. Remove the fresh air inlet tube and the air cleaner. Remove the heater hose and crankcase ventilation hoses. Remove valve rocker arm cover(s).
2. Remove the rocker arm stud nut or fulcrum bolts, fulcrum seat and rocker arm.
3. Make sure the push rod is in the valve tappet socket. Install a dial indicator D78P–4201–B (or equivalent) so that the actuating point of the indicator is in the push rod socket (or the indicator ball socket adapter Tool 6565–AB is on the end of the push rod) and in the same plane as the push rod movement.
4. Disconnect the I terminal and the S terminal at the starter relay. Install an auxiliary starter switch between the battery and S terminals of the starter relay. Crank the engine with the ignition switch off. Turn the crankshaft over until the tappet is on the base circle of the camshaft lobe. At this position, the push rod will be in its lowest position.
5. Zero the dial indicator. Continue to rotate the crankshaft slowly until the push rod is in the fully raised position.
6. Compare the total lift recorded on the dial indicator with the specification. To check the accuracy of the original indicator reading, continue to rotate the crankshaft until the indicator reads zero. If the lift on any lobe is below specified wear limits, the camshaft and the valve tappet operating on the worn lobe(s) must be replaced.
7. Remove the dial indicator and auxiliary starter switch.
8. Install the rocker arm, fulcrum seat and stud nut or fulcrum bolts.
9. Install the valve rocker arm covers and the air cleaner.

Camshaft End Play

♦ See Figure 201

2.3L/2.5L ENGINES

♦ See Figure 202

Remove the camshaft drive belt cover. Push the camshaft toward the rear of the engine. Install a dial indicator so that the indicator point is on the camshaft sprocket attaching screw or gear hub. Zero the dial indicator. Position a prybar between the camshaft sprocket or gear and the cylinder head. Pull the camshaft forward and release it. Compare the dial indicator reading with specifications. If the end play is excessive, replace the thrust plate at the rear of the cylinder head. Remove the dial indicator and install the camshaft drive belt cover. The camshaft end-play specification is 0.001–0.007 inch and the service limit is 0.003 inch. Camshaft specifications are sometimes modified by Mazda after production.

2.6L AND 3.0L (MPV) ENGINES

➡On engines with an aluminum or nylon camshaft sprocket, prying against the sprocket, with the valve train load on the camshaft, can break or damage the sprocket. Therefore, the rocker arm adjusting nuts must be backed off, or the rocker arm and shaft assembly must be loosened sufficiently to free the camshaft.

1. Push the camshaft toward the rear of the engine. Install a dial indicator so that the indicator point is on the camshaft sprocket attaching screw.
2. Zero the dial indicator. Position a prybar between the camshaft gear and the block. Pull the camshaft forward and release it. Compare the dial indicator reading with the specifications.
3. If the end play is excessive, check the spacer for correct installation before it is removed. If the spacer is correctly installed, replace the thrust plate.
4. Remove the dial indicator.

3.0L (B SERIES PICK-UP) AND 4.0L ENGINES

1. Push the camshaft toward the rear of the engine. Install a dial indicator (Tool D78P–4201–C or equivalent so that the indicator point is on the camshaft sprocket attaching screw.
2. Zero the dial indicator. Position a prybar between the camshaft gear and the block. Pull the camshaft forward and release it. Compare the dial indicator reading with the specification. The camshaft end-play specification is 0.0008–0.004 inch and the service limit is 0.009 inch (0.007 inch on 3.0L engine). Camshaft specifications are sometimes modified by Mazda after production.
3. If the end play is excessive, check the spacer for correct installation before it is removed. If the spacer is correctly installed, replace the thrust plate.

➡The spacer ring and thrust plate are available in two thicknesses to permit adjusting the end play.

4. Remove the dial indicator.

Camshaft Bearings

REMOVAL & INSTALLATION

Navajo and B Series Pick-up Models

If excessive camshaft wear is found, or if the engine is completely rebuilt, the camshaft bearings should be replaced. Use these service repair procedures as a guide.

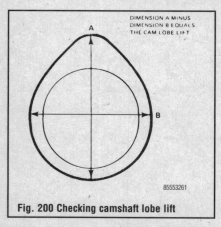

Fig. 200 Checking camshaft lobe lift

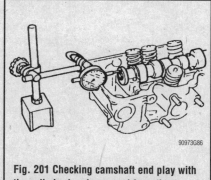

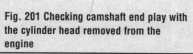

Fig. 201 Checking camshaft end play with the cylinder head removed from the engine

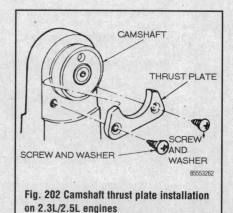

Fig. 202 Camshaft thrust plate installation on 2.3L/2.5L engines

2.3L AND 2.5L ENGINES

▶ **See Figure 203**

1. Remove the head and place it on a work stand.
2. Remove the camshaft.
3. Using a tool such as Bearing Replacer T71P–6250–A, remove the bearings.
4. Coat the new bearings with clean 50W engine oil and install them with the tool.

3.0L AND 4.0L ENGINES

1. Remove the engine and place it on a work stand.
2. Remove the flywheel.
3. Remove the camshaft.
4. Using a sharp punch and hammer, drive a hole in the rear bearing bore plug and pry it out.
5. Using the special tools and instructions in Cam Bearing Replacer Kit T65L–6250–A, or their equivalents, remove the bearings.
6. To remove the front bearing, install the tool from the rear of the block.

To install:

7. Following the instructions in the tool kit, install the bearings. Make sure that you follow the instructions carefully. Failure to use the correct expanding collets can cause severe bearing damage!

➡**Make sure that the oil holes in the bearings and block are aligned! Make sure that the front bearing is installed 0.51–0.89mm below the face of the block.**

8. Install a new bearing bore plug coated with sealer.
9. Install the camshaft.
10. Install the flywheel.
11. Install the engine.

MPV Models

On both of the MPV engines (2.6L and 3.0L), excessive oil clearance between the cylinder head/bearing caps-to-camshaft bearing surfaces, indicates that cylinder head and/or camshaft replacement is required.

Valve Lifters

➡**This procedure applies to hydraulic lash adjusters as well as valve lifters (tappets).**

BLEEDING

➡**The manufacturer does not recommend that the Hydraulic Lash Adjusters (HLA) be bled. Removing an HLA from its rocker arm will release its oil. If the HLAs are removed from the rocker arms, new ones should be installed using new O-rings.**

1. Before installing new HLAs, fill the rocker arm oil reservoir with fresh engine oil.

2. Apply fresh engine oil to the new HLA and its O-ring.
3. Install the new HLA into the rocker arm, taking care not to damage or distort its O-ring.

REMOVAL & INSTALLATION

2.3L and 2.5L Engines

➡**A special tool is required to compress the valve spring.**

1. Remove the valve cover and associated parts as required.
2. Rotate the camshaft so that the base circle of the cam is against the cam follower you intend to remove.

➡**If removing more than one cam follower, label them so they can be returned to their original position.**

3. Using special tool 49-UN01-135 or equivalent, depress the valve spring, as necessary, and slide the cam follower over the Hydraulic Lash Adjuster (HLA) and out from under the camshaft.
4. Remove each HLA.
5. Install the HLA and cam follower in the reverse order of removal. Lubricate the followers with SAE 50W engine oil meeting current API specification prior to installing.

2.6L and 3.0L (MPV) Engines

▶ **See Figures 204 and 205**

1. Disconnect the negative battery cable.
2. Remove the valve cover.
3. Remove the rocker arm/shaft assembly.
4. If necessary, disassemble the rocker arm/shaft assembly, noting the position of each component to ease reassembly.
5. Check the surface of the Hydraulic Lash Adjuster (HLA) for wear and damage. If the HLA is worn or damaged, it must be replaced.
6. Remove the HLA from the rocker arm. Don't remove the HLA unless necessary, because oil leakage will occur if the O-ring is damaged.

To install:

7. Follow these steps to install the HLA:
   a. Pour clean engine oil into the oil reservoir in the rocker arm.
   b. Coat the HLA with clean engine oil.
   c. Place the rocker arm and HLA into a tub filled with clean oil, and then insert the HLA into the rocker arm, taking care not to distort the O-ring.
8. Install the rocker arm/shaft assembly.
9. Install the valve cover.
10. Connect the negative battery cable, start the engine and check for leaks and proper operation.

3.0L (B Series Pick-up) and 4.0L Engines

1. Remove the upper and lower intake manifolds.
2. Remove the valve covers.
3. Remove the rocker arm/shaft assembly.

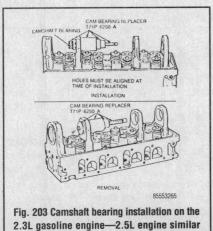

Fig. 203 Camshaft bearing installation on the 2.3L gasoline engine—2.5L engine similar

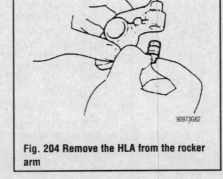

Fig. 204 Remove the HLA from the rocker arm

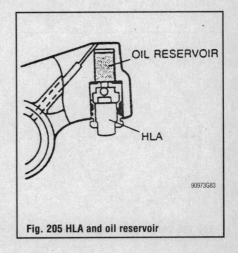

Fig. 205 HLA and oil reservoir

4. Remove and mark the pushrods for installation.
5. Remove the tappets with a magnet. If they are to be re-used, identify them.

➡️ **If the tappets are stuck in their bores, you'll need a claw-type removal tool.**

6. Coat the new tappets with clean engine oil and insert them in their bores.
7. Coat the pushrods with heavy engine oil and insert them into the bores from which they came.
8. Install the rocker arm/shaft assembly.
9. Install the valve covers.
10. Install the upper and lower manifold.

Auxiliary Shaft

REMOVAL & INSTALLATION

✳️✳️ CAUTION

When draining the coolant, keep in mind that cats and dogs are attracted by the ethylene glycol antifreeze, and are quite likely to drink any that is left in an uncovered container or in puddles on the ground. This will prove fatal in sufficient quantity. Always drain the coolant into a sealable container. Coolant should be reused unless it is contaminated or several years old.

2.3L Engines (1994 only)

▶ See Figure 206

1. Remove the timing belt cover.
2. Remove the timing belt. Remove the auxiliary shaft sprocket. A puller may be necessary to remove the sprocket.
3. Remove the inner timing belt cover.
4. Loosen the mounting bolts, then remove the auxiliary shaft cover and mounting gasket.
5. Loosen the mounting bolts and remove the auxiliary shaft thrust plate.

➡️ **Even though the 2.3L engine is equipped with a distributorless ignition system and an electronic fuel pump, the auxiliary shaft is still manufactured with a gear and eccentric to drive these components. The distributor drive gear and fuel pump eccentric on the auxiliary shaft must not be allowed to touch the auxiliary shaft bearings during removal and installation. Completely coat the shaft with oil before sliding it into place.**

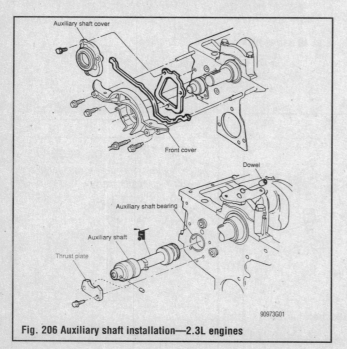

Fig. 206 Auxiliary shaft installation—2.3L engines

6. Carefully withdraw the auxiliary shaft from the block.
To install:
7. Slide the auxiliary shaft into the housing and insert the thrust plate to hold the shaft. Tighten the thrust plate mounting bolts to 6–8 ft. lbs. (8–12 Nm).
8. Install a new gasket and auxiliary shaft cover. Tighten the cover mounting bolts to 6–8 ft. lbs. (8–12 Nm).

➡️ **The auxiliary shaft cover and cylinder front cover share a gasket. Cut off the old gasket around the cylinder cover and use half of the new gasket on the auxiliary shaft cover.**

9. Install the inner timing belt cover.
10. Install the auxiliary shaft sprocket.
11. Align the timing marks and install the timing belt.
12. Install the timing belt cover.
13. Check the ignition timing.

2.6L Engines

▶ See Figures 207 thru 212

1. Disconnect the battery ground.
2. Drain the cooling system.
3. Remove the accessory drive belts.
4. Remove the fan and shroud.
5. Remove the water pump pulley.
6. Unbolt and remove the water pump.
7. Remove the crankshaft pulley.
8. Remove the oil pan.
9. Remove the timing chain cover.
10. Remove the oil pick-up tube.
11. Remove and discard the water inlet pipe gasket.
12. Remove the crankshaft sprocket spacer.
13. Remove the idler sprocket lockbolt.
14. Remove chain guides and mark them for correct assembly.
15. Remove the idler sprocket and crankshaft sprocket bolts and pull off the sprockets along with the balancer chain.
16. Remove the left balance shaft.
17. Remove the right balance shaft. Mark each balance shaft for correct assembly.
18. Remove the crankshaft timing gear bolt.
19. Remove the timing chain tensioner.
20. Pull the timing chain and sprockets off.
21. Remove the chain guide and lever.
To install:
22. Install the chain guide and lever. Torque the chain guide bolts to 78 in. lbs. (9 Nm); the lever bolts to 95 in. lbs. (11 Nm). Make sure that the lever moves smoothly.
23. Install the chain adjuster. Torque the bolts to 95 in. lbs. (11 Nm). Move the adjuster sleeve towards the left and install a pin to hold it in place.
24. Install the timing chain and sprocket.
25. Install the camshaft sprocket.
26. Install the balance shafts. Torque the thust plate bolts to 95 in. lbs. (11 Nm).
27. Install the crankshaft sprocket.
28. Install the idler shaft and sprocket.
29. Set the balance chain on the balance shaft sprocket so that it aligns with the brown link on the chain.
30. Install the balancer chain, aligning all the marks as shown.
31. Install chain guides **A** and **B**. Torque the bolts to 95 in. lbs. (11 Nm).
32. Install chain guide **C**. Tighten the bolt to 95 in. lbs. (11 Nm).
33. Torque the idler sprocket lockbolt to 38 ft. lbs. (52 Nm).
34. Install the spacer.
35. Loosen chain guide **C** adjusting bolt.
36. Push chain guide **C** with a force of about 10 lb., downward, against the chain, then, pull it back 3.2–3.8mm (0.126–0.149 in.) and tighten the bolt to 95 in. lbs. (11 Nm). When properly adjusted, there should be about 3mm (0.12 in.) of slack in the chain at the mid-point of the guide.

➡️ **If, when applying the downward force on the chain guide, it bottoms against the adjusting bolt, you should replace the balancer chain.**

37. Remove the tensioner adjuster retaining pin.
38. Install a new water inlet pipe gasket using adhesive sealer.

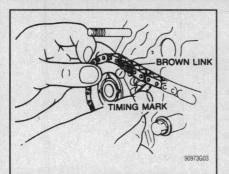

Fig. 207 When setting the balance chain onto the shaft sprocket, align the timing mark to the brown link on the chain

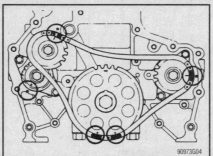

Fig. 208 When installing the balance shaft chain, be sure to match up the chain, sprocket and engine block alignment marks

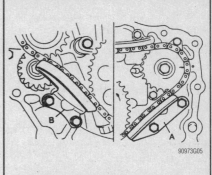

Fig. 209 Install the balance shaft chain guides A and B

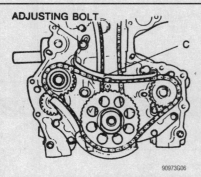

Fig. 210 Install balance shaft chain guide C and hand tighten the adjusting bolt

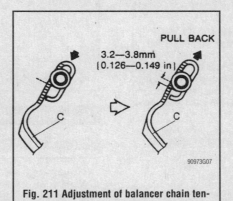

Fig. 211 Adjustment of balancer chain tension

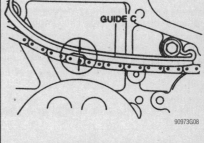

Fig. 212 When properly adjusted, there should be about 3mm (0.12 in.) of slack in the chain at the mid-point of the guide

39. Install the oil pick-up tube using a new gasket. Torque the bolts to 95 in. lbs. (11 Nm).
40. Using new gaskets coated with sealer, install the timing chain cover. Torque the bolts to 19 ft. lbs. (26 Nm).
41. Install the camshaft sprocket service cover.
42. Remove the wire from the camshaft sprocket.
43. Tighten the oil pick-up brace bolt to 95 in. lbs. (11 Nm).
44. Install the oil pan.
45. Install the crankshaft pulley.
46. Install the water pump.
47. Install the water pump pulley.
48. Install the fan and shroud.
49. Install the accessory drive belts.
50. Fill the cooling system.
51. Connect the battery ground.

Rear Main Oil Seal

REMOVAL & INSTALLATION

MPV Models

♦ **See Figures 213 and 214**

1. Disconnect the negative battery cable.
2. Raise and support the vehicle safely.
3. Remove the transmission.
4. If equipped with a manual transmission, remove the pressure plate, the clutch disc and the flywheel. If equipped with an automatic transmission, remove the drive plate from the crankshaft.
5. Using a razor blade, carefully cut the oil seal lip.
6. Using a small prying tool protected with a rag, remove the oil seal.
To install:
7. Apply clean engine oil to the new seal.

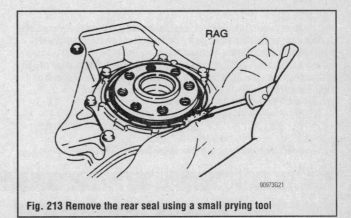

Fig. 213 Remove the rear seal using a small prying tool

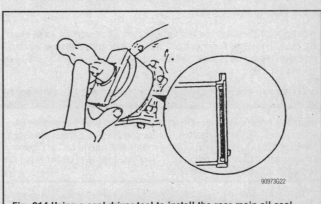

Fig. 214 Using a seal driver tool to install the rear main oil seal

8. Push the new oil seal slightly into place by hand.
9. Using a seal driver and a hammer, tap the oil seal in evenly.
10. Install the driveplate.
11. Install the transmission.
12. Lower the vehicle.
13. Connect the negative battery cable.

B Series Pick-up and Navajo Models

♦ **See Figure 215**

If the crankshaft rear oil seal replacement is the only operation being performed, it can be done in the vehicle as detailed in the following procedure. If the oil seal is being replaced in conjunction with a rear main bearing replacement, the engine must be removed from the vehicle and installed on a work stand.

1. Remove the transmission from the vehicle, following the procedures in Section 7.
2. On a manual shift transmission, remove the pressure plate and cover assembly and the clutch disc following the procedure in Section 7.
3. Remove the flywheel and engine rear cover plate.
4. Use an awl to punch two holes in the crankshaft rear oil seal. Punch the holes on opposite sides of the crankshaft and just above the bearing cap to cylinder block split line. Install a sheet metal screw in each hole. Use two large screwdrivers or small pry bars and pry against both screws at the same time to remove the crankshaft rear oil seal. It may be necessary to place small blocks of wood against the cylinder block to provide a fulcrum point for the pry bars. Use caution throughout this procedure to avoid scratching or otherwise damaging the crankshaft oil seal surface.

To install:

5. Clean the oil seal recess in the cylinder block and main bearing cap.
6. Clean, inspect and polish the rear oil seal rubbing surface on the crankshaft. Coat a new oil seal and the crankshaft with a light film of engine oil. Start the seal in the recess with the seal lip facing forward and install it with the following special seal driver tool, or equivalent:
   - 2.3L engine—49-UN01-070
   - 2.5L engine—49-UN01-170
   - 3.0L engine—49-UN01-064
   - 4.0L engine—49-UN01-009
7. Keep the tool straight with the centerline of the crankshaft and install the seal until the tool contacts the cylinder block surface. Remove the tool and inspect the seal to be sure it was not damaged during installation.
8. Inspect the installed height of the seal. The height should measure 0.02 inch (0.5mm) for the 2.3L, 2.5L and 3.0L engines, and 0.421–0.425 inch (10.7–10.9mm) for the 4.0L engine.
9. Install the engine rear cover plate.
10. Install the flywheel.
11. On a manual shift transmission, install the clutch disc and the pressure plate assembly following the procedure in Section 7.
12. Install the transmission, following the procedure in Section 7.

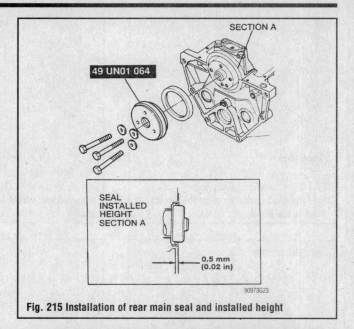

Fig. 215 Installation of rear main seal and installed height

Flywheel and Ring Gear

REMOVAL & INSTALLATION

1. Remove the transmission, following procedures in Section 7.
2. On a manual shift transmission, remove the clutch pressure plate and cover assembly and clutch disc, following the procedures in Section 7.
3. Remove the flywheel attaching bolts and remove the flywheel.

To install:

4. Position the flywheel on the crankshaft flange. Coat the threads of the flywheel attaching bolts with Loctite® or equivalent and install the bolts. Tighten the bolts in sequence across from each other to the following specifications:
   - 2.3L, 2.5L and 3.0L (B Series Pick-up) engines: 54–64 ft. lbs. (73–87 Nm)
   - 2.6L engine: 68–72 ft. lbs. (92–98 Nm)
   - 3.0L (MPV) engine: 76–81 ft. lbs. (103–109 Nm)
   - 4.0L engine: 50–55 ft. lbs. (68–74 Nm)
5. On a manual shift transmission, install the clutch disc and pressure plate and cover assembly following the procedure in Section 7.
6. Install the transmission following the procedure in Section 7.

EXHAUST SYSTEM

Inspection

♦ **See Figures 216 thru 222**

➡**Safety glasses should be worn at all times when working on or near the exhaust system. Older exhaust systems will almost always be covered with loose rust particles which are more than a nuisance and could injure your eye.**

✳ CAUTION

DO NOT perform exhaust repairs or inspection with the engine or exhaust hot. Allow the system to cool completely. Exhaust systems are noted for sharp edges, flaking metal and rusted bolts. Gloves and eye protection are required. A healthy supply of penetrating oil and rags is highly recommended.

Your vehicle must be raised and supported safely at four points to inspect the exhaust system properly. Start the inspection at the exhaust manifold where the header pipe is attached and work your way to the back of the vehicle. On dual

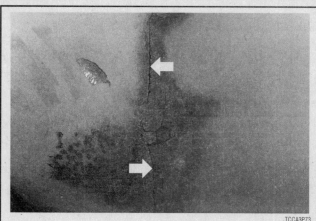

Fig. 216 Cracks in the muffler are a guaranteed leak

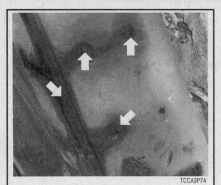

Fig. 217 Check the muffler for rotted spot welds and seams

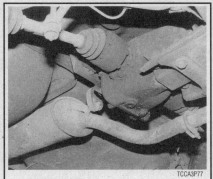

Fig. 218 Make sure the exhaust does contact the body or suspension

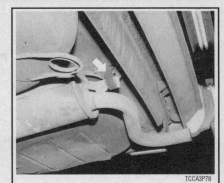

Fig. 219 Check for overstretched or torn exhaust hangers

Fig. 220 Example of a badly deteriorated exhaust pipe

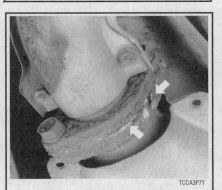

Fig. 221 Inspect flanges for gaskets that have deteriorated and need replacement

Fig. 222 Some systems, like this one, use large O-rings (donuts) in between the flanges

exhaust systems, remember to inspect both sides of the vehicle. Check the complete exhaust system for open seams, holes, loose connections, or other deterioration which could permit exhaust fumes to seep into the passenger compartment. Inspect all mounting brackets and hangers for deterioration, some may have rubber O-rings that can become overstretched and non-supportive (and should be replaced if worn). Many technicians use a pointed tool to poke up into the exhaust system at rust spots to see whether or not they crumble. Most models have heat shield(s) covering certain parts of the exhaust system, it is often necessary to remove these shields to visually inspect those components.

REPLACEMENT

▶ **See Figures 223, 224, 225, 226 and 227**

There are basically two types of exhaust systems. One is the flange type where the component ends are attached with bolts and a gasket in-between. The other exhaust system is the slip joint type. These components slip into one another using clamps to retain them together.

✳✳ CAUTION

Allow the exhaust system to cool sufficiently before spraying a solvent exhaust fasteners. Some solvents are highly flammable and could ignite when sprayed on hot exhaust components.

Before removing any component of the exhaust system, ALWAYS squirt a liquid rust dissolving agent onto the fasteners for ease of removal. A lot of knuckle skin will be saved by following this rule. It may even be wise to spray the fasteners and allow them to sit overnight.

✳✳ CAUTION

Do NOT perform exhaust repairs or inspection with the engine or exhaust hot. Allow the system to cool. Exhaust systems are noted for sharp edges, flaking metal and rusted bolts. Gloves and eye protection are required.

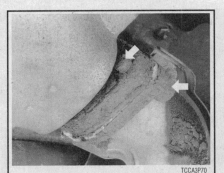

Fig. 223 Nuts and bolts will be extremely difficult to remove when deteriorated with rust

Fig. 224 Example of a flange type exhaust system joint

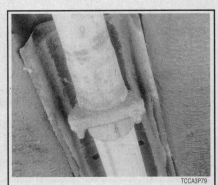

Fig. 225 Example of a common slip joint type system

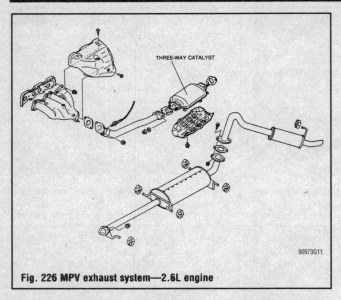

Fig. 226 MPV exhaust system—2.6L engine

90973G11

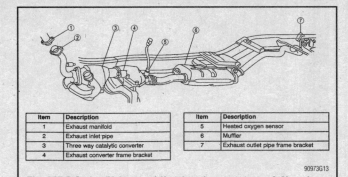

90973G13

Item	Description		Item	Description
1	Exhaust manifold		5	Heated oxygen sensor
2	Exhaust inlet pipe		6	Muffler
3	Three way catalytic converter		7	Exhaust outlet pipe frame bracket
4	Exhaust converter frame bracket			

Fig. 227 B Series Pick-up and Navajo exhaust system—3.0L and 4.0L engines

1. Raise and support the vehicle safely, as necessary, for access. Remember that some longer exhaust pipes may be difficult to wrestle out from under the vehicle if it is not supported high enough.

2. If you haven't already, apply a generous amount of penetrating oil or solvent to any rusted fasteners.

3. On flange joints, carefully loosen and remove the retainers at the flange. If bolts or nuts are difficult to break loose, apply more penetrating liquid and give it some additional time to set. If the fasteners still will not come loose an impact driver may be necessary to jar it loose (and keep the fastener from breaking).

➡When unbolting the headpipe from the manifold, make sure that the bolts are free before trying to remove them. If you snap a stud in the exhaust manifold, the stud will have to be removed with a bolt extractor, which often means removal of the manifold itself.

4. On slip joint components, remove the mounting U-bolts from around the exhaust pipe you are extracting from the vehicle. Don't be surprised if the U-bolts break while removing the nuts.

5. Loosen the exhaust pipe from any mounting brackets retaining it to the floor pan and separate the components. Slight twisting and turning may be required to remove the component completely from the vehicle. You may need to tap on the component with a rubber mallet to loosen it. If all else fails, use a hacksaw to separate the parts. An oxy-acetylene cutting torch may be faster but the sparks are DANGEROUS near the fuel tank, and at the very least, accidents could happen, resulting in damage to the under-vehicle parts, not to mention yourself.

6. When installing exhaust components, you should loosely position all components before tightening any of the joints. Once you are certain that the system is run correctly, begin tightening the fasteners at the front of the vehicle and work your way back.

ENGINE RECONDITIONING

Determining Engine Condition

Anything that generates heat and/or friction will eventually burn or wear out (ie. a light bulb generates heat, therefore its life span is limited). With this in mind, a running engine generates tremendous amounts of both; friction is encountered by the moving and rotating parts inside the engine and heat is created by friction and combustion of the fuel. However, the engine has systems designed to help reduce the effects of heat and friction and provide added longevity. The oiling system reduces the amount of friction encountered by the moving parts inside the engine, while the cooling system reduces heat created by friction and combustion. If either system is not maintained, a break-down will be inevitable. Therefore, you can see how regular maintenance can affect the service life of your vehicle. If you do not drain, flush and refill your cooling system at the proper intervals, deposits will begin to accumulate in the radiator, thereby reducing the amount of heat it can extract from the coolant. The same applies to your oil and filter; if it is not changed often enough it becomes laden with contaminants and is unable to properly lubricate the engine. This increases friction and wear.

There are a number of methods for evaluating the condition of your engine. A compression test can reveal the condition of your pistons, piston rings, cylinder bores, head gasket(s), valves and valve seats. An oil pressure test can warn you of possible engine bearing, or oil pump failures. Excessive oil consumption, evidence of oil in the engine air intake area and/or bluish smoke from the tail pipe may indicate worn piston rings, worn valve guides and/or valve seals. As a general rule, an engine that uses no more than one quart of oil every 1000 miles is in good condition. Engines that use one quart of oil or more in less than 1000 miles should first be checked for oil leaks. If any oil leaks are present, have them fixed before determining how much oil is consumed by the engine, especially if blue smoke is not visible at the tail pipe.

COMPRESSION TEST

♦ See Figure 228

A noticeable lack of engine power, excessive oil consumption and/or poor fuel mileage measured over an extended period are all indicators of internal engine wear. Worn piston rings, scored or worn cylinder bores, blown head gaskets, sticking or burnt valves, and worn valve seats are all possible culprits. A check of each cylinder's compression will help locate the problem.

➡A screw-in type compression gauge is more accurate than the type you simply hold against the spark plug hole. Although it takes slightly longer to use, it's worth the effort to obtain a more accurate reading.

1. Make sure that the proper amount and viscosity of engine oil is in the crankcase, then ensure the battery is fully charged.

2. Warm-up the engine to normal operating temperature, then shut the engine OFF.

3. Disable the ignition system.

4. Label and disconnect all of the spark plug wires from the plugs.

5. Thoroughly clean the cylinder head area around the spark plug ports, then remove the spark plugs.

6. Set the throttle plate to the fully open (wide-open throttle) position. You can block the accelerator linkage open for this, or you can have an assistant fully depress the accelerator pedal.

7. Install a screw-in type compression gauge into the No. 1 spark plug hole until the fitting is snug.

✶✶ WARNING

Be careful not to crossthread the spark plug hole.

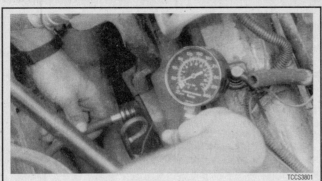

TCCS3801

Fig. 228 A screw-in type compression gauge is more accurate and easier to use without an assistant

8. According to the tool manufacturer's instructions, connect a remote starting switch to the starting circuit.

9. With the ignition switch in the **OFF** position, use the remote starting switch to crank the engine through at least five compression strokes (approximately 5 seconds of cranking) and record the highest reading on the gauge.

10. Repeat the test on each cylinder, cranking the engine approximately the same number of compression strokes and/or time as the first.

11. Compare the highest readings from each cylinder to that of the others. The indicated compression pressures are considered within specifications if the lowest reading cylinder is within 75 percent of the pressure recorded for the highest reading cylinder. For example, if your highest reading cylinder pressure was 150 psi (1034 kPa), then 75 percent of that would be 113 psi (779 kPa). So the lowest reading cylinder should be no less than 113 psi (779 kPa).

12. If a cylinder exhibits an unusually low compression reading, pour a tablespoon of clean engine oil into the cylinder through the spark plug hole and repeat the compression test. If the compression rises after adding oil, it means that the cylinder's piston rings and/or cylinder bore are damaged or worn. If the pressure remains low, the valves may not be seating properly (a valve job is needed), or the head gasket may be blown near that cylinder. If compression in any two adjacent cylinders is low, and if the addition of oil doesn't help raise compression, there is leakage past the head gasket. Oil and coolant in the combustion chamber, combined with blue or constant white smoke from the tail pipe, are symptoms of this problem. However, don't be alarmed by the normal white smoke emitted from the tail pipe during engine warm-up or from cold weather driving. There may be evidence of water droplets on the engine dipstick and/or oil droplets in the cooling system if a head gasket is blown.

OIL PRESSURE TEST

Check for proper oil pressure at the sending unit passage with an externally mounted mechanical oil pressure gauge (as opposed to relying on a factory installed dash-mounted gauge). A tachometer may also be needed, as some specifications may require running the engine at a specific rpm.

1. With the engine cold, locate and remove the oil pressure sending unit.

2. Following the manufacturer's instructions, connect a mechanical oil pressure gauge and, if necessary, a tachometer to the engine.

3. Start the engine and allow it to idle.

4. Check the oil pressure reading when cold and record the number. You may need to run the engine at a specified rpm, so check the specifications chart located earlier in this section.

5. Run the engine until normal operating temperature is reached (upper radiator hose will feel warm).

6. Check the oil pressure reading again with the engine hot and record the number. Turn the engine **OFF**.

7. Compare your hot oil pressure reading to that given in the chart. If the reading is low, check the cold pressure reading against the chart. If the cold pressure is well above the specification, and the hot reading was lower than the specification, you may have the wrong viscosity oil in the engine. Change the oil, making sure to use the proper grade and quantity, then repeat the test.

Low oil pressure readings could be attributed to internal component wear, pump related problems, a low oil level, or oil viscosity that is too low. High oil pressure readings could be caused by an overfilled crankcase, too high of an oil viscosity or a faulty pressure relief valve.

Buy or Rebuild?

Now that you have determined that your engine is worn out, you must make some decisions. The question of whether or not an engine is worth rebuilding is largely a subjective matter and one of personal worth. Is the engine a popular one, or is it an obsolete model? Are parts available? Will it get acceptable gas mileage once it is rebuilt? Is the car it's being put into worth keeping? Would it be less expensive to buy a new engine, have your engine rebuilt by a pro, rebuild it yourself or buy a used engine from a salvage yard? Or would it be simpler and less expensive to buy another car? If you have considered all these matters and more, and have still decided to rebuild the engine, then it is time to decide how you will rebuild it.

➡ **The editors at Chilton feel that most engine machining should be performed by a professional machine shop. Don't think of it as wasting money, rather, as an assurance that the job has been done right the first time. There are many expensive and specialized tools required to perform such tasks as boring and honing an engine block or having a valve job done on a cylinder head. Even inspecting the parts requires expensive micrometers and gauges to properly measure wear and clearances. Also, a machine shop can deliver to you clean, and ready to assemble parts, saving you time and aggravation. Your maximum savings will come from performing the removal, disassembly, assembly and installation of the engine and purchasing or renting only the tools required to perform the above tasks. Depending on the particular circumstances, you may save 40 to 60 percent of the cost doing these yourself.**

A complete rebuild or overhaul of an engine involves replacing all of the moving parts (pistons, rods, crankshaft, camshaft, etc.) with new ones and machining the non-moving wearing surfaces of the block and heads. Unfortunately, this may not be cost effective. For instance, your crankshaft may have been damaged or worn, but it can be machined undersize for a minimal fee.

So, as you can see, you can replace everything inside the engine, but, it is wiser to replace only those parts which are really needed, and, if possible, repair the more expensive ones. Later in this section, we will break the engine down into its two main components: the cylinder head and the engine block. We will discuss each component, and the recommended parts to replace during a rebuild on each.

Engine Overhaul Tips

Most engine overhaul procedures are fairly standard. In addition to specific parts replacement procedures and specifications for your individual engine, this section is also a guide to acceptable rebuilding procedures. Examples of standard rebuilding practice are given and should be used along with specific details concerning your particular engine.

Competent and accurate machine shop services will ensure maximum performance, reliability and engine life. In most instances it is more profitable for the do-it-yourself mechanic to remove, clean and inspect the component, buy the necessary parts and deliver these to a shop for actual machine work.

Much of the assembly work (crankshaft, bearings, piston rods, and other components) is well within the scope of the do-it-yourself mechanic's tools and abilities. You will have to decide for yourself the depth of involvement you desire in an engine repair or rebuild.

TOOLS

The tools required for an engine overhaul or parts replacement will depend on the depth of your involvement. With a few exceptions, they will be the tools found in a mechanic's tool kit (see Section 1 of this manual). More in-depth work will require some or all of the following:

- A dial indicator (reading in thousandths) mounted on a universal base
- Micrometers and telescope gauges
- Jaw and screw-type pullers
- Scraper
- Valve spring compressor
- Ring groove cleaner
- Piston ring expander and compressor
- Ridge reamer
- Cylinder hone or glaze breaker
- Plastigage®
- Engine stand

The use of most of these tools is illustrated in this section. Many can be rented for a one-time use from a local parts jobber or tool supply house specializing in automotive work.

Occasionally, the use of special tools is called for. See the information on Special Tools and the Safety Notice in the front of this book before substituting another tool.

OVERHAUL TIPS

Aluminum has become extremely popular for use in engines, due to its low weight. Observe the following precautions when handling aluminum parts:
- Never hot tank aluminum parts (the caustic hot tank solution will eat the aluminum.
- Remove all aluminum parts (identification tag, etc.) from engine parts prior to the tanking.
- Always coat threads lightly with engine oil or anti-seize compounds before installation, to prevent seizure.
- Never overtighten bolts or spark plugs especially in aluminum threads.

When assembling the engine, any parts that will be exposed to frictional contact must be prelubed to provide lubrication at initial start-up. Any product specifically formulated for this purpose can be used, but engine oil is not recommended as a prelube in most cases.

When semi-permanent (locked, but removable) installation of bolts or nuts is desired, threads should be cleaned and coated with Loctite® or another similar, commercial non-hardening sealant.

CLEANING

▶ See Figures 229, 230, 231 and 232

Before the engine and its components are inspected, they must be thoroughly cleaned. You will need to remove any engine varnish, oil sludge and/or carbon deposits from all of the components to insure an accurate inspection. A crack in the engine block or cylinder head can easily become overlooked if hidden by a layer of sludge or carbon.

Fig. 229 Use a gasket scraper to remove the old gasket material from the mating surfaces

Most of the cleaning process can be carried out with common hand tools and readily available solvents or solutions. Carbon deposits can be chipped away using a hammer and a hard wooden chisel. Old gasket material and varnish or sludge can usually be removed using a scraper and/or cleaning solvent. Extremely stubborn deposits may require the use of a power drill with a wire brush. If using a wire brush, use extreme care around any critical machined surfaces (such as the gasket surfaces, bearing saddles, cylinder bores, etc.). USE OF A WIRE BRUSH IS NOT RECOMMENDED ON ANY ALUMINUM COMPONENTS. Always follow any safety recommendations given by the manufacturer of the tool and/or solvent. You should always wear eye protection during any cleaning process involving scraping, chipping or spraying of solvents.

An alternative to the mess and hassle of cleaning the parts yourself is to drop them off at a local garage or machine shop. They will, more than likely, have the necessary equipment to properly clean all of the parts for a nominal fee.

✳✳ CAUTION

Always wear eye protection during any cleaning process involving scraping, chipping or spraying of solvents.

Remove any oil galley plugs, freeze plugs and/or pressed-in bearings and carefully wash and degrease all of the engine components including the fasteners and bolts. Small parts such as the valves, springs, etc., should be placed in a metal basket and allowed to soak. Use pipe cleaner type brushes, and clean all passageways in the components. Use a ring expander and remove the rings from the pistons. Clean the piston ring grooves with a special tool or a piece of broken ring. Scrape the carbon off of the top of the piston. You should never use a wire brush on the pistons. After preparing all of the piston assemblies in this manner, wash and degrease them again.

✳✳ WARNING

Use extreme care when cleaning around the cylinder head valve seats. A mistake or slip may cost you a new seat.

When cleaning the cylinder head, remove carbon from the combustion chamber with the valves installed. This will avoid damaging the valve seats.

REPAIRING DAMAGED THREADS

▶ See Figures 233, 234, 235, 236 and 237

Several methods of repairing damaged threads are available. Heli-Coil® (shown here), Keenserts® and Microdot® are among the most widely used. All involve basically the same principle—drilling out stripped threads, tapping the hole and installing a prewound insert—making welding, plugging and oversize fasteners unnecessary.

Two types of thread repair inserts are usually supplied: a standard type for most inch coarse, inch fine, metric course and metric fine thread sizes and a spark lug type to fit most spark plug port sizes. Consult the individual tool manufacturer's catalog to determine exact applications. Typical thread repair kits will contain a selection of prewound threaded inserts, a tap (corresponding to the outside diameter threads of the insert) and an installation tool. Spark plug inserts usually differ because they require a tap equipped with pilot threads and

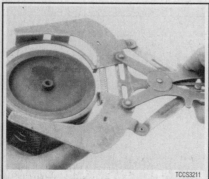

Fig. 230 Use a ring expander tool to remove the piston rings

Fig. 231 Clean the piston ring grooves using a ring groove cleaner tool, or . . .

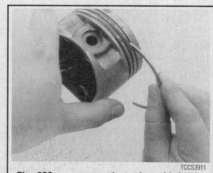

Fig. 232 . . . use a piece of an old ring to clean the grooves. Be careful, the ring can be quite sharp

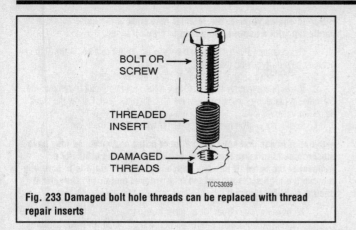

Fig. 233 Damaged bolt hole threads can be replaced with thread repair inserts

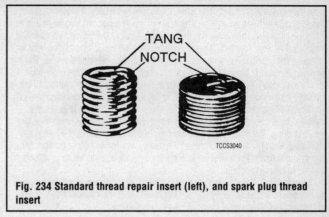

Fig. 234 Standard thread repair insert (left), and spark plug thread insert

Fig. 235 Drill out the damaged threads with the specified size bit. Be sure to drill completely through the hole or to the bottom of a blind hole

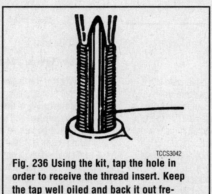

Fig. 236 Using the kit, tap the hole in order to receive the thread insert. Keep the tap well oiled and back it out frequently to avoid clogging the threads

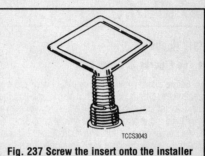

Fig. 237 Screw the insert onto the installer tool until the tang engages the slot. Thread the insert into the hole until it is ¼–½ turn below the top surface, then remove the tool and break off the tang using a punch

a combined reamer/tap section. Most manufacturers also supply blister-packed thread repair inserts separately in addition to a master kit containing a variety of taps and inserts plus installation tools.

Before attempting to repair a threaded hole, remove any snapped, broken or damaged bolts or studs. Penetrating oil can be used to free frozen threads. The offending item can usually be removed with locking pliers or using a screw/stud extractor. After the hole is clear, the thread can be repaired, as shown in the series of accompanying illustrations and in the kit manufacturer's instructions.

Engine Preparation

To properly rebuild an engine, you must first remove it from the vehicle, then disassemble and diagnose it. Ideally you should place your engine on an engine stand. This affords you the best access to the engine components. Follow the manufacturer's directions for using the stand with your particular engine. Remove the flywheel or flexplate before installing the engine to the stand.

Now that you have the engine on a stand, and assuming that you have drained the oil and coolant from the engine, it's time to strip it of all but the necessary components. Before you start disassembling the engine, you may want to take a moment to draw some pictures, or fabricate some labels or containers to mark the locations of various components and the bolts and/or studs which fasten them. Modern day engines use a lot of little brackets and clips which hold wiring harnesses and such, and these holders are often mounted on studs and/or bolts that can be easily mixed up. The manufacturer spent a lot of time and money designing your vehicle, and they wouldn't have wasted any of it by haphazardly placing brackets, clips or fasteners on the vehicle. If it's present when you disassemble it, put it back when you assemble, you will regret not remembering that little bracket which holds a wire harness out of the path of a rotating part.

You should begin by unbolting any accessories still attached to the engine, such as the water pump, power steering pump, alternator, etc. Then, unfasten any manifolds (intake or exhaust) which were not removed during the engine removal procedure. Finally, remove any covers remaining on the engine such as the rocker arm, front or timing cover and oil pan. Some front covers may require the vibration damper and/or crank pulley to be removed beforehand. The idea is

to reduce the engine to the bare necessities (cylinder head(s), valve train, engine block, crankshaft, pistons and connecting rods), plus any other 'in block' components such as oil pumps, balance shafts and auxiliary shafts.

Finally, remove the cylinder head(s) from the engine block and carefully place on a bench. Disassembly instructions for each component follow later in this section.

Cylinder Head

There are two basic types of cylinder heads used on today's automobiles: the Overhead Valve (OHV) and the Overhead Camshaft (OHC). The latter can also be broken down into two subgroups: the Single Overhead Camshaft (SOHC) and the Dual Overhead Camshaft (DOHC). Generally, if there is only a single camshaft on a head, it is just referred to as an OHC head. Also, an engine with an OHV cylinder head is also known as a pushrod engine.

Most cylinder heads these days are made of an aluminum alloy due to its light weight, durability and heat transfer qualities. However, cast iron was the material of choice in the past, and is still used on many vehicles today. Whether made from aluminum or iron, all cylinder heads have valves and seats. Some use two valves per cylinder, while the more hi-tech engines will utilize a multi-valve configuration using 3, 4 and even 5 valves per cylinder. When the valve contacts the seat, it does so on precision machined surfaces, which seals the combustion chamber. All cylinder heads have a valve guide for each valve. The guide centers the valve to the seat and allows it to move up and down within it. The clearance between the valve and guide can be critical. Too much clearance and the engine may consume oil, lose vacuum and/or damage the seat. Too little, and the valve can stick in the guide causing the engine to run poorly if at all, and possibly causing severe damage. The last component all cylinder heads have are valve springs. The spring holds the valve against its seat. It also returns the valve to this position when the valve has been opened by the valve train or camshaft. The spring is fastened to the valve by a retainer and valve locks (sometimes called keepers). Aluminum heads will also have a valve spring shim to keep the spring from wearing away the aluminum.

An ideal method of rebuilding the cylinder head would involve replacing all of the valves, guides, seats, springs, etc. with new ones. However, depending on how the engine was maintained, often this is not necessary. A major cause of valve, guide and seat wear is an improperly tuned engine. An engine that is running too rich, will often wash the lubricating oil out of the guide with gasoline, causing it to wear rapidly. Conversely, an engine which is running too lean will place higher combustion temperatures on the valves and seats allowing them to wear or even burn. Springs fall victim to the driving habits of the individual. A driver who often runs the engine rpm to the redline will wear out or break the springs faster then one that stays well below it. Unfortunately, mileage takes it toll on all of the parts. Generally, the valves, guides, springs and seats in a cylinder head can be machined and re-used, saving you money. However, if a valve is burnt, it may be wise to replace all of the valves, since they were all operating in the same environment. The same goes for any other component on the cylinder head. Think of it as an insurance policy against future problems related to that component.

Unfortunately, the only way to find out which components need replacing, is to disassemble and carefully check each piece. After the cylinder head(s) are disassembled, thoroughly clean all of the components.

DISASSEMBLY

OHV Heads

▶ See Figures 238 thru 243

Before disassembling the cylinder head, you may want to fabricate some containers to hold the various parts, as some of them can be quite small (such as keepers) and easily lost. Also keeping yourself and the components organized will aid in assembly and reduce confusion. Where possible, try to maintain a components original location; this is especially important if there is not going to be any machine work performed on the components.

1. If you haven't already removed the rocker arms and/or shafts, do so now.
2. Position the head so that the springs are easily accessed.
3. Use a valve spring compressor tool, and relieve spring tension from the retainer.

➡ Due to engine varnish, the retainer may stick to the valve locks. A gentle tap with a hammer may help to break it loose.

4. Remove the valve locks from the valve tip and/or retainer. A small magnet may help in removing the locks.
5. Lift the valve spring, tool and all, off of the valve stem.
6. If equipped, remove the valve seal. If the seal is difficult to remove with the valve in place, try removing the valve first, then the seal. Follow the steps below for valve removal.
7. Position the head to allow access for withdrawing the valve.

➡ Cylinder heads that have seen a lot of miles and/or abuse may have mushroomed the valve lock grove and/or tip, causing difficulty in removal of the valve. If this has happened, use a metal file to carefully remove the high spots around the lock grooves and/or tip. Only file it enough to allow removal.

8. Remove the valve from the cylinder head.
9. If equipped, remove the valve spring shim. A small magnetic tool or screwdriver will aid in removal.
10. Repeat Steps 3 though 9 until all of the valves have been removed.

OHC Heads

▶ See Figures 244 and 245

Whether it is a single or dual overhead camshaft cylinder head, the disassembly procedure is relatively unchanged. One aspect to pay attention to is careful labeling of the parts on the dual camshaft cylinder head. There will be an intake camshaft and followers as well as an exhaust camshaft and followers and they must be labeled as such. In some cases, the components are identical and could easily be installed incorrectly. DO NOT MIX THEM UP! Determining which is which is very simple; the intake camshaft and components are on the same side of the head as was the intake manifold. Conversely, the exhaust camshaft and components are on the same side of the head as was the exhaust manifold.

Fig. 238 When removing an OHV valve spring, use a compressor tool to relieve the tension from the retainer

TCCS3137

Fig. 239 A small magnet will help in removal of the valve locks

TCCS3138

Fig. 240 Be careful not to lose the small valve locks (keepers)

TCCS3139

Fig. 241 Remove the valve seal from the valve stem—O-ring type seal shown

TCCS3140

Fig. 242 Removing an umbrella/positive type seal

TCCS3252

Fig. 243 Invert the cylinder head and withdraw the valve from the valve guide bore

TCCS3141

Fig. 244 Exploded view of a valve, seal, spring, retainer and locks from an OHC cylinder head

Fig. 245 Example of a multi-valve cylinder head. Note how it has 2 intake and 2 exhaust valve ports

CUP TYPE CAMSHAFT FOLLOWERS

▶ See Figures 246, 247 and 248

Most cylinder heads with cup type camshaft followers will have the valve spring, retainer and locks recessed within the follower's bore. You will need a C-clamp style valve spring compressor tool, an OHC spring removal tool (or equivalent) and a small magnet to disassemble the head.

1. If not already removed, remove the camshaft(s) and/or followers. Mark their positions for assembly.

2. Position the cylinder head to allow use of a C-clamp style valve spring compressor tool.

➡It is preferred to position the cylinder head gasket surface facing you with the valve springs facing the opposite direction and the head laying horizontal.

3. With the OHC spring removal adapter tool positioned inside of the follower bore, compress the valve spring using the C-clamp style valve spring compressor.

4. Remove the valve locks. A small magnetic tool or screwdriver will aid in removal.

5. Release the compressor tool and remove the spring assembly.

6. Withdraw the valve from the cylinder head.

7. If equipped, remove the valve seal.

➡Special valve seal removal tools are available. Regular or needlenose type pliers, if used with care, will work just as well. If using ordinary pliers, be sure not to damage the follower bore. The follower and its bore are machined to close tolerances and any damage to the bore will effect this relationship.

8. If equipped, remove the valve spring shim. A small magnetic tool or screwdriver will aid in removal.

9. Repeat Steps 3 through 8 until all of the valves have been removed.

Fig. 246 C-clamp type spring compressor and an OHC spring removal tool (center) for cup type followers

Fig. 247 Most cup type follower cylinder heads retain the camshaft using bolt-on bearing caps

Fig. 248 Position the OHC spring tool in the follower bore, then compress the spring with a C-clamp type tool

ROCKER ARM TYPE CAMSHAFT FOLLOWERS

♦ **See Figures 249 thru 257**

Most cylinder heads with rocker arm-type camshaft followers are easily disassembled using a standard valve spring compressor. However, certain models may not have enough open space around the spring for the standard tool and may require you to use a C-clamp style compressor tool instead.

1. If not already removed, remove the rocker arms and/or shafts and the camshaft. If applicable, also remove the hydraulic lash adjusters. Mark their positions for assembly.
2. Position the cylinder head to allow access to the valve spring.
3. Use a valve spring compressor tool to relieve the spring tension from the retainer.

➡**Due to engine varnish, the retainer may stick to the valve locks. A gentle tap with a hammer may help to break it loose.**

4. Remove the valve locks from the valve tip and/or retainer. A small magnet may help in removing the small locks.
5. Lift the valve spring, tool and all, off of the valve stem.
6. If equipped, remove the valve seal. If the seal is difficult to remove with the valve in place, try removing the valve first, then the seal. Follow the steps below for valve removal.
7. Position the head to allow access for withdrawing the valve.

➡**Cylinder heads that have seen a lot of miles and/or abuse may have mushroomed the valve lock groove and/or tip, causing difficulty in removal of the valve. If this has happened, use a metal file to carefully remove the high spots around the lock grooves and/or tip. Only file it enough to allow removal.**

8. Remove the valve from the cylinder head.
9. If equipped, remove the valve spring shim. A small magnetic tool or screwdriver will aid in removal.
10. Repeat Steps 3 though 9 until all of the valves have been removed.

Fig. 249 Example of the shaft mounted rocker arms on some OHC heads

Fig. 250 Another example of the rocker arm type OHC head. This model uses a follower under the camshaft

Fig. 251 Before the camshaft can be removed, all of the followers must first be removed . . .

Fig. 252 . . . then the camshaft can be removed by sliding it out (shown), or unbolting a bearing cap (not shown)

Fig. 253 Compress the valve spring . . .

Fig. 254 . . . then remove the valve locks from the valve stem and spring retainer

Fig. 255 Remove the valve spring and retainer from the cylinder head

Fig. 256 Remove the valve seal from the guide. Some gentle prying or pliers may help to remove stubborn ones

Fig. 257 All aluminum and some cast iron heads will have these valve spring shims. Remove all of them as well

INSPECTION

Now that all of the cylinder head components are clean, it's time to inspect them for wear and/or damage. To accurately inspect them, you will need some specialized tools:

- A 0–1 in. micrometer for the valves
- A dial indicator or inside diameter gauge for the valve guides
- A spring pressure test gauge

If you do not have access to the proper tools, you may want to bring the components to a shop that does.

Valves

▶ See Figures 258 and 259

The first thing to inspect are the valve heads. Look closely at the head, margin and face for any cracks, excessive wear or burning. The margin is the best

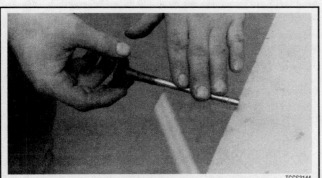

Fig. 258 Valve stems may be rolled on a flat surface to check for bends

place to look for burning. It should have a squared edge with an even width all around the diameter. When a valve burns, the margin will look melted and the edges rounded. Also inspect the valve head for any signs of tulipping. This will show as a lifting of the edges or dishing in the center of the head and will usually not occur to all of the valves. All of the heads should look the same, any that seem dished more than others are probably bad. Next, inspect the valve lock grooves and valve tips. Check for any burrs around the lock grooves, especially if you had to file them to remove the valve. Valve tips should appear flat, although slight rounding with high mileage engines is normal. Slightly worn valve tips will need to be machined flat. Last, measure the valve stem diameter with the micrometer. Measure the area that rides within the guide, especially towards the tip where most of the wear occurs. Take several measurements along its length and compare them to each other. Wear should be even along the length with little to no taper. If no minimum diameter is given in the specifications, then the stem should not read more than 0.001 in. (0.025mm) below the specification. Any valves that fail these inspections should be replaced.

Springs, Retainers and Valve Locks

▶ See Figures 260 and 261

The first thing to check is the most obvious, broken springs. Next check the free length and squareness of each spring. If applicable, insure to distinguish between intake and exhaust springs. Use a ruler and/or carpenters square to measure the length. A carpenters square should be used to check the springs for squareness. If a spring pressure test gauge is available, check each springs rating and compare to the specifications chart. Check the readings against the specifications given. Any springs that fail these inspections should be replaced.

The spring retainers rarely need replacing, however they should still be checked as a precaution. Inspect the spring mating surface and the valve lock retention area for any signs of excessive wear. Also check for any signs of cracking. Replace any retainers that are questionable.

Valve locks should be inspected for excessive wear on the outside contact area as well as on the inner notched surface. Any locks which appear worn or broken and its respective valve should be replaced.

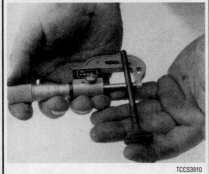

Fig. 259 Use a micrometer to check the valve stem diameter

Fig. 260 Use a caliper to check the valve spring free-length

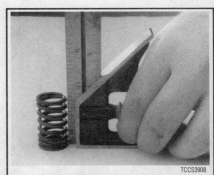

Fig. 261 Check the valve spring for squareness on a flat surface; a carpenter's square can be used

Cylinder Head

There are several things to check on the cylinder head: valve guides, seats, cylinder head surface flatness, cracks and physical damage.

VALVE GUIDES

◗ See Figure 262

Now that you know the valves are good, you can use them to check the guides, although a new valve, if available, is preferred. Before you measure anything, look at the guides carefully and inspect them for any cracks, chips or breakage. Also if the guide is a removable style (as in most aluminum heads), check them for any looseness or evidence of movement. All of the guides should appear to be at the same height from the spring seat. If any seem lower (or higher) from another, the guide has moved. Mount a dial indicator onto the spring side of the cylinder head. Lightly oil the valve stem and insert it into the cylinder head. Position the dial indicator against the valve stem near the tip and zero the gauge. Grasp the valve stem and wiggle towards and away from the dial indicator and observe the readings. Mount the dial indicator 90 degrees from the initial point and zero the gauge and again take a reading. Compare the two readings for a out of round condition. Check the readings against the specifications given. An Inside Diameter (I.D.) gauge designed for valve guides will give you an accurate valve guide bore measurement. If the I.D. gauge is used, compare the readings with the specifications given. Any guides that fail these inspections should be replaced or machined.

VALVE SEATS

A visual inspection of the valve seats should show a slightly worn and pitted surface where the valve face contacts the seat. Inspect the seat carefully for severe pitting or cracks. Also, a seat that is badly worn will be recessed into the cylinder head. A severely worn or recessed seat may need to be replaced. All cracked seats must be replaced. A seat concentricity gauge, if available, should be used to check the seat run-out. If run-out exceeds specifications the seat must be machined (if no specification is given use 0.002 in. or 0.051mm).

CYLINDER HEAD SURFACE FLATNESS

◗ See Figures 263 and 264

After you have cleaned the gasket surface of the cylinder head of any old gasket material, check the head for flatness.

Place a straightedge across the gasket surface. Using feeler gauges, determine the clearance at the center of the straightedge and across the cylinder head at several points. Check along the centerline and diagonally on the head surface. If the warpage exceeds 0.003 in. (0.076mm) within a 6.0 in. (15.2cm) span, or 0.006 in. (0.152mm) over the total length of the head, the cylinder head must be resurfaced. After resurfacing the heads of a V-type engine, the intake manifold flange surface should be checked, and if necessary, milled proportionally to allow for the change in its mounting position.

CRACKS AND PHYSICAL DAMAGE

Generally, cracks are limited to the combustion chamber, however, it is not uncommon for the head to crack in a spark plug hole, port, outside of the head or in the valve spring/rocker arm area. The first area to inspect is always the hottest: the exhaust seat/port area.

A visual inspection should be performed, but just because you don't see a crack does not mean it is not there. Some more reliable methods for inspecting for cracks include Magnaflux®, a magnetic process or Zyglo®, a dye penetrant. Magnaflux® is used only on ferrous metal (cast iron) heads. Zyglo® uses a spray on fluorescent mixture along with a black light to reveal the cracks. It is strongly recommended to have your cylinder head checked professionally for cracks, especially if the engine was known to have overheated and/or leaked or consumed coolant. Contact a local shop for availability and pricing of these services.

Physical damage is usually very evident. For example, a broken mounting ear from dropping the head or a bent or broken stud and/or bolt. All of these defects should be fixed or, if unrepairable, the head should be replaced.

Camshaft and Followers

Inspect the camshaft(s) and followers as described earlier in this section.

REFINISHING & REPAIRING

Many of the procedures given for refinishing and repairing the cylinder head components must be performed by a machine shop. Certain steps, if the inspected part is not worn, can be performed yourself inexpensively. However, you spent a lot of time and effort so far, why risk trying to save a couple bucks if you might have to do it all over again?

Valves

Any valves that were not replaced should be refaced and the tips ground flat. Unless you have access to a valve grinding machine, this should be done by a machine shop. If the valves are in extremely good condition, as well as the valve seats and guides, they may be lapped in without performing machine work.

It is a recommended practice to lap the valves even after machine work has been performed and/or new valves have been purchased. This insures a positive seal between the valve and seat.

LAPPING THE VALVES

➡ Before lapping the valves to the seats, read the rest of the cylinder head section to insure that any related parts are in acceptable enough condition to continue.

➡ Before any valve seat machining and/or lapping can be performed, the guides must be within factory recommended specifications.

1. Invert the cylinder head.
2. Lightly lubricate the valve stems and insert them into the cylinder head in their numbered order.
3. Raise the valve from the seat and apply a small amount of fine lapping compound to the seat.
4. Moisten the suction head of a hand-lapping tool and attach it to the head of the valve.
5. Rotate the tool between the palms of both hands, changing the position of the valve on the valve seat and lifting the tool often to prevent grooving.
6. Lap the valve until a smooth, polished circle is evident on the valve and seat.
7. Remove the tool and the valve. Wipe away all traces of the grinding compound and store the valve to maintain its lapped location.

TCCS3142

Fig. 262 A dial gauge may be used to check valve stem-to-guide clearance; read the gauge while moving the valve stem

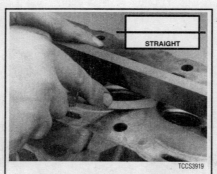

STRAIGHT

TCCS3919

Fig. 263 Check the head for flatness across the center of the head surface using a straightedge and feeler gauge

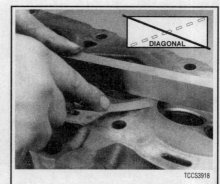

DIAGONAL

TCCS3918

Fig. 264 Checks should also be made along both diagonals of the head surface

Do not get the valves out of order after they have been lapped. They must be put back with the same valve seat with which they were lapped.

Springs, Retainers and Valve Locks

There is no repair or refinishing possible with the springs, retainers and valve locks. If they are found to be worn or defective, they must be replaced with new (or known good) parts.

Cylinder Head

Most refinishing procedures dealing with the cylinder head must be performed by a machine shop. Read the sections below and review your inspection data to determine whether or not machining is necessary.

VALVE GUIDE

➡ **If any machining or replacements are made to the valve guides, the seats must be machined.**

Unless the valve guides need machining or replacing, the only service to perform is to thoroughly clean them of any dirt or oil residue.

There are only two types of valve guides used on automobile engines: the replaceable-type (all aluminum heads) and the cast-in integral-type (most cast iron heads). There are four recommended methods for repairing worn guides.

- Knurling
- Inserts
- Reaming oversize
- Replacing

Knurling is a process in which metal is displaced and raised, thereby reducing clearance, giving a true center, and providing oil control. It is the least expensive way of repairing the valve guides. However, it is not necessarily the best, and in some cases, a knurled valve guide will not stand up for more than a short time. It requires a special knurlizer and precision reaming tools to obtain proper clearances. It would not be cost effective to purchase these tools, unless you plan on rebuilding several of the same cylinder head.

Installing a guide insert involves machining the guide to accept a bronze insert. One style is the coil-type which is installed into a threaded guide. Another is the thin-walled insert where the guide is reamed oversize to accept a split-sleeve insert. After the insert is installed, a special tool is then run through the guide to expand the insert, locking it to the guide. The insert is then reamed to the standard size for proper valve clearance.

Reaming for oversize valves restores normal clearances and provides a true valve seat. Most cast-in type guides can be reamed to accept an valve with an oversize stem. The cost factor for this can become quite high as you will need to purchase the reamer and new, oversize stem valves for all guides which were reamed. Oversizes are generally 0.003 to 0.030 in. (0.076 to 0.762mm), with 0.015 in. (0.381mm) being the most common.

To replace cast-in type valve guides, they must be drilled out, then reamed to accept replacement guides. This must be done on a fixture which will allow centering and leveling off of the original valve seat or guide, otherwise a serious guide-to-seat misalignment may occur making it impossible to properly machine the seat.

Replaceable-type guides are pressed into the cylinder head. A hammer and a stepped drift or punch may be used to install and remove the guides. Before removing the guides, measure the protrusion on the spring side of the head and record it for installation. Use the stepped drift to hammer out the old guide from the combustion chamber side of the head. When installing, determine whether or not the guide also seals a water jacket in the head, and if it does, use the recommended sealing agent. If there is no water jacket, grease the valve guide and its bore. Use the stepped drift, and hammer the new guide into the cylinder head from the spring side of the cylinder head. A stack of washers the same thickness as the measured protrusion may help the installation process.

VALVE SEATS

➡ **Before any valve seat machining can be performed, the guides must be within factory recommended specifications.**

➡ **If any machining or replacements were made to the valve guides, the seats must be machined.**

If the seats are in good condition, the valves can be lapped to the seats, and the cylinder head assembled. See the valves section for instructions on lapping.

If the valve seats are worn, cracked or damaged, they must be serviced by a machine shop. The valve seat must be perfectly centered to the valve guide, which requires very accurate machining.

CYLINDER HEAD SURFACE

If the cylinder head is warped, it must be machined flat. If the warpage is extremely severe, the head may need to be replaced. In some instances, it may be possible to straighten a warped head enough to allow machining. In either case, contact a professional machine shop for service.

➡ **Any OHC cylinder head that shows excessive warpage should have the camshaft bearing journals align bored after the cylinder head has been resurfaced.**

Failure to align bore the camshaft bearing journals could result in severe engine damage including but not limited to: valve and piston damage, connecting rod damage, camshaft and/or crankshaft breakage.

CRACKS AND PHYSICAL DAMAGE

Certain cracks can be repaired in both cast iron and aluminum heads. For cast iron, a tapered threaded insert is installed along the length of the crack. Aluminum can also use the tapered inserts, however welding is the preferred method. Some physical damage can be repaired through brazing or welding. Contact a machine shop to get expert advice for your particular dilemma.

ASSEMBLY

The first step for any assembly job is to have a clean area in which to work. Next, thoroughly clean all of the parts and components that are to be assembled. Finally, place all of the components onto a suitable work space and, if necessary, arrange the parts to their respective positions.

OHV Engines

1. Lightly lubricate the valve stems and insert all of the valves into the cylinder head. If possible, maintain their original locations.
2. If equipped, install any valve spring shims which were removed.
3. If equipped, install the new valve seals, keeping the following in mind:
- If the valve seal presses over the guide, lightly lubricate the outer guide surfaces.
- If the seal is an O-ring type, it is installed just after compressing the spring but before the valve locks.
4. Place the valve spring and retainer over the stem.
5. Position the spring compressor tool and compress the spring.
6. Assemble the valve locks to the stem.
7. Relieve the spring pressure slowly and insure that neither valve lock becomes dislodged by the retainer.
8. Remove the spring compressor tool.
9. Repeat Steps 2 through 8 until all of the springs have been installed.

OHC Engines

CUP TYPE CAMSHAFT FOLLOWERS

◗ See Figure 265

To install the springs, retainers and valve locks on heads which have these components recessed into the camshaft follower's bore, you will need a small screwdriver-type tool, some clean white grease and a lot of patience. You will also need the C-clamp style spring compressor and the OHC tool used to disassemble the head.

1. Lightly lubricate the valve stems and insert all of the valves into the cylinder head. If possible, maintain their original locations.
2. If equipped, install any valve spring shims which were removed.
3. If equipped, install the new valve seals, keeping the following in mind:

Fig. 265 Once assembled, check the valve clearance and correct as needed

• If the valve seal presses over the guide, lightly lubricate the outer guide surfaces.
• If the seal is an O-ring type, it is installed just after compressing the spring but before the valve locks.
4. Place the valve spring and retainer over the stem.
5. Position the spring compressor and the OHC tool, then compress the spring.
6. Using a small screwdriver as a spatula, fill the valve stem side of the lock with white grease. Use the excess grease on the screwdriver to fasten the lock to the driver.
7. Carefully install the valve lock, which is stuck to the end of the screwdriver, to the valve stem then press on it with the screwdriver until the grease squeezes out. The valve lock should now be stuck to the stem.
8. Repeat Steps 6 and 7 for the remaining valve lock.
9. Relieve the spring pressure slowly and insure that neither valve lock becomes dislodged by the retainer.
10. Remove the spring compressor tool.
11. Repeat Steps 2 through 10 until all of the springs have been installed.
12. Install the followers, camshaft(s) and any other components that were removed for disassembly.

ROCKER ARM TYPE CAMSHAFT FOLLOWERS

1. Lightly lubricate the valve stems and insert all of the valves into the cylinder head. If possible, maintain their original locations.
2. If equipped, install any valve spring shims which were removed.
3. If equipped, install the new valve seals, keeping the following in mind:
• If the valve seal presses over the guide, lightly lubricate the outer guide surfaces.
• If the seal is an O-ring type, it is installed just after compressing the spring but before the valve locks.
4. Place the valve spring and retainer over the stem.
5. Position the spring compressor tool and compress the spring.
6. Assemble the valve locks to the stem.
7. Relieve the spring pressure slowly and insure that neither valve lock becomes dislodged by the retainer.
8. Remove the spring compressor tool.
9. Repeat Steps 2 through 8 until all of the springs have been installed.
10. Install the camshaft(s), rockers, shafts and any other components that were removed for disassembly.

Engine Block

GENERAL INFORMATION

A thorough overhaul or rebuild of an engine block would include replacing the pistons, rings, bearings, timing belt/chain assembly and oil pump. For OHV engines also include a new camshaft and lifters. The block would then have the cylinders bored and honed oversize (or if using removable cylinder sleeves, new sleeves installed) and the crankshaft would be cut undersize to provide new wearing surfaces and perfect clearances. However, your particular engine may not have everything worn out. What if only the piston rings have worn out and the clearances on everything else are still within factory specifications? Well,

you could just replace the rings and put it back together, but this would be a very rare example. Chances are, if one component in your engine is worn, other components are sure to follow, and soon. At the very least, you should always replace the rings, bearings and oil pump. This is what is commonly called a "freshen up".

Cylinder Ridge Removal

Because the top piston ring does not travel to the very top of the cylinder, a ridge is built up between the end of the travel and the top of the cylinder bore.

Pushing the piston and connecting rod assembly past the ridge can be difficult, and damage to the piston ring lands could occur. If the ridge is not removed before installing a new piston or not removed at all, piston ring breakage and piston damage may occur.

➡ It is always recommended that you remove any cylinder ridges before removing the piston and connecting rod assemblies. If you know that new pistons are going to be installed and the engine block will be bored oversize, you may be able to forego this step. However, some ridges may actually prevent the assemblies from being removed, necessitating its removal.

There are several different types of ridge reamers on the market, none of which are inexpensive. Unless a great deal of engine rebuilding is anticipated, borrow or rent a reamer.
1. Turn the crankshaft until the piston is at the bottom of its travel.
2. Cover the head of the piston with a rag.
3. Follow the tool manufacturers instructions and cut away the ridge, exercising extreme care to avoid cutting too deeply.
4. Remove the ridge reamer, the rag and as many of the cuttings as possible. Continue until all of the cylinder ridges have been removed.

DISASSEMBLY

▶ See Figures 266 and 267

The engine disassembly instructions following assume that you have the engine mounted on an engine stand. If not, it is easiest to disassemble the engine on a bench or the floor with it resting on the bellhousing or transmission mounting surface. You must be able to access the connecting rod fasteners and turn the crankshaft during disassembly. Also, all engine covers (timing, front, side, oil pan, whatever) should have already been removed. Engines which are seized or locked up may not be able to be completely disassembled, and a core (salvage yard) engine should be purchased.

Pushrod Engines

If not done during the cylinder head removal, remove the pushrods and lifters, keeping them in order for assembly. Remove the timing gears and/or timing chain assembly, then remove the oil pump drive assembly and withdraw the camshaft from the engine block. Remove the oil pick-up and pump assembly. If equipped, remove any balance or auxiliary shafts. If necessary, remove the cylinder ridge from the top of the bore. See the cylinder ridge removal procedure earlier in this section.

OHC Engines

If not done during the cylinder head removal, remove the timing chain/belt and/or gear/sprocket assembly. Remove the oil pick-up and pump assembly and, if necessary, the pump drive. If equipped, remove any balance or auxiliary shafts. If necessary, remove the cylinder ridge from the top of the bore. See the cylinder ridge removal procedure earlier in this section.

All Engines

Rotate the engine over so that the crankshaft is exposed. Use a number punch or scribe and mark each connecting rod with its respective cylinder number. The cylinder closest to the front of the engine is always number 1. However, depending on the engine placement, the front of the engine could either be the flywheel or damper/pulley end. Generally the front of the engine faces the front of the vehicle. Use a number punch or scribe and also mark the main bearing caps from front to rear with the front most cap being number 1 (if there are five caps, mark them 1 through 5, front to rear).

✳✳ WARNING

Take special care when pushing the connecting rod up from the crankshaft because the sharp threads of the rod bolts/studs will score the crankshaft journal. Insure that special plastic caps are installed over them, or cut two pieces of rubber hose to do the same.

Again, rotate the engine, this time to position the number one cylinder bore (head surface) up. Turn the crankshaft until the number one piston is at the bottom of its travel, this should allow the maximum access to its connecting rod. Remove the number one connecting rods fasteners and cap and place two lengths of rubber hose over the rod bolts/studs to protect the crankshaft from damage. Using a sturdy wooden dowel and a hammer, push the connecting rod up about 1 in. (25mm) from the crankshaft and remove the upper bearing insert. Continue pushing or tapping the connecting rod up until the piston rings are out of the cylinder bore. Remove the piston and rod by hand, put the upper half

TCCS3803

Fig. 266 Place rubber hose over the connecting rod studs to protect the crankshaft and cylinder bores from damage

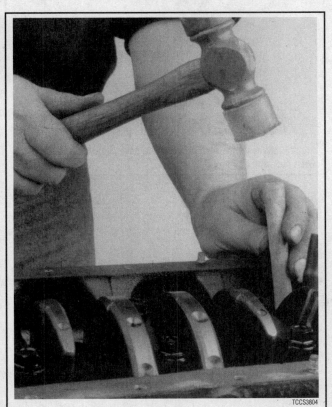

TCCS3804

Fig. 267 Carefully tap the piston out of the bore using a wooden dowel

of the bearing insert back into the rod, install the cap with its bearing insert installed, and hand-tighten the cap fasteners. If the parts are kept in order in this manner, they will not get lost and you will be able to tell which bearings came form what cylinder if any problems are discovered and diagnosis is necessary. Remove all the other piston assemblies in the same manner. On V-style engines, remove all of the pistons from one bank, then reposition the engine with the other cylinder bank head surface up, and remove that banks piston assemblies.

The only remaining component in the engine block should now be the crankshaft. Loosen the main bearing caps evenly until the fasteners can be turned by hand, then remove them and the caps. Remove the crankshaft from the engine block. Thoroughly clean all of the components.

INSPECTION

Now that the engine block and all of its components are clean, it's time to inspect them for wear and/or damage. To accurately inspect them, you will need some specialized tools:

- Two or three separate micrometers to measure the pistons and crankshaft journals
- A dial indicator
- Telescoping gauges for the cylinder bores
- A rod alignment fixture to check for bent connecting rods

If you do not have access to the proper tools, you may want to bring the components to a shop that does.

Generally, you shouldn't expect cracks in the engine block or its components unless it was known to leak, consume or mix engine fluids, it was severely overheated, or there was evidence of bad bearings and/or crankshaft damage. A visual inspection should be performed on all of the components, but just because you don't see a crack does not mean it is not there. Some more reliable methods for inspecting for cracks include Magnaflux®, a magnetic process or Zyglo®, a dye penetrant. Magnaflux® is used only on ferrous metal (cast iron). Zyglo® uses a spray on fluorescent mixture along with a black light to reveal the cracks. It is strongly recommended to have your engine block checked professionally for cracks, especially if the engine was known to have overheated and/or leaked or consumed coolant. Contact a local shop for availability and pricing of these services.

Engine Block

ENGINE BLOCK BEARING ALIGNMENT

Remove the main bearing caps and, if still installed, the main bearing inserts. Inspect all of the main bearing saddles and caps for damage, burrs or high spots. If damage is found, and it is caused from a spun main bearing, the block will need to be align-bored or, if severe enough, replacement. Any burrs or high spots should be carefully removed with a metal file.

Place a straightedge on the bearing saddles, in the engine block, along the centerline of the crankshaft. If any clearance exists between the straightedge and the saddles, the block must be align-bored.

Align-boring consists of machining the main bearing saddles and caps by means of a flycutter that runs through the bearing saddles.

DECK FLATNESS

The top of the engine block where the cylinder head mounts is called the deck. Insure that the deck surface is clean of dirt, carbon deposits and old gasket material. Place a straightedge across the surface of the deck along its centerline and, using feeler gauges, check the clearance along several points. Repeat the checking procedure with the straightedge placed along both diagonals of the deck surface. If the reading exceeds 0.003 in. (0.076mm) within a 6.0 in. (15.2cm) span, or 0.006 in. (0.152mm) over the total length of the deck, it must be machined.

CYLINDER BORES

▶ **See Figure 268**

The cylinder bores house the pistons and are slightly larger than the pistons themselves. A common piston-to-bore clearance is 0.0015–0.0025 in. (0.0381mm–0.0635mm). Inspect and measure the cylinder bores. The bore should be checked for out-of-roundness, taper and size. The results of this inspection will determine whether the cylinder can be used in its existing size and condition, or a rebore to the next oversize is required (or in the case of removable sleeves, have replacements installed).

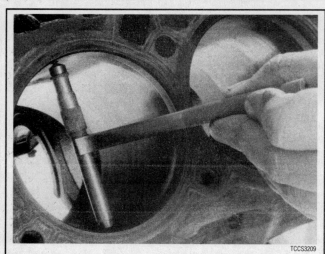

Fig. 268 Use a telescoping gauge to measure the cylinder bore diameter—take several readings within the same bore

The amount of cylinder wall wear is always greater at the top of the cylinder than at the bottom. This wear is known as taper. Any cylinder that has a taper of 0.0012 in. (0.305mm) or more, must be rebored. Measurements are taken at a number of positions in each cylinder: at the top, middle and bottom and at two points at each position; that is, at a point 90 degrees from the crankshaft centerline, as well as a point parallel to the crankshaft centerline. The measurements are made with either a special dial indicator or a telescopic gauge and micrometer. If the necessary precision tools to check the bore are not available, take the block to a machine shop and have them mike it. Also if you don't have the tools to check the cylinder bores, chances are you will not have the necessary devices to check the pistons, connecting rods and crankshaft. Take these components with you and save yourself an extra trip.

For our procedures, we will use a telescopic gauge and a micrometer. You will need one of each, with a measuring range which covers your cylinder bore size.

1. Position the telescopic gauge in the cylinder bore, loosen the gauges lock and allow it to expand.

➡Your first two readings will be at the top of the cylinder bore, then proceed to the middle and finally the bottom, making a total of six measurements.

2. Hold the gauge square in the bore, 90 degrees from the crankshaft centerline, and gently tighten the lock. Tilt the gauge back to remove it from the bore.

3. Measure the gauge with the micrometer and record the reading.

4. Again, hold the gauge square in the bore, this time parallel to the crankshaft centerline, and gently tighten the lock. Again, you will tilt the gauge back to remove it from the bore.

5. Measure the gauge with the micrometer and record this reading. The difference between these two readings is the out-of-round measurement of the cylinder.

6. Repeat steps 1 through 5, each time going to the next lower position, until you reach the bottom of the cylinder. Then go to the next cylinder, and continue until all of the cylinders have been measured.

The difference between these measurements will tell you all about the wear in your cylinders. The measurements which were taken 90 degrees from the crankshaft centerline will always reflect the most wear. That is because at this position is where the engine power presses the piston against the cylinder bore the hardest. This is known as thrust wear. Take your top, 90 degree measurement and compare it to your bottom, 90 degree measurement. The difference between them is the taper. When you measure your pistons, you will compare these readings to your piston sizes and determine piston-to-wall clearance.

Crankshaft

Inspect the crankshaft for visible signs of wear or damage. All of the journals should be perfectly round and smooth. Slight scores are normal for a used crankshaft, but you should hardly feel them with your fingernail. When measuring the crankshaft with a micrometer, you will take readings at the front and rear of each journal, then turn the micrometer 90 degrees and take two more readings, front and rear. The difference between the front-to-rear readings is the

journal taper and the first-to-90 degree reading is the out-of-round measurement. Generally, there should be no taper or out-of-roundness found, however, up to 0.0005 in. (0.0127mm) for either can be overlooked. Also, the readings should fall within the factory specifications for journal diameters.

If the crankshaft journals fall within specifications, it is recommended that it be polished before being returned to service. Polishing the crankshaft insures that any minor burrs or high spots are smoothed, thereby reducing the chance of scoring the new bearings.

Pistons and Connecting Rods

PISTONS

▸ See Figure 269

The piston should be visually inspected for any signs of cracking or burning (caused by hot spots or detonation), and scuffing or excessive wear on the skirts. The wristpin attaches the piston to the connecting rod. The piston should move freely on the wrist pin, both sliding and pivoting. Grasp the connecting rod securely, or mount it in a vise, and try to rock the piston back and forth along the centerline of the wristpin. There should not be any excessive play evident between the piston and the pin. If there are C-clips retaining the pin in the piston then you have wrist pin bushings in the rods. There should not be any excessive play between the wrist pin and the rod bushing. Normal clearance for the wrist pin is approx. 0.001–0.002 in. (0.025mm–0.051mm).

Use a micrometer and measure the diameter of the piston, perpendicular to the wrist pin, on the skirt. Compare the reading to its original cylinder measurement obtained earlier. The difference between the two readings is the piston-to-wall clearance. If the clearance is within specifications, the piston may be used as is. If the piston is out of specification, but the bore is not, you will need a new piston. If both are out of specification, you will need the cylinder rebored and oversize pistons installed. Generally if two or more pistons/bores are out of specification, it is best to rebore the entire block and purchase a complete set of oversize pistons.

Fig. 269 Measure the piston's outer diameter, perpendicular to the wrist pin, with a micrometer

CONNECTING ROD

You should have the connecting rod checked for straightness at a machine shop. If the connecting rod is bent, it will unevenly wear the bearing and piston, as well as place greater stress on these components. Any bent or twisted connecting rods must be replaced. If the rods are straight and the wrist pin clearance is within specifications, then only the bearing end of the rod need be checked. Place the connecting rod into a vice, with the bearing inserts in place, install the cap to the rod and torque the fasteners to specifications. Use a telescoping gauge and carefully measure the inside diameter of the bearings. Compare this reading to the rods original crankshaft journal diameter measurement. The difference is the oil clearance. If the oil clearance is not within specifications, install new bearings in the rod and take another measurement. If the clearance is still out of specifications, and the crankshaft is not, the rod will need to be reconditioned by a machine shop.

➡You can also use Plastigage® to check the bearing clearances. The assembling section has complete instructions on its use.

Camshaft

Inspect the camshaft and lifters/followers as described earlier in this section.

Bearings

All of the engine bearings should be visually inspected for wear and/or damage. The bearing should look evenly worn all around with no deep scores or pits. If the bearing is severely worn, scored, pitted or heat blued, then the bearing, and the components that use it, should be brought to a machine shop for inspection. Full-circle bearings (used on most camshafts, auxiliary shafts, balance shafts, etc.) require specialized tools for removal and installation, and should be brought to a machine shop for service.

Oil Pump

→ **The oil pump is responsible for providing constant lubrication to the whole engine and so it is recommended that a new oil pump be installed when rebuilding the engine.**

Completely disassemble the oil pump and thoroughly clean all of the components. Inspect the oil pump gears and housing for wear and/or damage. Insure that the pressure relief valve operates properly and there is no binding or sticking due to varnish or debris. If all of the parts are in proper working condition, lubricate the gears and relief valve, and assemble the pump.

REFINISHING

♦ **See Figure 270**

Almost all engine block refinishing must be performed by a machine shop. If the cylinders are not to be rebored, then the cylinder glaze can be removed with a ball hone. When removing cylinder glaze with a ball hone, use a light or penetrating type oil to lubricate the hone. Do not allow the hone to run dry as this may cause excessive scoring of the cylinder bores and wear on the hone. If new pistons are required, they will need to be installed to the connecting rods. This should be performed by a machine shop as the pistons must be installed in the correct relationship to the rod or engine damage can occur.

Fig. 270 Use a ball type cylinder hone to remove any glaze and provide a new surface for seating the piston rings

Pistons and Connecting Rods

♦ **See Figure 271**

Only pistons with the wrist pin retained by C-clips are serviceable by the home-mechanic. Press fit pistons require special presses and/or heaters to remove/install the connecting rod and should only be performed by a machine shop.

All pistons will have a mark indicating the direction to the front of the engine and the must be installed into the engine in that manner. Usually it is a notch or arrow on the top of the piston, or it may be the letter F cast or stamped into the piston.

ASSEMBLY

Before you begin assembling the engine, first give yourself a clean, dirt free work area. Next, clean every engine component again. The key to a good assembly is cleanliness.

Mount the engine block into the engine stand and wash it one last time using water and detergent (dishwashing detergent works well). While washing it, scrub

Fig. 271 Most pistons are marked to indicate positioning in the engine (usually a mark means the side facing the front)

the cylinder bores with a soft bristle brush and thoroughly clean all of the oil passages. Completely dry the engine and spray the entire assembly down with an anti-rust solution such as WD-40® or similar product. Take a clean lint-free rag and wipe up any excess anti-rust solution from the bores, bearing saddles, etc. Repeat the final cleaning process on the crankshaft. Replace any freeze or oil galley plugs which were removed during disassembly.

Crankshaft

♦ **See Figures 272, 273, 274 and 275**

1. Remove the main bearing inserts from the block and bearing caps.
2. If the crankshaft main bearing journals have been refinished to a definite undersize, install the correct undersize bearing. Be sure that the bearing inserts

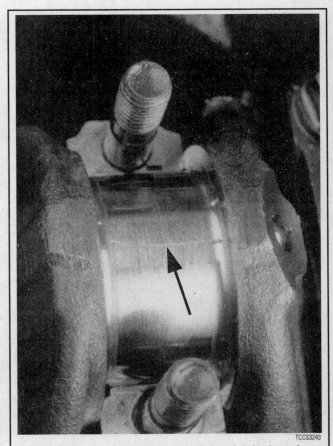

Fig. 272 Apply a strip of gauging material to the bearing journal, then install and torque the cap

Fig. 273 After the cap is removed again, use the scale supplied with the gauging material to check the clearance

Fig. 274 A dial gauge may be used to check crankshaft end-play

Fig. 275 Carefully pry the crankshaft back and forth while reading the dial gauge for end-play

and bearing bores are clean. Foreign material under inserts will distort bearing and cause failure.

3. Place the upper main bearing inserts in bores with tang in slot.

➡**The oil holes in the bearing inserts must be aligned with the oil holes in the cylinder block.**

4. Install the lower main bearing inserts in bearing caps.
5. Clean the mating surfaces of block and rear main bearing cap.
6. Carefully lower the crankshaft into place. Be careful not to damage bearing surfaces.
7. Check the clearance of each main bearing by using the following procedure:

　a. Place a piece of Plastigage® or its equivalent, on bearing surface across full width of bearing cap and about ¼ in. off center.

　b. Install cap and tighten bolts to specifications. Do not turn crankshaft while Plastigage® is in place.

　c. Remove the cap. Using the supplied Plastigage® scale, check width of Plastigage® at widest point to get maximum clearance. Difference between readings is taper of journal.

　d. If clearance exceeds specified limits, try a 0.001 in. or 0.002 in. undersize bearing in combination with the standard bearing. Bearing clearance must be within specified limits. If standard and 0.002 in. undersize bearing does not bring clearance within desired limits, refinish crankshaft journal, then install undersize bearings.

8. After the bearings have been fitted, apply a light coat of engine oil to the journals and bearings. Install the rear main bearing cap. Install all bearing caps except the thrust bearing cap. Be sure that main bearing caps are installed in original locations. Tighten the bearing cap bolts to specifications.
9. Install the thrust bearing cap with bolts finger-tight.
10. Pry the crankshaft forward against the thrust surface of upper half of bearing.
11. Hold the crankshaft forward and pry the thrust bearing cap to the rear. This aligns the thrust surfaces of both halves of the bearing.
12. Retain the forward pressure on the crankshaft. Tighten the cap bolts to specifications.

13. Measure the crankshaft end-play as follows:

　a. Mount a dial gauge to the engine block and position the tip of the gauge to read from the crankshaft end.

　b. Carefully pry the crankshaft toward the rear of the engine and hold it there while you zero the gauge.

　c. Carefully pry the crankshaft toward the front of the engine and read the gauge.

　d. Confirm that the reading is within specifications. If not, install a new thrust bearing and repeat the procedure. If the reading is still out of specifications with a new bearing, have a machine shop inspect the thrust surfaces of the crankshaft, and if possible, repair it.

14. Rotate the crankshaft so as to position the first rod journal to the bottom of its stroke.
15. Install the rear main seal.

Pistons and Connecting Rods

♦ **See Figures 276, 277, 278 and 279**

1. Before installing the piston/connecting rod assembly, oil the pistons, piston rings and the cylinder walls with light engine oil. Install connecting rod bolt protectors or rubber hose onto the connecting rod bolts/studs. Also perform the following:

　a. Select the proper ring set for the size cylinder bore.

　b. Position the ring in the bore in which it is going to be used.

　c. Push the ring down into the bore area where normal ring wear is not encountered.

　d. Use the head of the piston to position the ring in the bore so that the ring is square with the cylinder wall. Use caution to avoid damage to the ring or cylinder bore.

　e. Measure the gap between the ends of the ring with a feeler gauge. Ring gap in a worn cylinder is normally greater than specification. If the ring gap is greater than the specified limits, try an oversize ring set.

　f. Check the ring side clearance of the compression rings with a feeler gauge inserted between the ring and its lower land according to specification. The gauge should slide freely around the entire ring circumference without

Fig. 276 Checking the piston ring-to-ring groove side clearance using the ring and a feeler gauge

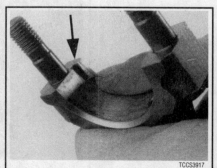

Fig. 277 The notch on the side of the bearing cap matches the tang on the bearing insert

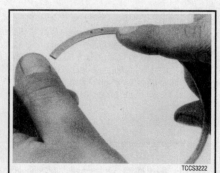

Fig. 278 Most rings are marked to show which side of the ring should face up when installed to the piston

Fig. 279 Install the piston and rod assembly into the block using a ring compressor and the handle of a hammer

binding. Any wear that occurs will form a step at the inner portion of the lower land. If the lower lands have high steps, the piston should be replaced.

2. Unless new pistons are installed, be sure to install the pistons in the cylinders from which they were removed. The numbers on the connecting rod and bearing cap must be on the same side when installed in the cylinder bore. If a connecting rod is ever transposed from one engine or cylinder to another, new bearings should be fitted and the connecting rod should be numbered to correspond with the new cylinder number. The notch on the piston head goes toward the front of the engine.

3. Install all of the rod bearing inserts into the rods and caps.

4. Install the rings to the pistons. Install the oil control ring first, then the second compression ring and finally the top compression ring. Use a piston ring expander tool to aid in installation and to help reduce the chance of breakage.

5. Make sure the ring gaps are properly spaced around the circumference of the piston. Fit a piston ring compressor around the piston and slide the piston and connecting rod assembly down into the cylinder bore, pushing it in with the wooden hammer handle. Push the piston down until it is only slightly below the top of the cylinder bore. Guide the connecting rod onto the crankshaft bearing journal carefully, to avoid damaging the crankshaft.

6. Check the bearing clearance of all the rod bearings, fitting them to the crankshaft bearing journals. Follow the procedure in the crankshaft installation above.

7. After the bearings have been fitted, apply a light coating of assembly oil to the journals and bearings.

8. Turn the crankshaft until the appropriate bearing journal is at the bottom of its stroke, then push the piston assembly all the way down until the connecting rod bearing seats on the crankshaft journal. Be careful not to allow the bearing cap screws to strike the crankshaft bearing journals and damage them.

9. After the piston and connecting rod assemblies have been installed, check the connecting rod side clearance on each crankshaft journal.

10. If equipped, install the auxiliary/balance shaft(s)/assembly(ies).

11. Prime and install the oil pump and the oil pump intake tube.

OHV Engines

CAMSHAFT, LIFTERS AND TIMING ASSEMBLY

1. Install the camshaft.
2. Install the lifters/followers into their bores.
3. Install the pushrods.
4. Install the timing gears/chain assembly.

CYLINDER HEAD(S)

1. Install the cylinder head(s) using new gaskets.
2. Assemble the rest of the valve train (pushrods and rocker arms and/or shafts).

OHC Engines

CYLINDER HEAD(S)

1. Install the cylinder head(s) using new gaskets.
2. Install the timing sprockets/gears and the belt/chain assemblies.

Engine Covers and Components

Install the timing cover(s) and oil pan. Refer to your notes and drawings made prior to disassembly and install all of the components that were removed. Install the engine into the vehicle.

Engine Start-up and Break-in

STARTING THE ENGINE

Now that the engine is installed and every wire and hose is properly connected, go back and double check that all coolant and vacuum hoses are connected. Check that you oil drain plug is installed and properly tightened. If not already done, install a new oil filter onto the engine. Fill the crankcase with the proper amount and grade of engine oil. Fill the cooling system with a 50/50 mixture of coolant/water.

1. Connect the vehicle battery.
2. Start the engine. Keep your eye on your oil pressure indicator; if it does not indicate oil pressure within 10 seconds of starting, turn the vehicle off.

✳✳ WARNING

Damage to the engine can result if it is allowed to run with no oil pressure. Check the engine oil level to make sure that it is full. Check for any leaks and if found, repair the leaks before continuing. If there is still no indication of oil pressure, you may need to prime the system.

3. Confirm that there are no fluid leaks (oil or other).
4. Allow the engine to reach normal operating temperature (the upper radiator hose will be hot to the touch).
5. If necessary, set the ignition timing.
6. Install any remaining components such as the air cleaner (if removed for ignition timing) or body panels which were removed.

BREAKING IT IN

Make the first miles on the new engine, easy ones. Vary the speed but do not accelerate hard. Most importantly, do not lug the engine, and avoid sustained high speeds until at least 100 miles. Check the engine oil and coolant levels frequently. Expect the engine to use a little oil until the rings seat. Change the oil and filter at 500 miles, 1500 miles, then every 3000 miles past that.

KEEP IT MAINTAINED

Now that you have just gone through all of that hard work, keep yourself from doing it all over again by thoroughly maintaining it. Not that you may not have maintained it before, heck you could have had one to two hundred thousand miles on it before doing this. However, you may have bought the vehicle used, and the previous owner did not keep up on maintenance. Which is why you just went through all of that hard work. See?

USING A VACUUM GAUGE

White needle = steady needle   *Dark needle = drifting needle*

The vacuum gauge is one of the most useful and easy-to-use diagnostic tools. It is inexpensive, easy to hook up, and provides valuable information about the condition of your engine.

Indication: Normal engine in good condition

Gauge reading: Steady, from 17–22 in./Hg.

Indication: Sticking valve or ignition miss

Gauge reading: Needle fluctuates from 15–20 in./Hg. at idle

Indication: Late ignition or valve timing, low compression, stuck throttle valve, leaking carburetor or manifold gasket.

Gauge reading: Low (15–20 in./Hg.) but steady

Indication: Improper carburetor adjustment, or minor intake leak at carburetor or manifold

NOTE: Bad fuel injector O-rings may also cause this reading.

Gauge reading: Drifting needle

Indication: Weak valve springs, worn valve stem guides, or leaky cylinder head gasket (vibrating excessively at all speeds).

NOTE: A plugged catalytic converter may also cause this reading.

Gauge reading: Needle fluctuates as engine speed increases

Indication: Burnt valve or improper valve clearance. The needle will drop when the defective valve operates.

Gauge reading: Steady needle, but drops regularly

Indication: Choked muffler or obstruction in system. Speed up the engine. Choked muffler will exhibit a slow drop of vacuum to zero.

Gauge reading: Gradual drop in reading at idle

Indication: Worn valve guides

Gauge reading: Needle vibrates excessively at idle, but steadies as engine speed increases

TCCS3C01

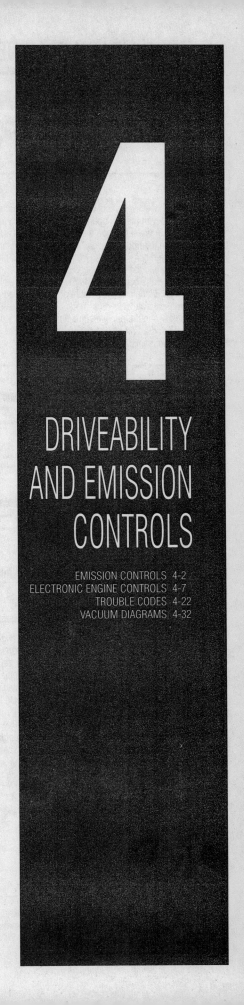

4

DRIVEABILITY AND EMISSION CONTROLS

EMISSION CONTROLS

Positive Crankcase Ventilation (PCV) System

OPERATION

▶ **See Figure 1**

The PCV valve system vents crankcase gases into the engine air intake where they are burned with the fuel and air mixture. The PCV valve system keeps pollutants from being released into the atmosphere, and also helps to keep the engine oil clean, by ridding the crankcase of moisture and corrosive fumes. The PCV valve system consists of the PCV valve, it's mounting grommet, the nipple in the air intake and the connecting hoses. On some engine applications, the PCV valve system is connected with the evaporative emission system.

The PCV valve controls the amount of vapors pulled into the intake manifold from the crankcase and acts as a check valve by preventing air flow from entering the crankcase in the opposite direction. The PCV valve also prevents combustion backfiring from entering the crankcase in order to prevent detonation of the accumulated crankcase gases.

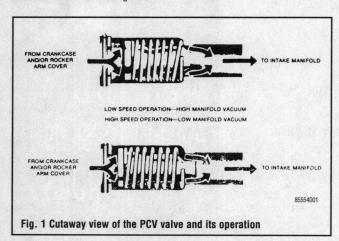

Fig. 1 Cutaway view of the PCV valve and its operation

TESTING

1. Remove the PCV valve from the valve cover or engine block mounting grommet. The PCV valve for the 2.3L and 2.5L engines is mounted in the crankcase oil vent separator in a rubber grommet near the lower intake manifold, or its ventilation hose before the connection to the throttle body. The PCV valve for the 3.0L (B Series Pick-up) and 4.0L engines is mounted in a rubber grommet, installed towards the rear of the left-hand valve cover. On the 2.6L engine, the PCV valve is located at the front of the engine, mounted in a rubber grommet on top of the valve cover. The PCV valve on the 3.0L engine (MPV) is located at the rear of the engine, mounted in a rubber grommet on the right side valve cover.
2. Shake the PCV valve. If the valve rattles when shaken, reinstall it and proceed to Step 3. If the valve does not rattle, it is sticking and must be replaced.
3. Start the engine and bring it to normal operating temperature.
4. Disconnect the closure (fresh air) hose from the air inlet tube (connects the air cleaner housing to the throttle body).
5. Place a stiff piece of paper over the hose end and wait 1 minute.
   a. If vacuum holds the paper in place, the system is OK; reconnect the hose.
   b. If the paper is not held in place, check for loose hose connections, vacuum leaks or blockage. Correct as necessary.

REMOVAL & INSTALLATION

1. Disconnect the vacuum hose from the PCV valve.
2. Remove the PCV valve from its mounting grommet.
3. To install, attach the PCV vacuum hose to the PCV valve, then insert the valve into its mounting grommet.

Evaporative Emission Control System

OPERATION

Fuel vapors trapped in the sealed fuel tank are vented through the fuel vapor valve assembly in the top of the tank, or vent cut valve at the fuel tank filler tube. The vapors leave the valve assembly through a single vapor line and continue to the carbon canister for storage until they are purged to the engine for burning.

Purging the carbon canister removes the fuel vapor stored in the carbon canister. The fuel vapor is purged via a purge control solenoid or vacuum controlled purge valve. Purging occurs when the engine is at normal operating temperature and off idle.

The evaporative emission control system consists of the following components: fuel vapor (charcoal) canister, fuel vapor valve (Navajo and 1994–97 B Series Pick-up), fuel separator (MPV), cut valve (MPV), check valve (MPV), fuel vapor canister purge solenoid, pressure/vacuum relief fuel tank filler cap, as well as, the fuel tank and fuel tank filler pipe, vapor tube and fuel vapor hoses.

Fuel Vapor (Charcoal) Canister

▶ **See Figure 2**

➡ **The fuel vapor canister is also referred to as evaporative emissions canister or charcoal canister.**

The fuel vapors from the fuel tank are stored in the fuel vapor canister until the vehicle is operated, at which time, the vapors will purge from the canister into the engine for consumption. The fuel vapor canister contains activated carbon, which absorbs the fuel vapor. The fuel vapor canister can be found in the following locations:
- 1994–95 MPV—right side rear of the engine compartment
- 1996–98 MPV—underneath the right side of the vehicle toward the front
- 1994–97 B Series Pick-up and Navajo—left side radiator support, under the hood
- 1998 B Series Pick-up—left side inner frame rail underneath the vehicle

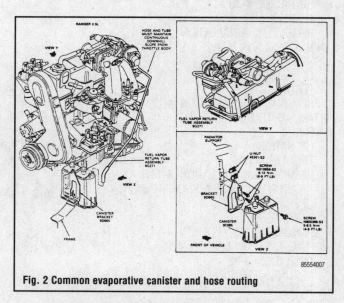

Fig. 2 Common evaporative canister and hose routing

Fuel Vapor Valve (Navajo and B Series Pick-up)

➡ **This component is also known as the evaporative emission valve on 1995–98 models.**

Fuel vapor in the fuel tank is vented to the carbon canister through the vapor valve assembly. The valve is mounted in a rubber grommet at a central location in the upper surface of the fuel tank. A vapor space between the fuel level and the tank upper surface is combined with a small orifice and float shut-off valve in the vapor valve assembly to prevent liquid fuel from passing to the carbon canister. The vapor space also allows for thermal expansion of the fuel.

Fuel Separator (MPV)

▶ See Figure 3

The fuel separator is the component that prevents fuel from flowing into the fuel vapor canister. The fuel separator is located on the right side rear wheelhouse behind the interior trim panel. The fuel separator is not serviceable and should be checked periodically for damage or leaking. Replace the separator if damage or leaking is evident.

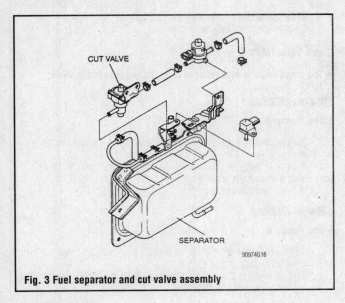

Fig. 3 Fuel separator and cut valve assembly

Cut Valve (MPV)

▶ See Figure 3

➡The cut valve was previously referred to as the check & cut valve on 1994–95 MPV models.

The cut valve is mounted on top of the fuel separator, which is located on the right side rear wheelhouse behind the interior trim panel. The cut valve when necessary, releases excessive pressure or vacuum in the fuel tank to the atmosphere.

Check Valve (MPV)

▶ See Figure 4

➡The check valve is also referred to as the two-way check valve.

On 1994–95 MPV models, the (two-way) check valve is mounted on top of the fuel separator, which is located on the right side rear wheelhouse behind the interior trim panel. On 1996–98 MPV models, the check valve is located on the right side of the engine compartment near the firewall. The check valve is used to control pressure in the fuel tank.

Canister Purge Control Solenoid

▶ See Figure 5

The canister purge control solenoid is inline with the carbon canister and controls the flow of fuel vapors out of the canister. It is normally closed. When the engine is shut **OFF**, the vapors from the fuel tank flow into the canister. After the engine is started, the solenoid is engaged and opens, purging the vapors into the engine. With the solenoid open, vapors from the fuel tank are routed directly into the engine. The canister purge control solenoid can be found in the following locations:
• 1994–95 MPV—right side front of the engine compartment next to the radiator
• 1996–98 MPV—right side of the engine compartment against the firewall

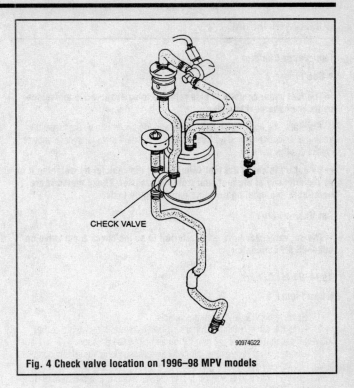

Fig. 4 Check valve location on 1996–98 MPV models

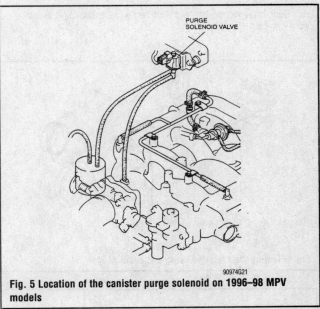

Fig. 5 Location of the canister purge solenoid on 1996–98 MPV models

• 1994–97 B Series Pick-up and Navajo—left side radiator support, under the hood
• 1998 B Series Pick-up—mounted on the fuel vapor canister

Pressure/Vacuum Relief Fuel Tank Filler Cap

The fuel cap contains an integral pressure and vacuum relief valve. The vacuum valve acts to allow air into the fuel tank to replace the fuel as it is used, while preventing vapors from escaping the tank through the atmosphere. The vacuum relief valve opens after a vacuum of approximately–0.25 psi (1.7 kPa). The pressure valve acts as a backup pressure relief valve in the event the normal venting system is overcome by excessive generation of internal pressure or restriction of the normal venting system. The pressure relief is approximately 2 psi (14 kPa). Fill cap damage or contamination that stops the pressure vacuum valve from working may result in deformation of the fuel tank.

COMPONENT TESTING

Fuel Vapor Canister

♦ See Figure 2

➡The fuel vapor canister is also referred to as evaporative emissions canister or charcoal canister.

Generally, the only testing done to the vapor canister is a visual inspection. Look the canister over and replace it with a new one if there is any evidence of cracks or other damage.

➡Do not try to check the fuel saturation of the canister by weighing it or by the intensity of the fuel odor from the canister. These methods are unreliable and inhaling gasoline fumes can be toxic.

Cut Valve (MPV)

➡The cut valve was previously referred to as the check & cut valve on 1994–95 MPV models.

1994–95 MODELS

♦ See Figure 6

1. Remove the cut valve from the vehicle.
2. Hold the valve in the horizontal position, otherwise the weight of the valve will cause it to move out of position and close the passage.
3. Connect a vacuum gauge in line to the passage which normally connects to the fuel tank — port **A**.
4. Blow air into port **A** and verify that the valve opens at a pressure of 0.79–0.99 psi (5.40-6.86kpa).
5. Remove the vacuum gauge and connect it to the passage to atmosphere— port **B**.

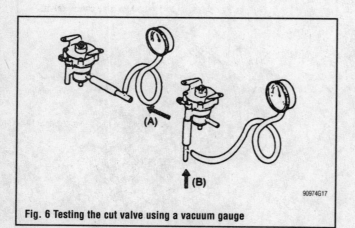

Fig. 6 Testing the cut valve using a vacuum gauge

6. Blow air into port **B** and verify that the valve opens at a pressure of 0.15–0.71 psi (0.99-4.91kpa).
7. If not as specified, replace the valve.

1996–98 MODELS

♦ See Figure 7

1. Remove the cut valve from the vehicle.
2. While holding the valve in the horizontal position, blow air into port **A** and verify that their is air flow through the valve.
3. Next, hold the valve in the tilted position and blow air through port **A** again.
4. Verify that air does not flow through the valve.
5. If not as specified, replace the cut valve.

Check Valve (MPV)

➡The check valve is also referred to as the two-way check valve.

1994–95 MODELS

♦ See Figure 8

1. Remove the check valve and blow air through port **A** and check that the air flows.
2. Blow air through the opposite side port (port **B**) and check that the air does not flow through the valve.
3. Replace the valve as required.

1996–98 MODELS

♦ See Figure 9

1. Remove the check valve and blow air through port **B** and check that the air flows smoothly through port **C**.
2. Blow air into port **C** and check that the air flows smoothly through port **A**.
3. Replace the valve as required.

Canister Purge Control Solenoid

1994 NAVAJO AND B SERIES PICK-UP MODELS

1. Remove the canister purge control solenoid.
2. Using an external voltage source, apply 9–14 DC volts to the purge solenoid electrical terminals. Then, use a hand-held vacuum pump and apply 16 in. Hg (53 kPa) vacuum to the manifold side nipple of the solenoid.
   a. If the solenoid opens and allows air to freely pass through it, the solenoid is working properly.
   b. If the solenoid does not allow air to pass freely while energized, replace the solenoid with a new one.

1995–98 B SERIES PICK-UP MODELS

1. Remove the canister purge control solenoid.
2. Measure the resistance between the two solenoid terminals.

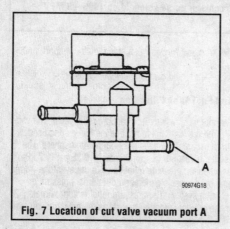

Fig. 7 Location of cut valve vacuum port A

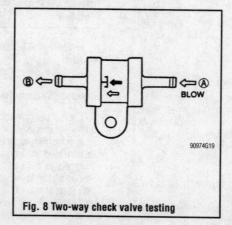

Fig. 8 Two-way check valve testing

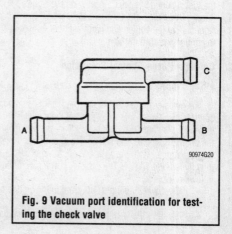

Fig. 9 Vacuum port identification for testing the check valve

a. If the resistance is between 30–90 ohms, proceed to the Step 3.

b. If the resistance is not between 30–90 ohms, replace the solenoid.

3. Attach a hand-held vacuum pump to the intake manifold vacuum side of the purge solenoid, then apply 16 in. Hg (53 kPa) of vacuum to the solenoid.

a. If the solenoid will not hold vacuum for at least 20 seconds replace it with a new one.

b. If the solenoid holds vacuum, proceed to Step 4. Keep the vacuum applied to the solenoid.

4. Using an external voltage source, apply 9–14 DC volts to the solenoid electrical terminals.

a. If the solenoid opens and the vacuum drops, the solenoid is working properly.

b. If the solenoid does not open and the vacuum remains, replace the solenoid with a new one.

MPV MODELS

▶ See Figure 10

1. Start the vehicle and warm the engine.

2. Disconnect the vacuum hose (usually white) closest to the wire connector from the solenoid valve.

3. Verify there is no vacuum at the solenoid valve at idle speed.

4. If there is vacuum at the solenoid valve, turn the engine OFF.

5. Disconnect the other vacuum hose and apply air pressure. Verify that no air flows through the valve.

6. Next, supply 12 volts to the terminals of the solenoid. Apply air pressure (port A) and verify that air does flow through the valve.

7. If not as specified, replace the solenoid valve.

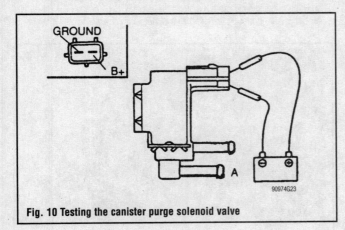

Fig. 10 Testing the canister purge solenoid valve

REMOVAL & INSTALLATION

Fuel Vapor Canister

➡The fuel vapor canister is also referred to as evaporative emissions canister or charcoal canister.

1. If the fuel vapor canister is mounted underneath the vehicle, raise and safely support the vehicle.

2. Disconnect the vapor hoses from the canister.

3. Remove the mounting screws, then remove the canister.

To install:

4. Position the canister in place, then install the mounting screws.

5. Attach all of the vapor hoses to the canister.

6. If the vehicle was raised, lower it to the ground.

Fuel Vapor Valve (Navajo and B Series Pick-up)

➡This component is also known as the evaporative emission valve on 1995–98 models.

1. Disconnect the negative battery cable.

2. Relieve the fuel system pressure.

3. Remove the fuel tank.

4. Remove the fuel vapor valve from the fuel tank by rotating the valve counterclockwise.

To install:

5. Install the fuel vapor valve into the fuel tank and secure it by rotating it clockwise.

6. Install the fuel tank in the vehicle.

7. Connect the negative battery cable.

Fuel Separator (MPV)

▶ See Figure 3

1. Disconnect the negative battery cable.

2. Remove the right rear interior side trim.

3. Remove the cover.

4. Label and disconnect the hoses from the separator.

5. Loosen the mounting fasteners and remove the fuel separator from the vehicle.

6. Installation is the reverse of the removal procedure.

Cut Valve (MPV)

▶ See Figure 3

➡The cut valve was previously referred to as the check & cut valve on 1994–95 MPV models.

1. Disconnect the negative battery cable.

2. Remove the right rear interior side trim.

3. Remove the cover.

4. Label and disconnect the evaporative gas hoses.

5. Loosen the mounting fasteners and remove the fuel separator/cut valve assembly from the vehicle.

6. Separate the cut valve from the fuel separator.

7. Installation is the reverse of the removal procedure.

Check Valve (MPV)

➡The check valve is also referred to as the two-way check valve.

1994–95 MODELS

▶ See Figure 3

1. Disconnect the negative battery cable.

2. Remove the right rear interior side trim.

3. Remove the cover.

4. Label and disconnect the evaporative gas hoses.

5. Loosen the mounting fasteners and remove the fuel separator/cut/check valve assembly from the vehicle.

6. Separate the (two-way) check valve from the fuel separator.

7. Installation is the reverse of the removal procedure.

1996–98 MODELS

▶ See Figure 4

1. Loosen each hose clamp to the check valve.

2. Pull each evaporative gas hose from the check valve.

3. Remove the check valve from the vehicle.

4. Installation is the reverse of the removal procedure.

Canister Purge Control Solenoid

1. If on the 1998 B Series Pick-up, raise and safely support the vehicle.

2. Disconnect the vapor hoses from the canister purge control solenoid.

3. Unplug the electrical connector from the purge solenoid.

➡The canister purge control solenoid is either secured into place with screw(s), or clipped onto a mounting bracket.

4. Remove the purge solenoid valve from the vehicle.

To install:

5. Install the purge solenoid, then attach the engine wiring harness connector to the solenoid.

6. Connect the vapor hoses to the solenoid.

7. If on the 1998 B Series Pick-up, lower the vehicle.

Exhaust Gas Recirculation (EGR) System

OPERATION

The Exhaust Gas Recirculation (EGR) system is designed to reintroduce exhaust gas into the combustion chambers, thereby lowering combustion temperatures and reducing the formation of Oxides of Nitrogen (NO_x).

The amount of exhaust gas that is reintroduced into the combustion cycle is determined by several factors, such as: engine speed, engine vacuum, exhaust system backpressure, coolant temperature, throttle position. All EGR valves are vacuum operated. The EGR vacuum diagram for your particular vehicle is displayed on the Vehicle Emission Control Information (VECI) label.

The EGR system is a Pressure Feedback EGR (PFE) or Differential PFE (DPFE) system, controlled by the Powertrain Control Module (PCM) and composed of the following components: PFE or DPFE sensor (also referred to as the backpressure transducer), EGR Vacuum Regulator (EVR) solenoid, EGR valve, and assorted hoses and tubing.

COMPONENT TESTING

♦ See Figure 11

System Integrity Inspection

Check the EGR system hoses and connections for looseness, pinching, leaks, splitting, blockage, etc. Ensure that the EGR valve mounting bolts are not loose, or that the flange gasket is not damaged. If the system appears to be in good shape, proceed to the EGR vacuum test, otherwise repair the damaged components.

EGR System Vacuum Test

➡The EVR solenoid has a constant internal leak; this is normal. There may be a small vacuum signal, however, it should be less than 1.0 in. Hg (3.4 kPa) of vacuum.

Start the engine and allow it to run until normal operating temperature is reached. With the engine running at idle, detach the vacuum supply hose from the EGR valve and install a vacuum gauge to the hose. The vacuum reading should be less than 1.0 in. Hg (3.4 kPa) of vacuum. If the vacuum is greater than that specified, the problem may lie with the EVR solenoid.

EVR Solenoid Test

1. Remove the EVR solenoid.
2. Attempt to lightly blow air into the EVR solenoid.
   a. If air blows through the solenoid, replace the solenoid with a new one.
   b. If air does not pass freely through the solenoid, continue with the test.

3. Apply battery voltage (approximately 12 volts) and a ground to the EVR solenoid electrical terminals. Attempt to lightly blow air, once again, through the solenoid.
   a. If air does not pass through the solenoid, replace the solenoid with a new one.
   b. If air does not flow through the solenoid, the solenoid is OK.

EGR Valve Function Test

♦ See Figure 12

1. Install a tachometer on the engine, following the manufacturer's instructions.
2. Detach the engine wiring harness connector from the Idle Air Control (IAC) solenoid.
3. Disconnect and plug the vacuum supply hose from the EGR valve.
4. Start the engine, then apply the parking brake, block the rear wheels and position the transmission in Neutral.
5. Observe and note the idle speed.

➡If the engine will not idle with the IAC solenoid disconnected, provide an air bypass to the engine by slightly opening the throttle plate or by creating an intake vacuum leak. Do not allow the idle speed to exceed typical idle rpm.

6. Using a hand-held vacuum pump, slowly apply 5–10 in. Hg (17–34 kPa) of vacuum to the EGR valve nipple.
   a. If the idle speed drops more than 100 rpm with the vacuum applied and returns to normal after the vacuum is removed, the EGR valve is OK.
   b. If the idle speed does not drop more than 100 rpm with the vacuum applied and return to normal after the vacuum is removed, inspect the EGR valve for a blockage; clean it if a blockage is found. Replace the EGR valve if no blockage is found, or if cleaning the valve does not remedy the malfunction.

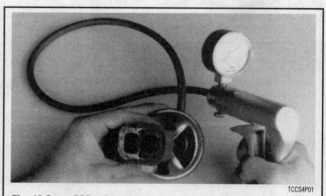

Fig. 12 Some EGR valves may be tested using a vacuum pump by watching for diaphragm movement

REMOVAL & INSTALLATION

PFE/DPFE Sensor

➡This component is found on all engines, and is also referred to as the backpressure transducer.

1. Disconnect the negative battery cable.
2. Detach and label the wiring harness connector from the PFE/DPFE sensor.
3. Disconnect all of the hoses from the sensor.
4. Remove the mounting nuts, then separate the sensor from the mounting bracket.
5. If necessary, remove the EVR solenoid and the PFE/DPFE mounting bracket from the upper intake manifold.
   To install:
6. If removed, install the EVR solenoid and mounting bracket onto the upper intake manifold.
7. If applicable, install the EGR tube heat shield.
8. Position the PFE/DPFE sensor on the mounting bracket, then install and tighten the mounting nuts until snug.

1. Throttle body
2. EGR valve
3. EGR valve bolts
4. EGR valve to exhaust manifold tube nut
5. EGR valve to exhaust manifold tube
6. EGR manifold (LH)
7. EGR valve to exhaust manifold

FRONT OF ENGINE

89684G09

Fig. 11 Exploded view of the EGR system and related components for the 3.0L engine—others similar

9. Attach all necessary hoses and wiring to the sensor.
10. Connect the negative battery cable.

EGR Vacuum Regulator (EVR) Solenoid

➡The EVR solenoid is mounted either on the same bracket as the PFE/DPFE sensor, attached to the upper intake manifold, or near the EGR valve on its own bracket.

1. Disconnect the negative battery cable.
2. Label and detach the wiring harness connector from the EVR solenoid.
3. Detach the main emission vacuum control connector from the solenoid.
4. Remove the retaining nuts, then separate the solenoid from the mounting bracket.

To install:

5. Position the solenoid on its mounting bracket and install the retaining nuts.
6. Attach the main emission vacuum control connector and the wiring harness connector to the EVR solenoid.
7. Connect the negative battery cable.

EGR Valve

1. Disconnect the negative battery cable.
2. If necessary, remove the air inlet tube from the throttle body and air cleaner housing.
3. Label and detach all vacuum hoses from the EGR valve.
4. Label and detach any electrical wiring harness connectors from the EGR valve.
5. Disconnect the EGR valve-to-exhaust manifold tube from the EGR valve.
6. Remove the EGR valve mounting fasteners, then separate the valve from the upper intake manifold.
7. Remove and discard the old EGR valve gasket, and clean the gasket mating surfaces on the valve and the intake manifold.

To install:

8. Install the EGR valve, along with a new gasket, on the upper intake manifold, then install and tighten the mounting bolts to 15–22 ft. lbs. (20–30 Nm).
9. Connect the EGR valve-to-exhaust manifold tube to the valve, then tighten the tube nut to 25–35 ft. lbs. (34–48 Nm) on 1994–97 models, or 15–20 ft. lbs. (20–28 Nm) on 1998 models.
10. Connect all wiring or hoses to the EGR valve.
11. Install the air inlet tube.
12. Connect the negative battery cable.

Emission Maintenance Warning Lights

RESETTING

Navajo and B Series Pick-up Models

All vehicles are equipped with a "CHECK ENGINE" or warning light located on the instrument cluster. This light should come on briefly when the ignition key is turned **ON**, but should turn off when the engine starts. If the light does not come ON when the ignition key is turned **ON** or if it comes ON and stays ON when the engine is running, there is a malfunction in the electronic engine control system. After the malfunction has been remedied, using the proper procedures, the "CHECK ENGINE" light will go out.

MPV Models

Federal and Canadian vehicles are equipped with a mileage sensor which is linked to the odometer. At every 80,000 miles (128,744 km), the mileage sensor will cause the Malfunction Indicator Light (MIL) to illuminate, indicating that the oxygen sensor must be replaced.

After replacing the oxygen sensor, remove the instrument cluster and reset the MIL by reversing the position of the MIL set screw.

ELECTRONIC ENGINE CONTROLS

All vehicles covered in this manual are utilize an electronic multi-port fuel injection system. The heart of this system is a micro-processor called the Powertrain Control Module (PCM) or Electronic Control Module (ECM). The PCM/ECM receives data from a number of sensors and other electronic components (switches, relay, etc.). Based on information received and information programmed in the PCM/ECM's memory, it generates output signals to control various relay, solenoids and other actuators. The PCM/ECM in this system has calibration modules located inside the assembly that contain calibration specifications for optimizing emissions, fuel economy and driveability. The calibration module is called a PROM.

The following are the electronic engine controls used by MPV, Navajo and B Series Pick-ups:

- Powertrain Control Module (PCM)
- Throttle Position (TP) sensor
- Mass Air Flow (MAF) sensor
- Intake Air Temperature (IAT) sensor
- Idle Air Control (IAC) valve
- Engine Coolant Temperature (ECT) sensor
- Heated Oxygen Sensor (HO2S)
- Camshaft Position (CMP) sensor
- Knock Sensor (KS)
- Vehicle Speed Sensor (VSS)
- Crankshaft Position (CKP) sensor

The MAF sensor (a potentiometer) senses the position of the airflow in the engine's air induction system and generates a voltage signal that varies with the amount of air drawn into the engine. The IAT sensor (a sensor in the area of the MAF sensor) measures the temperature of the incoming air and transmits a corresponding electrical signal. Another temperature sensor (the ECT sensor) inserted in the engine coolant tells if the engine is cold or warmed up. The TP sensor, a switch that senses throttle plate position, produces electrical signals that tell the PCM when the throttle is closed or wide open. A special probe (the HO2S) in the exhaust manifold measures the amount of oxygen in the exhaust gas, which is in indication of combustion efficiency, and sends a signal to the PCM. The sixth signal, camshaft position information, is transmitted by the CMP sensor, installed in place of the distributor (engines with distributorless ignition), or integral with the distributor.

The microcomputer circuit processes the input signals and produces output control signals to the fuel injectors to regulate fuel discharged to the injectors. It also adjusts ignition spark timing to provide the best balance between driveability and economy, and controls the IAC valve to maintain the proper idle speed.

➡Because of the complicated nature of this system, special tools and procedures are necessary for testing and troubleshooting.

Powertrain Control Module (PCM)/Electronic Control Module (ECM)

OPERATION

The PCM/ECM performs many functions on your car. The module accepts information from various engine sensors and computes the required fuel flow rate necessary to maintain the correct amount of air/fuel ratio throughout the entire engine operational range.

Based on the information that is received and programmed into the PCM's memory, the PCM generates output signals to control relays, actuators and solenoids. The PCM also sends out a command to the fuel injectors that meters the appropriate quantity of fuel. The module automatically senses and compensates for any changes in altitude when driving your vehicle.

REMOVAL & INSTALLATION

B Series Pick-up and Navajo Models

▶ See Figures 13 and 14

The module is mounted under the hood on the firewall. On 1994 models, it is mounted low on the firewall, near the left-hand fender (drivers side). On

1995–98 models, it is mounted high on the firewall offset to the right-hand side of center.

1. Disconnect the negative battery cable.
2. Disengage the wiring harness connector from the PCM by loosening the connector retaining bolt, then pulling the connector from the module.
3. Remove the two nuts and the PCM cover.
4. Remove the PCM from the bracket by pulling the unit outward.

To install:
5. Install the PCM in the mounting bracket.
6. Install the PCM cover and tighten the two nuts.
7. Attach the wiring harness connector to the module, then tighten the connector retaining bolt.
8. Connect the negative battery cable.

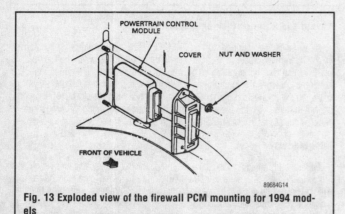

Fig. 13 Exploded view of the firewall PCM mounting for 1994 models

MPV Models

▶ See Figure 15

The PCM/ECM is mounted in the vehicle's interior, under the dashboard on the right (passenger) side.

1. Disconnect the negative battery cable.
2. Remove the right side scuff plate and right front side trim.
3. Lift up the front mat.
4. Remove the protector cover.
5. Unplug the wiring harness connector from the control module.
6. Loosen the mounting fasteners and remove the PCM/ECM from the vehicle.

To install:
7. Place the PCM into the vehicle in correct position.
8. Install the mounting fasteners and tighten to 70–95 inch lbs. (8–10 Nm).
9. Plug the wiring harness connector into the PCM/ECM.
10. Install the protector cover and place the mat back in proper position.
11. Install the right front side trim and the right side scuff plate.
12. Connect the negative battery cable.

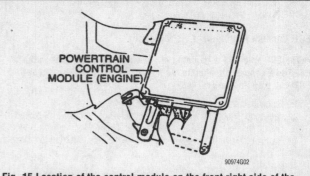

Fig. 15 Location of the control module on the front right side of the interior

OPERATION

The oxygen sensor supplies the computer with a signal which indicates a rich or lean condition during engine operation. The input information assists the computer in determining the proper air/fuel ratio. A low voltage signal from the sensor indicates too much oxygen in the exhaust (lean condition) and, conversely, a high voltage signal indicates too little oxygen in the exhaust (rich condition).

The oxygen sensors are threaded into the exhaust manifold and/or exhaust pipes on all vehicles. Heated oxygen sensors are used on some models to allow the engine to reach the closed loop faster.

TESTING

B Series Pick-up and Navajo Models

✵✵ WARNING

Do not pierce the wires when testing this sensor; this can lead to wiring harness damage. Back probe the connector to properly read the voltage of the HO2S.

1. Disconnect the HO2S.
2. Measure the resistance between PWR and GND terminals of the sensor. If the reading is approximately 6 ohms at 68°F (20°C), the sensor's heater element is in good condition.
3. With the HO2S connected and engine running, measure the voltage with a Digital Volt-Ohmmeter (DVOM) between terminals **HO2S** and **SIG RTN** (GND) of the oxygen sensor connector. If the voltage readings are swinging rapidly between 0.01–1.1 volts, the sensor is probably okay.

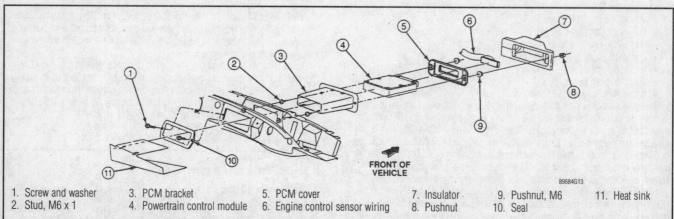

1. Screw and washer
2. Stud, M6 x 1
3. PCM bracket
4. Powertrain control module
5. PCM cover
6. Engine control sensor wiring
7. Insulator
8. Pushnut
9. Pushnut, M6
10. Seal
11. Heat sink

Fig. 14 Exploded view of the firewall PCM mounting for 1995–98 models

MPV Models w/2.6L Engine

▶ See Figure 16

➡MPV models equipped with the 2.6L engine do not have Heated Oxygen Sensors (HO2S), but instead, are equipped with Oxygen Sensors (O2S), which do not contain an integral heating element.

✳ WARNING

Do not pierce the wires when testing this sensor; this can lead to wiring harness damage. Back probe the connector to properly read the voltage of the O2S.

1. Warm up the engine and allow it to run at idle.
2. Disconnect the O2S.
3. Connect a voltmeter between the O2S and a good ground.
4. Run the engine at 4,500 rpm until the voltmeter reading indicates approximately 0.7V.
5. Increase and decrease the engine speed suddenly several times. Check to see that when the speed is increased, the voltmeter reads between 0.5V–1.0V and when the speed is decreased, the reading is between 0V–0.4V.
6. If the actual readings are out of specifications, replace the O2S.

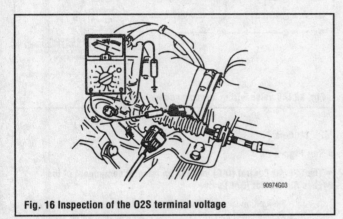

Fig. 16 Inspection of the O2S terminal voltage

MPV Models w/3.0L Engine

1994–95

▶ See Figures 17 and 18

✳ WARNING

Do not pierce the wires when testing this sensor; this can lead to wiring harness damage. Back probe the connector to properly read the voltage of the HO2S.

1. Warm up the engine and allow it to run at idle.
2. Disconnect the HO2S.

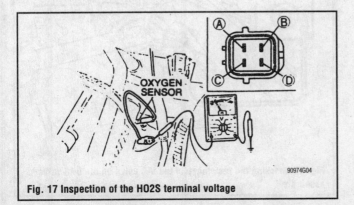

Fig. 17 Inspection of the HO2S terminal voltage

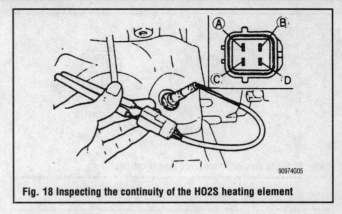

Fig. 18 Inspecting the continuity of the HO2S heating element

3. Connect a voltmeter between the HO2S connector terminals A and B on the sensor side.
4. Increase and decrease the engine speed suddenly several times. Check to see that when the speed is increased, the voltmeter reads between 0.5V–1.0V and when the speed is decreased, the reading is between 0V–0.4V.
5. If the actual readings are out of specifications, replace the O2S.
6. Inspect the continuity of the HO2S heating element by connecting an ohmmeter between connector terminals D and C on the sensor side.
7. If there is no continuity, replace the HO2S.

1996–98

▶ See Figures 19 and 20

✳ WARNING

Do not pierce the wires when testing this sensor; this can lead to wiring harness damage. Back probe the connector to properly read the voltage of the HO2S.

1. Connect NGS tester 49-T088-001 and 49-T088-002 scan tools or equivalent to the data link connector-2 located under the driver side dashboard.
2. Select the "PID/DATA MONITOR AND RECORD" function on the NGS tester display.
3. Select "FHO2S" and "RHO2S" on the NGS tester display. The NGS tester measures and displays the voltage.
4. The specifications should read as follows:
- With the ignition ON, or at idle: 0V–1.0V
- At deceleration: 0V–0.5V
- At acceleration: 0.5V–1.0V
5. If the readings are out of specifications, inspect the intake air, fuel and On-board diagnostic systems.
6. If these systems are working properly, replace the HO2S.
7. Disengage the HO2S wiring connector.
8. Inspect the continuity of the HO2S heating element by connecting an ohmmeter between connector terminals D and C on the sensor side.
9. If the reading is measures approximately 13 ohms at 68°F (20°C). the sensor's heating element is in good condition.
10. If there is no continuity, replace the HO2S.

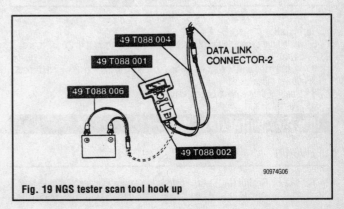

Fig. 19 NGS tester scan tool hook up

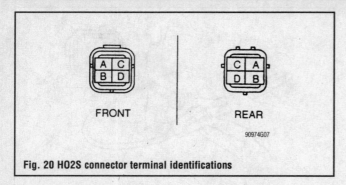

Fig. 20 HO2S connector terminal identifications

REMOVAL & INSTALLATION

♦ See Figure 21

➡1994–95 MPV models equipped with the 2.6L engine use 1 Oxygen Sensor (O2S). 1994–95 MPV models equipped with the 3.0L engine use 1 Heated Oxygen Sensor (HO2S). These sensors are located on the exhaust pipe between the exhaust manifold and the catalytic converter. 1996–98 MPV models use 2 HO2 sensors. V6 equipped B Series Pick-up models use three HO2S's, and 2.3L engines use two HO2S's for the engine control system. The heated sensors are located before and after the dual converters in the exhaust pipes. On 1994–95 V6 engines, there are two sensors, one is located in the left exhaust manifold and the other in the dual converter Y-pipe. The 1994–95 2.3L engines use only one sensor.

1. Disconnect the negative battery cable.
2. Raise and safely support the vehicle on jackstands.
3. Disconnect the HO2S from the engine control sensor wiring.

➡If excessive force is needed to remove the sensors, lubricate the sensor with penetrating oil prior to removal.

4. Remove the sensors with a sensor removal tool, such as Ford Tool T94P-9472-A.

Fig. 21 Using the proper wrench, loosen the oxygen sensor. Ensure that the wire and connector are unplugged

To install:
5. Install the sensor in the mounting boss, then tighten it to 27–33 ft. lbs. (37–45 Nm).
6. Reattach the sensor electrical wiring connector to the engine wiring harness.
7. Lower the vehicle.
8. Connect the negative battery cable.

Idle Air Control (IAC) Valve

OPERATION

The Idle Air Control (IAC) valve controls the engine idle speed and dashpot functions. The valve is located on the side of the throttle body. This valve allows air, determined by the Powertrain Control Module (PCM) and controlled by a duty cycle signal, to bypass the throttle plate in order to maintain the proper idle speed.

TESTING

B Series Pick-up and Navajo Models

♦ See Figure 22

1. Turn the ignition switch to the **OFF** position.
2. Disengage the wiring harness connector from the IAC valve .
3. Using an ohmmeter, measure the resistance between the terminals of the valve.

➡Due to the diode in the solenoid, place the ohmmeter positive lead on the VPWR terminal and the negative lead on the ISC terminal.

4. If the resistance is not 7–13 ohms, replace the IAC valve.

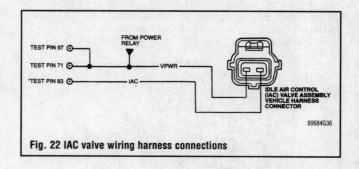

Fig. 22 IAC valve wiring harness connections

MPV Models

♦ See Figure 23

➡The Idle Air Control (IAC) valve is an integral component of the Bypass Air Control (BAC) valve.

1. Turn the ignition switch to the **OFF** position.
2. Disengage the wiring harness connector from the IAC valve .
3. Using an ohmmeter, measure the resistance between the terminals of the valve.
4. The resistance should measure 10.7–12.3 ohms at 68° F (20° C) for 3.0L equipped models and 7.7–9.3 ohms at 73° F (23° C) for 2.6L engine equipped models.
5. If the resistance does not measure within specifications, replace the BAC valve.

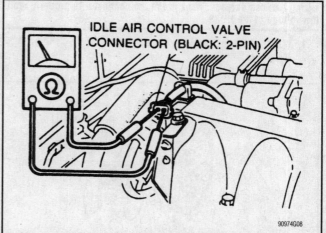

Fig. 23 Checking the resistance of the IAC valve on the BAC valve assembly

REMOVAL & INSTALLATION

B Series Pick-up Models

▶ **See Figures 24 and 25**

1. Disconnect the negative battery cable.
2. Disengage the wiring harness connector from the IAC valve.
3. Remove the two retaining screws, then remove the IAC valve and discard the old gasket.

To install:

4. Clean the IAC valve mounting surface on the throttle body of old gasket material.
5. Using a new gasket, position the IAC valve on the throttle body. Install and tighten the retaining screws to 71–106 inch lbs. (8–12 Nm).
6. Attach the wiring harness connector to the IAC valve.
7. Connect the negative battery cable.

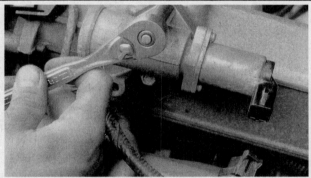

89684P04

Fig. 24 Next, remove the two IAC valve attaching bolts . . .

89684P05

Fig. 25 . . . and pull the valve from the intake manifold

MPV Models

▶ **See Figure 26**

➡ **The Idle Air Control (IAC) valve is an integral component of the Bypass Air Control (BAC) valve.**

1. Disconnect the negative battery cable.
2. Disconnect the water hoses (if equipped) and air hose from the BAC/IAC valve.
3. Disengage the wiring harness connector from the BAC/IAC valve.
4. Remove the mounting fasteners from the valve assembly.
5. Remove the BAC/IAC valve assembly, along with the mounting gasket and O-ring from the vehicle.

To install:

6. Remove any foreign material from the contact surface.
7. Install the BAC/IAC valve assembly, with a new mounting gasket and O-ring, onto the engine in correct position.

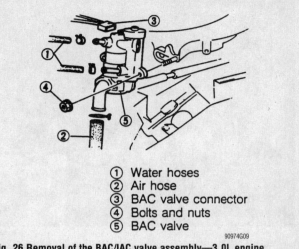

① Water hoses
② Air hose
③ BAC valve connector
④ Bolts and nuts
⑤ BAC valve

90974G09

Fig. 26 Removal of the BAC/IAC valve assembly—3.0L engine shown

8. Install and tighten the mounting fasteners to 14–18 ft. lbs. (19–25 Nm) on 3.0L engines, and 22–30 inch lbs. (2.5–3.4 Nm) on 2.6L engines.
9. Plug in the valve wiring harness connector.
10. Connect the air hose and water hoses (if equipped) to the valve assembly.
11. Connect the negative battery cable.
12. If equipped with water hoses, verify that the valve assembly does not leak.

Engine Coolant Temperature (ECT) Sensor

OPERATION

The engine coolant temperature sensor resistance changes in response to engine coolant temperature. The sensor resistance decreases as the surrounding temperature increases. This provides a reference signal to the PCM, which indicates engine coolant temperature.

The ECT sensor is mounted on the lower intake manifold near the water outlet/thermostat housing, except on 2.3L and 2.5L engines. On the 2.3L and 2.5L engine the ECT is mounted on the water outlet/thermostat housing.

TESTING

▶ **See Figures 27, 28, 29 and 30**

1. Disengage the engine wiring harness connector from the ECT sensor.
2. Connect an ohmmeter between the ECT sensor terminals, and set the ohmmeter scale on 200,000 ohms.
3. With the engine cold and the ignition switch in the **OFF** position, measure and note the ECT sensor resistance. Attach the engine wiring harness connector to the sensor.
4. Start the engine and allow the engine to warm up to normal operating temperature.
5. Once the engine has reached normal operating temperature, turn the engine **OFF**
6. Once again, detach the engine wiring harness connector from the ECT sensor.
7. Measure and note the ECT sensor resistance, then compare the cold and hot ECT sensor resistance measurements with the accompanying chart.
8. Replace the ECT sensor if the readings do not approximate those in the chart, otherwise reattach the engine wiring harness connector to the sensor.

REMOVAL & INSTALLATION

▶ **See Figure 31**

1. Partially drain the engine cooling system until the coolant level is below the ECT sensor mounting hole.

Fig. 27 Checking the resistance of the engine coolant temperature sensor still installed on the engine

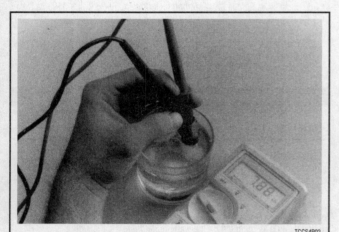

Fig. 28 If the sensor is removed, submerge the end of the coolant temperature sensor in cold or hot water and check resistance

IAT/ECT SENSOR VOLTAGE AND RESISTANCE SPECIFICATIONS

Temperature		Engine Coolant/Intake Air Temperature Sensor Values	
°C	°F	Voltage (volts)	Resistance (K ohms)
120	248	0.27	1.18
110	230	0.35	1.55
100	212	0.46	2.07
90	194	0.60	2.80
80	176	0.78	3.84
70	158	1.02	5.37
60	140	1.33	7.70
50	122	1.70	10.97
40	104	2.13	16.15
30	86	2.60	24.27
20	68	3.07	37.30
10	50	3.51	58.75

89684G37

Fig. 29 IAT and ECT sensor specifications chart—B Series Pick-up and Navajo models

Coolant	Resistance
−20°C (−4°F)	14.5 —17.8 kΩ
20°C (68°F)	2.2 — 2.7 kΩ
80°C (176°F)	0.28— 0.35 kΩ

90974G10

Fig. 30 ECT sensor specifications chart—MPV models

Fig. 31 Most ECT sensors (arrow) can be found on the intake manifold, near the water outlet housing

2. Disconnect the negative battery cable.
3. Detach the wiring harness connector from the ECT sensor.
4. Using an open-end wrench, remove the coolant temperature sensor from the intake manifold or thermostat housing.

To install:

5. Thread the sensor into the intake manifold, or thermostat housing, by hand, then tighten it securely.
6. Connect the negative battery cable.
7. Refill the engine cooling system.
8. Start the engine, check for coolant leaks and top off the cooling system.

Intake Air Temperature (IAT) Sensor

OPERATION

The Intake Air Temperature (IAT) sensor resistance changes in response to the intake air temperature. The sensor resistance decreases as the surrounding air temperature increases. This provides a signal to the PCM indicating the temperature of the incoming air charge.

Most engines mount the IAT sensor in the air cleaner-to-throttle body supply tube. However, some earlier engines have it mounted to the upper intake manifold.

TESTING

◊ **See Figures 29 and 32**

➡The 1994–95 MPV models equipped with the 3.0L engine utilize 2 IAT sensors. The one mounted in the upper intake manifold and the other, which is an integral component of the volume air flow sensor. The one covered here is mounted in the upper intake manifold.

Turn the ignition switch **OFF**.

1. Disengage the wiring harness connector from the IAT sensor.
2. Using a Digital Volt-Ohmmeter (DVOM), measure the resistance between the two sensor terminals.
3. Compare the resistance reading with the accompanying chart. If the reading for a given temperature is approximately that shown in the table, the IAT sensor is okay.
4. Attach the wiring harness connector to the sensor.

Temperature	Resistance (kΩ)
25°C (77°F)	29.7—36.3
85°C (185°F)	3.3—3.7

90974G11

Fig. 32 IAT sensor specifications chart—MPV models

REMOVAL & INSTALLATION

▶ **See Figures 33 and 34**

1. Disconnect the negative battery cable.
2. Disengage the wiring harness connector from the IAT sensor.
3. Remove the sensor from the air cleaner outlet tube.

To install:

4. Wipe down the IAT sensor mounting boss to clean the sensor area of all dirt and grime.
5. Install the sensor into the air cleaner outlet tube (B Series Pick-up and Navajo) or upper intake manifold assembly securely.
6. Attach the wiring harness connector to the IAT sensor.
7. Connect the negative battery cable.

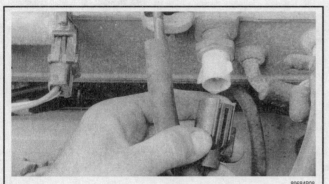

Fig. 33 To remove the IAT sensor, disconnect the wire harness plug . . .

Fig. 34 . . . then loosen and remove the sensor from its mounting boss

Mass Air Flow (MAF) Sensor

OPERATION

The Mass Air Flow (MAF) sensor directly measures the amount of the air flowing into the engine. The sensor is mounted between the air cleaner assembly and the air cleaner outlet tube.

The sensor utilizes a hot wire sensing element to measure the amount of air entering the engine. The sensor does this by sending a signal, generated by the sensor when the incoming air cools the hot wire down, to the PCM. The signal is used by the PCM to calculate the injector pulse width, which controls the air/fuel ratio in the engine. The sensor and plastic housing are integral and must be replaced if found to be defective.

The sensing element (hot wire) is a thin platinum wire wound on a ceramic bobbin and coated with glass. This hot wire is maintained at 392°F (200°C) above the ambient temperature as measured by a constant "cold wire".

TESTING

Navajo and B Series Pick-up Models

▶ **See Figure 35**

1. With the engine running at idle, use a DVOM to verify there is at least 10.5 volts between terminals **A** and **B** of the MAF sensor connector. This indicates the power input to the sensor is correct. Then, measure the voltage between MAF sensor connector terminals **C** and **D**. If the reading is approximately 0.34–1.96 volts, the sensor is functioning properly.

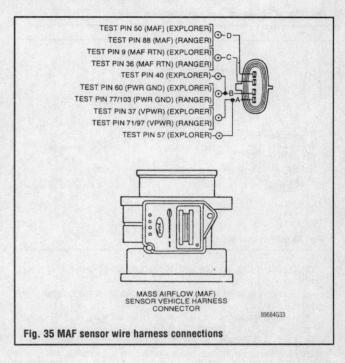

Fig. 35 MAF sensor wire harness connections

MPV Models

1994–95—2.6L ENGINE

▶ **See Figures 36, 37 and 38**

1. Remove the rubber boot from the Mass Air Flow (MAF) sensor wiring connector.
2. Using a voltmeter, measure the terminal voltages. Refer to the specifications chart.
3. If not as specified, inspect the wiring harness for an open or short circuit. If the wiring is okay, check the burn off operation as follows:
    a. Disconnect the negative battery cable for 20 seconds and reconnect it.
    b. Start the engine and allow it to warm up to operating temperature.

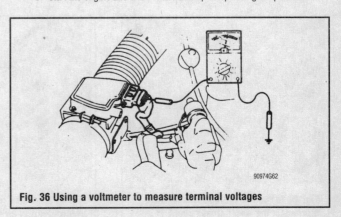

Fig. 36 Using a voltmeter to measure terminal voltages

Condition Terminal wire	Ignition switch ON	Engine running
B/W (Power supply)	B+	
G/O (Burn-off)	0V	
G/B (Airflow mass)	1.0—2.0V	1.9—5V
B/W (Ground)	0V	
B/O (Ground)	0V	

B+: Battery positive voltage

90974G63

Fig. 37 MAF sensor voltage specifications chart

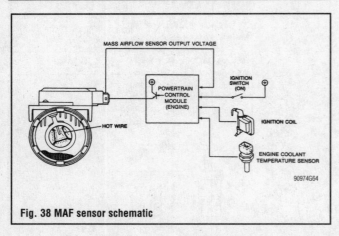

Fig. 38 MAF sensor schematic

c. Remove the rubber boot from the Mass Air Flow (MAF) sensor wiring connector.

d. Run the engine for more than 5 seconds at approximately 2000 rpm in neutral.

e. Turn the ignition switch OFF and check the voltage at the MAF sensor terminal wire (G/O) and terminal 2H of the powertrain control module. There should be 0 volts just after the ignition switch is turned OFF, then approximately 8 volts battery positive voltage momentarily 2–5 seconds after turning the ignition switch OFF.

4. If not as specified, replace the MAF sensor.

1996–98—3.0L ENGINE

▶ See Figure 39

1. Inspect the MAF sensor for damage and cracks.
2. Start the engine and allow it to warm up to operating temperature.
3. Shift the gear selector lever to the **P** (PARK) position.
4. Make sure that all electrical loads are turned OFF. (Ex. headlights, blower motor, etc.)
5. Connect the New Generation Star (NGS) tester, or equivalent scan tool, to the data link connector, located under the driver side dashboard.

90974G65

Fig. 39 Mass air flow sensor connector terminal identifications

6. Select the "PID/DATA MONITOR AND RECORD" function of the tester display.
7. Select "MAF V" on the tester display. The voltage should read as follows:
• Ignition switch ON: 0.5–1.0 Volts
• Engine at idle: 1.0–2.0 Volts
8. If not as specified, inspect the following:
• Harness continuity between PCM terminal 3B and MAF sensor connector terminal B
• Harness continuity between PCM terminal 4A and MAF sensor connector terminal E
• Harness continuity between main relay terminal D and MAF sensor connector terminal A
• Turn the ignition switch to the ON position and measure for battery positive voltage at MAF sensor connector terminal A.
9. Measure the resistance between MAF sensor connector terminals C and D. The resistance should measure 2.21–2.69k ohms at 68°F (20°C).
10. If there is incorrect terminal voltage, harness continuity or resistance measurements, replace the MAF sensor.

REMOVAL & INSTALLATION

▶ See Figures 40, 41, 42 and 43

✷✷ CAUTION

The mass air flow sensor hot wire sensing element and housing are calibrated as a unit and must be serviced as a complete assembly. Do not damage the sensing element or possible failure of the sensor may occur.

1. Disconnect the negative battery cable.
2. Disengage the wiring harness connector from the MAF sensor, and if necessary, the IAT sensor.
3. Loosen the engine air cleaner outlet tube clamps, then remove the tube from the engine.
4. Remove the MAF sensor from the air cleaner assembly by disengaging the retaining clips.

To install:

➡If necessary, be sure to align the arrow on the MAF sensor with the direction of the air flow.

5. Install the MAF sensor to the air cleaner assembly and ensure that the retaining clips are fully engaged.
6. Install the air cleaner outlet tube, then tighten the outlet tube clamps until snug.
7. Attach the engine wiring harness connectors to the IAT and MAF sensors.
8. Connect the negative battery cable.

89684P10

Fig. 40 To remove the MAF sensor, first disconnect the wire harness plug . . .

89684P11

Fig. 41 . . . then remove the air cleaner-to-throttle body air tube

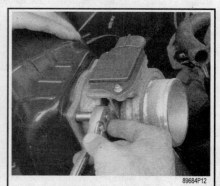

89684P12

Fig. 42 Remove the four MAF sensor attaching screws . . .

Fig. 43 . . . then remove the sensor from the air cleaner housing

Fig. 44 Checking the resistance of the volume airflow sensor with the shutter closed

Fig. 45 Checking the resistance of the volume airflow sensor while moving the shutter

Volume Air Flow Sensor

➡ Only 1994–95 MPV models equipped with the 3.0L engine utilize a volume air flow sensor.

OPERATION

The volume air flow sensor directly measures the amount of the air flowing into the engine. The sensor is mounted between the air cleaner assembly and the air cleaner outlet tube.

The sensor utilizes a shutter valve that measures the amount of air entering the engine. The sensor does this by sending a signal, generated by the sensor as the shutter opens and closes, to the PCM. The signal is used by the PCM to calculate the injector pulse width, which controls the air/fuel ratio in the engine. The sensor and plastic housing are integral and must be replaced if found to be defective.

The volume air flow sensor also contains an intake air temperature sensor and fuel pump switch.

TESTING

♦ See Figures 44 thru 49

➡ Testing of the volume air flow sensor also includes testing of the integral intake air temperature sensor.

1. Remove the volume air flow sensor from the vehicle.
2. Inspect the volume air flow sensor for cracks or any other signs of damage.
3. Check that the sensor shutter plate opens and closes smoothly.
4. Using an ohmmeter, open and close the sensor shutter plate while checking the resistance between the terminals.
5. Using a voltmeter with a temperature probe, an ohmmeter and a hairdryer for temperature variation, measure the resistance fluctuation of the integral intake air temperature sensor.
6. If the resistance does not measure within specifications, replace the volume air flow sensor.

REMOVAL & INSTALLATION

♦ See Figure 50

1. Disconnect the negative battery cable.
2. Loosen the air inlet duct hose clamp at the volume airflow sensor.
3. Release the metal volume airflow sensor connector retaining clip using a small tool such as a pick and pull the connector straight off of the sensor.
4. Loosen the five air cleaner housing cover fasteners and remove from the vehicle.
5. Remove the four mounting nuts, then remove the inner mounting plate.
6. After removing the mounting bolt, separate the volume airflow sensor from the air cleaner housing cover

To install:

7. Install the volume air flow sensor to the air cleaner housing cover and tighten the mounting bolt.

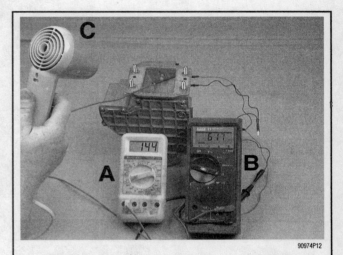

Fig. 46 Using a voltmeter with a temperature probe (A), an ohmmeter (B) and a hairdryer (C), measure the resistance fluctuation of the integral intake air temperature sensor

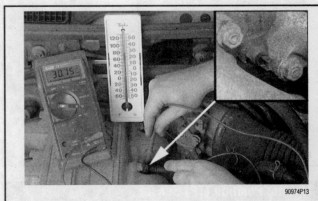

Fig. 47 Checking the resistance of the intake air temp sensor

8. Install the inner mounting plate and tighten the 4 mounting bolts.
9. Place the air cleaner housing cover and air flow sensor on top of the air cleaner box.
10. Connect the air inlet hose duct to the air flow sensor and tighten the hose clamp.
11. Attach the engine wiring harness connector to the volume air flow sensor and tighten down the air cleaner housing cover fasteners.
12. Connect the negative battery cable.

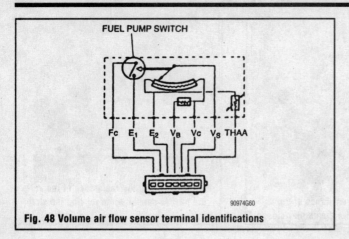

Fig. 48 Volume air flow sensor terminal identifications

Terminal	Resistance (Ω)	
	Closed throttle position	Wide open throttle
$E_2 \leftrightarrow Vs$	20—400	20—1,000
$E_2 \leftrightarrow Vc$	100—300	
$E_2 \leftrightarrow V_B$	200—400	
$E_2 \leftrightarrow THA_A$ (Intake air temperature sensor)	$-20\ ^\circ\text{C}$ {$-4\ ^\circ\text{F}$} $20\ ^\circ\text{C}$ { $68\ ^\circ\text{F}$ } $60\ ^\circ\text{C}$ { $140\ ^\circ\text{F}$ }	13,600—18,400 2,210— 2,690 493— 667
$E_1 \leftrightarrow Fc$	∞	0

90974G61

Fig. 49 Resistance specifications for the volume air flow sensor

Fig. 50 The volume airflow sensor is secured to the top of the air cleaner housing cover with four mounting nuts and one mounting bolt

Throttle Position (TP) Sensor

OPERATION

The Throttle Position (TP) sensor is a potentiometer that provides a signal to the PCM that is directly proportional to the throttle plate position. The TP sensor is mounted on the side of the throttle body and is connected to the throttle plate shaft. The TP sensor monitors throttle plate movement and position, and transmits an appropriate electrical signal to the PCM. These signals are used by the PCM to adjust the air/fuel mixture, spark timing and EGR operation according to engine load at idle, part throttle, or full throttle. The TPS is not adjustable.

TESTING

B Series Pick-up and Navajo Models

♦ See Figure 51

1. Disconnect the negative battery cable.
2. Disengage the wiring harness connector from the TP sensor.
3. Using a Digital Volt-Ohmmeter (DVOM) set on ohmmeter function, probe the terminals, which correspond to the Brown/White and the Gray/White connector wires, on the TP sensor. Do not measure the wiring harness connector terminals, rather the terminals on the sensor itself.
4. Slowly rotate the throttle shaft and monitor the ohmmeter for a continuous, steady change in resistance. Any sudden jumps, or irregularities (such as jumping back and forth) in resistance indicates a malfunctioning sensor.
5. Reconnect the negative battery cable.
6. Turn the DVOM to the voltmeter setting.

> **※ WARNING**
>
> **Ensuring the DVOM is on the voltmeter function is vitally important, because if you measure circuit resistance (ohmmeter function) with the battery cable connected, your DVOM will be destroyed.**

7. Detach the wiring harness connector from the PCM (located behind the lower right-hand kick panel in the passengers' compartment), then install a break-out box between the wiring harness connector and the PCM connector.
8. Turn the ignition switch **ON** and using the DVOM on voltmeter function, measure the voltage between terminals 89 and 90 of the breakout box. The specification is 0.9 volts.
9. If the voltage is outside the standard value or if it does not change smoothly, inspect the circuit wiring and/or replace the TP sensor.

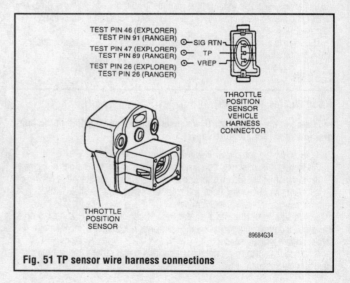

Fig. 51 TP sensor wire harness connections

MPV Models

♦ See Figures 52 and 53

1. Verify that the throttle valve is at the closed throttle position.
2. Disengage the wiring harness connector from the TP sensor.
3. Using a Digital Volt-Ohmmeter (DVOM) set on ohmmeter function, probe terminals C and D on the TP sensor.
4. Insert a 0.020 inch (0.50mm) feeler gauge between the throttle adjusting screw and the throttle lever. Verify that there is no continuity.
5. If there is no continuity, adjust the TPS as follows:
   a. Loosen the TPS mounting screws.
   b. Insert a feeler gauge between the throttle adjusting screw and the throttle lever.
   c. There should be continuity when inserting a 0.006 inch (0.15mm) feeler gauge and there should be NO continuity when inserting a 0.020 inch (0.50mm) feeler gauge.

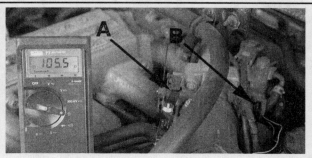

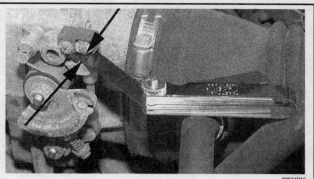

Fig. 52 Checking the resistance of the ignition switch within the TPS housing using a feeler gauge (A) and an ohmmeter on terminals C and D (B)

Fig. 53 Place a feeler gauge between the throttle lever and throttle lever stop

d. Tighten the mounting screws.

6. Replace the TPS if not as specified.

REMOVAL & INSTALLATION

▶ See Figures 54, 55 and 56

1. Disconnect the negative battery cable.
2. Disengage the wiring harness connector from the TP sensor.
3. Remove the two TP sensor mounting screws, then pull the TP sensor out of the throttle body housing.

To install:

4. Position the TP sensor against the throttle body housing, ensuring that the mounting screw holes are aligned. When positioning the TP sensor against the throttle body, slide the sensor straight onto the housing.
5. Install and tighten the sensor mounting screws until snug.

6. Attach the wiring harness connector to the sensor, then connect the negative battery cable.

Camshaft Position (CMP) Sensor

OPERATION

▶ See Figures 57 and 58

The CMP sensor provides the camshaft position information, called the CMP signal, which is used by the Powertrain Control Module (PCM) for fuel synchronization.

The following vehicles do not utilize a CMP sensor:

• 1994 B Series Pick-up equipped with 2.3L engine and automatic transmission.

Fig. 54 If the mounting holes of the sensor are slotted, mark its position. Note: factory sensors are not slotted

Fig. 55 Remove the two attaching screws . . .

Fig. 56 . . . then remove the sensor from the throttle body by lifting straight up to disengage the throttle blade (arrow)

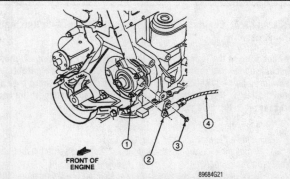

Fig. 57 Camshaft Position (CMP) sensor used on the 2.3L/2.5L engine

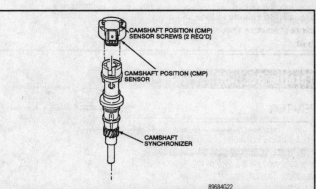

Fig. 58 Typical auxiliary drive mounted Camshaft Position (CMP) sensor used on 3.0L (B Series Pick-up) and 4.0L engines

- 1994 B Series Pick-up equipped with 4.0L engine.
- All 1994–95 MPV models.
- Navajo models.

1994 2.3L engines equipped with a manual transmission, all 1995–97 2.3L and 1998 2.5L engines utilize a CMP sensor that is located on the oil pump cover assembly, on the left-hand lower side of the engine block.

On the 1994 3.0L engine in the B Series Pick-up and 1996–98 MPV, the CMP sensor is an integral component of the distributor assembly, and it is a Hall effect magnetic switch.

On 1995–98 3.0L (B Series Pick-up) and 4.0L engines, the CMP sensor is mounted on an auxiliary shaft drive assembly, located towards the rear of the block. it is also a single hall effect magnetic switch and it is activated by a single vane, and is driven by the camshaft.

TESTING

B Series Pick-up Models

THREE WIRE SENSORS

▶ **See Figure 59**

1. With the ignition **OFF**, disconnect the CMP sensor. With the ignition **ON** and the engine **OFF**, measure the voltage between sensor harness connector **VPWR** and **PWR GND** terminals (refer to the accompanying illustration). If the reading is greater than 10.5 volts, the power circuit to the sensor is okay.

2. With the ignition **OFF**, install break-out box between the CMP sensor and the PCM. Using a Digital Volt-Ohmmeter (DVOM) set to the voltage function (scale set to monitor less than 5 volts), measure voltage between break-out box terminals **24** and **40** with the engine running at varying RPM. If the voltage reading varies more than 0.1 volt, the sensor is okay.

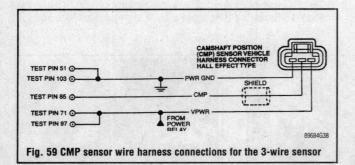

Fig. 59 CMP sensor wire harness connections for the 3-wire sensor

TWO WIRE SENSORS

▶ **See Figure 60**

1. With the ignition **OFF**, install a break-out box between the CMP sensor and PCM.

2. Using a Digital Volt-Ohmmeter (DVOM) set to the voltage function (scale set to monitor less than 5 volts), measure the voltage between break-out box terminals **24** and **46** with the engine running at varying RPM. If the voltage reading varies more than 0.1 volt AC, the sensor is okay.

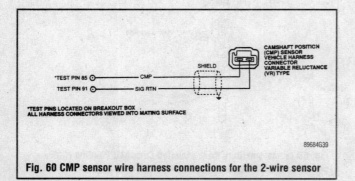

Fig. 60 CMP sensor wire harness connections for the 2-wire sensor

MPV Models

▶ **See Figures 61 and 62**

1. Disconnect the negative battery cable.
2. Remove the distributor assembly.
3. Unplug the fuel injector connector.
4. Connect ONLY the distributor 6-pin connector. Do NOT connect the 3-pin connector.
5. Turn the ignition switch to the ON position.
6. Turn the distributor drive by hand and check the output signal.
7. If not as specified, inspect the following:
- Harness continuity between PCM terminal 4G and distributor 6-pin connector terminal D
- Harness continuity between PCM terminal 4A and distributor 6-pin connector terminal A
- Harness continuity between main relay terminal D and distributor 6-pin connector terminal B
- Inspect and measure for battery positive voltage at distributor 6-pin connector terminal B

8. If there is incorrect terminal voltage or harness continuity, replace the distributor assembly.

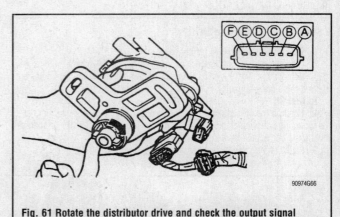

Fig. 61 Rotate the distributor drive and check the output signal

Signal	Terminal	Voltage
SGC	4G	Approx. 5 V (1 pulse/rev)

90974G67

Fig. 62 Output signal specification

REMOVAL & INSTALLATION

2.3L and 2.5L Engines (Except 1994 2.3L Engine With Automatic Transmission)

➡**According to the manufacturer, the A/C system, if equipped, must be discharged for this procedure. Have your A/C system refrigerant reclaimed by an MVAC certified repair shop. However, there may be enough flex or slack in the A/C lines to allow you to support the compressor off to the side without disconnecting the lines.**

1. Disconnect the negative battery cable.
2. Remove the accessory drive belt.
3. Remove the four bolts securing the A/C compressor to the mounting bracket and set aside.
4. Remove the three compressor/power steering bracket retaining bolts.
5. Pull the bracket, with the power steering pump attached, away from the engine and position it aside.

6. Disconnect the engine control sensor wiring from the camshaft position sensor.

7. Remove the two CMP mounting bolts and then pull the sensor from the oil pump.

To install:

8. Install the CMP sensor to the oil pump and tighten the two mounting screws to 45–61 inch lbs. (5–7 Nm).

9. Reconnect the engine control sensor wiring to the sensor.

10. Position the bracket, with the power steering pump attached, to the engine.

11. Install the three compressor/power steering bracket retaining bolts and tighten securely.

12. Install the A/C compressor to the mounting bracket and tighten the four mounting bolts.

13. Install the accessory drive belt.

14. Connect the negative battery cable. Start the engine and check for leaks.

1994 B Series Pick-up Equipped With the 3.0L Engine and All 1996–98 MPV Models

Refer to Section 2 in this manual for distributor removal and installation.

1995–98 3.0L and 4.0L Engines

♦ See Figures 63, 64 and 65

➡If the camshaft position sensor housing does not contain a plastic locator cover tool, a special service tool such as T89P-12200-A, or equivalent, must be obtained prior to installation. Failure to follow this procedure may result in improper stator alignment. This will result in the fuel system being out of time with the engine, possibly causing engine damage.

1. Disconnect the negative battery cable.
2. Remove the ignition coil, radio capacitor and ignition coil bracket.
3. Disengage the wiring harness connector from the CMP sensor.

➡Prior to removing the camshaft position sensor, set the No. 1 cylinder to 10° After Top Dead Center (ATDC) of the compression stroke. Note the position of the sensor electrical connection. When installing the sensor, the connection must be in the exact same position.

4. Position the No. 1 cylinder at 10° ATDC, then matchmark the CMP sensor terminal connector position with the engine assembly.
5. Remove the camshaft position sensor retaining screws and sensor.
6. Remove the retaining bolt and hold-down clamp.

➡The oil pump intermediate shaft should be removed with the camshaft sensor housing.

7. Remove the CMP sensor housing from the front engine cover.

To install:

8. If the plastic locator cover is not attached to the replacement camshaft position sensor, attach a synchro positioning tool, such as Ford Tool T89P-12200-A or equivalent. To do so, perform the following:

a. Engage the sensor housing vane into the radial slot of the tool.

b. Rotate the tool on the camshaft sensor housing until the tool boss engages the notch in the sensor housing.

➡The cover tool should be square and in contact with the entire top surface of the camshaft position sensor housing.

9. Transfer the oil pump intermediate shaft from the old camshaft position sensor housing to the replacement sensor housing.

10. Install the camshaft sensor housing so that the drive gear engagement occurs when the arrow on the locator tool is pointed approximately 30° counterclockwise (the sensor terminal connector should be aligned with its matchmarks) from the face of the cylinder block.

11. Install the hold-down clamp and bolt, then tighten the bolt to 15–22 ft. lbs. (20–30 Nm).

12. Remove the synchro positioning tool.

✳✳ CAUTION

If the sensor connector is positioned correctly, DO NOT reposition the connector by rotating the sensor housing. This will result in the fuel system being out of time with the engine. This could possibly cause engine damage. Remove the sensor housing and repeat the installation procedure beginning with step one.

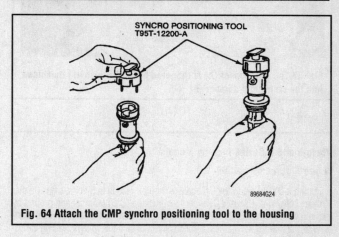

Fig. 64 Attach the CMP synchro positioning tool to the housing

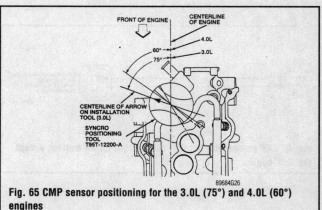

Fig. 65 CMP sensor positioning for the 3.0L (75°) and 4.0L (60°) engines

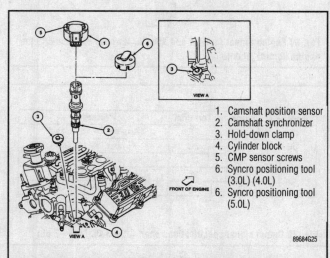

1. Camshaft position sensor
2. Camshaft synchronizer
3. Hold-down clamp
4. Cylinder block
5. CMP sensor screws
6. Syncro positioning tool (3.0L) (4.0L)
6. Syncro positioning tool (5.0L)

Fig. 63 Exploded view of the Camshaft Position (CMP) sensor mounting for the 3.0L engine—4.0L engine is similar

13. Install the sensor and retaining screws, tighten the screws to 22–31 inch lbs. (2–4 Nm).
14. Attach the engine control sensor wiring connector to the sensor.
15. Install the ignition coil bracket, radio ignition capacitor and ignition coil.
16. Connect the negative battery cable.

Crankshaft Position (CKP) Sensor

OPERATION

▶ See Figure 66

➡The crankshaft position sensor, on all 1994–95 MPV models, ia an integral component of the distributor assembly.

The Crankshaft Position (CKP) sensor, located on the front cover (near the crankshaft pulley) is used to determine crankshaft position and crankshaft rpm. The CKP sensor is a reluctance sensor which senses the passing of teeth on a sensor ring because the teeth disrupt the magnetic field of the sensor. This disruption creates a voltage fluctuation, which is monitored by the PCM.

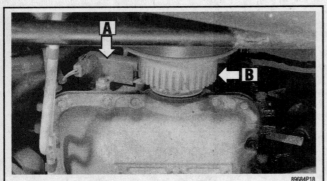

Fig. 66 The CKP sensor (A) is triggered by teeth which are machined into the crankshaft damper (B)

TESTING

Navajo and B Series Pick-up Models

▶ See Figures 67 and 68

Using a DVOM set to the DC scale to monitor less than 5 volts, measure the voltage between the sensor Cylinder Identification (CID) terminal and ground by backprobing the sensor connector. If the connector cannot be backprobed, fabricate or purchase a test harness. The sensor is okay if the voltage reading varies more than 0.1 volt with the engine running at varying RPM.

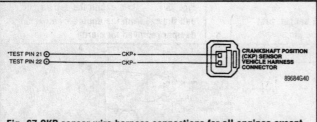

Fig. 67 CKP sensor wire harness connections for all engines except the 4.0L engine

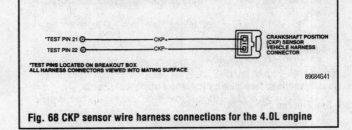

Fig. 68 CKP sensor wire harness connections for the 4.0L engine

1994–95 MPV Models

▶ See Figures 69 and 70

1. Disconnect the negative battery cable.
2. Remove the distributor assembly.
3. Plug in the distributor connector.
4. Unplug the fuel injector connector.
5. Turn the ignition switch to the ON position.
6. Connect the Engine Signal Monitor and Adapter Harness to the engine control module as illustrated.
7. Set the Engine Signal Monitor.
8. Turn the distributor drive by hand and measure the output voltage.
9. If not as specified, replace the distributor assembly.

1996–98 MPV Models

▶ See Figure 71

1. Disconnect the negative battery cable.
2. Unplug the crankshaft position sensor wiring harness connector.

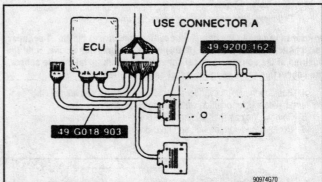

Fig. 69 Engine Signal Monitor and Adapter Harness connected to the engine control module

Engine	Signal	Terminal	Voltage
JE	NE	2E	Approx. 5V (6 pulses)
	G1	2G	Approx. 5V (1 pulse)
	G2	2H	Approx. 5V (1 pulse)
G6	NE	2E	Approx. 5V (4 pulses)
	G	2G	Approx. 5V (1 pulse)

Fig. 70 Output signal specifications chart (JE—3.0L / G6—2.6L)

3. Using an ohmmeter, measure the resistance between terminals A and B.
4. The measurement should read 950–1250 ohms at 68°F (20°C).
5. If not as specified, replace the crankshaft position sensor.

REMOVAL & INSTALLATION

Navajo and B Series Pick-up Models

▶ See Figures 72 and 73

1. Disconnect the negative battery cable.
2. Disengage the wiring harness connector from the CKP sensor.
3. Loosen the CKP sensor mounting stud/bolts, then separate the sensor form the engine front cover.

To install:

➡When installing a new sensor on the 4.0L engine, position the sensor against the crankshaft damper. There are small rub tabs which wear off and allow the sensor to be perfectly spaced from the damper.

4. Position the sensor against the engine front cover, then install the mounting stud/bolts. Tighten them until snug.
5. Install the CKP sensor cover and retaining nuts; tighten the nuts until snug.
6. Reattach the wiring harness connector to the CKP sensor.
7. Connect the negative battery cable.

1994–95 MPV Models

Refer to Section 2 in this manual for distributor removal and installation.

1996–98 MPV Models

▶ See Figure 74

1. Disconnect the negative battery cable.
2. Unplug the crankshaft position sensor connector.
3. Loosen the mounting bolt and remove the crankshaft position sensor from the engine.
4. Installation is the reverse of the removal procedure.

Vehicle Speed Sensor (VSS)

OPERATION

The Vehicle Speed Sensor (VSS) is a magnetic pick-up that sends a signal to the Powertrain Control Module (PCM). The sensor measures the rotation of the transmission and the PCM determines the corresponding vehicle speed.

TESTING

▶ See Figure 75

1. Turn the ignition switch to the **OFF** position.
2. Disengage the wiring harness connector from the VSS.
3. Using a Digital Volt-Ohmmeter (DVOM), measure the resistance (DVOM ohmmeter function) between the sensor terminals. If the resistance is 190–250 ohms, the sensor is okay.

REMOVAL & INSTALLATION

The VSS is located half-way down the right-hand side of the transmission assembly.

1. Apply parking brake, block the rear wheels, then raise and safely support the front of the vehicle on jackstands.
2. From under the right-hand side of the vehicle, disengage the wiring harness connector from the VSS.
3. Loosen the VSS hold-down bolt, then pull the VSS out of the transmission housing.

To install:

4. If a new sensor is being installed, transfer the driven gear retainer and gear to the new sensor.
5. Ensure that the O-ring is properly seated in the VSS housing.
6. For ease of assembly, engage the wiring harness connector to the VSS, then insert the VSS into the transmission assembly.
7. Install and tighten the VSS hold-down bolt to 62–88 inch lbs. (7–10 Nm).
8. Lower the vehicle and remove the wheel blocks.

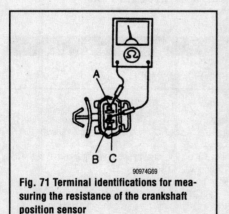
Fig. 71 Terminal identifications for measuring the resistance of the crankshaft position sensor

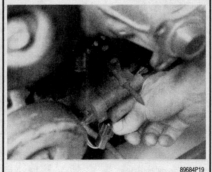
Fig. 72 To remove the CKP sensor, first disconnect the wire harness plug . . .

Fig. 73 . . . then unbolt the sensor and pull it away from the engine—crankshaft damper removed for clarity

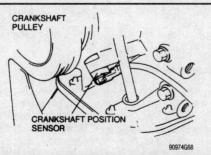
Fig. 74 Location of the crankshaft position sensor to the left of the crankshaft pulley

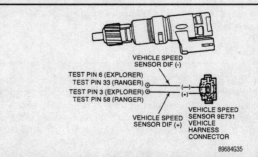
Fig. 75 Typical Vehicle Speed Sensor (VSS) and its wiring harness connections

TROUBLE CODES

General Description

Mazda Navajo, B Series Pick-up and MPV vehicles employ an electronic engine control system, to manage fuel, ignition and emissions on vehicle engines.

The Powertrain Control Module (PCM) is given responsibility for the operation of the emission control devices, ignition and advance and in some cases, automatic transmission functions. Because the control system oversees both the ignition timing and the fuel injector operation, a precise air/fuel ratio will be maintained under all operating conditions. The PCM is a microprocessor or small computer which receives electrical inputs from several sensors, switches and relays on and around the engine.

Based on combinations of these inputs, the PCM controls outputs to various devices concerned with engine operation and emissions. The engine control assembly relies on the signals to form a correct picture of current vehicle operation. If any of the input signals is incorrect, the PCM reacts to what ever picture is painted for it. For example, if the coolant temperature sensor is inaccurate and reads too low, the PCM may see a picture of the engine never warming up. Consequently, the engine settings will be maintained as if the engine were cold. Because so many inputs can affect one output, correct diagnostic procedures are essential on these systems.

One part of the PCM is devoted to monitoring both input and output functions within the system. This ability forms the core of the self-diagnostic system. If a problem is detected within a circuit, the controller will recognize the fault, assign it an identification code, and store the code in a memory section. Depending on the year and model, the fault code(s) may be represented by two or three digit numbers. The stored code(s) may be retrieved during diagnosis.

While the electronic engine control system is capable of recognizing many internal faults, certain faults will not be recognized. Because the computer system sees only electrical signals, it cannot sense or react to mechanical or vacuum faults affecting engine operation. Some of these faults may affect another component which will set a code. For example, the PCM monitors the output signal to the fuel injectors, but cannot detect a partially clogged injector. As long as the output driver responds correctly, the computer will read the system as functioning correctly. However, the improper flow of fuel may result in a lean mixture. This would, in turn, be detected by the oxygen sensor and noticed as a constantly lean signal by the PCM. Once the signal falls outside the pre-programmed limits, the engine control assembly would notice the fault and set an identification code.

Additionally, the electronic control system employs adaptive fuel logic. This process is used to compensate for normal wear and variability within the fuel system. Once the engine enters steady-state operation, the engine control assembly watches the oxygen sensor signal for a bias or tendency to run slightly rich or lean. If such a bias is detected, the adaptive logic corrects the fuel delivery to bring the air/fuel mixture towards a centered or 14.7:1 ratio. This compensating shift is stored in a non-volatile memory which is retained by battery power even with the ignition switched **OFF**. The correction factor is then available the next time the vehicle is operated.

➡️ **If the battery cable(s) is disconnected for longer than 5 minutes, the adaptive fuel factor will be lost. After repair it will be necessary to drive the vehicle at least 10 miles to allow the processor to relearn the correct factors. The driving period should include steady-throttle open road driving if possible. During the drive, the vehicle may exhibit driveability symptoms not noticed before. These symptoms should clear as the PCM computes the correction factor. The PCM will also store Code 19 indicating loss of power to the controller.**

MALFUNCTION INDICATOR LAMP (MIL)

The CHECK ENGINE or SERVICE ENGINE SOON dashboard warning lamp is referred to as the Malfunction Indicator Lamp (MIL). The lamp is connected to the engine control assembly and will alert the driver to certain malfunctions within the EEC system. When the lamp is lit, the PCM has detected a fault and stored an identity code in memory. The engine control system will usually enter either a failure or limited operation mode and driveability will be impaired.

The light will stay on as long as the fault causing it is present. Should the fault self-correct, the MIL will extinguish, but the stored code will remain in memory.

Under normal operating conditions, the MIL should light briefly when the ignition key is turned **ON**. As soon as the PCM receives a signal that the engine is cranking, the lamp will be extinguished. The dash warning lamp should remain out during the entire operating cycle.

Diagnostic Connector

▸ **See Figure 76**

To read Diagnostic Trouble Codes (DTC's), the test connector for the electronic engine control system must be used. The Data Link Connector (DLC) is also sometimes known as the Assembly Line Diagnostic Link (ALDL) connector. On 1994–95 vehicles, the DLC is located under the hood near the power distribution box. On 1996–98 vehicles, the DLC is located in the passenger compartment, under the driver side dashboard.

The connector is trapezoidal in shape and can accommodate up to 16 terminals.

89684P21

Fig. 76 To access the Navajo and 1994–95 B Series Pick-up diagnostic connector, unfasten it from its protective cover

Reading Codes

NAVAJO & 1994 B SERIES PICK-UP MODELS

Scan Tool Method

1. Connect the scan tool to the self-test connectors. Make certain the test button is unlatched or up.
2. Start the engine and run it until normal operating temperature is reached.
3. Turn the engine **OFF** and wait 10 seconds.
4. Activate the test button on the STAR tester.
5. Turn the ignition switch **ON** but do not start the engine.
6. The codes will be transmitted. Six to nine seconds after the last code, a single separator pulse will be transmitted. Six to nine seconds after this pulse, the codes from the Continuous Memory will be transmitted.
7. Record all service codes displayed. Do not depress the throttle during the test.
8. After the test, compare the DTC's retrieved with the accompanying DTC identification charts.

Analog Voltmeter Method

In the absence of a scan tool, an analog voltmeter may be used to retrieve stored fault codes. Set the meter range to read DC 0–15 volts. Connect the positive lead of the meter to the battery positive terminal and connect the negative lead of the meter to the Self-Test Output (STO) pin of the diagnostic connector.

Follow the directions given previously for performing the scan tool procedure. To activate the procedure, use a jumper wire to connect the signal return pin on the diagnostic connector to the self-test input connector. The self-test input line is the separate wire and connector with or near the diagnostic connector.

The codes will be transmitted as groups of needle sweeps. This method may be used to read either 2 or 3 digit codes. The Continuous Memory codes are separated from the other codes by 6 seconds, a single sweep and another 6 second delay.

1. After the test, compare the DTC's retrieved with the accompanying DTC identification charts.

Malfunction Indicator Lamp (MIL) Method

The Malfunction Indicator Lamp (MIL) on the dashboard may also be used to retrieve the stored codes. This method displays only the stored codes and does not allow any system investigation. It should only be used in field conditions where a quick check of stored codes is needed.

Follow the directions given previously for performing the scan tool procedure. To activate the tests, use a jumper wire to connect the signal return pin on the diagnostic connector to the Self-Test Input (STO) connector. The self-test input line is the separate wire and connector with or near the diagnostic connector.

Codes are transmitted by place value with a pause between the digits; Code 32 would be sent as 3 flashes, a pause and 2 flashes. A slightly longer pause divides codes from each other. Be ready to count and record codes; the only way to repeat a code is to recycle the system. This method may be used to read either 2 or 3 digit codes. The Continuous Memory codes are separated from the other codes by 6 seconds, a single flash and another 6 second delay.

1995–98 B SERIES PICK-UP MODELS

♦ See Figure 77

The 1995–98 B Series Pick-up models utilize On Board Diagnostic II (OBD-II) Diagnostic Trouble Codes (DTC's), which are alpha-numeric (they use letters and numbers). The letters in the OBD-II DTC's make it highly difficult to convey the codes through the use of anything but a scan tool. Therefore, to read the OBD-II DTC's on these vehicles it is necessary to utilize an OBD-II compatible scan tool.

1. Ensure that the ignition switch is in the **OFF** position.
2. Apply the parking brake.
3. Ensure that transmission gearshift is in either Park (automatic transmissions) or Neutral (manual transmissions).
4. Block the rear wheels.
5. Turn off all electrical loads, such as the heater blower motor, the radio, the rear defroster, etc.
6. Connect the scan tool to the Data Link Connector. Make certain the test button on the scan tool is unlatched or up.
7. Turn the ignition switch to the **ON** position without starting the engine (KOEO).
8. Using the scan tool, retrieve and record any continuous memory DTC's.
9. Turn the ignition switch to the **OFF** position.
10. Start the engine and run it until normal operating temperature is reached.
11. Turn the engine **OFF** and wait 10 seconds.
12. Turn the ignition switch **ON** but do not start the engine.
13. Activate the KOEO self-test. Retrieve and record any KOEO DTC's after the KOEO test is complete.
14. If any DTC's were present, refer to the accompanying OBD-II charts to locate the problem(s).

➡ Ignore DTC 1000.

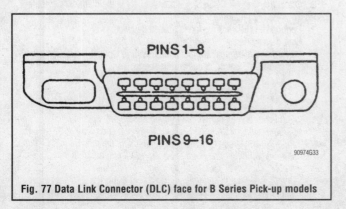

Fig. 77 Data Link Connector (DLC) face for B Series Pick-up models

MPV MODELS

1994–95

♦ See Figure 78

1. Connect System Selector Tool 49-B019-9A0 to the data link connector, located on the left side of the engine compartment.
2. Set switch **A** to position 1, then set TEST switch to SELF-TEST.
3. Connect Self-Diagnosis Checker Tool 49-H018-9A1 to the System Selector and a ground.
4. Set the select switch to position **A**.
5. Turn the ignition switch to the ON position, but do not start the engine. Check that number "88" flashes on the digital display and the buzzer sounds for 3 seconds after turning the ignition switch ON.
6. If the number "88" does not flash, check the main power relay, power supply circuit and check the DLC wiring.
7. If the number "88" flashes and the buzzer sounds continuously for more than 20 seconds, check for a short circuit between the engine control module terminal 1F and the data link connector. Replace the control module if necessary and perform steps 2–4 again.
8. Note the code numbers and check the causes. Repair as necessary. Be sure to clear the codes, then recheck for code numbers after repairing.

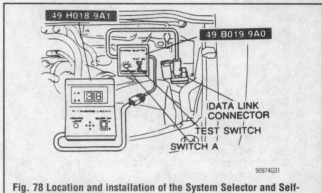

Fig. 78 Location and installation of the System Selector and Self-Diagnosis Checker tools

1996–98

♦ See Figure 79

The 1996–98 MPV models utilize On Board Diagnostic II (OBD-II) Diagnostic Trouble Codes (DTC's), which are alpha-numeric (they use letters and numbers). The letters in the OBD-II DTC's make it highly difficult to convey the codes through the use of anything but a scan tool. Therefore, to read the OBD-II DTC's on these vehicles it is necessary to utilize an OBD-II compatible scan tool.

1. Connect the New Generation Star (NGS) diagnostic tool, or equivalent, to the data link connector located under the driver side dashboard.

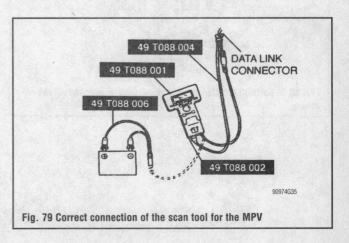

Fig. 79 Correct connection of the scan tool for the MPV

2. Read the manufacturer provided instruction manual for the correct operation of the scan tool.

➡**Some Diagnostic Trouble Codes (DTC) are detected only when the engine is running. Before checking the DTC's, start the engine.**

3. Start the engine, then select "DIAGNOSTIC TROUBLE CODES" function and press "TRIGGER".

4. When the scan tool displays the words "NO CODES RECIEVED/SYSTEM PASS-ED", all systems monitored are judged okay.

5. If any DTC'S are displayed, perform the troubleshooting according to the code.

6. When the scan tool displays "LINK MONITOR ERROR", check the connection of the scan tool.

7. After all the problems have been repaired, clear the DTC's.

Clearing Codes

NAVAJO & B SERIES PICK-UP MODELS

1994–95

▶ **See Figure 80**

1. Connect the Super Star II Tester 49-UN01-056, or equivalent scan tool, to the data link connectors, located in the engine compartment.

2. Set the switch select to the EEC-IV position.

3. Set the readout switch to the "FAST CODE" mode.

4. Set the "HOLD TEST" button to the "TEST" position.

5. Turn on the scan tool.

6. Turn the ignition switch to the "ON" position.

7. Verify that the pass code (111-10-111) is recieved.

8. Turn off the scan tool.

9. Start the engine and warm it up to operating temperature.

10. Turn off the engine.

11. Turn on the scan tool.

12. Start the engine and allow it to idle.

13. Within 2 seconds of starting the engine, depress the brake pedal and turn the steering wheel one complete turn.

14. Verify that the pass code (111) is recieved.

15. Perform the diagnostic trouble code (Reading Codes) inspection procedure again and verify that no codes are displayed.

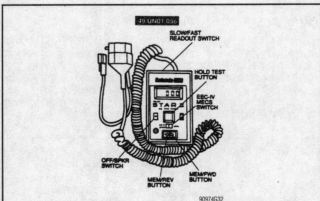

Fig. 80 To perform the clearing codes procedure, a scan tool is necessary

1996–98

1. After performing any necessary repairs, connect the New Generation Star (NGS) diagnostic tool, or equivalent, to the data link connector located under the driver side dashboard.

2. Select the "CLEAR CODES" function in GENERIC OBD II FUNCTIONS and erase the diagnostic trouble codes from the NGS memory.

3. Perform the "QUICK TEST" to ensure that the repair has been performed correctly. If diagnostic trouble code P1000 is present, perform the "OBD II DRIVE CYCLE TEST" using the scan tool.

4. Perform the diagnostic trouble code (Reading Codes) inspection procedure again and verify that no codes are displayed.

MPV MODELS

1994–95

▶ **See Figures 78 and 81**

1. Cancel the memory of malfunctions by disconnecting the negative battery cable for at least twenty seconds. Reconnect the negative battery cable.

2. Connect System Selector Tool 49-B019-9A0 to the data link connector, located on the left side of the engine compartment.

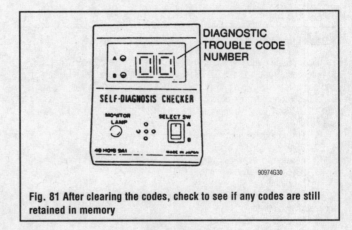

Fig. 81 After clearing the codes, check to see if any codes are still retained in memory

3. Set switch **A** to position 1, then set TEST switch to SELF-TEST.

4. Connect Self-Diagnosis Checker Tool 49-H018-9A1 to the System Selector and a ground.

5. Set the select switch to position **A**.

6. Turn the ignition switch to the ON position, but do not start the engine.

7. Start the engine and allow it to reach normal operating temperatures. Run the engine at 2000 rpm for three minutes. Check that no codes are displayed.

1996–98

1. After performing any necessary repairs, connect the New Generation Star (NGS) diagnostic tool, or equivalent, to the data link connector located under the driver side dashboard.

2. Select the "CLEAR CODES" function and erase the diagnostic trouble codes from the NGS memory.

3. Perform the OBD II drive mode procedure twice.

4. Start the engine.

5. Perform the diagnostic trouble code (Reading Codes) inspection procedure again and verify that no codes are displayed.

Code No.	Output devices	Open or short circuit
25	PRC solenoid valve	
26	Purge solenoid valve	
34	Idle air control valve (BAC valve)	
36	Heated oxygen sensor heater	
41	VRIS solenoid valve	

90974C04

Fig. 83 Diagnostic trouble code chart (2 of 2)—1994–95 MPV models

Code No.	Input devices	Malfunction
01	Ignition pulse (Igniter, Ignition coil)	Broken wire, short circuit
02	Distributor (NE signal)	Ne signal not input for 1.5 sec. during cranking
03	Distributor (G1 signal)	Broken wire, short circuit
04	Distributor (G2 signal)	Broken wire, short circuit
08	Volume airflow sensor	Broken wire, short circuit
09	Engine coolant temperature sensor	Broken wire, short circuit
10	Intake air temperature sensor (Volume air-flow sensor)	Broken wire, short circuit
11	Intake air temperature sensor (Dynamic chamber)	Broken wire, short circuit
12	Fuel pump relay or Throttle position sensor	Broken wire, short circuit
14	Barometric absolute pressure sensor	PCME
15	Heated oxygen sensor (Inactivation)	Heated oxygen sensor output below 0.55V 120 sec. after engine at 1,500 rpm
17	Heated oxygen sensor (Inversion)	Heated oxygen sensor output does not change from 0.55V 20 sec. after engine at 1,500 rpm

90974C03

Fig. 82 Diagnostic trouble code chart (1 of 2)—1994–95 MPV models

DTC No.	Condition
P0745	Pressure control solenoid malfunction
P0750	Shift solenoid A malfunction
P0755	Shift solenoid B malfunction
P1110	Intake air temperature sensor (Dynamic chamber) open or short
P1170	Heated oxygen sensor (Front) (Inversion)
P1195	Barometric pressure sensor circuit open or short
P1196	Ignition switch (Start) open or short
P1250	PRC solenoid valve open or short
P1252	PRC solenoid valve No. 2 open or short
P1345	No SGC signal
P1449	Canister drain cut valve (CDCV) open or short
P1450	Evaporative emission control system malfunction
P1455	Fuel gauge sender unit circuit malfunction
P1521	VRIS solenoid valve open or short
P1527	AWS control system malfunction (California 2WD only)
P1566	Backup power supply circuit malfunction
P1601	Communication line error (PCM — TCM)
P1608	PCM malfunction (CPU)
P1720	Vehicle speedometer sensor circuit malfunction
P1743	Torque converter clutch control solenoid valve
P1770	Overrunning clutch solenoid valve open or short
P1790	Throttle position sensor open or short
P1792	Barometric pressure signal circuit malfunction
P1794	Battery or circuit malfunction
P1795	Closed throttle position switch malfunction
P1797	P or N range or neutral/clutch switch signal open or short

*1 : DC signifies the Number of consecutive drive cycles required to store the DTC.

*2 : Appropriate OBD II Monitor.

90974C02

Fig. 85 OBD-II system diagnostic trouble code chart (2 of 2)—1996–98 MPV models

DTC No.	Condition
P0100	Mass airflow circuit malfunction
P0110	Intake air temperature circuit malfunction
P0115	Engine coolant temperature malfunction
P0120	Throttle position circuit malfunction
P0125	Excessive time to enter closed loop fuel control
P0130	Front O₂ sensor circuit malfunction
P0134	Front O₂ sensor circuit no activity detected
P0135	Front O₂ sensor heater circuit malfunction
P0140	Rear O₂ sensor circuit no activity detected
P0141	Rear O₂ sensor heater circuit malfunction
P0170	Fuel trim malfunction
P0300	Random misfire detected
P0301	Cylinder 1 misfire detected
P0302	Cylinder 2 misfire detected
P0303	Cylinder 3 misfire detected
P0304	Cylinder 4 misfire detected
P0305	Cylinder 5 misfire detected
P0306	Cylinder 6 misfire detected
P0335	Crankshaft position sensor circuit malfunction
P0420	Catalyst system efficiency below threshold
P0442	Evaporative emission control system malfunction (Leak check)
P0443	Evaporative emission control system purge control valve malfunction
P0446	Evaporative emission control system malfunction (Vent control malfunction)
P0450	Evaporative emission control system pressure sensor malfunction
P0455	Evaporative emission control system malfunction (con. Leak detected)
P0500	Vehicle speed sensor malfunction
P0505	Idle control system malfunction
P0510	Closed throttle position switch malfunction
P0550	P/S pressure input malfunction
P0703	Brake switch input malfunction
P0705	Transmission range switch circuit malfunction
P0706	Transmission range switch circuit malfunction (Open circuit)
P0710	Transmission fluid temperature sensor circuit malfunction
P0711	Transmission fluid temperature sensor circuit malfunction (Stuck)
P0720	Output speed sensor circuit malfunction
P0725	Engine speed input circuit malfunction
P0740	Torque converter clutch system malfunction

90974C01

Fig. 84 OBD-II system diagnostic trouble code chart (1 of 2)—1996–98 MPV models

No.	Diagnosed circuit	Condition
111	Pass	—
112	Intake air temperature sensor	Sensor output voltage below 0.2V (indicates 123°C [254°F])
113	Intake air temperature sensor	Sensor output voltage above 4.6V (indicates -40°C [-40°F])
114	Intake air temperature sensor	Sensor output voltage less than or greater than expected
116	Engine coolant temperature sensor	Sensor output voltage less than or greater than expected
117	Engine coolant temperature sensor	Sensor output voltage below 0.2V (indicates 123°C [254°F])
118	Engine coolant temperature sensor	Sensor output voltage above 4.6V (indicates -40°C [-40°F])
121	Throttle position sensor	Sensor output voltage less than or greater than expected
122	Throttle position sensor	Sensor output voltage below 0.5V
123	Throttle position sensor	Sensor output voltage above 4.6V
129	Mass air flow sensor	Incorrect change in sensor output voltage during Dynamic Response Test
136	Heated oxygen sensor (LH)	Sensor output continues lean condition
137	Heated oxygen sensor (LH)	Sensor output continues rich condition
139	Heated oxygen sensor (LH)	Open or short circuit
144	Heated oxygen sensor (RH)	Open or short circuit
157	Mass air flow sensor	Sensor output voltage below 0.4V
158	Mass air flow sensor	Sensor output voltage above 4.5V
159	Mass air flow sensor	Sensor output voltage less than or greater than expected

90974C05

Fig. 86 Diagnostic trouble code chart (1 of 4)—Navajo and 1994 B Series Pick-up models

No.	Diagnosed circuit	Condition
167	Throttle position sensor	Incorrect change in sensor output voltage during Dynamic Response Test
171	Adaptive fuel control (RH)	Exceeds adaptive fuel control limits
172	Heated oxygen sensor (RH)	Sensor output continues lean condition
173	Heated oxygen sensor (RH)	Sensor output continues rich condition
175	Adaptive fuel control (LH)	Exceeds adaptive fuel control limits
176	Heated oxygen sensor (LH)	Sensor output continues lean condition
177	Heated oxygen sensor (LH)	Sensor output continues rich condition
179	Adaptive fuel control (RH)	Fuel system at lean adaptive limit with throttle valve open
181	Adaptive fuel control (RH)	Fuel system at rich adaptive limit with throttle valve open
182	Adaptive fuel control (RH)	Fuel system at lean adaptive limit at idle
183	Adaptive fuel control (RH)	Fuel system at rich adaptive limit at idle
188	Adaptive fuel control (LH)	Fuel system at lean adaptive limit with throttle valve open
189	Adaptive fuel control (LH)	Fuel system at rich adaptive limit with throttle valve open
191	Adaptive fuel control (LH)	Fuel system at lean adaptive limit at idle
192	Adaptive fuel control (LH)	Fuel system at rich adaptive limit at idle
211	Camshaft position signal (from ignition control module)	No camshaft position signal
212	Ignition diagnostic monitor (in ignition control module)	No ignition diagnostic monitor signal
213	Spark output	Open
214	Camshaft position sensor	Open or short

90974C06

Fig. 87 Diagnostic trouble code chart (2 of 4)—Navajo and 1994 B Series Pick-up models

NO.	DIAGNOSED CIRCUIT	CONDITION
P0102	Mass Airflow Sensor (MAF)	MAF signal went below 0.39 volts sometime during normal engine operation or KOER self-test.
P0103		MAF signal went above 3.90 volts during KOEO or KOFR self-test.(1)
P0112	Intake Air Temperature (IAT) Sensor	• IAT signal is less than 0.2 volt (250°F (121°C)). • IAT signal was not received during KOEO/KOER self-test, but was output during Retrieve/Clear Continuous DTC Self-Test.
P0113		• IAT signal is greater than 4.6 volts (-46°F (-50°C)). • IAT signal was not received during KOEO/KOER self-test, but was output during Retrieve/Clear Continuous DTC Self-Test.
P0117	Engine Coolant Temperature (ECT) Sensor	• ECT signal is less than 0.2 volt (250°F (121°C)). • ECT signal was not received during KOEO/KOER self-test, but was output during Retrieve/Clear Continuous DTC Self-Test.
P0118		• ECT signal is greater than 4.6 volts (-46°F (-50°C)). • ECT signal was not received during KOEO/KOER self-test, but was output during Retrieve/Clear Continuous DTC Self-Test.
P0121	Throttle Position (TP) Sensor	TP signal is an in-range operating TP sensor circuit failure.
P0122		TP signal is less than self-test minimum value of 0.17 volt (3.43%).
P0123		TP signal is greater than self-test maximum value of 4.60 volts (92.27%).
P0125	Engine Coolant Temperature (ECT) Sensor	ECT signal has not achieved required temperature level to enter closed loop operating conditions within a specified amount of time after starting engine.
P0131	Heated Oxygen Sensor (HO2S)-11	HO2S-11 generates a negative voltage.
P0133		Response rate of HO2S-11 is below calibrated window.
P0135	HO2S HTR 11	HO2S-11 heater circuit has a short to ground, open, or short to VPWR.
P0136	Heated Oxygen Sensor (HO2S)-12	HO2S-12 output voltage is less than calibrated functional window.
P1137		Any exhaust leaks between engine and end of catalyst may cause this DTC.
P1138		
P0141	HO2S HTR 12	HO2S-12 heater circuit has a short to ground, open, or short to VPWR.
P0151	Heated Oxygen Sensor (HO2S)-21	HO2S-21 generates a negative voltage.
P0153		Response rate of HO2S-21 is below calibrated window.
P0155	HO2S HTR 21	HO2S-21 heater circuit has a short to ground, open, or short to VPWR.
P0171	Adaptive Fuel Control	Fuel adaptive system is at rich correction limit due to fuel/air ratio too lean (#1 cylinder bank).
P0172		Fuel adaptive system is at lean correction limit due to fuel/air ratio too rich (#1 cylinder bank).
P0174		Fuel adaptive system is at rich correction limit due to fuel/air ratio too lean (opposite bank).
P0175		Fuel adaptive system is at lean correction limit due to fuel/air ratio too rich (opposite bank).
P0230	Fuel Pump Relay	Fuel pump primary circuit failure.
P0231		Fuel pump secondary circuit failure between B+ supply and fuel pump monitor (test pin 40) connection to power-to-pump circuit.
P0232		Fuel pump monitor circuit voltage was high when fuel pump was commanded off.
P0300	Misfire Detection Monitor	Multiple cylinders misfiring, or cannot identify cylinder due to camshaft position sensor failure.
P0301		Cylinder #1 misfiring.
P0302		Cylinder #2 misfiring.
P0303		Cylinder #3 misfiring.

Fig. 89 Diagnostic trouble code chart (4 of 4)—Navajo and 1994 B Series Pick-up models

No.	Diagnosed circuit	Condition
215	Coil #1 primary circuit	Open or short
216	Coil #2 primary circuit	Open or short
217	Coil #3 primary circuit	Open or short
218	Ignition diagnostic monitor (left) (in ignition control module)	No ignition diagnostic monitor (left) signal
219	Spark output	Open
222	Ignition diagnostic monitor (right) (in ignition control module)	No ignition diagnostic monitor (right) signal
223	Dual plug control	No dual plug operation
224	Coil #1, #2, #3 or #4 primary circuit	Open or short
226	Ignition diagnostic monitor (in ignition control module)	No ignition diagnostic monitor signal
232	Coil #1, #2, or #3 primary circuit	Open or short
326	Differential pressure feedback EGR sensor	Sensor output less than expected
327	Differential pressure feedback EGR sensor	Sensor output voltage below 0.2V
335	Differential pressure feedback EGR sensor	Sensor output less than or greater than expected during Key On Engine Off test
336	Differential pressure feedback EGR sensor	Sensor output greater than expected
337	Differential pressure feedback EGR sensor	Sensor output voltage above 4.8V
332	Differential pressure feedback EGR sensor	Insufficient EGR flow
341	Octane adjust circuit	Open
411	Idle air control solenoid	Failed low RPM test during Key On Engine Running test
412	Idle air control solenoid	Failed high RPM test during Key On Engine Running test

Fig. 88 Diagnostic trouble code chart (3 of 4)—Navajo and 1994 B Series Pick-up models

NO.	DIAGNOSED CIRCUIT	CONDITION
P0304	Misfire Detection Monitor	Cylinder #4 misfiring.
P0305		Cylinder #5 misfiring.
P0306		Cylinder #6 misfiring.
P0320	Powertrain Control Module (PCM)	Erratic Profile Ignition Pickup (PIP) signal
P0340	Camshaft Position (CMP) Sensor	Self-test has detected a Camshaft Position (CMP) sensor circuit failure.
P0350	Ignition Coil	Ignition coil primary circuit malfunction.
P0351		Ignition coil A primary circuit malfunction.
P0352		Ignition coil B primary circuit malfunction.
P0353		Ignition coil C primary circuit malfunction.
P0400	Exhaust Gas Recirculation (EGR) System	Self-test has detected an EGR system malfunction. • Continuous DTC P0400 indicates that self-test has detected an EGR system malfunction sometime during vehicle operation.
P0401		Continuous self-test has detected insufficient EGR flow.
P0402		Self-test has detected EGR flow at idle.
P0420	Catalyst Efficiency Monitor	Bank 1 catalyst system efficiency is below acceptable threshold.
P0443	EVAP Purge Solenoid	Failure in solenoid circuit.
P0500	Vehicle Speed Sensor (VSS)	PCM detected loss of VSS signal during operation.
P0503		VSS circuit intermittent.
P0505	Idle Air Control (IAC) System	Self-test has detected IAC system malfunction.
P0603	Powertrain Control Module (PCM)	PCM has experienced a power interrupt in Keep Alive Power (KAPWR) circuit.
P0605		Read Only Memory (ROM) test error.
P0703	Brake On/Off (BOO) Switch	BOO signal did not cycle high and low when brake pedal was pressed and released during KOER.
P0704	Clutch Pedal Position (CPP) Switch	Switch is malfunctioning.
P0705	Transmission Range (TR) Sensor	TR sensor circuit failure.
P0708		TR signal is high or open.
P0712	Transmission Fluid Temperature (TFT) Sensor	TFT signal exceeds scale set for temperature of 157°C (315°F).
P0713		TFT signal exceeds scale set for temperature of -40°C (-40°F).
P0715	Turbine Shaft Speed (TSS) Sensor	PCM detected a loss of TSS signal during operation.
P0720	Output Shaft Speed (OSS) Sensor	PCM detected a loss of OSS signal during operation.
P0721		PCM detected an erratic OSS signal.
P0731	AT Solenoid	Gear #1 incorrect ratio (no first gear).
P0732		Gear #2 incorrect ratio (no second gear).
P0733		Gear #3 incorrect ratio (no third gear).
P0734		Gear #4 incorrect ratio (no fourth gear).
P0735		Gear #5 incorrect ratio (no fifth gear).
P0736		An incorrect ratio for reverse.
P0741	Torque Converter Clutch (TCC) Solenoid	PCM picked up an excessive amount of TCC slippage during normal vehicle operation.
P0743		TCC circuit fails to provide voltage drop across solenoid during on-board diagnostic.

90974C10

Fig. 91 OBD-II system diagnostic trouble code chart (2 of 5)—1995–98 B Series Pick-up models

No.	Diagnosed circuit	Condition
415	Idle air control	Adaptive idle air control at minimum limit
416	Idle air control	Adaptive idle air control at maximum limit
452	Vehicle speed sensor	No vehicle speed sensor signal
511	PCM	PCM read only memory test failure during Key On Engine Off test
512	Power	PCM keep alive memory test failure
513	PCM	Internal voltage problem
519	Power steering pressure switch	Open during Key On Engine Off test
521	Power steering pressure switch	Open during Key On Engine Running test
522	Park/Neutral position switch (AT)	Vehicle not in Park or Neutral during Key On Engine Off test
525	A/C switch	A/C on during Key On Engine Off test
528	Clutch pedal position switch or park/neutral position switch (MT)	Open or short
536	Stoplight switch	Open or short
538	Dynamic response test	Incorrect RPM change during Dynamic Response Test
539	A/C switch	A/C switch on during Key On Engine Off test or Key On Engine Running test
542	Fuel pump	Open or short
543	Fuel pump	Open
556	Fuel pump	Open or short
558	EGR vacuum regulator solenoid	Open or short
565	Purge solenoid valve	Open or short
586	3-4 shift solenoid valve (AT only)	Open or short
629	Torque converter clutch solenoid (AT only)	Open or short
998	PCM	PCM is in fail safe mode
No codes	Data link connector	Open or short

90974C09

Fig. 90 OBD-II system diagnostic trouble code chart (1 of 5)—1995–98 B Series Pick-up models

NO.	DIAGNOSED CIRCUIT	CONDITION
P1260	Anti-Theft System	Anti-theft system has detected a break in the onboard security test due to an attempted theft or system hardware failure.
P1270	Over-Revving	Engine RPM or vehicle speed limit reached.
P1351	Powertrain Control Module (PCM)	Loss of Ignition Diagnostic Monitor (IDM).
P1358		
P1352	Ignition Coil	Ignition coil A primary circuit malfunction.
P1353		Ignition coil B primary circuit malfunction.
P1354		Ignition coil C primary circuit malfunction.
P1359	Powertrain Control Module (PCM)	Loss of Spark Output (SPOUT) signal.
P1360	Ignition Coil	Ignition coil A secondary circuit malfunction.
P1361		Ignition coil B secondary circuit malfunction.
P1362		Ignition coil C secondary circuit malfunction.
P1364		Ignition coil primary circuit malfunction.
P1365		Ignition coil secondary circuit malfunction.
P1390	OCT ADJ Shorting Bar	OCT ADJ shorting bar is not in or OCT ADJ circuit is open.
P1400	Differential Pressure Feedback EGR (DPFE) Sensor	Self-test has detected DPFE SIG circuit input below minimum.
P1401		Self-test has detected DPFE SIG circuit input above maximum.
P1405		Continuous self-test has detected that exhaust manifold side (upstream) DPFE pressure hose is off or plugged.
P1406		Continuous self-test has detected that intake manifold side (downstream) DPFE pressure hose is off or plugged.
P1408	EGR System	KOER self-test has detected EGR flow out of range.
P1409	EGR Vacuum Regulator (EVR) Solenoid	• Self-test has detected an electrical malfunction in EVR circuit. • Continuous DTC P1409 indicates that continuous self-test has detected an electrical malfunction in EVR circuit sometime during vehicle operation.
P1443	Evaporator System	Purge flow malfunction.
P1444	Purge Flow (PF) Sensor	PF SIG circuit input below minimum.
P1445		PF SIG circuit input above maximum.
P1460	Wide-Open Throttle A/C Cut-Off (WAC) Relay	• A/C was on during self-test or WAC circuit fault. • Continuous DTC P1460 indicates that WAC circuit failure has occurred during vehicle operation.
P1464	A/C Control Signal (ACCS)	ACCS input to PCM was high during self-test.
P1500	Vehicle Speed Sensor (VSS)[3]	PCM detected an erratic VSS signal during operation.
P1501		VSS signal has been detected out of self-test range.
P1504	Idle Air Control (IAC) Solenoid	Self-test has detected IAC circuit malfunction.
P1505		IAC system has reached adaptive clip.
P1506		Self-test has detected IAC over-speed error.
P1507		Self-test has detected IAC under-speed error.
P1605	Powertrain Control Module (PCM)	PCM has experienced a power interrupt in Keep Alive Power (KAPWR) circuit.
P1650	Power Steering Pressure (PSP) Switch[4]	PSP circuit open during KOEO (2.3L only).
P1651		PSP signal not changing state during KOER (2.3L only).
P1701	AT Solenoid	EPC pressure is low, no drop in TSS rpm, TR indicates reverse.

Fig. 93 OBD-II system diagnostic trouble code chart (4 of 5)—1995-98 B Series Pick-up models

NO.	DIAGNOSED CIRCUIT	CONDITION
P0746	Electrical Pressure Control (EPC) Solenoid	EPC solenoid malfunction.
P0750	Shift Solenoid 1 (SS1)	SS1 circuit open or shorted or PCM driver failure during on-board diagnostic.
P0751		SS1 function failure (mechanical or hydraulic failure).
P0755	Shift Solenoid 2 (SS2)	SS2 circuit open or shorted or PCM driver failure during on-board diagnostic.
P0756		SS2 functional failure (mechanical or hydraulic failure).
P0760	Shift Solenoid 3 (SS3)	SS3 circuit open or shorted or PCM driver failure during on-board diagnostic.
P0761		SS3 functional failure (mechanical or hydraulic failure).
P0765	Shift Solenoid 4 (SS4)	SS4 circuit open or shorted or PCM driver failure during OBD.
P0781	AT Solenoid	Gear #1 incorrect ratio.
P0782		Gear #2 incorrect ratio.
P0783		Gear #3 incorrect ratio.
P0784		Gear #4 incorrect ratio.
P1000	OBD II Drive Cycle	OBD II monitor testing not complete.
P1001	Data Link Connector (DLC)	KOER self-test not able to complete or aborted.
P1100	Mass Airflow Sensor (MAF)	MAF signal went below 0.39 volt or above 3.90 volts sometime during last 40 warm-up cycles.
P1101[2]	Mass Airflow Sensor (MAF)	• MAF signal was greater than 0.20 volt during KOEO self-test (outputs KOEO DTC P1101). • MAF signal was not between 0.34-1.96 volts during KOER self-test (outputs KOER DTC P1101).
P1112	Intake Air Temperature (IAT) Sensor	IAT signal was not received during KOEO and KOER self-test, but was output during Retrieve/Clear Continuous DTC self-test.
P1116	Engine Coolant Temperature (ECT) Sensor	ECT signal went below 0.3 volt or above 3.7 volts during KOEO or KOER self-test.
P1117		ECT signal was not received during KOEO and KOER self-test, but was output during Retrieve/Clear Continuous DTC self-test.
P1120	Throttle Position (TP) Sensor	TP signal is within self-test range but below closed throttle position range of 0.17 to 0.49 volts (3.43 to 9.80%).
P1121		TP signal is inconsistent with MAF sensor signal.
P1124		TP rotational setting and signal are not in self-test range of 0.66 to 1.20 volts (13.23 to 24.02%).
P1125		TP signal went below 0.49 volts (9.80%) or above 4.60 volts (92.27%) sometime during last 80 warm-up cycles.
P1127	Heated Oxygen Sensor (HO2S)-12	HO2S-12 heater was not on during KOER self-test.
P1127	Heated Oxygen Sensor (HO2S)	Upstream HO2S signal(s) are swapped from bank to bank during KOER.
P1130	Heated Oxygen Sensor (HO2S)-11	Fuel control has reached its maximum compensation for lean or rich and HO2S is not switching.
P1131		Fuel/air ratio is correcting rich for overly lean condition (HO2S voltage is less than 0.45 volts).
P1132		Fuel/air ratio is correcting lean for overly rich condition (HO2S voltage is greater than 0.45 volts).
P1150	Heated Oxygen Sensor (HO2S)-21	Fuel control has reached its maximum compensation for lean or rich and HO2S is not switching.
P1151		Fuel/air ratio is correcting rich for overly lean condition (HO2S voltage is less than 0.45 volts).
P1152	Heated Oxygen Sensor (HO2S)-11	Fuel/air ratio is correcting lean for overly rich condition (HO2S voltage is greater than 0.45 volts).

Fig. 92 OBD-II system diagnostic trouble code chart (3 of 5)—1995-98 B Series Pick-up models

NO.	DIAGNOSED CIRCUIT	CONDITION
P1703	Brake On/Off (BOO) Switch	Brake not cycled during KOER or BOO circuit failure during KOEO.
P1704	Transmission Range (TR) Sensor	TR sensor misaligned or failed electrically.
P1705		TR signal is not in PARK during KOEO self-test.
P1709	Clutch Pedal Position (CPP) Switch	Voltage is high or CPP is open when voltage should be low or switch should be closed grounding.
P1711	Transmission Fluid Temperature (TFT) Sensor	TFT signal went either low or high end of acceptable range during self-test.
P1714	Shift Solenoid 1 (SS1)	SS1 malfunction (mechanical failure).
P1715	Shift Solenoid 2 (SS2)	SS2 malfunction (mechanical failure).
P1716	Shift Solenoid 3 (SS3)	SS3 malfunction (mechanical failure).
P1717	Shift Solenoid 4 (SS4)	SS4 malfunction (mechanical failure).
P1719	Overdrive Drum Speed (ODS)	PCM detected loss of ODS signal during operation.
P1729	4x4 Low SW	Switch error.
P1740	Torque Control Clutch (TCC) Control	TCC control error.
P1741		
P1742	Torque Control Clutch (TCC) Solenoid	TCC solenoid has failed ON (turn on MIL).
P1743		TCC solenoid has failed ON by electric, mechanical or hydraulic concern (turn on TCIL).
P1744	Torque Control Clutch (TCC) System	TCC system mechanically stuck in OFF position.
P1746	Electronic Pressure Control (EPC) Solenoid	EPC circuit open.
P1747		EPC circuit shorted.
P1749		EPC solenoid failed low.
P1751	Shift Solenoid 1 (SS1)	SS1 functional failure (mechanical or hydraulic failure).
P1754	Coast Clutch Solenoid (CCS)	CCS circuit open or shorted or PCM driver failure during on-board diagnostic.
P1756	Shift Solenoid 2 (SS2)	SS2 functional failure (mechanical or hydraulic failure).
P1761	Shift Solenoid 3 (SS3)	SS3 functional failure (mechanical or hydraulic failure).
P1762	Transmission	SS3/SS4/OD band failure
P1780	Transmission Control Switch (TCS)	TCS was not cycled during KOER self-test. TCS circuit open or shorted.
P1781	4x4 Low SW	Out of self-test range.
P1783	Transmission	Transmission fluid temperature exceeds 127°C (270°F).

90974C13

Fig. 94 OBD-II system diagnostic trouble code chart (5 of 5)—1995–98 B Series Pick-up models

VACUUM DIAGRAMS

Following are vacuum diagrams for most of the engine and emissions package combinations covered by this manual. Because vacuum circuits will vary based on various engine and vehicle options, always refer first to the vehicle emission control information label, if present. Should the label be missing, or should vehicle be equipped with a different engine from the vehicle's original equipment, refer to the diagrams below for the same or similar configuration.

If you wish to obtain a replacement emissions label, most manufacturers make the labels available for purchase. The labels can usually be ordered from a local dealer.

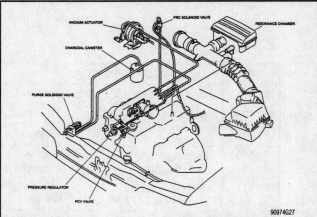

Fig. 98 Vacuum hose routing for 1994–95 MPV models equipped with the 2.6L engine

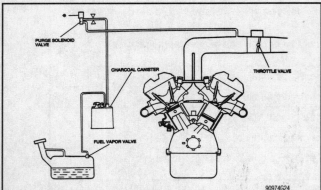

Fig. 95 Vacuum hose routing for the Navajo and 1994 B Series Pick-up models equipped with the 4.0L engine

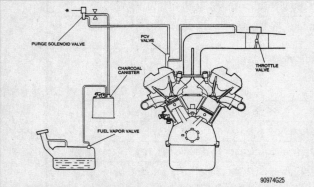

Fig. 96 Vacuum hose routing for 1994 B Series Pick-up models equipped with the 3.0L engine

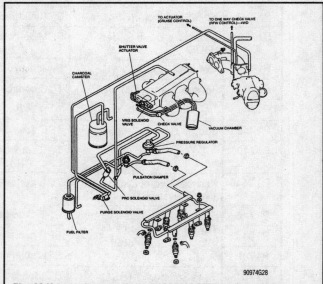

Fig. 99 Vacuum hose routing for 1994–95 MPV models equipped with the 3.0L engine

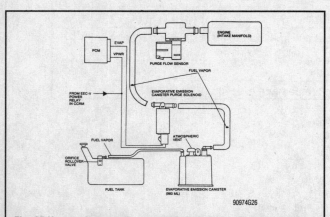

Fig. 97 Vacuum hose routing for 1995–97 B Series Pick-up models

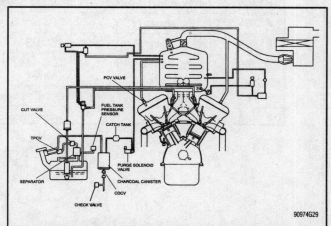

Fig. 100 Vacuum hose routing for 1996–98 MPV models equipped with the 3.0L engine

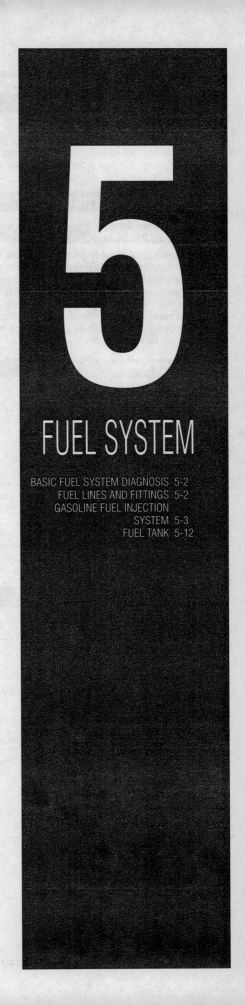

5

FUEL SYSTEM

BASIC FUEL SYSTEM DIAGNOSIS

When there is a problem starting or driving a vehicle, two of the most important checks involve the ignition and the fuel systems. The questions most mechanics attempt to answer first, "is there spark?" and "is there fuel?" will often lead to solving most basic problems. For ignition system diagnosis and testing, please refer to the information on engine electrical components and ignition systems found earlier in this manual. If the ignition system checks out (there is spark), then you must determine if the fuel system is operating properly (is there fuel?).

FUEL LINES AND FITTINGS

General Information

→Quick-connect (push type) fuel line fittings must be disconnected using proper procedure or the fitting may be damaged. There are two types of retainers used on the push connect fittings. Line sizes of ⅜ and ⁵/₁₆ in. diameter use a hairpin clip retainer. The ¼ in. diameter line connectors use a duck-bill clip retainer. In addition, some engines use spring-lock connections, secured by a garter spring, which require Special Spring Lock Coupling Tools 49 UN01 051 and 49 UN01 052 (or equivalent) for removal.

Hairpin Clip Fitting

REMOVAL & INSTALLATION

▶ See Figures 1 and 2

1. Clean all dirt and grease from the fitting. Spread the two clip legs about ⅛ in. (3mm) each to disengage from the fitting and pull the clip outward from the fitting. Use finger pressure only; do not use any tools.
2. Grasp the fitting and hose assembly and pull away from the steel line. Twist the fitting and hose assembly slightly while pulling, if the assembly sticks.
3. Inspect the hairpin clip for damage, replacing the clip if necessary. Reinstall the clip in position on the fitting.
4. Inspect the fitting and inside of the connector to ensure freedom from dirt or obstruction. Install the fitting into the connector and push together. A click will be heard when the hairpin snaps into the proper connection. Pull on the line to insure full engagement.

Duckbill Clip Fitting

REMOVAL & INSTALLATION

▶ See Figures 2 and 3

1. Special tools are available from Mazda and other manufacturers for removng retaining clips. Use Mazda Tools 49-UN01-053 and 49-UN01-054 or

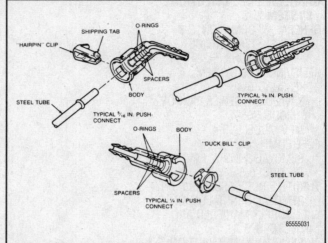

Fig. 2 Exploded views of the hairpin and duckbill clip type fuel fittings

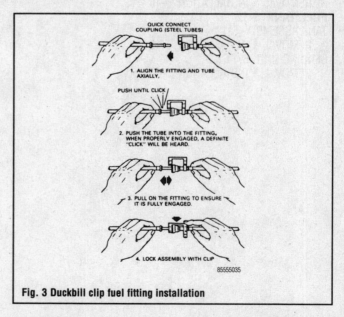

Fig. 3 Duckbill clip fuel fitting installation

equivalent. If the tool is not on hand, go onto step 2. Align the slot on the push connector disconnect tool with either tab on the retaining clip. Pull the line from the connector.

2. If the special clip tool is not available, use a pair of narrow 6-inch slip-jaw pliers with a jaw width of 0.2 in (5mm) or less. Align the jaws of the pliers with the openings of the fitting case and compress the part of the retaining clip that engages the case. Compressing the retaining clip will release the fitting, which may be pulled from the connector. Both sides of the clip must be compressed at the same time to disengage.

3. Inspect the retaining clip, fitting end and connector. Replace the clip if any damage is apparent.

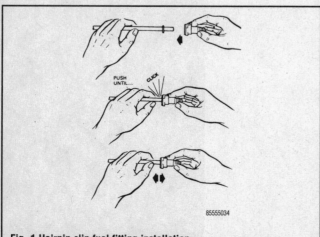

Fig. 1 Hairpin clip fuel fitting installation

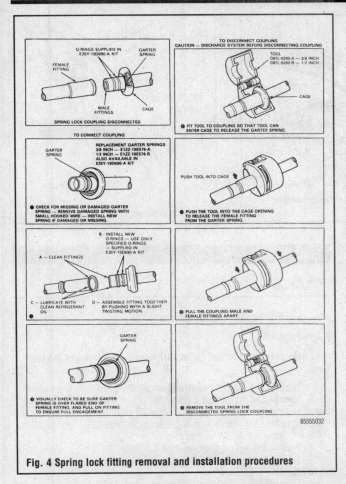

Fig. 4 Spring lock fitting removal and installation procedures

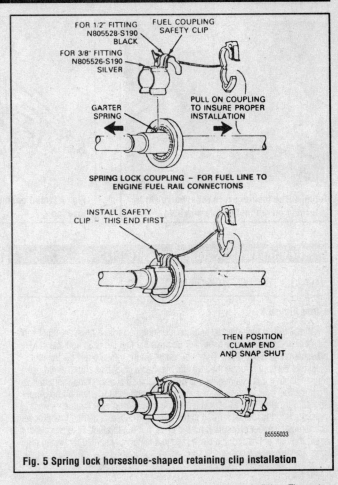

Fig. 5 Spring lock horseshoe-shaped retaining clip installation

4. Push the line into the steel connector until a click is heard, indicating the clip is in place. Pull on the line to check engagement.

Spring Lock Coupling

♦ See Figures 4 and 5

The spring lock coupling is held together by a garter spring inside a circular cage. When the coupling is connected together, the flared end of the female fit-ting slips behind the garter spring inside the cage of the male fitting. The garter spring and cage then prevent the flared end of the female fitting from pulling out of the cage. As an additional locking feature, most vehicles have a horseshoe-shaped retaining clip that improves the retaining reliability of the spring lock coupling.

GASOLINE FUEL INJECTION SYSTEM

General Information

The Multi-port Fuel Injection (MFI) system includes a high pressure, inline electric fuel pump mounted in the fuel tank, a fuel supply manifold, a throttle body (meters the incoming air charge for the correct mixture with the fuel), a pressure regulator, fuel filters and both solid and flexible fuel lines. The fuel supply manifold includes 4 or 6 electronically-controlled fuel injectors, each mounted directly above an intake port in the lower intake manifold. Each injec-tor fires once every other crankshaft revolution, in sequence with the engine fir-ing order.

FUEL SYSTEM SERVICE PRECAUTIONS

Safety is the most important factor when performing not only fuel system maintenance, but any type of maintenance. Failure to conduct maintenance and repairs in a safe manner may result in serious personal injury or death. Work on a vehicle's fuel system components can be accomplished safely and effectively by adhering to the following rules and guidelines.

• To avoid the possibility of fire and personal injury, always disconnect the negative battery cable unless the repair or test procedure requires that battery voltage by applied.

• Always relieve the fuel system pressure prior to disconnecting any fuel system component (injector, fuel rail, pressure regulator, etc.) fitting or fuel line connection. Exercise extreme caution whenever relieving fuel system pressure to avoid exposing skin, face and eyes to fuel spray. Please be advised that fuel under pressure may penetrate the skin or any part of the body that it contacts.

• Always place a shop towel or cloth around the fitting or connection prior to loosening to absorb any excess fuel due to spillage. Ensure that all fuel spillage is quickly remove from engine surfaces. Ensure that all fuel-soaked cloths or towels are deposited into a flame-proof waste container with a lid.

• Always keep a dry chemical (Class B) fire extinguisher near the work area.

• Do not allow fuel spray or fuel vapors to come into contact with a spark or open flame.

• Always use a second wrench when loosening or tightening fuel line con-nections fittings. This will prevent unnecessary stress and torsion to fuel piping. Always follow the proper torque specifications.

• Always replace fuel fitting O-rings with new ones. Do not substitute fuel hose where rigid pipe is installed.

Fig. 6 The fuel pressure relief valve (A) is located on the fuel supply manifold

89685P14

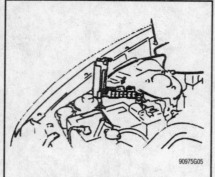

90975G05

Fig. 7 Circuit opening relay connector location

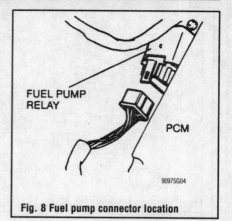

FUEL PUMP RELAY

PCM

90975G04

Fig. 8 Fuel pump connector location

Relieving Fuel System Pressure

NAVAJO & B SERIES PICK-UP MODELS

♦ See Figure 6

All multi-port fuel injected engines are equipped with a pressure relief valve located on the fuel supply manifold. Remove the fuel tank cap and attach fuel pressure gauge T80L-9974-B, or equivalent, to the valve to release the fuel pressure. Be sure to drain the fuel into a suitable container and to avoid gasoline spillage. If a pressure gauge is not available, disconnect the vacuum hose from the fuel pressure regulator and attach a hand-held vacuum pump. Apply about 25 in. Hg (84 kPa) of vacuum to the regulator to vent the fuel system pressure into the fuel tank through the fuel return hose. Note that this procedure will remove the fuel pressure from the lines, but not the fuel. Take precautions to avoid the risk of fire and use clean rags to soak up any spilled fuel when the lines are disconnected.

MPV MODELS

2.6L Engine

♦ See Figure 7

1. Start the engine.
2. Remove the circuit opening relay connector from the relay box, located in the right side of the engine compartment.
3. After the engine stalls, turn the ignition switch **OFF** and reinstall the relay connector.

3.0L Engine

♦ See Figure 8

❊❊ CAUTION

Fuel injection systems remain under pressure after the engine has been turned OFF. Properly relieve fuel pressure before disconnecting any fuel lines. Failure to do so may result in fire or personal injury.

❊❊ CAUTION

Do not allow fuel spray or fuel vapors to come in contact with a spark or open flame. Keep a dry chemical fire extinguisher nearby. Never store fuel in an open container due to risk of fire or explosion.

1. Start the engine.
2. Disconnect the fuel pump relay connector, located at the ECM.
3. After the engine stalls, turn the ignition switch **OFF**.
4. Connect the fuel pump relay connector.

Fuel Pump

REMOVAL & INSTALLATION

Navajo and B Series Pick-up Models

♦ See Figure 9

➡ To gain access to the fuel pump, it is necessary to remove the fuel tank.

1. Depressurize the fuel system and remove the fuel tank from the vehicle.
2. Remove any dirt that has accumulated around the fuel pump attaching flange, to prevent it from entering the tank during service.
3. Turn the fuel pump locking ring counterclockwise using a locking ring removal tool and remove the locking ring.
4. Remove the fuel pump and bracket assembly.
5. Remove the seal gasket and discard it.
To install:
6. Put a light coating of heavy grease on a new seal ring to hold it in place during assembly. Install it in fuel tank ring groove.
7. Insert the fuel pump assembly into the fuel tank, then secure it in place with the locking ring. Tighten the ring until secure.
8. Install the tank in the vehicle.

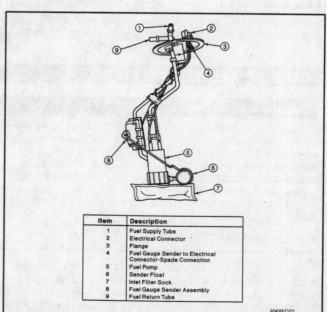

Item	Description
1	Fuel Supply Tube
2	Electrical Connector
3	Flange
4	Fuel Gauge Sender to Electrical Connector-Spade Connection
5	Fuel Pump
6	Sender Float
7	Inlet Filter Sock
8	Fuel Gauge Sender Assembly
9	Fuel Return Tube

89685G02

Fig. 9 Fuel pump and sending unit used on the B Series Pick-up regular cab

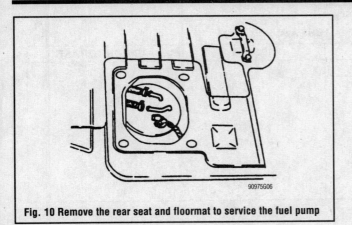

Fig. 10 Remove the rear seat and floormat to service the fuel pump

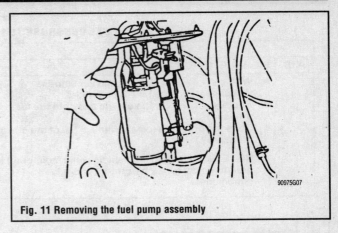

Fig. 11 Removing the fuel pump assembly

9. Install a minimum of 10 gallons of fuel and check for leaks.

10. Install a pressure gauge on the throttle body valve and turn the ignition **ON** for 3 seconds. Turn the key **OFF**, then repeat the key cycle five to ten times until the pressure gauge shows at least 30 psi. Reinspect for leaks at the fittings.

11. Remove the pressure gauge. Start the engine and check for fuel leaks.

MPV Models

▶ **See Figures 10 and 11**

1. Relieve the fuel system pressure and disconnect the negative battery cable.

2. Remove the rear seat and lift up the rear floormat. Remove the fuel pump cover.

3. Disconnect the sending unit/fuel pump assembly electrical connector and the fuel lines.

4. Remove any dirt that has accumulated around the sending unit/fuel pump assembly so it will not enter the fuel tank during removal and installation.

5. Remove the attaching screws and remove the sending unit/fuel pump assembly.

6. If necessary, disconnect the electrical connectors and the fuel hose and remove the pump from the sending unit assembly.

7. Installation is the reverse of the removal procedure. Be sure to install a new seal rubber gasket.

TESTING

Navajo and B Series Pick-up Models

▶ **See Figures 12, 13 and 14**

※ CAUTION

Fuel pressure must be relieved before attempting to disconnect any fuel lines.

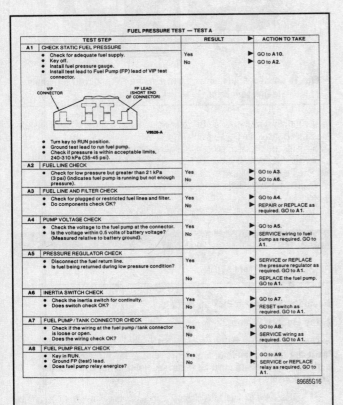

Fig. 12 Fuel pressure test chart–part 1

FUEL PRESSURE TEST — TEST A			
TEST STEP	**RESULT**	▶	**ACTION TO TAKE**
A1 CHECK STATIC FUEL PRESSURE • Check for adequate fuel supply. • Key off. • Install fuel pressure gauge. • Install test lead to Fuel Pump (FP) lead of VIP test connector. • Turn key to RUN position. • Ground test lead to run fuel pump. • Check if pressure is within acceptable limits, 240-310 kPa (35-45 psi).	Yes No	▶ ▶	GO to A10. GO to A2.
A2 FUEL LINE CHECK • Check for low pressure but greater than 21 kPa (3 psi) (indicates fuel pump is running but not enough pressure).	Yes No	▶ ▶	GO to A3. GO to A6.
A3 FUEL LINE AND FILTER CHECK • Check for plugged or restricted fuel lines and filter. • Do components check OK?	Yes No	▶ ▶	GO to A4. REPAIR or REPLACE as required. GO to A1.
A4 PUMP VOLTAGE CHECK • Check the voltage to the fuel pump at the connector. • Is the voltage within 0.5 volts of battery voltage? (Measured relative to battery ground).	Yes No	▶ ▶	GO to A5. SERVICE wiring to fuel pump as required. GO to A1.
A5 PRESSURE REGULATOR CHECK • Disconnect the fuel return line. • Is fuel being returned during low pressure condition?	Yes No	▶ ▶	SERVICE or REPLACE the pressure regulator as required. GO to A1. REPLACE the fuel pump. GO to A1.
A6 INERTIA SWITCH CHECK • Check the inertia switch for continuity. • Does switch check OK?	Yes No	▶ ▶	GO to A7. RESET switch as required. GO to A1.
A7 FUEL PUMP / TANK CONNECTOR CHECK • Check if the wiring at the fuel pump / tank connector is loose or open. • Does the wiring check OK?	Yes No	▶ ▶	GO to A8. SERVICE wiring as required. GO to A1.
A8 FUEL PUMP RELAY CHECK • Key in RUN. • Ground FP (test) lead. • Does fuel pump relay energize?	Yes No	▶ ▶	GO to A9. SERVICE or REPLACE relay as required. GO to A1.

89685G16

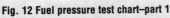

Fig. 13 Fuel pressure test chart–part 2

FUEL PRESSURE TEST — TEST A (Continued)			
TEST STEP	**RESULT**	▶	**ACTION TO TAKE**
A9 PCM RELAY CHECK • Key in RUN. • Does PCM relay energize?	Yes No	▶ ▶	REPLACE fuel pump. GO to A1. SERVICE or REPLACE PCM relay as required. GO to A1.
A10 CHECK VALVE TEST • Remove ground from test lead and note pressure on gauge. • Does the pressure remain within 14 kPa (2 psi) for 3 minutes after the ground is removed?	Yes No	▶ ▶	GO to A14. GO to A11.
A11 FUEL LINE AND CONNECTOR LEAK CHECK • Check all fuel lines and connectors for leaks. • Do lines and connectors check OK?	Yes No	▶ ▶	GO to A12. SERVICE or REPLACE fuel lines and connectors as required. GO to A1.
A12 CHECK VALVE TEST, RETURN LINE PLUGGED • Disconnect the return line and plug engine side. • Ground test lead to momentarily activate the fuel pump. • Raise pressure to normal operating pressure, 240-310 kPa (35-45 psi). • Remove ground from test lead and note pressure on gauge. • Does the pressure remain within 14 kPa (2 psi) for 3 minutes after the ground is removed?	Yes No	▶ ▶	If pressure holds, REPLACE regulator and REPEAT last two parts of Test Step. REPLACE the fuel pump. GO to A1.
A13 CHECK VALVE TEST, REGULATOR REPLACED • With the return line still disconnected and regulator plugged, ground the test lead to momentarily activate the fuel pump. • Raise the pressure to normal operating pressure, 240-310 kPa (35-45 psi). • Remove ground from test lead and note pressure on gauge. • Does the pressure remain within 14 kPa (2 psi) for 3 minutes after the ground is removed?	Yes No	▶ ▶	GO to A1. REPLACE fuel pump and GO to A1. If unit still fails Step A10, there may be a leaking fuel injector or fuel rail. Correct these concerns and GO to A10.
A14 ENGINE ON TEST • Disconnect and plug the vacuum line connected to the pressure regulator. • Key ON, engine running at idle. • Is fuel pressure 240-310 kPa (35-45 psi)?	Yes No	▶ ▶	GO to A18. GO to A15.
A15 FUEL LINE AND FILTER CHECK • Check for plugged or restricted fuel lines and filter. • Do components check OK?	Yes No	▶ ▶	GO to A16. REPAIR or REPLACE as required. GO to A1.
A16 PUMP VOLTAGE CHECK • Check the voltage to the fuel pump at the connector. • Is the voltage within 0.5 volts of battery voltage? (Measured relative to battery ground).	Yes No	▶ ▶	GO to A17. SERVICE wiring to fuel pump as required. CHECK for poor or dirty connections on ground side of pump. GO to A1.
A17 PRESSURE REGULATOR CHECK • Disconnect the fuel return line. • Is fuel being returned during low pressure condition?	Yes No	▶ ▶	SERVICE or REPLACE the pressure regulator as required. GO to A1. REPLACE the fuel pump.

89685G17

FUEL PRESSURE TEST — TEST A (Continued)

TEST STEP	RESULT	▶	ACTION TO TAKE
A18 HIGH SPEED TEST • With engine running at idle and vacuum line disconnected, note fuel rail pressure. • Rapidly accelerate the engine and note the fuel pressure. • Does the pressure remain within 5 psi of the starting pressure? NOTE: Road testing the vehicle while monitoring the pressure may give a better test under load conditions.	Yes No	▶ ▶	Fuel pump is OK. GO to A15.

89685G18

Fig. 14 Fuel pressure test chart–part 3

The diagnostic pressure valve (Schrader valve) is located on the fuel supply manifold (rail). This valve provides a convenient point for service personnel to monitor fuel pressure, release the system pressure prior to maintenance, and to bleed out air which may become trapped in the system during pressure replacement. A pressure gauge with an adapter is required to perform pressure tests.

If the pressure tap is not installed or an adapter is not available, use a T-fitting to install the pressure gauge between the fuel filter line and the throttle body fuel inlet or fuel rail.

To test the fuel pump, follow the accompanying diagnostic charts. Testing fuel pressure requires the use of a special pressure gauge (Ford Tool T80L-9974-B, Rotunda Fuel Pressure Testing Kit 014–00447, or equivalent) that attaches to the diagnostic pressure tap fitting. To perform the fuel system test a scan tool is necessary to access the different test modes.

➡**Depressurize the fuel system before disconnecting any lines.**

MPV Models

◆ **See Figures 15 and 16**

1. Relieve the fuel system pressure and disconnect the negative battery cable.
2. Disconnect the fuel line from the fuel filter outlet. Connect a fuel pressure gauge to the fuel filter outlet.
3. Connect the negative battery cable. Connect the data link connector terminals F/P and GND (Ground) with a jumper wire.

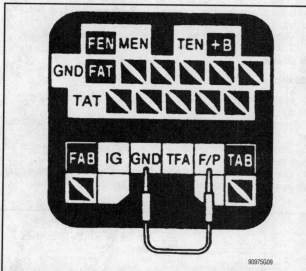

Fig. 16 Connect a jumper wire between the F/P and GND terminals of the data link connector

4. Turn the ignition switch **ON** to operate the fuel pump and check the fuel pressure. It should be 64–92 psi.
5. If the fuel pressure is not as specified, replace the fuel pump.
6. Turn the ignition switch **OFF** and disconnect the negative battery cable. Remove the jumper wire from the test connector.
7. Remove the fuel pressure gauge and reconnect the fuel line to the fuel filter outlet.
8. Connect the negative battery cable.

Throttle Body Assembly

REMOVAL & INSTALLATION

Navajo and B Series Pick-up Models

◆ **See Figures 17 thru 22**

➡**The 3.0L engine's throttle body is a 1 piece casting which includes the upper intake manifold. In order to remove the throttle body, the entire upper manifold must be removed. Refer to Section 3 for the proper procedures.**

1. Loosen the air inlet tube clamps, then separate the tube from the throttle body and air cleaner housing. Remove the tube from the vehicle.

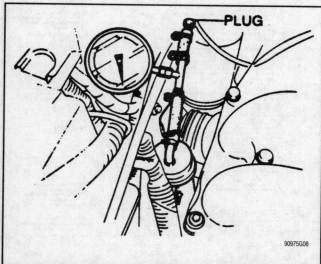

Fig. 15 Install a fuel pressure gauge to the outlet of the fuel filter

Fig. 17 To remove the throttle body, first remove the air intake hose, then the linkage shield

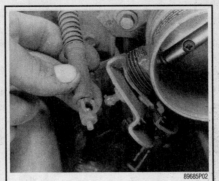

Fig. 18 Next, disconnect the throttle control cable(s) from the throttle body . . .

Fig. 19 . . . as well as any electrical connections. . .

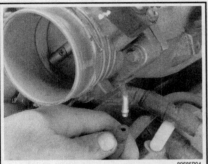

Fig. 20 . . . and vacuum fittings. Make sure to label them to assure proper installation

Fig. 21 Remove the throttle body-to-upper intake attaching bolts . . .

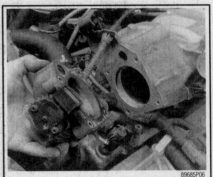

Fig. 22 . . . then remove the throttle body assembly

2. If equipped, remove the throttle linkage shield.

3. Detach the accelerator and speed control (if equipped) cables from the throttle body lever.

4. Label and disengage the engine wiring harness connectors from the Throttle Position (TP) sensor and the Idle Air Control (IAC) valve; both are mounted on the throttle body.

5. Remove the four mounting nuts, then carefully separate the throttle body from the upper intake manifold.

6. Remove and discard the old throttle body-to-intake manifold gasket.

To install:

➡️ If scraping is necessary to clean the remaining gasket material off of the mating surfaces, take care to avoid scratching or gouging the soft aluminum.

7. Clean the gasket mating surfaces of any residual gasket material.

8. Install the throttle body, along with a new gasket, onto the upper intake manifold. Install and tighten the mounting nuts in a crisscross pattern to specifications.

9. Engage the TP sensor and IAC valve wiring connectors and remove the temporary labels.

10. Reattach the accelerator and speed control cables, if applicable, to the throttle body lever.

11. If removed, install the throttle linkage shield.

12. Install the air inlet tube between the air cleaner housing and the throttle body. Tighten the tube clamps until snug.

MPV Models

2.6L ENGINE

▶ See Figure 23

1. Disconnect the battery ground.
2. Disconnect the air hose.
3. Disconnect the ventilation hose.

4. Remove the air pipe and resonance chamber.
5. Disconnect the accelerator cable from the throttle lever.
6. Drain the engine coolant.

✱✱ CAUTION

When draining the coolant, keep in mind that cats and dogs are attracted by the ethylene glycol antifreeze, and are quite likely to drink any that is left in an uncovered container or in puddles on the ground. This will prove fatal in sufficient quantity. Always drain the coolant into a sealable container. Coolant should be reused unless it is contaminated or several years old.

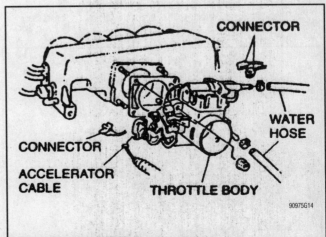

Fig. 23 Removal of throttle body components

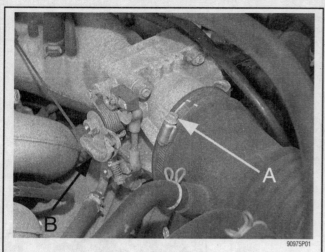

Fig. 24 Loosen the air cleaner-to-throttle body hose clamps (A) and remove hose, then disconnect the accelerator cable (B)

7. Disconnect the coolant lines at the manifold.
8. Tag and disconnect all vacuum hoses.
9. Tag and disconnect all wiring.
10. Unbolt and remove the throttle body.
11. Always use a new mounting gasket. Place the new gasket and throttle body in position. Install and torque the fasteners to 14–18 ft. lbs. (19–25 Nm). Connect the vacuum lines, hoses and intake system components. Fill the cooling system.

3.0L ENGINE (1994–95)

▶ See Figures 24 and 25

1. Disconnect battery negative cable.
2. Drain approximately 2 qts. of coolant from the engine.
3. Loosen air cleaner-to-throttle body hose clamps and remove hose.
4. Remove accelerator cable.
5. Remove harness connector from throttle position sensor (TPS).
6. Disconnect the water hoses.
7. Label and remove vacuum hoses necessary.
8. Remove throttle body mounting nuts and remove throttle body and gasket.
9. Install throttle body using a new gasket on air intake plenum. Secure with mounting nuts. Tighten the mounting nuts to 14–18 ft. lbs. (19–25 Nm).
10. Reconnect water hoses and TPS connector.
11. Reconnect accelerator cable.
12. Install air cleaner to throttle body hose and tighten clamps.
13. Add the necessary amount of engine coolant.
14. Reconnect battery negative cable. Adjust the idle speed, if necessary.

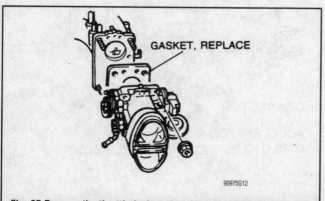

Fig. 25 Remove the throttle body and replace the mounting gasket

3.0L ENGINE (1996–98)

1. Disconnect the negative battery cable.
2. Remove the clamps and remove the air intake hose from the throttle body and the MAF sensor.
3. Disconnect the accelerator cable and if equipped, the cruise control cable.
4. Disconnect the throttle position sensor connector.
5. Remove the 2 bolts and the 2 nuts and remove the throttle body unit and gasket.

To install:

6. Using a new gasket, install the throttle body assembly with the 2 bolts and the 2 nuts. Torque the bolts and nuts to 14–18 ft. lbs. (19–25 Nm).
7. Reconnect the throttle position sensor connector.
8. Reconnect the accelerator cable and if equipped, the cruise control cable.
9. Install the air intake hose to the throttle body assembly and the MAF sensor with the 2 clamps.
10. Connect the negative battery cable, start the engine and operate until normal temperature, check for proper operation.

Fuel Supply Manifold and Injectors

REMOVAL & INSTALLATION

Navajo and B Series Pick-up Models

▶ See Figures 26 thru 33

1. Remove the upper intake manifold. Be sure to depressurize the fuel system before disconnecting any fuel lines.
2. Disconnect the fuel supply and return line retaining clips.
3. Detach the vacuum line from the fuel pressure regulator.
4. Disconnect the fuel chassis inlet and outlet fuel hoses from the fuel supply manifold.
5. Label and disconnect the fuel injector wire harness plugs.
6. On the 2.3L engine, remove the two fuel supply manifold retaining bolts.
7. On the 4.0L engine, remove the six upper intake manifold attaching studs.
8. On all other engines, remove the four fuel supply manifold retaining bolts.
9. Carefully disengage the fuel rail assembly from the fuel injectors by lifting and gently rocking the rail.
10. Remove the fuel injectors from the intake manifold by lifting while gently rocking them from side to side
11. Place all removed components on a clean surface to prevent contamination by dirt or grease.

➥Never use silicone grease; it will clog the injector. All injectors and the fuel rail must be handled with extreme care to prevent damage to sealing areas and sensitive fuel metering orifices.

12. Examine the injector O-rings for deterioration damage, replacing them as needed.

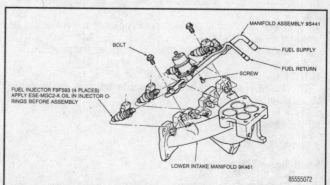

Fig. 26 Exploded view of the 2.3L engine fuel supply rail and injectors—2.5L engine similar

Fig. 27 For fuel supply manifold removal, unbolt the upper intake, then disconnect the injector wire harness plugs

Fig. 28 On the 4.0L engine, remove the 6 manifold mounting studs which retain the supply manifold

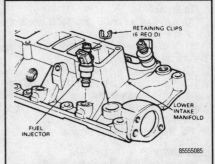

Fig. 29 Some models use small retaining clips to secure the injectors in the supply manifold

Fig. 30 Lift upwards with a rocking motion to disengage the injectors, then remove the supply manifold

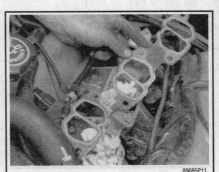

Fig. 31 On the 4.0L engine, remove the old fuel supply manifold gasket and clean the mating surfaces

Fig. 32 Remove the injectors from the engine by gently rocking it while pulling upwards

Fig. 33 The injector has O-rings at the nozzle (A) and at the fuel supply manifold (B). Replace any damaged seals

13. Make sure the injector caps are clean and free from contamination or damage.

To install:

14. Lubricate all O-rings with clean engine oil, then install the injectors into the fuel rail using a light twisting/pushing motion.

15. On the 4.0L engine, position a new fuel rail gasket to the lower intake manifold.

16. Carefully install the fuel rail assembly and injectors into the lower intake manifold. Make certain to correctly position the insulators. Push down on the fuel rail to make sure the O-rings are seated.

17. Hold the fuel rail assembly in place and install the retaining bolts finger tight. Then tighten the bolts to specifications.

18. Connect the fuel supply and return lines.

19. Attach the vacuum hose to the fuel pressure regulator.

20. Connect the fuel injector wiring harness at the injectors.

21. Connect the vacuum line to the fuel pressure regulator, if removed.

22. Install the air intake and throttle body assembly.

23. Run the engine and check for fuel leaks.

MPV Models

2.6L ENGINE

> **CAUTION**
>
> Fuel injection systems remain under pressure after the engine has been turned OFF. Properly relieve fuel pressure before disconnecting any fuel lines. Failure to do so may result in fire or personal injury. Do not allow fuel spray or fuel vapors to come in contact with a spark or open flame. Keep a dry chemical fire extinguisher nearby. Never store fuel in an open container due to risk of fire or explosion.

1. Relieve the fuel system pressure.
2. Disconnect the negative battery cable.
3. Remove the upper intake manifold (dynamic chamber) as follows:
   a. Remove the manifold brackets.
   b. Disconnect and label the PCV hose, intake temperature sensor and ground wire.
   c. Remove the fuel injector harness bracket, and then remove the upper intake manifold.
4. Label and disconnect the vacuum and fuel hoses from the fuel rail.
5. Remove the fuel rail with the pressure regulator attached.
6. Disconnect the injector harness from injectors.
7. Invert fuel injector rail assembly.
8. Remove lock rings securing injectors to fuel rail receiver cups. Pull injectors upward from receiver cups.
9. If injectors are to be reused, place a protective cap on injector nozzle to prevent dirt or other damage.

To install:

10. Lubricate the new O-ring of each injectors with a clean drop of engine oil prior to installation.

11. Assemble each injector into the fuel rail receiver cups. Be careful not to damage the O-rings.

12. Install lock ring between receiver cup ridge and injector slot.

13. Install the fuel rail. Connect the vacuum and fuel hoses.

14. Install the upper intake manifold (dynamic chamber). Tighten the mounting bolts for the manifold and brackets to 14–18 ft. lbs. (19–25 Nm).

15. Connect the negative battery cable.

16. Start the engine and examine for leaks.

3.0L ENGINE

▶ See Figure 34

❊❊ CAUTION

Fuel injection systems remain under pressure after the engine has been turned OFF. Properly relieve fuel pressure before disconnecting any fuel lines. Failure to do so may result in fire or personal injury.

1. Disconnect the negative battery cable.
2. Drain the coolant system.
3. Remove the air and water hoses.
4. Remove the air cleaner assembly.
5. Disconnect the accelerator cable.
6. Disengage the throttle position sensor connector.
7. Remove the throttle body and gasket.
8. Remove the Bypass Air Control (BAC) valve and intake air pipe.
9. Remove the extension manifolds.
10. Remove the dynamic chamber.
11. Disconnect the fuel lines and electrical connectors.
12. Remove the fuel rail.
13. Disconnect the injector harness from injectors.
14. Invert the fuel injector rail assembly.
15. Remove the lock rings securing the injectors to the fuel rail receiver cups. Pull the injectors upward from the receiver cups.
16. If the injectors are to be reused, place a protective cap on the injector nozzle to prevent dirt or other damage.

To install:

17. Lubricate the new O-ring of each injectors with a clean drop of engine oil prior to installation.

18. Assemble each injector into the fuel rail receiver cups. Be careful not to damage the O-rings.

19. Install a lock ring between the receiver cup ridge and injector slot.

20. Install the fuel rail.

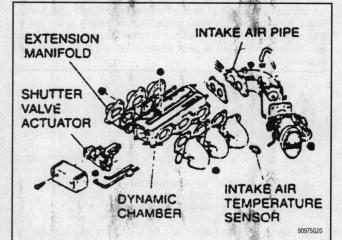

EXTENSION MANIFOLD

INTAKE AIR PIPE

SHUTTER VALVE ACTUATOR

DYNAMIC CHAMBER

INTAKE AIR TEMPERATURE SENSOR

90975G20

Fig. 34 Dynamic chamber and related components—3.0L engines

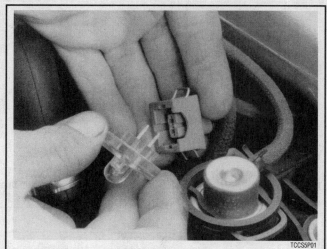

TCCS5P01

Fig. 35 A noid light can be attached to the fuel injector harness in order to test for injector pulse

21. Connect the fuel lines and electrical connectors.
22. Install the dynamic chamber.
23. Install the extension manifolds.
24. Install the intake air pipe, with a new gasket, and BAC valve.
25. Install the throttle body with a new gasket.
26. Engage the throttle position sensor connector.
27. Connect and adjust the accelerator cable.
28. Install the air cleaner assembly.
29. Install the air and water hoses.
30. Fill and bleed the coolant system.
31. Connect the negative battery cable.

TESTING

▶ See Figure 35

The fuel injectors can be tested with a Digital Volt-Ohmmeter (DVOM). To test an injector, detach the engine wiring harness connector from it. This may require removing the upper intake manifold or other engine components.

Once access to the injector is gained and the wiring is disconnected from it, set the DVOM to measure resistance (ohms). Measure the resistance of the injector by probing one terminal with the positive DVOM lead and the other injector terminal with the negative lead. The resistance measured should be between 12–16 ohms. If the resistance is not within this range, the fuel injector is faulty and must be replaced with a new one.

Fuel Pressure Regulator

REMOVAL & INSTALLATION

B Series Pick-up and Navajo Models

▶ See Figures 36 thru 42

❊❊ CAUTION

Observe all applicable safety precautions when working around fuel. Whenever servicing the fuel system, always work in a well ventilated area. Do not allow fuel spray or vapors to come in contact with a spark or open flame. Keep a dry chemical fire extinguisher near the work area. Always keep fuel in a container specifically designed for fuel storage; also, always properly seal fuel containers to avoid the possibility of fire or explosion.

1. Depressurize the fuel system; remove shielding as needed.
2. Remove the vacuum line at the pressure regulator.
3. If necessary, disconnect the fuel return line from the regulator.

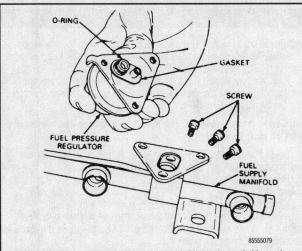

Fig. 36 Fuel pressure regulator on the 2.3L engine—3.0L engines are similar

➡ Some engines use two standard hex head bolts to retain the regulator instead of the Allen® head screws.

4. Remove the three Allen® head retaining screws from the regulator housing.

5. Remove the pressure regulator assembly, gasket and O-ring. Discard the gasket and check the O-ring for signs of cracks or deterioration.

To install:

6. Clean the gasket mating surfaces. If scraping is necessary, be careful not to damage the fuel pressure regulator or supply line gasket mating surfaces.

7. Lubricate the pressure regulator O-ring with light engine oil. Do not use silicone grease; it will clog the injectors.

8. Install the O-ring and a new gasket on the pressure regulator.

9. Install the pressure regulator on the fuel manifold and tighten the retaining screws to 27–40 inch lbs. (3–4 Nm) for all engines except the 4.0L engine, which is tightened to 70–97 inch lbs. (8–11 Nm).

➡ On the 2.3L engine, install the fuel manifold shield and tighten the bolts to 15–22 ft. lbs. (20–30 Nm).

10. Install the vacuum line at the pressure regulator.

11. If removed, connect the fuel return line.

12. Build fuel pressure in the system by turning the ignition **ON** and **OFF** (without starting the engine) at least five times. Leave the ignition **ON** at least 5 seconds each time. Check for fuel leaks.

MPV Models

※ **CAUTION**

Observe all applicable safety precautions when working around fuel. Whenever servicing the fuel system, always work in a well ventilated area. Do not allow fuel spray or vapors to come in contact with a spark or open flame. Keep a dry chemical fire extinguisher near the work area. Always keep fuel in a container specifically designed for fuel storage; also, always properly seal fuel containers to avoid the possibility of fire or explosion.

1. Relieve the fuel system pressure.
2. Disconnect the negative battery cable.
3. Disconnect the vacuum hose.
4. Disconnect the fuel hose.
5. Unbolt and remove the unit.
6. Install in the reverse order. Tighten the bolts to 70–95 inch lbs. (8–10 Nm).
7. Connect the negative battery cable.

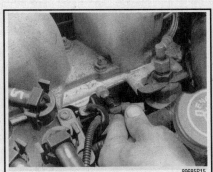

Fig. 37 To remove the fuel pressure regulator, first remove the vacuum line from the regulator . . .

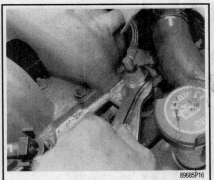

Fig. 38 . . . then loosen the fuel return line fitting . . .

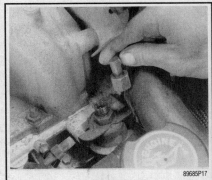

Fig. 39 . . . and disconnect it from the regulator

Fig. 40 Remove the regulator attaching bolts . . .

Fig. 41 . . . then pull the regulator from the supply manifold using a slight rocking motion to unseat the O-ring seal

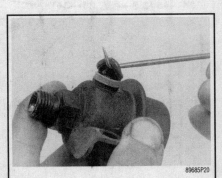

Fig. 42 Inspect the regulator O-ring seal and replace it if needed. A small pick will aid in removing the old seal

FUEL TANK

Tank Assembly

REMOVAL & INSTALLATION

B Series Pick-up and Navajo

▶ **See Figure 43**

1. Disconnect the negative battery cable and relieve the fuel system pressure.

2. Siphon or pump as much fuel as possible out through the fuel filler pipe.

➡**Fuel injected vehicles have reservoirs inside the fuel tank to maintain fuel near the fuel pick-up during cornering or low-fuel operation. These reservoirs could block siphon hoses or tubes from reaching the bottom of the fuel tank. Repeated attempts, using different hose orientations, can overcome this obstacle.**

3. Raise and safely support the vehicle.

4. If equipped, remove the skid plate attaching bolts, then lower the plate and remove it.

➡**On Navajo models, the front fuel tank strap is bolted to the skid plate and will be disconnected when the plate is removed.**

5. Disconnect the fuel fill and vent hoses connecting the filler pipe to the tank.

6. On vehicles equipped with a metal retainer fastening the filler pipe to the fuel tank, remove the screw holding the retainer to the fuel tank flange.

7. Disengage the fuel lines and the electrical connections to the fuel tank sending unit/fuel pump assembly. On some vehicles, these are inaccessible on top of the tank. In this case, they must be disconnected when the tank is partially lowered. To disconnect the lines from the sending unit/fuel pump assembly, refer to "FUEL LINES and FITTINGS' earlier in this section.

8. Place a safety support (such as a floor jack) under the fuel tank and remove the bolts from the fuel tank straps. Allow the straps to swing out of the way. Be careful not to deform the fuel tank.

➡**On B Series Pick-up vehicles, the rear fuel tank strap has two connections which must be unbolted.**

9. Lower the tank a few inches, then detach the fuel lines and electrical connection from the sending unit/fuel pump assembly, if required.

10. Remove the tank from the vehicle.

To install:

11. Before installation, it would be wise to perform the following:

   a. Double-check the tightness of the sending unit/fuel pump locking ring. If it is already loose, now would be a good time to remove it and check the condition of the gasket underneath.

   b. Ensure that all metal shields are reinstalled in their original positions and that the fasteners are secure.

   c. Be sure that the fuel vapor valve is completely installed on top of the fuel tank.

   d. Make all necessary fuel line or wiring connections which will be inaccessible after the fuel tank is installed.

12. Raise the fuel tank into position in the vehicle. If necessary, attach the fuel lines and sending unit electrical connector before the tank is in its final position.

13. Lubricate the fuel filler pipe with a water-based lubricant. Install the tank onto the filler pipe, then bring the tank into final position. Be careful not to deform the tank.

14. Position the tank straps around the tank and start the retaining nut or

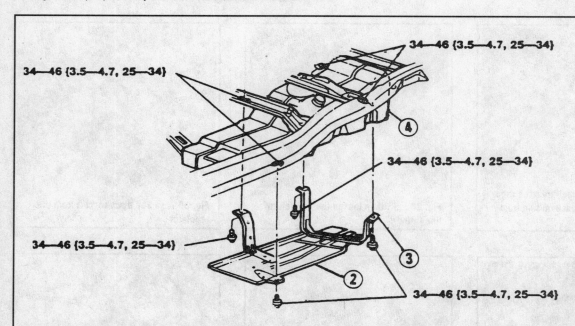

34—46 {3.5—4.7, 25—34}

34—46 {3.5—4.7, 25—34}

34—46 {3.5—4.7, 25—34}

34—46 {3.5—4.7, 25—34}

34—46 {3.5—4.7, 25—34}

1. Filler hose (not shown)
2. Heat shield
3. Fuel tank strap
4. Fuel tank

N·m {kgf·m, ft·lbf}

90975G03

Fig. 43 Exploded view of the 1996–97 B Series Cab Plus fuel tank assembly—other models similar

bolt. Align the tank with the straps. If equipped, be sure the fuel tank shields are installed with the straps and are positioned correctly.

15. Check the hoses and wiring on top of the tank. Make sure they are correctly routed and will not be pinched between the tank and body.

16. Tighten the fuel tank strap retaining nuts or bolts to 25–34 ft. lbs. (34–46 Nm).

17. If not already attached, connect the fuel hoses and lines. Make sure the fuel supply, fuel return (if present) and the vapor vent attachments are made properly. If not already attached, connect the sending unit.

18. If removed, install the fuel tank skid plate.

19. Lower the vehicle.

20. Connect the negative battery cable.

21. Fill the tank with fuel and check all connections for leaks.

MPV Models

▶ See Figure 44

✶✶ CAUTION

Observe all applicable safety precautions when working around fuel. Whenever servicing the fuel system, always work in a well ventilated area. Do not allow fuel spray or vapors to come in contact with a spark or open flame. Keep a dry chemical fire extinguisher near the work area. Always keep fuel in a container

specifically designed for fuel storage; also, always properly seal fuel containers to avoid the possibility of fire or explosion.

1. Relieve the fuel system pressure and disconnect the negative battery cable.

2. Remove the fuel filler cap. Raise and safely support the vehicle.

3. If equipped, remove the fuel pipe protector and tank under guard.

4. Position a suitable container under the fuel tank. Remove the drain plug and drain the tank.

5. Disconnect the fuel pump electrical connector.

6. Disconnect the fuel lines, evaporative hoses, breather hose and fuel filler hose.

7. If equipped, remove the nonreturn valve from the fuel filler pipe and inspect its condition. Replace, if necessary.

8. Support the tank with a jack. Remove the retaining bolts and the fuel tank straps.

9. Lower the fuel tank from the vehicle.

To install:

10. Raise the fuel tank into position and install the straps and retaining bolts. Tighten to 32–44 ft. lbs. (44–60 Nm). Remove the jack.

11. If equipped, install the nonreturn valve into the fuel filler pipe until the stopper portion of the valve completely fits the pipe.

12. Connect the fuel and evaporative hoses, making sure they are pushed onto the fuel tank fittings at least 1 in. (25mm). Connect the breather hose.

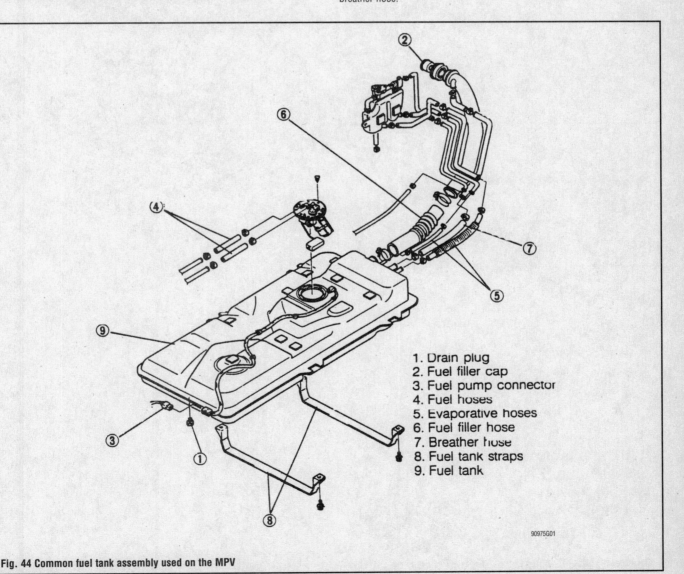

1. Drain plug
2. Fuel filler cap
3. Fuel pump connector
4. Fuel hoses
5. Evaporative hoses
6. Fuel filler hose
7. Breather hose
8. Fuel tank straps
9. Fuel tank

90975G01

Fig. 44 Common fuel tank assembly used on the MPV

13. Connect the fuel filler hose, making sure the hose is pushed onto the fuel tank pipe and filler pipe at least 1.4 in. (35mm).

14. Connect the fuel pump electrical connector.

15. If equipped, install the fuel tank under guard and the fuel pipe protector. Tighten the fuel pipe protector retaining bolts to 14–19 ft. lbs. (19–26 Nm).

16. Install the drain plug and lower the vehicle.

17. Fill the fuel tank and install the filler cap. Check for leaks.

18. Connect the negative battery cable.

19. Start the engine and check for leaks.

Sending Unit

REMOVAL & INSTALLATION

Please refer to the fuel pump removal and installation procedure in this section.

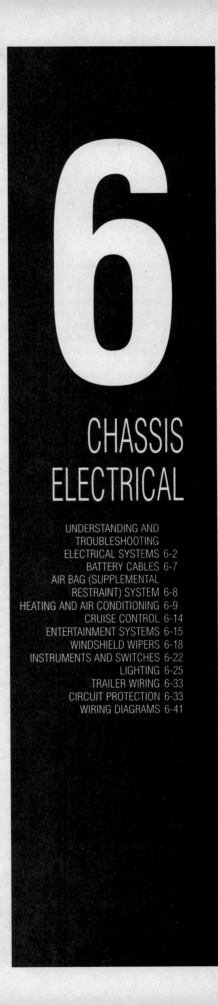

6

CHASSIS ELECTRICAL

UNDERSTANDING AND TROUBLESHOOTING ELECTRICAL SYSTEMS

Basic Electrical Theory

♦ **See Figure 1**

For any 12 volt, negative ground, electrical system to operate, the electricity must travel in a complete circuit. This simply means that current (power) from the positive (+) terminal of the battery must eventually return to the negative (ñ) terminal of the battery. Along the way, this current will travel through wires, fuses, switches and components. If, for any reason, the flow of current through the circuit is interrupted, the component fed by that circuit will cease to function properly.

Perhaps the easiest way to visualize a circuit is to think of connecting a light bulb (with two wires attached to it) to the battery—one wire attached to the negative (ñ) terminal of the battery and the other wire to the positive (+) terminal. With the two wires touching the battery terminals, the circuit would be complete and the light bulb would illuminate. Electricity would follow a path from the battery to the bulb and back to the battery. It's easy to see that with longer wires on our light bulb, it could be mounted anywhere. Further, one wire could be fitted with a switch so that the light could be turned on and off.

The normal automotive circuit differs from this simple example in two ways. First, instead of having a return wire from the bulb to the battery, the current travels through the frame of the vehicle. Since the negative (ñ) battery cable is attached to the frame (made of electrically conductive metal), the frame of the vehicle can serve as a ground wire to complete the circuit. Secondly, most automotive circuits contain multiple components which receive power from a single circuit. This lessens the amount of wire needed to power components on the vehicle.

HOW DOES ELECTRICITY WORK: THE WATER ANALOGY

Electricity is the flow of electrons—the subatomic particles that constitute the outer shell of an atom. Electrons spin in an orbit around the center core of an atom. The center core is comprised of protons (positive charge) and neutrons (neutral charge). Electrons have a negative charge and balance out the positive charge of the protons. When an outside force causes the number of electrons to unbalance the charge of the protons, the electrons will split off the atom and look for another atom to balance out. If this imbalance is kept up, electrons will continue to move and an electrical flow will exist.

Many people have been taught electrical theory using an analogy with water. In a comparison with water flowing through a pipe, the electrons would be the water and the wire is the pipe.

The flow of electricity can be measured much like the flow of water through a pipe. The unit of measurement used is amperes, frequently abbreviated as amps (a). You can compare amperage to the volume of water flowing through a pipe.

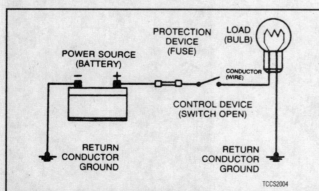

Fig. 1 This example illustrates a simple circuit. When the switch is closed, power from the positive (+) battery terminal flows through the fuse and the switch, and then to the light bulb. The light illuminates and the circuit is completed through the ground wire back to the negative (ñ) battery terminal. In reality, the two ground points shown in the illustration are attached to the metal frame of the vehicle, which completes the circuit back to the battery

When connected to a circuit, an ammeter will measure the actual amount of current flowing through the circuit. When relatively few electrons flow through a circuit, the amperage is low. When many electrons flow, the amperage is high.

Water pressure is measured in units such as pounds per square inch (psi); The electrical pressure is measured in units called volts (v). When a voltmeter is connected to a circuit, it is measuring the electrical pressure.

The actual flow of electricity depends not only on voltage and amperage, but also on the resistance of the circuit. The higher the resistance, the higher the force necessary to push the current through the circuit. The standard unit for measuring resistance is an ohm. Resistance in a circuit varies depending on the amount and type of components used in the circuit. The main factors which determine resistance are:

• Material—some materials have more resistance than others. Those with high resistance are said to be insulators. Rubber materials (or rubber-like plastics) are some of the most common insulators used in vehicles as they have a very high resistance to electricity. Very low resistance materials are said to be conductors. Copper wire is among the best conductors. Silver is actually a superior conductor to copper and is used in some relay contacts, but its high cost prohibits its use as common wiring. Most automotive wiring is made of copper.

• Size—the larger the wire size being used, the less resistance the wire will have. This is why components which use large amounts of electricity usually have large wires supplying current to them.

• Length—for a given thickness of wire, the longer the wire, the greater the resistance. The shorter the wire, the less the resistance. When determining the proper wire for a circuit, both size and length must be considered to design a circuit that can handle the current needs of the component.

• Temperature—with many materials, the higher the temperature, the greater the resistance (positive temperature coefficient). Some materials exhibit the opposite trait of lower resistance with higher temperatures (negative temperature coefficient). These principles are used in many of the sensors on the engine.

OHM'S LAW

There is a direct relationship between current, voltage and resistance. The relationship between current, voltage and resistance can be summed up by a statement known as Ohm's law.

Voltage (E) is equal to amperage (I) times resistance (R): $E = I \times R$

Other forms of the formula are $R = E/I$ and $I = E/R$

In each of these formulas, E is the voltage in volts, I is the current in amps and R is the resistance in ohms. The basic point to remember is that as the resistance of a circuit goes up, the amount of current that flows in the circuit will go down, if voltage remains the same.

The amount of work that the electricity can perform is expressed as power. The unit of power is the watt (w). The relationship between power, voltage and current is expressed as:

Power (w) is equal to amperage (I) times voltage (E): $W = I \times E$

This is only true for direct current (DC) circuits; The alternating current formula is a tad different, but since the electrical circuits in most vehicles are DC type, we need not get into AC circuit theory.

Electrical Components

POWER SOURCE

Power is supplied to the vehicle by two devices: The battery and the alternator. The battery supplies electrical power during starting or during periods when the current demand of the vehicle's electrical system exceeds the output capacity of the alternator. The alternator supplies electrical current when the engine is running. Just not does the alternator supply the current needs of the vehicle, but it recharges the battery.

The Battery

In most modern vehicles, the battery is a lead/acid electrochemical device consisting of six 2 volt subsections (cells) connected in series, so that the unit is capable of producing approximately 12 volts of electrical pressure. Each subsection consists of a series of positive and negative plates held a short distance apart in a solution of sulfuric acid and water.

The two types of plates are of dissimilar metals. This sets up a chemical reaction, and it is this reaction which produces current flow from the battery when its positive and negative terminals are connected to an electrical load. The power removed from the battery is replaced by the alternator, restoring the battery to its original chemical state.

The Alternator

On some vehicles there isn't an alternator, but a generator. The difference is that an alternator supplies alternating current which is then changed to direct current for use on the vehicle, while a generator produces direct current. Alternators tend to be more efficient and that is why they are used.

Alternators and generators are devices that consist of coils of wires wound together making big electromagnets. One group of coils spins within another set and the interaction of the magnetic fields causes a current to flow. This current is then drawn off the coils and fed into the vehicles electrical system.

GROUND

Two types of grounds are used in automotive electric circuits. Direct ground components are grounded to the frame through their mounting points. All other components use some sort of ground wire which is attached to the frame or chassis of the vehicle. The electrical current runs through the chassis of the vehicle and returns to the battery through the ground (ñ) cable; if you look, you'll see that the battery ground cable connects between the battery and the frame or chassis of the vehicle.

➡ **It should be noted that a good percentage of electrical problems can be traced to bad grounds.**

PROTECTIVE DEVICES

▶ **See Figure 2**

It is possible for large surges of current to pass through the electrical system of your vehicle. If this surge of current were to reach the load in the circuit, the surge could burn it out or severely damage it. It can also overload the wiring, causing the harness to get hot and melt the insulation. To prevent this, fuses, circuit breakers and/or fusible links are connected into the supply wires of the electrical system. These items are nothing more than a built-in weak spot in the system. When an abnormal amount of current flows through the system, these protective devices work as follows to protect the circuit:

• Fuse—when an excessive electrical current passes through a fuse, the fuse "blows" (the conductor melts) and opens the circuit, preventing the passage of current.

• Circuit Breaker—a circuit breaker is basically a self-repairing fuse. It will open the circuit in the same fashion as a fuse, but when the surge subsides, the circuit breaker can be reset and does not need replacement.

• Fusible Link—a fusible link (fuse link or main link) is a short length of special, high temperature insulated wire that acts as a fuse. When an excessive electrical current passes through a fusible link, the thin gauge wire inside the link melts, creating an intentional open to protect the circuit. To repair the circuit, the link must be replaced. Some newer type fusible links are housed in plug-in modules, which are simply replaced like a fuse, while older type fusible links must be cut and spliced if they melt. Since this link is very early in the electrical path, it's the first place to look if nothing on the vehicle works, yet the battery seems to be charged and is properly connected.

✴ CAUTION

Always replace fuses, circuit breakers and fusible links with identically rated components. Under no circumstances should a component of higher or lower amperage rating be substituted.

SWITCHES & RELAYS

▶ **See Figures 3 and 4**

Switches are used in electrical circuits to control the passage of current. The most common use is to open and close circuits between the battery and the various electric devices in the system. Switches are rated according to the amount of amperage they can handle. If a sufficient amperage rated switch is not used in a circuit, the switch could overload and cause damage.

Some electrical components which require a large amount of current to operate use a special switch called a relay. Since these circuits carry a large amount of current, the thickness of the wire in the circuit is also greater. If this large wire were connected from the load to the control switch, the switch would have to carry the high amperage load and the fairing or dash would be twice as large to accommodate the increased size of the wiring harness. To prevent these problems, a relay is used.

Relays are composed of a coil and a set of contacts. When the coil has a current passed though it, a magnetic field is formed and this field causes the contacts to move together, completing the circuit. Most relays are normally open, preventing current from passing through the circuit, but they can take any electrical form depending on the job they are intended to do. Relays can be considered "remote control switches." They allow a smaller current to operate devices that require higher amperages. When a small current operates the coil, a larger current is allowed to pass by the contacts. Some common circuits which may use relays are the horn, headlights, starter, electric fuel pump and other high draw circuits.

Fig. 2 Most vehicles use one or more fuse panels. This one is located on the driver's side kick panel

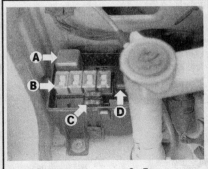

A. Relay
B. Fusible link
C. Fuse
D. Flasher

Fig. 3 The underhood fuse and relay panel usually contains fuses, relays, flashers and fusible links

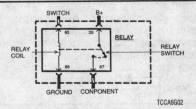

TCCA6G02

Fig. 4 Relays are composed of a coil and a switch. These two components are linked together so that when one operates, the other operates at the same time. The large wires in the circuit are connected from the battery to one side of the relay switch (B+) and from the opposite side of the relay switch to the load (component). Smaller wires are connected from the relay coil to the control switch for the circuit and from the opposite side of the relay coil to ground

LOAD

Every electrical circuit must include a "load" (something to use the electricity coming from the source). Without this load, the battery would attempt to deliver its entire power supply from one pole to another. This is called a "short circuit." All this electricity would take a short cut to ground and cause a great amount of damage to other components in the circuit by developing a tremendous amount of heat. This condition could develop sufficient heat to melt the insulation on all the surrounding wires and reduce a multiple wire cable to a lump of plastic and copper.

WIRING & HARNESSES

The average vehicle contains meters and meters of wiring, with hundreds of individual connections. To protect the many wires from damage and to keep them from becoming a confusing tangle, they are organized into bundles, enclosed in plastic or taped together and called wiring harnesses. Different harnesses serve different parts of the vehicle. Individual wires are color coded to help trace them through a harness where sections are hidden from view.

Automotive wiring or circuit conductors can be either single strand wire, multi-strand wire or printed circuitry. Single strand wire has a solid metal core and is usually used inside such components as alternators, motors, relays and other devices. Multi-strand wire has a core made of many small strands of wire twisted together into a single conductor. Most of the wiring in an automotive electrical system is made up of multi-strand wire, either as a single conductor or grouped together in a harness. All wiring is color coded on the insulator, either as a solid color or as a colored wire with an identification stripe. A printed circuit is a thin film of copper or other conductor that is printed on an insulator backing. Occasionally, a printed circuit is sandwiched between two sheets of plastic for more protection and flexibility. A complete printed circuit, consisting of conductors, insulating material and connectors for lamps or other components is called a printed circuit board. Printed circuitry is used in place of individual wires or harnesses in places where space is limited, such as behind instrument panels.

Since automotive electrical systems are very sensitive to changes in resistance, the selection of properly sized wires is critical when systems are repaired. A loose or corroded connection or a replacement wire that is too small for the circuit will add extra resistance and an additional voltage drop to the circuit.

The wire gauge number is an expression of the cross-section area of the conductor. Vehicles from countries that use the metric system will typically describe the wire size as its cross-sectional area in square millimeters. In this method, the larger the wire, the greater the number. Another common system for expressing wire size is the American Wire Gauge (AWG) system. As gauge number increases, area decreases and the wire becomes smaller. An 18 gauge wire is smaller than a 4 gauge wire. A wire with a higher gauge number will carry less current than a wire with a lower gauge number. Gauge wire size refers to the size of the strands of the conductor, not the size of the complete wire with insulator. It is possible, therefore, to have two wires of the same gauge with different diameters because one may have thicker insulation than the other.

It is essential to understand how a circuit works before trying to figure out why it doesn't. An electrical schematic shows the electrical current paths when a circuit is operating properly. Schematics break the entire electrical system down into individual circuits. In a schematic, usually no attempt is made to represent wiring and components as they physically appear on the vehicle; switches and other components are shown as simply as possible. Face views of harness connectors show the cavity or terminal locations in all multi-pin connectors to help locate test points.

CONNECTORS

▶ See Figures 5 and 6

Three types of connectors are commonly used in automotive applications—weatherproof, molded and hard shell.

• Weatherproof—these connectors are most commonly used where the connector is exposed to the elements. Terminals are protected against moisture and dirt by sealing rings which provide a weathertight seal. All repairs require the use of a special terminal and the tool required to service it. Unlike standard blade type terminals, these weatherproof terminals cannot be straightened once they are bent. Make certain that the connectors are properly seated and all of the sealing rings are in place when connecting leads.

• Molded—these connectors require complete replacement of the connector if found to be defective. This means splicing a new connector assembly into the harness. All splices should be soldered to insure proper contact. Use care when prob-

Fig. 5 Hard shell (left) and weatherproof (right) connectors have replaceable terminals

ing the connections or replacing terminals in them, as it is possible to create a short circuit between opposite terminals. If this happens to the wrong terminal pair, it is possible to damage certain components. Always use jumper wires between connectors for circuit checking and NEVER probe through weatherproof seals.

• Hard Shell—unlike molded connectors, the terminal contacts in hard-shell connectors can be replaced. Replacement usually involves the use of a special terminal removal tool that depresses the locking tangs (barbs) on the connector terminal and allows the connector to be removed from the rear of the shell. The connector shell should be replaced if it shows any evidence of burning, melting, cracks, or breaks. Replace individual terminals that are burnt, corroded, distorted or loose.

Fig. 6 Weatherproof connectors are most commonly used in the engine compartment or where the connector is exposed to the elements

Test Equipment

Pinpointing the exact cause of trouble in an electrical circuit is most times accomplished by the use of special test equipment. The following describes different types of commonly used test equipment and briefly explains how to use them in diagnosis. In addition to the information covered below, the tool manufacturer's instructions booklet (provided with the tester) should be read and clearly understood before attempting any test procedures.

JUMPER WIRES

✳✳ CAUTION

Never use jumper wires made from a thinner gauge wire than the circuit being tested. If the jumper wire is of too small a gauge, it may overheat and possibly melt. Never use jumpers to bypass high resistance loads in a circuit. Bypassing resistances, in effect, creates a

short circuit. This may, in turn, cause damage and fire. Jumper wires should only be used to bypass lengths of wire or to simulate switches.

Jumper wires are simple, yet extremely valuable, pieces of test equipment. They are basically test wires which are used to bypass sections of a circuit. Although jumper wires can be purchased, they are usually fabricated from lengths of standard automotive wire and whatever type of connector (alligator clip, spade connector or pin connector) that is required for the particular application being tested. In cramped, hard-to-reach areas, it is advisable to have insulated boots over the jumper wire terminals in order to prevent accidental grounding. It is also advisable to include a standard automotive fuse in any jumper wire. This is commonly referred to as a "fused jumper". By inserting an in-line fuse holder between a set of test leads, a fused jumper wire can be used for bypassing open circuits. Use a 5 amp fuse to provide protection against voltage spikes.

Jumper wires are used primarily to locate open electrical circuits, on either the ground (ñ) side of the circuit or on the power (+) side. If an electrical component fails to operate, connect the jumper wire between the component and a good ground. If the component operates only with the jumper installed, the ground circuit is open. If the ground circuit is good, but the component does not operate, the circuit between the power feed and component may be open. By moving the jumper wire successively back from the component toward the power source, you can isolate the area of the circuit where the open is located. When the component stops functioning, or the power is cut off, the open is in the segment of wire between the jumper and the point previously tested.

You can sometimes connect the jumper wire directly from the battery to the "hot" terminal of the component, but first make sure the component uses 12 volts in operation. Some electrical components, such as fuel injectors or sensors, are designed to operate on about 4 to 5 volts, and running 12 volts directly to these components will cause damage.

TEST LIGHTS

▸ See Figure 7

The test light is used to check circuits and components while electrical current is flowing through them. It is used for voltage and ground tests. To use a 12 volt test light, connect the ground clip to a good ground and probe wherever necessary with the pick. The test light will illuminate when voltage is detected. This does not necessarily mean that 12 volts (or any particular amount of voltage) is present; it only means that some voltage is present. It is advisable before using the test light to touch its ground clip and probe across the battery posts or terminals to make sure the light is operating properly.

❊❊ WARNING

Do not use a test light to probe electronic ignition, spark plug or coil wires. Never use a pick-type test light to probe wiring on computer controlled systems unless specifically instructed to do so. Any wire insulation that is pierced by the test light probe should be taped and sealed with silicone after testing.

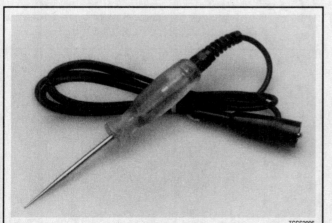

TCCS2006

Fig. 7 A 12 volt test light is used to detect the presence of voltage in a circuit

Like the jumper wire, the 12 volt test light is used to isolate opens in circuits. But, whereas the jumper wire is used to bypass the open to operate the load, the 12 volt test light is used to locate the presence of voltage in a circuit. If the test light illuminates, there is power up to that point in the circuit; if the test light does not illuminate, there is an open circuit (no power). Move the test light in successive steps back toward the power source until the light in the handle illuminates. The open is between the probe and a point which was previously probed.

The self-powered test light is similar in design to the 12 volt test light, but contains a 1.5 volt penlight battery in the handle. It is most often used in place of a multimeter to check for open or short circuits when power is isolated from the circuit (continuity test).

The battery in a self-powered test light does not provide much current. A weak battery may not provide enough power to illuminate the test light even when a complete circuit is made (especially if there is high resistance in the circuit). Always make sure that the test battery is strong. To check the battery, briefly touch the ground clip to the probe; if the light glows brightly, the battery is strong enough for testing.

➡A self-powered test light should not be used on any computer controlled system or component. The small amount of electricity transmitted by the test light is enough to damage many electronic automotive components.

MULTIMETERS

Multimeters are an extremely useful tool for troubleshooting electrical problems. They can be purchased in either analog or digital form and have a price range to suit any budget. A multimeter is a voltmeter, ammeter and ohmmeter (along with other features) combined into one instrument. It is often used when testing solid state circuits because of its high input impedance (usually 10 megaohms or more). A brief description of the multimeter main test functions follows:

• Voltmeter—the voltmeter is used to measure voltage at any point in a circuit, or to measure the voltage drop across any part of a circuit. Voltmeters usually have various scales and a selector switch to allow the reading of different voltage ranges. The voltmeter has a positive and a negative lead. To avoid damage to the meter, always connect the negative lead to the negative (ñ) side of the circuit (to ground or nearest the ground side of the circuit) and connect the positive lead to the positive (+) side of the circuit (to the power source or the nearest power source). Note that the negative voltmeter lead will always be black and that the positive voltmeter will always be some color other than black (usually red).

• Ohmmeter—the ohmmeter is designed to read resistance (measured in ohms) in a circuit or component. Most ohmmeters will have a selector switch which permits the measurement of different ranges of resistance (usually the selector switch allows the multiplication of the meter reading by 10, 100, 1,000 and 10,000). Some ohmmeters are "auto-ranging" which means the meter itself will determine which scale to use. Since the meters are powered by an internal battery, the ohmmeter can be used like a self-powered test light. When the ohmmeter is connected, current from the ohmmeter flows through the circuit or component being tested. Since the ohmmeter's internal resistance and voltage are known values, the amount of current flow through the meter depends on the resistance of the circuit or component being tested. The ohmmeter can also be used to perform a continuity test for suspected open circuits. In using the meter for making continuity checks, do not be concerned with the actual resistance readings. Zero resistance, or any ohm reading, indicates continuity in the circuit. Infinite resistance indicates an opening in the circuit. A high resistance reading where there should be none indicates a problem in the circuit. Checks for short circuits are made in the same manner as checks for open circuits, except that the circuit must be isolated from both power and normal ground. Infinite resistance indicates no continuity, while zero resistance indicates a dead short.

❊❊ WARNING

Never use an ohmmeter to check the resistance of a component or wire while there is voltage applied to the circuit.

• Ammeter—an ammeter measures the amount of current flowing through a circuit in units called amperes or amps. At normal operating voltage, most circuits have a characteristic amount of amperes, called "current draw" which can be measured using an ammeter. By referring to a specified current draw rating, then measuring the amperes and comparing the two values, one can determine what is happening within the circuit to aid in diagnosis. An open circuit, for example, will not allow any current to flow, so the ammeter reading will be zero. A damaged component or circuit will have an increased current draw, so the reading will be high. The ammeter is always connected in series with the circuit being tested. All of the current that normally flows through the circuit must also flow through the ammeter; if there is any other path for the current to follow, the ammeter reading will not be accurate. The ammeter itself has very little resistance to current flow and, therefore, will not affect the circuit, but it will measure current draw only when the circuit is closed and electricity is flowing. Excessive current draw can blow fuses and drain the battery, while a reduced current draw can cause motors to run slowly, lights to dim and other components to not operate properly.

Troubleshooting Electrical Systems

When diagnosing a specific problem, organized troubleshooting is a must. The complexity of a modern automotive vehicle demands that you approach any problem in a logical, organized manner. There are certain troubleshooting techniques, however, which are standard:

• Establish when the problem occurs. Does the problem appear only under certain conditions? Were there any noises, odors or other unusual symptoms? Isolate the problem area. To do this, make some simple tests and observations, then eliminate the systems that are working properly. Check for obvious problems, such as broken wires and loose or dirty connections. Always check the obvious before assuming something complicated is the cause.

• Test for problems systematically to determine the cause once the problem area is isolated. Are all the components functioning properly? Is there power going to electrical switches and motors. Performing careful, systematic checks will often turn up most causes on the first inspection, without wasting time checking components that have little or no relationship to the problem.

• Test all repairs after the work is done to make sure that the problem is fixed. Some causes can be traced to more than one component, so a careful verification of repair work is important in order to pick up additional malfunctions that may cause a problem to reappear or a different problem to arise. A blown fuse, for example, is a simple problem that may require more than another fuse to repair. If you don't look for a problem that caused a fuse to blow, a shorted wire (for example) may go undetected.

Experience has shown that most problems tend to be the result of a fairly simple and obvious cause, such as loose or corroded connectors, bad grounds or damaged wire insulation which causes a short. This makes careful visual inspection of components during testing essential to quick and accurate troubleshooting.

Testing

OPEN CIRCUITS

▶ See Figure 8

This test already assumes the existence of an open in the circuit and it is used to help locate the open portion.

1. Isolate the circuit from power and ground.
2. Connect the self-powered test light or ohmmeter ground clip to the ground side of the circuit and probe sections of the circuit sequentially.
3. If the light is out or there is infinite resistance, the open is between the probe and the circuit ground.
4. If the light is on or the meter shows continuity, the open is between the probe and the end of the circuit toward the power source.

SHORT CIRCUITS

➡ **Never use a self-powered test light to perform checks for opens or shorts when power is applied to the circuit under test. The test light can be damaged by outside power.**

1. Isolate the circuit from power and ground.
2. Connect the self-powered test light or ohmmeter ground clip to a good ground and probe any easy-to-reach point in the circuit.

Fig. 8 The infinite reading on this multimeter indicates that the circuit is open

3. If the light comes on or there is continuity, there is a short somewhere in the circuit.
4. To isolate the short, probe a test point at either end of the isolated circuit (the light should be on or the meter should indicate continuity).
5. Leave the test light probe engaged and sequentially open connectors or switches, remove parts, etc. until the light goes out or continuity is broken.
6. When the light goes out, the short is between the last two circuit components which were opened.

VOLTAGE

This test determines voltage available from the battery and should be the first step in any electrical troubleshooting procedure after visual inspection. Many electrical problems, especially on computer controlled systems, can be caused by a low state of charge in the battery. Excessive corrosion at the battery cable terminals can cause poor contact that will prevent proper charging and full battery current flow.

1. Set the voltmeter selector switch to the 20V position.
2. Connect the multimeter negative lead to the battery's negative (ñ) post or terminal and the positive lead to the battery's positive (+) post or terminal.
3. Turn the ignition switch **ON** to provide a load.
4. A well charged battery should register over 12 volts. If the meter reads below 11.5 volts, the battery power may be insufficient to operate the electrical system properly.

VOLTAGE DROP

▶ See Figure 9

When current flows through a load, the voltage beyond the load drops. This voltage drop is due to the resistance created by the load and also by small resistances created by corrosion at the connectors and damaged insulation on the wires. The maximum allowable voltage drop under load is critical, especially if there is more than one load in the circuit, since all voltage drops are cumulative.

Fig. 9 This voltage drop test revealed high resistance (low voltage) in the circuit

1. Set the voltmeter selector switch to the 20 volt position.
2. Connect the multimeter negative lead to a good ground.
3. Operate the circuit and check the voltage prior to the first component (load).
4. There should be little or no voltage drop in the circuit prior to the first component. If a voltage drop exists, the wire or connectors in the circuit are suspect.
5. While operating the first component in the circuit, probe the ground side of the component with the positive meter lead and observe the voltage readings. A small voltage drop should be noticed. This voltage drop is caused by the resistance of the component.
6. Repeat the test for each component (load) down the circuit.
7. If a large voltage drop is noticed, the preceding component, wire or connector is suspect.

RESISTANCE

▶ See Figures 10 and 11

✳✳ WARNING

Never use an ohmmeter with power applied to the circuit. The ohmmeter is designed to operate on its own power supply. The normal 12 volt electrical system voltage could damage the meter!

1. Isolate the circuit from the vehicle's power source.
2. Ensure that the ignition key is **OFF** when disconnecting any components or the battery.
3. Where necessary, also isolate at least one side of the circuit to be checked, in order to avoid reading parallel resistances. Parallel circuit resistances will always give a lower reading than the actual resistance of either of the branches.

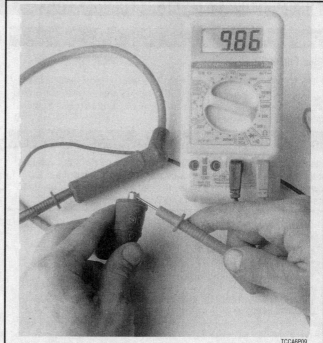

Fig. 11 Spark plug wires can be checked for excessive resistance using an ohmmeter

4. Connect the meter leads to both sides of the circuit (wire or component) and read the actual measured ohms on the meter scale. Make sure the selector switch is set to the proper ohm scale for the circuit being tested, to avoid misreading the ohmmeter test value.

Wire and Connector Repair

Almost anyone can replace damaged wires, as long as the proper tools and parts are available. Wire and terminals are available to fit almost any need. Even the specialized weatherproof, molded and hard shell connectors are now available from aftermarket suppliers.

Be sure the ends of all the wires are fitted with the proper terminal hardware and connectors. Wrapping a wire around a stud is never a permanent solution and will only cause trouble later. Replace wires one at a time to avoid confusion. Always route wires exactly the same as the factory.

➡**If connector repair is necessary, only attempt it if you have the proper tools. Weatherproof and hard shell connectors require special tools to release the pins inside the connector. Attempting to repair these connectors with conventional hand tools will damage them.**

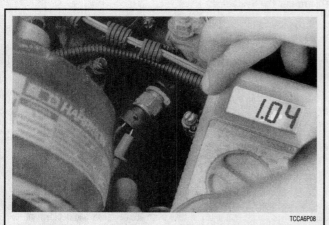

Fig. 10 Checking the resistance of a coolant temperature sensor with an ohmmeter. Reading is 1.04 kilohms

BATTERY CABLES

Disconnecting the Cables

When working on any electrical component on the vehicle, it is always a good idea to disconnect the negative (-) battery cable. This will prevent potential damage to many sensitive electrical components such as the Powertrain Control Module (PCM), radio, alternator, etc.

➡**Any time you disengage the battery cables, it is recommended that you disconnect the negative (-) battery cable first. This will prevent your accidentally grounding the positive (+) terminal to the body of the vehicle when disconnecting it, thereby preventing damage to the above mentioned components.**

Before you disconnect the cable(s), first turn the ignition to the **OFF** position. This will prevent a draw on the battery which could cause arcing (electricity trying to ground itself to the body of a vehicle, just like a spark plug jumping the gap) and, of course, damaging some components such as the alternator diodes.

When the battery cable(s) are reconnected (negative cable last), be sure to check that your lights, windshield wipers and other electrically operated safety components are all working correctly. If your vehicle contains an Electronically Tuned Radio (ETR), don't forget to also reset your radio stations. Ditto for the clock.

Also, anytime the battery cables have been disconnected and then reconnected, some abnormal drive symptoms could occur. The is due to the PCM losing the memory voltage and its learned adaptive strategy. The vehicle will need to be driven for 10 miles (16Km) or more until the PCM relearns its adaptive strategy, and acclimates the engine and transmission functions to your driving style.

AIR BAG (SUPPLEMENTAL RESTRAINT) SYSTEM

General Information

▶ **See Figure 12**

The 1995–98 B Series Pick-up and all MPV vehicles are available with an air bag Supplemental Restraint System (SRS). The SRS is designed to work in conjunction with the standard three-point safety belts to reduce injury in a head-on collision.

✳ WARNING

The SRS can actually cause physical injury or death if the safety belts are not used, or if the manufacturer's warnings are not followed. The manufacturer's warnings can be found in your owner's manual, or, in some cases, on your sun visors.

The SRS is comprised of the following components:
- Driver's side air bag module
- Passenger's side air bag module
- Right-hand and left-hand primary crash front air bag sensors
- Air bag diagnostic monitor computer
- Electrical wiring

The SRS primary crash front air bag sensors are hard-wired to the air bag modules and determine when the air bags are deployed. During a frontal collision, the sensors quickly inflate the two air bags to reduce injury by cushioning the driver and front passenger from striking the dashboard, windshield, steering wheel and any other hard surfaces. The air bag inflates so quickly (in a fraction of a second) that in most cases it is fully inflated before you actually start to move during an automotive collision.

Since the SRS is a complicated and essentially important system, its components are constantly being tested by a diagnostic monitor computer, which illuminates the air bag indicator light on the instrument cluster for approximately 6 seconds when the ignition switch is turned to the **RUN** position when the SRS is functioning properly. After being illuminated for the 6 seconds, the indicator light should then turn off.

If the air bag light does not illuminate at all, stays on continuously, or flashes at any time, a problem has been detected by the diagnostic monitor computer.

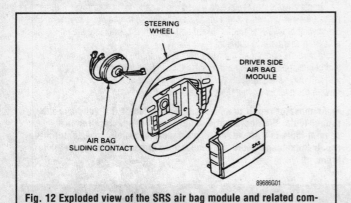

Fig. 12 Exploded view of the SRS air bag module and related components

✳ WARNING

If at any time the air bag light indicates that the computer has noted a problem, have your vehicle's SRS serviced immediately by a qualified automotive technician. A faulty SRS can cause severe physical injury or death.

SERVICE PRECAUTIONS

Whenever working around, or on, the air bag supplemental restraint system, ALWAYS adhere to the following warnings and cautions.

- Always wear safety glasses when servicing an air bag vehicle and when handling an air bag module.
- Carry a live air bag module with the bag and trim cover facing away from your body, so that an accidental deployment of the air bag will have a small chance of personal injury.
- Place an air bag module on a table or other flat surface with the bag and trim cover pointing up.
- Wear gloves, a dust mask and safety glasses whenever handling a deployed air bag module. The air bag surface may contain traces of sodium hydroxide, a by-product of the gas that inflates the air bag and which can cause skin irritation.
- Ensure to wash your hands with mild soap and water after handling a deployed air bag.
- All air bag modules with discolored or damaged cover trim must be replaced, not repainted.
- All component replacement and wiring service must be made with the negative and positive battery cables disconnected from the battery for a minimum of one minute prior to attempting service or replacement.
- NEVER probe the air bag electrical terminals. Doing so could result in air bag deployment, which can cause serious physical injury.
- If the vehicle is involved in a fender-bender which results in a damaged front bumper or grille, have the air bag sensors inspected by a qualified automotive technician to ensure that they were not damaged.
- If at any time, the air bag light indicates that the computer has noted a problem, have your vehicle's SRS serviced immediately by a qualified automotive technician. A faulty SRS can cause severe physical injury or death.

1995–98 B SERIES PICK-UP MODELS

Disarming The System

1. Disconnect the negative battery cable from the battery.
2. Disconnect the positive battery cable from the battery.
3. Wait one minute. This time is required for the back-up power supply in the air bag diagnostic monitor to completely drain. The system is now disarmed.

If you are disarming the system with the intent of testing the system, do not! The SRS is a sensitive, complex system and should only be tested or serviced by a qualified automotive technician. Also, specific tools are needed for SRS testing.

Arming The System

1. Connect the positive battery cable.
2. Connect the negative battery cable.
3. Stand outside the vehicle and carefully turn the ignition to the **RUN** position. Be sure that no part of your body is in front of the air bag module on the steering wheel, to prevent injury in case of an accidental air bag deployment.
4. Ensure the air bag indicator light turns off after approximately 6 seconds. If the light does not illuminate at all, does not turn off, or starts to flash, have the system tested by a qualified automotive technician. If the light does turn off after 6 seconds and does not flash, the SRS is working properly.

MPV MODELS

Disarming The System

▶ **See Figures 13 and 14**

1. Turn the ignition switch to the **LOCK** position.
2. Disconnect the negative battery cable from the battery.
3. Wait one minute. This time is required for the back-up power supply in the air bag diagnostic monitor to completely drain.
4. If disarming the driver side air bag, remove the lower steering column cover, then disengage the orange and blue clock spring connector. If disarming the passenger side air bag (if equipped), remove the glove compartment cover and disengage the air bag module connector.
5. The air bag system is now disarmed.

If you are disarming the system with the intent of testing the system, do not!

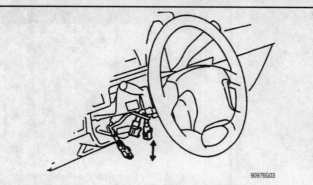

Fig. 13 Disengage the orange and blue clock spring connector located behind the lower steering column cover

Fig. 14 Disengage the air bag module connector located behind the glove compartment cover

The SRS is a sensitive, complex system and should only be tested or serviced by a qualified automotive technician. Also, specific tools are needed for SRS testing.

Arming The System

♦ See Figure 15

1. If equipped, plug in the passenger side air bag module connector, then install the glove compartment cover.
2. Plug in the orange and blue clock spring connector, then install the lower steering column cover.
3. Connect the negative battery cable.
4. Stand outside the vehicle and carefully turn the ignition to the **ON** position. Be sure that no part of your body is in front of the driver or passenger side air bag module, to prevent injury in case of an accidental air bag deployment.
5. Ensure the air bag indicator light turns off after approximately 6 seconds. If the light does not illuminate at all, does not turn off, or starts to flash, have the system tested by a qualified automotive technician. If the light does turn off after 6 seconds and does not flash, the SRS is working properly.

Fig. 15 Check to make sure that the air bag indicator light turns off after approximately 6 seconds

HEATING AND AIR CONDITIONING

Blower Motor

REMOVAL & INSTALLATION

Navajo and 1994–97 B Series Pick-up Models

WITHOUT AIR CONDITIONING

♦ See Figures 16, 17, 18 and 19

1. Disconnect the negative battery cable.
2. Remove the air cleaner or air inlet duct, as necessary.
3. If necessary, remove the speed control module and the washer fluid reservoir.
4. Disconnect the wire harness connector from the blower motor by pushing down on the connector tabs and pulling the connector off of the motor.
5. Disconnect the blower motor cooling tube at the blower motor.
6. Remove the 3 screws attaching the blower motor and wheel to the heater blower assembly.
7. Holding the cooling tube aside, pull the blower motor and wheel from the heater blower assembly and remove it from the vehicle.
8. Remove the blower wheel push-nut and/or clamp from the motor shaft and pull the blower wheel from the motor shaft.

To install:
9. Install the blower wheel on the blower motor shaft.
10. Install the hub clamp and/or push-nut.
11. Holding the cooling tube aside, position the blower motor and wheel on the heater blower assembly and install the 3 attaching screws.
12. Connect the blower motor cooling tube and the wire harness connector.
13. Install the vacuum reservoir on the hoses with the 2 screws.

14. If removed, install the speed control module and the washer fluid reservoir.
15. Install the air cleaner or air inlet duct, as necessary.
16. Connect the negative battery cable and check the system for proper operation.

WITH AIR CONDITIONING

1. Disconnect the negative battery cable.
2. In the engine compartment, disconnect the wire harness from the motor by pushing down on the tab while pulling the connection off at the motor.
3. Remove the air cleaner or air inlet duct, as necessary.
4. If necessary, remove the solenoid box cover retaining bolts and the solenoid box cover.

Fig. 16 To remove the blower motor, first disconnect the electrical wire harness plug . . .

Fig. 17 . . . then remove the blower motor cooling tube from the motor

89686P02

Fig. 18 Remove the blower motor attaching screws and the washer fluid reservoir . . .

89686P03

Fig. 19 . . . then slide the blower motor from the housing. Take care to not damage the blower wheel (arrow)

89686P04

5. Disconnect the blower motor cooling tube from the blower motor.

6. Remove the blower motor mounting plate attaching screws and remove the motor and wheel assembly from the evaporator assembly blower motor housing.

7. Remove the blower motor hub clamp from the motor shaft and pull the blower wheel from the shaft.

To install:

8. Install the blower motor wheel on the blower motor shaft and install a new hub clamp.

9. Install a new motor mounting seal on the blower housing before installing the blower motor.

10. Position the blower motor and wheel assembly in the blower housing and install the attaching screws.

11. Connect the blower motor cooling tube.

12. Connect the electrical wire harness hard shell connector to the blower motor by pushing into place.

13. If removed, position the solenoid box cover into place and install the 3 retaining screws.

14. Install the air cleaner or air inlet duct, as necessary.

15. Connect the negative battery cable and check the blower motor in all speeds for proper operation.

1998 B Series Pick-up Models

1. Disconnect the negative battery cable.

2. Remove the retaining screw and reposition the cruise control servo out of the way.

3. In the engine compartment, disconnect the wire harness from the motor by lifting up on the tab while pulling the connection off at the motor.

4. Disconnect the blower motor cooling tube from the blower motor.

5. Remove the blower motor mounting plate attaching screws and remove the motor and wheel assembly from the blower motor housing.

6. Remove the blower motor hub clamp from the motor shaft and pull the blower wheel from the shaft.

To install:

7. Install the blower motor wheel on the blower motor shaft and install a new hub clamp.

8. Position the blower motor and wheel assembly in the blower housing and install the attaching screws.

9. Connect the blower motor cooling tube.

10. Connect the electrical wire harness hard shell connector to the blower motor by pushing into place.

11. Install the cruise control servo back into position and tighten the retaining screw.

12. Connect the negative battery cable and check the blower motor in all speeds for proper operation.

MPV Models

FRONT BLOWER MOTOR

♦ See Figure 20

1. Disconnect the negative battery cable.

2. Remove the passenger's side lower instrument panel and cover.

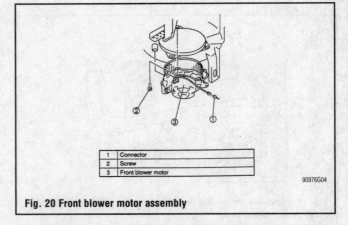

1	Connector
2	Screw
3	Front blower motor

90976G04

Fig. 20 Front blower motor assembly

3. Unplug the wiring at the motor connector.

4. Remove the mounting nuts and lift out the blower motor.

To install:

5. Place the blower motor assembly up into position in the housing, then install and tighten the mounting nuts.

6. Plug in the wiring at the motor connector.

7. Install the passenger's side lower instrument panel and cover.

8. Connect the negative battery cable and check the blower motor in all speeds for proper operation.

REAR HEATER BLOWER MOTOR

♦ See Figure 21

1. Disconnect the battery ground.

2. Set the rear heater temperature control knob to WARM.

3. Drain the engine coolant.

4. Remove the driver's seat.

5. Disconnect the heater hoses at the core tubes.

6. Unplug the wiring at the connector.

7. Remove the mounting bolts and lift out the heater case.

8. Remove the mounting screws and lift out the blower motor.

To install:

➡**During the course of the installation procedure, replace any damaged sealer.**

9. Place the blower motor assembly into position in the heater case, then install and tighten the mounting screws.

10. Place the heater case into position and tighten the mounting bolts.

11. Plug the wiring into the connector.

12. Connect the heater hoses to the core tubes along with new hose clamps.

13. Install the driver's seat.

14. Refill the engine coolant.

15. Connect the negative battery cable and check the blower motor in all speeds for proper operation.

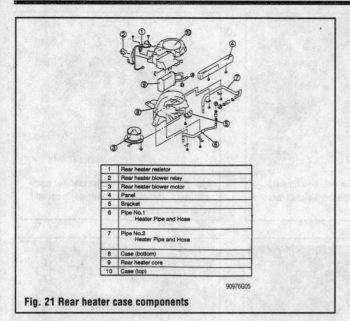

1	Rear heater resistor
2	Rear heater blower relay
3	Rear heater blower motor
4	Panel
5	Bracket
6	Pipe No.1 Heater Pipe and Hose
7	Pipe No.2 Heater Pipe and Hose
8	Case (bottom)
9	Rear heater core
10	Case (top)

90976G05

Fig. 21 Rear heater case components

REAR BLOWER MOTOR

▶ **See Figure 22**

1. Disconnect the battery ground.
2. Remove the rear interior left side trim panel.
3. Unplug the wiring at the connector.
4. Remove the mounting fasteners and lift out the rear blower unit.
5. Remove the mounting screws and lift out the blower motor assembly.

To install:

6. Place the blower motor assembly into position in the rear blower unit, then install and tighten the mounting screws.
7. Place the rear blower unit into position at the rear of the vehicle and tighten the mounting fasteners.
8. Plug the wiring into the connector.
9. Install the rear interior left side trim panel.
10. Connect the negative battery cable and check the blower motor in all speeds for proper operation.

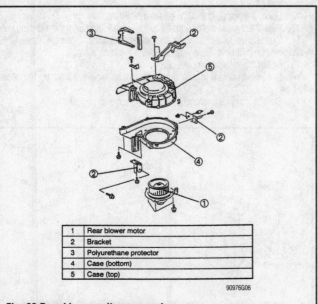

1	Rear blower motor
2	Bracket
3	Polyurethane protector
4	Case (bottom)
5	Case (top)

90976G06

Fig. 22 Rear blower unit components

Blower Motor Resistor

REMOVAL & INSTALLATION

▶ **See Figure 23**

1. Disconnect the negative battery cable.
2. Disconnect the wire connector from the resistor assembly.
3. Remove the 2 screws attaching the resistor assembly to the blower or evaporator case and remove the resistor.
4. Installation is the reverse of the removal procedure. Check the blower motor for proper operation in all blower speeds.

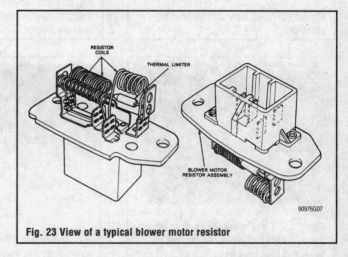

90976G07

Fig. 23 View of a typical blower motor resistor

Heater Core

REMOVAL & INSTALLATION

✷ CAUTION

When draining the coolant, keep in mind that cats and dogs are attracted by the ethylene glycol antifreeze, and are quite likely to drink any that is left in an uncovered container or in puddles on the ground. This will prove fatal in sufficient quantity. Always drain the coolant into a sealable container. Coolant should be reused unless it is contaminated or several years old.

Navajo and 1994 B Series Pick-up Models

▶ **See Figures 24 thru 30**

1. Disconnect the negative battery cable. Allow the engine to cool down. Drain the cooling system to a level below the heater core fittings on the firewall.
2. Disconnect the heater hoses from the heater core tubes and plug hoses.
3. In the passenger compartment, remove the four screws attaching the heater core access cover to the plenum assembly and remove the access cover.
4. Pull the heater core rearward and down, removing it from the plenum assembly.

To install:

5. Position the heater core and seal in the plenum assembly.
6. Install the heater core access cover to the plenum assembly and secure with four screws.
7. Install the heater hoses to the heater core tubes at the dash panel in the engine compartment. Do not over-tighten hose clamps.
8. Check the coolant level and add coolant as required. Connect the negative battery cable.
9. Start the engine and check the system for coolant leaks.

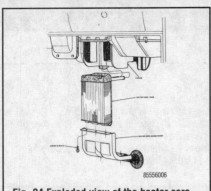

Fig. 24 Exploded view of the heater core assembly

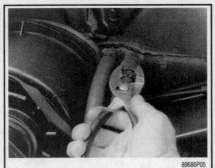

Fig. 25 From inside the engine compartment, disconnect the heater hoses from the core fittings . . .

Fig. 26 . . . then, in the passenger compartment, remove the under dash cover retaining screws . . .

Fig. 27 . . . and allow the cover to drop down. If necessary, you can remove the cover if it is in your way

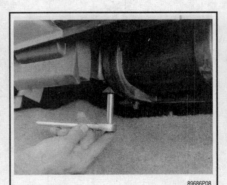

Fig. 28 Remove the heater core access panel attaching screws . . .

Fig. 29 . . . then remove the cover by pulling downward and straight back to disengage the drain tube (arrow)

Fig. 30 Pull the heater core rearward and down to remove it from the plenum assembly

1995–98 B Series Pick-up Models

▶ See Figure 31

1. Disconnect the negative battery cable. Allow the engine to cool down. Drain the cooling system to a level below the heater core fittings on the firewall.
2. Disconnect the heater hoses from the heater core tubes and plug hoses.
3. Remove the five nuts that secure the blower motor housing to the firewall.
4. Pull the housing away from the firewall. Disconnect any wire harness plugs which inhibit the housing.
5. Remove the remaining nuts which secure the heater air plenum (inside the passenger compartment) to the firewall.
6. In the passenger compartment, remove the instrument panel. Refer to Section 10.

7. Pull the heater air plenum rearward from the firewall and remove it from the vehicle.
8. Remove the heater core from the heater air plenum.
9. Inspect all air seals on the components and firewall and replace any that are damaged.
To install:
10. Install the heater core into the air plenum chamber.
11. Position the heater air plenum against the firewall from the passenger compartment.
12. Under the hood, install the plenum retaining nuts.
13. Install the blower motor housing to the firewall and install the attaching nuts.
14. Connect the heater hoses to the heater core tubes at the dash panel in the engine compartment. Do not over-tighten the hose clamps.
15. Install the instrument panel.
16. Check the coolant level and add coolant as required. Connect the negative battery cable.
17. Start the engine and check the system for coolant leaks.

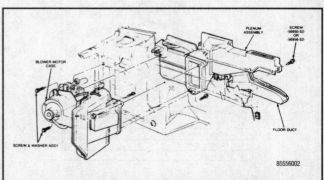

Fig. 31 Exploded view of the blower motor housing and the heater air plenum assemblies

MPV Models

FRONT HEATER CORE

♦ **See Figure 32**

1. Disconnect the negative battery cable.
2. Drain the engine cooling system.
3. Remove the instrument panel. Refer to Section 10.
4. Disconnect the heater hoses at the core tubes.
5. Unbolt and remove the instrument panel brace.
6. Support the heater case and remove the mounting nuts.
7. Carefully lift off the case and remove it from the vehicle. Be Careful! There will be a substantial amount of coolant left in the core.
8. Lift out the heater core.
9. Installation is the reverse of removal. Use new sealer around the case and core. Refill the cooling system.
10. Connect the negative battery cable. Check for leaks.

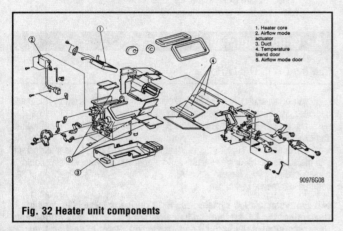

1. Heater core
2. Airflow mode actuator
3. Duct
4. Temperature blend door
5. Airflow mode door

90976G08

Fig. 32 Heater unit components

REAR HEATER CORE

♦ **See Figure 21**

1. Disconnect the negative battery cable.
2. Set the rear heater temperature control knob to WARM.
3. Drain the engine coolant.
4. Remove the driver's seat.
5. Disconnect the heater hoses at the core tubes.
6. Disconnect the wiring at the connector.
7. Remove the mounting bolts and lift out the heater case.
8. Separate the case halves and lift out the core.
9. Installation is the reverse of removal. Replace any damaged sealer.
10. Connect the negative battery cable. Check for leaks.

Control Cables

ADJUSTMENT

Navajo and B Series Pick-up Models

To check the temperature cable adjustment, move the temperature control lever all the way to the left, then move it all the way to the right. At the extreme ends of lever travel, the door should be heard to firmly seat, indicated by a loud thumping sound, allowing either maximum or no air flow through the heater core. To check the function cable adjustment, see that the function lever will reach the detents at the far left and right of its travel. In addition, check that the air flow is correct when the function lever is moved through each detent provided in the control assembly. If cable adjustment is needed, proceed as follows:

1. Disengage the glove compartment door by squeezing its sides together. Allow the door to hang free.
2. Working through the glove compartment opening, remove the cable

jacket from the metal attaching clip on the top of the plenum by depressing the clip tab and pulling the cable out of the clip.

➡ **The adjustable end should remain attached to the door cams.**

3. To adjust the temperature control cable, set the temperature lever at COOL and hold. With the cable end attached to the temperature door cam, push gently on the cable jacket to seat the blend door. Push until resistance is felt. Reinstall the cable to the clip by pushing the cable jacket into the clip from the top until it snaps in.
4. To adjust the function control cable, set the function selector lever in the DEFROST detent and hold. With the cable end attached to the function cam, pull on the cam jacket until cam travel stops. Reinstall the cable to the clip by pushing the cable jacket into the clip from the top until it snaps in place.
5. Install the glove compartment.
6. Run the system blower on HIGH and actuate the levers, checking for proper adjustment.

MPV Models

1. To adjust the temperature control cable (air mix): Set the temperature control lever to the MAX-HOT position. Install the cable and secure the attaching clip with the heater unit shutter lever all the way to the right. Make sure the temperature control lever moves easily from the HOT to COLD position.
2. To adjust the airflow mode cable: Set the airflow mode control lever to the DEFROST position. Install the cable and attaching clip with the heater unit shutter lever at its closest point. Make sure the control lever moves easily between the DEFROST and VENT positions.
3. To adjust the rec/fresh control cable (air intake): Set the rec/fresh lever to the RECIRCULATE position. Install the cable and attaching clip with the blower unit shutter lever at its closest point. Make sure the control lever moves easily from the RECIRCULATE to the FRESH position.

REMOVAL & INSTALLATION

♦ **See Figures 33 and 34**

Navajo and B Series Pick-up Models

1. Disconnect the negative battery cable.
2. Remove the control assembly from the instrument panel.
3. Disengage the glove compartment door by squeezing the sides together and allowing the door to hang free.
4. Working through the glove compartment and/or control opening, remove the temperature and function cable jackets from their clips on top of the plenum by compressing the clip tangs and pulling the cables upward.
5. Reach through the glove compartment opening and disconnect the function and temperature cables from their separate cams. The cable ends are secured to the cams under a retention finger.
6. The cables are routed inside the instrument panel with 2 routing aids. Remove the cables from these devices. Reaching through the control opening, pull the cables upward out of the wiring shield cut-out. Reaching through the glove box opening, pull the cables out of the plastic clip up inside the instrument panel.

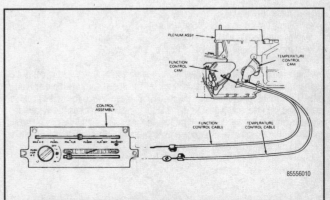

85556010

Fig. 33 Control cable connections at the head and the air plenum

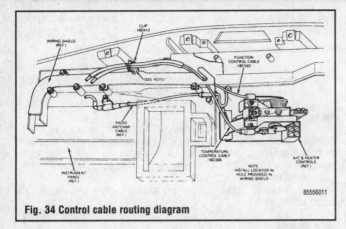

Fig. 34 Control cable routing diagram

7. Pull the cables from the instrument panel through the control assembly opening.

To install:

8. Working through the glove compartment opening and the control opening in the instrument panel, feed the end of the cables to the cam area. Feed the cables in from the glove compartment opening, making sure the coiled end of the white function cable and the round hole diecast end of the temperature cable go in first.

9. Attach the coiled end of the function cable to the function cam, making sure the cable is routed under the cable hold-down feature on the cam assembly. The pigtail coil may be facing either up or down.

10. Attach the diecast end of the temperature cable to the temperature cam making sure the cable is routed under the cable hold-down feature on the cam assembly.

11. Route the control end of the cable through the instrument panel until the ends stick out of the control opening. It is not necessary to insert the cable into any routing devices previously used. The routing aids are only necessary when the entire instrument panel is removed and reinstalled.

12. Attach the function and temperature cables to the control. Install the control assembly in the instrument panel.

13. Adjust the cables in their clips on top of the plenum.

➥Make sure the radio antenna cable does not become disengaged from its mounting and fall into the plenum cam area where it could cause an increase in control assembly operating effort or a faulty selection of system functions.

14. Connect the negative battery cable and make a final check of the system for proper control cable operation.

MPV Models

1. Remove the control head unit.
2. Disconnect the air intake wire from the front blower unit.
3. Disconnect the air mix and airflow mode wires from the front heater unit.
4. Disconnect the control wires from the control unit.

To install:

5. Connect the control wires to the control unit.
6. Connect the air mix and airflow mode wires to the front heater unit, then adjust.
7. Connect the air intake wire to the front blower unit and adjust.
8. Install the control head unit into the dashboard.

Air Conditioning Components

REMOVAL & INSTALLATION

Repair or service of air conditioning components is not covered by this manual, because of the risk of personal injury or death, and because of the legal ramifications of servicing these components without the proper EPA certification and experience. Cost, personal injury or death, environmental damage, and legal considerations (such as the fact that it is a federal crime to vent refrigerant into the atmosphere), dictate that the A/C components on your vehicle should be serviced only by a Motor Vehicle Air Conditioning (MVAC) trained, and EPA certified automotive technician.

➥If your vehicle's A/C system uses R-12 refrigerant and is in need of recharging, the A/C system can be converted over to R-134a refrigerant (less environmentally harmful and expensive). Refer to Section 1 for additional information on R-12 to R-134a conversions, and for additional considerations dealing with your vehicle's A/C system.

CRUISE CONTROL

Vacuum Controlled Systems

♦ **See Figures 35 and 36**

The vacuum controlled cruise control system consists of the following components:

- Control switches
- Servo or vacuum actuator (throttle actuator)
- Speed sensor
- Stoplamp/brake switch
- Actuator cable
- Cruise control unit
- Clutch switch (manual transmissions)
- Vacuum dump valve (B Series Pick-up and Navajo)
- Amplifier assembly (B Series Pick-up and Navajo)
- Transmission range switch (MPV)

The throttle actuator is mounted in the engine compartment and is connected to the throttle linkage with an actuator cable. The speed control amplifier regulates the throttle actuator to keep the requested speed. When the brake pedal is depressed, an electrical signal from the stoplamp switch returns the system to stand-by mode. The vacuum dump valve also mechanically releases the vacuum in the throttle actuator, thus releasing the throttle independently of the amplifier control. This feature is used as a safety backup.

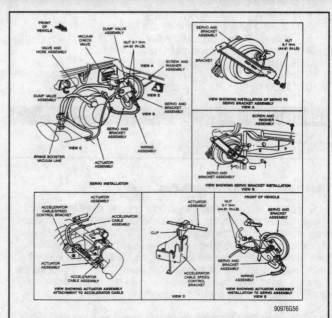

Fig. 35 Typical vacuum operated cruise control system components—Navajo shown

Fig. 36 The cruise control vacuum servo unit is mounted on top of the right side strut tower in the engine compartment of the MPV

Fig. 37 Electronic cruise control system components—2.3L B Series Pick-up shown, others similar

Electronic Systems

▶ See Figure 37

The electronic cruise control system consists of the following components:
- Control switches
- Actuator cable
- Servo/control unit (throttle actuator)
- Cruise control module
- Speed sensor
- Stoplamp and deactivator switches

The throttle actuator/control unit is mounted in the engine compartment and is connected to the throttle linkage with an actuator cable. The control unit regulates the throttle actuator to keep the requested speed. When the brake pedal is depressed, an electrical signal from the stoplamp and deactivator switches return the system to stand-by mode. This system operates independently of engine vacuum, therefore no vacuum lines are required.

CRUISE CONTROL TROUBLESHOOTING

Problem	Possible Cause
Will not hold proper speed	Incorrect cable adjustment
	Binding throttle linkage
	Leaking vacuum servo diaphragm
	Leaking vacuum tank
	Faulty vacuum or vent valve
	Faulty stepper motor
	Faulty transducer
	Faulty speed sensor
	Faulty cruise control module
Cruise intermittently cuts out	Clutch or brake switch adjustment too tight
	Short or open in the cruise control circuit
	Faulty transducer
	Faulty cruise control module
Vehicle surges	Kinked speedometer cable or casing
	Binding throttle linkage
	Faulty speed sensor
	Faulty cruise control module
Cruise control inoperative	Blown fuse
	Short or open in the cruise control circuit
	Faulty brake or clutch switch
	Leaking vacuum circuit
	Faulty cruise control switch
	Faulty stepper motor
	Faulty transducer
	Faulty speed sensor
	Faulty cruise control module

Note: Use this chart as a guide. Not all systems will use the components listed.

ENTERTAINMENT SYSTEMS

Radio Receiver/Tape Player

REMOVAL & INSTALLATION

Navajo and B Series Pick-up Models

▶ See Figures 38, 39, 40 and 41

1. Disconnect the negative battery cable.
2. Insert the radio removal tool 49-UN01-050 or equivalent, into the radio face.

3. Press in 1 inch (25.4mm) to release the retaining clips, then using the tool as handles, pull the radio out of the instrument panel.
4. Disconnect the antenna and wiring connectors from the radio.
To install:
5. Connect the wiring and slide the radio into the instrument panel. Ensure that the rear mounting bracket is engaged on the mounting track in the panel.
6. If removed, install the finish panel
7. Connect the battery cable.
8. Check the operation of the radio.

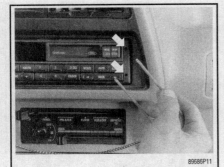

Fig. 38 To remove the radio, insert the removal tool prongs into the release clip access holes (arrows)

Fig. 39 Push in approximately 1 inch (25.4mm) to release the retainer clips, then pull straight out to remove

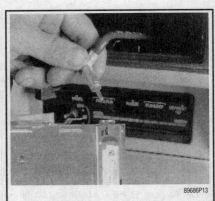

Fig. 40 Disconnect the antenna . . .

Fig. 41 . . . and the electrical wire harness plugs from the back of the radio

1994–95 MPV Models

▶ **See Figures 42 thru 48**

1. Disconnect the negative battery cable.
2. Remove the ashtray by pushing down on the inside metal flap and then pulling straight out.
3. Remove the two lower center bezel mounting screws.
4. Carefully pull out the center bezel, disengaging the metal retaining clips.
5. Remove the five radio mounting screws.
6. Carefully pull the radio out of the instrument panel far enough to unplug the antenna leads and wiring connectors from the radio.
7. Remove the radio from the vehicle.

To install:

8. Connect the antenna leads and wiring connectors to the back of the radio, then slide into the instrument panel.

9. Install and tighten the five mounting screws.
10. Install the center bezel and tighten the two mounting screws.
11. Install the ashtray.
12. Connect the negative battery cable.

1996–98 MPV Models

1. Disconnect the negative battery cable.
2. Remove the hole covers by inserting a small, tape wrapped, prying tool into the slot and carefully prying them off without scratching the center lower panel. Pry upward and pull off the hole covers carefully to prevent the posts from breaking off.
3. Insert the radio removal tool 49-UN01-050 or equivalent, into the radio face with the beveled parts of the tool facing inward.
4. Press in to release the retaining clips, then using the tool as handles, pull the radio out of the instrument panel.
5. Disconnect the antenna and wiring connectors from the radio.

To install:

6. Connect the wiring and slide the radio into the instrument panel until each retaining clip clicks.
7. Install the hole covers.
8. Connect the negative battery cable.
9. Check the operation of the radio.

Speakers

REMOVAL & INSTALLATION

✷✷ WARNING

Never operate the radio with one of the speaker disconnected. Damage to the radio can occur.

Fig. 42 Push down on the upper retaining flap and pull out the ashtray

Fig. 43 Remove the two center bezel retaining screws located at the bottom edge of the bezel

Fig. 44 Pull the bezel away from the dashboard disengaging the metal clips around the bezel

Fig. 45 Remove the five radio unit mounting screws

Fig. 46 Carefully pull the radio unit out of the center dash . . .

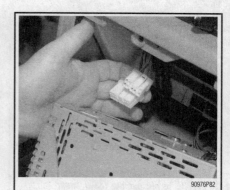

Fig. 47 . . . then unplug the wiring harness connectors from behind the radio . . .

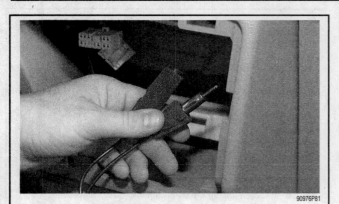

Fig. 48 . . . then disconnect the radio antenna leads

90976P81

Door Mounted Speakers

◗ See Figures 49, 50 and 51

1. Remove the door trim panel.
2. If necessary, peel away the plastic inner liner.
3. Remove the speaker attaching screws.
4. Pull the speaker out from the door frame and disconnect the wire harness plug.
5. Installation is the reverse of the removal procedure.

Body Mounted Rear Speakers

B SERIES PICK-UP AND NAVAJO MODELS

1. On B Series Pick-up models, remove the four speaker grille attaching screws and remove the grille.
2. On Navajo models, gently pry the speaker grille from the trim panel.
3. On CabPlus models, remove the four speaker mounting screws.
4. Pull the speaker out from the trim panel and disconnect the wire harness plug.
5. Installation is the reverse of the removal procedure.

MPV MODELS

1. Remove the rear interior side trim.
2. Remove the three speaker mounting screws.
3. Carefully pull the speaker out and disconnect the wire harness plug.
4. Installation is the reverse of the removal procedure.

Dash Mounted Speakers (1994–95 MPV only)

◗ See Figures 52, 53, 54, 55 and 56

➡This procedure applies to both right and left side dash mounted speakers.

1. Remove the dashboard end panel by carefully prying outward to disengage the retaining clips.
2. Remove all of the dashboard lower panel mounting screws.
3. Carefully pull the lower panel outward and unplug the speaker wiring connector.
4. Remove the speaker mounting fasteners and remove from the vehicle.
5. Installation is the reverse of the removal procedure.

Fig. 49 Carefully peel away the inner door liner to access the speaker mounting bolts

90976P52

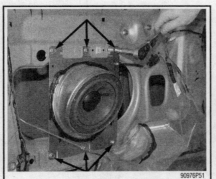

Fig. 50 Remove the door speaker mounting bolts

90976P51

Fig. 51 Disengage the door mounted speaker wiring connector and remove from the vehicle

90976P50

Fig. 52 Disengage the metal clips and remove the side dashboard end cover . . .

90976P84

Fig. 53 . . . then remove the lower cover end mounting screw

90976P85

Fig. 54 Remove the lower dash panel cover mounting screws

90976P83

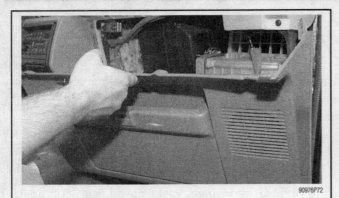

Fig. 55 Carefully pull away the lower dash cover . . .

Fig. 56 . . . then unplug the wire from the lower dash cover speaker, loosen the mounting fasteners and remove from the vehicle

WINDSHIELD WIPERS

Wiper Arm and Blade

REMOVAL & INSTALLATION

Front Wipers

NAVAJO AND B SERIES PICK-UP MODELS

◆ See Figures 57, 58 and 59

1. Raise the blade end of the arm off of the windshield.
2. Move the slide latch away from the pivot shaft. The wiper arm can now be removed from the shaft without the use of any tools.

Fig. 57 While holding the wiper arm off of the windshield, slide the latch out and away from the pivot shaft . . .

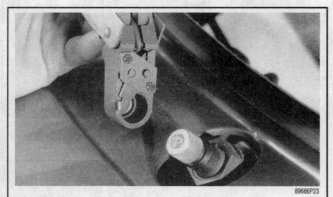

Fig. 58 . . . then lift it straight up and off of the shaft to remove

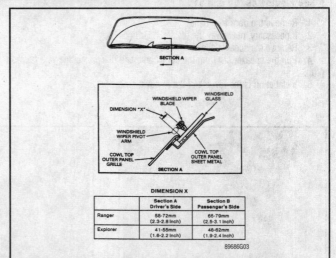

Fig. 59 Windshield wiper arm positioning for the Ranger, Explorer and Mountaineer models

DIMENSION X

	Section A Driver's Side	Section B Passenger's Side
Ranger	58-72mm (2.3-2.8 Inch)	65-79mm (2.5-3.1 Inch)
Explorer	41-55mm (1.6-2.2 Inch)	48-62mm (1.9-2.4 Inch)

To install:
3. Be sure the wipers are in the parked position, and the blade assembly is in its correct position.
4. Push the main head over the pivot shaft.
5. Hold the main arm head onto the pivot shaft while raising the blade end of the wiper arm and push the slide latch into the lock under the pivot shaft head.
6. Lower the blade to the windshield. If the blade does not lower to the windshield, the slide latch is not completely in place.

MPV MODELS

◆ See Figure 60

1. To remove the blade and arm, remove cap, unscrew the retaining nut and pry the blade and arm from the pivot shaft. The shaft and arm are serrated to provide for adjustment of the wiper pattern on the glass.
2. To set the arms back in the proper park position, turn the wiper switch on and allow the motor to cycle three or four times. Then turn off the wiper switch (do not turn off the wiper motor with the ignition key). This will place the wiper shafts in the proper park position.

➡Using a wire brush, clean the wiper arm connector shafts before installing the wiper arms.

3. Install the blade and arm on the shaft and install the retaining nut. Install the caps. The blades and arms should be positioned according to the illustration.

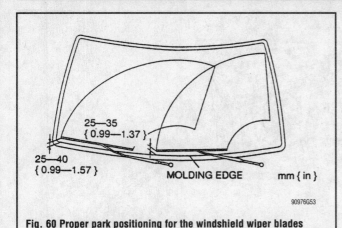

Fig. 60 Proper park positioning for the windshield wiper blades

Rear Wiper

MPV MODELS

▶ See Figures 61, 62, 63 and 64

1. To remove the blade and arm, unscrew the retaining nut and pry the blade and arm from the pivot shaft. The shaft and arm are serrated to provide for adjustment of the wiper pattern on the glass.

2. To set the arm back in the proper park position, turn the wiper switch on and allow the motor to cycle three or four times. Then turn off the wiper switch (do not turn off the wiper motor with the ignition key). This will place the wiper shafts in the proper park position.

3. Install the blade and arm on the shaft and install the retaining nut. The blades and arms should be positioned according to the illustration.

NAVAJO MODELS

▶ See Figure 65

☼ WARNING

Use a towel or similar device to protect the vehicle finish when performing this procedure.

1. Raise the windshield wiper blade/arm off of the glass and place it into the service position.
2. Using a small, flat bladed prytool, release the retaining clip at the base of the windshield wiper pivot arm.
3. Carefully pry the wiper arm from the shaft.
To install:
4. Ensure that the wiper motor pivot shaft is in the park position.
5. Position the wiper arm over the shaft and firmly push it on until it stops.
6. Lower the wiper blade/arm against the glass.

➡The blade is properly positioned when it firmly contacts the windshield wiper arm stop. If it does not, remove the arm again and reposition it so that it does.

Windshield Wiper Motor

REMOVAL & INSTALLATION

Front Wiper Motor

NAVAJO AND B SERIES PICK-UP MODELS

▶ See Figure 66

1. Turn the wiper switch on. Turn the ignition switch on until the blades are straight up and then turn ignition off to keep them there.

Fig. 61 Lift up the plastic wiper arm pivot nut cover and carefully remove from the wiper arm

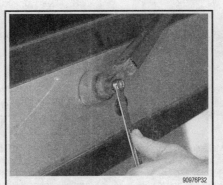

Fig. 62 Using a 10mm box wrench, remove the rear wiper arm pivot nut

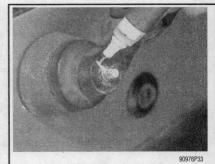

Fig. 63 To aid in correct installation of the rear wiper arm, matchmark the wiper arm to the pivot shaft

Fig. 64 If the wiper arm is difficult to remove, use a small puller tool such as the one shown

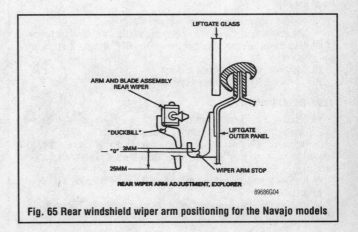

Fig. 65 Rear windshield wiper arm positioning for the Navajo models

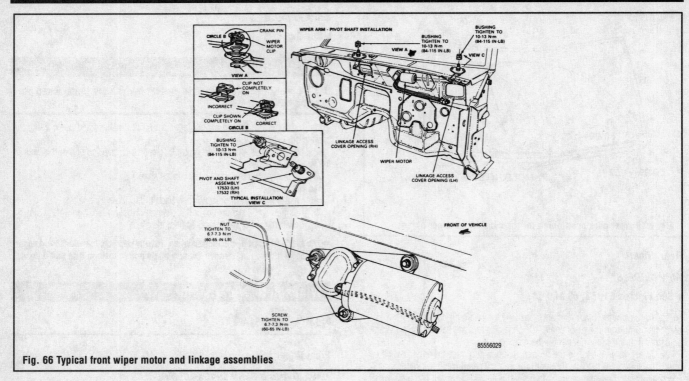

Fig. 66 Typical front wiper motor and linkage assemblies

2. Remove the right wiper arm and blade.

3. Remove the negative battery cable.

4. Remove the right pivot nut and allow the linkage to drop into the cowl.

5. Remove the linkage access cover, located on the right side of the dash panel near the wiper motor.

6. Reach through the access cover opening and unsnap the wiper motor clip.

7. Push the clip away from the linkage until it clears the nib on the crank pin. Then, push the clip off the linkage.

8. Remove the wiper linkage from motor crank pin.

9. Disconnect the wiper motor's wiring connector.

10. Remove the wiper motor's three attaching screws and remove the motor.

To install:

11. Install the motor and attach the three attaching screws. Tighten to 60–65 inch lbs. (6.7–7.3 Nm).

12. Connect the wiper motor's wiring connector.

13. Install the clip completely on the right linkage. Make sure the clip is completely on.

14. Install the left linkage on the wiper motor crank pin.

15. Install the right linkage on the wiper motor crank pin and pull the linkage on to the crank pin until it snaps.

➡The clip is properly installed if the nib is protruding through the center of the clip.

16. Reinstall the right wiper pivot shaft and nut.

17. Reconnect the battery and turn the ignition **ON**. Turn the wiper switch off so the wiper motor will park, then turn the ignition **OFF**. Replace the right linkage access cover.

18. Install the right wiper blade and arm.

19. Check the system for proper operation.

1994–95 MPV MODELS

1. Disconnect the negative battery cable.

2. Unplug the electrical connector from the wiper motor.

3. Disconnect the wiper linkage from the motor crank arm. If necessary to remove the crank arm from the motor, matchmark the arm to the bracket prior to removal.

4. Remove the mounting bolts and remove the wiper motor.

To install:

5. Position the wiper motor and install the mounting bolts. Tighten to 61–87 inch lbs. (6.9–9.8 Nm).

6. If removed, install the motor crank arm, aligning the marks that were made during removal.

7. Connect the wiper linkage to the motor crank arm. Plug in the electrical connector.

8. Make sure when in the park position, the wiper blades are 0.98–1.38 in. (25–35mm) from the lower windshield moulding.

1996–98 MPV MODELS

▶ See Figure 67

1. Make sure the wipers are in the parked position.

2. Disconnect the negative battery cable and wait at least 90 seconds before performing any work.

3. Remove the 2 nuts and remove the 2 wiper arms.

4. Remove the 2 nuts and the 2 seal rings securing the wiper transmission to the cowl.

5. Remove the 2 bolts securing the wiper motor bracket and disconnect the wiper motor connector.

6. Disconnect the wiper transmission from the wiper motor bell crank by carefully prying the transmission link from the bell crank.

7. Remove the nut and the O-ring and remove the bell crank from the wiper motor.

8. Remove the 3 wiper motor mounting bolts and the wiper motor.

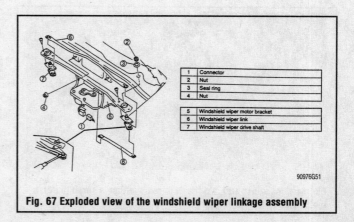

1	Connector
2	Nut
3	Seal ring
4	Nut
5	Windshield wiper motor bracket
6	Windshield wiper link
7	Windshield wiper drive shaft

Fig. 67 Exploded view of the windshield wiper linkage assembly

To install:

9. Install the wiper motor with the 3 mounting bolts and torque the bolts to 61–86 inch lbs. (6.9–9.8 Nm).

10. Install the bell crank to the wiper motor with the seal and the nut.

11. Install the wiper transmission to the bell crank.

12. Install the wiper transmission assembly through the openings in the cowl panel. Reconnect the wiper motor connector and install the 2 bolts securing the wiper motor bracket.

13. Install the wiper pivot seal rings and secure with the 2 nuts. Torque the nuts to 61–86 inch lbs. (6.9–9.8 Nm).

2. Remove the wiper arm and blade.

3. Remove the liftgate interior trim.

4. Remove the motor attaching bolts (3). Disconnect the electrical leads.

5. Remove the wiper motor from the vehicle.

To install:

6. Install the wiper motor in position and connect the electrical leads.

7. Install the liftgate trim. Connect the negative battery cable.

Fig. 68 Ater removing the wiper arm, pull the bushing off of the motor shaft

Fig. 69 Use a 29mm wrench to loosen the motor shaft-to-tailgate retaining nut

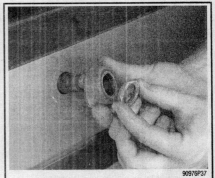

Fig. 70 Remove the motor shaft retaining nut and shaft grommet

Fig. 71 Disengage the black rear wiper motor electrical connector

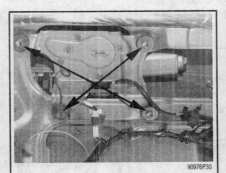

Fig. 72 Location of the rear wiper motor assembly mounting bolts. Remove these bolts using a 10mm socket

Fig. 73 Remove the rear wiper motor assembly from the tailgate door

14. Reinstall the wiper arms and secure with the 2 nuts. Torque the nuts to 86.8–120 inch lbs. (9.81–13.7 Nm).

15. Reconnect the negative battery cable and check for proper operation.

Rear Window Wiper Motor

MPV MODELS

▶ **See Figures 68 thru 73**

1. Disconnect the battery ground cable.

2. Remove the protective cap and wiper arm nut and pull off the wiper arm, seal and bushing.

3. Remove the liftgate inner trim panels.

4. Remove the weathershield.

5. Disconnect the wiper motor wiring.

6. Remove the motor mounting bolts and lift out the motor.

7. Installation is the reverse of removal.

NAVAJO MODELS

▶ **See Figure 74**

1. Disconnect the negative battery cable.

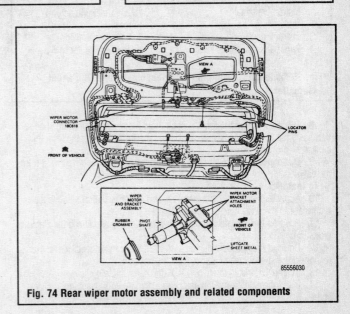

Fig. 74 Rear wiper motor assembly and related components

INSTRUMENTS AND SWITCHES

Instrument Cluster

REMOVAL & INSTALLATION

1994 B Series Pick-up and Navajo Models

♦ **See Figure 75**

1. Disconnect the negative battery cable.
2. Open the ash tray and remove the two retaining screws. Remove the ash tray assembly from the dash.
3. If necessary, remove the left and right A/C register vents from the dash.
4. Unsnap the instrument cluster trim panel by pulling rearwards around the edge of the panel. Depress the hazard warning switch (4-way flashers) and remove the trim panel.
5. Remove the four screws securing the instrument cluster to the dash mounting.
6. On vehicles equipped with an automatic transmission, perform the following:
    a. Remove the two screws attaching the PRNDL indicator to the cluster.
    b. If necessary for clearance, block the wheels and apply the parking brake, then turn the ignition switch to unlock the steering wheel and pull the gear select lever into the Low (L) range.
7. Pull the cluster assembly rearward to gain access to the speedometer cable.

➡ **If there is insufficient slack in the cable for gaining access, disconnect the cable from the transmission. Once disconnected pull the cluster out gently until enough clearance is gained.**

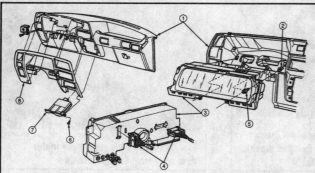

1. Instrument panel
2. Nut
3. Instrument cluster
4. Wire harness connectors
5. Cluster retaining screws
6. Screws
7. Ash tray assembly
8. Instrument cluster trim panel

89686G08

Fig. 75 Exploded view of the instrument cluster and trim panel assemblies

8. Disconnect the speedometer cable from the cluster. The cable connection has a flat surface clip; press the clip inward and pull the cable from the cluster.
9. Disconnect the wire harness plugs from the cluster and remove it from the dash.

To install:

10. Apply approximately 3/16 inch (4.8mm) diameter ball of silicone dielectric grease in the drive hole of the speedometer head.
11. Position the instrument cluster near its opening and attach the electrical plugs to it.
12. Connect the speedometer cable to the speedometer head. If necessary, reconnect the speedometer cable to the transmission.
13. If removed, install the two PRNDL indicator retaining screws.
14. Insert the cluster into the dash and install the four attaching screws.

15. Ensure that the hazard warning switch is depressed and install the cluster trim panel.
16. Connect the negative battery cable. Start the vehicle and check all gauges, lamps and signals for proper operation.

1995–98 B Series Pick-up Models

♦ **See Figure 76**

1. Disconnect the negative battery cable.
2. Remove the radio.
3. Remove the center finish panel to access and remove the lower trim and knee bolster attaching screws.
4. Remove the lower trim and knee bolster.
5. Remove the cluster finish panel and unplug the headlamp and dimmer switch harnesses from it.
6. Remove the four instrument cluster retaining screws.
7. If equipped with an automatic transmission, remove the two PRNDL indicator attaching screws and remove the indicator by sliding it straight down.
8. Disconnect the electrical wire harness plugs and remove the cluster.

To install:

9. Connect the electrical wire harness plugs and install the instrument cluster.
10. If equipped with an automatic transmission, install the two PRNDL indicator attaching screws and remove the indicator by sliding it straight down.
11. Install the four instrument cluster retaining screws.
12. Connect the headlamp and dimmer switch harnesses to the cluster finish panel then install it.
13. Install the lower trim and knee bolster panels and the attaching screws.
14. Install the center finish panel.
15. Install the radio.
16. Connect the negative battery cable. Start the vehicle and check all gauges, lamps and signals for proper operation.

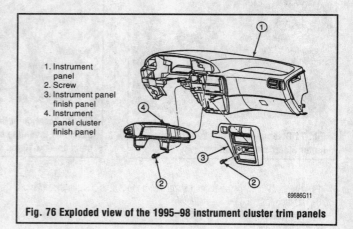

1. Instrument panel
2. Screw
3. Instrument panel finish panel
4. Instrument panel cluster finish panel

89686G11

Fig. 76 Exploded view of the 1995–98 instrument cluster trim panels

1994–95 MPV Models

♦ **See Figures 77 thru 82**

1. Disconnect the negative battery cable.
2. Using a small prying tool, remove the trim panel at the front edge of the instrument cluster hood, near the bottom edge of the windshield.
3. Remove the three instrument cluster hood mounting screws underneath the trim panel.
4. Remove the two instrument cluster hood mounting screws located under the bootom edge of the hood assembly.
5. Carefully pull the instrument cluster hood assembly away from the dashboard far enough to unplug the wiring harness connectors from behind the switches on each side.
6. Remove the 4 cluster assembly retaining screws and pull the cluster towards you slowly and carefully, until you can reach behind it and unplug the electrical connectors, speedometer cable and unhook the transmission range indicator wire from the steering column.
7. Remove the cluster.

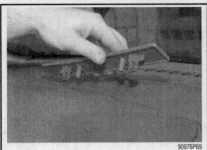

Fig. 77 Lift up the trim panel from the front edge of the instrument cluster hood assembly to access and remove the three mounting screws

Fig. 78 Remove the lower instrument cluster hood mounting screws

Fig. 79 Carefully pull the instrument cluster hood assembly away from the dashboard . . .

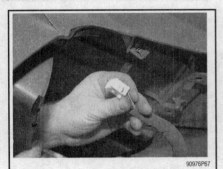

Fig. 80 . . . then unplug the wiring connectors from behind the switches on the instrument cluster hood assembly

Fig. 81 Remove the four instrument cluster assembly mounting screws

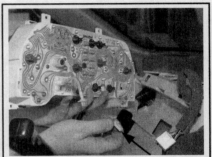

Fig. 82 When removing the instrument cluster, disconnect the transmission selector cable from the steering column

To install:

8. Hold the instrument cluster close to the dashboard and route the transmission range indicator wire through the dashboard.

9. Connect the speedometer cable to the back of the cluster assembly and plug in the electrical connectors.

10. Place the cluster into correct position, then install and tighten the four cluster retaining screws. Attach the transmission range indicator wire from the steering column.

11. Hold the instrument cluster hood assembly close to the dashboard and plug in wiring harness connectors.

12. Place the instrument cluster hood assembly onto the dashboard. Install and tighten the five mounting screws.

13. Install the trim panel cover.

14. Connect the negative battery cable. Check the operation of the instrument cluster gauges.

1996–98 MPV Models

▶ **See Figures 83 and 84**

1. Disconnect the negative battery cable.
2. Shift the selector lever to the **L** range.
3. Remove the instrument cluster hood mounting screws.
4. Pull the instrument cluster hood forward to disengage the retaining clips from the dashboard.
5. Unplug the wiring harness connectors from behind the cluster hood and remove from the vehicle.
6. Remove the four instrument cluster mounting screws.
7. Remove the speedometer cable from the clips.
8. Insert your hand into the dashboard from the bottom right of the instrument cluster and disconnect the speedometer cable.
9. Pull the instrument cluster out far enough to unplug the wiring harness

connectors from the back of the cluster assembly. Remove the cluster from the vehicle.

To install:

10. Hold the instrument cluster assembly close to the dashboard, then connect the speedometer cable to the back of the cluster assembly and plug in the electrical connectors.

11. Position the cluster assembly onto the dashboard, then install and tighten the four cluster mounting screws.

12. Hold the instrument cluster hood assembly close to the dashboard and plug in wiring harness connectors.

13. Place the instrument cluster hood assembly onto the dashboard. Install and tighten the mounting screws. Make sure that the retaining clips are fully engaged.

14. Place the selector lever into **P** range.

15. Connect the negative battery cable.

Gauges

REMOVAL & INSTALLATION

Each of the gauges can be removed in the same manner, once the instrument cluster is removed.

1. Disconnect the negative battery cable.
2. Remove the instrument cluster assembly.
3. Remove the lens from the instrument cluster.
4. Remove the gauge mounting screws, then pull the gauge from the cluster.

To install:

5. Install the gauge, by pushing it firmly into position. Secure with mounting screws.

6. Install the cluster lens and install the cluster into the instrument panel.

Fig. 83 Instrument cluster hood assembly removal

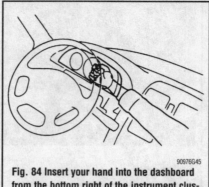

Fig. 84 Insert your hand into the dashboard from the bottom right of the instrument cluster and disconnect the speedometer cable

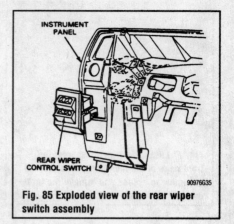

Fig. 85 Exploded view of the rear wiper switch assembly

Rear Wiper Switch

REMOVAL & INSTALLATION

Navajo Models

▶ See Figure 85

1. Disconnect the negative battery cable.
2. Loosen the two mounting screws and remove the ashtray.
3. Disengage the retaining clips and remove the instrument cluster finish panel.
4. Unsnap and remove the mounting bezel that contains the rear wiper switch.
5. Disconnect the electrical lead from the switch.
6. Remove the switch from the mounting bezel by pushing on the switch from the connector side until the mounting clips unsnap.

To install:

7. Connect the wiring and install the switch in the instrument panel.
8. Install the instrument cluster finish panel.
9. Install the ashtray and tighten the two mounting screws.
10. Connect the negative battery cable. Check the operation of the switch.

1994–95 MPV Models

1. Disconnect the negative battery cable.
2. Using a small prying tool, remove the trim panel at the front edge of the instrument cluster hood, near the bottom edge of the windshield.
3. Remove the three instrument cluster hood mounting screws underneath the trim panel.
4. Remove the two instrument cluster hood mounting screws located under the bootom edge of the hood assembly.
5. Carefully pull the instrument cluster hood assembly away from the dashboard far enough to unplug the wiring harness connectors from behind the switches on each side.
6. Remove the mounting screws, then separate the rear wiper and washer switch from the left side of the cluster hood.

To install:

7. Place the rear wiper and washer switch onto the cluster hood and tighten the mounting screws.
8. Hold the instrument cluster hood assembly close to the dashboard and plug in wiring harness connectors.
9. Place the instrument cluster hood assembly onto the dashboard. Install and tighten the five mounting screws.
10. Install the trim panel cover.

11. Connect the negative battery cable. Check the operation of the switch.

1996–98 MPV Models

▶ See Figure 86

1. Disconnect the negative battery cable.
2. Remove the side panel on the left side of the dashboard.
3. Remove the left side lower panel.
4. Remove the glove compartment.
5. Remove the side panel on the right side of the dashboard, then remove the glove compartment cover.
6. Remove the center lower panel.
7. Remove the center upper panel.
8. Press the stoppers on the switch to remove the rear wiper and washer switch.
9. Disconnect the electrical lead from the switch.

To install:

10. Connect the wiring and install the switch in the instrument panel.
11. Install the center upper panel.
12. Install the center lower panel.
13. Install the glove compartment cover.
14. Install the glove compartment.
15. Install the lower panel.
16. Install the side panel.
17. Connect the negative battery cable. Check the operation of the switch.

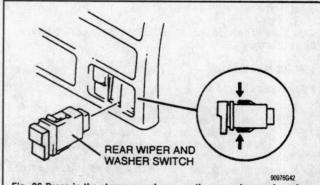

Fig. 86 Press in the stoppers and remove the rear wiper and washer switch

LIGHTING

Headlights

REMOVAL & INSTALLATION

B Series Pick-up, Navajo and 1994–95 MPV Models

▶ **See Figures 87, 88, 89 and 90**

1. Make sure that the headlight switch is turned **OFF**.
2. Disconnect the negative battery cable.
3. Open the vehicle's hood and secure it in an upright position.
4. If equipped with a bulb access panel, open by depressing the latch then lifting.
5. Unfasten the locking ring which secures the bulb and wire harness plug assembly, then withdraw the assembly rearward.
6. Disconnect the electrical wire harness plug from the bulb and remove the locking ring as well.

To install:

7. Before connecting a light bulb to the wire harness plug, ensure that all electrical contact surfaces are free of corrosion or dirt.
8. Install the locking ring onto the bulb, then line up the replacement headlight bulb with the harness plug. Firmly push the bulb onto the plug until the spring clip latches over the bulb's projection.

✷✷ WARNING

Do not touch the glass bulb with your fingers. Oil from your fingers can severely shorten the life of the bulb. If necessary, wipe off any dirt or oil from the bulb with rubbing alcohol before completing installation.

9. Position the headlight bulb and secure it with the locking ring.
10. Connect the negative battery cable.
11. To ensure that the replacement bulb functions properly, activate the applicable switch to illuminate the bulb which was just replaced. (If this is a combination low and high beam bulb, be sure to check both intensities.) If the replacement light bulb does not illuminate, either it too is faulty or there is a problem in the bulb circuit or switch. Correct if necessary.
12. Close the bulb access panel and the vehicle's hood.

1996–98 MPV Models

▶ **See Figures 91 and 92**

1. Make sure that the headlight switch is turned **OFF**.
2. Disconnect the negative battery cable.
3. Open the vehicle's hood and secure it in an upright position.
4. Unplug the electrical connector from the bulb by compressing the tabs and pulling it to the rear.
5. Remove the sealing ring.
6. Unhook the headlight bulb retaining spring and turn it counterclockwise approximately ⅛ of a turn.
7. Carefully remove the bulb assembly from the socket by pulling it straight back.

To install:

8. Before connecting a light bulb to the wire harness plug, ensure that all electrical contact surfaces are free of corrosion or dirt.

✷✷ WARNING

Do not touch the glass bulb with your fingers. Oil from your fingers can severely shorten the life of the bulb. If necessary, wipe off any dirt or oil from the bulb with rubbing alcohol before completing installation.

Fig. 87 If equipped, open the headlight access panel by sliding the latch and lifting the panel upwards

Fig. 88 Push down the upper retaining tab on the headlight bulb connector plug and pull straight off of the bulb

Fig. 89 Turn the headlight bulb retaining ring counterclockwise and pull off of the back of the bulb

Fig. 90 Pull the headlight bulb straight out of the headlight housing. Under any circumstance, never touch the glass of the light bulb with your fingers

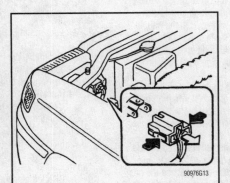

Fig. 91 Unplug the electrical connector by compressing the outer tabs

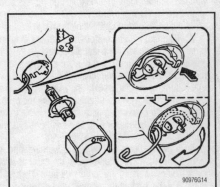

Fig. 92 Pull off the sealing cover and unhook the retaining spring

9. Carefully install the new bulb assembly into the socket and secure it with the headlight bulb retaining spring.

10. Install the sealing ring.

11. Plug the electrical connector into the rear of the bulb and make sure that the locking tabs engage.

12. Connect the negative battery cable.

13. To ensure that the replacement bulb functions properly, activate the applicable switch to illuminate the bulb which was just replaced. (If this is a combination low and high beam bulb, be sure to check both intensities.) If the replacement light bulb does not illuminate, either it too is faulty or there is a problem in the bulb circuit or switch. Correct if necessary.

AIMING THE HEADLIGHTS

▶ **See Figures 93 and 94**

The headlights must be properly aimed to provide the best, safest road illumination. The lights should be checked for proper aim and adjusted as necessary. Certain state and local authorities have requirements for headlight aiming; these should be checked before adjustment is made.

✳✳ CAUTION

About once a year, when the headlights are replaced or any time front end work is performed on your vehicle, the headlight should be accurately aimed by a reputable repair shop using the proper equipment. Headlights not properly aimed can make it virtually impossible to see and may blind other drivers on the road, possibly causing an accident. Note that the following procedure is a temporary fix, until you can take your vehicle to a repair shop for a proper adjustment.

Headlight adjustment may be temporarily made using a wall, as described below, or on the rear of another vehicle. When adjusted, the lights should not glare in oncoming car or truck windshields, nor should they illuminate the passenger compartment of vehicles driving in front of you. These adjustments are rough and should always be fine-tuned by a repair shop which is equipped with headlight aiming tools. Improper adjustments may be both dangerous and illegal.

For most of the vehicles covered by this manual, horizontal and vertical aiming of each sealed beam unit is provided by two adjusting screws which move the retaining ring and adjusting plate against the tension of a coil spring. There is no adjustment for focus; this is done during headlight manufacturing.

➡Because the composite headlight assembly is bolted into position, no adjustment should be necessary or possible. Some applications, however, may be bolted to an adjuster plate or may be retained by adjusting screws. If so, follow this procedure when adjusting the lights, BUT always have the adjustment checked by a reputable shop.

Before removing the headlight bulb or disturbing the headlamp in any way, note the current settings in order to ease headlight adjustment upon reassembly. If the high or low beam setting of the old lamp still works, this can be done using the wall of a garage or a building:

1. Park the vehicle on a level surface, with the fuel tank about ½ full and with the vehicle empty of all extra cargo (unless normally carried). The vehicle should be facing a wall which is no less than 6 feet (1.8m) high and 12 feet (3.7m) wide. The front of the vehicle should be about 25 feet from the wall.

2. If aiming is to be performed outdoors, it is advisable to wait until dusk in order to properly see the headlight beams on the wall. If done in a garage, darken the area around the wall as much as possible by closing shades or hanging cloth over the windows.

3. Turn the headlights **ON** and mark the wall at the center of each light's low beam, then switch on the brights and mark the center of each light's high beam. A short length of masking tape which is visible from the front of the vehicle may be used. Although marking all four positions is advisable, marking one position from each light should be sufficient.

4. If neither beam on one side is working, and if another like-sized vehicle is available, park the second one in the exact spot where the vehicle was and mark the beams using the same-side light. Then switch the vehicles so the one to be aimed is back in the original spot. It must be parked no closer to or farther away from the wall than the second vehicle.

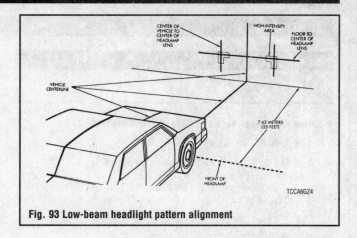

Fig. 93 Low-beam headlight pattern alignment

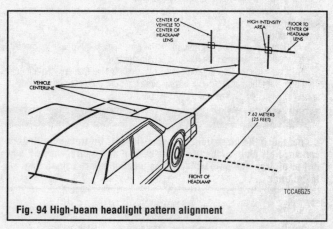

Fig. 94 High-beam headlight pattern alignment

5. Perform any necessary repairs, but make sure the vehicle is not moved, or is returned to the exact spot from which the lights were marked. Turn the headlights **ON** and adjust the beams to match the marks on the wall.

6. Have the headlight adjustment checked as soon as possible by a reputable repair shop.

Signal and Marker Lights

REMOVAL & INSTALLATION

Front Marker and Turn Signal

NAVAJO AND 1994–97 B SERIES PICK-UP MODELS

▶ **See Figure 95**

1. Loosen the two mounting nuts and remove the parking/turn signal lamp assembly.

2. Loosen the one mounting screw and remove the side marker lamp housing.

3. To remove the side marker, parking/turn signal bulbs and sockets from their housings, simply turn the socket(s) counterclockwise and pull straight out.

4. Remove the bulb from the socket by pulling straight out of the socket.

To install:

5. Install the new bulb straight into the socket.

6. Install the socket into the rear of the housing and turn clockwise to lock into place.

7. Install the side marker lamp housing and tighten the one mounting screw.

8. Place the parking/turn signal lamp assembly into position and tighten the two mounting nuts.

9. Check the operation of the lights.

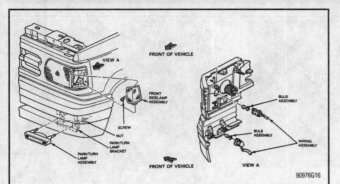

Fig. 95 Front turn signal and side marker lens assembly for the Navajo and 1994–97 B Series Pick-up

1998 B SERIES PICK-UP MODELS

♦ See Figure 96

1. Remove the marker/turn signal lens retaining screws or nut.
2. Gently pull outward on the lens assembly to disengage the barbed retainers.
3. Twist the lamp socket and remove it from the lens.
4. Pull the bulb from the socket.

To install:

5. Install the bulb into the lamp socket.
6. Install the lamp socket to the lens and twist it to lock it in position.
7. Position the lens assembly, ensure that the barbed retainers are aligned

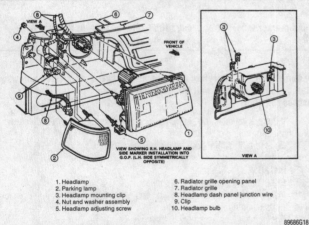

1. Headlamp
2. Parking lamp
3. Headlamp mounting clip
4. Nut and washer assembly
5. Headlamp adjusting screw
6. Radiator grille opening panel
7. Radiator grille
8. Headlamp dash panel junction wire
9. Clip
10. Headlamp bulb

Fig. 96 1998 B Series Pick-up models front signal and marker lens assembly

with their mounting clips, and press the assembly until fully seated.

8. Install the marker/turn signal lens retaining screws or nut.
9. Check the operation of the lights.

1994–95 MPV MODELS

♦ See Figures 97 thru 103

1. Disconnect the battery ground cable.
2. Remove the grille side moldings.

➡The grille side molding pieces are retained by both screws and snap-clips. The snap-clips can be freed by depressing the tabs with a small screwdriver.

3. Remove the lens mounting screws and pull off the lens.
4. Turn the socket counterclockwise and pull it straight out of the back of the housing.
5. Carefully push in on the bulb and twist it counterclockwise to remove it from the socket.
6. Installation is the reverse of removal.

1996–98 MPV MODELS

♦ See Figure 104

1. Disconnect the battery ground cable.
2. Remove the top lens mounting bolt pull off the lens.
3. Turn the socket counterclockwise and pull it straight out of the back of the housing.
4. Carefully push in on the bulb and twist it counterclockwise to remove it from the socket.
5. Installation is the reverse of removal.

Rear Marker and Rear Lamps

NAVAJO AND B SERIES PICK-UP MODELS

♦ See Figure 105

1. Remove the 2 (Navajo models) or 4 (B Series Pick-up models) screws retaining the lamp assembly to the vehicle.
2. Remove the lamp assembly from the vehicle by pulling it outward. On the Navajo models, make sure the 2 barbed retainers at the bottom of the assembly release.
3. Remove the lamp sockets from the lens housing by twisting it, then pulling outward.
4. Remove the bulb from the socket by pulling it straight outward.

To install:

5. Install the bulb into the lamp socket.
6. Install the lamp socket to the lens and twist it to lock it in position.
7. Position the lens assembly to the body. On Navajo models, ensure that the barbed retainers are aligned with their mounting clips, and press the assembly until fully seated.
8. Install the lens assembly retaining screws (four screws used on the B Series Pick-up and 2 on the Navajo).
9. Check the operation of the lights.

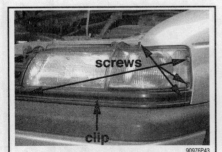

Fig. 97 To change the front turn signal/side marker bulb, five mounting screws must be removed and one clip disengaged

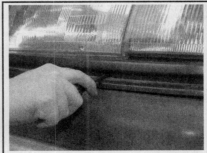

Fig. 98 Disengage the retaining clip in the middle of the trim panel below the headlight and turn signal housing

Fig. 99 Pull out the trim panel to aid in turn signal/side marker light housing removal

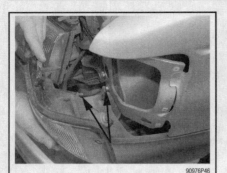

Fig. 100 When removing the turn signal housing, pull firm enough to disengage the locating pin from the location hole

Fig. 101 To remove the turn signal light bulb socket from the housing, turn the socket counterclockwise

Fig. 102 Pull the socket straight out of the turn signal housing . . .

Fig. 103 . . . then press in and turn to remove the front turn signal bulb from the socket

Fig. 104 Front turn signal and marker lens assembly for 1996–98 MPV

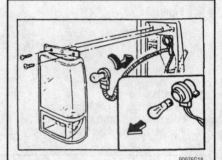

Fig. 105 Exploded view of the rear light assembly used on the Navajo model

MPV MODELS

♦ See Figures 106 thru 121

1. Remove the lens mounting screws and pull off the lens.
2. Carefully push in on the bulb and twist it counterclockwise to remove it.
3. Installation is the reverse of removal.

High Mount Brake Light

B SERIES PICK-UP AND NAVAJO MODELS

♦ See Figures 122 and 123

1. Remove the screws retaining the lamp to the liftgate (Navajo models) or the cab (B Series Pick-up models).
2. Pull the lamp away from the vehicle and disconnect the wiring connector.

➡Some later models retain the lamp socket to the lens with a screw. Remove the screw and pull the lamp socket away from the lens to access the bulbs.

3. If there is no retaining screw, remove the lamp socket from the lens by twisting it and pulling outward.
4. Pull the bulb straight out from the lamp socket to remove it.

To install:
5. Install the bulb into the lamp socket.
6. Install the lamp socket to the lens and either twist it to lock it in position or install its retaining screw.
7. Position the lens assembly to the body.
8. Install the lens assembly retaining screws.
9. Check the operation of the lights.

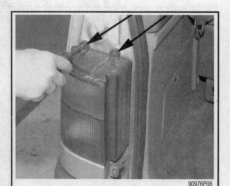

Fig. 106 Remove the two rear combination light assembly mounting screws

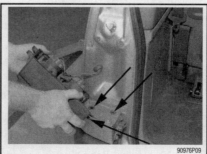

Fig. 107 When removing the rear combination light housing, be careful not to brake the locating pegs that fit into the mounting holes of the body

Fig. 108 To remove the socket from the back of the combination light housing, turn the socket counterclockwise . . .

Fig. 109 . . . then carefully pull the socket out of the opening in the housing unit

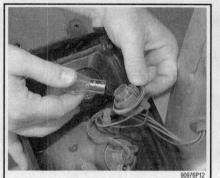

Fig. 110 Gently press in and turn the bulb, then pull it out of the socket

Fig. 111 Remove the two inboard combination light retaining screws . . .

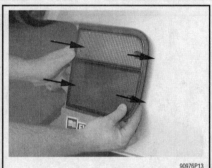

Fig. 112 . . . then gently push the assembly inward of the door to free it from the retaining tabs

Fig. 113 Part of the inboard combination light assembly is held in place by retaining tabs secured against the door metal

Fig. 114 Hold the inboard combination light assembly fimly and turn the socket counterclockwise . . .

Fig. 115 . . . then pull the bulb and socket out of the housing

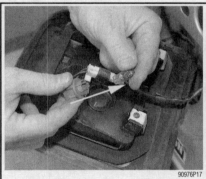

Fig. 116 While holding the socket, pull the light bulb straight out

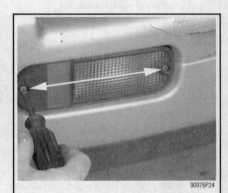

Fig. 117 Remove the two reverse light housing mounting screws . . .

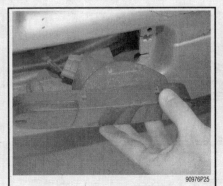

Fig. 118 . . . then pull the reverse light housing straigh out of the rear bumper

Fig. 119 Turn the reverse light bulb socket counterclockwise to release the retaining tabs . . .

Fig. 120 . . . then pull the socket straight out from behind the housing

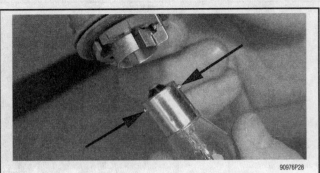

Fig. 121 When replacing bulbs (reverse light bulb shown) of any kind, be sure to note the type of bulb retaining ears exist on each side–they can be different

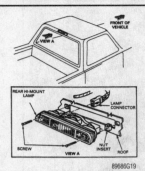

Fig. 122 Exploded view of the Ranger high mount brake and cargo light assembly–Explorer/Mountaineer models are similar, but without cargo light

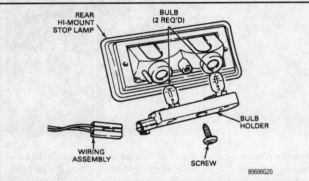

Fig. 123 Example of the screw retained lamp socket used on some high mount brake light assemblies

MPV MODELS

▶ See Figure 124

1. Open the liftgate.
2. Using a small prying tool, lift out the center pin of the plastic pushpin fasteners, then remove the fasteners from the housing cover.
3. Remove the high mount brake light housing cover.
4. Remove the lamp socket(s) from the lens housing by twisting it and pulling outward.
5. Remove by pulling the bulb(s) straight out from the lamp socket(s).
To install:
6. Install the bulb(s) into the lamp socket(s).
7. Install the lamp socket(s) into the lens housing and twist it to lock it in position.
8. Place the plastic housing cover into position and secure into place by installing the pushpin fasteners making sure that the center pins are pushed in all the way.
9. Check the operation of the lights.

License Plate Light

NAVAJO AND B SERIES PICK-UP MODELS

▶ See Figures 125, 126 and 127

1. From underneath the rear of the vehicle, grasp the lamp socket and rotate it ¼ turn.
2. Pull the lamp socket from the lens.
3. Pull the bulb from the socket
4. Installation is the reverse of the removal procedure.

MPV MODELS

1. Remove the lens mounting screws and pull off the lens.
2. Carefully push in on the bulb and twist it counterclockwise to remove it.
3. Installation is the reverse of removal.

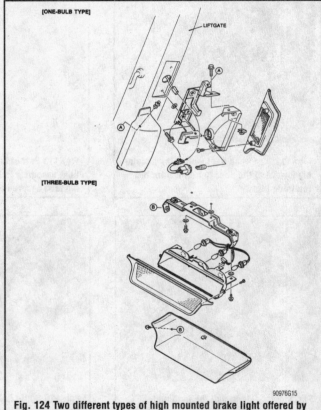

Fig. 124 Two different types of high mounted brake light offered by the MPV

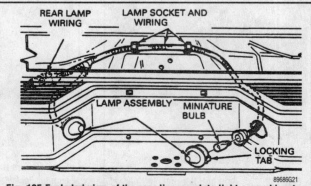

Fig. 125 Exploded view of the rear license plate light assembly–step bumper shown, other styles are similar

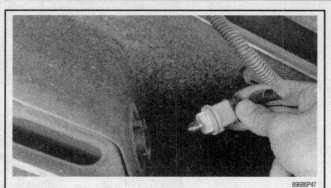

Fig. 126 To change the license plate bulb, first remove the socket from the lens housing by twisting then pulling

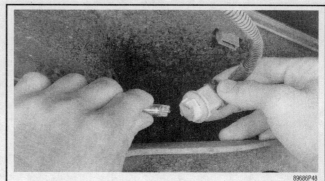

Fig. 127 Next, remove the bulb from the socket by pulling it straight out

Dome and Map Lights

♦ See Figures 128, 129 and 130

1. Remove the plastic cover.
2. Pull the map and/or area bulb from the dome light assembly.
3. Installation is the reverse of the removal procedure.

Cargo Light

♦ See Figures 131, 132 and 133

The B Series Pick-up has a rear cargo light which illuminates the pick-up bed. It is incorporated with the high mount brake light. For removal & installation procedures refer to the high mount brake light procedures earlier in this Section and remove the cargo lamp socket and bulb instead of the brake lamp components.

The Navajo has a cargo light mounted on the roof headliner near the tailgate, while the MPV has a cargo light located on the liftgate door. To replace the bulbs, simply pry off the lens and pull out the bulb. Install the new bulb.

1. Test to make sure the lights work correctly, and the light pattern is even.

Fig. 128 Using slight hand pressure, release the tabs . . .

Fig. 129 . . . then pull the dome lamp lens away from the light fixture

Fig. 130 Pull the bulb out from the contacts

Fig. 131 Using a small prying tool, release the tabs of the tailgate inner door light lens

Fig. 132 Pull off the tailgate inner door light lens . . .

Fig. 133 . . . then pull the glass bulb out from between the bulb holder/connectors

Light Bulb	Wattage	Bulb Trade Number
Parking lights, Side marker light, and turn signal	27/8	1157
Brake light and taillight	27/8	1157
Turn signal light	27	1156
Backup light	27	1156
Taillight	4.9	168
High-mount brake light	18.4	921

Fig. 136 Light bulb chart for 1994–95 MPV

Light bulb	Wattage	Bulb Trade Number
Parking lights, and Front turn-signal lights	27/8	1157NA
Brake light and taillights	27/8	1157
Rear turn-signal lights	27	1156
Backup light	21	1156
High-mount brake light (one bulb)	21	1156
High-mount brake light (3 bulbs)	18.4 × 2	921
Liftgate light	5	—
License plate light	5	194
Interior lights	10	—
Map light	5	—

Fig. 137 Light bulb chart for 1996–98 MPV

LIGHT BULB	NUMBER OF BULBS REQUIRED	BULB TRADE NUMBER	LIGHT BULB	NUMBER OF BULBS REQUIRED	BULB TRADE NUMBER
A/C control illumination (optional)	1	161	Heater control illumination	1	161
Ashtray lamp	1	161	Hi-beam indicator	1	194
Back-up lamp	2	3156	Hi-mount stop lamp	2	912
Brake warning light	1	194	Instrument panel gauge illumination	5	194
Cargo lamp (optional)	1	211-2	License plate lamp — rear bumper	2	194
Charging system warning	1	194	Oil pressure indicator light	1	194
Dome lamp	1	912	Rear tail/brake/turn lamp	2	3157
Door courtesy lamp	1	168	Turn signal indicator light	2	194
Engine coolant temperature warning	1	194	RABS warning light	1	194
4x4 indicator light	1	194	Deluxe map reading lamp/dome	2	168 / 906
Check engine warning light	1	194	Under hood lamp	1	906
Fasten safety belt warning light	1	194	Map lamps	2	168
Front parking lamp and turn signal	2	3157			
Front side marker lamp	2	194			
Glove compartment lamp	1	194			
Headlamps	2	9004			
Headlamp switch illumination	1	1815			

Fig. 134 Light bulb chart—Navajo

Light bulb	Number of Bulbs Required	Bulb number
Headlights	2	9007
Front turn signal lights	2	3157
Front parking lights	2	3157
Rear turn signal lights	2	3156
Rear brake/Taillights	2	3157
Back-up lights	2	3156
License plate light (with bumper)	1	194
License plate light (without bumper)	2	194
Interior light	1	912
High-mount stoplight	2	906
Cargo light	1	922
Underhood light	1	906
Map/Interior light (Cab Plus)	1	212-2
Map/Interior light (Regular Cab)	2	906

Fig. 135 Light bulb chart—B Series Pick-up

RAILER WIRING

Wiring the vehicle for towing is fairly easy. There are a number of good wiring kits available and these should be used, rather than trying to design your own.

All trailers will need brake lights and turn signals as well as tail lights and side marker lights. Most areas require extra marker lights for overwide trailers. Also, most areas have recently required back-up lights for trailers, and most trailer manufacturers have been building trailers with back-up lights for several years.

Additionally, some Class I, most Class II and just about all Class III trailers will have electric brakes. Add to this number an accessories wire, to operate trailer internal equipment or to charge the trailer's battery, and you can have as many as seven wires in the harness.

Determine the equipment on your trailer and buy the wiring kit necessary. The kit will contain all the wires needed, plus a plug adapter set which includes the female plug, mounted on the bumper or hitch, and the male plug, wired into, or plugged into the trailer harness.

When installing the kit, follow the manufacturer's instructions. The color coding of the wires is usually standard throughout the industry. One point to note: some domestic vehicles, and most imported vehicles, have separate turn signals. On most domestic vehicles, the brake lights and rear turn signals operate with the same bulb. For those vehicles with separate turn signals, you can purchase an isolation unit so that the brake lights won't blink whenever the turn signals are operated, or, you can go to your local electronics supply house and buy four diodes to wire in series with the brake and turn signal bulbs. Diodes will isolate the brake and turn signals. The choice is yours. The isolation units are simple and quick to install, but far more expensive than the diodes. The diodes, however, require more work to install properly, since they require the cutting of each bulb's wire and soldering in place of the diode.

One, final point, the best kits are those with a spring loaded cover on the vehicle mounted socket. This cover prevents dirt and moisture from corroding the terminals. Never let the vehicle socket hang loosely; always mount it securely to the bumper or hitch.

IRCUIT PROTECTION

uses

♦ **See Figures 138 thru 153**

REPLACEMENT

Fuse Panel

Located inside the passenger compartment, under the drivers-side of the instrument panel.
1. Turn the ignition switch **OFF**.
2. If equipped, remove the fuse panel access cover.

3. If equipped, remove the fuse puller tool from the cover.
4. Grasp the push-in type fuse with the provided tool, or a pair of needle-nose pliers.
5. Look through the side of the fuse body to determine if the fuse element is blown.

To install:
6. Check the amperage rating of the fuse which was removed and obtain a new fuse of the same rating.

❊ WARNING

Never replace a blown fuse with a new fuse of a higher rating. Severe electrical damage, as well as possible electrical fire could result.

	DESCRIPTION	FUSE RATING	COLOR	PROTECTED COMPONENT
A	Flash	15A	Light Blue	4 way flash, stoplamps
B	Circuit Breaker	6A	—	Front windshield washer/wiper
C	Dome	15A	Light Blue	Dome, courtesy lamps, radio memory, power mirror (2-door only)
D	Horn	20A	Yellow	Horn
E	Cluster Warning Lamps	15A	Light Blue	Cluster warning, electric all wheel drive
F	Speed Control	10A	Red	Speed control
G	Turn/Back-Up Lamps/ Rear Def/DRL	15A	Light Blue	Turn lamps, back-up lamps, rear defrost control, blower
H	Instrument Panel	10A	Red	Instrument panel illumination
I	Circuit Breaker	20A	Yellow	Cigarette lighter, flash to pass, lumbar
J	Radio	15A	Light Blue	Radio, speed control
K	Park/Lic/Trailer	15A	Light Blue	Park lights, license lights, trailer towing
L	A/C	10A	Red	A/C switches, A/C clutch coil
M	Amplifier	20A	Yellow	Radio amplifier
N	ABS	10A	Red	Anti-lock brake system control unit
P	Circuit Breaker	30A	Light Green	Power windows
Q	HEGO	15A	Light Blue	HEGO heater
R	Rear Window Washer/Wiper	15A	Light Blue	Rear window washer/wiper

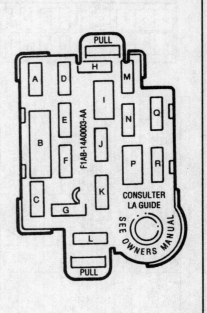

90976G19

Fig. 138 Fuse panel and identification chart for the Navajo

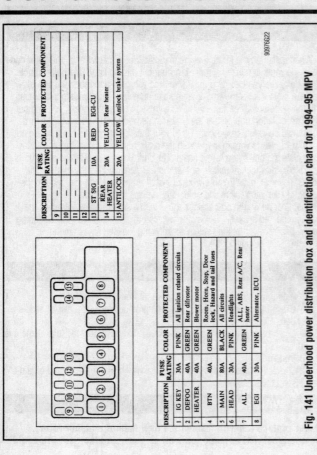

DESCRIPTION	FUSE RATING	COLOR	PROTECTED COMPONENT
9			
10			
11			
12			
13 ST SIG	10A	RED	EGI-CU
14 REAR HEATER	20A	YELLOW	Rear heater
15 ANTILOCK	20A	YELLOW	Antilock brake system

DESCRIPTION	FUSE RATING	COLOR	PROTECTED COMPONENT
1 IG KEY	30A	PINK	All ignition related circuits
2 DEFOG	40A	GREEN	Rear difroster
3 HEATER	40A	GREEN	Blower motor
4 BTN	40A	GREEN	Room, Horn, Stop, Door lock, Hazard and tail fuses
5 MAIN	80A	BLACK	All circuits
6 HEAD	30A	PINK	Headlights
7 ALL	40A	GREEN	ALL, ABS, Rear A/C, Rear heater
8 EGI	30A	PINK	Alternator, ECU

Fig. 141 Underhood power distribution box and identification chart for 1994–95 MPV

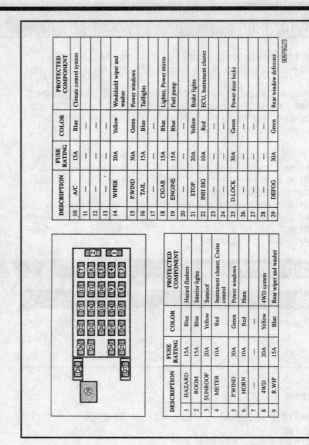

DESCRIPTION	FUSE RATING	COLOR	PROTECTED COMPONENT
10 A/C	15A	Blue	Climate control system
11			
12			
13			
14 WIPER	20A	Yellow	Windshield wiper and washer
15 PWIND	30A	Green	Power windows
16 TAIL	15A	Blue	Taillights
17			
18 CIGAR	15A	Blue	Lighter, Power mirror
19 ENGINE	15A	Blue	Fuel pump
20			
21 STOP	20A	Yellow	Brake lights
22 INH SIG	10A	Red	ECU, Instrument cluster
23			
24			
25 D LOCK	30A	Green	Power door locks
26			
27			
28			
29 DEFOG	30A	Green	Rear window defroster

DESCRIPTION	FUSE RATING	COLOR	PROTECTED COMPONENT
1 HAZARD	15A	Blue	Hazard flashers
2 ROOM	15A	Blue	Interior lights
3 SUNROOF	20A	Yellow	Sunroof
4 METER	10A	Red	Instrument cluster, Cruise control
5 PWIND	30A	Green	Power windows
6 HORN	10A	Red	Horn
7			
8 4WD	20A	Yellow	4WD system
9 R.WIP	15A	Blue	Rear wiper and washer

Fig. 142 Fuse panel and identification chart for 1996-98 MPV

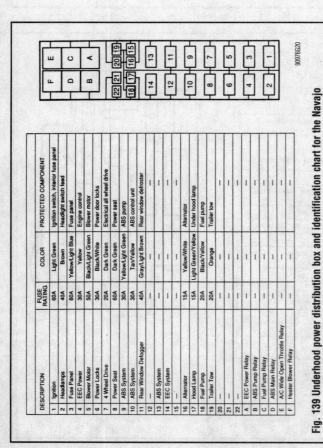

DESCRIPTION	FUSE RATING	COLOR	PROTECTED COMPONENT
1 Ignition	60A	Light Green	Ignition switch, interior fuse panel
2 Headlamps	40A	Brown	Headlight switch feed
3 Fuse Panel	60A	Yellow/Light Blue	Fuse panel
4 EEC Power	30A	Yellow	Engine control
5 Blower Motor	50A	Black/Light Green	Blower motor
6 Power Locks	30A	Black/White	Power door locks
7 4 Wheel Drive	20A	Dark Green	Electrical all wheel drive
8 Power Seat	60A	Dark Green	Power seat
9 ABS System	30A	Yellow/Light Green	ABS pump
10 ABS System	30A	Tan/Yellow	ABS control unit
11 Rear Window Defogger	40A	Gray/Light Brown	Rear window defroster
12 ABS System			
13 ABS System			
14 EEC System			
15 EEC System			
16 Alternator	15A	Yellow/White	Alternator
17 Hood Lamp	15A	Light Green/Yellow	Under hood lamp
18 Fuel Pump	20A	Black/Yellow	Fuel pump
19 Trailer Tow	20A	Orange	Trailer tow
20			
21			
22			
A EEC Power Relay			
B ABS Pump Relay			
C Fuel Pump Relay			
D ABS Main Relay			
E A/C Wide Open Throttle Relay			
F Heater Blower Relay			

Fig. 139 Underhood power distribution box and identification chart for the Navajo

DESCRIPTION	FUSE RATING	COLOR	PROTECTED COMPONENT
H FOG	15A	BLUE	Fog lights
I METER	10A	RED	Instrument cluster, Cruise control
J DOOR LOCK	30A	GREEN	Power door locks
K AIR CON	15A	BLUE	A/C switch, ALL, Rear heater main switch
L WIPER	20A	YELLOW	Windshield wiper and washer
M			
N HAZARD	15A	BLUE	Hazard flashers
P HORN STOP	15A	BLUE	Horn, Brake lights, Cruise control, ALL
Q ENGINE	15A	BLUE	Fuel pump
R SUNROOF	20A	BLUE	Sunroof

DESCRIPTION	FUSE RATING	COLOR	PROTECTED COMPONENT
A INH SIG	10A	RED	ECU, Instrument cluster
B POWER WINDOW	30A	GREEN	Power windows
C TAIL	15A	BLUE	Instrument panel light control, Taillights
D ROOM	15A	BLUE	Interior lights, Key reminder
E 4WD	20A	YELLOW	4WD
F REAR WIPER	15A	BLUE	Rear wiper and washer
G CIGAR	15A	BLUE	Lighter, Power mirror, CPU, Clock (audio)

Fig. 140 Fuse panel and identification chart for 1994–95 MPV

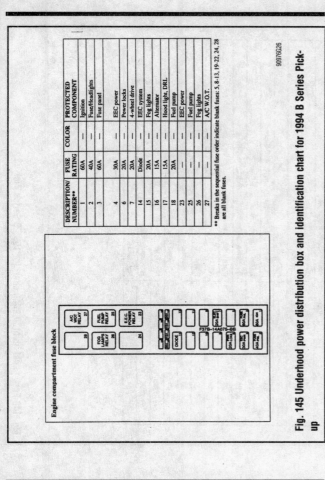

Engine compartment fuse block

DESCRIPTION/NUMBER**	FUSE RATING	COLOR	PROTECTED COMPONENT
1	60A	—	Ignition
2	40A	—	Fuse/Headlights
3	60A	—	Fuse panel
4	30A	—	EEC power
6	20A	—	Power locks
7	20A	—	4-wheel drive
14	Diode	—	EEC system
15	20A	—	EEC system
16	15A	—	Alternator
17	15A	—	Hood light, DRL
18	20A	—	EEC power
23	—	—	Fuel pump
25	—	—	EEC power
26	—	—	Fog lights
27	—	—	Fog lights
	—	—	A/C W.O.T.

** Breaks in the sequential fuse order indicate blank fuses. 5, 8-13, 19-22, 24, 28 are all blank fuses.

Fig. 145 Underhood power distribution box and identification chart for 1994 B Series Pick-up

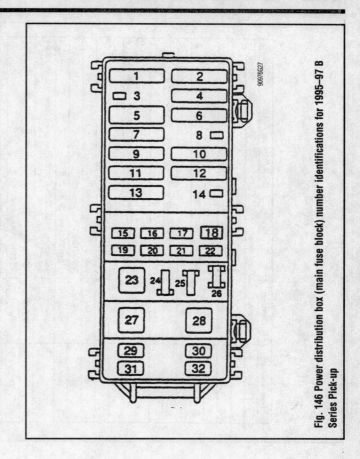

Fig. 146 Power distribution box (main fuse block) number identifications for 1995-97 B Series Pick-up

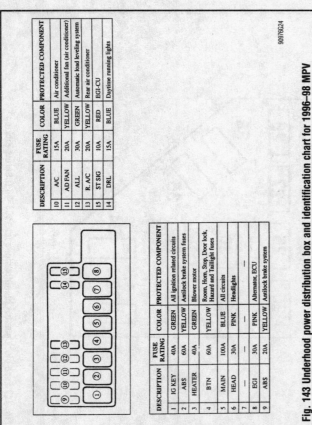

	DESCRIPTION	FUSE RATING	COLOR	PROTECTED COMPONENT
10	A/C	15A	BLUE	Air conditioner
11	AD FAN	20A	YELLOW	Additional fan (air conditioner)
12	ALL	30A	GREEN	Automatic load leveling system
13	R. A/C	20A	YELLOW	Rear air conditioner
15	ST SIG	10A	RED	EGI-CU
14	DRL	15A	BLUE	Daytime running lights

DESCRIPTION	FUSE RATING	COLOR	PROTECTED COMPONENT
1	IG KEY	40A	GREEN	All ignition related circuits
2	ABS	60A	YELLOW	Antilock brake system fuses
3	HEATER	40A	GREEN	Blower motor
4	BTN	60A	YELLOW	Room, Horn, Stop, Door lock, Hazard and Taillight fuses
5	MAIN	10A	BLUE	All circuits
6	HEAD	30A	PINK	Headlights
7	—	—	—	
8	EGI	30A	PINK	Alternator, ECU
9	ABS	20A	YELLOW	Antilock brake system

Fig. 143 Underhood power distribution box and identification chart for 1996-98 MPV

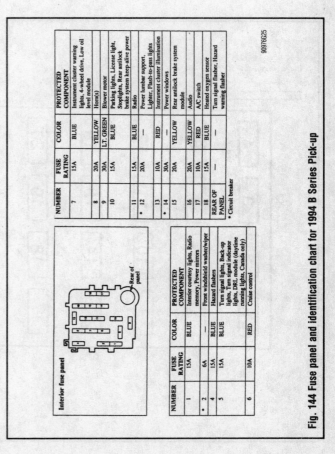

Rear of panel

NUMBER	FUSE RATING	COLOR	PROTECTED COMPONENT
7	15A	BLUE	Instrument cluster warning lights, 4-wheel drive, Low oil level module
8	20A	YELLOW	Horn(s)
9	30A	LT. GREEN	Blower motor
10	15A	BLUE	Parking lights, License light, Stoplights, Rear antilock brake system keep-alive power
11	15A	BLUE	Radio
• 12	20A	—	Power lumbar support, Lighter, Flash-to-pass lights
13	10A	RED	Instrument cluster illumination
• 14	30A	—	Power windows
15	20A	YELLOW	Rear antilock brake system module
16	20A	YELLOW	Audio
17	10A	RED	A/C switch
18	15A	BLUE	Heated oxygen sensor
REAR OF PANEL	—	—	Turn signal flasher, Hazard warning flasher

• Circuit breaker

Interior fuse panel

NUMBER	FUSE RATING	COLOR	PROTECTED COMPONENT
1	15A	BLUE	Interior courtesy lights, Radio memory, Power mirrors
• 2	6A	—	Front windshield washer/wiper
4	15A	BLUE	Hazard flashers
5	15A	BLUE	Turn signal lights, Back-up lights, Turn signal indicator lights, DRL module (daytime running lights, Canada only)
6	10A	RED	Cruise control

Fig. 144 Fuse panel and identification chart for 1994 B Series Pick-up

Fuse Position	Rating	Circuit Protected
1	10 Amp	Power Mirror
2	10 Amp	Air Bag/Blower Motor Relay
3	15 Amp	Main Light Switch, All Unlock Relay
4	15 Amp	Left Headlamp
5	10 Amp	Data Link Connector (DLC)
6	—	Not Used
7	10 Amp	Park Lamps, GEM, License Lights, Stoplamps, Main Light Switch
8	15 Amp	Right Headlamp/DRL
9	10 Amp	RABS Test Connector
10	10 Amp	Cruise Control/GEM/Brake Interlock Module/Blend Door Actuator
11	10 Amp	Instrument Cluster, Main Light Switch
12	10 Amp	Power Window Relay, Washer Pump Relay
13	15 Amp	Brake On/Off (BOO) Switch
14	10 / 20 Amp	RABS/4WABS
15	15 Amp	Air Bags/Instrument Cluster
16	30 Amp	RABS Diode, RABS/Low Fluid Resistor, Instrument Cluster, DRL, Park Brake Switch
17	30 Amp	Cigar Lighter
18	15 Amp	A/C Mode Selector Switch
19	25 Amp	PCM Power Diode
20	10 Amp	Radio/GEM/RAP Module
21	15 Amp	Turn Signals
22	15 Amp	Turn Signals
23	—	Not Used
24	15 Amp	Clutch Pedal Position (CPP) Switch, RAP System
25	10 Amp	GEM/Instrument Cluster
26	15 Amp	Overdrive Cancel Switch/Backup Lights/DRL
27	15 Amp	Electric Shift/Interior Lights
28	10 Amp	GEM
29	15 Amp	Radio/CD
30	—	Not Used
31	—	Not Used
32	—	Not Used
33	20 Amp	Headlights/DRL
34	—	Not Used

Fig. 148 Fuse panel identification chart for 1995 B Series Pick-up

90976G29

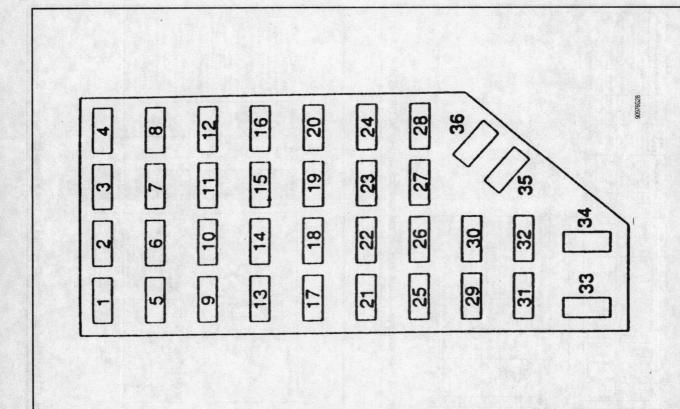

Fig. 147 Fuse block number identifications for 1995–98 B Series Pick-up

90976G28

Fuse	Amps	Circuit Protected
1	7.5A	Power Mirror Switch
2	—	Blower Motor Relay, PAD Module, Air Bag Diagnostic Monitor
3	7.5A	Trailer Tow Connector
4	10A	Left Headlamp
5	10A	Data Link Connector (DLC)
6	—	NOT USED
7	7.5A	Trailer Tow Connector
8	10A	Right Headlamp, Daytime Running Lamps (DRL), Fog Lamp Relay
9	7.5A	Brake Pedal Position (BPP) Switch
10	7.5A	Cruise Control Servo/Amplifier Assembly, Generic Electronic Module (GEM), Shift Lock Actuator, Blend Door Actuator, A/C – Heater Assembly, Flasher
11	7.5A	Instrument Cluster, Main Light Switch, RABS Resistor
12	—	NOT USED
13	20A	Brake Pressure Switch, Brake Pedal Posision (BPP) Switch
14	20A	Rear Anti-Lock Brake System (RABS) Module
14	10A	4 Wheel Anti-Lock Brake System (4WABS) Module, 4WABS Main Relay
15	7.5A	Instrument Cluster
16	30A	Windshield Wiper Motor, Wiper Hi-LO Relay, Wiper Run/Park Relay
17	25A	Cigar Lighter
18	15A	Driver's Unlock Relay, All-Unlock Relay, All-Lock Relay
19	25A	PCM Power Diode
20	7.5A	RAP Module, Generic Electronic Module (GEM), Relay
21	15A	Flasher (Hazard)
22	20A	Auxiliary Power Socket
23	—	NOT USED
24	7.5A	Anti-theft
25	7.5A	Generic Electronic Module (GEM), Instrument Cluster
26	10A	Battery Saver Relay, Electronic Shift Relay, Interior Lamp Relay, Power Window Relay, Electronic Shift Control Module, Transmission Control Switch, DRL, Backup Lamp Switch, DTR Sensor, Instrument Illumination Dimming Module, Dome/Map Lamp, GEM
27	15A	Electronic Shift, DRL, PLSE Vacuum Hublock Solenoid
28	7.5A	Generic Electronic Module (GEM), Radio
29	15A	Radio
30	15A	Park Lamp/Trailer Tow Relay
31	—	NOT USED
32	—	NOT USED
33	15A	Headlamps, Daytime Running Lamps (DRL) Module, Instrument Cluster
34	—	NOT USED
35	10A	RABS Test Connector
36	—	NOT USED

90976631

Fig. 150 Fuse panel and identification chart for 1998 B Series Pick-up

Fuse Position	Rating	Circuit Protected
1	7.5 Amp	Power Mirror Switch
2	—	Not Used
3	15 Amp	Main Light Switch, Park Lamps Relay
4	10 Amp	Left Headlamp
5	10 Amp	Data Link Connector (DLC)
6	7.5 Amp	Air Bag Diagnostic Monitor, Blower Motor Relay, Passive Deactivation (PAD) Module
7	7.5 Amp	Instrument Illumination Dimming Module
8	10 Amp	Right Headlamp, Daytime Running Lamps (DRL) Module
9	10 Amp	RABS Test Connector
10	7.5 Amp	Cruise Control/GEM/Brake Interlock Module/Blend Door Actuator
11	7.5 Amp	Instrument Cluster, Main Light Switch, RABS Resistor
12	10 Amp	Power Window Relay, Washer Pump Relay
13	—	Brake On/Off (BOO) Switch
14	10/20 Amp	RABS Module/4WABS Module, 4WABS Main Relay
15	7.5 Amp	Air Bag Diagnostic Monitor, Instrument Cluster
16	30 Amp	Windshield Wiper Motor, Wiper Hi-Lo Relay, Wiper Relay
17	25 Amp	Cigar Lighter
18	15 Amp	A/C Mode Selector Switch
19	25 Amp	PCM Power Diode, Noise Capacitor, Ignition Coil, Primary and Secondary Coil
20	7.5 Amp	Radio, GEM, RAP Module
21	15 Amp	Turn Signals
22	10 Amp	Turn Signals
23	—	Not Used
24	10 Amp	Clutch Pedal Position (CPP) Switch, Starter Interrupt Relay
25	7.5 Amp	GEM, Instrument Cluster
26	10 Amp	Backup Lights, DRL, DTR Sensor, Transmission Control Switch
27	10 Amp	Electric Shift, Interior Lights
28	7.5 Amp	GEM
29	10 Amp	Radio, CD Changer, Amplifier
30	—	Not Used
31	—	Not Used
32	—	Not Used
33	15 Amp	Headlamps, Daytime Running Lamps (DRL) Module, Instrument Cluster
34	—	Not Used
35	—	Not Used
36	—	Not Used

90976630

Fig. 149 Fuse panel identification chart for 1996–97 B Series Pick-up

Fuse Position	Rating	Color	Circuit Protected
1	50 Amp	Red	Ignition
2	50 Amp	Red	Instrument Panel Fuse Panel
3	—	—	Not Used
4	20 Amp	Yellow	Horn
5	20 Amp	Yellow	Power Windows/Seats/Door Locks
6	40 Amp	Orange	Blower Motor
7	20 Amp	Yellow	Parking Lamps
8	—	—	Not Used
9	30 Amp	Green	ABS System Main Relay
10	30 Amp	Green	ABS System Pump Relay
11	20 Amp	Yellow	Headlamps
12	20 Amp	Yellow	Fuel System/Anti-Theft System
13	30 Amp	Green	PCM Power
14	—	—	Not Used
15	15 Amp	Blue	Daylight Running Lamps
16	10 Amp	Red	Air Bag System
17	15 Amp	Blue	Alternator
18	15 Amp	Blue	PCM Memory Power
19	20 Amp	Yellow	Four-Wheel Drive System
20	15 Amp	Blue	PCM HO2S System
21	30 Amp	Green	Power Point
22	20 Amp	Yellow	Audio System
23	Relay	—	Fuel Pump
24	Diode	—	PCM
25	Diode	—	ABS
26	Resistor	—	RABS/Low Fluid
27	Relay	—	PCM Power
28	Relay	—	W.A.C.
29	—	—	Not Used
30	Relay	—	Wiper Hi-Low
31	Relay	—	Horn
32	Relay	—	Wiper Run/Park

Fig. 152 Power distribution box identification chart for the 1997 B Series Pick-up

90976G33

Fuse Position	Rating	Color	Circuit Protected
1	50 Amp	Red	Ignition
2	50 Amp	Red	Instrument Panel Fuse Panel
3	—	—	Not Used
4	20 Amp	Yellow	Horn/PCM Memory Power
5	20 Amp	Yellow	Power Windows/Seats/Door Locks
6	40 Amp	Orange	Blower Motor
7	20 Amp	Yellow	Parking Lamps
8	—	—	Not Used
9	30 Amp	Green	ABS System Main Relay
10	30 Amp	Green	ABS System Pump Relay
11	20 Amp	Yellow	Headlamps
12	20 Amp	Yellow	Fuel System/Anti-Theft System
13	30 Amp	Green	PCM Power
14	—	—	Not Used
15	15 Amp	Blue	Daylight Running Lamps/Fog Lamps
16	20 Amp	Yellow	Four-Wheel Drive System
17	15 Amp	Blue	Alternator
18	—	—	Not Used
19	10 Amp	Red	Air Bag System
20	15 Amp	Blue	PCM HO2S System
21	30 Amp	Green	Power Point
22	20 Amp	Yellow	JBL System
23	Relay	—	Fuel Pump
24	Diode	—	PCM
25	Diode	—	ABS
26	Resistor	—	RABS/Low Fluid
27	Relay	—	PCM Power
28	Relay	—	W.A.C.
29	Relay	—	Fog Lamp
30	Relay	—	Wiper Hi-Low
31	Relay	—	Horn
32	Relay	—	Wiper Run/Park

Fig. 151 Power distribution box identification chart for 1995–96 B Series Pick-up

90976G32

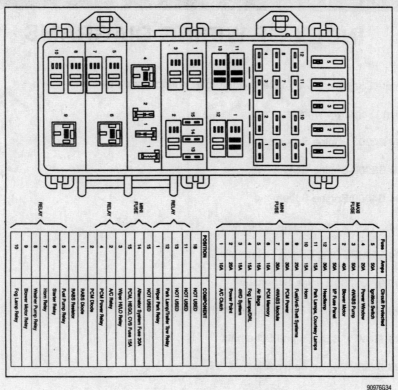

POSITION	COMPONENT
10	Fog Lamp Relay
9	Blower Motor Relay
8	Washer Pump Relay
7	Horn Relay
6	Starter Relay
5	Fuel Pump Relay
1	RABS Diode
2	RABS Resistor
4	PCM Power Relay
3	PCM Diode
2	A/C Relay
15	Wiper HI/LO Relay
14	PCM, HEGO, CYS Fuse 15A
15	Alternator System Fuse 30A
1	Wiper Park Relay
12	Park Lamp/Trailer Tow Relay
11	NOT USED
13	NOT USED
18	NOT USED

Fuse	Amps	Circuit Protected
1	10A	A/C Clutch
2	20A	Power Point
3	15A	4WD System
4	15A	Fog Lamps/DRL
5	10A	PCM Memory
6	10A	4WABS Module
7	30A	PCM Power
8	20A	Fuel/Anti-Theft Systems
9	15A	Horn
10	15A	Park Lamps, Courtesy Lamps
11	30A	Headlamp
12	50A	I/P Fuse Panel
1	40A	4WABS Pump
2	50A	Blower Motor
3	50A	Power Window
4	20A	Ignition Switch
5	50A	

90976G34

Fig. 153 Power distribution box and identification chart for the 1998 B Series Pick-up

7. Align the fuse with its mounting position and push it into place until fully seated in the panel.

8. Turn the ignition switch on and operate the accessory that was protected by that fuse.

✳ WARNING

If the fuse continues to blow, inspect and test the wire harness and component or components which are protected by that fuse.

Power Distribution Box

Located under the hood, in the engine compartment. It houses the fuses and relays for most of the under hood components which are not controlled by a dash mounted switch (such as the alternator, fuel pump, ECM, etc.). The fuses and relays are replaced in the same manner as the fuse panel inside the vehicle. The power distribution box cover is hinged on one end and utilizes a retaining latch on the other. Simply release the latch and lift the cover up to gain access to the fuses and relays.

Fusible Links

The fusible link is a short length of special, Hypalon (high temperature) insulated wire, integral with the engine compartment wiring harness and should not be confused with standard wire. It is several wire gauges smaller than the circuit which it protects. Under no circumstances should a fuse link replacement repair be made using a length of standard wire cut from bulk stock or from another wiring harness.

The fusible links are located near the starter solenoid and shares the terminal with the battery-to-starter solenoid cable.

Circuit Breakers

The B Series Pick-up, Navajo and MPV models use circuit breakers for components which have a high start-up amperage pull (such as power windows). All breakers will automatically reset if they have been tripped. The circuit breakers are replaceable (should one go bad or not reset) and can be found on the fuse panel.

REPLACEMENT

The circuit breakers are replaced in the same manner as a fuse. Simply pull the breaker from the fuse panel to remove.

Flasher Locations

The hazard warning flasher is mounted on the fuse panel, located in the passenger compartment of the vehicle. The fuse panel is positioned under the driver's side of the instrument panel. The flasher is replaced in the same manner as a regular fuse, simply pull it from the fuse panel to remove.

WIRING DIAGRAMS

INDEX OF WIRING DIAGRAMS

90976W01

SAMPLE DIAGRAM: HOW TO READ & INTERPRET WIRING DIAGRAMS

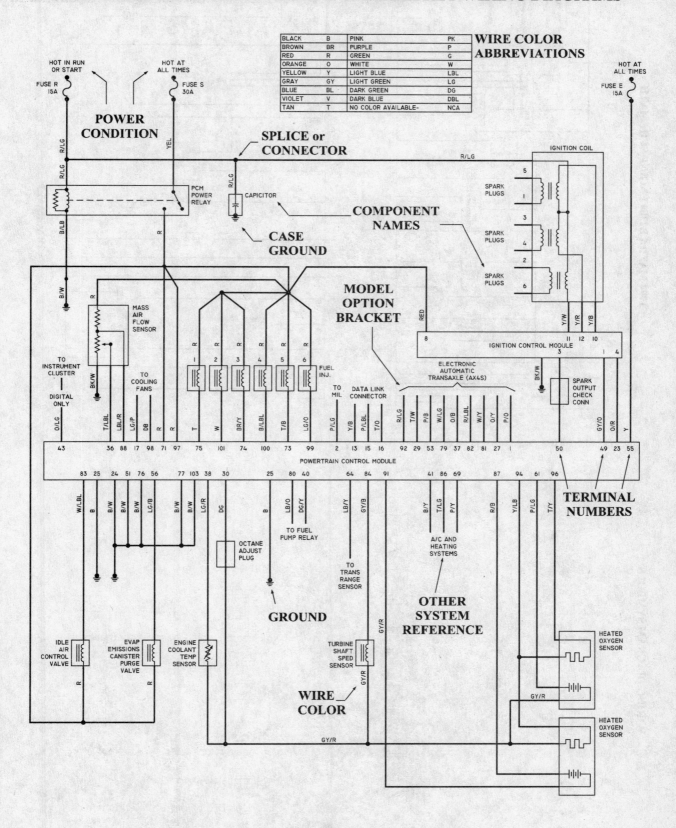

DIAGRAM 1

TCCA6W01

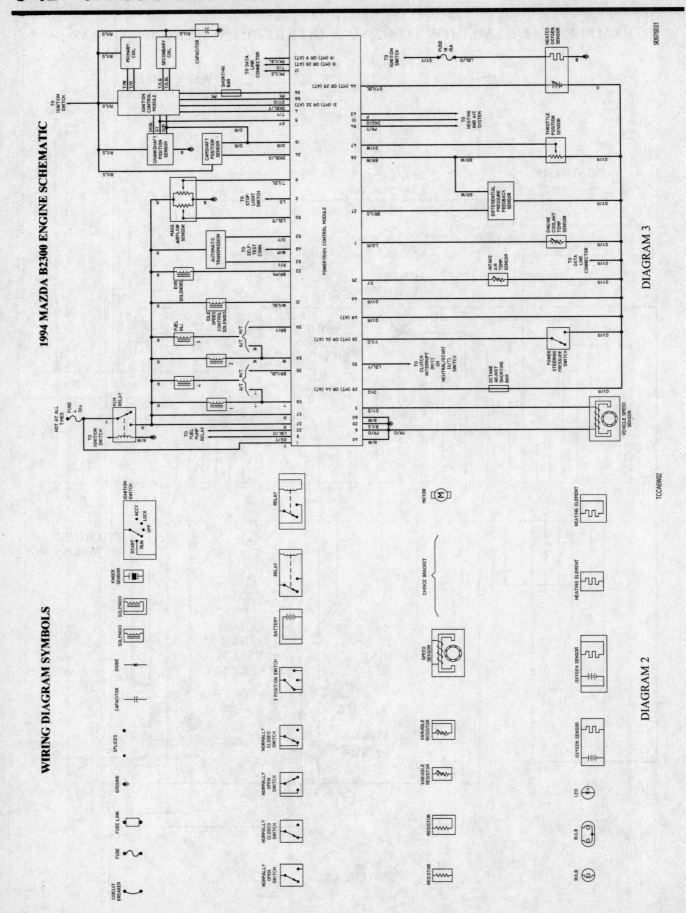

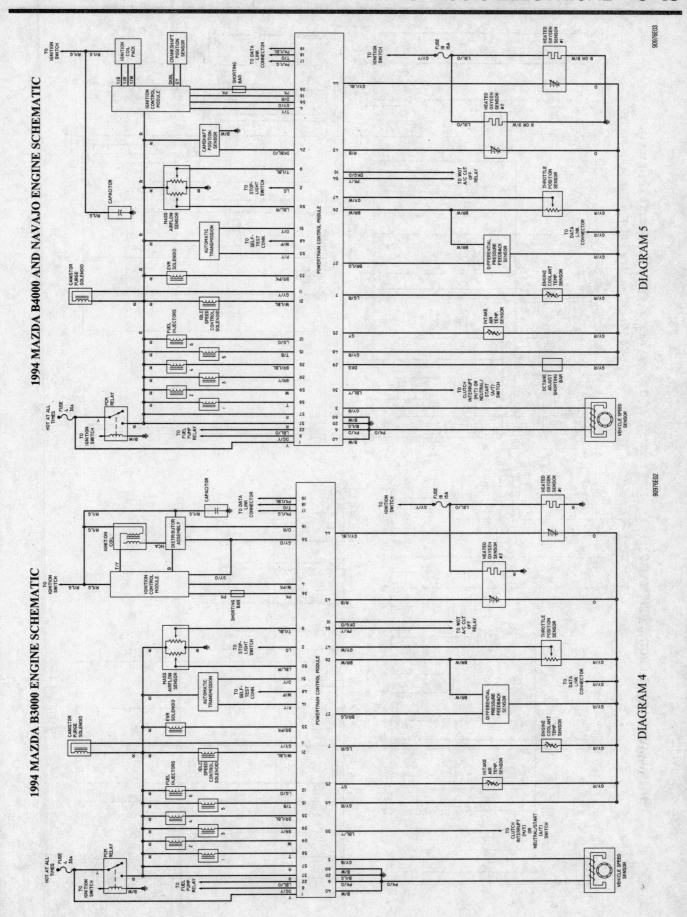

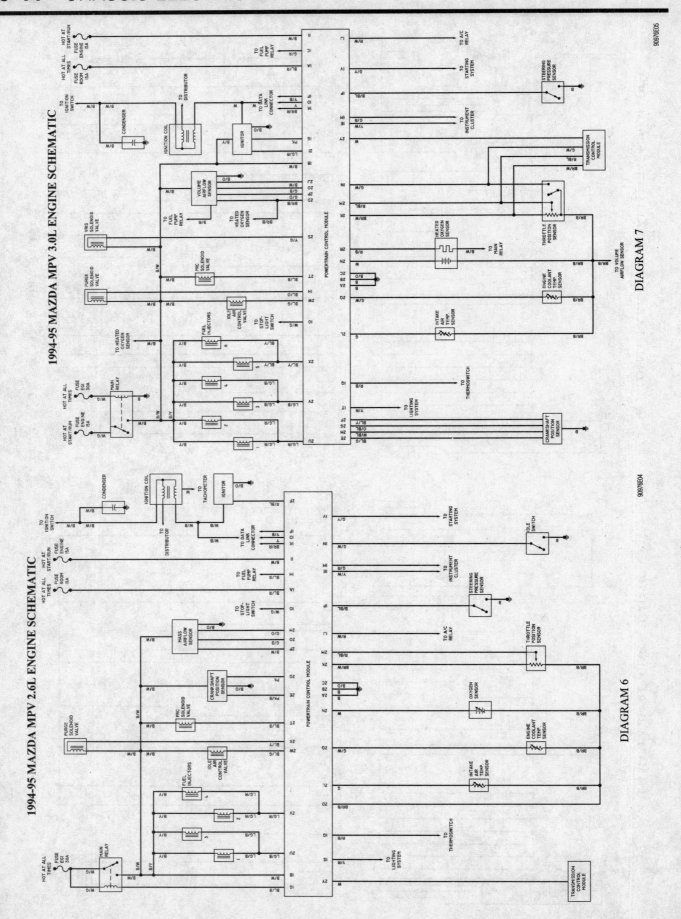

1994-95 MAZDA MPV 3.0L ENGINE SCHEMATIC

DIAGRAM 7

1994-95 MAZDA MPV 2.6L ENGINE SCHEMATIC

DIAGRAM 6

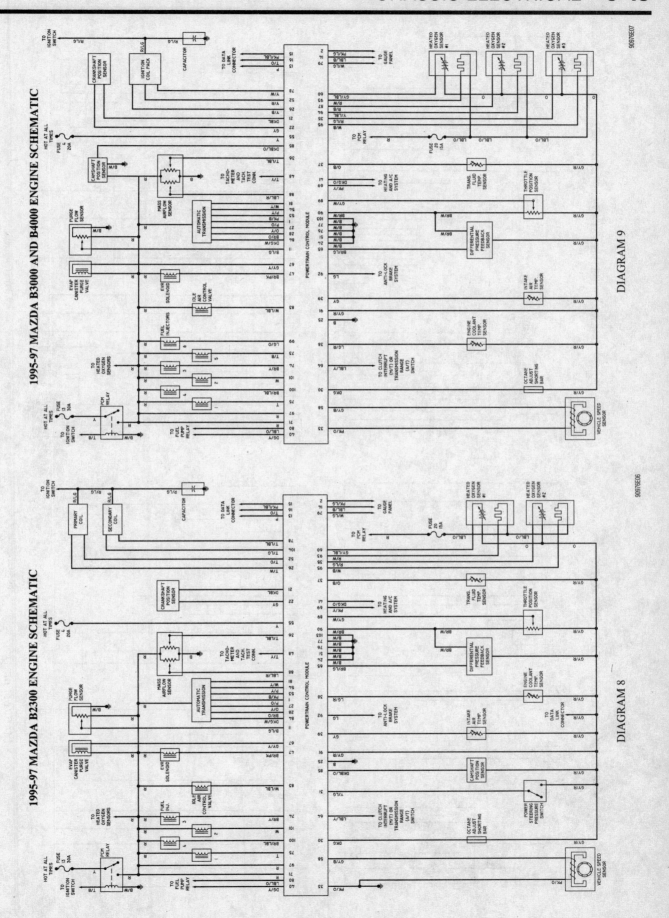

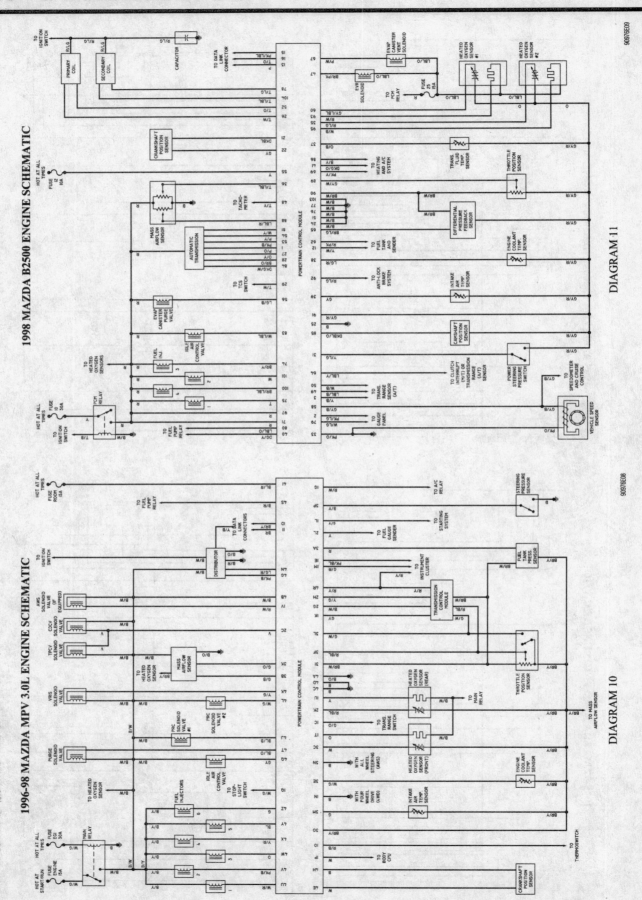

1998 MAZDA B2500 ENGINE SCHEMATIC

1996-98 MAZDA MPV 3.0L ENGINE SCHEMATIC

DIAGRAM 11

DIAGRAM 10

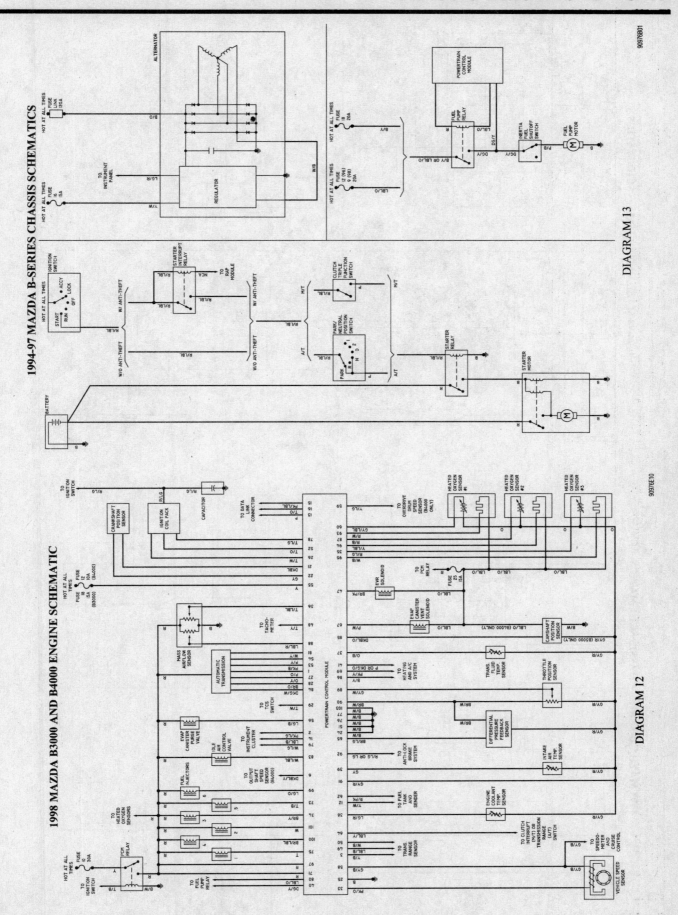

1994-97 MAZDA B-SERIES CHASSIS SCHEMATICS

DIAGRAM 13

1998 MAZDA B3000 AND B4000 ENGINE SCHEMATIC

DIAGRAM 12

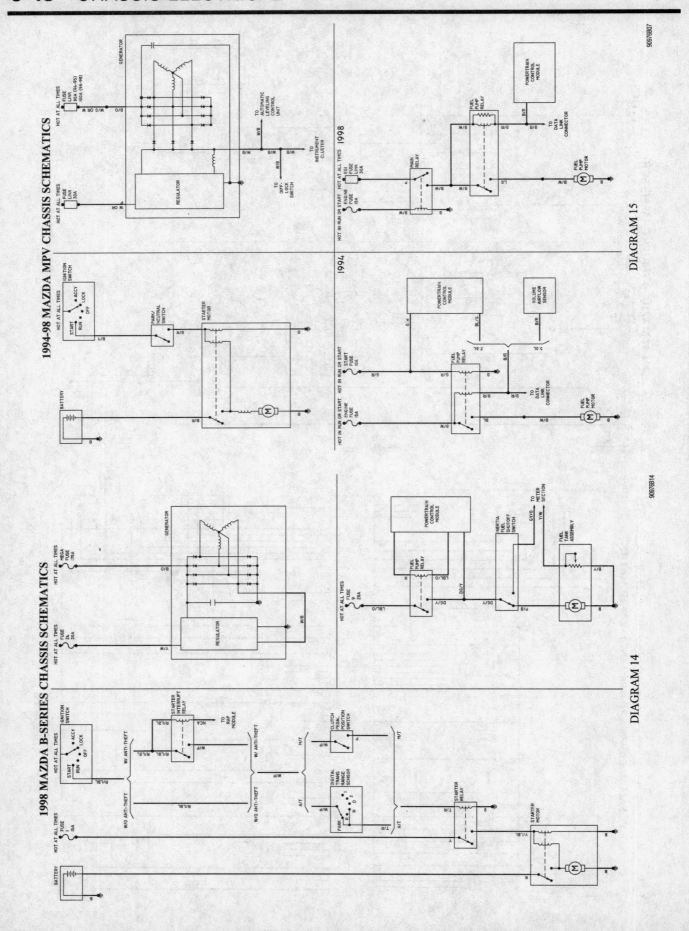

1994-98 MAZDA MPV CHASSIS SCHEMATICS

1998 MAZDA B-SERIES CHASSIS SCHEMATICS

DIAGRAM 15

DIAGRAM 14

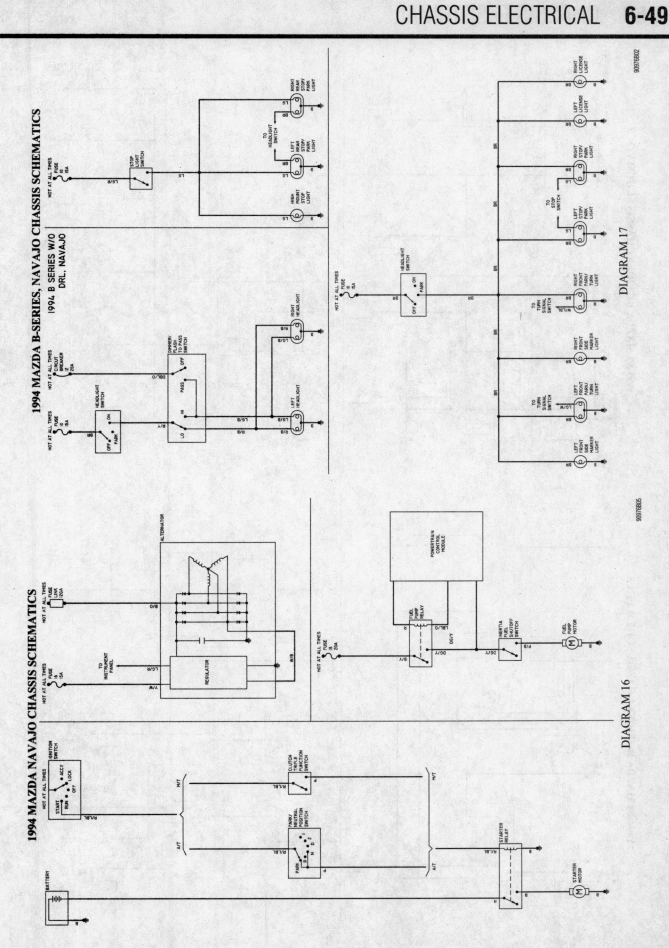

1994 MAZDA B-SERIES, NAVAJO CHASSIS SCHEMATICS

1994 MAZDA NAVAJO CHASSIS SCHEMATICS

DIAGRAM 17

DIAGRAM 16

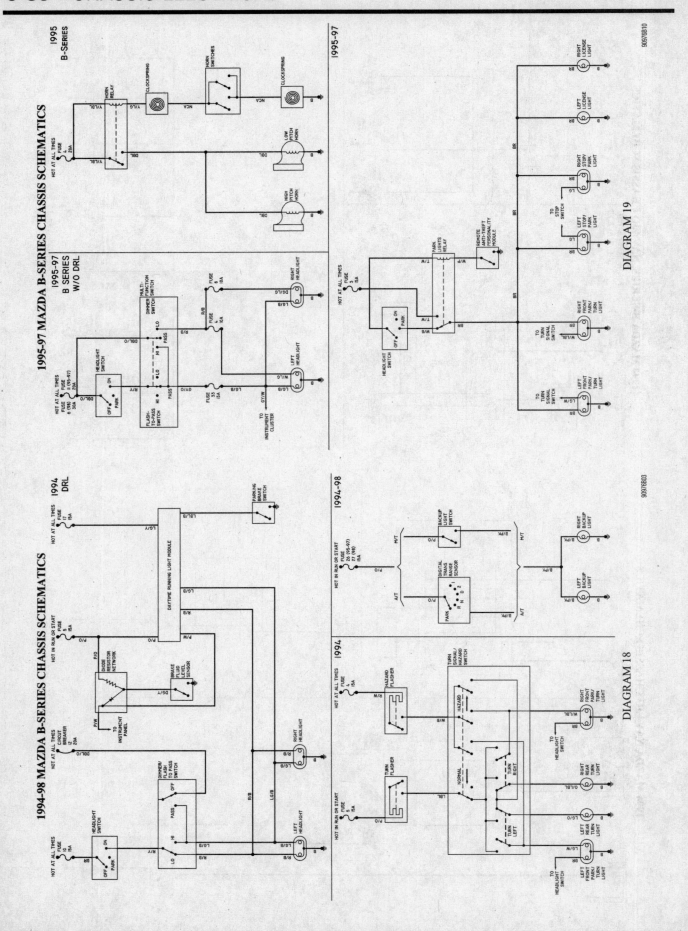

1994-98 MAZDA B-SERIES CHASSIS SCHEMATICS

1995-97 MAZDA B-SERIES CHASSIS SCHEMATICS

DIAGRAM 18

DIAGRAM 19

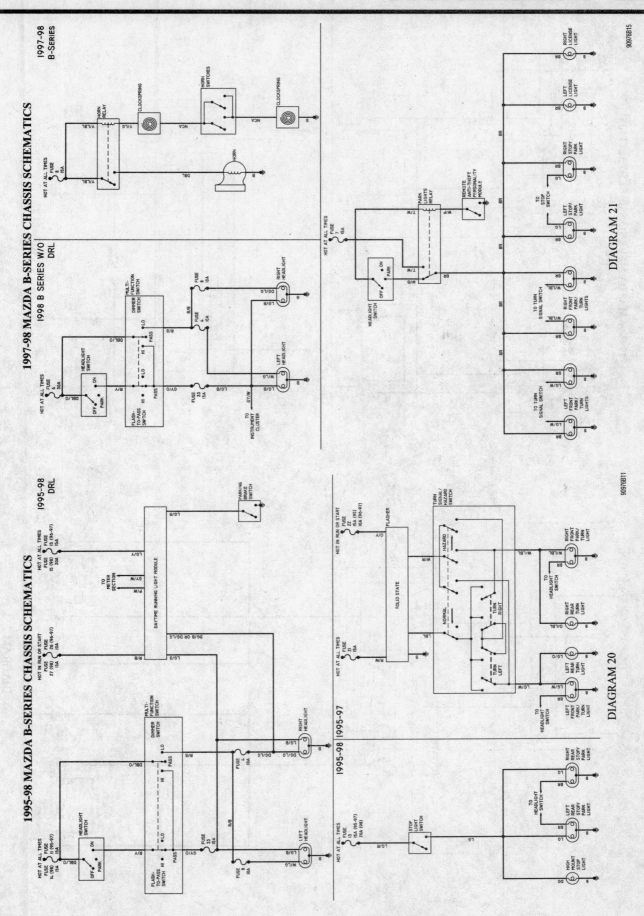

1997-98 MAZDA B-SERIES CHASSIS SCHEMATICS

1995-98 MAZDA B-SERIES CHASSIS SCHEMATICS

DIAGRAM 21

DIAGRAM 20

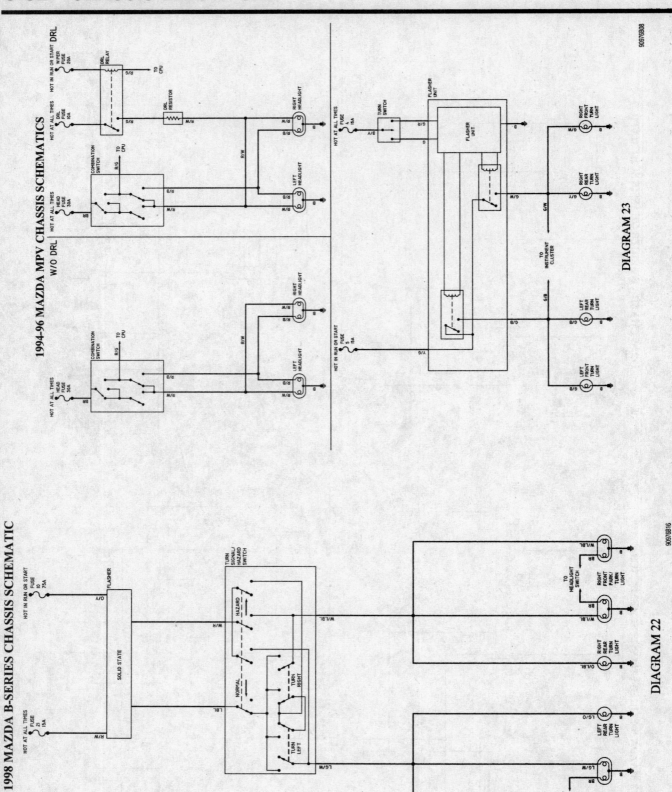

1994-96 MAZDA MPV CHASSIS SCHEMATICS

DIAGRAM 23

1998 MAZDA B-SERIES CHASSIS SCHEMATIC

DIAGRAM 22

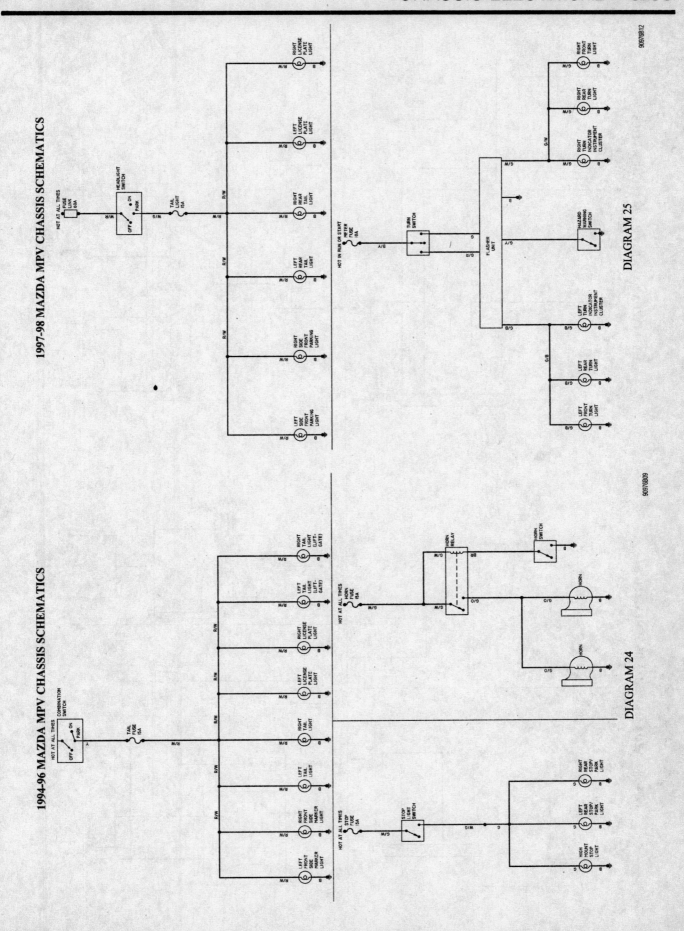

1997-98 MAZDA MPV CHASSIS SCHEMATICS

1994-96 MAZDA MPV CHASSIS SCHEMATICS

DIAGRAM 25

DIAGRAM 24

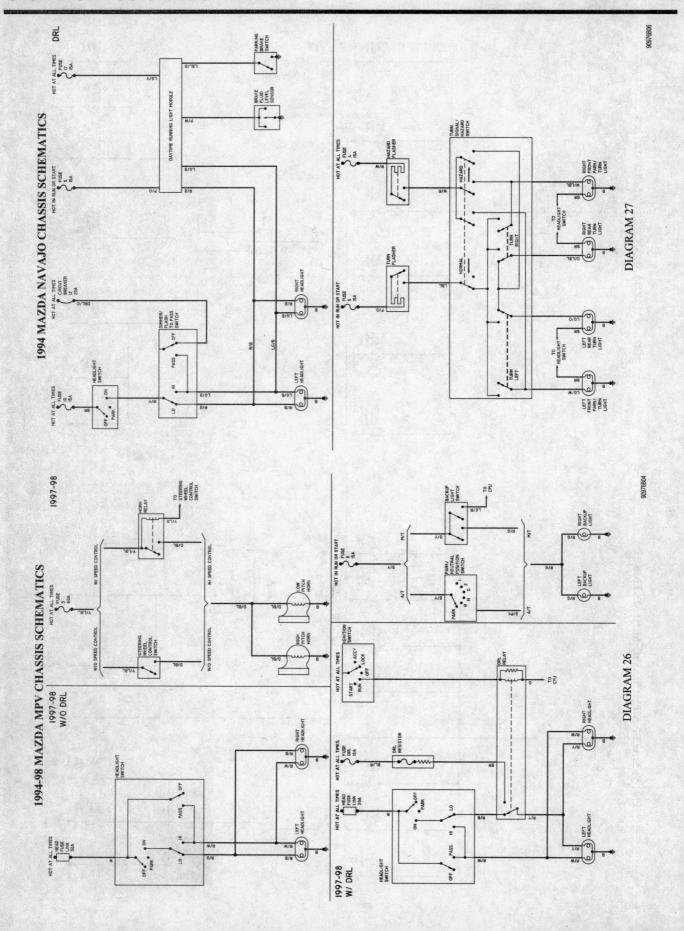

1994 MAZDA NAVAJO CHASSIS SCHEMATICS

1994-98 MAZDA MPV CHASSIS SCHEMATICS

DIAGRAM 27

DIAGRAM 26

7

DRIVE TRAIN

MANUAL TRANSMISSION

Understanding the Manual Transmission

Because of the way an internal combustion engine breathes, it can produce torque (or twisting force) only within a narrow speed range. Most overhead valve pushrod engines must turn at about 2500 rpm to produce their peak torque. Often by 4500 rpm, they are producing so little torque that continued increases in engine speed produce no power increases.

The torque peak on overhead camshaft engines is, generally, much higher, but much narrower.

The manual transmission and clutch are employed to vary the relationship between engine RPM and the speed of the wheels so that adequate power can be produced under all circumstances. The clutch allows engine torque to be applied to the transmission input shaft gradually, due to mechanical slippage. The vehicle can, consequently, be started smoothly from a full stop.

The transmission changes the ratio between the rotating speeds of the engine and the wheels by the use of gears. 4-speed or 5-speed transmissions are most common. The lower gears allow full engine power to be applied to the rear wheels during acceleration at low speeds.

The clutch driveplate is a thin disc, the center of which is splined to the transmission input shaft. Both sides of the disc are covered with a layer of material which is similar to brake lining and which is capable of allowing slippage without roughness or excessive noise.

The clutch cover is bolted to the engine flywheel and incorporates a diaphragm spring which provides the pressure to engage the clutch. The cover also houses the pressure plate. When the clutch pedal is released, the driven disc is sandwiched between the pressure plate and the smooth surface of the flywheel, thus forcing the disc to turn at the same speed as the engine crankshaft.

The transmission contains a mainshaft which passes all the way through the transmission, from the clutch to the driveshaft. This shaft is separated at one point, so that front and rear portions can turn at different speeds.

Power is transmitted by a countershaft in the lower gears and reverse. The gears of the countershaft mesh with gears on the mainshaft, allowing power to be carried from one to the other. Countershaft gears are often integral with that shaft, while several of the mainshaft gears can either rotate independently of the shaft or be locked to it. Shifting from one gear to the next causes one of the gears to be freed from rotating with the shaft and locks another to it. Gears are locked and unlocked by internal dog clutches which slide between the center of the gear and the shaft. The forward gears usually employ synchronizers; friction members which smoothly bring gear and shaft to the same speed before the toothed dog clutches are engaged.

Adjustments

SHIFTER & LINKAGE ADJUSTMENTS

The 5-speed transmission is directly controlled with a floor shift mechanism built into the transmission extension housing. There are no adjustments necessary on this transmission.

Shift Handle

REMOVAL & INSTALLATION

▸ **See Figure 1**

1. Disconnect the negative battery cable.

➡ **Do not remove the shift knob, unless the shift knob or boot is to be replaced. Otherwise, remove the shift knob, boot and lever as an assembly.**

2. Place the gearshift lever in **N** position.
3. Remove the shifter boot retainer screws and slide the boot up the lever.
4. Remove the shift lever-to-extension housing/transfer case adapter housing retaining bolts. Pull the gearshift lever straight up and away from the gearshift lever retainer.

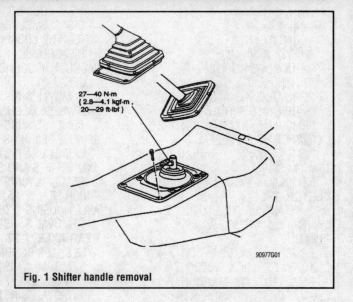

27—40 N·m
{ 2.8—4.1 kgf·m ,
20—29 ft-lbf }

90977G01

Fig. 1 Shifter handle removal

To install:

5. Prior to installing the shift lever, lubricate the shift lever ball stud, using C1AZ-19590-B (ESA-M1C75-B) or equivalent.
6. Fit the shift lever into place and install the retaining bolt(s). Tighten the retaining bolt(s) to 20–29 ft. lbs. (27–40 Nm).
7. Install the rubber boot and retaining screws.
8. Place the shift lever in **N** position. Then, align the shift pattern plastic insert with the vehicle centerline and install it to the shift lever knob.

Back-up Light Switch

REMOVAL & INSTALLATION

▸ **See Figure 2**

1. Disconnect the negative battery cable.
2. Raise and support the vehicle safely.
3. Place the transmission in any position other than **N**.
4. Clean the area around the switch, then remove the switch.

To install:

5. Install the switch and tighten 8–12 ft. lbs. (11– 16Nm).
6. Reconnect the harness connector to the switch.
7. Lower the vehicle.
8. Reconnect the negative battery cable.

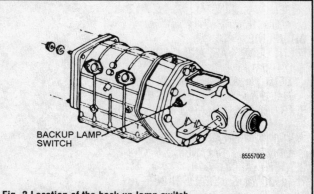

BACKUP LAMP
SWITCH

85557002

Fig. 2 Location of the back-up lamp switch

Extension Housing Seal

REMOVAL & INSTALLATION

Two Wheel Drive Models

▶ **See Figures 3 and 4**

1. Disconnect the negative battery cable.
2. Raise and support the vehicle safely.
3. Place a suitable drain pan beneath the extension housing. Clean the area around the extension housing seal.
4. Matchmark the driveshaft to the rear axle flange. Disconnect the driveshaft and pull it rearward from the unit.
5. Remove the extension housing seal using tool T74P-77248-A or equivalent, remove the extension housing seal.

To install:

6. Lubricate the inside diameter of the oil seal and install the seal into the extension housing using tool T74P-77052-A. Check to ensure that the oil seal drain hole faces downward.
7. Install the driveshaft to the extension housing. Connect the driveshaft to the rear axle flange. Make sure the marks made during removal are in alignment. Fit the attaching washer, lockwasher and nuts.
8. Check and adjust the transmission fluid level, using Ford manual transmission lube D8DZ-19C547-A (ESP-M2C83-C) or equivalent.
9. Lower the vehicle.
10. Reconnect the negative battery cable.

Four Wheel Drive Models

Refer to the transfer case procedures for the front and/or rear output shaft seals.

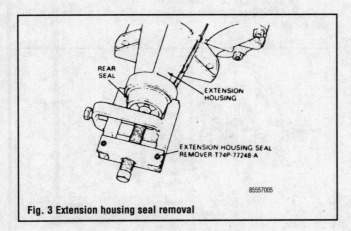

Fig. 3 Extension housing seal removal

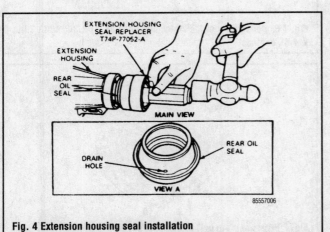

Fig. 4 Extension housing seal installation

Transmission

REMOVAL & INSTALLATION

▶ **See Figures 5 and 6**

1. Disconnect the negative battery cable.
2. Remove the gearshift lever assembly from the control housing.
3. Cover the opening in the control housing with a cloth to prevent dirt from falling into the unit.
4. Raise the vehicle and support it safely.
5. On 2WD vehicles, matchmark the driveshaft to the rear axle flange. Position a drain pan under the tailend of the transmission. Remove the driveshaft-to-rear axle flange fasteners and pull the driveshaft rearward to disconnect it from the transmission.
6. Disconnect the clutch hydraulic line a the clutch housing. Plug the lines.
7. Disconnect the speedometer from the transfer case/extension housing.
8. Disconnect the starter motor, back-up lamp and, if equipped, neutral sensing switch harness connector.
9. Place a wood block on a service jack and position the jack under the engine oil pan.
10. On 4WD vehicles, remove the transfer case from the vehicle.
11. Remove the starter motor.
12. Position a transmission jack, under the transmission.
13. Remove the transmission-to-engine retaining bolts and washers.
14. Remove the nuts and bolts attaching the transmission mount and damper to the crossmember.
15. Remove the nuts and bolts attaching the crossmember to the frame side rails and remove the crossmember.
16. Lower the engine jack slightly to angle the transmission assembly. Work the clutch housing off the locating dowels and slide the clutch housing and the transmission rearward until the input shaft clears the clutch disc.
17. Lower the transmission jack and remove the transmission from the vehicle.

To install:

18. Check that the mating surfaces of the clutch housing, engine rear and dowel holes are free of burrs, dirt and paint.
19. Place the transmission on the transmission jack. Position the transmission under the vehicle, then raise it into position. Align the input shaft splines with the clutch disc splines and work the transmission forward into the locating dowels.
20. Install the transmission-to-engine retaining bolts and washers. Tighten the retaining bolts to specifications. Remove the transmission jack.
21. Install the starter motor. Tighten the attaching nuts.
22. Raise the engine and install the rear crossmember, insulator and damper and attaching nuts and bolts. Tighten and torque the bolts to specification.

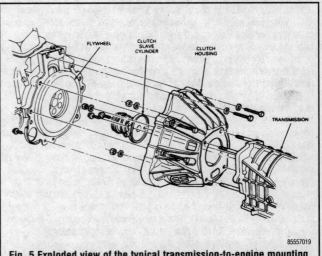

Fig. 5 Exploded view of the typical transmission-to-engine mounting and related components

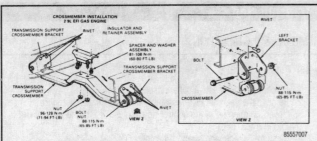

Fig. 6 Exploded view of a typical transmission crossmember assembly

23. On 4WD vehicles, install the transfer case.
24. On 2WD vehicles, insert the driveshaft into the transmission extension housing and install the center bearing attaching nuts, washers and lockwashers. Connect the driveshaft to the rear axle drive flange.
25. Connect the starter motor, back-up lamp and, if equipped, neutral sensing switch connectors.
26. Connect the hydraulic clutch line and bleed the system.
27. Install the speedometer cable.
28. Check and adjust the fluid level.
29. Lower the vehicle.
30. Install the gearshift lever assembly. Install the boot cover and bolts.
31. Reconnect the negative battery cable.
32. Check for proper shifting and operation of the transmission.

CLUTCH

Understanding the Clutch

The purpose of the clutch is to disconnect and connect engine power at the transmission. A vehicle at rest requires a lot of engine torque to get all that weight moving. An internal combustion engine does not develop a high starting torque (unlike steam engines) so it must be allowed to operate without any load until it builds up enough torque to move the vehicle. To a point, torque increases with engine rpm. The clutch allows the engine to build up torque by physically disconnecting the engine from the transmission, relieving the engine of any load or resistance.

The transfer of engine power to the transmission (the load) must be smooth and gradual; if it weren't, drive line components would wear out or break quickly. This gradual power transfer is made possible by gradually releasing the clutch pedal. The clutch disc and pressure plate are the connecting link between the engine and transmission. When the clutch pedal is released, the disc and plate contact each other (the clutch is engaged) physically joining the engine and transmission. When the pedal is pushed in, the disc and plate separate (the clutch is disengaged) disconnecting the engine from the transmission.

Most clutch assemblies consists of the flywheel, the clutch disc, the clutch pressure plate, the throw out bearing and fork, the actuating linkage and the pedal. The flywheel and clutch pressure plate (driving members) are connected to the engine crankshaft and rotate with it. The clutch disc is located between the flywheel and pressure plate, and is splined to the transmission shaft. A driving member is one that is attached to the engine and transfers engine power to a driven member (clutch disc) on the transmission shaft. A driving member (pressure plate) rotates (drives) a driven member (clutch disc) on contact and, in so doing, turns the transmission shaft.

There is a circular diaphragm spring within the pressure plate cover (transmission side). In a relaxed state (when the clutch pedal is fully released) this spring is convex; that is, it is dished outward toward the transmission. Pushing in the clutch pedal actuates the attached linkage. Connected to the other end of this is the throw out fork, which hold the throw out bearing. When the clutch pedal is depressed, the clutch linkage pushes the fork and bearing forward to contact the diaphragm spring of the pressure plate. The outer edges of the spring are secured to the pressure plate and are pivoted on rings so that when the center of the spring is compressed by the throw out bearing, the outer edges bow outward and, by so doing, pull the pressure plate in the same direction — away from the clutch disc. This action separates the disc from the plate, disengaging the clutch and allowing the transmission to be shifted into another gear. A coil type clutch return spring attached to the clutch pedal arm permits full release of the pedal. Releasing the pedal pulls the throw out bearing away from the diaphragm spring resulting in a reversal of spring position. As bearing pressure is gradually released from the spring center, the outer edges of the spring bow outward, pushing the pressure plate into closer contact with the clutch disc. As the disc and plate move closer together, friction between the two increases and slippage is reduced until, when full spring pressure is applied (by fully releasing the pedal) the speed of the disc and plate are the same. This stops all slipping, creating a direct connection between the plate and disc which results in the transfer of power from the engine to the transmission. The clutch disc is now rotating with the pressure plate at engine speed and, because it is splined to the transmission shaft, the shaft now turns at the same engine speed.

The clutch is operating properly if:
1. It will stall the engine when released with the vehicle held stationary.
2. The shift lever can be moved freely between 1st and reverse gears when the vehicle is stationary and the clutch disengaged.

Driven Disc and Pressure Plate

⁂ CAUTION

The clutch driven disc may contain asbestos, which has been determined to be a cancer causing agent. Never clean clutch surfaces with compressed air! Avoid inhaling any dust from any clutch surface! When cleaning clutch surface, use a commercially available brake cleaning fluid.

REMOVAL & INSTALLATION

◆ See Figures 7 thru 14

1. Disconnect the negative battery cable.
2. Disconnect the clutch hydraulic system master cylinder from the clutch pedal and remove.

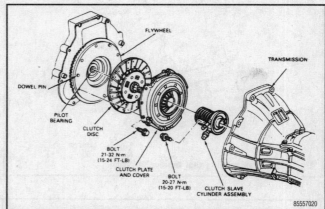

Fig. 7 Exploded view of the clutch components for 2.3L, 2.5L, 3.0L & 4.0L engines

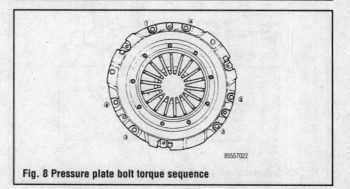

Fig. 8 Pressure plate bolt torque sequence

Fig. 9 Loosen and remove the clutch and pressure plate bolts evenly, a little at a time . . .

Fig. 10 . . . then carefully remove the pressure plate and clutch assembly from the flywheel

Fig. 11 Check the flywheel surface for flatness and, if necessary, remove it from the engine for truing

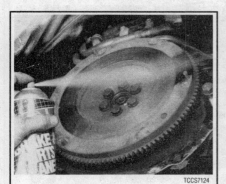

Fig. 12 Be sure that the flywheel surface is clean before installing the clutch

Fig. 13 Typical clutch alignment tool, note how the splines match the transmission's input shaft

Fig. 14 Be sure to use a torque wrench to tighten all of the bolts

3. Raise the vehicle and support it safely.
4. Remove the starter.
5. Disconnect the hydraulic coupling at the transmission.

➠Clean the area around the hose and slave cylinder to prevent fluid contamination.

6. Remove the transmission from the vehicle.
7. Mark the assembled position of the pressure plate and cover the flywheel, to aid during re-assembly.
8. Loosen the pressure plate and cover attaching bolts evenly until the pressure plate springs are expanded, and remove the bolts.
9. Remove the pressure plate and cover assembly and the clutch disc from the flywheel. Remove the pilot bearing only for replacement.

To install:
10. Position the clutch disc on the flywheel so that the Clutch Alignment Shaft Tool T74P-7137-K or equivalent can enter the clutch pilot bearing and align the disc.
11. When reinstalling the original pressure plate and cover assembly, align the assembly and flywheel according to the marks made during the removal operations. Position the pressure plate and cover assembly on the flywheel, align the pressure plate and disc, and install the retaining bolts that fasten the assembly to the flywheel. Tighten the bolts to 15–25 ft. lbs. (21–35 Nm) in the proper sequence. Remove the clutch disc pilot tool.
12. Install the transmission into the vehicle.
13. Connect the coupling by pushing the male coupling into the slave cylinder.
14. Connect the hydraulic clutch master cylinder pushrod to the clutch pedal.

Clutch Interlock Switch

The clutch interlock switch has 3-functions. It is also known as the Clutch Pedal Position (CPP) switch and provides the 3 following functions:
• It requires the clutch pedal to be depressed to the floor in order to start the engine.
• If cuts off the speed control system when the clutch pedal is depressed.
• It provides a fuel control signal to the EEC system.

REMOVAL & INSTALLATION

♦ See Figure 15

1. Disconnect the negative battery cable.
2. Disconnect the connector at the switch by flexing the retaining tab on the switch housing and withdraw the connector.
3. Rotate the switch ½ turn to expose the plastic retainer.
4. Push the tabs together to allow the retainer to slide rearward and separate from the switch.
5. Remove the switch from the pushrod.

To install:
6. Fit the switch to the master cylinder pushrod.
7. Install the plastic retainer.
8. Rotate the switch into the position to attach the clip. Reconnect the switch connector.
9. Reconnect the negative battery cable.

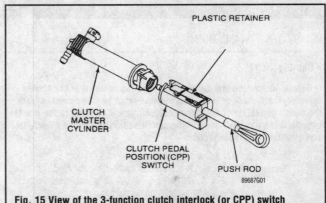

Fig. 15 View of the 3-function clutch interlock (or CPP) switch

Clutch Master Cylinder

REMOVAL & INSTALLATION

▶ **See Figure 16**

1. Disconnect the negative battery cable.
2. Disconnect the clutch master cylinder pushrod from the clutch pedal.
3. Remove the switch from the master cylinder assembly, if equipped.
4. Remove the screw retaining the fluid reservoir to the cowl access cover.
5. Disconnect the tube from the slave cylinder and plug both openings.
6. Remove the bolts retaining the clutch master cylinder to the dash panel and remove the clutch master cylinder assembly.

To install:

7. Install the pushrod through the hole in the engine compartment. Make certain it is located on the correct side of the clutch pedal. Place the master cylinder assembly in position and install the retaining bolts. Tighten to 8–12 ft. lbs. (11–16Nm).
8. Insert the coupling end into the slave cylinder and install the tube into the clips.
9. Fit the reservoir on the cowl access cover and install the retaining screws.
10. Replace the retainer bushing in the clutch master cylinder pushrod if worn or damaged. Install the retainer and pushrod on the clutch pedal pin. Make certain the bushing is fitted correctly with the flange of the bushing against the pedal blade.
11. Install the switch.
12. Bleed the system.
13. Reconnect the negative battery cable.

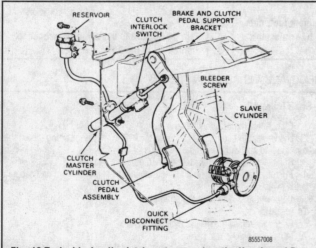

Fig. 16 Typical hydraulic clutch system used on the Navajo and B Series Pick-up models

Slave Cylinder

REMOVAL & INSTALLATION

▶ **See Figure 17**

➡ **Before performing any service that requires removal of the slave cylinder, the master cylinder and pushrod must be disconnected from the clutch pedal. If not disconnected, permanent damage to the master cylinder assembly will occur if the clutch pedal is depressed while the slave cylinder is disconnected.**

1. Disconnect the negative battery cable.
2. Disconnect the coupling at the transmission, using the clutch coupling removal tool T88T-70522-A or equivalent. Slide the white plastic sleeve toward the slave cylinder while applying a slight tug on the tube.
3. Remove the transmission assembly.

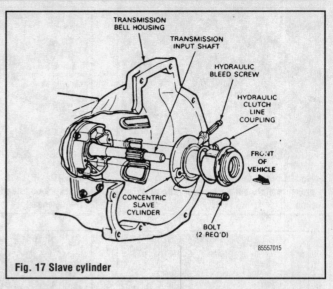

Fig. 17 Slave cylinder

4. Remove the slave cylinder-to-transmission retaining bolts.
5. Remove the slave cylinder from the transmission input shaft.

To install:

6. Fit the slave cylinder over the transmission input shaft with the bleed screws and coupling facing the left side of the transmission.
7. Install the slave cylinder retaining bolts. Torque to 13–19 ft. lbs. (18–26Nm).
8. Install the transmission.
9. Reconnect the coupling to the slave cylinder.
10. Bleed the system.
11. Reconnect the negative battery cable.

BLEEDING THE SYSTEM

The following procedure is recommended for bleeding a hydraulic system installed on the vehicle. The largest portion of the filling is carried out by gravity. It is recommended that the original clutch tube with quick connect be replaced when servicing the hydraulic system because air can be trapped in the quick connect and prevent complete bleeding of the system. The replacement tube does not include a quick connect.

1. Clean the dirt and grease from the dust cap.
2. Remove the cap and diaphragm and fill the reservoir to the top with approved brake fluid FMVSS116 DOT 3 or equivalent.

➡ **To keep brake fluid from entering the clutch housing, route a suitable rubber tube of appropriate inside diameter from the bleed screw to a container.**

3. Loosen the bleed screw, located in the slave cylinder body, next to the inlet connection. Fluid will now begin to move from the master cylinder down the tube to the slave cylinder.

➡ **The reservoir must be kept full at all time during the bleeding operation, to ensure no additional air enters the system.**

4. Notice the bleed screw outlet. When the slave is full, a steady stream of fluid comes from the slave outlet. Tighten the bleed screw.
5. Depress the clutch pedal to the floor and hold for 1–2 seconds. Release the pedal as rapidly as possible. The pedal must be released completely. Pause for 1–2 seconds. Repeat 10 times.
6. Check the fluid level in the reservoir. The fluid should be level with the step when the diaphragm is removed.
7. Repeat Step 5 and 6 five times. Replace the reservoir diaphragm and cap.
8. Hold the pedal to the floor, crack open the bleed screw to allow any additional air to escape. Close the bleed screw, then release the pedal.
9. Check the fluid in the reservoir. The hydraulic system should now be fully bled and should release the clutch.
10. Check the vehicle by starting, pushing the clutch pedal to the floor and selecting reverse gear. There should be no grating of gears. If there is, and the hydraulic system still contains air, repeat the bleeding procedure from Step 5.

AUTOMATIC TRANSMISSION

Understanding Automatic Transmissions

The automatic transmission allows engine torque and power to be transmitted to the rear wheels within a narrow range of engine operating speeds. It will allow the engine to turn fast enough to produce plenty of power and torque at very low speeds, while keeping it at a sensible rpm at high vehicle speeds (and it does this job without driver assistance). The transmission uses a light fluid as the medium for the transmission of power. This fluid also works in the operation of various hydraulic control circuits and as a lubricant.

Neutral Start Switch/Back-up Switch

REMOVAL & INSTALLATION

A4LD Transmission

▶ See Figure 18

The Park/Neutral Position (PNP) switch, mounted on the transmission, allows the vehicle to start only in **P** or **N**. The switch has a dual purpose, in that it is also the back-up lamp switch.
1. Disconnect the negative battery cable.
2. Raise and support the vehicle safely.
3. Disconnect the harness connector from the neutral start switch.
4. Clean the area around the switch. Remove the switch and O-ring, using a thin wall socket (tool T74P-77247-A or equivalent).
To install:
5. Fit a new O-ring to the switch. Install the switch.
6. Reconnect the harness connector to the switch.
7. Lower the vehicle.
8. Reconnect the negative battery cable.
9. Check the operation of the switch, with the parking brake engaged. The engine should only start in **N** or **P**. The back-up lamps should come ON only in **R**.

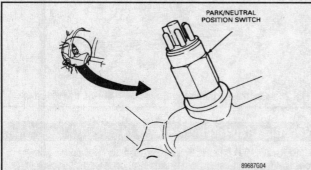

Fig. 18 View of the Park/Neutral Position (PNP) switch used on the A4LD transmission

4R44E, 4R55E and 5R55E Transmissions

▶ See Figures 19, 20 and 21

Starting in 1995, the switch was used not only for neutral start sensing and back-up light activation, but also as a gear position range sensor. The Powertrain Control Module reads the sensor to determine which gear position the transmission is in, and adjusts fuel and spark timing accordingly. The new switch is called the Transmission Range (TR) sensor.

➡ To install the Transmission Range (TR) sensor requires a special Transmission Range Sensor Alignment Tool T97L-70010-AH, or equivalent.

1. Disconnect the negative battery cable, block the rear wheels and apply the parking brake.
2. Place the transmission shift lever in the Neutral (N) position.
3. Raise and safely support the front of the vehicle
4. Disconnect the shift control cable from the transmission manual control lever.
5. Disconnect the electrical wire harness plug from the TR sensor.
6. Remove the manual control lever retaining nut as well as the lever.
7. Remove the two retaining bolts and the sensor.
To install:
8. Ensure that the transmission shift lever is in the Neutral (N) position.
9. Install the TR sensor and loosely install the retaining bolts.
10. Align TR sensor slots using the Transmission Range Sensor Alignment Tool T97L-70010-AH, or equivalent.
11. Tighten the retaining bolts to 7–9 ft. lbs. (9–12 Nm).
12. Install the manual control lever to the sensor and tighten the retaining nut to 22–26 ft. lbs. (30–35 Nm).
13. Connect the TR sensor electrical wire harness plug.
14. Install the shift control cable to the transmission manual control lever.
15. Lower the vehicle and connect the negative battery cable.
16. Ensure that the wheels are still blocked and the parking brake is applied.
17. Check for proper operation of the switch. The engine should only start in Park (P) or Neutral (N).

RA4A-EL and RA4AX-EL (Electronically Controlled) Transmissions

1. Disconnect the negative battery cable.
2. Raise and safely support the vehicle.
3. Disconnect the control linkage from the transmission manual shaft.
4. Disconnect the park/neutral switch harness connector, remove the switch mounting bolts, and remove the park/neutral switch.
To install:
5. Install the park/neutral switch over the manual shaft.
6. Install the switch mounting bolts but do not tighten.
7. Make sure the transmission manual shaft lever is positioned at the **L** position (fully forward). Turn the manual shaft lever fully rearward, then return it 2 notches (**N** position).
8. Insert a 0.157 inch (4.0mm) pin through the holes of the switch and the manual shaft lever.

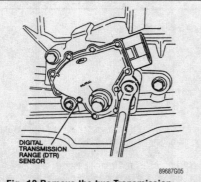

Fig. 19 Remove the two Transmission Range (TR) sensor retaining bolts

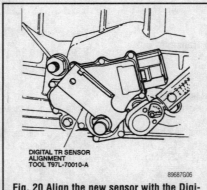

Fig. 20 Align the new sensor with the Digital TR Sensor Alignment Tool

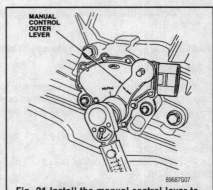

Fig. 21 Install the manual control lever to the sensor and tighten the retaining bolt

9. Tighten the switch mounting bolts to 22–35 inch lbs. (2.5–3.9 Nm). Remove the pin.

10. Connect the electrical connector.

11. Reinstall the shift control linkage.

12. Safely lower the vehicle, connect the negative battery cable, and check for proper operation.

NA4A-HL (Hydraulically Controlled) Transmission

1. Disconnect the negative battery cable.

2. Raise and safely support the vehicle.

3. Disconnect the control linkage from the transmission manual shaft.

4. Disconnect the wiring harness connector and remove the park/neutral switch mounting bolts. Remove the switch from the manual shaft lever.

To install:

5. Position the park/neutral switch over the manual shaft lever and install the mounting bolts. Do not fully tighten the mounting bolts.

6. Move the manual shaft lever to the **N** position.

7. Remove the screw on the switch body and move the switch so the screw hole is aligned with the small hole inside the switch. Check their alignment by inserting a 0.079 in. (2.0mm) diameter pin through the holes.

8. Tighten the switch mounting bolts to 43–61 inch lbs. (4.9–6.9 Nm).

9. Install the screw in the park/neutral switch body and reconnect the wiring harness connector.

10. Reinstall the control linkage.

11. Safely lower the vehicle, connect the negative battery cable, and check for proper operation.

ADJUSTMENT

A4LD Transmission

No adjustment is necessary or possible on the A4LD transmission Park Neutral Position (PNP) switch.

4R44E, 4R55E and 5R55E Transmissions

▶ See Figures 20 and 21

➡To adjust the Transmission Range (TR) sensor requires a special Transmission Range Sensor Alignment Tool T97L-70010-AH, or equivalent.

1. Raise and safely support the vehicle.

2. Block the rear wheels and apply the parking brake.

3. Place the transmission shift control lever in the Neutral (N) position.

4. Remove the nut securing the transmission control manual lever to the TR sensor.

5. Loosen the two TR sensor retaining bolts.

6. Align the TR sensor slots using the Transmission Range Sensor Alignment Tool T97L-70010-AH, or equivalent.

7. Tighten the TR sensor retaining bolts to 7–9 ft. lbs. (9–12 Nm).

8. Install the nut retaining the transmission manual control lever to the TR sensor. Tighten to 12–16 ft. lbs. (16–22 Nm).

9. Lower the vehicle. Leave the wheels blocked and the parking brake applied.

10. Check the TR sensor operation. The engine should only start in Park (P) or Neutral (N).

RA4A-EL and RA4AX-EL (Electronically Controlled) Transmissions

▶ See Figure 22

1. Install the park/neutral switch over the manual shaft.

2. Make sure the transmission manual shaft lever is positioned at the **L** position (fully forward). Turn the manual shaft lever fully rearward, then return it 2 notches (**N** position).

3. Insert a 0.157 inch (4.0mm) pin through the holes of the switch and the manual shaft lever.

4. Tighten the switch mounting bolts to 22–35 inch lbs. (2.5–3.9 Nm). Remove the pin.

5. Connect the electrical connector.

6. Reinstall the shift control linkage.

7. Connect the negative battery cable, and check for proper operation.

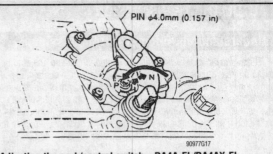

Fig. 22 Adjusting the park/neutral switch—RA4A-EL/RA4AX-EL transmissions

NA4A-HL (Hydraulically Controlled) Transmission

▶ See Figure 23

1. Position the park/neutral switch over the manual shaft lever and install the mounting bolts.

2. Move the manual shaft lever to the **N** position.

3. Remove the screw on the switch body and move the switch so the screw hole is aligned with the small hole inside the switch. Check their alignment by inserting a 0.079 in. (2.0mm) diameter pin through the holes.

4. Tighten the switch mounting bolts to 43–61 inch lbs. (4.9–6.9 Nm).

5. Install the screw in the park/neutral switch body and reconnect the wiring harness connector.

6. Reinstall the control linkage.

7. Safely lower the vehicle, reconnect the negative battery cable, and check for proper operation.

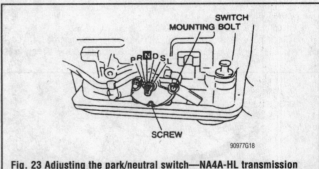

Fig. 23 Adjusting the park/neutral switch—NA4A-HL transmission

Vacuum Diaphragm

Only Navajo, 1994 B Series Pick-up and 1994–95 MPV models (with the hydraulically controlled automatic transmission) use a vacuum diaphragm (or modulator). All other automatic transmissions are PCM controlled and do not require vacuum supply from the engine.

REMOVAL & INSTALLATION

Navajo and 1994 B Series Pick-up Models

▶ See Figure 24

1. Disconnect the negative battery cable.

2. Raise and support the vehicle safely.

3. Disconnect the hose from the vacuum diaphragm.

4. Remove the vacuum diaphragm retaining clamp bolt and clamp. Do not pry on the clamp.

5. Pull the vacuum diaphragm from the transmission case and remove the vacuum diaphragm control rod from the transmission case.

To install:

6. Install the vacuum diaphragm control rod from the transmission case.

7. Push the vacuum diaphragm into the case and secure it with the clamp and bolt. Tighten to 80–106 inch lbs. (9–12Nm).

8. Fit the vacuum hose to the diaphragm.

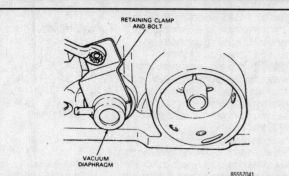

Fig. 24 Remove the vacuum diaphragm retaining clamp and bolt, then pull the diaphragm out of the transmission

9. Lower the vehicle.
10. Reconnect the negative battery cable.

MPV Models Equipped with the Hydraulically Controlled Transmission

▶ See Figure 25

1. Disconnect the negative battery cable.
2. Raise and support the vehicle safely. Place a fluid drain pan under the transmission oil pan.
3. Loosen the transmission oil pan mounting bolts and drain approximately 1 quart of transmission oil. After draining the oil, tighten the oil pan bolts back up again.
4. Disconnect the hose from the vacuum diaphragm.
5. Remove the vacuum diaphragm, O-ring seal and vacuum diaphragm rod.

To install:
6. Apply ATF to a new O-ring seal and install it onto the vacuum diaphragm.
7. Apply ATF to the vacuum diaphragm and rod, then install them into the transmission.
8. Fit the vacuum hose to the diaphragm.
9. Lower the vehicle.
10. Add approximately 1 quart of ATF to the transmission, then check the level.
11. Reconnect the negative battery cable.
12. Warm up the engine to normal operating temperature and check the system for fluid and vacuum leakage.

Extension Housing Seal

REMOVAL & INSTALLATION

▶ See Figures 3, 4 and 26

1. Disconnect the negative battery cable.
2. Raise and support the vehicle safely. Drain the ATF.

3. Matchmark the driveshaft end yoke and rear axle companion flange to assure proper positioning during assembly. Remove the driveshaft.
4. Remove the oil seal from the extension housing, using seal remover T71P-7657-A or equivalent.

To install:
Before install the replacement seal, inspect the sealing surface of the universal joint yoke for scores. If scoring is found, replace the yoke.
5. Install the new seal, using seal installer T74P-77052-A or equivalent. Coat the inside diameter at the end of the rubber boot portion of the seal with long-life lubricant (C1AZ-19590-BA or equivalent).
6. Align the matchmarks and install the driveshaft.
7. Lower the vehicle. Fill the transmission with the correct type and amount of ATF.
8. Reconnect the negative battery cable.

Transmission Assembly

REMOVAL & INSTALLATION

▶ See Figures 27, 28, 29 and 30

1. Disconnect the negative battery cable.
2. Raise the vehicle and support it safely.
3. Position a drain pan under the transmission pan and drain the transmission fluid.
4. Remove the converter access cover from the lower right side of the converter housing on the 3.0L engine. Remove the cover from the bottom of the engine oil pan on the 2.3L engine. Remove a bolt on the access cover of the 2.9L engine and swing the cover open. Remove the access cover and adapter plate bolts from the lower left side of the converter housing on all other applications.
5. Remove the flywheel to converter attaching nuts. Use a socket and breaker bar on the crankshaft pulley attaching bolt. Rotate the pulley clockwise as viewed from the front to gain access to each of the nuts.

➡ **On belt driven overhead cam engines, never rotate the pulley in a counterclockwise direction as viewed from the front.**

6. Remove the speedometer cable and/or vehicle speed sensor from the transfer case (4WD) or extension housing (2WD).
7. On 2WD vehicles, scribe a mark indexing the driveshaft to the rear axle flange. Remove the driveshaft.
8. On 4WD vehicles, remove the transfer case.
9. Disconnect the shift rod or cable at the transmission manual lever and retainer bracket.
10. Disconnect the downshift cable from the downshift lever. Depress the tab on the retainer and remove the kickdown cable from the bracket.
11. Disconnect all of the transmission wire harness plugs.
12. Remove the starter mounting bolts and the ground cable. Remove the starter.
13. If equipped, remove the vacuum line from the transmission vacuum modulator.
14. Remove the filler tube from the transmission.

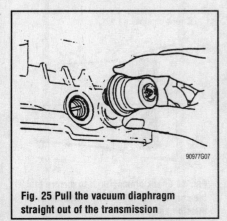

Fig. 25 Pull the vacuum diaphragm straight out of the transmission

Fig. 26 Examine the overall condition of the transmission extension housing seal and replace it if necessary

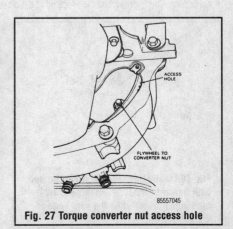

Fig. 27 Torque converter nut access hole

15. Position a transmission jack under the transmission and raise it slightly.

16. Remove the engine rear support to crossmember bolts.

17. Remove the crossmember to frame side support attaching nuts and bolts. Remove the crossmember.

18. Remove the converter housing to engine bolts.

19. Slightly lower the jack to gain access to the oil cooler lines. Disconnect the oil cooler lines at the transmission. Plug all openings to keep dirt and contamination out.

20. Move the transmission to the rear so it disengages from the dowel pins and the converter is disengaged from the flywheel. Lower the transmission from the vehicle.

21. If necessary, remove the torque converter from the transmission.

➡**If the transmission is to be removed for a period of time, support the engine with a safety stand and wood block.**

To install:

✳✳ WARNING

Before installing an automatic transmission, always check that the torque converter is fully seated into the transmission. Typically, the converter has notches or tangs on the hub which must engage the transmission fluid pump. If they are not engaged in the pump, the transmission will not mate to the engine properly, as the converter will be holding it away. Severe damage to the pump, converter or transmission casing can occur if the transmission-to-engine bolts are tightened as if to force the transmission to mate to the engine.

Proper installation of the converter requires full engagement of the converter hub in the pump gear. To accomplish this, the converter must be pushed and at the same time rotated through what feels like 2 notches or bumps. When fully installed, rotation of the converter will usually result in a clicking noise heard, caused by the converter surface touching the housing to case bolts.

This should not be a concern, but an indication of proper converter installation since, when the converter is attached to the engine flywheel, it will be pulled slightly forward away from the bolt heads. Besides the clicking sound, the converter should rotate freely with no binding.

For reference, a properly installed converter will have a distance from the converter pilot nose from face to converter housing outer face of $^{13}/_{32}$–$^{7}/_{16}$ in. (10.5–14.5mm).

22. Install the converter on the transmission.

23. With the converter properly installed, position the transmission on the jack.

24. Rotate the converter so that the drive studs are in alignment with the holes in the flywheel.

25. Move the converter and transmission assembly forward into position, being careful not to damage the flywheel and converter pilot. The converter housing is piloted into position by the dowels in the rear of the engine block.

➡**During this move, to avoid damage, do not allow the transmission to get into a nose down position as this will cause the converter to move forward and disengage from the pump gear.**

26. Install the converter housing to engine attaching bolts and tighten to specification. The 2 longer bolts are located at the dowel holes.

27. Remove the jack supporting the engine.

28. The rest of the installation procedure is the reverse of removal. Tighten all fasteners to the following specifications:

Navajo and B Series Pick-up Models
- Transmission-to-engine mounting bolts: 30–41 ft. lbs. (40–55 Nm)
- Torque converter-to-flywheel mounting bolts: 22–30 ft. lbs. (30–40 Nm)
- Transmission mount-to-transmission: 64–81 ft. lbs. (87–110 Nm)
- Transmission crossmember mounting bolts: 63–87 ft. lbs. (85–118 Nm)
- Transmission mount-to-crossmember: 60–82 ft. lbs. (82–111 Nm)

MPV Models
- Transmission-to-engine mounting bolts: 28–38 ft. lbs. (38–51 Nm)
- Torque converter-to-flywheel mounting bolts: 27–39 ft. lbs. (37–53 Nm)
- Transmission mount-to-transmission: 32–44 ft. lbs. (44–60 Nm)
- Transmission crossmember mounting bolts: 32–44 ft. lbs. (44–60 Nm)
- Transmission mount-to-crossmember: 32–44 ft. lbs. (44–60 Nm)

29. Follow the procedures outlined in Section 1 when filling the transmission with fluid.

ADJUSTMENTS

Navajo and B Series Pick-up Models

SHIFT/MANUAL LINKAGE—SHIFT SELECT LEVER

♦ See Figure 31

➡Before performing the linkage adjustment, confirm that the shift indicator is properly adjusted.

1. Turn the vehicle **OFF**, block the rear wheels and engage the parking brake.

2. From inside the vehicle, place the gear shift lever in the overdrive position (shown as a circle with the letter D in the middle). Hang a 3 lb. (1.4Kg) weight on the lever.

3. Raise and safely support the vehicle.

4. From underneath, use a prytool to remove the shift control cable end from the transmission manual control lever ball stud.

5. Unlock the cable adjuster body by pushing down on the two tangs and releasing the lock tab.

6. Move the shift cable back and forth the full adjustment length four or five times to remove any accumulated dirt. Ensure that the adjuster body moves freely.

7. Move the transmission manual control lever all the way rearward (counterclockwise) to its last position, then move it forward three detent positions. The transmission is now set in the overdrive position.

8. Holding the cable end fitting, push it rearward until the fitting lines up with the lever ball stud. Connect the cable end to the ball stud.

9. Push up on the lock tab to lock the adjuster body into position. Ensure that the locator tab is properly seated.

10. Ensure that the shift cable is properly clipped to the floorpan and that is routed into the tunnel.

11. Lower the vehicle.

12. Remove the weight from the gear select lever.

13. After adjustment, check for Park (P) engagement. Start the engine and check all the lever positions for proper operation.

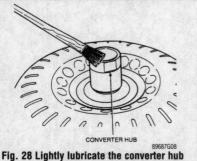
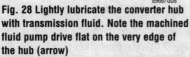

Fig. 28 Lightly lubricate the converter hub with transmission fluid. Note the machined fluid pump drive flat on the very edge of the hub (arrow)

CONVERTER HUB
89687G08

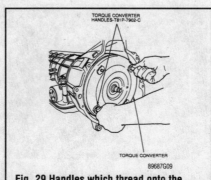

TORQUE CONVERTER HANDLES-T81P-7902-C

TORQUE CONVERTER
89687G09

Fig. 29 Handles which thread onto the converter-to-flywheel studs can be use to ease the installation process

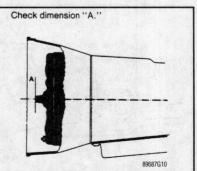

Check dimension "A."

89687G10

Fig. 30 Check dimension A to ensure that the converter is fully seated into the transmission and pump

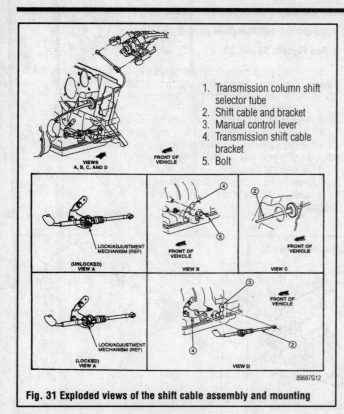

1. Transmission column shift selector tube
2. Shift cable and bracket
3. Manual control lever
4. Transmission shift cable bracket
5. Bolt

Fig. 31 Exploded views of the shift cable assembly and mounting

SHIFT/MANUAL LINKAGE—SHIFT SELECT INDICATOR

▶ See Figures 32, 33 and 34

To test the shift select indicator:

1. Turn the engine **OFF**, apply the parking brake and place the transmission select lever in the OD (overdrive) position.
2. Hang a 3 lb. (1.4Kg) weight on the select lever.
3. Look at the selector indicator on the instrument panel. The pointer should be centered on the D within the overdrive (circle with a letter D in the middle) graphic. If it is not, adjust as follows.

To adjust the indicator:

4. Remove the steering wheel.
5. Remove the lower steering column trim panel from the dash board.
6. Remove the lower steering column shroud by removing the two securing screws.
7. Lift off the upper steering column shroud.
8. On 1996–98 vehicles, remove the ignition switch lock cylinder.
9. With the engine **OFF** and the parking brake set, move the transmission select lever into the overdrive position. Hang a 3 lb. (1.4Kg) weight on the lever.
10. Turn the adjuster thumb wheel to properly position the pointer until it is centered on the overdrive graphic.
11. If removed, install the ignition switch lock cylinder.
12. Install the upper and lower steering column shrouds and the steering wheel.
13. Remove the weight from the lever.
14. Operate the shift select lever in all positions and ensure that the indicator pointer aligns with all of the position graphics.

KICKDOWN CABLE

▶ See Figure 35

The kickdown cable is self-adjusting over a tolerance range of 1 in. (25mm). If the cable requires readjustment, reset the by depressing the semi-circular metal tab on the self-adjuster mechanism and pulling the cable forward (toward the front of the vehicle) to the "Zero" position setting. The cable will then automatically readjust to the proper length when kicked down.

MPV Model

SELECTOR LEVER POSITION

▶ See Figures 36 and 37

1. Move the selector lever to the **P** range.
2. Remove the column covers.
3. Pull the selector lever rearward, toward the driver and insert a 0.197 in. (5mm) outer diameter pin into the gearshift rod assembly.
4. Remove the air intake tube.
5. Loosen the shift lever and the top lever mounting bolts.
6. Shift the transmission manual shaft to the **P** range position.
7. Adjust the clearance between the lower bracket and the shift lever bushing by sliding the shift lever assembly until there is no clearance.

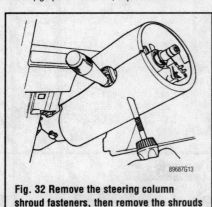

Fig. 32 Remove the steering column shroud fasteners, then remove the shrouds

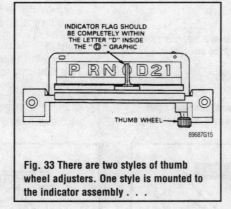

Fig. 33 There are two styles of thumb wheel adjusters. One style is mounted to the indicator assembly . . .

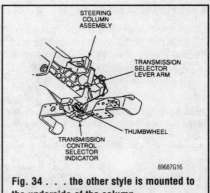

Fig. 34 . . . the other style is mounted to the underside of the column

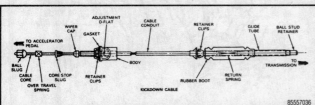

Fig. 35 View of the transmission kickdown cable assemble and its adjusting points

8. Tighten the shift lever mounting bolts to 12–17 ft. lbs. (16–23 Nm).
9. Make sure the detent ball is positioned in the center of the **P** range detent. If not, loosen the linkage bolts and turn the bracket to adjust the position, then retighten the bolts to 61–87 inch lbs. (7–10 Nm).
10. Adjust the clearance between the lower bracket and the shift lever bushing by turning the top lever until there is no clearance. Tighten the top lever mounting bolt, then retighten the remaining bolt to 12–17 ft. lbs. (16–23 Nm).
11. Remove the pin from the gear shift rod assembly and install the column covers. Check selector lever operation.

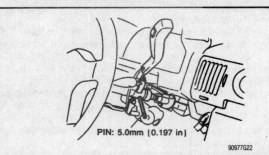

Fig. 36 Pull the selector lever rearward, toward the driver and insert a 0.197 in. (5mm) outer diameter pin into the gearshift rod assembly

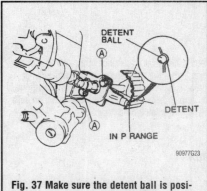

Fig. 37 Make sure the detent ball is positioned in the center of the P range detent

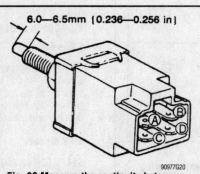

Fig. 38 Measure the continuity between terminals C and D with the switch depressed

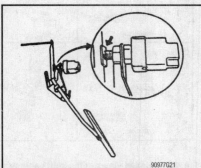

Fig. 39 With the pedal held down, turn the kick-down switch clockwise until a click is heard, then, turn it ¼ turn further

KICK-DOWN SWITCH (N4A-HL ONLY)

◆ See Figures 38 and 39

1. Connect an ohmmeter across terminals C and D of the kick-down switch. Make sure that there is continuity when the tip of the switch is depressed 0.236–0.256 inch (6.0–6.5mm). If not, proceed:
2. Disconnect the wiring.
3. Loosen the switch locknut and back the switch out fully.
4. Depress the accelerator pedal fully and hold it.
5. With the pedal held down, turn the kick-down switch clockwise until a click is heard, then, turn it ¼ turn further.
6. Tighten the locknut.
7. Release the pedal and reconnect the wiring.
8. Depress the accelerator pedal fully and verify that a click is heard. If not, replace the solenoid.

TRANSFER CASE

Rear Output Shaft Seal

REMOVAL & INSTALLATION

◆ See Figures 40 and 41

1. Raise and safely support the vehicle.
2. Matchmark the rear driveshaft to the transfer case yoke then disconnect the shaft from the yoke. Wire the driveshaft up and out of the way.
3. Drain the transfer case oil.
4. Using a thin-wall socket, remove the rear output shaft yoke retaining nut.

➡Some fluid may dribble out as the yoke is removed, and then again when the seal is removed. While an old rag should suffice for catching the fluid, a small catch can may be better, especially if the vehicle is not parked level.

5. Remove the output shaft yoke washer, rubber seal and the yoke from the output shaft. On MPV models, use companion flange puller tool 49-0839-425C, or equivalent.
6. Remove the rear output shaft seal by prying and pulling on the curved outer lip of the seal. On the 1998 B Series Pick-up, use seal removal tool 49-0223-630B. Take care to not damage the bearing, bearing cage or case.

To install:

7. Ensure that the output housing bore is free of any dirt, burrs or nicks. Apply molybdenum grease to the seal lip.
8. Position the new seal to the output housing and using an appropriate driver, such as the Output Shaft Seal Installer tool 49-U027-003 and Driver Handle 49-F027-003 (B Series Pick-up/Navajo) or 49-G030-797 (MPV), press the seal into the housing until fully seated.

Fig. 40 Remove the rear output shaft seal—puller tool shown

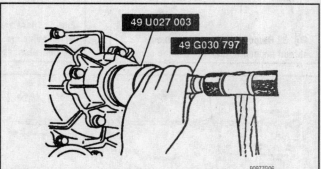

Fig. 41 Drive the new seal into the case housing using the appropriate seal installation tool

9. Install the rear out put shaft yoke, rubber seal and washer.

10. Install the output shaft yoke retaining nut and tighten to 184–203 ft. lbs. (250–275 Nm).

11. Connect the rear driveshaft to the transfer case.

12. Add transfer case oil to the correct level.

13. Lower the vehicle.

14. Drive the vehicle and check for leaks.

Front Output Shaft Seal

REMOVAL & INSTALLATION

♦ **See Figure 42**

1. Place the transfer case in 4WD mode. If automatic transmission, place it in the **P** position. If manual transmission, place it in gear.

2. Raise and safely support the vehicle.

3. If equipped, remove the skid plate from the frame.

4. If equipped, remove the damper from the transfer case.

5. Place a drain pan under the transfer case, remove the drain plug and drain the fluid.

6. Matchmark the front driveshaft to the transfer case yoke then disconnect the shaft from the yoke. Wire the driveshaft up and out of the way.

7. Using a 30mm (1.18 in.) thin-wall socket, remove the rear output shaft yoke retaining nut.

8. Remove the output shaft yoke washer, rubber seal and the yoke from the output shaft.

9. Remove the front output shaft seal by prying and pulling on the curved outer lip of the seal. Take care to not damage the bearing, bearing cage or case.

To install:

10. Ensure that the output housing bore is free of any dirt, burrs or nicks. Apply molybdenum grease to the seal lip.

11. Position the new seal to the output housing and using an appropriate driver, such as the Output Shaft Seal Installer 49-U027-003 and Driver Handle 49-F027-003 (B Series Pick-up/Navajo) or 49-G030-797 (MPV), press the seal into the housing until fully seated.

12. Install the front output shaft yoke, rubber seal and washer.

13. Install the output shaft yoke retaining nut and tighten to 184–203 ft. lbs. (250–275 Nm).

14. Connect the front driveshaft to the transfer case.

15. If removed, install the damper using new bolts. Be sure to apply threadlock to the bolts. Tighten the bolts to 25–35 ft. lbs. (34–48 Nm).

16. Remove the oil fill plug and add the proper amount of Dexron/Mercon® automatic transmission fluid.

17. If removed, install the skid plate. Tighten the skid plate mounting nuts and bolts to 15–20 ft. lbs. (20–27 Nm).

18. Lower the vehicle.

19. Drive the vehicle and check for leaks.

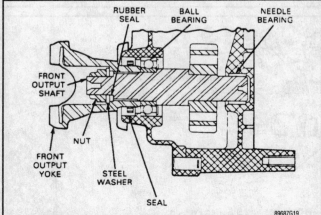

Fig. 42 Cutaway view of the front output shaft , seal and yoke assembly—rear components are similar

Transfer Case Assembly

REMOVAL & INSTALLATION

♦ **See Figure 43**

☀ CAUTION

The catalytic converter is located beside the transfer case. Be careful when working around the catalytic converter because of the extremely high temperatures generated by the converter.

1. Disconnect the negative battery cable.

2. Raise the vehicle and support it safely.

3. If so equipped, remove the skid plate from frame.

4. Drain the transfer case.

5. Remove the damper from the transfer case, if so equipped.

6. On electronic shift models, remove the wire connector from the feed wire harness at the rear of the transfer case. Be sure to squeeze the locking tabs, then pull the connectors apart.

7. Disconnect the front driveshaft from the axle input yoke.

8. If equipped, loosen the clamp retaining the front driveshaft boot to the transfer case, and pull the driveshaft and front boot assembly out of the transfer case front output shaft.

9. Disconnect the rear driveshaft from the transfer case output shaft yoke.

10. If equipped, disconnect the speedometer driven gear from the transfer case rear cover.

11. If equipped, disconnect the electrical wire harness plug from the Vehicle Speed Sensor (VSS).

12. Disconnect the vent hose from the mounting bracket.

13. On manual shift models, perform the following:

   a. Remove the shift lever retaining nut and remove the lever.

   b. Remove the bolts that retains the shifter to the extension housing. Note the size and location of the bolts to aid during installation. Remove the lever assembly and bushing.

14. If equipped, remove the heat shield from the transfer case.

15. Support the transfer case with a transmission jack.

16. Remove the mounting bolts retaining the transfer case to the transmission.

17. Slide the transfer case rearward off the transmission output shaft and lower the transfer case from the vehicle. Remove the gasket or any old sealer from between the transfer case and the transmission.

To install:

18. Install the heat shield onto the transfer case, if equipped, and place a new gasket or silicone sealer between the transfer case and adapter.

19. Raise the transfer case with a suitable transmission jack or equivalent, raise it high enough so that the transmission output shaft aligns with the splined transfer case input shaft.

20. Slide the transfer case forward on to the transmission output shaft and onto the dowel pin. Install transfer case retaining bolts and torque them to specification. Tighten the mounting bolts to 35–46 ft. lbs. (47–63 Nm) on Navajo/B Series Pick-ups and 27–39 ft. lbs. (37–52 Nm) on MPV models.

21. The remainder of the installation procedure is the reverse of removal. Check the fluid level and, if necessary, top off with the correct amount and type of transfer case fluid.

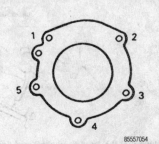

Fig. 43 Case-to-extension bolt torque sequence—Navajo and B Series Pick-up

ADJUSTMENTS

Manual Shift Models

♦ See Figure 44

The following procedure should be used, if a partial or incomplete engagement of the transfer case shift lever detent is experienced or if the control assembly requires removal.

1. Disconnect the negative battery cable.
2. Raise the shift boot to expose the top surface of the cam plates.
3. Loosen the 1 large and 1 small bolt, approximately 1 turn. Move the transfer case shift lever to the **4L** position (lever down).
4. Move the cam plate rearward until the bottom chamfered corner of the neutral lug just contacts the forward right edge of the shift lever.
5. Hold the cam plate in this position and torque the larger bolt first to 70–90 ft. lbs. (95–122 Nm) and torque the smaller bolt to 31–42 ft. lbs. (42–57 Nm).
6. Move the transfer case in cab shift lever to all shift positions to check for positive engagement. There should be a clearance between the shift lever and the cam plate in the **2H** front and **4H** rear (clearance not to exceed 3.3mm) and **4L** shift positions.

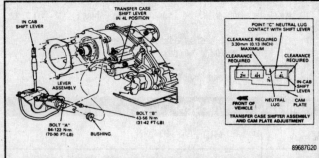

Fig. 44 Exploded view of the manual shift transfer case controls

7. Install the shift boot assembly.
8. Reconnect the negative battery cable.

Except Manual Shift Models

Both of the electronic shift and the AWD model transfer cases do not require any linkage adjustments, nor are any possible.

DRIVELINE

Front Driveshaft and U-Joints (4x4)

REMOVAL & INSTALLATION

Navajo and B Series Pick-up Models

♦ See Figure 45

1. Raise and safely support the vehicle.
2. Remove the bolts and straps or the flange bolts retaining the driveshaft to the transfer case. If necessary, remove the boot from the transfer case to gain access to the slip yoke.
3. Remove the bolts and straps retaining the front U-joint to the front axle and remove the front driveshaft.
To install:
4. If equipped, lubricate the slip yoke splines and the edge of the inner diameter of the rubber boot. Slide the driveshaft into the transfer case, making sure the wide-tooth splines are properly indexed. Reposition the boot and install the clamp.
5. If equipped, install the driveshaft to the transfer case flange and install the retaining bolts. Tighten to 12–16 ft. lbs. (17–22 Nm).
6. Install the driveshaft to the front axle flange with the straps and bolts. Tighten to 10–15 ft. lbs. (14–20 Nm).
7. Lower the vehicle.

MPV Models

♦ See Figure 46

1. Raise and safely support the vehicle.
2. Matchmark the flanges and remove the mounting nuts and bolts at the front differential.

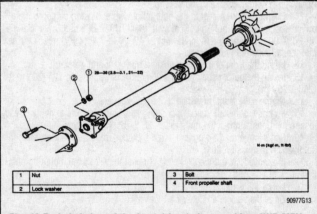

| 1 | Nut | | 3 | Bolt |
| 2 | Lock washer | | 4 | Front propeller shaft |

Fig. 46 Exploded view of the front driveshaft assembly—4WD MPV

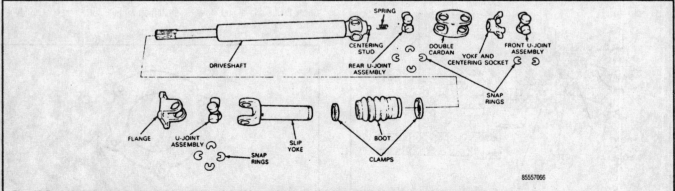

Fig. 45 Exploded view of the front driveshaft and double cardan type U-joint—4WD Navajo and B Series Pick-up

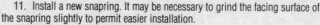

3. Slide the shaft out of the transfer case. Cap the opening to prevent fluid loss.

4. Installation is the reverse of removal. Align the flange marks. Torque the nuts and bolts to 21–22 ft. lbs. (28–30 Nm).

U-JOINT REPLACEMENT

Single Cardan Type U-Joint

▶ **See Figures 47 and 48**

1. Remove the driveshaft.

2. If the front yoke is to be disassembled, matchmark the driveshaft and sliding splined yoke (transmission yoke) so that driveline balance is preserved upon reassembly. Remove the snaprings which retain the bearing caps.

3. Select two sockets, one small enough to pass through the yoke holes for the bearing caps, the other large enough to receive the bearing cap.

4. Using a vise or a press, position the small and large sockets on either side of the U-joint. Press in on the smaller socket so that it presses the opposite bearing cap out of the yoke and into the larger socket. If the cap does not come all the way out, grasp it with a pair of pliers and work it out.

5. Reverse the position of the sockets so that the smaller socket presses on the cross. Press the other bearing cap out of the yoke.

6. Repeat the procedure on the other bearings.

7. To install, grease the bearing caps and needles thoroughly if they are not pregreased. Start a new bearing cap into one side of the yoke. Position the cross in the yoke.

8. Select two sockets small enough to pass through the yoke holes. Put the sockets against the cross and the cap, and press the bearing cap ¼ in. (6mm) below the surface of the yoke. If there is a sudden increase in the force needed to press the cap into place, or if the cross starts to bind, the bearings are cocked, They must be removed and restarted in the yoke. Failure to do so will greatly reduce the life of the bearing.

9. Install a new snapring.

10. Start a new bearing into the opposite side. Place a socket on it and press in until the opposite bearing contacts the snapring.

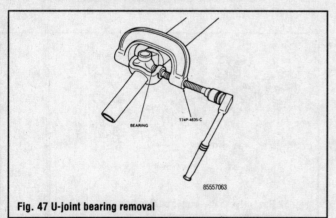

85557063

Fig. 47 U-joint bearing removal

11. Install a new snapring. It may be necessary to grind the facing surface of the snapring slightly to permit easier installation.

12. Install the other bearings in the same manner.

13. Check the joint for free movement. If binding exists, smack the yoke ears with a brass or plastic faced hammer to seat the bearing needles. Do not strike the bearings, and support the shaft firmly. Do not install the driveshaft until free movement exists at all joints.

Double Cardan Type U-Joint

▶ **See Figures 45, 49 and 50**

1. Place the driveshaft on a suitable workbench.

2. Matchmark the positions of the spiders, the center yoke and the centering socket yoke as related to the stud yoke which is welded to the front of the driveshaft tube.

➡**The spiders must be assembled with the bosses in their original position to provide proper clearance.**

3. Remove the snaprings that secure the bearings in the front of the center yoke.

4. Position the U-joint tool, T74P–4635–C or equivalent, on the center yoke. Thread the tool clockwise until the bearing protrudes approximately ⅜ in. (10mm) out of the yoke.

5. Position the bearing in a vice and tap on the center yoke to free it from the bearing. Lift the 2 bearing cups from the spider.

6. Re-position the tool on the yoke and move the remaining bearing in the opposite direction so that it protrudes approximately ⅜ in. (10mm) out of the yoke.

7. Position the bearing in a vice. Tap on the center yoke to free it from the bearing. Remove the spider from the center yoke.

8. Pull the centering socket yoke off the center stud. Remove the rubber seal from the centering ball stud.

9. Remove the snaprings from the center yoke and from the driveshaft yoke.

10. Position the tool on the driveshaft yoke and press the bearing outward until the inside of the center yoke almost contacts the slinger ring at the front of the driveshaft yoke. Pressing beyond this point can distort the slinger ring interference point.

11. Clamp the exposed end of the bearing in a vice and drive on the center yoke with a soft-faced hammer to free it from the bearing.

12. Reposition the tool and press on the spider to remove the opposite bearing.

13. Remove the center yoke from the spider. Remove the spider form the driveshaft yoke.

14. Clean all serviceable parts in cleaning solvent. If using a repair kit, install all of the parts supplied in the kit.

15. Remove the clamps on the driveshaft boot seal. Discard the clamps.

16. Note the orientation of the slip yoke to the driveshaft tube for installation during assembly. Mark the position of the slip yoke to the driveshaft tube.

17. Carefully pull the slip yoke from the driveshaft. Be careful not to damage the boot seal.

18. Clean and inspect the spline area of the driveshaft.

To assemble:

19. Lubricate the driveshaft slip splines with Multi-purpose Long-Life lubricant C1AZ–19490–B or equivalent.

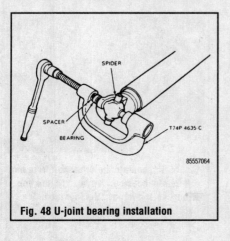

85557064

Fig. 48 U-joint bearing installation

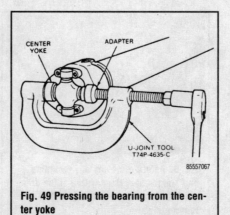

85557067

Fig. 49 Pressing the bearing from the center yoke

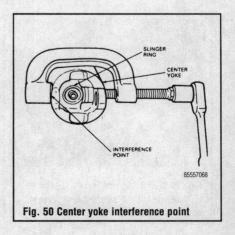

85557068

Fig. 50 Center yoke interference point

20. With the boot loosely installed on the driveshaft tube, install the slip yoke into the driveshaft splines in their original orientation.

21. Using new clamps, install the driveshaft boot in its original position.

22. To assemble the double cardan joint, position the spider in the driveshaft yoke. Make certain the spider bosses (or lubrication plugs on kits) will be in the same position as originally installed. Press in the bearing using the U-joint tool. Then, install the snaprings.

23. Pack the socket relief and the ball with Multi-purpose Long-Life lubricant C1AZ–19490–B or equivalent, then position the center yoke over the spider ends and press in the bearing. Install the snaprings.

24. Install a new seal on the centering ball stud. Position the centering socket yoke on the stud.

25. Place the front spider in the center yoke. Make certain the spider bosses (or lubrication plugs on kits) are properly positioned.

26. With the spider loosely positioned on the center stop, seat the first pair of bearings into the centering socket yoke. Then, press the second pair into the centering yoke. Install the snaprings.

27. Apply pressure on the centering socket yoke and install the remaining bearing cup.

28. If a kit was used, lubricate the U-joint through the grease fitting, using Multi-purpose Long-Life lubricant C1AZ–19490–B or equivalent.

Rear Driveshaft and U-Joints

REMOVAL & INSTALLATION

Navajo and B Series Pick-up Models

▶ **See Figures 51 and 52**

1. Raise and safely support the vehicle.

2. Mark the driveshaft in relation to the rear axle flange. If necessary, mark the relation of the driveshaft to the transfer case flange.

3. If equipped with a center bearing assembly, remove the retaining bolts and the spacers under the center bearing bracket, if installed.

4. Remove the attaching bolts and disconnect the driveshaft from the rear axle flange.

5. On 2WD models, slide the driveshaft rearward until the slip yoke clears the transmission extension housing and remove the driveshaft. Plug the extension housing to prevent fluid leakage.

6. On 4WD models, remove the bolts attaching the driveshaft to the transfer case flange and remove the driveshaft.

To install:

7. On 2WD models, lubricate the splines of the slip yoke. Remove the plug from the extension housing and install the driveshaft assembly. Do not allow the slip yoke to bottom on the output shaft with excessive force.

8. On 4WD models, install the driveshaft to the transfer case flange, aligning the marks that were made during removal. Install the attaching bolts and tighten to 61–87 ft. lbs. (83–118 Nm) if equipped with constant velocity U-joints or 12–16 ft. lbs. (17–22 Nm) if equipped with double cardan U-joints.

9. Connect the driveshaft to the rear axle flange, aligning the marks that were made during removal. Install the retaining bolts and tighten to 70–95 ft. lbs. (95–129 Nm).

10. If equipped, install the center bearing attachment bolts and tighten to 27–37 ft. lbs. (37–50 Nm). Make sure the center bearing bracket is installed "square" to the vehicle. If spacers were installed under the center bearing bracket, make sure they are reinstalled.

11. Lower the vehicle.

MPV Models

▶ **See Figures 53 thru 62**

1. Raise and safely support the vehicle.

2. Stuff a rag into the CV U-joint to hold the driveshaft straight and prevent damage to the boot.

3. Matchmark the flanges and remove the mounting nuts and bolts at the differential.

4. Remove the bolts at the center bearing support assembly.

5. If rear wheel drive only, remove the driveshaft from the transmission. If equipped with 4WD, remove the driveshaft from the transfer case. Cap the opening to prevent spillage of fluid.

6. Installation is the reverse of removal. Align the flange marks when installing. Torque the mounting bolts at the differential to 37–43 ft. lbs. (50–58 Nm). Torque the bolts for the center support to 27–39 ft. lbs. (37–53 Nm).

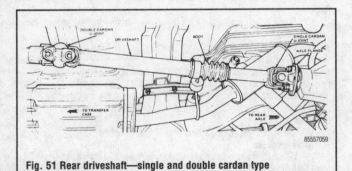

Fig. 51 Rear driveshaft—single and double cardan type

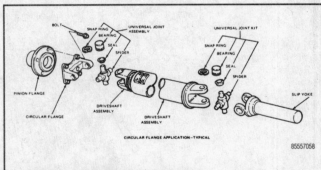

Fig. 52 Rear driveshaft—single cardan type

Fig. 53 Stuff a rag into the CV U-joint to hold the driveshaft straight and prevent damage to the boot

Fig. 54 Before removing any mounting nuts, matchmark the position of the driveshaft to the differential for correct reassembly

Fig. 55 To separate the driveshaft from the differential housing, use two, 14 mm box wrenches and remove the four mounting nuts

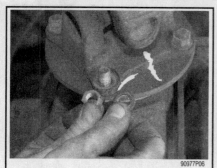

Fig. 56 Be careful not to lose the washer when removing the driveshaft-to-differential mounting nuts

Fig. 57 Using a 14mm socket, loosen the ground wire retaining bolt . . .

Fig. 58 . . . then remove the bolt, separating the ground wire from the driveshaft center bearing

Fig. 59 Remove the driveshaft center bearing mounting bolts

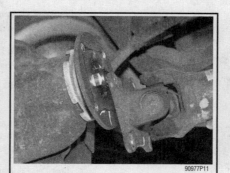

Fig. 60 After removing the center bearing mounting bolts, separate the driveshaft from the differntial housing . . .

Fig. 61 . . . then, while supporting the driveshaft assembly, slide the driveshaft straight out of the extension housing

Fig. 62 After removing the driveshaft, install a plug such as the one pictured, into the opening of the extension housing to prevent transmission fluid from dripping out

U-JOINT REPLACEMENT

Single Cardan Type U-Joint

For replacement procedures for the single cardan U-joint, refer to U-JOINT REPLACEMENT under "Front Driveshaft and U-Joints" earlier in this section.

Double Cardan Type U-Joint

For replacement procedures for the double cardan U-joint, refer to U-JOINT REPLACEMENT under "Front Driveshaft and U-Joints" earlier in this section.

Constant Velocity (CV) Type U-Joint

The CV U-joint is found on all MPV model rear driveshafts. This U-joint is not a servicable component. If the CV U-joint requires service, the driveshaft must be replaced.

DRIVESHAFT BALANCING

▶ See Figures 63, 64 and 65

Unbalance

Propeller shaft vibration increases as the vehicle speed is increased. A vibration that occurs within a specific speed range is not usually caused by a propeller shaft being unbalanced. Defective universal joints, or an incorrect propeller shaft angle, are usually the cause of such a vibration.

If propeller shaft is suspected of being unbalanced, it can be verified with the following procedure.

➡Removing and re-indexing the propeller shaft 180° relative to the yoke may eliminate some vibrations.

1. Raise and safely support the vehicle securely on jackstands.
2. Clean all the foreign material from the propeller shaft and the universal joints.
3. Inspect the propeller shaft for missing balance weights, broken welds, and bent areas. If the propeller shaft is dented or bent, it must be replaced.
4. Inspect the universal joints to ensure that they are not worn, are properly installed, and are correctly aligned with the shaft.
5. Check the universal joint clamp bolt torque.
6. Remove the wheels and tires. Install the wheel lug nuts to retain the brake drums or rotors.
7. Mark and number the shaft six inches (15.24cm) from the yoke end at four positions 90° apart.
8. Run and accelerate the vehicle until vibration occurs. Note the intensity and speed the vibration occurred. Stop the engine.
9. Install a screw clamp at any position.

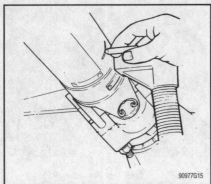

Fig. 63 Mark and number the shaft (yoke end) at four positions 90° apart.

90977G15

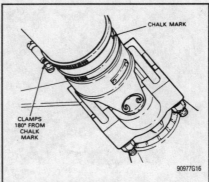

Fig. 64 If the vibration decreases, install a second clamp

90977G16

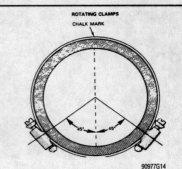

Fig. 65 If the second clamp causes additional vibration, rotate the clamps in opposite directions

90977G14

10. Start the engine and re-check for vibration. If there is little or no change in vibration, move the clamp to one of the other three positions. Repeat the vibration test.

11. If there is no difference in vibration at the other positions, the source of the vibration may not be propeller shaft.

12. If the vibration decreased, install a second clamp and repeat the test.

13. If the additional clamp causes additional vibration, rotate the clamps (¼ inch above and below the mark). Repeat the vibration test.

14. Increase distance between the clamp screws and repeat the test until the amount of vibration is at the lowest level. Bend the slack end of the clamps so the screws will not loosen.

15. If the vibration remains unacceptable, apply the same steps to the front end of the propeller shaft.

16. Install the wheel and tires.

17. Lower the vehicle.

Run-out

1. Remove dirt, rust, paint, and undercoating from the propeller shaft surface where the dial indicator will contact the shaft.

2. The dial indicator must be installed perpendicular to the shaft surface.

➡ **Measure front/rear run-out approximately 3 inches (76mm) from the weld seem at each end of the shaft tube for tube lengths over 30 inches (76.2cm).**

3. Measure run-out at the center and ends of the shaft sufficiently far away from weld areas to ensure that the effects of the weld process will not enter into the measurements.

4. Replace the propeller shaft if the run-out exceeds 0.035 inch (0.89mm) on Navajo and B Series Pick-up models, and 0.016 inch (0.40mm) on MPV models.

Center Bearing

REMOVAL & INSTALLATION

Navajo and B Series Pick-up Models

▶ **See Figure 66**

1. Remove the driveshaft from the vehicle.

2. Separate the driveshaft from the coupling shaft maintaining proper orientation.

3. Remove the nut retaining the half round yoke to the coupling shaft and remove the yoke.

4. Check the center bearing support for wear by rotating the outer area while holding the coupling shaft. If any wear or roughness is evident, replace the bearing.

5. Inspect the rubber insulator for evidence of hardness, cracking or deterioration. Replace if damaged in any way.

6. Re-install the coupling shaft yoke.

➡ **Be sure the yoke is re-installed on the coupling shaft in the same orientation as it was originally installed. The orientation is critical so that proper driveshaft balance and U-joint phasing is maintained. Tighten the retaining nut to 100–120 ft. lbs. (135–162 Nm).**

7. Re-assemble the driveshaft to the coupling shaft, maintaining proper orientation.

MPV Models

▶ **See Figures 66, 67 and 68**

The center support bearing is a sealed unit which requires no periodic maintenance. The following procedure should be used if it becomes necessary to replace the bearing. You will need a pair of snapring pliers for this job.

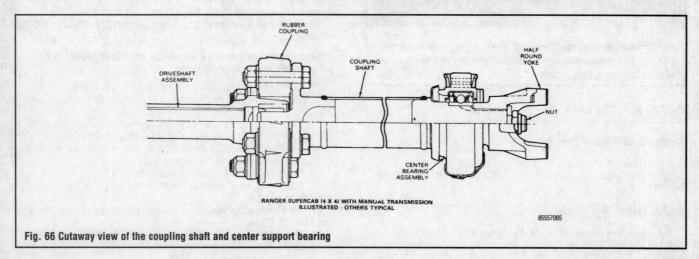

RANGER SUPERCAB (4 X 4) WITH MANUAL TRANSMISSION ILLUSTRATED - OTHERS TYPICAL

85557065

Fig. 66 Cutaway view of the coupling shaft and center support bearing

Fig. 67 Before separating the two halves of the rear driveshaft assembly, matchmark the positioning of the halves for correct reassembly

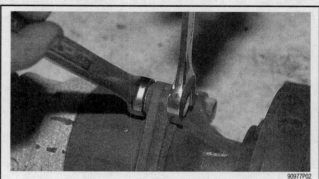

Fig. 68 When separating the front half from the rear half, use two, 14 mm box wrenches and remove the four mounting nuts

1. Remove the driveshaft assembly.
2. To maintain driveline balance, matchmark the rear driveshaft, the center yoke and the front driveshaft so that they may be installed in their original positions.
3. Remove the center universal joint from the center yoke, leaving it attached to the rear driveshaft. See the following section for the correct procedure.
4. Remove the nut and washer securing the center yoke to the front driveshaft.
5. Slide the center yoke off the splines. The rear oil seal should slide off with it.
6. If the oil has remained on top of the snapring, remove and discard the seal. Remove the snapring from its groove. Remove the bearing.
7. Slide the center support and front oil seal from the front driveshaft. Discard the seal.

8. Install the new bearing into the center support. Secure it with the snapring.
9. Apply a coat of grease to the lips of the new oil seals, and install them into the center support on either side of the bearing.
10. Coat the splines of the front driveshaft with grease. Install the center support assembly and the center yoke onto the front driveshaft, being sure to match up the marks made during disassembly.
11. Install the washer and nut. Tighten the nut to 120–130 ft. lbs. (163–177 Nm).
12. Check that the center support assembly rotates smoothly around the driveshaft.
13. Align the mating marks on the center yoke and the rear driveshaft, and assemble the center universal joint.
14. Install the driveshaft. Be sure that the rear yoke and the axle flange re aligned properly.

FRONT DRIVE AXLE

Manual Locking Hubs

DISASSEMBLY & ASSEMBLY

▶ **See Figures 69, 70, 71 and 72**

1. Loosen the front wheel lug nuts.
2. Raise and safely support the front of the vehicle.
3. Remove the lug nuts and wheel/tire assembly.
4. If equipped, remove the lug nut retainer washers from the wheel studs.

➡**Some gentle tapping with a soft faced hammer may help to loosen the locking hub if it seems stuck.**

5. Remove the manual locking hub assembly from the rotor by pulling straight outward.
6. Inspect the O-ring seal on the back side of the hub assembly and, if damaged, replace it.
7. Installation is the reverse of the removal procedure. Ensure that the rotor mounting face is flat and free of burrs, dirt or grease, especially where the O-ring seal makes contact.

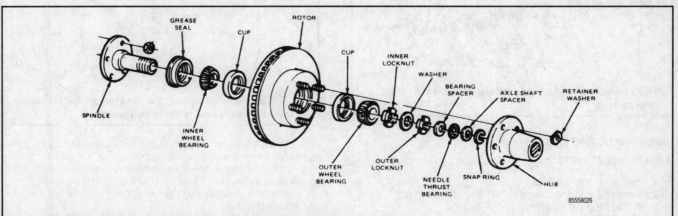

Fig. 69 Exploded view of the manual locking hub assembly and related components

Fig. 70 To remove the manual locking hub, remove the wheel and stud retainers (if equipped), then pull the hub off

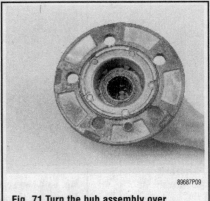

Fig. 71 Turn the hub assembly over . . .

Fig. 72 . . . and inspect this rubber O-ring seal for damage. Replace as needed

Automatic Locking Hubs

DISASSEMBLY & ASSEMBLY

Navajo and 1994–97 B Series Pick-up Models

OUTER HUB COVER

♦ See Figure 73

1. Loosen the front wheel lug nuts.
2. Raise and safely support the front of the vehicle.
3. Remove the lug nuts and wheel/tire assembly.
4. If equipped, remove the lug nut retainer washers from the wheel studs.

➡Some gentle tapping with a soft faced hammer may help to loosen the locking hub cover if it seems stuck.

5. Remove the automatic locking hub cover assembly from the rotor by pulling straight outward.
6. Inspect the O-ring seal on the back side of the hub assembly and, if damaged, replace it.
7. Installation is the reverse of the removal procedure. Ensure that the rotor mounting face is flat and free of burrs, dirt or grease, especially where the O-ring seal makes contact.

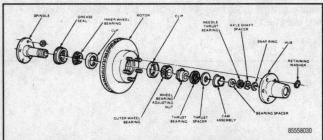

Fig. 73 Exploded view of the automatic locking hubs and related components

INNER HUB LOCKING CAM

♦ See Figures 74 and 75

1. Remove the outer hub cover.
2. Remove the snap-ring from the end of the splined axle shaft.
3. Remove the axle shaft spacer(s).

✳✳ WARNING

Do not pry on the locking cam or thrust spacers during removal. Prying may damage the cam or spacers.

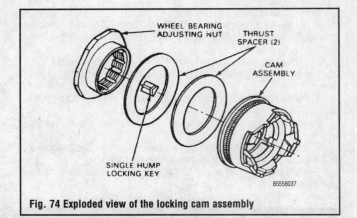

Fig. 74 Exploded view of the locking cam assembly

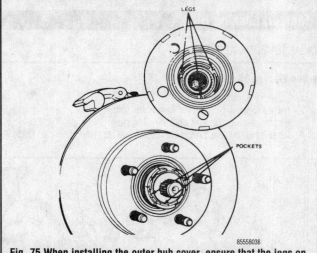

Fig. 75 When installing the outer hub cover, ensure that the legs on the cover seat in the pockets on the locking cam

4. Pull the locking cam assembly and the two thrust spacers (behind cam assembly) from the wheel bearing adjusting nut.
5. Installation is the reverse of the removal procedure. Make sure to install the two thrust spacers first. Also, when pushing or pressing the locking cam into position, ensure that the key in the cam assembly is aligned with the keyway of the front spindle.

✳✳ WARNING

Extreme care must be taken when aligning the locking cam key with the keyway on the front spindle to prevent damage to the fixed cam.

1998 B Series Pick-up Models

While the 1998 B Series Pick-up is technically equipped with automatic locking hubs, the system is mounted to the axle housing itself and is called a vacuum disconnect axle lock. Refer to the procedures in this section.

MPV Models

While the MPV models are technically equipped with automatic locking hubs, the system is mounted to the axle housing itself and referred to as a freewheel mechanism. Refer to the procedures in this section.

Vacuum Disconnect Axle Lock

The vacuum disconnect axle locking system is used on the 1998 B Series Pick-up models only. The axle locking controls are mounted to the axle housing. Most other models use manual or automatic locking hubs at the wheel ends.

REMOVAL & INSTALLATION

◗ **See Figure 76**

1. Raise and safely support the front of the vehicle.

➡**If possible, support the right side of the vehicle slighly higher than the left. This will minimize the amount of axle fluid lost when the center disconnect shift motor cover is removed.**

2. Position a drain pan beneath the center disconnect shift motor cover.
3. Label and disconnect the vacuum lines at the shift motor.
4. Unplug the electrical wire harness connectors from the shift motor.
5. Remove the four shift motor cover-to-axle housing retaining bolts.
6. Pull the cover and shift motor assembly straight out from the axle housing.
7. To disassemble the shift fork and shift motor from the cover, proceed as follows:

   a. Note the position of the shift fork to assure proper assembly.

   b. Remove the outboard snapring that retains the shift fork to the motor shaft and slide the fork off of the shaft.

   c. Remove the inboard snapring that located the shift fork.

   d. Remove the snapring from the motor shaft where the shaft comes through the cover then slide the motor and shaft out from the cover.

To install:

8. Inspect all gaskets and O-ring seals for damage and replace them as required.
9. Inspect the nylon bushings on the shift fork and if worn, replace them.
10. To assemble the shift motor and fork to the cover, proceed as follows:

    a. Lightly lubricate the O-ring on the motor shaft and slide it into the cover until it is fully seated.

b. Install the motor shaft-to-cover snapring.

c. Install the inboard shift fork snapring.

d. Install the shift fork in the same position as was removed.

e. Install the outboard shift fork snapring.

11. Ensure that the locking collar inside the axle assembly slides freely back and forth. Position the locking collar so that the shift fork will engage it when installing.
12. Install the center disconnect assembly into the axle housing. Ensure that the shift fork is engaging the locking collar.
13. Install and tighten the four cover retaining bolts.
14. Connect the vacuum fittings and electrical harness plugs to the shift motor assembly.
15. Ensure that the vehicle is level and check the axle fluid level. Top off the fluid as needed.
16. Lower the vehicle, road test and check for leaks.

Freewheel Mechanism

REMOVAL & INSTALLATION

◗ **See Figure 77**

➡**The Automatic Freewheel Mechanism on 4WD MPV models are used in place of automatic locking hubs.**

1. Disconnect the negative battery cable. Raise and safely support the vehicle. Remove the left front wheel and tire assembly.
2. Drain the fluid from the front differential.
3. Remove the left side halfshaft assembly.
4. Tag and disconnect the vacuum hoses and electrical connector from the control box assembly.
5. Remove and discard the snap pin at the control box assembly.
6. Remove the attaching bolts and remove the joint shaft assembly.
7. Remove the attaching bolts and remove the control box assembly.
8. Remove the gear sleeve from the side of the differential, if necessary.
9. If necessary, remove the output shaft from the differential using a slide hammer.

To install:

10. If removed, install a new clip on the end of the output shaft and install in the differential. Install the gear sleeve, if removed.
11. Install the control box and tighten the attaching bolts to 17–20 ft. lbs. (23–26 Nm).
12. Install the joint shaft assembly and tighten the attaching bolts to 27–40 ft. lbs. (36–54 Nm). Install the attaching nut and tighten to 49–72 ft. lbs. (67–97 Nm).
13. Install a new snap pin at the control box assembly.

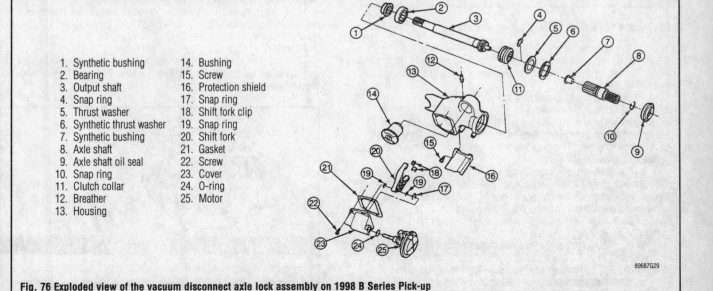

1. Synthetic bushing
2. Bearing
3. Output shaft
4. Snap ring
5. Thrust washer
6. Synthetic thrust washer
7. Synthetic bushing
8. Axle shaft
9. Axle shaft oil seal
10. Snap ring
11. Clutch collar
12. Breather
13. Housing
14. Bushing
15. Screw
16. Protection shield
17. Snap ring
18. Shift fork clip
19. Snap ring
20. Shift fork
21. Gasket
22. Screw
23. Cover
24. O-ring
25. Motor

89687G29

Fig. 76 Exploded view of the vacuum disconnect axle lock assembly on 1998 B Series Pick-up

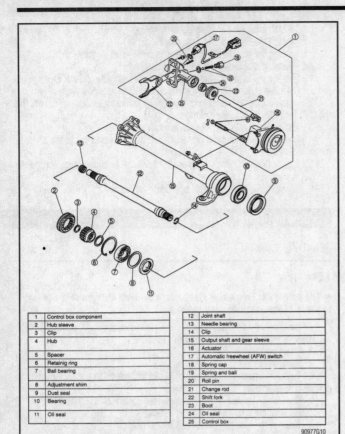

1	Control box component
2	Hub sleeve
3	Clip
4	Hub
5	Spacer
6	Retainig ring
7	Ball bearing
8	Adjustment shim
9	Dust seal
10	Bearing
11	Oil seal

12	Joint shaft
13	Needle bearing
14	Clip
15	Output shaft and gear sleeve
16	Actuator
17	Automatic freewheel (AFW) switch
18	Spring cap
19	Spring and ball
20	Roll pin
21	Change rod
22	Shift fork
23	Boot
24	Oil seal
25	Control box

90977G10

Fig. 77 Exploded view of the components to the automatic freewheel mechanism—MPV

14. Connect the electrical connector and vacuum hoses at the control box assembly.
15. Install the left side halfshaft assembly.
16. Fill the differential with the proper type and quantity of fluid.
17. Install the wheel and tire assembly and lower the vehicle.

Spindle Bearings

REMOVAL & INSTALLATION

Navajo and 1994–97 B Series Pick-up Models

1. Loosen the front wheel lug nuts.
2. Raise and support the vehicle safely. Remove the wheel and tire assembly.
3. Remove the disc brake calipers and support the caliper on the vehicle's frame rail.
4. Remove the hub locks and lock nuts.
5. Remove the hub and rotor.
6. Remove the nuts retaining the spindle to the steering knuckle. Tap the spindle with a plastic or rawhide hammer to jar the spindle from the knuckle.
7. Inspect the needle bearings inside the spindle bore. If worn or damaged, replace as follows:
   a. Place the spindle in a vise on the second step of the spindle. Wrap a shop towel around the spindle or use a brass–jawed vise to protect the spindle.
   b. Remove the oil seal and needle bearing from the spindle with a slide hammer and seal remover tool, 1175–AC or equivalent.
   c. Clean all dirt and grease from the spindle bearing bore. Bearing bore must be free from nicks and burrs.
   d. Place the bearing in the bore with the manufacturer's identification facing outward. Drive the bearing into the bore using spindle bearing replacer tool, T83T–3123–A and drive handle T80T–4000–W or equivalent.
   e. Install the grease seal in the bearing bore with the lip side of the seal

facing towards the tool. Drive the seal in the bore using spindle bearing replacer tool, T83T–3123–A and drive handle T80T–4000–W or equivalent. Coat the bearing seal lip with Multi–Purpose Long Life Lubricant C1AZ–19590–B or equivalent.

To install:
8. Inspect the seal on the axle shaft, and if damaged or worn replace it. Refer to front axle shaft removal & installation procedure in this Section.
9. Install the splash shield and spindle onto the steering knuckle. Install and tighten the spindle nuts to 35–45 ft. lbs. (47–61Nm).

➡**Since the rotor is removed, check that the wheel bearings are properly greased and that the rotor grease seal is in acceptable condition.**

10. Install the rotor on the spindle.
11. Install the wheel bearing, locknut, thrust bearing, snapring and locking hubs.
12. Install the disc brake calipers. Install the wheel and tire assembly.
13. Lower the vehicle. Tighten the lug nuts to specification.

1998 B Series Pick-up Models

The 1998 B Series Pick-up models do not use spindles. Instead they use an internally splined wheel hub which is pressed into a sealed bearing. If the assembly goes bad, it must be replaced as an entire unit. For removal & installation procedures, refer to Section 8.

MPV Models

▶ **See Figure 78**

1. Raise and safely support the vehicle. Remove the wheel and tire assembly.
2. Remove and discard the locknut from the end of the halfshaft.
3. Remove the brake caliper and disc brake rotor. Support the caliper aside with rope or mechanics wire; do not let the caliper hang by the brake hose.
4. Remove the cotter pin and nut and, using a suitable tool, disconnect the tie rod end from the knuckle.
5. Remove the cotter pin and loosen the lower ball joint nut. Separate lower arm from the knuckle using a suitable tool.
6. Remove the knuckle-to-strut bolts and nuts and remove the knuckle/hub assembly from the vehicle.
7. Pry out the inner oil seal from the knuckle.
8. Position the knuckle/hub assembly in a press and, using a suitable driver, press the hub from the knuckle.

➡**If the inner bearing race remains on the hub, position the hub in a vise, secured by the flange. Move the race away from the hub using a hammer and chisel, then position the hub in a press and press the race off of the hub.**

9. Pry out the outer oil seal from the knuckle.
10. Remove the retaining ring and position the knuckle in a press. Using a suitable driver, press the wheel bearing from the knuckle.
11. If necessary, mark the position of the dust shield on the knuckle and remove the dust shield, using a hammer and chisel. Do not reuse the dust cover, if removed.

To install:
12. If the dust cover was removed, mark the new cover in the same place as the old was marked during removal. Align the cover and knuckle marks and press the cover onto the knuckle.

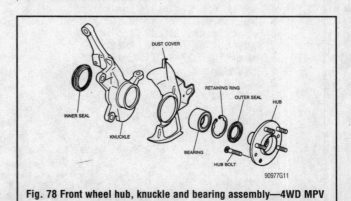

90977G11

Fig. 78 Front wheel hub, knuckle and bearing assembly—4WD MPV

13. Press a new wheel bearing into the knuckle, using a suitable driver. Install the retaining ring and a new outer seal. Apply grease to the seal lip.

14. Press the hub into the knuckle, using a suitable driver. Install a new inner seal and lubricate the seal lip with grease.

15. Install the knuckle/hub assembly onto the strut, install the bolts and nuts and tighten to 69–86 ft. lbs. (93–117 Nm).

16. Install the lower ball joint into the knuckle and tighten the nut to 115–137 ft. lbs. (157–187 Nm). Install a new cotter pin.

17. Connect the tie rod to the knuckle and install the nut. Tighten to 43–58 ft. lbs. (59–78 Nm) and install a new cotter pin.

18. Install the brake rotor and caliper.

19. Install a new locknut on the end of the halfshaft and tighten to 174–231 ft. lbs. (235–314 Nm). After tightening, stake the nut with a blunt chisel.

20. Install the wheel and tire assembly and lower the vehicle. Check the front end alignment.

Axle Shafts and Seals

REMOVAL & INSTALLATION

Navajo and 1994–97 B Series Pick-up Models

▶ **See Figure 79**

1. Loosen the front wheel lug nuts.
2. Raise and support the vehicle safely. Remove the wheel and tire assembly.
3. Remove the disc brake calipers and support the caliper on the vehicle's frame rail.
4. Remove the hub locks and lock nuts.
5. Remove the hub and rotor.
6. Remove the nuts retaining the spindle to the steering knuckle. Tap the spindle with a plastic or rawhide hammer to jar the spindle from the knuckle.
7. Remove the front disc brake rotor shield.

➡ **The left-hand axle shaft is engaged inside of the front carrier assembly. Depending on how the truck is sitting (especially if it is not level), some fluid may leak out of the front carrier assembly. A small drip pan should can be placed underneath the front carrier as a precautionary measure.**

8. Remove the left-hand side axle shaft by pulling the assembly out of the carrier and through the hole in the steering knuckle (spindle mount).
9. Remove the right-hand axle shaft by performing the following:
   a. Remove and discard the right front axle joint boot clamp from the outer axle assembly.
   b. Pull the right-hand axle shaft out of the axle joint boot and stub shaft and through the hole in the steering knuckle (spindle mount).

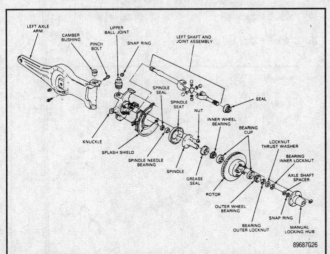

LEFT AXLE ARM
CAMBER BUSHING
PINCH BOLT
UPPER BALL JOINT
SNAP RING
LEFT SHAFT AND JOINT ASSEMBLY
SPINDLE SEAL
SPINDLE SEAT
NUT
SEAL
INNER WHEEL BEARING
BEARING CUP
KNUCKLE
SPLASH SHIELD
SPINDLE NEEDLE BEARING
SPINDLE
GREASE SEAL
ROTOR
OUTER WHEEL BEARING
BEARING OUTER LOCKNUT
LOCKNUT THRUST WASHER
BEARING INNER LOCKNUT
AXLE SHAFT SPACER
SNAP RING
MANUAL LOCKING HUB

89687G26

Fig. 79 Exploded view of the left-hand axle shaft assembly and related components

10. Inspect the seals on the outer axle shaft ends, and replace them if necessary. Replace the seals as follows:
   a. Remove the old seal from the axle shaft by driving them off with a hammer.
   b. Thoroughly clean the axle seal area of the shaft.
   c. Place the shaft in a press and install the new seal using the Spindle/Axle Seal Installer Tool T83T-3132-A, or equivalent.

To install:
11. Install the right-hand axle shaft as follows:
   a. Ensure that the rubber boot is properly installed on the carrier stub shaft. Slide a new outer axle shaft boot clamp onto the rubber boot.

➡ **The model 35 front axle does not use blind, or master, splines. Therefore, special attention should be made to ensure that the yoke ears are in line (in phase) during assembly.**

   b. Slide the right axle shaft assemble through the hole in the steering knuckle, into the rubber boot and engage the splines of the stub shaft. Ensure the splines are fully engaged.
   c. Position the rubber boot and clamp onto the outer axle shaft and crimp the clamp securely on the rubber boot using Keystone Clamp Pliers T63P-9171-A.

12. Install the left-hand axle shaft by sliding it through the hole in the steering knuckle and engaging it into the carrier. Ensure that the shaft is fully seated into the carrier and engage to the splines inside.

13. Install the front disc brake rotor shield, spindle and retaining nuts.
14. Install the front brake rotors, bearings, locknuts and hubs.
15. Install the brake caliper and wheel assembly.
16. Lower the vehicle. Tighten the lug nuts to specification.

1998 B Series Pick-up Models

▶ **See Figures 80, 81, 82, 83 and 84**

❋❋ **WARNING**

Do not perform this procedure unless a new wheel hub nut and washer assembly and a new axle shaft circlip are available. Once removed, these parts must never be reused during assembly.

1. Loosen the front wheel lug nuts.
2. Raise and safely support the vehicle.
3. Remove the wheels.
4. Remove and discard the center wheel hub nut and washer.

❋❋ **WARNING**

Never reuse the wheel hub nut and washer. This nut is a torque prevailing design and cannot be reused.

5. Remove the disc brake caliper and position it aside.

➡ **The hub shaft is a slip fit into the wheel hub and bearing; a press is not normally required.**

6. Ensure that the wheel hub shaft can be pushed inwards. If not, assemble a press to the front wheel studs and press the wheel hub shaft inwards slightly to break it loose.
7. Place a jack under the lower control arm to support it.
8. Remove the upper ball joint-to-steering knuckle retaining bolt and separate the joint from the knuckle.

❋❋ **WARNING**

Support the steering knuckle and do not allow it to drop or swing downwards. This can overstress the CV-boot and joint, causing damage.

9. Remove the outboard CV-joint from the wheel hub by slightly rotating the steering knuckle down, taking care not to overstress the joint or boot, and pulling the CV-joint out from the hub.
10. Use a CV-joint puller and impact slide hammer to pull the inboard CV-joint from the axle housing. You can also use a prytool to carefully pry the CV-joint outward to disengage the internal circlip. Take care to not damage the axle housing seal.

Fig. 80 Remove the wheel hub nut (arrow) and discard it. NEVER reuse the wheel hub nut

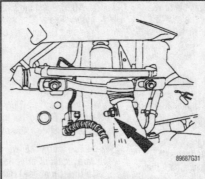

Fig. 81 Remove the upper ball joint-to-steering knuckle retaining bolt

Fig. 82 Rotate the knuckle (1) downward and pull the CV-joint (2) out of the wheel hub by compressing the axle shaft (3) inward

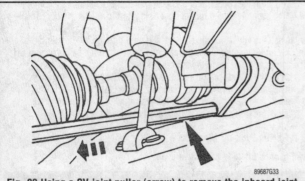

Fig. 83 Using a CV-joint puller (arrow) to remove the inboard joint from the axle housing

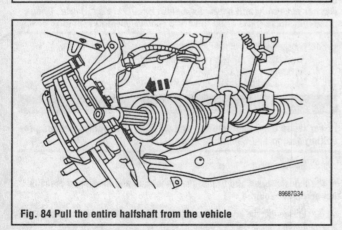

Fig. 84 Pull the entire halfshaft from the vehicle

11. Remove the halfshaft from the vehicle. Remove the circlip from the inboard CV-joint end and discard it.

To install:

12. Install a new circlip to the inboard CV-joint end.

13. Position the halfshaft into the vehicle. Slide the inboard CV-joint end into the axle housing until it is fully seated. Ensure that the circlip is engaged in the housing by attempting to pull the joint outwards.

14. Install the outboard CV-joint end into the wheel hub.

15. Position the upper ball joint to the steering knuckle and install the retaining bolt.

16. Install the disc brake caliper back onto the rotor.

17. Install a new wheel hub nut and washer and tighten to 157–213 ft. lbs. (212–288 Nm).

18. Install the wheel and lug nuts.

19. Lower the vehicle and tighten the lug nuts.

MPV Models

▶ See Figure 85

1. Raise and safely support the vehicle. Remove the wheel and tire assembly.

2. Remove and discard the halfshaft locknut.

3. Disconnect the tie rod end from the knuckle.

4. Remove the caliper and brake rotor from the knuckle. Support the caliper aside with rope or mechanics wire; do not let it hang by the brake hose.

5. Remove the nut and bolts and remove the lower ball joint. Remove the bolts and nuts and remove the knuckle/hub assembly from the strut.

➡ If the halfshaft is stuck to the hub, install a used locknut so it is flush with the end of the shaft, then tap the nut with a soft mallet.

6. Remove the splash shield.

7. Using a suitable prybar, pry out the halfshaft from the differential and remove the halfshaft from the vehicle. Be careful not to damage the dust cover or oil seal.

To install:

8. Install a new clip on the halfshaft. Coat the differential seal with clean transmission fluid.

9. Install the halfshaft in the differential, being careful not to damage the seal. After installation, attempt to pull the halfshaft outward to make sure it does not come out.

10. Install the knuckle/hub assembly to the strut and tighten the nuts to 69–86 ft. lbs. (93–117 Nm).

11. Install the lower ball joint. Tighten the bolts to 75–101 ft. lbs. (102–137 Nm) and the nut to 115–137 ft. lbs. (157–187 Nm). Install a new cotter pin.

12. Install the brake rotor and caliper.

13. Connect the tie rod end to the knuckle.

14. Install a new locknut and tighten to 174–231 ft. lbs. (235–314 Nm). After tightening, stake the locknut using a blunt chisel.

15. Install the splash shield. Install the wheel and tire assembly and lower the vehicle.

16. Check the front end alignment.

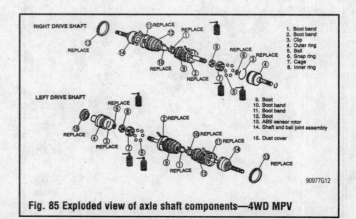

Fig. 85 Exploded view of axle shaft components—4WD MPV

Pinion Seal

➡This service procedure disturbs the pinion bearing preload and this preload must be carefully reset when assembling.

1. Raise the vehicle and support it safely.
2. Drain the differential oil.
3. Remove the wheels and the brake rotors.
4. Mark the driveshaft and the axle companion flange so the driveshaft can be reinstalled in the same position. Remove the driveshaft.
5. Using an inch pound torque wrench on the pinion nut, record the torque required to maintain rotation of the pinion through several revolutions.
6. While holding the companion flange with a suitable tool, remove the pinion nut. Mark the companion flange in relation to the pinion shaft so the flange can be reinstalled in the same position.
7. Using a 3-jawed puller tool or equivalent, remove the rear axle companion flange. Use a small prybar to remove the seal from the carrier.

To install:

8. Make sure the splines of the pinion shaft are free of burrs.
9. Apply grease to the lips of the pinion seal and install, using a seal installation tool.
10. Check the seal surface of the companion flange for scratches, nicks or a groove. Replace the companion flange, as necessary. Apply a small amount of lubricant to the splines. Align the mark on the flange with the mark on the pinion shaft and install the companion flange.

➡The companion flange must never be hammered on or installed with power tools.

11. Install a new nut on the pinion shaft. Hold the companion flange with a suitable tool while tightening the nut.
12. Tighten the pinion nut, rotating the pinion occasionally to ensure proper bearing seating. Take frequent pinion bearing torque preload readings until the original recorded preload reading is obtained.

➡Under no circumstances should the pinion nut be backed off to reduce preload. If reduced preload is required, a new collapsible pinion spacer and pinion nut must be installed.

13. Install the driveshaft and add the correct amount and type of differential fluid to the carrier. Lower the vehicle.

Axle Housing

REMOVAL & INSTALLATION

Navajo and 1994–97 B Series Pick-up Models

▶ See Figure 86

1. Disconnect the negative battery cable.
2. Raise and support the vehicle safely. Remove the wheel and tire assembly.

➡Before removing the driveshaft from the front axle yoke, mark the yoke and driveshaft so that they can be reassembled in the same relative position, thus eliminating driveshaft imbalance.

3. Disconnect the driveshaft from the front axle yoke.
4. Remove the disc brake calipers and support the caliper on the vehicle's frame rail.
5. Remove the cotter pin and nut retaining the steering linkage to the spindle. Disconnect the linkage from the spindle.

➡The axle arm assembly must be supported on the jack throughout spring removal and installation and must not be permitted to hang by the brake hose. If the length of the brake hose is not sufficient to provide adequate clearance for the removal and installation of the spring, the caliper must be removed.

6. Remove the bolt and nut and disconnect the shock absorber from the radius arm bracket.
7. Remove the stud and bolts that connect the radius arm bracket and radius arm to the axle arm. Remove the bracket and radius arm.
8. Remove the pivot bolt securing the right handle axle arm assembly to the crossmember. Remove the keystone clamps securing the axle shaft boot

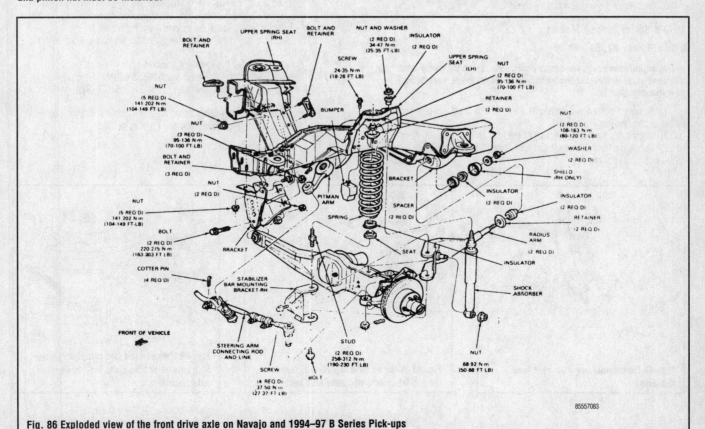

Fig. 86 Exploded view of the front drive axle on Navajo and 1994–97 B Series Pick-ups

85557083

from the axle shaft slip yoke and axle shaft and slide the rubber boot over. Disconnect the right driveshaft from the slip yoke assembly. Lower the jack and remove the right axle arm assembly.

9. Position another jack under the differential housing. Remove the bolt that connects the left axle arm to the crossmember. Lower the jacks and remove the left axle arm assembly.

To install:

10. Position the under the left axle arm assembly. Raise the axle arm until the arm is in position in the left pivot bracket. Install the nut and bolt and tighten to 120–150 ft. lbs. (163–203 Nm).

➡**Do not remove the jack from under the differential housing at this time.**

11. Place new keystone clamps for the axle shaft boot on the axle shaft assembly. Position the right axle arm on a jack and raise the right axle arm so the right driveshaft slides onto the slip yoke stub shaft and the axle arm is in position in the right pivot bracket. Install the nut and bolt and tighten to 120–150 ft. lbs. (163–203 Nm).

➡**Do not remove the jack from the right axle arm at this time.**

12. Position the radius arm and front bracket on the axle arms. Install a new stud and nut on the top of the axle and radius arm assembly and tighten to 160–220 ft. lbs. (217–298 Nm). Install the bolts in the front of the bracket and tighten to 27–37 ft. lbs. (37–50 Nm).

13. Install the seat, spacer retainer and coil spring on the stud and nut. Raise the jack to compress the coil spring. Install the nut and tighten to 70–100 ft. lbs. (95–135 Nm).

14. Connect the shock absorber to the axle arm assembly. Install the nut and tighten to 42–72 ft. lbs. (57–97 Nm).

15. Connect the tie rod ball joint to the spindle. Install the nut and tighten to 50–75 ft. lbs. (68–101 Nm).

16. Lower the jacks from the axle arms.

17. Install the disc brake calipers. Install the wheel and tire assembly. Install the lug nuts and tighten to 85–115 ft. lbs. (115–155 Nm).

18. Connect the front output shaft to the front axle yoke. Install the U-bolts and tighten to 8–15 ft. lbs. (11–20 Nm).

19. Remove the jacks and lower the vehicle.

20. Reconnect the negative battery cable.

1998 B Series Pick-up Models

▸ **See Figures 87, 88 and 89**

➡**The manufacturer recommends using new fasteners when installing the front axle. Before beginning this procedure, make sure to acquire new mounting bolts.**

1. Remove the front axle halfshafts. Refer to axle shaft and seal procedures earlier in this Section.

2. Matchmark the front driveshaft to the front axle companion flange.

3. Unbolt the front driveshaft retaining straps from the front axle assembly and support it out of the way.

⁜⁜ WARNING

Do not allow the driveshaft to hang unsupported, damage to the shaft and or U-joint can occur.

4. Disconnect the axle vent tube.

5. Place a jack under the front axle to support it.

6. Remove the left front axle-to-frame attaching bolt.

7. Remove the remaining two axle-to-frame bolts.

8. Lower the axle assembly and remove it from under the vehicle.

To install:

9. Place the axle assembly on a jack and position it under the vehicle.

10. Raise the axle assembly up and align the three mounting holes.

11. Install the three mounting bolts and tighten them to 45–59 ft. lbs. (60–80 Nm).

12. Connect the axle vent tube.

13. Install the front driveshaft to the axle companion flange, aligning the matchmarks made earlier, then install the retaining straps and tighten the bolts.

14. Install the axle halfshafts.

MPV Models

▸ **See Figure 90**

➡**The differential is removed as a unit with the freewheel mechanism. After removal, the differential can then be separated from the freewheel mechanism, if necessary.**

1. Raise and safely support the vehicle. Remove the wheel and tire assemblies.

2. Remove the splash shield and drain the differential fluid.

3. Remove the halfshafts.

4. Mark the position of the driveshaft on the axle flange and remove the driveshaft.

5. Tag and disconnect the vacuum hoses and electrical connector from the freewheel mechanism control box.

6. Support the differential with a jack.

7. Remove the bolts/nuts attaching the differential/freewheel mechanism assembly in 3 places and lower the assembly from the vehicle.

8. If necessary, separate the freewheel mechanism from the differential.

To install:

9. If removed, install the freewheel mechanism.

10. Raise the differential/freewheel mechanism assembly into position and install the attaching bolts/nuts. Tighten to 49–72 ft. lbs. (67–97 Nm). Remove the jack.

11. Install the remaining components in the reverse order of their removal. Fill the differential with the proper type and quantity of fluid.

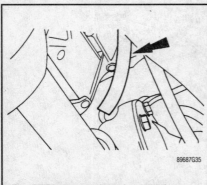

89687G35

Fig. 87 Disconnect the axle vent tube at the axle

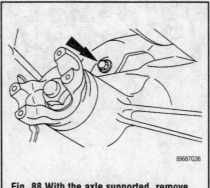

89687G36

Fig. 88 With the axle supported, remove the left front axle-to-frame bolt first

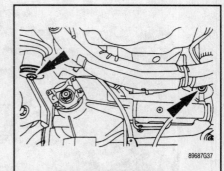

89687G37

Fig. 89 Remove the two remaining axle-to-frame attaching bolts then lower the axle housing

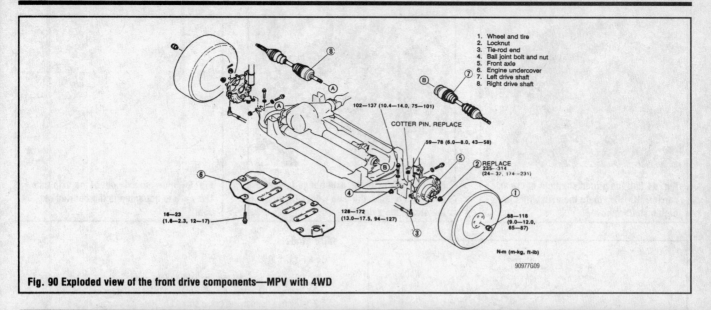

1. Wheel and tire
2. Locknut
3. Tie-rod end
4. Ball joint bolt and nut
5. Front axle
6. Engine undercover
7. Left drive shaft
8. Right drive shaft

102—137 (10.4—14.0, 75—101)

COTTER PIN, REPLACE

59—78 (6.0—8.0, 43—58)

REPLACE
235—314
(24—32, 174—231)

16—23
(1.6—2.3, 12—17)

128—172
(13.0—17.5, 94—127)

88—118
(9.0—12.0,
65—87)

N-m (m-kg, ft-lb)

90977G09

Fig. 90 Exploded view of the front drive components—MPV with 4WD

REAR AXLE

Axle Shaft, Bearing and Seal

REMOVAL & INSTALLATION

Navajo and B Series Pick-up Models

▶ **See Figures 91 thru 98**

1. Disconnect the negative battery cable.
2. Raise and support the vehicle safely.
3. Remove the rear wheels and brake drums.
4. Drain the rear axle lubricant.
5. For all axles except 3.73:1 and 4.10:1 ratio:
   a. Remove the differential pinion shaft lock bolt and differential pinion shaft.

➡**The pinion gears may be left in place. Once the axle shafts are removed, reinstall the pinion shaft and lock bolt.**

   b. Push the flanged end of the axle shafts toward the center of the vehicle and remove the C-lockwasher from the end of the axle shaft.
   c. Remove the axle shafts from the housing. If the seals and/or bearing are not being replaced, be careful not to damage the seals with the axle shaft splines upon removal.
6. For 3.73:1 and 4.10:1 ratio axles:
   a. Remove the pinion shaft lock bolt. Place a hand behind the differential case and push out the pinion shaft until the step contacts the ring gear.

   b. Remove the C-lockwasher from the axle shafts.
   c. Remove the axle shafts from the housing. If the seals and/or bearing are not being replaced, be careful not to damage the seals with the axle shaft splines upon removal.
7. Insert the wheel bearing and seal remover, T85L-1225-AH or equivalent, and a slide hammer into the axle bore and position it behind the bearing so the tanks on the tool engage the bearing outer race. Remove the bearing and seal as a unit.

To install:

8. If removed, lubricate the new bearing with rear axle lubricant and install the bearing into the housing bore. Use axle tube bearing replacer, T78P-1225-A or equivalent.
9. Apply Multi-Purpose Long-Life Lubricant, or equivalent, between the lips of the axle shaft seal.
10. Install a new axle shaft seal using axle tube seal replacer T78P-1177-A or equivalent.

➡**To permit axle shaft installation on 3.73:1 and 4.10:1 ratio axles, make sure the differential pinion shaft contacts the ring gear before performing Step 11.**

11. Carefully slide the axle shaft into the axle housing, making sure not to damage the oil seal. Start the splines into the side gear and push firmly until the button end of the axle shaft can be seen in the differential case.
12. Install the C-lockwasher on the end of the axle shaft splines, then pull the shaft outboard until the shaft splines engage the C-lockwasher seats in the counterbore of the differential side gear.

89687P03

Fig. 91 To remove the axle, first remove the rear axle cover and drain the fluid

89687P04

Fig. 92 Next, loosen the pinion shaft lock bolt . . .

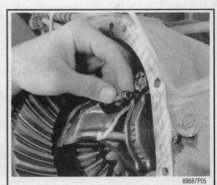

89687P05

Fig. 93 . . . and remove it from the axle carrier

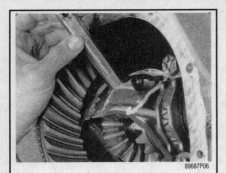

Fig. 94 Pull the pinion shaft out of the axle carrier. DO NOT rotate the axle with the pinion shaft removed!

Fig. 95 Push in on the axle flange (wheel side) and remove the axle C-lock (A) from the end of the axle (B)

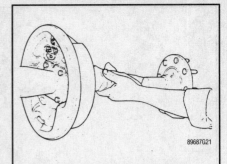

Fig. 96 Slide the axle out of the axle tube. Use care to not damage the bearing or seal

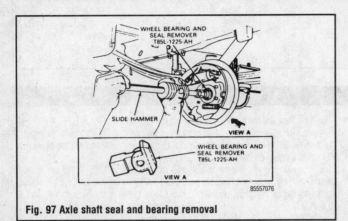

Fig. 97 Axle shaft seal and bearing removal

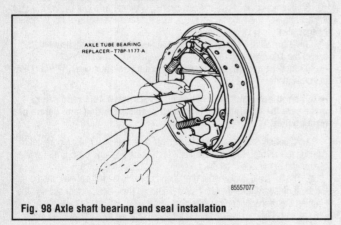

Fig. 98 Axle shaft bearing and seal installation

13. Position the differential pinion shaft through the case and pinion gears, aligning the hole in the shaft with the lock screw hole. Install the lock bolt and tighten to 15–22 ft. lbs. (21–29Nm).

14. Clean the gasket mounting surface on the rear axle housing and cover. Apply a continuous bead of Silicone Rubber Sealant ESE-M4G195-A or equivalent to the carrier casting face.

15. Install the cover and tighten the retaining bolts to 25–35 ft. lbs. (20–34 Nm).

➡The cover assembly must be installed within 15 minutes of application of the silicone sealant.

16. Add lubricant until it is ¼ in. (6mm) below the bottom of the filler hole in the running position. Install the filler plug and tighten to 15–30 ft. lbs. (20–41Nm).

MPV Models

▶ See Figure 99

1. Raise and support the rear end on jackstands.
2. Remove the wheel, then the brake caliper and rotor assemblies.
3. Remove the parking brake shoes.
4. Remove the parking brake cable retainer.
5. Remove the bolts securing the backing plate and bearing housing.
6. Slide the axle shaft from the axle housing. Be careful to avoid damaging the oil seal with the shaft.
7. If the seal in the axle housing is damaged in any way, it must be replaced. The seal can be removed using a slide hammer and adapter.
8. Remove two of the backing plate bolts, diagonally from each other.
9. Using a grinding wheel, grind down the bearing retaining collar in one spot, until about 5mm remains before you get to the axle shaft. Place a chisel at this point and break the collar. Be careful to avoid damaging the shaft.

✳✳ CAUTION

Wear some kind of protective goggles when grinding the collar and breaking the collar from the shaft!

10. Using a press or puller, remove the hub and bearing assembly from the shaft. Remove the spacer from the shaft.
11. Remove the bearing and seal from the hub.
12. Using a drift, tap the race from the hub.
13. Check all parts for wear or damage. If either race is to be replaced, both must be replaced. The race in the axle housing can be removed with a slide hammer and adapter. It's a good idea to replace the bearing and races as a set. It's also a good idea to replace the seals, regardless of what other service is being performed.
14. The outer race must be installed using an arbor press. The inner race can be driven into place in the axle housing.

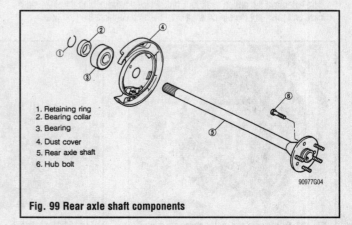

1. Retaining ring
2. Bearing collar
3. Bearing
4. Dust cover
5. Rear axle shaft
6. Hub bolt

Fig. 99 Rear axle shaft components

15. Pack the hub with lithium based wheel bearing grease.

16. Tap a new oil seal into the axle housing until it is flush with the end of the housing. Coat the seal lip with wheel bearing grease.

17. Install a new spacer on the shaft with the larger flat surface up.

18. Install a new seal in the hub.

19. Thoroughly pack the bearing with clean, lithium based, wheel bearing grease. If one is available, use a grease gun adapter meant for packing bearings. These are available at all auto parts stores.

20. Place the bearing in the hub, and, using a press, press the hub and bearing assembly onto the shaft.

21. Press the new collar onto the shaft. The press pressure for the collar is critical. Press pressures should be 9,240-13,420 lb. (4,200-6,100 kg).

22. Install one shaft in the housing being very careful to avoid damaging the inner seal.

23. If only on shaft was being serviced, the other must now be removed to check bearing play on the serviced axle. If both shafts were removed, leave the other one out for now.

24. Tighten the backing plate bolts on the one installed axle to 80 ft. lbs. (108 Nm).

25. Mount a dial indicator on the backing plate, with the pointer resting on the axle shaft flange. Check the axial play. Standard bearing play should be 0.0224 inches (0.57mm).

26. If play is not within specifications, shims are available for correcting it.

27. Install the other shaft and torque the backing plate bolts. Check the play as on the first shaft.

28. Install the regular and parking brake system components. Install the wheels. Bleed the brake system.

Pinion Oil Seal

REMOVAL & INSTALLATION

♦ **See Figures 100 and 101**

1. Disconnect the negative battery cable.

2. Raise and support the vehicle safely. Allow the axle to drop to rebound position for working clearance.

3. Remove the rear wheels and brake drums, or calipers if equipped with rear disc brakes. No drag must be present on the axle.

4. Mark the companion flanges and U-joints for correct reinstallation position.

5. Remove the driveshaft.

6. Using an inch pound torque wrench and socket on the pinion yoke nut measure the amount of torque needed to maintain differential rotation through several clockwise revolutions. Record the measurement.

7. Use a suitable tool to hold the companion flange. Remove the pinion nut.

8. Place a drain pan under the differential. Clean the area around the seal and mark the yoke-to-pinion relation.

9. Use a 2-jawed puller to remove the companion flange.

10. Remove the seal with a small prybar and/or locking pliers and hammer.

To install:

11. Thoroughly clean the oil seal bore.

➡**If you are not absolutely certain of the proper seal installation depth, the proper seal driver must be used. If the seal is misaligned or damaged during installation, it must be removed and a new seal installed.**

12. Drive the new seal into place with a seal driver such as T83T-4676-A. Coat the seal lip with clean, waterproof wheel bearing grease.

13. Coat the splines with a small amount of wheel bearing grease and install the yoke, aligning the matchmarks. Never hammer the yoke onto the pinion!

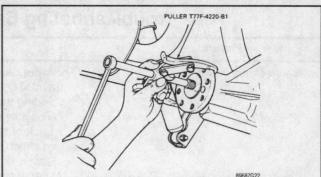

Fig. 100 Use a 2-jawed puller to remove the driveshaft companion flange

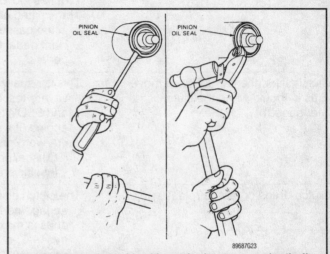

Fig. 101 Remove the seal by either prying it out, or grasping the lip edge with locking pliers and tapping it out of the housing

14. Install a new nut on the pinion.

15. Hold the yoke with a holding tool. Tighten the pinion nut, taking frequent turning torque readings until the original preload reading is attained. If the original preload reading, that you noted before disassembly, is lower than the specified reading of 8–14 inch lbs. (1–2 Nm) for used bearings; 16–29 inch lbs. (2–3 Nm) for new bearings, keep tightening the pinion nut until the specified reading is reached. If the original preload reading is higher than the specified values, torque the nut just until the original reading is reached.

✳✳ WARNING

Under no circumstances should the nut be backed off to reduce the preload reading! If the preload is exceeded, the yoke and bearing must be removed and a new collapsible spacer must be installed. The entire process of preload adjustment must be repeated.

16. Install the driveshaft using the matchmarks. Torque the nuts to 15 ft. lbs. (20 Nm).

17. Lower the vehicle.

18. Reconnect the negative battery cable.

Troubleshooting Basic Clutch Problems

Problem	Cause
Excessive clutch noise	Throwout bearing noises are more audible at the lower end of pedal travel. The usual causes are: • Riding the clutch • Too little pedal free-play • Lack of bearing lubrication A bad clutch shaft pilot bearing will make a high pitched squeal, when the clutch is disengaged and the transmission is in gear or within the first 2″ of pedal travel. The bearing must be replaced. Noise from the clutch linkage is a clicking or snapping that can be heard or felt as the pedal is moved completely up or down. This usually requires lubrication. Transmitted engine noises are amplified by the clutch housing and heard in the passenger compartment. They are usually the result of insufficient pedal free-play and can be changed by manipulating the clutch pedal.
Clutch slips (the car does not move as it should when the clutch is engaged)	This is usually most noticeable when pulling away from a standing start. A severe test is to start the engine, apply the brakes, shift into high gear and SLOWLY release the clutch pedal. A healthy clutch will stall the engine. If it slips it may be due to: • A worn pressure plate or clutch plate • Oil soaked clutch plate • Insufficient pedal free-play
Clutch drags or fails to release	The clutch disc and some transmission gears spin briefly after clutch disengagement. Under normal conditions in average temperatures, 3 seconds is maximum spin-time. Failure to release properly can be caused by: • Too light transmission lubricant or low lubricant level • Improperly adjusted clutch linkage
Low clutch life	Low clutch life is usually a result of poor driving habits or heavy duty use. Riding the clutch, pulling heavy loads, holding the car on a grade with the clutch instead of the brakes and rapid clutch engagement all contribute to low clutch life.

86747G58

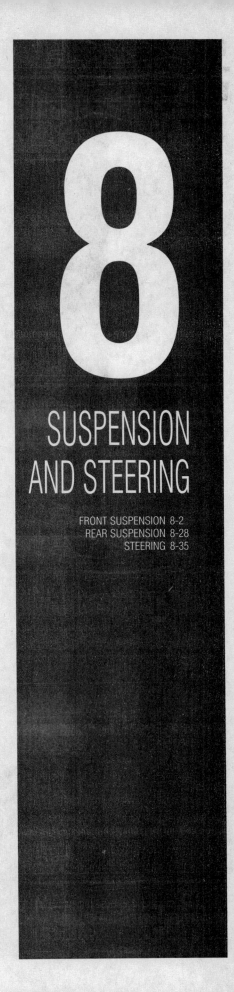

8

SUSPENSION AND STEERING

FRONT SUSPENSION

FRONT SUSPENSION COMPONENTS—EXCEPT MPV

1. Lower ball joint and steering knuckle
2. Shock absorber
3. Radius arm
4. I-beam
5. Outer tie rod end
6. Adjusting sleeve
7. Drag link
8. Stabilizer bar
9. Stabilizer bar link

FRONT SUSPENSION COMPONENTS—MPV

1. Struts
2. Lower ball joints
3. Steering knuckle
4. Compression rods
5. Sway bar (stabilizer bar)
6. Sway bar links
7. Lower control arms
8. Tie rod ends
9. Steering rack assembly

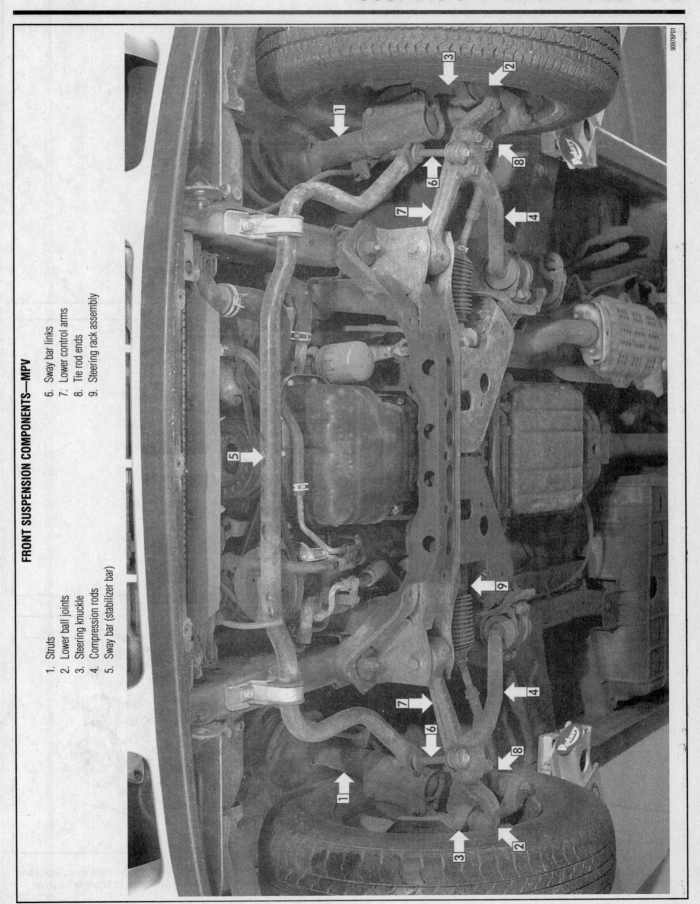

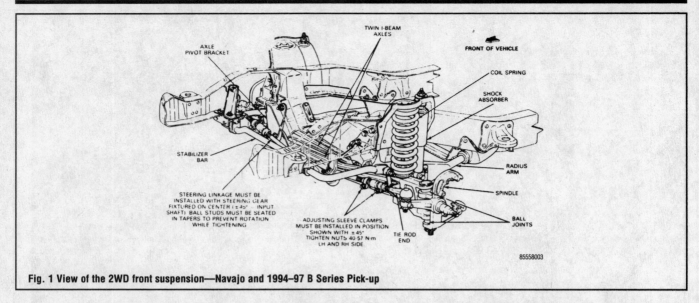

Fig. 1 View of the 2WD front suspension—Navajo and 1994-97 B Series Pick-up

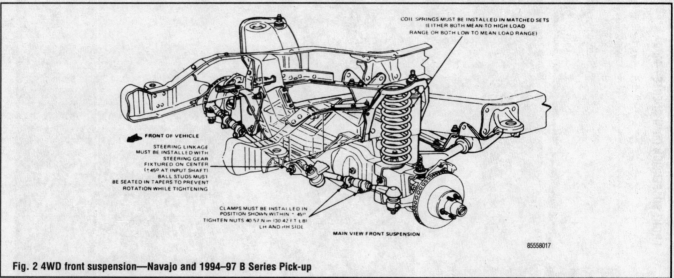

Fig. 2 4WD front suspension—Navajo and 1994-97 B Series Pick-up

1. Front suspension arm bushing joint
2. Frame
3. Nut
4. Front wheel hub and spindle (RH)
5. Front wheel hub and spindle (LH)
6. Hub washer and nut assembly
7. Nut
8. Cotter pin
9. Cotter pin
10. Nut
11. Front wheel driveshaft and joint (RH)
12. Front wheel driveshaft and joint (RH)
13. Front suspension lower arm (RH)
14. Front suspension lower arm (LH)

FRONT OF VEHICLE

Fig. 3 Exploded view of the 4WD 1998 B Series Pick-up front suspension

All Navajo and 1994-97 B Series Pick-up, use a twin I-beam front suspension which utilizes coil springs to support the vehicle and radius rods to locate the I-beam.

1998 B Series Pick-up models use unequal length control arms (Short/Long Arm—SLA) which utilize torsion bars (4WD) or coil springs over the shock absorbers (2WD) to support the vehicle.

All MPV models use a MacPherson-type strut front suspension to support the vehicle and compression rods to locate the lower control arms.

Coil Springs

➡All Navajo and 1994–97 B Series Pick-up and 1998 B Series Pick-up (rear wheel drive only) models utilize coil springs.

REMOVAL & INSTALLATION

Navajo and 1994–97 B Series Pick-up

REAR WHEEL DRIVE

▶ See Figures 4 and 5

1. Raise the front of the vehicle and place jackstands under the frame and a jack under the axle.

�֎ WARNING

The axle must not be permitted to hang by the brake hose. If the length of the brake hoses is not sufficient to provide adequate clearance for removal and installation of the spring, the disc brake caliper must be removed from the spindle. A Strut Spring Compressor, T81P-5310-A or equivalent may be used to compress the spring sufficiently, so that the caliper does not have to be removed. After removal, the caliper must be placed on the frame or otherwise supported to prevent suspending the caliper from the caliper hose. These precautions are absolutely necessary to prevent serious damage to the tube portion of the caliper hose assembly!

2. Disconnect the shock absorber at the lower shock stud. Remove the nut securing the lower retainer to spring seat. Remove the lower retainer.

3. Lower the axle as far as it will go without stretching the brake hose and tube assembly. The axle should now be unsupported without hanging by the brake hose. If not, then either remove the caliper or use Strut Spring Compressor Tool, T81P-5310-A or equivalent. Remove the spring.

4. If there is a lot of slack in the brake hose assembly, a pry bar can be used to lift the spring over the bolt that passes through the lower spring seat.

5. Rotate the spring so the built-in retainer on the upper spring seat is cleared.

6. Remove the spring from the vehicle.

To install:

7. If removed, install the bolt in the axle arm and install the nut all the way down. Install the spring lower seat and lower insulator. On the 1994 Navajo, also install the stabilizer bar mounting bracket and spring spacer.

8. With the axle in the lowest position, install the top of the spring in the upper seat. Rotate the spring into position.

9. Lift the lower end of the spring over the bolt.

10. Raise the axle slowly until the spring is seated in the lower spring upper seat. Install the lower retainer and nut.

11. Connect the shock absorber to the lower shock stud.

12. Remove the jack and jackstands and lower vehicle.

FOUR WHEEL DRIVE

▶ See Figure 6

1. Raise the vehicle and install jackstands under the frame. Position a jack beneath the spring under the axle. Raise the jack and compress the spring.

2. Remove the nut retaining the shock absorber to the radius arm. Slide the shock out from the stud.

3. Remove the nut that retains the spring to the axle and radius arm. Remove the retainer.

4. Slowly lower the axle until all spring tension is released and adequate clearance exists to remove the spring from its mounting.

5. Remove the spring by rotating the upper coil out of the tabs in the upper spring seat. Remove the spacer and the seat.

✖ WARNING

The axle must be supported on the jack throughout spring removal and installation, and must not be permitted to hang by the brake hose. If the length of the brake hose is not sufficient to provide adequate clearance for removal and installation of the spring, the disc brake caliper must be removed from the spindle. After removal, the caliper must be placed on the frame or otherwise supported to prevent suspending the caliper from the brake line hose. These precautions are absolutely necessary to prevent serious damage to the tube portion of the caliper hose assembly!

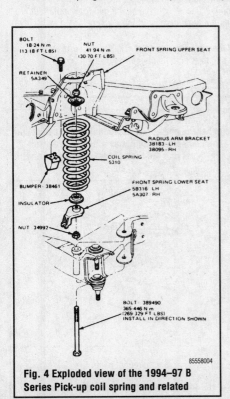

Fig. 4 Exploded view of the 1994–97 B Series Pick-up coil spring and related

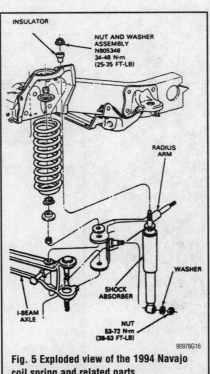
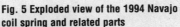

Fig. 5 Exploded view of the 1994 Navajo coil spring and related parts

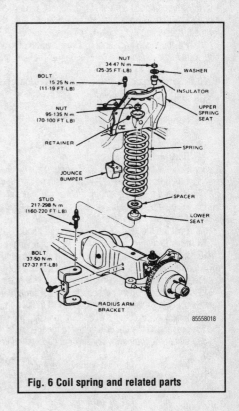

Fig. 6 Coil spring and related parts

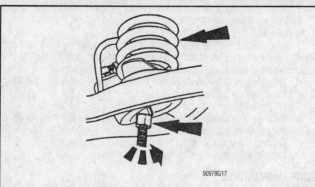

90978G17

Fig. 7 Use a coil spring compressor tool to compress the coil spring

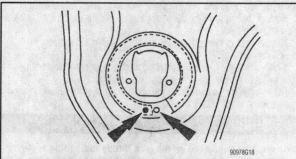

90978G18

Fig. 8 The end of the coil spring must cover the first hole and should not be visible in the second hole

6. If required, remove the stud from the axle assembly.

To install:

7. If removed, install the stud on the axle and torque to 190–230 ft. lbs. Install the lower seat and spacer over the stud.

8. Place the spring in position and slowly raise the front axle. Ensure springs are positioned correctly in the upper spring seats.

9. Position the spring lower retainer over the stud and lower seat and torque the attaching nut to 70–100 ft. lbs.

10. Position the shock absorber to the lower stud and install the attaching nut. Tighten the nut to 41–63 ft. lbs. Lower the vehicle.

1998 B Series Pick-up (rear wheel drive only)

♦ **See Figures 7 and 8**

1. Raise and safely support the vehicle.
2. Remove the front wheel.
3. Remove the front disc brake rotor shield.
4. Remove the front shock absorber.
5. Remove the front sway bar link nut.
6. Compress the front coil spring using a spring comressor tool.
7. Remove the lower ball joint cotter pin and castle nut.
8. Using a pitman arm puller or equivalent puller tool, separate the lower ball joint from the front wheel steering knuckle.
9. Position the knuckle to one side and remove the coil spring.

To install:

10. Install the coil spring (with spring compressor tool installed) into the lower control arm. Be sure that the end of the coil spring covers the first hole on the lower control arm and is not visible in the second hole.

11. Install the front wheel spindle into the lower ball joint and install the castle nut. Tighten the castle nut to 83–113 ft. lbs. (113–153 Nm).

12. Install a new cotter pin. Be sure to install the cotter pin with the loop of the pin pointing to the tire or damage to the tire could result.

13. Install the front sway bar link nut and tighten to 15–21 ft. lbs. (21–29 Nm).

14. Remove the coil spring compressor tool.

15. Install the shock absorber.

16. Install the front disc brake rotor shield.
17. Install the front wheel.
18. Lower the vehicle.

Torsion Bars

Only the 1998 B Series Pick-up models equipped with 4WD use torsion bars.

REMOVAL & INSTALLATION

♦ **See Figures 9 and 10**

➡ **A special tool (Torsion Bar Tool T95T-5310-A) is required for removing the torsion bar. Also, anytime the torsion bar or its adjuster is removed, the vehicle ride height must be checked.**

1. Raise and safely support the front of the vehicle. Place the jackstands so as to support the frame of the vehicle. Do not position the jackstands under the lower control arms and do not use car ramps. The lower control arms must be free to hang unhindered.

2. Remove the torsion bar protector/skid plate from the frame.

3. Remove the torsion bar adjuster bolt from the support nut. Count the number of turns required to remove the bolt and record it for installation.

4. Use Torsion Bar Tool T95T-5310-A, or equivalent, to raise the adjuster lever.

5. Remove the support nut then lower the adjuster lever completely.

6. Slide the torsion bar forward, into the lower control arm, to allow the adjuster lever to be removed.

7. Lower the torsion bar and pull it from the lower control arm.

➡ **Ensure that you do not mix up the right and left-hand torsion bars. They must be installed to the side they were originally removed. If installing a new torsion bar, ensure to order the bar for the proper side of the vehicle.**

To install:

8. Raise the torsion bar and slide it forward into the lower control arm.

9. Slide the torsion bar rearward and engage it into the adjuster lever.

10. Use Torsion Bar Tool T95T-5310-A, or equivalent, to raise the adjuster lever.

11. Install the support nut and remove the tool.

12. Lubricate the tip of the adjuster bolt and start it into the support nut.

13. Tighten the adjuster the same number of turns you recorded earlier, then rotate two additional turns.

14. Install the torsion bar protector/skid plate. Tighten the bolts securely.

15. Lower the vehicle and check the ride height adjustment.

RIDE HEIGHT ADJUSTMENT

♦ **See Figures 11 and 12**

➡ **To perform the ride height check and adjustment requires the use of special slip plates under the front wheels. These plates allow the front suspension to properly settle by bypassing the tires adhesion to the ground.**

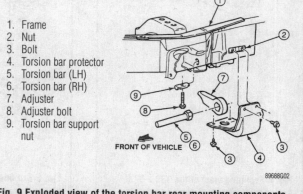

1. Frame
2. Nut
3. Bolt
4. Torsion bar protector
5. Torsion bar (LH)
6. Torsion bar (RH)
7. Adjuster
8. Adjuster bolt
9. Torsion bar support nut

FRONT OF VEHICLE

89688G02

Fig. 9 Exploded view of the torsion bar rear mounting components

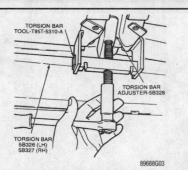

Fig. 10 Use the torsion bar tool to relieve the tension from the bar

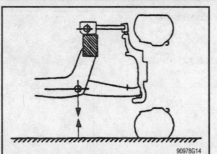

Fig. 11 Measure the distance between the center of the lower control arm bushing bolt and the ground

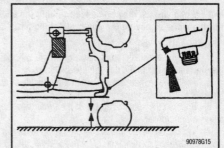

Fig. 12 Measure the distance between the lowest point of the steering knuckle (but not the ball joint) and the ground

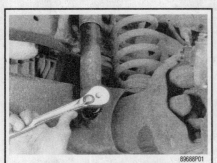

Fig. 13 To remove the front shock absorber, remove the lower radius arm shock retaining nut . . .

Fig. 14 . . . then pull the lower shock mount from the stud

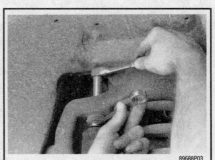

Fig. 15 Next, unbolt the upper shock mount using a second wrench on the mount stud to keep it from spinning . . .

1. Raise and support the vehicle.
2. Position frictionless slip plates under the tires then lower the vehicle onto the slip plates.
3. Bounce the vehicles front and rear suspensions several times to normalize the vehicle static ride height.
4. Measure the distance between the center of the lower control arm bushing bolt and the ground. Record the measurement as dimension A.
5. Measure the distance between the lowest point of the steering knuckle (but not the ball joint) and the ground. Record the measurement as dimension B.
6. Subtract dimension B from dimension A for ride height.
7. Ride height should be 4.33–4.56 in. (110–116mm).
8. To increase the ride height, raise the vehicle and tighten the torsion bar adjuster bolt. Recheck the ride height.
9. To decrease the ride height, raise the vehicle and loosen the torsion bar adjuster bolt. Recheck the ride height.
10. Once proper ride height is established, raise and support the vehicle.
11. Remove the slip plates from under the wheels.
12. Lower the vehicle.

Shock Absorbers

REMOVAL & INSTALLATION

➡Low pressure gas shocks are charged with Nitrogen gas. Do not attempt to open, puncture or apply heat to them. Prior to installing a new shock absorber, hold it upright and extend it fully. Invert it and fully compress and extend it at least 3 times. This will bleed trapped air.

Navajo and 1994–97 B Series Pick-up

♦ See Figures 13, 14, 15 and 16

1. Raise the vehicle, as required to provide additional access and remove the nut attaching the shock absorber to the lower mounting stud on the radius arm.
2. Slide the lower shock absorber end off of the stud.
3. Remove the nut, washer and insulator from the upper shock absorber mount at the frame bracket and remove the shock absorber.

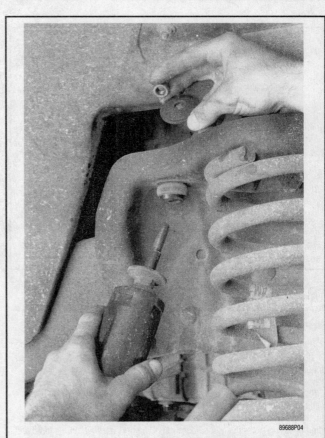

Fig. 16 . . . then pull the shock assembly from the upper spring mount

➡A second wrench may be needed to hold the shock absorber from turning while removing the upper attaching nut.

To install:

4. Position the washer and insulator on the shock absorber rod and position the shock absorber to the upper frame bracket mount.

5. Position the insulator and washer on the shock absorber rod and install the attaching nut loosely.

6. Position the shock absorber to the lower mounting stud and install the attaching nut loosely.

7. Tighten the lower shock attaching bolts to 39–53 ft. lbs. (53–72 Nm), and the upper shock attaching bolts to 25–34 ft. lbs. (34–46 Nm).

1998 B Series Pick-up

▶ See Figure 17

1. Raise the front of the vehicle and place jackstands under the lower control arms. Ensure that the lower shock attaching nuts do not become obstructed by the jackstands.

2. Remove the upper shock-to-frame attaching nut, washer and insulator assembly.

3. Remove the two lower shock-to-control arm attaching nuts.

4. Slightly compress the shock absorber by hand and remove it from the vehicle.

To install:

5. Position the lower washer and insulator on the shock absorber rod and position the shock absorber to the upper frame bracket mount.

6. Position the upper insulator and washer on the shock absorber rod and install the attaching nut loosely.

7. Position the lower shock absorber mounting studs into the control arm and install the attaching nuts loosely.

8. Tighten the lower shock attaching nuts to 15–21 ft. lbs. (21–29 Nm), and the upper shock attaching bolts to 30–40 ft. lbs. (40–55 Nm).

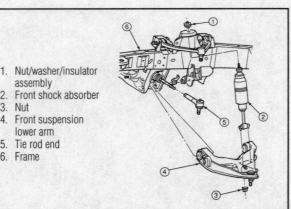

1. Nut/washer/insulator assembly
2. Front shock absorber
3. Nut
4. Front suspension lower arm
5. Tie rod end
6. Frame

89688G05

Fig. 17 Exploded view of the 1998 B Series Pick-up 4WD front shock absorber—rear wheel drive similar

TESTING

▶ See Figure 18

The purpose of the shock absorber is simply to limit the motion of the spring during compression and rebound cycles. If the vehicle is not equipped with these motion dampers, the up and down motion would multiply until the vehicle was alternately trying to leap off the ground and to pound itself into the pavement.

Countrary to popular rumor, the shocks do not affect the ride height of the vehicle. This is controlled by other suspension components such as springs and tires. Worn shock absorbers can affect handling; if the front of the vehicle is rising or falling excessively, the ïfootprintï of the tires changes on the pavement and steering is affected.

The simplest test of the shock absorber is simply push down on one corner of the unladen vehicle and release it. Observe the motion of the body as it is

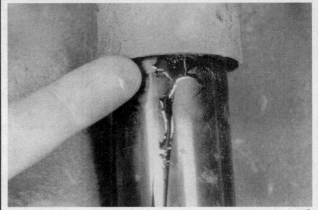

TCCA8P73ï

Fig. 18 When fluid is seeping out of the shock absorber, itís time to replace it

released. In most cases, it will come up beyond it original rest position, dip back below it and settle quickly to rest. This shows that the damper is controlling the spring action. Any tendency to excessive pitch (up-and-down) motion or failure to return to rest within 2-3 cycles is a sign of poor function within the shock absorber. Oil-filled shocks may have a light film of oil around the seal, resulting from normal breathing and air exchange. This should NOT be taken as a sign of failure, but any sign of thick or running oil definitely indicates failure. Gas filled shocks may also show some film at the shaft; if the gas has leaked out, the shock will have almost no resistance to motion.

While each shock absorber can be replaced individually, it is recommended that they be changed as a pair (both front or both rear) to maintain equal response on both sides of the vehicle. Chances are quite good that if one has failed, its mate is weak also.

Struts

Only MPV models utilize a MacPherson-type strut front suspension.

REMOVAL & INSTALLATION

▶ See Figures 19 thru 26

1. Raise and safely support the vehicle. Remove the wheel and tire assembly.

2. Support the lower control arm with a jack.

3. Remove the clip attaching the brake hose to the strut and disconnect the hose from the strut.

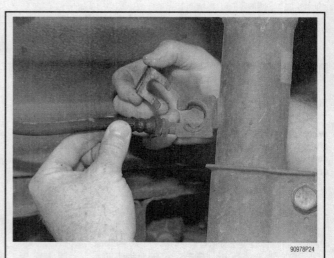

90978P24

Fig. 19 Remove the retaining clip securing the rubber brake hose to the strut

Fig. 20 Using a socket and a backup wrench, remove the two strut-to-steering knuckle nuts and bolts

Fig. 21 Separate the lower portion of the strut from the steering knuckle

Fig. 22 After separating the strut from the knuckle, support the knuckle with a strong piece of wire to prevent possible stress damage to the rubber brake hose

Fig. 23 Remove the igniter, ignition coil and mounting bracket assembly from the top of the strut tower to access the upper strut mounting nuts

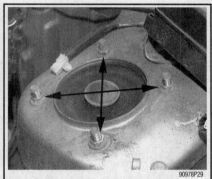

Fig. 24 Remove the four upper strut mounting nuts while supporting the strut assembly

Fig. 25 Carefully remove the strut assembly from the vehicle through the fender well

4. If equipped with 4 wheel ABS, remove the wheel sensor wiring harness bracket mounting bolt from the strut.

5. Remove the strut-to-knuckle attaching bolts and nuts.

6. Working in the engine compartment, remove the 4 attaching nuts from the strut tower and remove the strut assembly from the vehicle. If necessary, remove any components that can hinder the removal of the strut mounting nuts.

7. If the strut must be disassembled, or the coil spring removed, refer to the overhaul procedure later in this section.

To install:

8. Assemble the strut according to the overhaul procedure, if necessary.

9. Install the strut assembly in the strut tower, making sure the white mark on the upper mounting block is in the front-inside direction. Install the attaching nuts and tighten to 34–46 ft. lbs. (47–62 Nm).

10. Install the strut to the knuckle and tighten the attaching bolts and nuts to 69–86 ft. lbs. (93–117 Nm).

11. Position the brake hose on the strut and install the clip. Remove the jack from under the lower control arm.

12. Install the wheel and tire assembly and lower the vehicle. Check the front end alignment.

OVERHAUL

▶ **See Figures 27 thru 36**

1. Secure the strut assembly firmly in a bench vise. Remove the rubber cap from the upper mounting block. Loosen the upper attaching nut, but do not remove it.

Fig. 26 Note the marking to indicate how the strut assembly is installed into the vehicle (OUT w/arrow)

Fig. 27 Mount the complete strut assembly firmly in a bench vise, then remove the top plastic cap from the strut bearing plate

Fig. 28 Before attempting to compress the strut coil spring, loosen the top srut retaining nut a couple of turns, but do NOT remove

Fig. 29 Install a coil spring compressor tool as shown, then use a box wrench and socket to compress the coil . . .

Fig. 30 . . . to the compressed size as shown . . .

Fig. 31 . . . then remove the top retaining nut and two washers

Fig. 32 Pull the bearing plate straight off the top of the strut assembly. Note during installation that it may be necessary to pull up the strut rod through the bumper stop by installing the nut and using two screwdrivers to pry upward (arrows)

Fig. 33 Pull the spring seat/bumper stop/dust boot assembly up off of the strut rod

Fig. 34 Remove the coil spring with the compressor still installed

Fig. 35 Remove the rubber ring from the strut

Fig. 36 Strut assembly components

2. Install a suitable spring compressor and compress the coil spring.

3. Remove the upper attaching nut and slowly relieve the tension on the coil spring, using the spring compressor. When the spring is no longer under tension, remove the spring compressor.

4. Remove the upper mounting block, upper spring seat, spring seat, coil spring, bump stopper and ring rubber from the strut.

5. Apply a suitable rubber grease to the ring rubber and install it on the bump stopper. Install the bump stopper on the strut.

6. Attach the spring compressor to the coil spring and compress the spring.

7. Install the compressed spring on the strut and install the spring seat.

8. Install the upper spring seat. The flat of the strut rod must fit correctly into the upper spring seat.

9. Install the upper mounting block. Install and loosely tighten the upper attaching nut.

10. Remove the spring compressor. Make sure the spring is properly seated in the upper and lower spring seats.

11. Secure the upper spring seat in a vise and tighten the upper attaching nut to 47–59 ft. lbs. (64–80 Nm). Install the rubber cap on the upper mounting block.

Ball Joints

INSPECTION

Navajo and B Series Pick-up Models

♦ See Figure 37

1. Check and adjust the front wheel bearings. Raise and support the vehicle.
2. Have a helper grasp the lower edge of the tire and move the wheel assembly in and out.
3. While the wheel is being moved, observe the lower spindle arm and the lower part of the axle jaw.
4. A 1/32 in. (0.8mm) or greater movement between the lower part of the axle jaw and the lower spindle arm indicates that the lower ball joint must be replaced
5. To check the upper ball joints, while the wheel is being moved, observe the upper spindle arm and the upper part of the axle jaw.
6. A 1/32 in. (0.8mm) or greater movement between the upper part of the axle jaw and the upper spindle arm indicates that the upper ball joint must be replaced

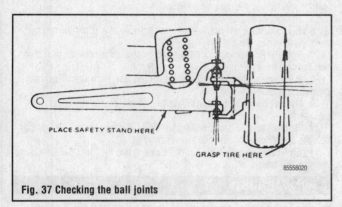

Fig. 37 Checking the ball joints

MPV Models

♦ See Figure 38

Defective ball joints are determined by checking the rotational torque with a special preload attachment and spring scale.
1. Remove the lower control arm from the vehicle.
2. Inspect the control arm for damage and the boots for cracks. Replace them if necessary.
3. Inspect the ball joint for looseness and replace, if necessary.
4. Shake the ball joint stud at least 5 times.
5. Install tool 49 0180 510B or equivalent to the ball joint stud and attach a suitable pull scale to the stud.
6. After shaking the ball joint stud back and forth 5 times, measure the rotational torque while the ball joint stud is rotating. The rotational torque should be 18–30 inch lbs. (2–3 Nm). The pull scale reading should be 4.4–7.7 lbs.

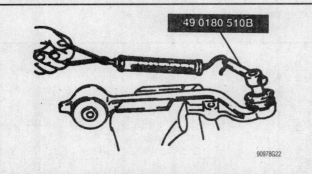

Fig. 38 Inspecting the rotational torque of the ball joint using a spring scale

7. If the reading is not as specified, replace the lower ball joint (4WD) or control arm assembly (rear wheel drive).

REMOVAL & INSTALLATION

Navajo and 1994–97 B Series Pick-up

♦ See Figures 39 and 40

➡The ball joints are arranged such that if the upper ball joint is to be removed, the lower ball joint must be removed first. Conversely, on rear wheel drive vehicles, the upper ball joint must be installed first, before the lower ball joint. On 4WD vehicles, when installing the upper ball joint, the lower ball joint must be installed first. Failure to install the ball joints in the correct order will result in a lack of clearance for the installation tool.

1. Remove the steering knuckle.
2. Place knuckle in vise and remove snapring from bottom ball joint socket if so equipped.
3. Assemble the C-frame, T74P-4635-C, forcing screw, D79T-3010-AE and ball joint remover T83T-3050-A or equivalent on the lower ball joint.

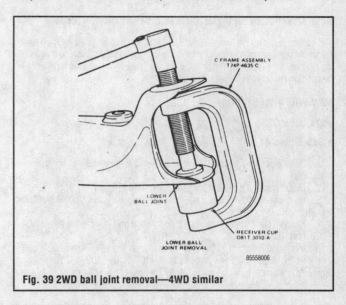

Fig. 39 2WD ball joint removal—4WD similar

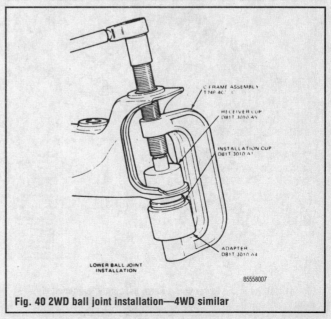

Fig. 40 2WD ball joint installation—4WD similar

4. Turn forcing screw clockwise until the lower ball joint is removed from the steering knuckle.

5. Repeat these steps for the upper ball joint.

➡**Always remove the lower ball joint first**

To install:

6. Clean the steering knuckle bore and insert lower ball joint in knuckle as straight as possible. The lower ball joint doesn't have a cotter pin hole in the stud.

7. Assemble the C-frame, T74P-4635-C, forcing screw, D790T-3010-AE, ball joint installer, T83T-3050-A and receiver cup T80T-3010-A3 or equivalent tools, to install the upper ball joint (on rear wheel drive) or the lower ball joint (on 4WD).

8. Turn the forcing screw clockwise until the upper (rear wheel drive) or lower (4WD) ball joint is firmly seated.

➡**If the ball joint cannot be installed to the proper depth, realignment of the receiver cup and ball joint installer will be necessary.**

9. Repeat these steps for the remaining ball joint.

10. Be sure to install the snapring on the lower ball joint.

11. Install the steering knuckle.

Rear Wheel Drive MPV and All 1998 B Series Pick-up Models

The ball joints on rear wheel drive MPV and all 1998 B Series Pick-up models are integral with the control arms. If the ball joint is defective, the entire control arm must be replaced. Refer to the appropriate control arm removal and installation procedures later in the section.

MPV With 4-Wheel Drive

BALL JOINT

▶ **See Figure 41**

1. Raise and safely support the vehicle. Remove the wheel and tire assembly.

2. Disconnect the sway bar from the lower control arm.

3. Remove the cotter pin and nut from the lower ball joint stud. Separate the ball joint from the knuckle.

4. Remove the 2 upper bolts, one through-bolt and remove the ball joint.

To install:

5. Install the ball joint to the lower control arm. Tighten the two upper ball joint-to-control arm bolts and washers to 75–101 ft. lbs. (102–137 Nm). Tighten the through-bolt and nut to 94–127 ft. lbs. (128–172 Nm).

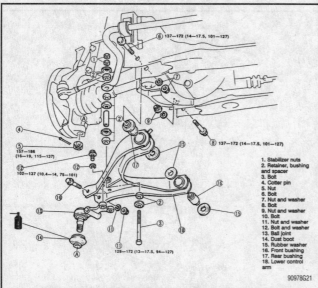

1. Stabilizer nuts
2. Retainer, bushing and spacer
3. Bolt
4. Cotter pin
5. Nut
6. Bolt
7. Nut and washer
8. Bolt
9. Nut and washer
10. Bolt
11. Nut and washer
12. Bolt and washer
13. Ball joint
14. Dust boot
15. Rubber washer
16. Front bushing
17. Rear bushing
18. Lower control arm

90978G21

Fig. 41 Ball joint and lower control arm assembly, exploded view—4WD

6. Install the ball stud into the steering knuckle. Torque the nut to 115–137 ft. lbs. (157–186 Nm) and install a new cotter pin.

7. Connect the sway bar to the lower control arm.

8. Install the wheel and tire assembly and lower the vehicle.

Knuckle and Spindle

REMOVAL & INSTALLATION

Navajo and 1994–97 B Series Pick-up

REAR WHEEL DRIVE

▶ **See Figure 42**

1. Raise the front of the vehicle and install jackstands.

2. Remove the wheel and tire assembly.

3. Remove the caliper assembly from the rotor and hold it out of the way with wire.

4. Remove the dust cap, cotter pin, nut, nut retainer, washer, and outer bearing, and remove the rotor from the spindle.

5. Remove brake dust shield.

6. Disconnect the steering linkage from the spindle and spindle arm by removing the cotter pin and nut.

7. With Tie Rod removal tool 3290-D or equivalent remove the tie rod end from the spindle arm.

8. If equipped, unbolt the front wheel ABS sensor and wire harness from the steering knuckle.

9. Remove the cotter pin and the castellated nut from the lower ball joint stud.

10. Remove the axle clamp bolt from the axle. Remove the camber adjuster from the upper ball joint stud and axle beam.

11. Strike the area inside the top of the axle to pop the lower ball joint loose from the axle beam.

✳ WARNING

Do not use a ball joint fork to separate the ball joint from the spindle, as this will damage the seal and the ball joint socket!

12. Remove the spindle and the ball joint assembly from the axle.

To install:

➡**A 3 step sequence for tightening ball joint stud nuts must be followed to avoid excessive turning effort of spindle about axle.**

13. Prior to assembly of the spindle, make sure the upper and lower ball joints seals are in place.

14. Place the spindle and the ball joint assembly into the axle.

15. Install the camber adjuster in the upper over the upper ball joint. If camber adjustment is necessary, special adapters must be installed.

16. Tighten the lower ball joint stud to 104–146 ft. lbs. (141–198 Nm) for 1994 models and 89–133 ft. lbs. (120–180 Nm) for 1995–97 models. Continue tightening the castellated nut until it lines up with the hole in the ball joint stud. Install the cotter pin. Install the dust shield.

17. If removed, install the front wheel ABS sensor and wire harness to the steering knuckle.

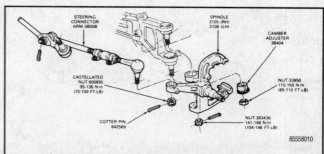

85558010

Fig. 42 Navajo spindle removal–B Series Pick-up similar

18. Install the hub and rotor on the spindle.
19. Install the outer bearing cone, washer, and nut. Adjust bearing end-play and install the cotter pin and dust cap.
20. Install the caliper.
21. Connect the steering linkage to the spindle. Tighten the nut to 52–74 ft. lbs. (70–100 Nm) and advance the nut as required for installation of the cotter pin.
22. Install the wheel and tire assembly. Lower the vehicle. Check, and if necessary, adjust the toe setting.

4-WHEEL DRIVE

1. Raise the vehicle and support on jackstands.
2. Remove the wheel and tire assembly.
3. Remove the caliper.
4. Remove hub locks and locknuts.
5. Remove the hub and rotor. Ensure that the wheel bearings do not fall out.
6. Remove the nuts retaining the spindle to the steering knuckle. Tap the spindle with a plastic or rawhide hammer to jar the spindle from the knuckle. Remove the splash shield.
7. Remove the axle shaft for the side of the vehicle you are working on. Refer to Section 7 for axle shaft removal procedures.
8. Remove the cotter pin from the tie rod nut and then remove the nut. Tap on the tie rod stud to free it from the steering arm.
9. Remove the upper ball joint cotter pin and nut. Loosen the lower ball joint nut to the end of the stud.
10. Strike the inside of the spindle near the upper and lower ball joints to break the spindle loose from the ball joint studs.
11. Remove the camber adjuster sleeve. If required, use pitman arm puller, T64P-3590-F or equivalent to remove the adjuster out of the spindle. Remove the lower ball joint nut.
12. Remove the steering knuckle from the I-beam end.

To install:

13. Install the steering knuckle to the I-beam end, engaging both upper and lower ball joints studs in their respective holes.
14. Install the camber adjuster into the support arm. Position the slot in its original position.

❊❊ CAUTION

The following torque sequence must be followed exactly when securing the spindle. Excessive spindle turning effort may result in reduced steering returnability if this procedure is not followed.

15. Install a new nut on the bottom of the ball joint stud and torque to 90 ft. lbs. (minimum). Tighten to align the nut to the next slot in the nut with the hole in the ball joint stud. Install a new cotter pin.
16. Install the snapring on the upper ball joint stud. Install the upper ball joint pinch bolt and torque the nut to 48–65 ft. lbs.

➡**The camber adjuster will seat itself into the knuckle at a predetermined position during the tightening sequence. Do not attempt to adjust this position.**

17. Install the axle shaft or shafts that were removed.
18. Install the splash shield and spindle onto the steering knuckle. Install and tighten the spindle nuts to 40–50 ft. lbs.
19. Install the rotor on the spindle and push the outer wheel bearing inwards to seat it..
20. Install the locknuts and adjust the wheel bearings. Install the remainder of the locking hub assemblies.

1998 B Series Pick-up

REAR WHEEL DRIVE

◆ **See Figure 43**

➡**The steering knuckle and spindle are an integral assembly.**

1. Position the steering wheel to the on-center position.
2. Loosen the wheel lug nuts then raise and safely support the front of the vehicle.
3. Remove the wheels.
4. Remove the front disc brake caliper, bracket and rotor. Also remove the rotor splash shield.

1. Bolt
2. Nut
3. Front wheel spindle (RH)
4. Front wheel spindle (LH)
5. Nut
6. Cotter pin
7. Cotter pin
8. Nut
9. Tie rod end
10. Front suspension lower arm (LH)
11. Front suspension lower arm (RH)

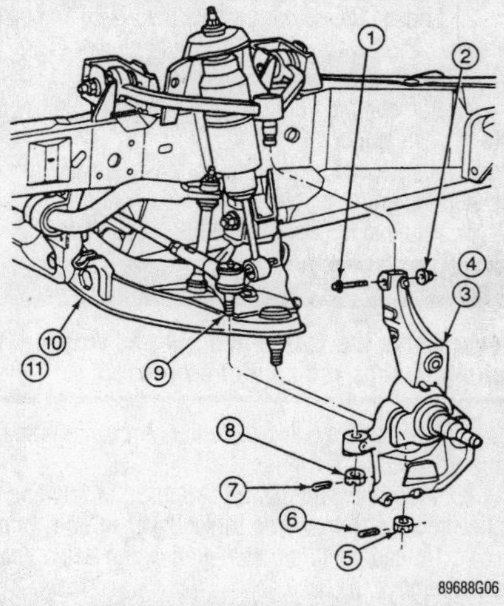

89688G06

Fig. 43 Exploded view of the 1998 B Series Pick-up steering knuckle

5. Remove the cotter pin and nut retaining the tie rod end to the steering knuckle.
6. Disconnect the tie rod end from the steering knuckle using a jawed puller, such as Pitman Arm Puller T64P-3590-F, or equivalent.
7. If equipped, unbolt the front wheel ABS sensor and wire harness from the steering knuckle.
8. Support the lower control arm with a jack. Remove the cotter pin and loosen the nut retaining the lower ball joint to the steering knuckle.
9. Disconnect the lower ball joint from the steering knuckle using a jawed puller, such as Pitman Arm Puller T64P-3590-F, or equivalent.
10. Remove the lower ball joint retaining nut and slowly raise the lower control arm until the ball joint stud is disengaged from the steering knuckle.
11. Remove the upper ball joint retaining bolt and nut from the steering knuckle then disconnect the joint from the knuckle.
12. Remove the steering knuckle/spindle assembly from the vehicle.

To install:

13. Inspect the upper and lower ball joints and seals for damage and replace as needed.
14. Position the steering knuckle onto the upper ball joint and install the retaining bolt and nut. Tighten the bolt to 30–41 ft. lbs. (40–55 Nm).
15. Install the lower ball joint stud into the steering knuckle until the stud protrudes through the knuckle.
16. Install the retaining nut to the lower ball joint stud and tighten to 84–113 ft. lbs. (113–153 Nm). Install the cotter pin, advancing (tightening) the nut as needed. Never loosen the ball joint nut in order to install the cotter pin.
17. Connect the tie rod end to the steering knuckle and install the retaining nut. Tighten to 57–77 ft. lbs. (77–104 Nm) and install the cotter pin, advancing (tightening) the nut as needed. Never loosen the ball joint nut in order to install the cotter pin.
18. Install the front disc brake splash shield, rotor, bracket and caliper.
19. Install the wheel and snug all of the lug nuts.
20. Lower the vehicle and tighten the wheel lug nuts to 100 ft. lbs. (135 Nm).

4-WHEEL DRIVE

❊❊ WARNING

Do not perform this procedure unless a new wheel hub nut and washer assembly is available. Once removed, these parts must never be reused during assembly.

1. Position the steering wheel to the on-center position.

❊❊ WARNING

If equipped, always turn off the Automatic Ride Control (ARC) service switch before lifting the vehicle off of the ground. Failure to do so could damage the ARC system components. Refer to Section 1 for jacking procedures.

2. Loosen the wheel lug nuts then raise and safely support the front of the vehicle.

3. Remove the wheels.

4. Remove the front disc brake caliper, bracket and rotor. Also remove the rotor splash shield.

5. If equipped, unbolt the front wheel ABS sensor and wire harness from the steering knuckle.

6. Remove the front wheel hub nut and washer.

❄❄ WARNING

Never reuse the wheel hub nut and washer. This nut is a torque prevailing design and cannot be reused.

7. Remove the cotter pin and nut retaining the tie rod end to the steering knuckle.

8. Disconnect the tie rod end from the steering knuckle using a jawed puller, such as Pitman Arm Puller T64P-3590-F, or equivalent.

9. Unload the torsion bar. Follow the torsion bar removal procedures, but do not remove the bar.

10. Support the lower control arm with a jack. Remove the cotter pin and loosen the nut retaining the lower ball joint to the steering knuckle.

11. Disconnect the lower ball joint from the steering knuckle using a jawed puller, such as Pitman Arm Puller T64P-3590-F, or equivalent.

12. Remove the lower ball joint retaining nut and slowly raise the lower control arm until the ball joint stud is disengaged from the steering knuckle.

➡ The hub shaft is a slip fit into the wheel hub and bearing; a press is not normally required.

13. Ensure that the wheel hub shaft can be pushed inwards. If not, assemble a press to the front wheel studs and press the wheel hub shaft inwards slightly to break it loose.

14. Remove the upper ball joint retaining bolt and nut from the steering knuckle then disconnect the joint from the knuckle.

15. Remove the steering knuckle/spindle assembly from the vehicle.

To install:

16. Inspect the upper and lower ball joints and seals for damage and replace as needed.

17. Position the steering knuckle onto the upper ball joint, while aligning the axle shaft with the wheel hub, and install the retaining bolt and nut. Tighten the bolt to 30–41 ft. lbs. (40–55 Nm).

18. Install the lower ball joint stud into the steering knuckle until the stud protrudes through the knuckle.

19. Install the retaining nut to the lower ball joint stud and tighten to 84–113 ft. lbs. (113–153 Nm). Install the cotter pin, advancing (tightening) the nut as needed. Never loosen the ball joint nut in order to install the cotter pin.

20. Connect the tie rod end to the steering knuckle and install the retaining nut. Tighten to 57–77 ft. lbs. (77–104 Nm) and install the cotter pin, advancing (tightening) the nut as needed. Never loosen the ball joint nut in order to install the cotter pin.

21. If removed, install the ABS sensor to the wheel hub.

22. Install the hub washer and nut then tighten to 157–213 ft. lbs. (212–288 Nm).

23. Install the front disc brake splash shield, rotor, bracket and caliper.

24. Install the wheel and snug all of the lug nuts.

25. Reload the torsion bar pressure. Refer to the torsion bar installation procedures. Check and, if necessary, set the vehicle ride height.

26. Lower the vehicle and tighten the wheel lug nuts to 100 ft. lbs. (135 Nm).

MPV Models

REAR WHEEL DRIVE

1. Raise and safely support the vehicle.
2. Remove the wheel assembly.
3. Remove the wheel hub/bearing assembly, if necessary.
4. Remove the brake caliper.
5. Remove the disc plate.
6. Disconnect the tie-rod end from the knuckle/spindle.
7. Disconnect the lower arm.
8. Remove the knuckle/spindle assembly.

To install:

9. Install the knuckle/spindle assembly. Torque the strut mounting nut to 69–86 ft. lbs. (94–116 Nm).

10. Install the lower arm, ball joint to the knuckle/spindle assembly. Torque the ball joint nut to 87–115 ft. lbs. (118–156 Nm).

11. Connect the tie-rod end, torque the nut to 44–57 ft. lbs. (59–78 Nm).

12. Install wheel hub/bearing assembly, if removed.

13. Install the disc plate.

14. Install the brake caliper, torque the mounting bolts to 66–79 ft. lbs. (89–107 Nm).

15. Install the locknut, torque to 131–173 ft. lbs. (117–235 Nm).

16. Install the hub dust cap.

17. Install the wheel assembly.

18. Lower the vehicle.

4-WHEEL DRIVE

1. Raise and safely support the vehicle.
2. Remove the wheel assembly.
3. Remove the locknut.
4. Remove the brake caliper.
5. Remove the disc plate retaining screw(s).
6. Disconnect the tie-rod end from the knuckle.
7. Disconnect the lower ball joint.
8. Remove the disc plate.
9. Remove the ball joint mounting nuts and bolts.
10. Remove the knuckle, wheel hub and dustplate as an assembly.
11. Remove the wheel bearings from the hub assembly, if needed.

To install:

12. Install wheel bearings to the hub assembly, if removed.

13. Install the knuckle assembly. Torque the strut mounting nut to 69–86 ft. lbs. (94–116 Nm).

14. Install the ball joint mounting nuts and bolts. Torque the upper mounting bolts to 76–101 ft. lbs. (102–137 Nm). Torque the through-bolt nut to 95–106 ft. lbs. (128–171 Nm).

15. Replace the disc plate.

16. Install ball joint to the knuckle assembly. Torque the ball joint nut to 116–137 ft. lbs. (157–186 Nm).

17. Connect the tie-rod end, torque the nut to 44–57 ft. lbs. (59–78 Nm).

18. Install the brake caliper, torque the mounting bolts to 66–79 ft. lbs. (89–107 Nm).

19. Install the disc plate retaining nut.

20. Install the locknut, torque to 174–231 ft. lbs. (236–313 Nm).

21. Install the wheel assembly.

22. Lower the vehicle.

Radius Arm

Radius arms are found only on Navajo and 1994–97 B Series Pick-up models.

REMOVAL & INSTALLATION

Rear Wheel Drive

▶ See Figure 44

1. Raise the front of the vehicle, place jackstands under the frame. Place a jack under the axle.

❄❄ WARNING

The axle must be supported on the jack throughout spring removal and installation, and must not be permitted to hang by the brake hose. If the length of the brake hose is not sufficient to provide adequate clearance for removal and installation of the spring, the disc brake caliper must be removed from the spindle. After removal, the caliper must be placed on the frame or otherwise supported to prevent suspending the caliper from the caliper hose. These precautions are absolutely necessary to prevent serious damage to the tube portion of the caliper hose assembly.

2. Disconnect the lower end of the shock absorber from the shock lower bracket (bolt and nut).

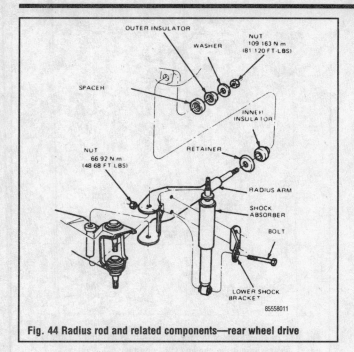

Fig. 44 Radius rod and related components—rear wheel drive

3. Remove the front spring. Loosen the axle pivot bolt.

4. Remove the spring lower seat from the radius arm, and then remove the bolt and nut that attaches the radius arm to the axle and front bracket.

5. Remove the nut, rear washer and insulator from the rear side of the radius arm rear bracket.

6. Remove the radius arm from the vehicle, and remove the inner insulator and retainer from the radius arm stud.

To install:

7. Position the front end of the radius arm to the axle. Install the attaching bolt from underneath, and install the nut finger tight.

8. Install the retainer and inner insulator on the radius arm stud and insert the stud through the radius arm rear bracket.

9. Install the rear washer, insulator and nut on the arm stud at the rear side of the arm rear bracket. Tighten the nut to 82–113 ft. lbs. (113–153 Nm).

10. Tighten the nut on the radius arm-to-axle bolt to 188–254 ft. lbs. (255–345 Nm).

11. Install the spring lower seat and spring insulator on the radius arm so that the hole in the seat goes over the arm-to-axle bolt.

12. Install the front spring.

13. Connect the lower end of the shock absorber to the stud on the radius arm with the retaining nut and tighten to specifications.

4-Wheel Drive

▶ See Figure 45

1. Raise the front of the vehicle, place jackstands under the frame. Place a jack under the axle.

✳✳ WARNING

The axle must be supported on the jack throughout spring removal and installation, and must not be permitted to hang by the brake hose. If the length of the brake hose is not sufficient to provide adequate clearance for removal and installation of the spring, the disc brake caliper must be removed from the spindle. After removal, the caliper must be placed on the frame or otherwise supported to prevent suspending the caliper from the caliper hose. These precautions are absolutely necessary to prevent serious damage to the tube portion of the caliper hose assembly.

2. Disconnect the lower stud. Remove the front spring from the vehicle.

3. Remove the spring lower seat and stud from the radius arm. Remove the bolts that attach the radius arm to the axle and front bracket.

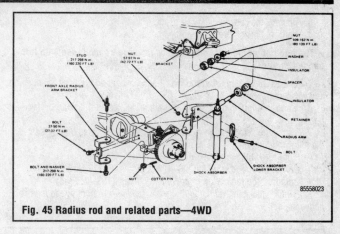

Fig. 45 Radius rod and related parts—4WD

4. Remove the nut, rear washer and insulator from the rear side of the radius arm rear bracket.

5. Remove the radius arm from the vehicle. Remove the inner insulator and retainer from the radius arm stud.

To install:

6. Position the front end of the radius arm from bracket to axle. Install the retaining bolts and stud in the bracket finger tight.

7. Install the retainer and inner insulator on the radius arm stud and insert the stud through the radius arm rear bracket.

8. Install the rear washer, insulator and nut on the arm stud at the rear side of the arm rear bracket. Tighten the nut to 80–120 ft. lbs.

9. Tighten the stud to 190–230 ft. lbs. Tighten the front bracket to axle bolts to 37–50 ft. lbs. and the lower bolt and washer to 190–230 ft. lbs.

10. Install the spring lower seat and spring insulator on the radius arm so that the hole in the seat goes over the arm to axle bolt. Tighten the axle pivot bolt to 120–150 ft. lbs.

11. Install the front spring. Connect the lower stud of the radius arm and torque the retaining nut to 39–53 ft. lbs. on 1991–94 vehicles.

Compression Rods

All rear wheel drive MPV models are equipped with compression rods on each side of the front suspension.

REMOVAL & INSTALLATION

▶ See Figures 46 and 47

1. Raise and support the front end on jackstands.
2. Disconnect the stabilizer link at the compression rod.

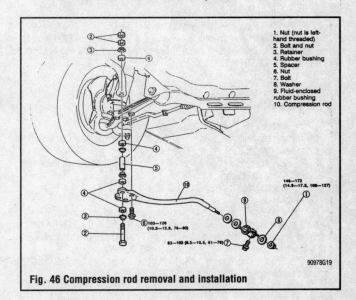

1. Nut (nut is left-hand threaded)
2. Bolt and nut
3. Retainer
4. Rubber bushing
5. Spacer
6. Nut
7. Bolt
8. Washer
9. Fluid-enclosed rubber bushing
10. Compression rod

Fig. 46 Compression rod removal and installation

3. Remove the compression rod-to-lower arm bolts.
4. Remove the compression rod end nut and washer.

➡The end nut on the left compression rod may be equipped with left handed threads.

5. Unbolt the compression rod fluid-filled bushing and remove the bushing and washers.
6. Check the bushing for signs of leakage. Replace it if leaking or damaged.
7. Install the compression rod and components in reverse order. Observe the following torques:
- Fluid-filled bushing bolts: 61–76 ft. lbs. (83–103 Nm)
- Compression rod end nut: 108–127 ft. lbs. (146–172 Nm)
- Compression rod-to-lower arm: 76–93 ft. lbs. (103–126 Nm)
8. Tighten the stabilizer bar end link bolt until 9–11mm of thread is visible above the nut.

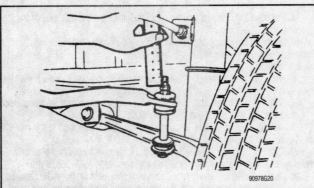

Fig. 47 Tighten the stabilizer bar end link bolt until 9–11mm of thread is visible above the nut

Stabilizer Bar

REMOVAL & INSTALLATION

1994–97 B Series Pick-up

1. As required, raise and support the vehicle safely.
2. Remove the nuts and bolts retaining the stabilizer bar to the end links.
3. Remove the retainers and the stabilizer bar and bushings from the vehicle.

To install:
4. Position the stabilizer bar to the axles and brackets.
5. Install the retainer and the end link bolts.
6. Torque the retainer bolts to 35–50 ft. lbs. (47–67 Nm) on 1994 models and 22–30 ft. lbs. (30–40 Nm) on 1995–97 models. Torque the end link nuts to 30–41 ft. lbs. (40–55 Nm).

Navajo

▸ See Figure 48

1. As required, raise and support the vehicle safely.
2. Remove the nuts and washer and disconnect the stabilizer link assembly from the front I-beam axle.
3. Remove the mounting bolts and remove the stabilizer bar retainers from the stabilizer bar assembly.
4. Remove the stabilizer bar from the vehicle.

To install:
5. Place stabilizer bar in position on the frame mounting brackets.
6. Install retainers and tighten retainer bolt to 35–50 ft. lbs. (47–67 Nm). If removed, install the stabilizer bar link assembly to the stabilizer bar. Install the nut and washer and tighten to 30–41 ft. lbs. (40–55 Nm).
7. Position the stabilizer bar link in the I-beam mounting bracket. Install the bolt and tighten to 30–41 ft. lbs. (40–55 Nm).

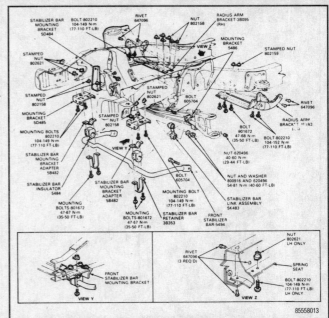

Fig. 48 Exploded view of the Navajo stabilizer bar and related parts—rear wheel drive shown, 4WD similar

1998 B Series Pick-up

▸ See Figure 49

1. Raise and safely support the vehicle.
2. Remove the nut, washer and bushing (on underside of the lower control arm) linking the stabilizer bar end to the lower control arm.
3. Lift up on the bar and remove the remaining bushings and the spacer and bolt assembly (called the end link) from the stabilizer bar end.
4. Remove the bar mounting bracket-to-frame bolts.
5. Remove the stabilizer bar from the vehicle. If necessary, remove the mounting brackets and insulators from the bar.

To install:
6. Inspect all of the stabilizer bar mounting and end link bushings. Replace any that are cracked, squashed, swollen or damaged.
7. Position the stabilizer bar mounting brackets to the frame and install the retaining bolts loosely.
8. Install the end link assembly to the bar end and the lower control arm. Install the end link retaining bolt loosely.
9. Tighten the mounting bracket bolts to 25–34 ft. lbs. (34–46 Nm).

➡The end link assembly must be tightened with the vehicle weight on the front wheels.

10. Lower the vehicle then tighten the end link retaining nut to 15–21 ft. lbs. (21–29 Nm).

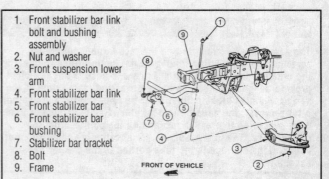

1. Front stabilizer bar link bolt and bushing assembly
2. Nut and washer
3. Front suspension lower arm
4. Front stabilizer bar link
5. Front stabilizer bar
6. Front stabilizer bar bushing
7. Stabilizer bar bracket
8. Bolt
9. Frame

FRONT OF VEHICLE

Fig. 49 Exploded view of the Mountaineer and 1995–97 Explorer stabilizer bar mounting

MPV Models

▶ See Figures 47, 50, 51 and 52

1. Raise and support the front end on jackstands.
2. If equipped with 4 wheel ABS, remove the front wheel speed sensor and fix it to an appropriate place where the sensor will not be damaged while servicing the vehicle.
3. Remove the splash shield.
4. Disconnect the end links at the compression rods (2WD) or lower control arms (4WD).
5. Remove the clamp bolts. Lift out the stabilizer bar.
6. Inspect all parts for wear and/or damage. Replace as necessary.

To install:

7. Place the sway bar on the frame and install the U-brackets finger-tight. Be sure that the bracket bushing is aligned with the mark on the stabilizer bar. Install the bracket so that the **F** mark on the bracket faces the front of the vehicle.

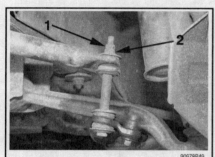

Fig. 50 Use a box wrench and a backup wrench, remove the locking nut (1) and then the retaining nut (2)

Fig. 51 Remove the top bushing and retainer from the top of the sway bar link

8. Install the end links to the control arms, or compression rods, and tighten until, on 2WD, 0.35–0.43 in. (9–11mm) of thread is visible above the nut; on 4WD, 0.20–0.28 in. (5–7mm) of thread is visible above the nut.
9. If equipped with 4-wheel ABS, install the front wheel speed sensors.
10. Lower the vehicle to the floor and tighten the U-bracket bolts to 37–44 ft. lbs. (51–60 Nm) on 2WD or 14–18 ft. lbs. (19–25 Nm) on 4WD.
11. Install the splash shield.
12. Lower the vehicle.

I-Beam Axle

Al Navajo and 1994–97 B Series Pick-up models use an I-beam axle front suspension.

REMOVAL & INSTALLATION

Rear Wheel Drive

▶ See Figure 53

1. Raise and safely support the vehicle. Remove the front wheel spindle. Remove the front spring. Remove the front stabilizer bar, if equipped.
2. Remove the spring lower seat from the radius arm, and then remove the bolt and nut that attaches the stabilizer bar bracket, if equipped, and the radius arm to the (I-Beam) front axle.
3. Remove the axle-to-frame pivot bracket bolt and nut.

To install:

4. Position the axle to the frame pivot bracket and install the bolt and nut finger tight.
5. Position the opposite end of the axle to the radius arm, install the attaching bolt from underneath through the bracket, the radius arm and the axle. Install the nut and tighten to 188–254 ft. lbs. (255–345 Nm).
6. Install the spring lower seat on the radius arm so that the hole in the seat indexes over the arm-to-axle bolt.

7. Install the front spring.

➡ Lower the vehicle on its wheels or properly support the vehicle at the front springs before tightening the axle pivot bolt and nut.

8. Tighten the axle-to-frame pivot bracket bolt to 111–148 ft. lbs. (150–200 Nm).
9. Install the front wheel spindle.

4-Wheel Drive

The I-beam axle is part of the front drive axle assembly. Refer to Section 7 for front drive axle housing removal and installation procedures.

Upper Control Arm

Only the 1998 B Series Pick-up models have control arms.

Fig. 52 Remove the two sway bar bushing retainer mounting bolts

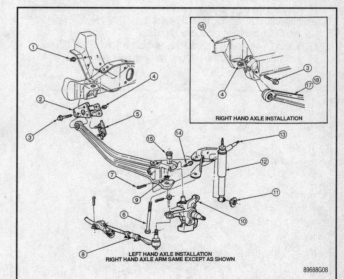

1. Nut
2. Right front axle pivot bracket
3. Bolt
4. Nut
5. Bolt and retainer
6. Bolt
7. Cotter pin
8. Steering connecting arm
9. Nut
10. Front wheel spindle
11. Nut and washer assembly
12. Front shock absorber
13. Radius arm
14. Bolt
15. Camber adjuster
16. Crossmember reference
17. Front right hand axle
18. Left axle

Fig. 53 Exploded view of the front I-beam axle assembly

REMOVAL & INSTALLATION

◗ See Figure 54

➥After performing this procedure, it will be necessary to have the wheel alignment checked and adjusted by a professional shop.

1. Position the steering wheel to the on-center position. Loosen the wheel lug nuts.
2. Raise and safely support the vehicle. Position the jack stands under the lower control arms.
3. Remove the wheel lug nuts and wheel.

➥Before removing the steering knuckle-to-upper ball joint retaining (pinch) bolt, secure the steering knuckle from tilting.

4. Remove the steering knuckle-to-upper ball joint retaining (pinch) bolt and separate the two components.
5. Make alignment marks on the control arm pivot bolt cam assemblies.
6. To remove the left side control arm proceed as follows:
   a. Remove the nuts and cam bolts from the control arm pivot points.
   b. Pull the control arm from the vehicle frame.
7. To remove the right side control arm, proceed as follows:
   a. If only the ball joint is to be removed, make alignment marks on the control arm and ball joint assembly then remove the two retaining nuts and the ball joint. Skip to the installation procedures.
   b. Remove the nuts and cam bolts from the control arm pivot points.
   c. Pull the control arm from the vehicle frame.

To install:
8. For right-side control arm, if removed, install the ball joint assembly and retaining nuts to the control arm and tighten the nuts to 95–128 ft. lbs. (128–173 Nm).
9. Install the control arm pivot points into the frame pockets.
10. Install the cam bolts and nuts, align the matchmarks and tighten the nuts to 83–112 ft. lbs. (113–153 Nm).
11. Connect the upper ball joint shaft to the steering knuckle. Install the retaining (pinch) bolt and tighten to 35–46 ft. lbs. (47–63 Nm).
12. Install the wheel and snug the lug nuts.
13. Lower the vehicle and tighten the lug nuts to 100 ft. lbs. (135 Nm).
14. Have the alignment checked by a professional repair shop.

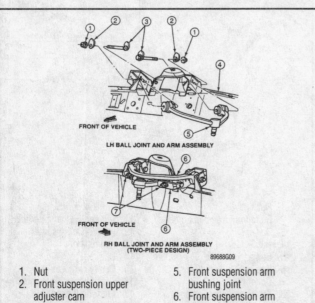

1. Nut
2. Front suspension upper adjuster cam
3. Front suspension upper adjuster cam bolt
4. Frame
5. Front suspension arm bushing joint
6. Front suspension arm bushing joint
7. Nut

Fig. 54 Exploded views of the right and left upper control arms

CONTROL ARM BUSHING REPLACEMENT

The control arm bushings are not serviced separately. If the bushings require service, the front suspension upper control arm will have to be replaced.

Lower Control Arm

Only the MPV and 1998 B Series Pick-up models have control arms.

REMOVAL & INSTALLATION

1998 B Series Pick-up

◗ See Figure 55

➥To remove the lower control arm, the torsion bar must be removed. Anytime the torsion bar is disturbed, the ride height must be checked and adjusted.

1. Position the steering wheel to the on-center position. Loosen the wheel lug nuts.
2. Raise and safely support the vehicle.
3. Remove the wheel lug nuts and wheel.
4. Disconnect the stabilizer bar link bolt from the lower control arm.
5. Remove the front shock absorber.
6. If 4WD, remove the torsion bar. If rear wheel drive, remove the coil spring.
7. Remove the lower ball joint retaining nut cotter pin and loosen the nut but do not remove it.
8. Disconnect the lower ball joint stud from the steering knuckle using a jawed puller, such as Pitman Arm Puller T64P-3590-F, or equivalent.

✳ WARNING

Fasten a support, either out of a block of wood or wire wrapped around the frame, and support the weight of the steering knuckle/brake assembly. Do not allow the steering knuckle/brake assembly to hang from the upper ball joint as this may damage the joint.

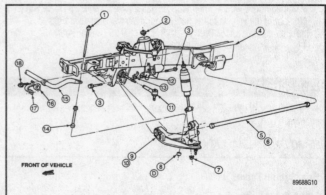

1. Stabilizer bar stud and bushing
2. Nut, washer, and insulator assembly
3. Bolt
4. Frame
5. Torsin bar (LH)
6. Torsion bar (RH)
7. Nut
8. Nut and washer
9. Front suspension lower arm (LH)
10. Front suspension lower arm (RH)
11. Tie rod end
12. Nut
13. Nut
14. Front stabilizer bar link
15. Front stabilizer bar
16. Front stabilizer bar bushing
17. Stabilizer bar bracket
18. Bolt

Fig. 55 Exploded view of the lower control arm assembly—4WD shown, rear wheel drive does not have torsion bars, but has coil springs over the shock absorbers

9. Position a jack under the lower control arm then remove the lower ball joint retaining nut.

10. Raise the lower control arm until the lower ball joint stud is free from the steering knuckle.

11. Remove the two nuts and bolts retaining the lower arm pivot points to the frame crossmember.

12. Remove the lower control arm from the frame pockets. Some careful prying may ease the removal of the arm.

To install:

13. Inspect the lower ball joint, boot and pivot bushings. If any inspected components are worn or damaged, the entire control arm must be replaced.

➡**Do not tighten the lower control arm mounting bolts to the final torque until the end of the installation procedure.**

14. Position the lower control arm pivot points into the frame and crossmember pockets. Install the bolts and nuts and snug the bolts.

15. Position a jack under the lower control arm.

16. If 4WD, install the torsion bar. If rear wheel drive, install the coil spring.

17. Raise the lower control arm to allow the lower ball joint stud to be inserted into the steering knuckle.

18. Lower the control arm assembly and ensure that the lower ball joint stud protrudes through the steering knuckle bore.

19. Install the lower ball joint attaching nut and tighten to 83–113 ft. lbs. (113–153 Nm). Install a new cotter pin, advancing (tightening) the nut as required. Never loosen the retaining nut in order to install the cotter pin.

20. Install the shock absorber.

21. Install the wheel and snug the lug nuts.

22. Lower the vehicle and tighten the lug nuts to 100 ft. lbs. (135 Nm).

➡**The lower control arm-to-frame bolts must be tightened with the weight of the vehicle resting on the wheels. If clearance permits, allow the vehicle to sit on the ground while tightening the bolts.**

23. If necessary, raise the vehicle again and position either car ramps under the wheels or jackstands on the lower control arms, as close to the wheels as possible.

24. Tighten the control arm-to-frame bolts to 111–148 ft. lbs. (150–200 Nm).

25. Lower the vehicle.

26. Check and adjust the ride height.

27. While it should not be necessary, have the wheel alignment checked by a professional shop.

MPV Models

REAR WHEEL DRIVE

♦ See Figures 56, 57 and 58

1. Raise and safely support the vehicle. Remove the wheel and tire assembly.

2. Remove the brake caliper and support it aside with mechanics wire, do not let it hang by the brake hose.

3. Remove the nuts, bolts, spacer, washers and bushings and remove the compression rod from the lower control arm and chassis and disconnect the stabilizer bar from the lower control arm.

4. Remove the cotter pin and nut and separate the tie rod end from the knuckle.

5. Remove the bolts and nuts and disconnect the strut from the knuckle.

6. Remove the cotter pin and nut from the lower ball joint stud and separate the lower ball joint from the knuckle.

7. Remove the mounting bolt and nut and remove the lower control arm from the vehicle.

To install:

8. Position the lower control arm to the chassis and install the bolt and nut, but do not tighten at this time.

9. Install the knuckle to the lower control arm. Tighten the lower ball joint stud nut to 87–115 ft. lbs. (118–156 Nm) and install a new cotter pin.

10. Connect the strut to the knuckle and tighten the attaching bolts and nuts to 69–86 ft. lbs. (94–116 Nm).

11. Connect the tie rod end to the knuckle. Tighten the tie rod end stud nut to 43–58 ft. lbs. (59–78 Nm) and install a new cotter pin.

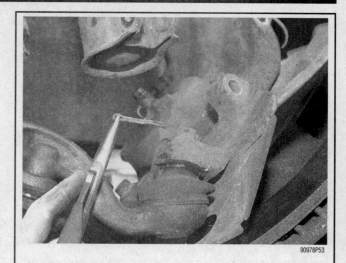

Fig. 56 Remove and discard the lower ball joint stud cotter pin

90978P53

Fig. 57 Using a ball joint separator tool, separate the steering knuckle from the lower ball joint

90978P52

Fig. 58 After separating the ball joint from the steering knuckle and sway bar link from the lower control arm, remove the 3 compression rod-to-control arm bolts (B), control arm bushing nut and through bolt (C) and 4 tailing arm-to-frame rail bolts (A)

90978P54

12. Install the compression rod to the lower control arm and chassis. Tighten the compression rod-to-lower control arm mounting bolts to 76–93 ft. lbs. (103–126 Nm) and the compression rod bushing-to-chassis bolts to 61–76 ft. lbs. (83–103 Nm). Install the compression rod nut but do not tighten at this time.

➡**The left-hand compression rod nut has left-hand threads.**

13. Connect the stabilizer bar to the control arm with the bolt, washers, bushings, spacer and nuts. Tighten the nuts so 0.24 in. (6mm) of thread is exposed at the end of the bolt.

14. Install the caliper and the wheel and tire assembly. Lower the vehicle.

15. With the vehicle unloaded, tighten the lower control arm-to-chassis bolt and nut to 94–108 ft. lbs. (146–172 Nm). Tighten the compression rod nut to 108–126 ft. lbs. (147–171 Nm).

16. Lower the vehicle.

17. Check the front end alignment.

4-WHEEL DRIVE

1. Raise and safely support the vehicle. Remove the wheel and tire assembly.

2. Remove the bolt, retainers, bushings, spacer and nuts and disconnect the stabilizer bar from the lower control arm.

3. Remove the cotter pin and nut from the lower ball joint stud. Separate the ball joint from the knuckle.

4. Remove the lower control arm-to-chassis nuts and bolts and remove lower control arm.

To install:

5. Position the lower control arm to the chassis and install the bolts and nuts. Do not tighten at this time.

6. Connect the lower ball joint to the knuckle and tighten the ball joint stud nut to 116–137 ft. lbs. (157–186 Nm). Install a new cotter pin.

7. Install the bolt, retainers, bushings, spacer and nuts and connect the stabilizer bar to the lower control arm. Tighten the nuts so 0.20–0.28 in. (5–7mm) of thread is exposed at the end of the bolt.

8. Install the wheel and tire assembly and lower the vehicle. With the vehicle unloaded, tighten the lower control arm-to-chassis nuts and bolts to 102–126 ft. lbs. (138–171 Nm).

9. Lower the vehicle.

10. Check the front end alignment.

4. Remove the front bushing from the control arm by using special bushing press tools 49-G033-102, 49-F027-009 and a press.

5. Using special press tools 49-U034-202, 49-G026-103 and a press, remove the rear lower control arm bushing.

6. Apply soapy water to the outside surface of the new front lower control arm bushing.

7. Using special tools 49-G033-102, 49-F027-009 and a press, install the new front bushing into the lower control arm.

8. Set a new rear control arm bushing into the lower control arm with the direction marks on the bushing aligned with marks on the control arm.

9. Using special tools 49-U034-202, 49-G026-103 and a press, install the new rear bushing into the lower control arm.

Front Wheel Bearings

REMOVAL & INSTALLATION

Navajo and 1994–97 B Series Pick-up Models (Rear Wheel Drive)

▶ **See Figures 63 thru 70**

1. Raise and support the vehicle safely. Remove the tire and wheel assembly from the hub and rotor.

2. Remove the caliper from its mounting and position it to the side with mechanics wire in order to prevent damage to the brake line hose.

3. Remove the grease cap from the hub. Remove the cotter pin, retainer, adjusting nut and flatwasher from the spindle.

4. Remove the outer bearing cone and roller assembly from the hub. Remove the hub and rotor from the spindle.

5. Using seal removal tool 1175-AC or equivalent remove and discard the grease seal. Remove the inner bearing cone and roller assembly from the hub.

6. Clean the inner and outer bearing assemblies in solvent. Inspect the bearings and the cones for wear and damage. Replace defective parts, as required.

7. If the cups are worn or damaged, remove them with front hub remover tool T81P-1104-C and tool T77F-1102-A or equivalent.

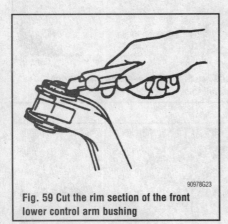

90978G23

Fig. 59 Cut the rim section of the front lower control arm bushing

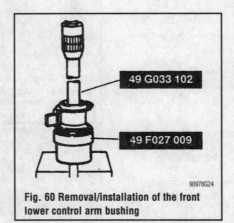

49 G033 102

49 F027 009

90978G24

Fig. 60 Removal/installation of the front lower control arm bushing

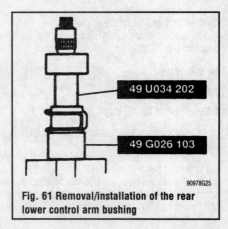

49 U034 202

49 G026 103

90978G25

Fig. 61 Removal/installation of the rear lower control arm bushing

CONTROL ARM BUSHING REPLACEMENT

Rear Wheel Drive MPV and All 1998 B Series Pick-up Models

The control arm bushings are not serviced separately. If the bushings require service, the front suspension upper control arm will have to be replaced.

MPV Models With 4WD

▶ **See Figures 59, 60, 61 and 62**

1. Remove the lower control arm.

2. Secure the lower control arm in a bench vise protected with brass mounting pads.

3. Cut the rim section of the front lower arm bushing.

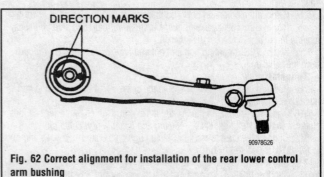

DIRECTION MARKS

90978G26

Fig. 62 Correct alignment for installation of the rear lower control arm bushing

Fig. 63 Remove the nut and washer from the spindle . . .

Fig. 64 . . . then remove the outer bearing

Fig. 65 Pull the hub and rotor assembly from the spindle

Fig. 66 Use a small prytool to remove the old seal

Fig. 67 With the seal removed, the inner bearing may be withdrawn from the hub

Fig. 68 Thoroughly pack the bearing with fresh, high temperature wheel bearing grease

8. Wipe the old grease from the spindle. Check the spindle for excessive wear or damage. Replace defective parts, as required.

To install:

9. If the inner and outer cups were removed, use bearing driver handle tool T80-4000-W or equivalent and replace the cups. Be sure to seat the cups properly in the hub.

10. Use a bearing packer tool and properly repack the wheel bearings with the proper grade and type grease. If a bearing packer is not available work as much of the grease as possible between the rollers and cages. Also, grease the cone surfaces.

11. Position the inner bearing cone and roller assembly in the inner cup. A light film of grease should be included between the lips of the new grease retainer (seal).

12. Install the retainer using the proper installer tool. Be sure that the retainer is properly seated.

13. Install the hub and rotor assembly onto the spindle. Keep the hub centered on the spindle to prevent damage to the spindle and the retainer.

14. Install the outer bearing cone and roller assembly and flatwasher on the spindle. Install the adjusting nut. Adjust the wheel bearings.

15. Install the retainer, a new cotter pin and the grease cap. Install the caliper.

16. Lower the vehicle and tighten the lug nuts to 100 ft. lbs. Before driving the vehicle pump the brake pedal several times to restore normal brake pedal travel.

✷✷ CAUTION

Retighten the wheel lug nuts to specification after about 500 miles of driving. Failure to do this could result in the wheel coming off while the vehicle is in motion possibly causing loss of vehicle control or collision.

Navajo and 1994–97 B Series Pick-up Models (4-Wheel Drive)

WITH MANUAL LOCKING HUBS

◗ See Figures 71 thru 86

1. Raise the vehicle and install jackstands.
2. Remove the wheel and tire assembly.

Fig. 69 Apply a thin coat of fresh grease to the new seal lip

Fig. 70 Use a suitably sized driver to install the inner bearing seal to the hub

Fig. 71 Before beginning the wheel bearing removal, and after the outer hub is removed, wipe off any excess grease

Fig. 72 After the grease is wiped off, remove the axle shaft snaping . . .

Fig. 73 . . . then pull the splined spacer from the axle shaft end

Fig. 74 Use a 4 pronged socket to loosen the outer wheel bearing locknut . . .

Fig. 75 . . . then remove the outer lock-nut

Fig. 76 Remove the lockwasher from behind the outer locknut . . .

Fig. 77 . . . then loosen and remove the inner locknut—note the lockwasher engagement pin (arrow)

Fig. 78 While pushing inwards on the rotor/hub assembly, remove the outer wheel bearing . . .

Fig. 79 . . . then pull the rotor/hub assembly from the spindle, taking care not to scratch the bearing cups in the hub

Fig. 80 Pry out the grease seal on the back of the rotor/hub assembly . . .

Fig. 81 . . . then remove the inner wheel bearing. Thoroughly clean and inspect all of the parts for wear or damage

Fig. 82 After packing the bearing with grease, position a new seal to the rotor/hub assembly . . .

Fig. 83 . . . then, using the correct seal installer, drive the seal into the rotor/hub until it is fully seated

3. Remove the retainer washers from the lug nut studs and remove the manual locking hub assembly from the spindle.

4. Remove the snaping and spacer from the end of the spindle shaft.

5. Remove the outer wheel bearing locknut from the spindle using 4 prong spindle nut spanner wrench, T86T-1197-A or equivalent. Make sure the tabs on the tool engage the slots in the locknut.

6. Remove the locknut washer from the spindle.

7. Remove the inner wheel bearing locknut from the spindle using 4 prong spindle nut spanner wrench, T86T-1197-A or equivalent. Make sure the tabs on the tool engage the slots in the locknut.

8. Remove the outer bearing cone and roller assembly from the hub. Remove the hub and rotor from the spindle.

9. Using seal removal tool 1175-AC or equivalent remove and discard the grease seal. Remove the inner bearing cone and roller assembly from the hub.

10. Clean the inner and outer bearing assemblies in solvent. Inspect the bearings and the cones for wear and damage. Replace defective parts, as required.

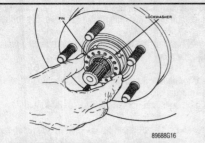

Fig. 84 Ensure that the pin on the inner locknut engages one of the holes of the lock washer

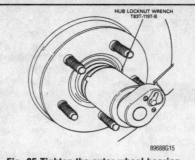

Fig. 85 Tighten the outer wheel bearing locknut to specification

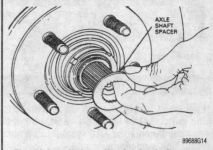

Fig. 86 Install the splined axle shaft spacer then the snapring

11. If the cups are worn or damaged, remove them with front hub remover tool T81P-1104-C and tool T77F-1102-A or equivalent.

12. Wipe the old grease from the spindle. Check the spindle for excessive wear or damage. Replace defective parts, as required.

To install:

13. If the inner and outer cups were removed, use bearing driver handle tool T80-4000-W or equivalent and replace the cups. Be sure to seat the cups properly in the hub.

14. Use a bearing packer tool and properly repack the wheel bearings with the proper grade and type grease. If a bearing packer is not available work as much of the grease as possible between the rollers and cages. Also, grease the cone surfaces.

15. Position the inner bearing cone and roller assembly in the inner cup. A light film of grease should be included between the lips of the new grease seal.

16. Install the grease seal by driving in place with hub seal replacer tool T83T-1175-B and Driver Handle T80T-4000-W.

17. Install the hub and rotor assembly onto the spindle. Keep the hub centered on the spindle to prevent damage to the spindle and the retainer.

18. Install the outer bearing cone and roller assembly.

19. Carefully install the rotor onto the spindle. Install the outer wheel bearing in the rotor.

20. Install the inner adjusting nut with the pin facing out. Tighten the inner adjusting nut to 35 ft. lbs. (47 Nm) to seat the bearings.

21. Follow the appropriate wheel bearing adjustment procedures.

WITH AUTOMATIC LOCKING HUBS

▶ See Figures 87, 88 and 89

1. Raise the vehicle and install jackstands.
2. Remove the wheel and tire assembly.
3. Remove the retainer washers from the lug nut studs and remove the automatic locking hub assembly from the spindle.
4. Remove the snapring and spacer from the end of the spindle shaft.
5. Pull the locking cam assembly and the two plastic spacers off of the wheel bearing adjusting nut.
6. Use a magnet and remove the locking key from under the adjusting nut. If required, rotate the adjusting nut slightly to relieve pressure against the locking key.

❋❋ WARNING

To prevent damage to the adjusting nut and spindle threads on vehicles equipped with automatic hubs, look into the spindle keyway under the adjusting nut and remove the separate locking key before removing the adjusting nut.

7. Remove the wheel bearing locknut using a 2-⅜ inch (60.3mm) hex socket, such as Hex Locknut Wrench T70T-4252-B.

8. Remove the outer bearing cone and roller assembly from the hub. Remove the hub and rotor from the spindle.

9. Using seal removal tool 1175-AC or equivalent remove and discard the grease seal. Remove the inner bearing cone and roller assembly from the hub.

10. Clean the inner and outer bearing assemblies in solvent. Inspect the bearings and the cones for wear and damage. Replace defective parts, as required.

11. If the cups are worn or damaged, remove them with front hub remover tool T81P-1104-C and tool T77F-1102-A or equivalent.

12. Wipe the old grease from the spindle. Check the spindle for excessive wear or damage. Replace defective parts, as required.

To install:

13. If the inner and outer cups were removed, use bearing driver handle tool T80-4000-W or equivalent and replace the cups. Be sure to seat the cups properly in the hub.

14. Use a bearing packer tool and properly repack the wheel bearings with the proper grade and type grease. If a bearing packer is not available work as much of the grease as possible between the rollers and cages. Also, grease the cone surfaces.

15. Position the inner bearing cone and roller assembly in the inner cup. A light film of grease should be included between the lips of the new grease seal.

16. Install the grease seal by driving in place with hub seal replacer tool T83T-1175-B and Driver Handle T80T-4000-W.

17. Install the hub and rotor assembly onto the spindle. Keep the hub centered on the spindle to prevent damage to the spindle and the retainer.

18. Install the outer bearing cone and roller assembly.

19. Carefully install the rotor onto the spindle. Install the outer wheel bearing in the rotor.

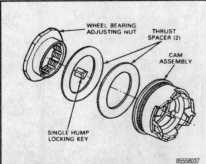

Fig. 87 Exploded view of the locking cam, thrust washers, locking key and bearing adjuster nut

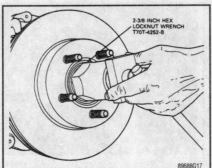

Fig. 88 Remove the wheel bearing adjusting nut after removing the locking key from under it

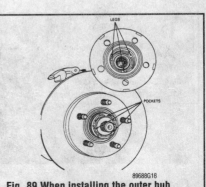

Fig. 89 When installing the outer hub cover, align the cam pockets with the legs on the cover

20. Install the adjusting nut and tighten 35 ft. lbs. (47 Nm) to seat the bearings.
21. Follow the appropriate wheel bearing adjustment procedures.

1998 B Series Pick-up

♦ See Figure 90

❊❊ WARNING

If equipped, always turn off the Automatic Ride Control (ARC) service switch before lifting the vehicle off of the ground. Failure to do so could damage the ARC system components. Refer to Section 1 for jacking procedures.

1. Loosen the wheel lug nuts then raise and safely support the front of the vehicle.
2. Remove the wheels.
3. Remove the front disc brake caliper, bracket and rotor. Also remove the rotor splash shield.
4. If equipped, unbolt the front wheel ABS sensor and wire harness from the steering knuckle.
5. Remove the front wheel hub nut and washer.

❊❊ WARNING

Never reuse the wheel hub nut and washer. This nut is a torque prevailing design and cannot be reused.

➡The hub shaft is a slip fit into the wheel hub and bearing; a press is not normally required.

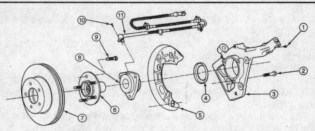

1. Hex tapping screw
2. Flange head screw
3. Steering knuckle
4. Hub oil slinger
5. Brake dust shield
6. Flange hub
7. Rotor
8. Bearing assembly
9. Wheel bolt
10. Front brake anti-lock sensor screw
11. Front brake anti-lock sensor

89688G19

Fig. 90 Exploded view of the Mountaineer and 1995–97 Explorer sealed front wheel bearing and related components

6. Ensure that the wheel hub shaft can be pushed inwards. If not, assemble a press to the front wheel studs and press the wheel hub shaft inwards slightly to break it loose.
7. Remove the three wheel hub/bearing to steering knuckle retaining bolts. Remove the hub and bearing assembly.

To install:

8. Install the ABS sensor to the wheel hub then position the hub to the front axle shaft and steering knuckle.
9. Install the three retaining bolts and tighten them to 70–80 ft. lbs. (95–108 Nm).
10. Install the hub washer and nut and tighten to 157–213 ft. lbs. (212–288 Nm).
11. Install the ABS sensor retaining bolt.
12. Install the front brake rotor shield, rotor, bracket and caliper.
13. Install the wheel and snug the lug nuts.
14. Lower the vehicle and tighten the lug nuts to 100 ft. lbs. (135 Nm).

MPV Models

REAR WHEEL DRIVE

♦ See Figures 91 thru 98

1. Raise and safely support the vehicle.
2. Remove the wheel assembly.
3. Remove the hub dust cap.
4. Remove the locknut.
5. Remove the brake caliper.
6. Remove the disc plate.
7. Remove the hub assembly.

90978P55

Fig. 91 Remove the dust cap from the wheel hub, using pliers, if necessary

90978P56

Fig. 92 Installing the dust cap onto the wheel hub using a hammer and a 2 3/8 inch socket

90978P57

Fig. 93 If the wheel hub retaining nut was staked previously, open it up using a hammer and a punch or drift

90978P58

Fig. 94 Using a 34mm deep well socket, remove the wheel hub retaining nut

Fig. 95 Remove the wheel hub/bearing assembly by sliding straight off of the spindle

Fig. 96 Be sure to clean the spindle area of any debris using a towel

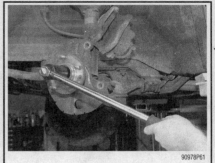

Fig. 97 After installing the wheel hub/bearing assembly and retaining nut, use a torque wrench to tighten the nut

To install:

8. Install the hub assembly.
9. Install the disc plate.
10. Install the brake caliper, torque the mounting bolts to 66–79 ft. lbs. (89–107 Nm).
11. Install the locknut, torque to 131–173 ft. lbs. (117–235 Nm).
12. Using a hammer and a punch or drift, stake the hub/bearing retaining nut onto the spindle.
13. Install the hub dust cap.
14. Install the wheel assembly.
15. Lower the vehicle.

4-WHEEL DRIVE

▶ See Figure 99

1. Raise and safely support the vehicle.
2. Remove the wheel assembly.
3. Remove the locknut.
4. Remove the brake caliper.
5. Remove the disc plate retaining screw(s).
6. Disconnect the tie-rod end from the knuckle.
7. Disconnect the lower ball joint.
8. Remove the disc plate.
9. Remove the ball joint mounting nuts and bolts.
10. Remove the knuckle, wheel hub and dustplate as an assembly.
11. Remove the wheel hub/bearing assembly from the knuckle.

To install:

12. Install wheel hub/bearing assembly to the knuckle.
13. Install the knuckle assembly. Torque the strut mounting nut to 69–86 ft. lbs. (94–116 Nm).
14. Install the ball joint mounting nuts and bolts. Torque the upper mounting bolts to 76–101 ft. lbs. (102–137 Nm). Torque the through-bolt nut to 95–106 ft. lbs. (128–171 Nm).
15. Replace the disc plate.
16. Install ball joint to the knuckle assembly. Torque the ball joint nut to 116–137 ft. lbs. (157–186 Nm).
17. Connect the tie-rod end, torque the nut to 44–57 ft. lbs. (59–78 Nm).
18. Install the brake caliper, torque the mounting bolts to 66–79 ft. lbs. (89–107 Nm).
19. Install the disc plate retaining nut.
20. Install the locknut, torque to 174–231 ft. lbs. (236–313 Nm).
21. Install the wheel assembly.
22. Lower the vehicle.

ADJUSTMENT

Navajo and B Series Pick-up Models (Rear Wheel Drive)

▶ See Figure 100

1. Raise and support the vehicle safely. Remove the wheel cover. Remove the grease cap from the hub.

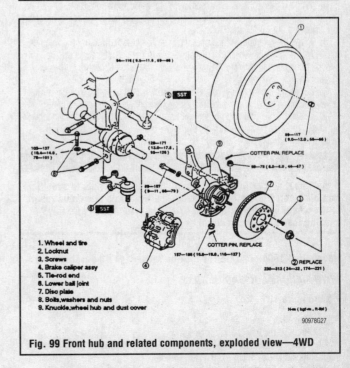

Fig. 98 Using a hammer and a punch or drift, stake the hub/bearing retaining nut onto the spindle

1. Wheel and tire
2. Locknut
3. Screws
4. Brake caliper assy
5. Tie-rod end
6. Lower ball joint
7. Disc plate
8. Bolts, washers and nuts
9. Knuckle, wheel hub and dust cover

COTTER PIN, REPLACE

COTTER PIN, REPLACE

REPLACE

Fig. 99 Front hub and related components, exploded view—4WD

2. Wipe the excess grease from the end of the spindle. Remove the cotter pin and retainer. Discard the cotter pin.
3. Loosen the adjusting nut 3 turns.

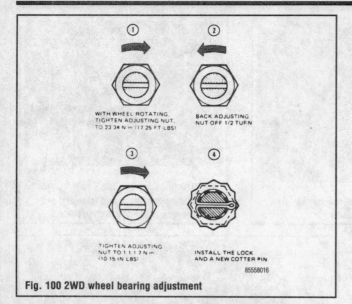

Fig. 100 2WD wheel bearing adjustment

❄ WARNING

Obtain running clearance between the disc brake rotor surface and shoe linings by rocking the entire wheel assembly in and out several times in order to push the caliper and brake pads away from the rotor. An alternate method to obtain proper running clearance is to tap lightly on the caliper housing. Be sure not to tap on any other area that may damage the disc brake rotor or the brake lining surfaces. Do not pry on the phenolic caliper piston. The running clearance must be maintained throughout the adjustment procedure. If proper clearance cannot be maintained, the caliper must be removed from its mounting.

4. While rotating the wheel assembly, tighten the adjusting nut to 17–25 ft. lbs. in order to seat the bearings. Loosen the adjusting nut a half turn. Retighten the adjusting nut 18–20 inch lbs.

5. Place the retainer on the adjusting nut. The castellations on the retainer must be in alignment with the cotter pin holes in the spindle. Once this is accomplished install a new cotter pin and bend the ends to insure its being locked in place.

6. Check for proper wheel rotation. If correct, install the grease cap and wheel cover. If rotation is noisy or rough recheck your work and correct as required.

7. Lower the vehicle and tighten the lug nuts to 100 ft. lbs., if the wheel was removed. Before driving the vehicle pump the brake pedal several times to restore normal brake pedal travel.

❄ CAUTION

If the wheel was removed, retighten the wheel lug nuts to specification after about 500 miles of driving. Failure to do this could result in the wheel coming off while the vehicle is in motion possibly causing loss of vehicle control or collision.

Navajo and 1994–97 B Series Pick-up Models (4-Wheel Drive)

WITH MANUAL LOCKING HUBS

♦ See Figure 101

1. Raise the vehicle and install jackstands.
2. Remove the wheel and tire assembly.
3. Remove the retainer washers from the lug nut studs and remove the manual locking hub assembly from the spindle.
4. Remove the snapring and spacer from the end of the spindle shaft.
5. Remove the outer wheel bearing locknut from the spindle using 4 prong spindle nut spanner wrench, T86T-1197-A or equivalent. Make sure the tabs on the tool engage the slots in the locknut.

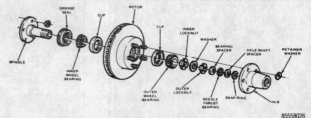

Fig. 101 Exploded view of the manual locking hubs and wheel bearings

6. Remove the locknut washer from the spindle.
7. Loosen the inner wheel bearing locknut using 4 prong spindle nut spanner wrench, tool T86T-1197-A or equivalent. Make sure that the tabs on the tool engage the slots in the locknut and that the slot in the tool is over the pin on the locknut.
8. Tighten the inner locknut to 35 ft. lbs. (47 Nm) to seat the bearings.
9. Spin the rotor and back off the inner locknut ¼ turn. Install the lockwasher on the spindle. Retighten the inner locknut to 16 inch lbs. (1.8 Nm). It may be necessary to turn the inner locknut slightly so that the pin on the locknut aligns with the closest hole in the lockwasher.
10. Install the outer wheel bearing locknut using 4 prong spindle nut spanner wrench, tool T86T-1197-A or equivalent. Tighten locknut to 150 ft. lbs.
11. Install the axle shaft spacer.
12. Clip the snapring onto the end of the spindle.
13. Install the manual hub assembly over the spindle. Install the retainer washers.
14. Install the wheel and tire assembly. Install and torque lug nuts to specification.
15. Check the end-play of the wheel and tire assembly on the spindle. End-play should be 0.001–0.003 in. (0.025–0.076mm) and the maximum torque to rotate the hub should be 25 inch lbs. (2.8Nm).

WITH AUTOMATIC LOCKING HUBS

♦ See Figure 102

1. Raise the vehicle and install jackstands.
2. Remove the wheel and tire assembly.
3. Remove the retainer washers from the lug nut studs and remove the automatic locking hub assembly from the spindle.
4. Remove the snapring and spacer from the end of the spindle shaft.
5. Pull the locking cam assembly and the two plastic spacers off of the wheel bearing adjusting nut.
6. Use a magnet and remove the locking key from under the adjusting nut. If required, rotate the adjusting nut slightly to relieve pressure against the locking key.

❄ WARNING

To prevent damage to the adjusting nut and spindle threads on vehicles equipped with automatic hubs, look into the spindle keyway under the adjusting nut and remove the separate locking key before removing the adjusting nut.

7. Loosen the wheel bearing locknut using a 2-³⁄₈ inch (60.3mm) hex socket, such as Hex Locknut Wrench T70T-4252-B.

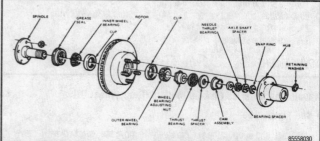

Fig. 102 Exploded view of the automatic locking hubs and wheel bearings

8. Tighten the inner locknut to 35 ft. lbs. (47 Nm) to seat the bearings.

9. Spin the rotor and back off the inner locknut ¼ turn (90°). Retighten the locknut to 16 inch lbs. (1.8 Nm).

10. Align the closest lug in the bearing adjusting nut with the center of the spindle keyway slot. Advance the nut to the next if required.

11. Install the separate locking key in the spindle keyway under the adjusting nut.

> ### ✳✳ CAUTION
>
> **Extreme care must be taken when aligning the adjusting nut with the center of the spindle keyway slot to prevent damage to the separate locking key. The wheel and tire assembly may come off while the vehicle is in motion if the key is damaged.**

12. Install the two plastic thrust spacers and push or press the cam assembly onto the adjusting nut by lining up the keyway in the cam assembly with the separate locking key.

> ### ✳✳ WARNING
>
> **Do not damage the locking key when installing the cam assembly.**

13. Install the axle shaft spacer.

14. Clip the snapring onto the end of the spindle.

15. Install the manual hub assembly over the spindle. Install the retainer washers.

16. Install the wheel and tire assembly. Install and torque lug nuts to specification.

17. Check the endplate of the wheel and tire assembly on the spindle. Endplay should be 0.001–0.003 in. (0.025–0.076mm) and the maximum torque to rotate the hub should be 25 inch lbs. (2.8Nm).

1998 B Series Pick-up (4-Wheel Drive)

The 1998 B Series Pick-up uses non-adjustable wheel bearings. If the endplate is not within specifications, the wheel bearings must be replaced. End-play should be 0.000–0.003 in. (0.00–0.08mm).

MPV Models

The wheel hub/bearing assembly used on both rear- and 4-wheel drive models is a non-adjustable component. No adjustments can be made, nor are any possible. However, the wheel bearing can be inspected as follows:

1. Raise and support the vehicle safely. Remove the tire and wheel assembly.

2. Remove and properly support the caliper assembly.

3. Position a dial indicator gauge against the dust cap. Push and pull the disc brake rotor or brake drum in and out in the axial direction and measure the end-play of the wheel bearing.

4. End-play should not exceed 0.002 in. (0.05mm).

5. If end-play is excessive, check the hub nut torque or replace the bearing.

Wheel Alignment

If the tires are worn unevenly, if the vehicle is not stable on the highway or if the handling seems uneven in spirited driving, the wheel alignment should be checked. If an alignment problem is suspected, first check for improper tire inflation and other possible causes. These can be worn suspension or steering components, accident damage or even unmatched tires. If any worn or damaged components are found, they must be replaced before the wheels can be properly aligned. Wheel alignment requires very expensive equipment and involves minute adjustments which must be accurate; it should only be performed by a trained technician. Take your vehicle to a properly equipped shop.

Following is a description of the alignment angles which are adjustable on most vehicles and how they affect vehicle handling. Although these angles can apply to both the front and rear wheels, usually only the front suspension is adjustable.

CASTER

▶ See Figure 103

Looking at a vehicle from the side, caster angle describes the steering axis rather than a wheel angle. The steering knuckle is attached to a control arm or strut at the top and a control arm at the bottom. The wheel pivots around the line between these points to steer the vehicle. When the upper point is tilted back, this is described as positive caster. Having a positive caster tends to make the wheels self-centering, increasing directional stability. Excessive positive caster makes the wheels hard to steer, while an uneven caster will cause a pull to one side. Overloading the vehicle or sagging rear springs will affect caster, as will raising the rear of the vehicle. If the rear of the vehicle is lower than normal, the caster becomes more positive.

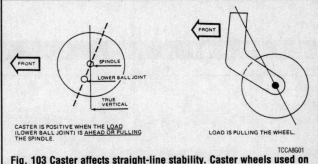

Fig. 103 Caster affects straight-line stability. Caster wheels used on shopping carts, for example, employ positive caster

CAMBER

▶ See Figure 104

Looking from the front of the vehicle, camber is the inward or outward tilt of the top of wheels. When the tops of the wheels are tilted in, this is negative

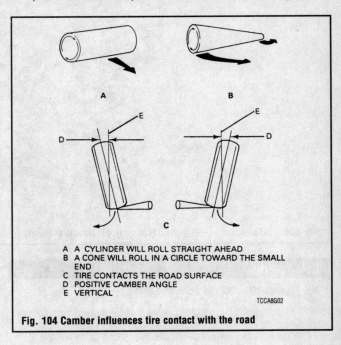

A   A CYLINDER WILL ROLL STRAIGHT AHEAD
B   A CONE WILL ROLL IN A CIRCLE TOWARD THE SMALL END
C   TIRE CONTACTS THE ROAD SURFACE
D   POSITIVE CAMBER ANGLE
E   VERTICAL

TCCA8G02

Fig. 104 Camber influences tire contact with the road

camber; if they are tilted out, it is positive. In a turn, a slight amount of negative camber helps maximize contact of the tire with the road. However, too much negative camber compromises straight-line stability, increases bump steer and torque steer.

TOE

▶ **See Figure 105**

Looking down at the wheels from above the vehicle, toe angle is the distance between the front of the wheels, relative to the distance between the back of the wheels. If the wheels are closer at the front, they are said to be toed-in or to have negative toe. A small amount of negative toe enhances directional stability and provides a smoother ride on the highway.

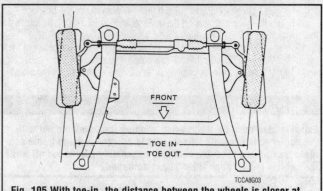

Fig. 105 With toe-in, the distance between the wheels is closer at the front than at the rear

REAR SUSPENSION

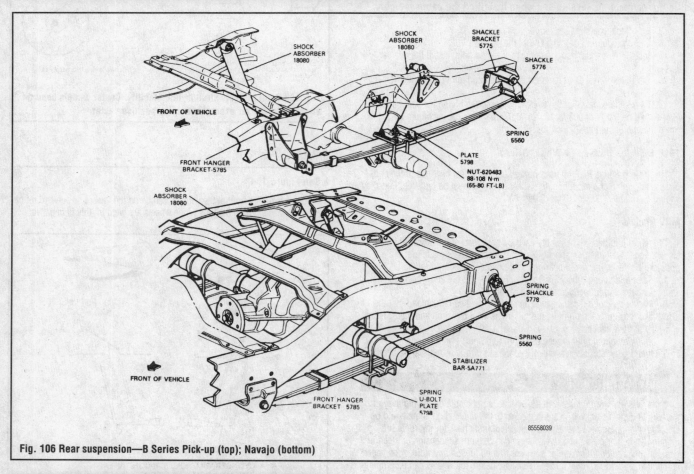

Fig. 106 Rear suspension—B Series Pick-up (top); Navajo (bottom)

Coil Springs

▶ **See Figures 107, 108, 109 and 110**

MPV models are the only vehicles covered in this manual with coil spring rear suspension.

1. Raise and safely support the vehicle. Remove the splash shield.
2. Remove the stabilizer bar.
3. Remove the nut and disconnect the height sensor from the rear axle.
4. Remove the bolt attaching the parking brake cable bracket.

5. Support the rear axle housing with a jack. Raise the jack slightly to take the load off the shock absorbers.
6. Remove the attaching bolts and nuts and disconnect the shock absorbers from the lower axle housing.
7. Slowly lower the axle housing until the spring tension is relieved.
8. Remove the bump stopper.
9. Remove the coil springs.
10. Remove the spring seats, if equipped.

To install:
11. Install the upper and lower spring seats, if removed.

REAR SUSPENSION COMPONENTS—EXCEPT MPV

1. Leaf springs
2. Stabilizer bar links
3. Stabilizer bar
4. Shock absorbers
5. Spring shackles

REAR SUSPENSION COMPONENTS—MPV

1. Coil springs
2. Upper control arms
3. Lower control arms
4. Sway bar (stabilizer bar)
5. Sway bar link

Fig. 107 Using a 14mm deep well socket, loosen the rubber coil spring bump stopper mounting bolt

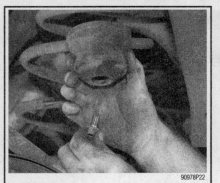

Fig. 108 Remove the bump stopper and mounting bolt

Fig. 109 Remove the rear coil spring and upper rubber mount from the vehicle

Fig. 110 Remove the lower coil spring mount from the top of the differential housing

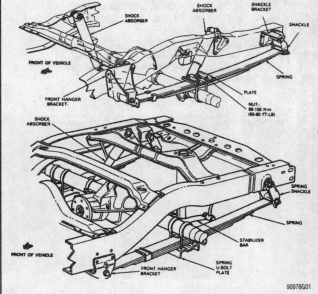

Fig. 111 Exploded view of the B Series Pick-up U-bolt and spring plate assembly—Navajo similar

12. Install the coil springs, making sure the larger diameter coil is toward the axle housing.

13. Install the bump stopper.

14. Raise the axle housing enough to connect the shock absorbers. Install the attaching bolts and nuts and tighten to 56–76 ft. lbs. (76–103 Nm). Remove the jack.

15. Install the bolt attaching the parking brake cable bracket and the nut attaching the height sensor.

16. Install the stabilizer bar. Tighten the link bolt nut until 0.28 in. (7mm) of thread is exposed at the top of the link bolt. Do not tighten the stabilizer bar bushing bracket bolts at this time.

17. Lower the vehicle. With the vehicle unladen, tighten the stabilizer bar bushing bracket bolts to 23–38 ft. lbs. (34–51 Nm).

18. Install the splash shield.

Leaf Springs

REMOVAL & INSTALLATION

◆ See Figure 111

1. Raise the vehicle and install jackstands under the frame. The vehicle must be supported in such a way that the rear axle hangs free with the tires still touching the ground.

2. Remove the nuts from the spring U-bolts and drive the U-bolts from the U-bolt plate.

3. Remove the spring to bracket nut and bolt at the front of the spring.

4. Remove the shackle upper and lower nuts and bolts at the rear of the spring.

5. Remove the spring and shackle assembly from the rear shackle bracket.

To install:

6. Position the spring in the shackle. Install the upper shackle spring bolt and nut with the bolt head facing outward.

7. Position the front end of the spring in the bracket and install the bolt and nut.

8. Position the shackle in the rear bracket and install the nut and bolt.

9. Position the spring on top of the axle with the spring tie bolt centered in the hole provided in the seat.

10. Lower the vehicle to the floor. Torque the spring U-bolt nuts to 65–75 ft. lbs. (88–102 Nm). Torque the front spring bolt to 74–115 ft. lbs. (100–155 Nm). Torque the rear shackle nuts and bolts to 74–115 ft. lbs. (100–155 Nm).

Shock Absorbers

REMOVAL & INSTALLATION

▶ **See Figures 112 thru 119**

1. Raise and safely support the vehicle.

2. In order to take the load off of the shock absorber, support the rear axle assembly by placing a jack stand underneath the lower shock absorber mounting bracket, then using a 21mm box wrench, loosen the mounting nut

3. If equipped with a load levelling system, remove the height sensor.

4. If equipped with ABS, remove the wheel speed sensor to prevent possible damage.

5. Remove the shock absorber lower retaining nut and bolt. Swing the lower end free of the mounting bracket on the axle housing.

6. Remove the retaining nut(s) from the upper shock absorber mounting.

7. Remove the shock absorber from the vehicle.

8. Installation is the reverse of the removal procedure.

9. On the Navajo, tighten the upper shock absorber retaining nuts to 15–21 ft. lbs. (21–29 Nm) and the lower shock absorber retaining bolt to 39–53 ft. lbs. (53–72 Nm).

10. On the B Series Pick-up, tighten the upper and lower shock absorber retaining nuts to 39–53 ft. lbs. (53–72 Nm).

11. On the MPV, tighten the upper and lower shock absorber retaining nuts to 56–75 ft. lbs. (76–102 Nm).

Fig. 112 Support the rear axle assembly by placing a jack stand underneath the lower shock absorber mounting bracket, then using a 21mm box wrench, loosen the mounting nut

Fig. 113 Remove the mounting nut, washer and retaining plate from the bottom of the shock absorber

Fig. 114 Place the nut onto the end of the retaining bolt to prevent the bolt from being damaged by the hammer blows

Fig. 115 Pull out the lower shock absorber-to-rear axle retaining bolt

Fig. 116 The top rear shock absorber mounting nut is accessible through a hole in the inner fenderwell splash shield

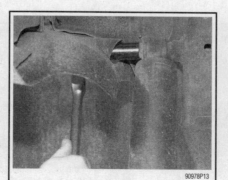

Fig. 117 Loosen the upper shock absorber mounting bolt using a 21mm socket

Fig. 118 Remove the mounting nut, washer and retaining plate from the top of the shock absorber

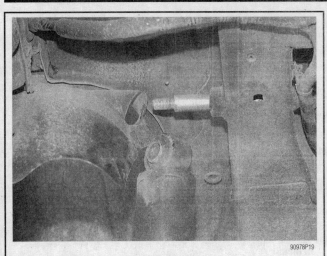

Fig. 119 Separate the top of the rear shock absorber from the top mounting stud

TESTING

1. Visually check the shock absorbers for the presence of fluid leakage. A thin film of fluid is acceptable. Anything more than that means that the shock absorber must be replaced.

2. Disconnect the lower end of the shock absorber. Compress and extend the shock fully as fast as possible. If the action is not smooth in both directions, or there is no pressure resistance, replace the shock absorber. Shock absorbers should be replaced in pairs. In the case of relatively new shock absorbers, where one has failed, that one, alone, may be replaced.

Rear Control Arms

REMOVAL & INSTALLATION

Lateral Rod

▶ See Figure 120

1. Raise and safely support the vehicle.
2. Support the axle housing with a jack.
3. Remove the lateral rod-to-chassis stud bolt and nut and the lateral rod-to-axle housing nut.

4. Remove the lateral rod.
5. Place the lateral rod in position and secure it with the mounting hardware. Make sure the lateral rod is installed with the identification mark toward the body.
6. Tighten the lateral rod-to-axle housing nut to 108–127 ft. lbs. (146–167 Nm). Tighten the lateral rod-to-chassis stud bolt and nuts to 94–127 ft. lbs. (128–167 Nm).

Upper Control Arms

▶ See Figure 121

1. Raise and safely support the vehicle.
2. Support the axle housing with a jack.
3. Remove the upper control arm-to-chassis bolt and nut and the upper control arm-to-axle housing bolt and nut.
4. Remove the upper control arm.
5. Place the control arm in position and secure it with the mounting bolts. Tighten the upper control arm attaching bolts and nuts to 94–127 ft. lbs. (128–167 Nm).

Lower Control Arms

▶ See Figure 122

1. Raise and safely support the vehicle.
2. Support the axle housing with a jack.
3. Remove the lower control arm-to-chassis bolt and nut and the lower control arm-to-axle housing bolt and nut.
4. Remove the lower control arm.
5. Position the lower control arm and install the mounting bolts. Tighten the upper control arm attaching bolts and nuts to 101–127 ft. lbs. (137–167 Nm).

Stabilizer Bar

REMOVAL & INSTALLATION

Navajo and B Series Pick-up Models

▶ See Figure 123

❊❊ WARNING

If equipped, always turn off the Automatic Ride Control (ARC) service switch before lifting the vehicle off of the ground. Failure to do so could damage the ARC system components. Refer to Section 1 for jacking procedures.

1. As required, raise and support the vehicle.
2. Remove the nuts, bolts and washers and disconnect the stabilizer bar from the links.

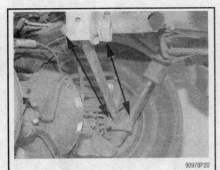

Fig. 120 Using a backup wrench, remove the nuts and bolts securing the lateral rod to the vehicle underbody and rear axle

Fig. 121 Remove the nuts and bolts to the upper trailing arm

Fig. 122 Remove the nuts and bolts to the lower trailing arm

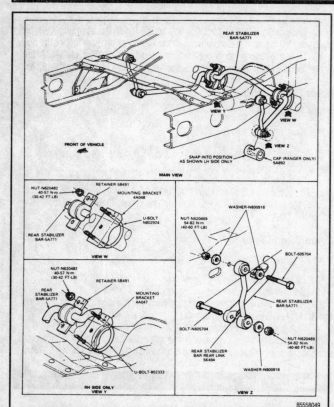

Fig. 123 Common rear stabilizer bar mounting—B Series Pick-up shown, other models are similar

3. Remove the U-bolts and nuts from the mounting bracket and retainers. Remove the mounting brackets, retainers and stabilizer bars.

To install:

4. Position the U-bolts and mounting brackets on the axle with the brackets having the **UP** marking in the proper position.

5. Install the stabilizer bar and retainers on the mounting brackets with the retainers having the **UP** marking in the proper position.

6. Connect the stabilizer bar to the rear links. Install the nuts, bolts, and washers and tighten.

7. Tighten the mounting bracket U-bolt nuts to 30–42 ft. lbs.

MPV Models

◆ **See Figures 124 thru 129**

1. Raise and safely support the vehicle.

2. Remove the stabilizer bar links from both sides of the stabilizer bar.

3. Remove the stabilizer bar bracket and bushing from the axle and remove the stabilizer bar.

To install:

4. Install the bushing on the bar and install the bar finger-tight on the axle housing.

5. Install the stabilizer bar links to the frame brackets.

6. Lower the vehicle to the floor and tighten the stabilizer bar to axle bolts to 26–37 ft. lbs. (35–50 Nm).

Rear Wheel Bearings

REMOVAL AND INSTALLATION

For replacement of the rear wheel bearing, please refer to the axle shaft removal and installation procedure, located in Section 7.

Fig. 124 Using a 12mm box wrench and a 12mm open end wrench as a backup wrench, loosen then remove the sway bar link locking nut

Fig. 125 Holding the sway bar link bolt with a 12mm box wrench, remove the retaining nut

Fig. 126 After removing the sway bar link retaining nut, remove the top bushing washer and rubber bushing

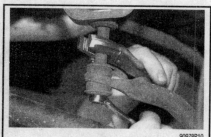

Fig. 127 The sway bar link may be corroded to the metal sleeve. If this is so, secure the sleeve in a pair of locking pliers while using a box wrench to loosen the corrosion bond between the two components

Fig. 128 Spray the sway bar link with a rust penetrating lubricant to aid in the removal of the sway bar link from the sleeve

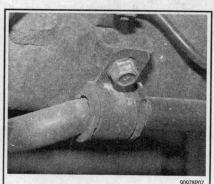

Fig. 129 Remove the sway bar bushing retainer mounting bolt

STEERING

Steering Wheel

REMOVAL & INSTALLATION

Navajo and 1994 B Series Pick-up

▶ See Figures 130 thru 137

1. Disconnect the negative battery cable.
2. Center the steering wheel to the straight ahead position.
3. From the underside of the steering wheel, remove the screws that hold the steering wheel pad to the steering wheel spokes.

4. Lift up the steering wheel pad and disconnect the horn wires from the steering wheel pad by pulling the spade terminal from the blade connectors.
5. Remove the steering wheel pad. Loosen the bolt 2 or 3 turns from the steering shaft.

✳✳ CAUTION

Tilt columns have a compression spring under the steering wheel that can unexpectantly "pop up" the steering wheel if the bolt is removed completely.

6. Using the proper steering wheel removal tool, loosen the steering wheel on the steering column.

Fig. 130 To remove the steering wheel, first remove the horn pad retaining screws from the backside of the wheel

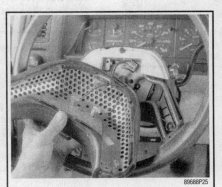

Fig. 131 Next, lift up and turn over the horn pad . . .

Fig. 132 . . . then disconnect the horn pad electrical plug from the column

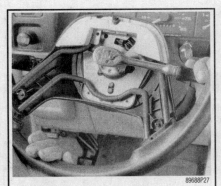

Fig. 133 Loosen the steering wheel-to-shaft retaining bolt a couple of turns . . .

Fig. 134 . . . then assemble a puller to the wheel and loosen the wheel from the shaft

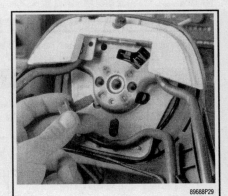

Fig. 135 Finally, remove the retaining bolt

Fig. 136 Before pulling the wheel from the shaft, make a matchmark on the shaft and wheel

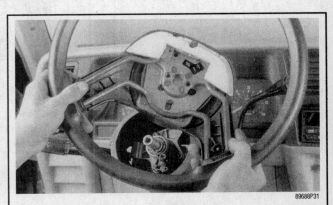

Fig. 137 Finish by pulling the steering wheel from the column shaft

❋❋ WARNING

Do not hammer on the steering wheel or the steering shaft or use a knock off type steering wheel puller as damage to the steering column will occur.

7. Remove the tool and the steering wheel retaining bolt then lift off the steering wheel.

8. Installation is the reverse of the removal procedure. Be sure that the steering wheel is properly aligned before installing the lock bolt. Torque the steering wheel lock bolt to 23–33 ft. lbs. (31–45 Nm).

1995–98 B Series Pick-up Models

♦ **See Figures 138, 139 and 140**

❋❋ CAUTION

Whenever working on a vehicle equipped with an air bag, always refer to Section 6 for disarming procedures. Follow the procedures outlined or severe injury, or even death may occur.

➥The manufacturer recommends installing the steering wheel using a new wheel-to-shaft retaining bolt. Before beginning this procedure, obtain a new bolt.

1. Follow the procedures in Section 6 and disarm the air bag.
2. Pry out the two plugs covering the drivers side air bag module screws on the sides of the steering wheel.
3. Remove the two air bag module retaining screws and carefully lift the module away from the steering wheel.
4. Disconnect the air bag electrical harness plug at the sliding contact. Also unplug the horn and, if equipped, cruise control wire harness connectors.

❋❋ CAUTION

Always carry the air bag with the horn pad facing away from your body.

5. Remove the air bag module and set it on a clean, dry and stable bench with the horn pad facing upwards.

❋❋ CAUTION

Tilt columns have a compression spring under the steering wheel that can unexpectedly "pop up" the steering wheel if the bolt is removed completely.

6. Loosen but do not remove the steering wheel retaining bolt approximately 2 to 3 turns.
7. Using the proper steering wheel removal tool, loosen the steering wheel on the steering column.

❋❋ WARNING

Do not hammer on the steering wheel or the steering shaft or use a knock off type steering wheel puller as damage to the steering column will occur.

8. Remove the tool and the steering wheel retaining bolt. Discard the steering wheel retaining bolt.

❋❋ WARNING

Ensure that the air bag sliding contact wire harness does not get caught on the steering wheel assembly when lifting the wheel from the shaft.

9. Remove the steering wheel while routing the wire harness through the wheel opening.

To install:

10. Ensure that the vehicleís front wheels are in the straight-ahead position.
11. Route the air bag sliding contact wire harnesses through the steering wheel opening (at the 3 oíclock position).
12. Align the steering wheel and shaft and press the wheel onto the shaft. Ensure that the sliding contact wire harness does not get pinched by the wheel.
13. Install the new lock bolt and tighten to 25–34 ft. lbs. (34–46 Nm).
14. Position the air bag module and connect all of the wire harness plugs to it.
15. Carefully install the module to the wheel and loosely install the side retaining bolts.
16. Hold the module in position while tightening the retaining bolts to 67–92 inch lbs. (7.6–10.4 Nm).
17. Install the two cover plugs by snapping them into the holes on the side of the steering wheel.
18. Arm the air bag system by following the procedures in Section 6.

MPV Models

♦ **See Figure 141**

❋❋ CAUTION

The air bag system must be disarmed before removing the steering wheel. Failure to do so may cause accidental deployment, property damage or personal injury.

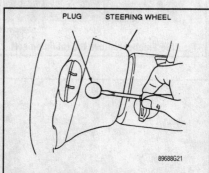

Fig. 138 After disarming the air bag, pry out the retaining screw covers on the sides of the steering wheel

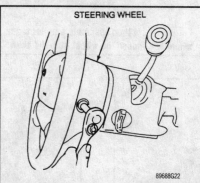

Fig. 139 Remove the two air bag module retaining screws

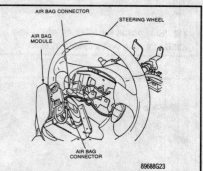

Fig. 140 Pull the module away from the steering wheel and disconnect all of the wire harness plugs

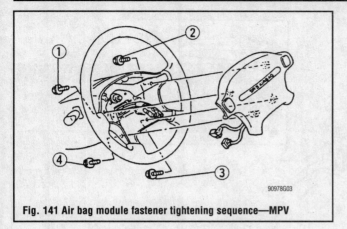

Fig. 141 Air bag module fastener tightening sequence—MPV

1. Set the steering wheel so the front wheels are straight ahead.
2. Disconnect the negative battery cable.
3. Disarm the air bag.
4. At the back of the steering wheel hub, remove the fasteners that hold the air bag assembly and remove the air bag. Place it in a safe place, pad side up.

CAUTION

Always carry an air bag assembly with the bag and trim cover away from your body. Store the assembly facing upward; never place the assembly face down on any surface.

5. Remove the steering wheel attaching bolt or nut. Check to see if the steering wheel and steering shaft have alignment marks or flats. If there are no steering wheel-to-steering column shaft alignment marks or flats, matchmark the steering wheel and column shaft so they can be reassembled in the same position.
6. Using a steering wheel puller, remove the steering wheel from the steering column shaft.

➡ **Do not hammer on the steering wheel or steering shaft or use a knock-off type steering wheel puller, as either will damage the steering column.**

To install:
7. Double check that the front wheels are in the straight-ahead position and mount the steering wheel. Make sure the matchmarks are aligned.
8. Tighten the steering wheel nut to 29–36 ft. lbs. (40–49 Nm). Install the air bag unit and tighten the retaining fasteners in a clockwise sequence to 35–52 inch lbs. (4–6 Nm) for 1994–95 MPV, and 70–104 inch lbs. (8–12 Nm) for 1996–98 MPV.
9. Arm the air bag system by following the procedures in Section 6.
10. Connect the negative battery and check the steering column for proper operation.

Combination Switch

REMOVAL & INSTALLATION

Navajo and B Series Pick-up
▶ **See Figures 142 and 143**

1. Disconnect the negative battery cable. Remove the steering wheel.
2. On vehicles equipped with tilt wheel, remove the tilt lever.
3. On vehicles equipped with tilt wheel, remove the steering column collar by pressing on the collar from the top and bottom while removing the collar.

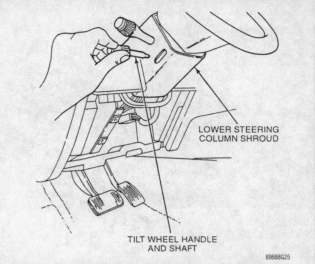

Fig. 142 To remove the tilt column control lever, simply rotate it counterclockwise until removed

4. Remove the instrument panel trim cover retaining screws. Remove the trim cover.
5. Remove the 2 screws from the bottom of the steering column shroud. Remove the bottom half of the shroud by pulling the shroud down and toward the rear of the vehicle.
6. If the vehicle is equipped with automatic transmission, move the shift lever as required to aid in removal of the shroud. Lift the top half of the shroud from the column.
7. Remove the 2 self tapping screws that retain the combination switch to the steering column casting. Disengage the switch from the casting.
8. Disconnect the 3 electrical connectors, using caution not to damage the locking tabs. Be sure not to damage the PRNDL cable.
9. Installation is the reverse of the removal procedure. Torque the combination switch retaining screws to 18–27 inch lbs. (2–3 Nm).

1994–95 MPV
▶ **See Figures 144 and 145**

CAUTION

The air bag system must be disarmed before removing the steering wheel. Failure to do so may cause accidental deployment, property damage or personal injury.

CAUTION

Always carry an air bag assembly with the bag and trim cover away from your body. Store the assembly facing upward; never place the assembly face down on any surface.

1. Disconnect the battery.
2. Remove the steering wheel.
3. Remove the attaching screws, and remove the upper and lower steering column covers.
4. Disconnect the electrical connectors.
5. Remove the combination retaining screw, and remove the switch.
To install:
6. Install the combination switch and secure with the retaining screw.

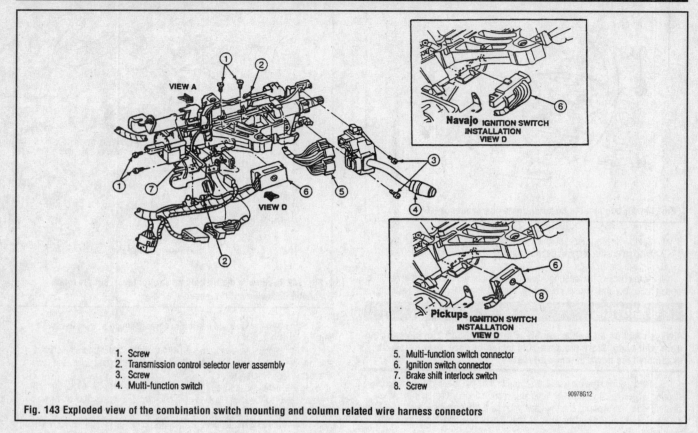

1. Screw
2. Transmission control selector lever assembly
3. Screw
4. Multi-function switch
5. Multi-function switch connector
6. Ignition switch connector
7. Brake shift interlock switch
8. Screw

90978G12

Fig. 143 Exploded view of the combination switch mounting and column related wire harness connectors

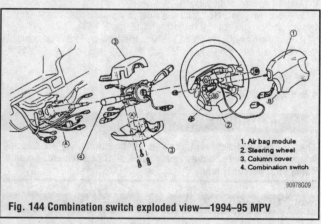

1. Air bag module
2. Steering wheel
3. Column cover
4. Combination switch

90978G09

Fig. 144 Combination switch exploded view—1994–95 MPV

7. Connect all combination switch connectors.
8. Install the steering column covers with retaining screws.
9. Make sure the front wheels are aligned straight ahead and set the clock spring connector by turning it clockwise until it stops, then return the connector 2¾ turns. Align the marks on the clock spring connector and the outer housing.
10. Install the steering wheel.
11. Connect the negative battery cable.
12. Check all the functions of the combination switch for proper operation.

1996–98 MPV

▶ See Figure 146

❋❋ CAUTION

The air bag system must be disarmed before removing the steering wheel. Failure to do so may cause accidental deployment, property damage or personal injury.

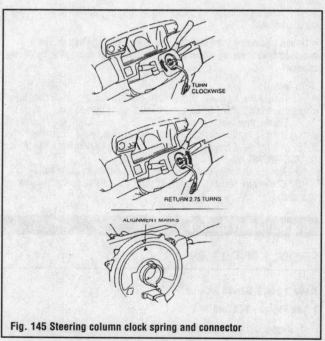

TURN CLOCKWISE

RETURN 2.75 TURNS

ALIGNMENT MARKS

Fig. 145 Steering column clock spring and connector

❋❋ CAUTION

Always carry an air bag assembly with the bag and trim cover away from your body. Store the assembly facing upward; never place the assembly face down on any surface.

1. Disconnect the negative battery cable and wait at least 90 seconds before performing any work.

2. Remove the service caps and remove the bolts securing the air bag module to the steering wheel. Disconnect the air bag connector and remove the air bag module.

3. Remove the steering wheel nut and remove the steering wheel.

4. Remove the screws and the upper and lower steering column covers.

5. Disconnect the clock spring connector, remove the mounting screws, and remove the clock spring.

6. Disconnect the combination switch connector, remove the mounting screws and remove the combination switch.

To install:

7. Install the combination switch with the mounting screws and reconnect the connector.

8. Install the clock spring with its screws and reconnect the connector. The clock spring must be adjusted in the following manner:

   a. Turn the clock spring clockwise until it stops.

   b. Turn the clock spring counterclockwise 2¾ turns.

   c. Align the marks on the clock spring connector with that on the outer housing.

9. Reinstall the steering column upper and lower covers with the mounting screws.

10. Reinstall the steering wheel and tighten with the nut.

11. Reconnect the air bag module connector and install the air bag with its mounting bolts. Reinstall the service caps.

12. Reconnect the negative battery cable and check for proper operation.

Ignition Switch

REMOVAL & INSTALLATION

Navajo and B Series Pick-up

▶ See Figure 143

1. Disconnect the negative battery cable.

2. Remove the steering wheel.

3. As necessary, remove all under dash panels in order to gain access to the ignition switch.

4. As necessary, lower the steering column to gain working clearance.

5. Disconnect the ignition switch electrical connectors.

6. Remove the ignition switch retaining screws from the studs. Disengage the ignition switch from switch rod. Remove the switch from the vehicle.

To install:

7. Position the lock cylinder in the **LOCK** position.

8. To set the switch, position a wire in the opening in the outer surface of the switch through its positions until the wire drops down into the slot.

➥The slot is in the bottom of the switch where the rod must be inserted to allow full movement through the switch positions.

9. Position the ignition switch on the column studs and over the actuating rod. Torque the retaining nuts to 40–64 inch lbs. (4.5–7.2 Nm).

10. Remove the wire from the slot in the housing. Continue the installation in the reverse order of the removal procedure.

MPV

▶ See Figure 147

1. Disconnect the negative battery cable. Wait at least 90 seconds before performing any work.

2. Remove the steering column cover and the lower dash panel.

3. Remove the screw and disconnect the connector.

4. Extract the key-reminder switch terminals from the ignition switch and remove the ignition switch.

5. Installation is the reverse of removal.

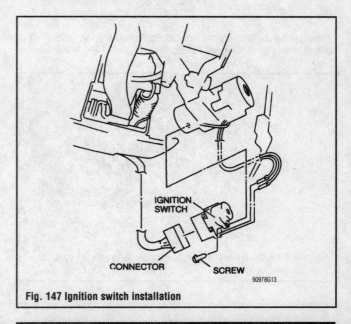

Fig. 147 Ignition switch installation

Ignition Lock Cylinder Assembly

REMOVAL & INSTALLATION

Navajo and B Series Pick-up

▶ See Figure 148

1. Disconnect the negative battery cable. Remove the steering wheel.

2. On vehicles equipped with tilt wheel, remove the tilt lever.

3. On vehicles equipped with tilt wheel, remove the steering column collar by pressing on the collar from the top and bottom while removing the collar.

4. Remove the instrument panel trim cover retaining screws. Remove the trim cover.

5. Remove the 2 screws from the bottom of the steering column shroud. Remove the bottom half of the shroud by pulling the shroud down and toward the rear of the vehicle.

6. Turn the lock cylinder with the ignition key in it to the **ON** position. On vehicles equipped with automatic transmission be sure that the selector lever is in the **P** position.

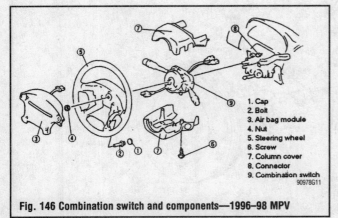

1. Cap
2. Bolt
3. Air bag module
4. Nut
5. Steering wheel
6. Screw
7. Column cover
8. Connector
9. Combination switch
90978G11

Fig. 146 Combination switch and components—1996–98 MPV

7. Push up on the lock cylinder retaining pin with a ⅛ in. (3mm) diameter wire pin or small punch. Pull the lock cylinder from the column housing. Disconnect the lock cylinder wiring plug from the horn brush wiring connector.

To install:

8. Prior to installation of the lock cylinder, lubricate the cylinder cavity, including the drive gear, with Lubriplate® or equivalent.

9. To install the lock cylinder, turn the lock cylinder to the **ON** position, depress the retaining pin. Insert the lock cylinder housing into its housing in the flange casting. Be sure that the tab at the end of the cylinder aligns with the slot in the ignition drive gear.

10. Turn the key to the **OFF** position. This action will permit the cylinder retaining pin to extend into the cylinder casting housing hole.

11. Using the ignition key rotate the lock cylinder to ensure correct mechanical operation in all positions. Connect the key warning wire plug.

12. Install the steering column lower shroud. Install the steering wheel.

13. Check for proper vehicle operation in **P** and **N**. Also be sure that the start circuit cannot be actuated in **D** or **R**.

MPV

The ignition lock is an integral part of the ignition switch. The ignition lock is serviced only as the ignition switch is replaced.

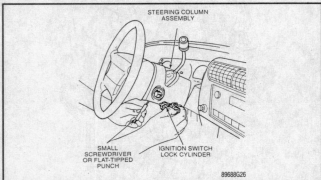

Fig. 148 Push the lock cylinder retaining pin then pull the cylinder from the column

Steering Linkage

▶ See Figure 149

REMOVAL & INSTALLATION

Navajo and 1994–97 B Series Pick-up

PITMAN ARM

1. As required, raise and safely support the vehicle using jackstands.
2. Remove the cotter pin and nut from the drag link ball stud at the pitman arm.
3. Remove the drag link ball stud from the pitman arm using pitman arm removal tool T64P-3590-F or equivalent.
4. Remove the pitman arm retaining nut and washer. Remove the pitman arm from the steering gear sector shaft using tool T64P-3590-F or equivalent.

To install:

5. Installation is the reverse of the removal procedure. Torque the pitman arm attaching washer and nut to 170–228 ft. lbs. (230–310 Nm). Torque the drag link ball stud nut to 51–73 ft. lbs. (70–100 Nm) and install a new cotter pin.
6. Check and adjust front end alignment, as required.

TIE ROD

▶ See Figures 150 thru 156

1. Raise and support the vehicle using jackstands. Be sure that the front wheels are in the straight ahead position.
2. Remove the nut and cotter pin from the ball stud on the drag link. Remove the ball stud from the drag link using pitman arm removal tool T64P-3590-F or equivalent.
3. Loosen the bolts on the tie rod adjusting sleeve. Be sure to count and record the number of turns it takes to remove the tie rod from the tie rod adjusting sleeve. Remove the tie rod from the vehicle.

To install:

4. Install the tie rod in the tie rod sleeve in the same number of turns it took to remove it. Torque the tie rod adjusting sleeve nuts to 30–42 ft. lbs. (40–57 Nm).
5. Be sure that the adjusting sleeve clamps are pointed down ±45°. Tighten the tie rod ball stud to drag link retaining bolt to 51–73 ft. lbs. (70–100 Nm). Install a new cotter pin.
6. Check and adjust front end alignment, as required.

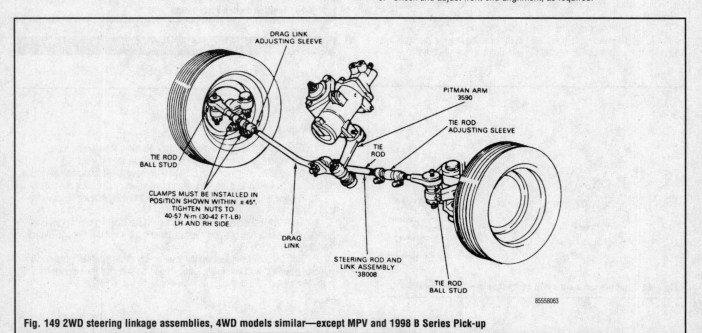

Fig. 149 2WD steering linkage assemblies, 4WD models similar—except MPV and 1998 B Series Pick-up

Fig. 150 To remove the tie rod end, first remove the cotter pin and discard it. A new pin will be used for installation

Fig. 151 Loosen and remove the tie rod end retaining nut . . .

Fig. 152 . . . then, using a jawed puller, loosen the tie rod stud-to-steering knuckle connection

Fig. 153 Loosen the tie rod sleeve clamp bolts . . .

Fig. 154 . . . and before unthreading the tie rod from the sleeve, make an installation mark on the threads

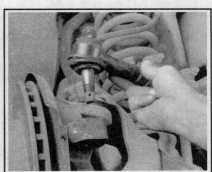

Fig. 155 Lift the tie rod end out of the steering knuckle bore . . .

Fig. 156 . . . and unthread the tie rod end from the adjusting sleeve

DRAG LINK

1. Raise and support the vehicle using jackstands. Be sure that the front wheels are in the straight ahead position.

2. Remove the nuts and cotter pins from the ball stud at the pitman arm and steering tie rod. Remove the ball studs from the linkage using pitman arm removal tool T64P-3590-F or equivalent.

3. Loosen the bolts on the drag link adjusting sleeve. Be sure to count and record the number of turns it takes to remove the drag link.

To install:

4. Install the drag link in the same number of turns it took to remove it. Tighten the adjusting sleeve nuts to 30–42 ft. lbs. (40–57 Nm). Be sure that the adjusting sleeve clamps are pointed down ±45°.

5. Position the drag link ball stud in the pitman arm. Position the steering tie rod ball stud in the drag link. With the vehicle wheels in the straight ahead position install and torque the nuts to 51–73 ft. lbs. (70–100 Nm). Install a new cotter pin.

6. Check and adjust front end alignment, as required.

1998 B Series Pick-up

❊❊ WARNING

If equipped, always turn off the Automatic Ride Control (ARC) service switch before lifting the vehicle off of the ground. Failure to do so could damage the ARC system components. Refer to Section 1 for jacking procedures.

OUTER TIE ROD END

1. Position the front wheels in the straight ahead position.

2. Raise and safely support the vehicle, as necessary.

3. Remove and discard the outer tie rod end retaining nut cotter pin.

4. Remove the nut and install a puller to separate the tie rod end from the steering knuckle.

5. Hold the tie rod end with a wrench and loosen the jam nut.

6. Mark the exact position of the outer tie rod on the inner tie rod threads. Grip the tie rod end with a pair of pliers and unscrew the outer end from the inner tie rod.

To install:

7. Ensure that the inner tie rod threads are clean.

8. Thread the outer tie rod end onto the inner tie rod to the same location as marked earlier.

9. Install the out tie rod end stud into the steering knuckle then install and tighten the attaching nut to 57–77 ft. lbs. (77–104 Nm). Install new cotter pins, advancing (tightening) the nut as required. NEVER loosen the nut to install the cotter pin.

10. Tighten the jam nut, while holding the outer tie rod, to 50–68 ft. lbs. (68–92 Nm).

11. Have the toe alignment checked and adjusted by a professional shop.

MPV

OUTER TIE ROD END

▶ **See Figures 157 thru 163**

1. Raise and support the front end on jackstands.
2. Remove the wheels.
3. Matchmark the tie rod end and tie rod and loosen the locknut.
4. Loosen the tie rod end ball stud nut and separate the tie rod end from the knuckle arm with a separator tool.
5. Unscrew the tie rod end, counting the number of turns until it's off, for installation purposes.

To install:

6. Install the tie rod end onto the tie rod the same number of turns that it took to remove it. Tighten the locknut to 51–57 ft. lbs. (69–78 Nm).

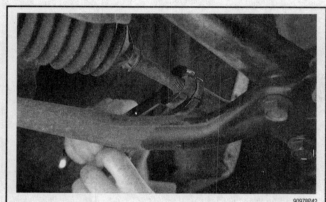

Fig. 157 Using a backup wrench, loosen the jam nut from the tie rod

7. Install the ball stud into the steering knuckle. Tighten the ball stud nut to 44–57 ft. lbs. (59–78 Nm) and install the cotter pin.
8. Lower the vehicle and install a new cotter pin. Always advance the nut to align the cotter pin hole. Never back it off. Check the front alignment.

Manual Steering Gear

REMOVAL & INSTALLATION

▶ **See Figure 164**

1. Raise and safely support the vehicle using jackstands. Disengage the flex coupling shield from the steering gear input shaft shield and slide it up the intermediate shaft.
2. Remove the bolt that retains the flex coupling to the steering gear.
3. Remove the steering gear input shaft shield.
4. Remove the nut and washer that secures the pitman arm to the sector shaft. Remove the pitman arm using pitman arm puller tool, T64P-3590-F or equivalent. Do not hammer on the end of the puller as this can damage the steering gear.
5. Remove the bolts and washers that attach the steering gear to the side rail. Remove the gear.

To install:

6. Rotate the gear input shaft (wormshaft) from stop to stop, counting the total number of turns. Then turn back exactly half-way, placing the gear on center.
7. Slide the steering gear input shaft shield on the steering gear input shaft.
8. Position the flex coupling on the steering gear input shaft. Ensure that the flat on the gear input shaft is facing straight up and aligns with the flat on the flex coupling. Install the steering gear to side rail with bolts and washers. Torque the bolts to 66 ft. lbs. (89 Nm).
9. Place the pitman arm on the sector shaft and install the attaching washer and nut. Align the 2 blocked teeth on the Pitman arm with 4 missing teeth on

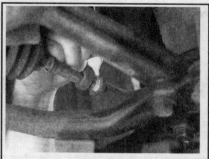

Fig. 158 Matchmark the location of the tie rod end on the tie rod. This will help during installation

Fig. 159 Remove and discard the cotter pin from tie rod ball stud

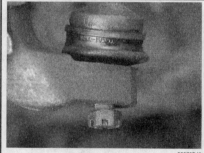

Fig. 160 Install the castle nut onto the end of the ball stud to prevent the stud from ìmushroomingî during removal

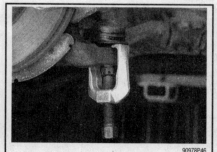

Fig. 161 Using a puller tool with the castle nut on the end of the ball stud, separate the tie rod end ball joint from the steering knuckle

Fig. 162 Remove the castle nut and pull the tie rod end ball stud straight out of the steering knuckle

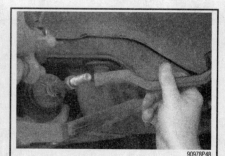

Fig. 163 Count the number of turns required to remove the tie rod end from the tie rod. This will help during the installation process

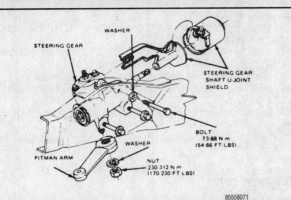

Fig. 164 View of the 1994–97 B Series Pick-up manual steering gear and related parts

the steering gear sector shaft. Tighten the nut to 170–228 ft. lbs. (230–310 Nm).

10. Install the flex coupling to steering gear input shaft attaching bolt and tighten to 50–62 ft. lbs. (68–84 Nm).

11. Snap the flex coupling shield to the steering gear input shield.

12. Check the system to ensure equal turns from center to each lock position.

Power Steering Gear

REMOVAL & INSTALLATION

▶ **See Figure 165**

1. Disconnect the pressure and return lines from the steering gear. Plug the lines and the ports in the gear to prevent entry of dirt.

2. Remove the upper and lower steering gear shaft U-joint shield from the flex coupling. Remove the bolts that secure the flex coupling to the steering gear and to the column steering shaft assembly.

3. Raise the vehicle and remove the pitman arm attaching nut and washer.

4. Remove the pitman arm from the sector shaft using tool T64P-3590-F. Remove the tool from the pitman arm. Do not damage the seals.

5. Support the steering gear, and remove the steering gear attaching bolts.

6. Work the steering gear free of the flex coupling. Remove the steering gear from the vehicle.

To install:

7. Install the lower U-joint shield onto the steering gear lugs. Slide the upper U-joint shield into place on the steering shaft assembly.

8. Slide the flex coupling into place on the steering shaft assembly. Turn the steering wheel so that the spokes are in the horizontal position. Center the steering gear input shaft.

9. Slide the steering gear input shaft into the flex coupling and into place on the frame side rail. Install the attaching bolts and tighten to 50–62 ft. lbs. (68–84 Nm). Tighten the flex coupling bolt 30–40 ft. lbs. (41–54 Nm).

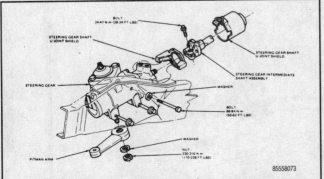

Fig. 165 View of the power steering gear and related parts used on Navajo and 1994–97 B Series Pick-up

10. Be sure the wheels are in the straight ahead position, then install the pitman arm on the sector shaft. Install the pitman arm attaching washer and nut. Tighten nut to 170–228 ft. lbs. (230–310 Nm).

11. Connect and tighten the pressure and the return lines to the steering gear.

12. Disconnect the coil wire. Fill the reservoir. Turn on the ignition and turn the steering wheel from left to right to distribute the fluid.

13. Recheck fluid level and add fluid, if necessary. Connect the coil wire, start the engine and turn the steering wheel from side to side. Inspect for fluid leaks.

Power Rack and Pinion Steering Gear

REMOVAL & INSTALLATION

1998 B Series Pick-up

▶ **See Figures 166 and 167**

⁑ WARNING

If equipped, always turn off the Automatic Ride Control (ARC) service switch before lifting the vehicle off of the ground. Failure to do so could damage the ARC system components. Refer to Section 1 for jacking procedures.

1. Raise and safely support the front of the vehicle, block the rear wheels and apply the parking brake.

2. Start the engine then rotate the steering wheel from lock-to-lock and record the number of rotations.

3. Divide the number of rotations by two. This gives the number of rotations to achieve true center of the steering. Turn the wheel in one direction to the full lock.

4. Turn the wheel in the opposite direction the number of turns equal to true steering (lock-to-lock number divided by two).

⁑ WARNING

Do not rotate the steering wheel when the shaft is disconnected from the steering gear as damage to the clock spring could occur.

5. Remove the bolt retaining the lower steering column shaft to the steering gear input shaft and disconnect the two.

6. Remove the stabilizer bar.

7. Unscrew the quick-connect fittings for the power steering pressure and return hoses at the steering gear housing.

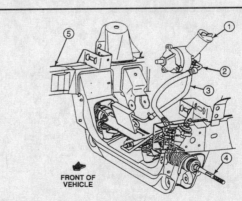

FRONT OF VEHICLE

1. Power steering pump
2. Power steering pressure hose
3. Power steering cooler and hose assembly
4. Steering gear
5. Frame

Fig. 166 View of the power steering hose connections for the power rack and pinion steering gear

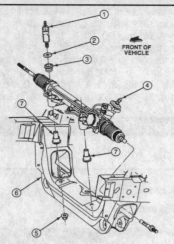

1. Bolt
2. Washer
3. Steering gear mounting housing insulator
4. Steering gear
5. Nut
6. Front crossmember
7. Steering gear insulator

89688G30

Fig. 167 Exploded view of the power rack and pinion steering gear mounting

8. Plug the ends of the lines and the fitting in the rack to avoid dirt contamination.

9. Remove the two nuts securing the power steering cooler and remove the cooler.

10. Remove the outer tie rod ends.

11. Remove the two nuts, bolts and washer assemblies retaining the steering gear housing to the front crossmember.

To install:

12. Position the steering gear to the front crossmember and install the nuts, bolts and washer assemblies. Tighten to 94–127 ft. lbs. (128–172 Nm).

13. Install the power steering cooler and two retaining bolts.

14. Connect the power steering lines to the steering gear housing and tighten the fittings to 20–25 ft. lbs. (27–34 Nm).

15. Install the outer tie rod ends.

16. Ensure that the steering shaft or gear input shaft has not been rotated, then connect the two.

17. Install the intermediate shaft-to-steering input shaft retaining (pinch) bolt and tighten to 30–42 ft. lbs. (41–56 Nm).

18. Lower the vehicle and refill the power steering pump reservoir.

19. Bleed the air from the power steering system. Follow the procedures in this Section.

20. Ensure that there are no leaks and the fluid is maintained at the proper level.

21. Have the alignment checked and adjusted by a professional repair shop.

MPV

REAR WHEEL DRIVE

◆ **See Figure 168**

1. Place the front wheels in the straight-ahead position. Raise and safely support the vehicle.

2. Remove the wheel and tire assemblies. Remove the splash shield.

3. Remove the cotter pins and nuts from both tie rod end studs. Separate the tie rod ends from the knuckles.

4. Remove the pinch bolt from the intermediate shaft-to-pinion shaft coupling.

5. Disconnect and plug the pressure line from the rack and pinion assembly. Loosen the clamp and disconnect the return line from the rack and pinion assembly. Plug the line.

6. If equipped with automatic transmission, remove the change counter assembly to remove the protector plate mounting bolt.

7. Remove the steering bracket mounting bolts and remove the rack and pinion assembly and brackets.

8. If necessary, remove the brackets.

To install:

9. If removed, install the brackets and tighten the mounting bolts, in sequence, to 54–69 ft. lbs. (74–93 Nm).

10. Install the rack and pinion assembly and brackets in the vehicle. Tighten the bracket-to-chassis bolts to 46–69 ft. lbs. (63–93 Nm).

11. If equipped with automatic transmission, install the change counter assembly.

12. Connect the return line and tighten the clamp. Connect the pressure line and tighten the nut to 23–35 ft. lbs. (31–47 Nm).

13. Install the pinch bolt in the intermediate shaft-to-pinion shaft coupling and tighten to 13–20 ft. lbs. (18–26 Nm).

14. Position the tie rod end studs in the knuckles and install the nuts. Tighten the nuts to 43–58 ft. lbs. (59–78 Nm) and install new cotter pins.

15. Install the splash shield and the wheel and tire assemblies. Lower the vehicle and bleed the power steering system.

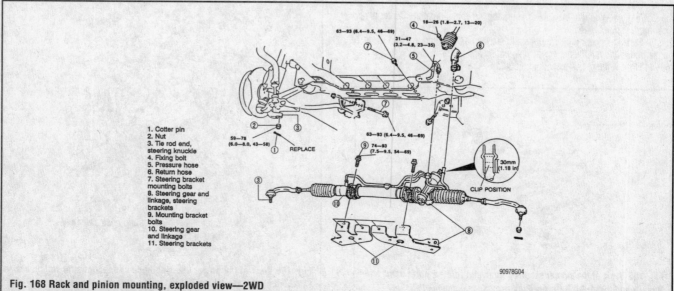

1. Cotter pin
2. Nut
3. Tie rod end, steering knuckle
4. Fixing bolt
5. Pressure hose
6. Return hose
7. Steering bracket mounting bolts
8. Steering gear and linkage, steering brackets
9. Mounting bracket bolts
10. Steering gear and linkage
11. Steering brackets

90978G04

Fig. 168 Rack and pinion mounting, exploded view—2WD

4WD

♦ **See Figure 169**

1. Place the front wheels in the straight-ahead position. Raise and safely support the vehicle.
2. Remove the wheel and tire assemblies. Remove the splash shield.
3. Remove the cotter pins and nuts from both tie rod end studs. Separate the tie rod ends from the knuckles.
4. Disconnect and plug the pressure and return hoses at the pressure and return lines.
5. Remove the pressure and return lines from the rack and pinion assembly.
6. Remove the pinch bolt from the intermediate shaft-to-pinion shaft coupling.
7. Working inside the vehicle, remove the lower panel and column cover from under the steering column. Remove the steering column mounting bolts and nuts and pull the column and intermediate shaft rearward to separate the intermediate shaft from the pinion shaft.
8. Mark the position of the front driveshaft on the axle flange and remove the front driveshaft.
9. Remove the rack and pinion assembly mounting bracket bolts and the front differential/joint shaft assembly mounting bolts.
10. Slide the differential/joint shaft assembly rearward. Slide the rack and pinion assembly rearward and turn it 90 degrees, then remove it from the left side of the vehicle.

To install:

11. Install the rack and pinion assembly from the left side of the vehicle, turn it 90 degrees and move it forward into position. Install the mounting bolts and tighten, in sequence, to 54–69 ft. lbs. (74–93 Nm).
12. Move the differential/joint shaft assembly forward, install the mounting bolts and tighten to 49–72 ft. lbs. (67–97 Nm).
13. Install the driveshaft, aligning the marks made during removal.
14. Working inside the vehicle, move the steering column and intermediate shaft forward to engage the intermediate shaft with the pinion shaft. Install and tighten the steering column nuts and bolts to 12–17 ft. lbs. (16–23 Nm). Install the lower panel and column cover.
15. Install the pinch bolt in the intermediate shaft-to-pinion shaft coupling and tighten to 13–20 ft. lbs. (18–26 Nm).
16. Install the pressure and return lines on the rack and pinion assembly. Connect the pressure and return hoses to the lines.
17. Position the tie rod end studs in the knuckles and install the nuts. Tighten the nuts to 43–58 ft. lbs. (59–78 Nm) and install new cotter pins.

18. Install the splash shield and the wheel and tire assemblies. Lower the vehicle and bleed the power steering system.

Power Steering Pump

REMOVAL & INSTALLATION

Navajo and B Series Pick-up

♦ **See Figure 170**

1. Disconnect the negative battery cable.
2. Remove some power steering fluid from the reservoir by disconnecting the fluid return line hose at the reservoir. Drain the fluid into a container and discard it.
3. Remove the pressure hose from the pump. If equipped, disconnect the power steering pump pressure switch.
4. On the 2.3L, 2.5L and 3.0L engines, loosen the idler pulley assembly pivot and adjusting bolts to slacken the belt tension.
5. On the 4.0L engine, slacken belt tension by lifting the tensioner pulley in a clockwise direction. Remove the drive belt from under the tensioner pulley and slowly lower the pulley to its stop.
6. Remove the drive belt from the pulley. If necessary, remove the oil dipstick tube.
7. If equipped, remove the power steering pump bracket support brace.
8. Install power steering pump pulley removal tool T69L-10300-B or equivalent. Hold the pump and rotate the tool counterclockwise to remove the pulley. Do not apply in and out pressure to the pump shaft, as internal pump damage will occur.
9. Remove the power steering retaining bolts. Remove the power steering pump from the vehicle.

To install:

10. Position the pump on the bracket. Install and tighten the retaining bolts.
11. Install the pulley removal tool and install the power steering pump pulley to the power steering pump.

➡Fore and aft location of the pulley on the power steering pump shaft is critical. Incorrect belt alignment may cause belt squeal or chirp. Be sure that the pull off groove on the pulley is facing front and flush with the end of the shaft ± 0.010 in. (0.25mm).

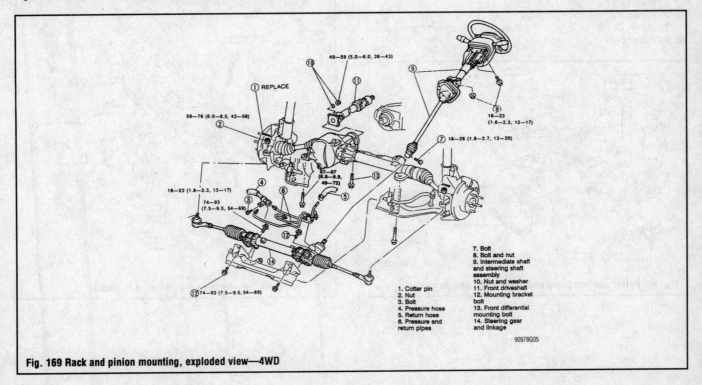

Fig. 169 Rack and pinion mounting, exploded view—4WD

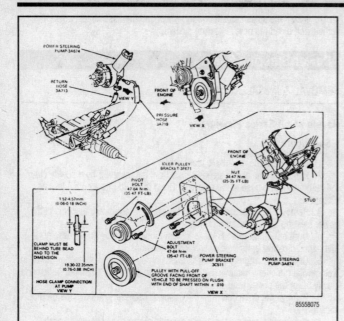

Fig. 170 Exploded view of a common power steering pump used on Mazda trucks

12. Continue the installation in the reverse order of the removal procedure. Adjust the belt tension to specification.

13. On the 2.3L, 2.5L and 3.0L engines torque the idler pivot pulley bolts 30–40 ft. lbs. for the 2.3L/2.5L engines and 35–47 ft. lbs. for the 3.0L engine

14. On the 4.0L while lifting the tensioner pulley in a clockwise direction, slide the belt under the tensioner pulley and lower the pulley to the belt.

MPV

2.6L ENGINE

▶ See Figure 171

1. Disconnect the negative battery cable.
2. Place a drain pan under the pump.
3. Loosen the idler pulley locknut and the pump adjusting bolt and remove the pump drive belt.

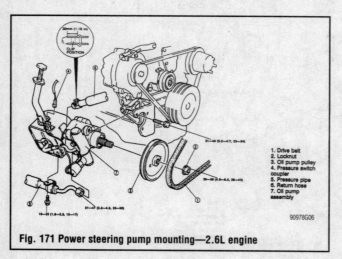

Fig. 171 Power steering pump mounting—2.6L engine

4. Remove the pump pulley nut.
5. Remove the pulley.
6. Unplug the pressure switch coupler.
7. Matchmark the high pressure line coupling and disconnect the line.
8. Remove the return hose.
9. Remove the pump-to-bracket bolts and lift out the pump.

To install:

10. Place the pump in position and install and tighten the mounting bolts. Connect the return and pressure lines. Install the drive pulley. Install and adjust the drive belt. Fill and bleed the system. Tighten the high pressure coupling to 23-35 ft. lbs. (31–48 Nm), aligning the high pressure coupling matchmarks. Tighten the pump mounting bolts to 23-34 ft. lbs. (31–48 Nm). Tighten the pulley nut to 29-43 ft. lbs. (39–58 Nm). Tighten the idler pulley locknut to 27-38 ft. lbs. (37–52 Nm). Connect the negative battery cable.

3.0L ENGINE

▶ See Figure 172

1. Disconnect the negative battery cable.
2. Loosen the idler pulley locknut.
3. Loosen the pump adjusting bolt.
4. Remove the drive belt.
5. Remove the pump pulley nut.
6. Using a puller, remove the pulley.
7. Disconnect the pressure switch wiring connector.
8. Place a drain pan under the pump.
9. Matchmark the pressure line connection and disconnect it.
10. Remove the pressure line bracket bolt.
11. Disconnect the return line.
12. Remove the pump-to-bracket bolts and lift out the pump.

To install:

13. Place the pump in position and install the mounting bolts. Connect the return and pressure line. Install the drive pulley and belt. Adjust the drive belt to the proper tension. Fill and bleed the system. Connect the negative battery cable. Observe the following torques:
   • mounting bolts to 34 ft. lbs. (46 Nm).
   • pressure line connection to 35 ft. lbs. (47 Nm).
   • pressure line bracket bolt: 17 ft. lbs. (23 Nm).

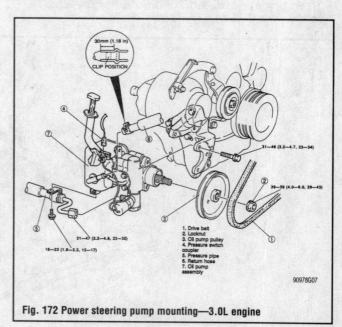

Fig. 172 Power steering pump mounting—3.0L engine

- pulley bolt: 43 ft. lbs. (58 Nm).
- adjusting bolt: 35 ft. lbs.
- idler pulley locknut: 38 ft. lbs. (52 Nm).

BLEEDING

Navajo and 1994–97 B Series Pick-up

1. Disconnect the coil wire.
2. Crank the engine and continue adding fluid until the level stabilizes.
3. Continue to crank the engine and rotate the steering wheel about 30° to either side of center.
4. Check the fluid level and add as required.
5. Connect the coil wire and start the engine. Allow it to run for several minutes.
6. Rotate the steering wheel from stop to stop.
7. Shut of the engine and check the fluid level. Add fluid as necessary.

1998 B Series Pick-up

♦ See Figure 173

1. Remove the power steering fluid reservoir cap. Check the fluid level and top off, if necessary.
2. Tightly install the stopper of a vacuum pump into the filler neck of the reservoir.
3. Start the vehicle.
4. Apply the maximum amount of vacuum possible and maintain it for a minimum of 3 minutes with the engine running at idle.
5. Release the vacuum and remove the vacuum pump from the vehicle.
6. Check the fluid level in the reservoir and fill up to the correct level, if necessary.
7. Install the vacuum pump again. Apply and maintain maximum vacuum.
8. Rotate the steering wheel fully to the left and right every 30 seconds. Do this for approximately 5 minutes. Do NOT hold the steering wheel against the stops for more than 3–5 seconds at a time or damage to the power steering pump could occur.
9. Turn off the engine, release the vacuum and remove the vacuum pump.
10. Install the fluid reservoir cap.
11. Check the entire system for leaks. If the system shows signs of air, repeat this procedure.

MPV

1. Check the fluid level.
2. With the engine OFF, turn the steering wheel fully to the left and right several times. If the vehicle is elevated to do this, make certain the vehicle is level before rechecking the fluid level.
3. Recheck the fluid level, and add fluid (Dexron®II or M-III) if necessary.
4. Repeat the previous 2 steps until the fluid level stabilizes.
5. Start the engine and let it idle.
6. Turn the steering wheel fully to the left and right several times.
7. Verify that the fluid level has not dropped, and that the fluid is smooth, not foamy.
8. If necessary, repeat the previous 2 steps until the fluid level stabilizes.

QUICK-CONNECT PRESSURE LINE

♦ See Figure 174

If a leak occurs between the tubing and the tube nut, replace the hose assembly. If a leak occurs between the tube nut and the pump outlet replace the plastic washer.

1. Check the fitting to determine whether the leak is between the tube and tube nut or between the tube nut and pump outlet.
2. If the leak is between the tube nut and pump outlet check to be sure the nut is tightened to 30–40 ft. lbs. Do not overtighten this nut.
3. If the leak continues or if the leak is between the tube and tube nut, remove the line.
4. Unscrew the tube nut and inspect the plastic seal washer. Replace the plastic seal washer when the line is removed.
5. To aid in the assembly of the new plastic seal washer, a tapered shaft may be required to stretch the washer so that it may be slipped over the tube nut threads.
6. If the rubber O-ring is damaged it cannot be serviced and the hose assembly will have to be replaced.
7. Connect the tube nut and torque to 30–40 ft. lbs.

☀ CAUTION

The quick connect fitting may disengage if not fully assembled, if the snapring is missing or if the tube nut or hose end is not machined properly. If the fitting disengages replace the hose assembly. The fitting is fully engaged when the hose will not pull out. To test for positive engagement the system should be properly filled, the engine started and the steering wheel turned from stop to stop.

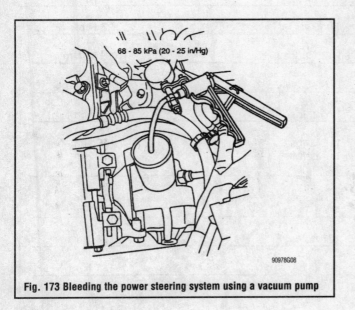

Fig. 173 Bleeding the power steering system using a vacuum pump

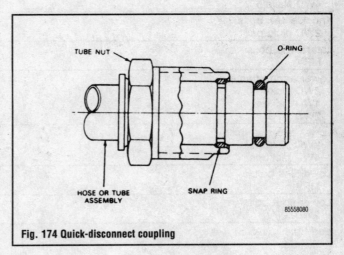

Fig. 174 Quick-disconnect coupling

TORQUE SPECIFICATIONS

Component	U.S.	Metric
WHEELS AND SUSPENSION		
Axle pivot bolt		
4WD Navajo	120-150 ft. lbs.	163-204 Nm
Axle-to-radius arm nut		
2WD Navajo	120-150 ft. lbs.	163-204 Nm
Axle-to-frame pivot bracket bolt		
2WD Navajo	120-150 ft. lbs.	163-204 Nm
Ball joint stud nut		
Lower, 2WD pickups	116 ft. lbs.	158 Nm
Lower, 2WD MPV	116 ft. lbs.	158 Nm
4WD pickups	70 ft. lbs.	95 Nm
4WD pickups	115 ft. lbs.	156 Nm
2WD Navajo	85-110 ft. lbs.	116-149 Nm
Ball joint-to-arm bolts		
2WD pickups		
old	15-20 ft. lbs.	21-27 Nm
New	70 ft. lbs.	95 Nm
4WD pickups	15-20 ft. lbs.	21-27 Nm
Cap nut		
2WD MPV	36-43 ft. lbs.	49-58 Nm
Clamp bolts		
4WD pickups	19 ft. lbs.	26 Nm
2WD MPV	45 ft. lbs.	61 Nm
Compression rod end nuts		
2WD MPV	127 ft. lbs.	173 Nm
Compression rod-to-lower arm		
2WD MPV	93 ft. lbs.	126 Nm
Fluid-filled bushing bolts		
2WD MPV	76 ft. lbs.	103 Nm
Front bracket-to-axle bolts		
4WD Navajo	37-50 ft. lbs.	50-68 Nm
Height sensor link		
MPV	104 inch lbs.	12 Nm
Height sensor bolts		
MPV	20 ft. lbs.	27 Nm
Insulator-to-arm stud nut		
4WD Navajo	80-120 ft. lbs.	109-163 Nm
Knuckle arm bolts		
2WD pickups	70-74 ft. lbs.	95-100 Nm
Lateral rod bolts		
MPV	127 ft. lbs.	173 Nm
Lower arm-to-frame nut		
2WD pickups	115 ft. lbs.	156 Nm
4WD pickups	115 ft. lbs.	156 Nm
2WD MPV	108 ft. lbs.	147 Nm
Lower arm end bolts		
2WD pickups	85 ft. lbs.	116 Nm
4WD pickups	85 ft. lbs.	116 Nm
Lower link bolts		
MPV	127 ft. lbs.	173 Nm
Lower strut bolts		
2WD MPV	86 ft. lbs.	117 Nm
Lug nuts		
Pickups		
non-styled wheels	65-87 ft. lbs.	89-118 Nm
styled wheels	87-108 ft. lbs.	119-146 Nm
MPV	65-87 ft. lbs.	89-118 Nm
Navajo	100 ft. lbs.	136 Nm

89688C01

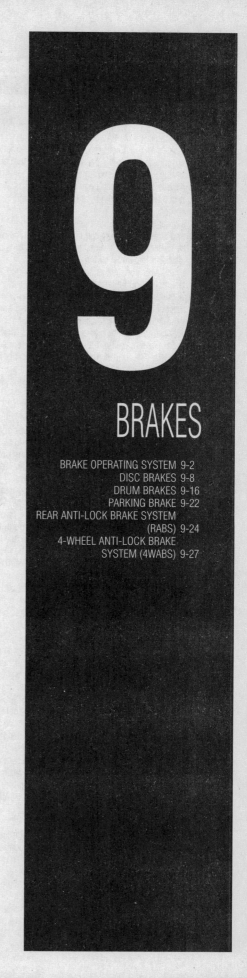

9

BRAKES

BRAKE OPERATING SYSTEM

Basic Operating Principles

Hydraulic systems are used to actuate the brakes of all modern automobiles. The system transports the power required to force the frictional surfaces of the braking system together from the pedal to the individual brake units at each wheel. A hydraulic system is used for two reasons.

First, fluid under pressure can be carried to all parts of an automobile by small pipes and flexible hoses without taking up a significant amount of room or posing routing problems.

Second, a great mechanical advantage can be given to the brake pedal end of the system, and the foot pressure required to actuate the brakes can be reduced by making the surface area of the master cylinder pistons smaller than that of any of the pistons in the wheel cylinders or calipers.

The master cylinder consists of a fluid reservoir along with a double cylinder and piston assembly. Double type master cylinders are designed to separate the front and rear braking systems hydraulically in case of a leak. The master cylinder coverts mechanical motion from the pedal into hydraulic pressure within the lines. This pressure is translated back into mechanical motion at the wheels by either the wheel cylinder (drum brakes) or the caliper (disc brakes).

Steel lines carry the brake fluid to a point on the vehicle's frame near each of the vehicle's wheels. The fluid is then carried to the calipers and wheel cylinders by flexible tubes in order to allow for suspension and steering movements.

In drum brake systems, each wheel cylinder contains two pistons, one at either end, which push outward in opposite directions and force the brake shoe into contact with the drum.

In disc brake systems, the cylinders are part of the calipers. At least one cylinder in each caliper is used to force the brake pads against the disc.

All pistons employ some type of seal, usually made of rubber, to minimize fluid leakage. A rubber dust boot seals the outer end of the cylinder against dust and dirt. The boot fits around the outer end of the piston on disc brake calipers, and around the brake actuating rod on wheel cylinders.

The hydraulic system operates as follows: When at rest, the entire system, from the piston(s) in the master cylinder to those in the wheel cylinders or calipers, is full of brake fluid. Upon application of the brake pedal, fluid trapped in front of the master cylinder piston(s) is forced through the lines to the wheel cylinders. Here, it forces the pistons outward, in the case of drum brakes, and inward toward the disc, in the case of disc brakes. The motion of the pistons is opposed by return springs mounted outside the cylinders in drum brakes, and by spring seals, in disc brakes.

Upon release of the brake pedal, a spring located inside the master cylinder immediately returns the master cylinder pistons to the normal position. The pistons contain check valves and the master cylinder has compensating ports drilled in it. These are uncovered as the pistons reach their normal position. The piston check valves allow fluid to flow toward the wheel cylinders or calipers as the pistons withdraw. Then, as the return springs force the brake pads or shoes into the released position, the excess fluid reservoir through the compensating ports. It is during the time the pedal is in the released position that any fluid that has leaked out of the system will be replaced through the compensating ports.

Dual circuit master cylinders employ two pistons, located one behind the other, in the same cylinder. The primary piston is actuated directly by mechanical linkage from the brake pedal through the power booster. The secondary piston is actuated by fluid trapped between the two pistons. If a leak develops in front of the secondary piston, it moves forward until it bottoms against the front of the master cylinder, and the fluid trapped between the pistons will operate the rear brakes. If the rear brakes develop a leak, the primary piston will move forward until direct contact with the secondary piston takes place, and it will force the secondary piston to actuate the front brakes. In either case, the brake pedal moves farther when the brakes are applied, and less braking power is available.

All dual circuit systems use a switch to warn the driver when only half of the brake system is operational. This switch is usually located in a valve body which is mounted on the firewall or the frame below the master cylinder. A hydraulic piston receives pressure from both circuits, each circuit's pressure being applied to one end of the piston. When the pressures are in balance, the piston remains stationary. When one circuit has a leak, however, the greater pressure in that circuit during application of the brakes will push the piston to one side, closing the switch and activating the brake warning light.

In disc brake systems, this valve body also contains a metering valve and, in some cases, a proportioning valve. The metering valve keeps pressure from traveling to the disc brakes on the front wheels until the brake shoes on the rear wheels have contacted the drums, ensuring that the front brakes will never be used alone. The proportioning valve controls the pressure to the rear brakes to lessen the chance of rear wheel lock-up during very hard braking.

Warning lights may be tested by depressing the brake pedal and holding it while opening one of the wheel cylinder bleeder screws. If this does not cause the light to go on, substitute a new lamp, make continuity checks, and, finally, replace the switch as necessary.

The hydraulic system may be checked for leaks by applying pressure to the pedal gradually and steadily. If the pedal sinks very slowly to the floor, the system has a leak. This is not to be confused with a springy or spongy feel due to the compression of air within the lines. If the system leaks, there will be a gradual change in the position of the pedal with a constant pressure.

Check for leaks along all lines and at wheel cylinders. If no external leaks are apparent, the problem is inside the master cylinder.

DISC BRAKES

Instead of the traditional expanding brakes that press outward against a circular drum, disc brake systems utilize a disc (rotor) with brake pads positioned on either side of it. An easily-seen analogy is the hand brake arrangement on a bicycle. The pads squeeze onto the rim of the bike wheel, slowing its motion. Automobile disc brakes use the identical principle but apply the braking effort to a separate disc instead of the wheel.

The disc (rotor) is a casting, usually equipped with cooling fins between the two braking surfaces. This enables air to circulate between the braking surfaces making them less sensitive to heat buildup and more resistant to fade. Dirt and water do not drastically affect braking action since contaminants are thrown off by the centrifugal action of the rotor or scraped off the by the pads. Also, the equal clamping action of the two brake pads tends to ensure uniform, straight line stops. Disc brakes are inherently self-adjusting. There are three general types of disc brake:

1. A fixed caliper.
2. A floating caliper.
3. A sliding caliper.

The fixed caliper design uses two pistons mounted on either side of the rotor (in each side of the caliper). The caliper is mounted rigidly and does not move.

The sliding and floating designs are quite similar. In fact, these two types are often lumped together. In both designs, the pad on the inside of the rotor is moved into contact with the rotor by hydraulic force. The caliper, which is not held in a fixed position, moves slightly, bringing the outside pad into contact with the rotor. There are various methods of attaching floating calipers. Some pivot at the bottom or top, and some slide on mounting bolts. In any event, the end result is the same.

DRUM BRAKES

Drum brakes employ two brake shoes mounted on a stationary backing plate. These shoes are positioned inside a circular drum which rotates with the wheel assembly. The shoes are held in place by springs. This allows them to slide toward the drums (when they are applied) while keeping the linings and drums in alignment. The shoes are actuated by a wheel cylinder which is mounted at the top of the backing plate. When the brakes are applied, hydraulic pressure forces the wheel cylinder's actuating links outward. Since these links bear directly against the top of the brake shoes, the tops of the shoes are then forced against the inner side of the drum. This action forces the bottoms of the two shoes to contact the brake drum by rotating the entire assembly slightly (known as servo action). When pressure within the wheel cylinder is relaxed, return springs pull the shoes back away from the drum.

Most modern drum brakes are designed to self-adjust themselves during application when the vehicle is moving in reverse. This motion causes both shoes to rotate very slightly with the drum, rocking an adjusting lever, thereby causing rotation of the adjusting screw. Some drum brake systems are designed to self-adjust during application whenever the brakes are applied. This on-board adjustment system reduces the need for maintenance adjustments and keeps both the brake function and pedal feel satisfactory.

Brake Light Switch

REMOVAL & INSTALLATION

Navajo and B Series Pick-up Models

♦ See Figure 1

1. Lift the locking tab on the switch connector and disconnect the wiring.
2. Remove the hairpin retainer, slide the stoplamp switch, pushrod and nylon washer off of the pedal. Remove the washer, then the switch by sliding it up or down.

➡On some vehicles equipped with speed control, the spacer washer is replaced by the dump valve adapter washer.

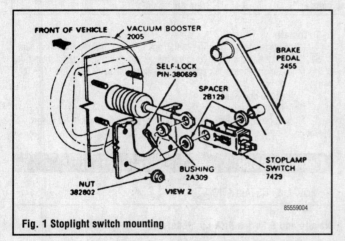

Fig. 1 Stoplight switch mounting

Fig. 2 To remove the master cylinder, first disconnect the fluid level sensor wire

To install:

3. Position it so that the U-shaped side is nearest the pedal and directly over/under the pin.
4. Slide the switch up or down, trapping the master cylinder pushrod and bushing between the switch side plates.
5. Push the switch and pushrod assembly firmly towards the brake pedal arm. Assemble the outside white plastic washer to the pin and install the hairpin retainer.

➡Don't substitute any other type of retainer. Use only the Ford specified hairpin retainer.

6. Assemble the connector on the switch.
7. Check stoplamp operation.

➡Make sure that the stoplamp switch wiring has sufficient travel during a full pedal stroke.

MPV Models

The switch is located at the top of the brake pedal.
1. Disconnect the wiring from the switch.
2. Loosen the locknut and adjusting nut and unscrew the switch from the bracket.
3. Install the new switch. Adjust the brake pedal. Tighten the locknut.

Master Cylinder

REMOVAL & INSTALLATION

Navajo and B Series Pick-up Models

♦ See Figures 2 thru 8

✳✳ WARNING

Vehicles with 4-wheel anti-lock brakes require an Anti-lock Brake Adapter (T90P-50-ALA) and Jumper (T93T-50-ALA) in order to bleed the master cylinder and the Hydraulic Control Unit (HCU). Failure to do so will trap air in the HCU unit, eventually causing a spongy pedal.

➡Before performing this procedure, ensure that you have the tools necessary to bleed the master cylinder and the HCU unit. If the tools are not available, you can still perform the procedure. However, you will need to tow the vehicle to a professional garage capable of bleeding the ABS system.

1. With the engine turned off, push the brake pedal down to expel vacuum from the brake booster system.
2. Disconnect the brake fluid level sensor wire from the reservoir.
3. Disconnect the hydraulic lines (use correct tool, a Line Wrench) from the brake master cylinder.

Fig. 3 Next, loosen the fluid line fittings at the master cylinder with a flarenut wrench . . .

Fig. 4 . . . then disconnect the lines

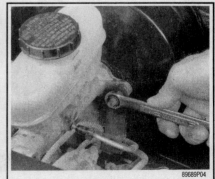

Fig. 5 If equipped, remove any bracket retaining nuts . . .

Fig. 6 . . . and pull the bracket from the mounting stud

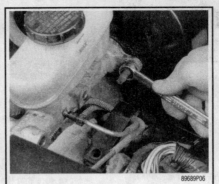

Fig. 7 Remove the master cylinder-to-power booster attaching bolts . . .

Fig. 8 . . . then pull the master cylinder off of the mounting studs and remove it from the vehicle

4. Remove the brake booster-to-master cylinder retaining nuts and lock washers. Remove the master cylinder from the brake booster.

To install:

5. Before installing the master cylinder, check the distance from the outer end of the booster assembly push rod to the front face of the brake booster assembly. Turn the push rod adjusting screw in or out as required to obtain the length shown. Refer to illustration in this Section.

6. Position the master cylinder assembly over the booster push rod and onto the 2 studs on the booster assembly. Install the attaching nuts and lock-washers and tighten to 13–25 ft. lbs. (18–34 Nm).

7. Connect the hydraulic brake system lines to the master cylinder.

8. Bleed the hydraulic brake system (refer to procedure in this Section). Centralize the differential valve. Then, fill the dual master cylinder reservoirs with DOT 3 brake fluid to within ¼ in. (6mm) of the top. Install the gasket and reservoir cover. Roadtest the vehicle for proper operation.

When replacing the master cylinder it is best to BENCH BLEED the master cylinder before installing it to the vehicle. Mount the master cylinder into a vise or suitable equivalent (do not damage the cylinder). Fill the cylinder to the correct level with the specified fluid. Block off all the outer brake line holes but one, then, using a long tool such as rod position it in the cylinder to actuate the brake master cylinder. Pump (push tool in and out) the brake master cylinder 3 or 4 times till brake fluid is release out and no air is in the brake fluid. Repeat this procedure until all brake fluid is released out of every hole and no air is expelled.

MPV Models

▶ See Figure 9

1. Clean all dirt and grease from the master cylinder and lines. Disconnect and cap the brake lines from the master cylinder.

2. Disconnect the fluid level sensor connector.

3. Unbolt and remove the master cylinder from the power booster.

Fig. 9 Disconnect the brake lines from the master cylinder using a flare nut wrench and a box wrench

To install:

4. Place the master cylinder in position and loosely install the mounting nuts.

5. Connect the hydraulic lines to the master cylinder, but do not tighten fully at this time. Tighten the master cylinder mounting nuts to 7–12 ft. lbs. (10–16 Nm).

6. Tighten the brake lines.

7. Connect the sensor connector.

8. Fill and properly bleed the brake system. Check the system for proper operation.

Power Booster

REMOVAL & INSTALLATION

Navajo and B Series Pick-up Models

▶ See Figure 10

➡Make sure that the booster rubber reaction disc is properly installed if the master cylinder push rod is removed or accidentally pulled out. A dislodged disc may cause excessive pedal travel and extreme operation sensitivity. The disc is black compared to the silver colored valve plunger that will be exposed after the push rod and front seal is removed. The booster unit is serviced as an assembly and must be replaced if the reaction disc cannot be properly installed and aligned, or if it cannot be located within the unit itself.

1. Disconnect the stop lamp switch wiring to prevent running the battery down.

2. Support the master cylinder from the underside with a prop.

3. Remove the master cylinder-to-booster retaining nuts.

4. Loosen the clamp that secures the manifold vacuum hose to the booster check valve, and remove the hose. Remove the booster check valve.

5. Pull the master cylinder off the booster and leave it supported by the prop, far enough away to allow removal of the booster assembly.

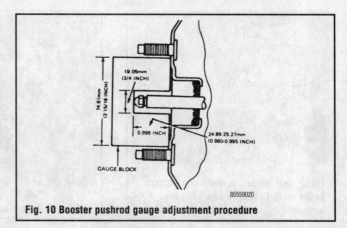

Fig. 10 Booster pushrod gauge adjustment procedure

6. From inside the cab on vehicles equipped with push rod mounted stop lamp switch, remove the retaining pin and slide the stop lamp switch, push rod, spacers and bushing off the brake pedal arm.

7. From the engine compartment remove the bolts that attach the booster to the dash panel.

To install:

8. Mount the booster assembly on the engine side of the dash panel by sliding the bracket mounting bolts and valve operating rod in through the holes in the dash panel.

➡**Make certain that the booster push rod is positioned on the correct side of the master cylinder to install onto the push pin prior to tightening the booster assembly to the dash.**

9. From inside the cab, install the booster mounting bracket-to-dash panel retaining nuts.

10. Position the master cylinder on the booster assembly, install the retaining nuts, and remove the prop from underneath the master cylinder.

11. Install the booster check valve. Connect the manifold vacuum hose to the booster check valve and secure with the clamp.

12. From inside the cab on vehicles equipped with push rod mounted stop lamp switch, install the bushing and position the switch on the end of the push rod. Then install the switch and rod on the pedal arm, along with spacers on each side, and secure with the retaining pin.

13. Connect the stop lamp switch wiring.

14. Start the engine and check brake operation.

MPV Models

2.6L ENGINE

▶ **See Figure 11**

1. Disconnect the fluid sensor line.
2. Remove the master cylinder.
3. Disconnect the pushrod at the pedal.
4. Disconnect the vacuum line at the booster.
5. Unbolt and remove the power booster from the bulkhead.

To install:

6. Check the clearance between the master cylinder piston and the power booster pushrod. Clearance should be 0, but the piston should not depress the pushrod. Adjust the clearance at the pushrod.
7. Position a new mounting gasket, coated with sealant, on the bulkhead.
8. Position the vacuum unit on the bulkhead and install the nuts. Torque the mounting nuts to 14–19 ft. lbs. (19–25 Nm).
9. Connect the pushrod at the pedal.
10. Connect the vacuum line.
11. Install the master cylinder.
12. Bleed the brakes.

3.0L ENGINE

▶ **See Figure 11**

1. Remove the wiper arms.
2. Remove the drive link nuts from the top of the cowl.
3. Working under the hood, disconnect the battery ground cable.
4. Remove the wiper motor and linkage mounting bolts and lift out the assembly.
5. Remove the master cylinder.
6. Disconnect the pushrod at the pedal.
7. Disconnect the vacuum line at the booster.
8. Unbolt and remove the power booster from the bulkhead.

To install:

9. Check the clearance between the master cylinder piston and the power booster pushrod. Clearance should be 0, but the piston should not depress the pushrod. Adjust the clearance at the pushrod.
10. Position a new mounting gasket, coated with sealant, on the bulkhead.
11. Position the vacuum unit on the bulkhead and install the nuts. Torque the mounting nuts to 14–19 ft. lbs. (19–25 Nm).
12. Connect the pushrod at the pedal.
13. Connect the vacuum line.
14. Install the master cylinder.
15. Install the wiper motor and linkage. When installing the wiper arms,

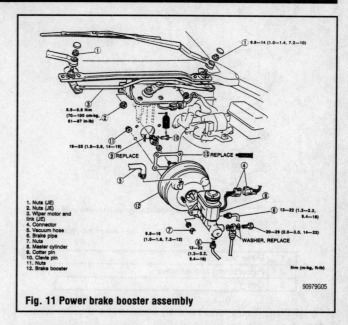

1. Nuts (JE)
2. Nuts (JE)
3. Wiper motor and link (JE)
4. Connector
5. Vacuum hose
6. Brake pipe
7. Nuts
8. Master cylinder
9. Cotter pin
10. Clevis pin
11. Nuts
12. Brake booster

Fig. 11 Power brake booster assembly

make sure that the at-rest position gives a gap of 30mm between the blade tips and the lower windshield molding.

16. Bleed the brakes.

Proportioning Valve

REMOVAL & INSTALLATION

All Models Except 1996–98 MPV

▶ **See Figure 12**

1. Raise and support the front end on jackstands.
2. Unplug the pressure differential switch connector.
3. Disconnect and cap the brake lines at the valve.
4. Remove the attaching bolts.
5. Installation is the reverse of removal.
6. Tighten the proportioning valve mounting bolt to 14–18 ft. lbs. (19–25 Nm).
7. Bleed the system.

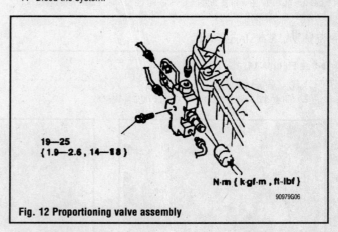

Fig. 12 Proportioning valve assembly

1996–98 MPV Models

▶ **See Figure 13**

The proportioning valve on 1996–98 MPV models is located on the master cylinder where the brake line threads in.

1. Using a flare nut wrench, with another one as a backup, disconnect the brake line to the master cylinder.

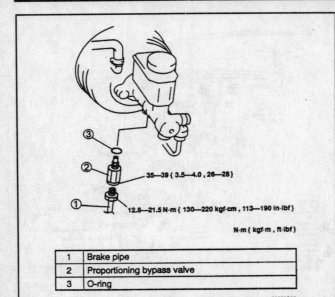

1	Brake pipe
2	Proportioning bypass valve
3	O-ring

90979G07

Fig. 13 Proportioning valve assembly mounted on the master cylinder

2. Remove the proportioning valve from the master cylinder. Replace the O-ring seal with a new one.
3. Installation is the reverse of removal.
4. Tighten the proportioning valve to 26–28 ft. lbs. (35–39 Nm).
5. Bleed the brake system.

Brake Hoses and Lines

Metal lines and rubber brake hoses should be checked frequently for leaks and external damage. Metal lines are particularly prone to crushing and kinking under the vehicle. Any such deformation can restrict the proper flow of fluid and therefore impair braking at the wheels. Rubber hoses should be checked for cracking or scraping; such damage can create a weak spot in the hose and it could fail under pressure.

Any time the lines are removed or disconnected, extreme cleanliness must be observed. Clean all joints and connections before disassembly (use a stiff bristle brush and clean brake fluid); be sure to plug the lines and ports as soon as they are opened. New lines and hoses should be flushed clean with brake fluid before installation to remove any contamination.

REMOVAL & INSTALLATION

▶ See Figures 14, 15, 16 and 17

1. Disconnect the negative battery cable.
2. Raise and safely support the vehicle on jackstands.

3. Remove any wheel and tire assemblies necessary for access to the particular line you are removing.
4. Thoroughly clean the surrounding area at the joints to be disconnected.
5. Place a suitable catch pan under the joint to be disconnected.
6. Using two wrenches (one to hold the joint and one to turn the fitting), disconnect the hose or line to be replaced.
7. Disconnect the other end of the line or hose, moving the drain pan if necessary. Always use a back-up wrench to avoid damaging the fitting.
8. Disconnect any retaining clips or brackets holding the line and remove the line from the vehicle.

➡**If the brake system is to remain open for more time than it takes to swap lines, tape or plug each remaining clip and port to keep contaminants out and fluid in.**

To install:
9. Install the new line or hose, starting with the end farthest from the master cylinder. Connect the other end, then confirm that both fittings are correctly threaded and turn smoothly using finger pressure. Make sure the new line will not rub against any other part. Brake lines must be at least 1/2 in. (13mm) from the steering column and other moving parts. Any protective shielding or insulators must be reinstalled in the original location.

✳✳ WARNING

Make sure the hose is NOT kinked or touching any part of the frame or suspension after installation. These conditions may cause the hose to fail prematurely.

10. Using two wrenches as before, tighten each fitting.
11. Install any retaining clips or brackets on the lines.
12. If removed, install the wheel and tire assemblies, then carefully lower the vehicle to the ground.
13. Refill the brake master cylinder reservoir with clean, fresh brake fluid, meeting DOT 3 specifications. Properly bleed the brake system.
14. Connect the negative battery cable.

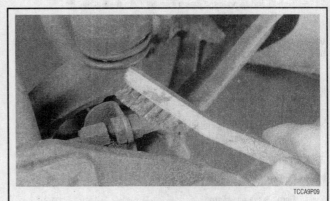

TCCA9P09

Fig. 14 Use a brush to clean the fittings of any debris

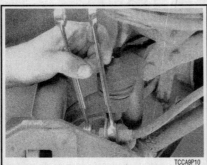

TCCA9P10

Fig. 15 Use two wrenches to loosen the fitting. If available, use flare nut type wrenches

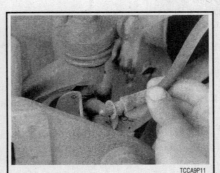

TCCA9P11

Fig. 16 Any gaskets/crush washers should be replaced with new ones during installation

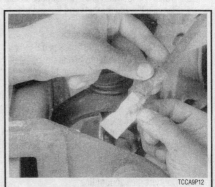

TCCA9P12

Fig. 17 Tape or plug the line to prevent contamination

Bleeding The Brakes

NAVAJO & B SERIES PICK-UP MODELS

▶ See Figures 18 and 19

✳ WARNING

Vehicles with 4-wheel anti-lock brakes require an Anti-lock Brake Adapter (T90P-50-ALA) and Jumper (T93T-50-ALA) in order to bleed the master cylinder and the Hydraulic Control Unit (HCU). Failure to do so will trap air in the HCU unit, eventually causing a spongy pedal. The tools are not required for caliper or wheel cylinder bleeding procedures.

When any part of the hydraulic system has been disconnected for repair or replacement, air may get into the lines and cause spongy pedal action (because air can be compressed and brake fluid cannot). To correct this condition, it is necessary to bleed the hydraulic system after it has been properly connected to be sure all air is expelled from the brake cylinders and lines.

When bleeding the brake system, bleed one brake cylinder at a time, beginning at the cylinder with the longest hydraulic line (farthest from the master cylinder) first. ALWAYS Keep the master cylinder reservoir filled with brake fluid during the bleeding operation. Never use brake fluid that has been drained from the hydraulic system, no matter how clean it is.

It will be necessary to centralize the pressure differential value after a brake system failure has been corrected and the hydraulic system has been bled.

The primary and secondary hydraulic brake systems are individual systems and are bled separately. During the entire bleeding operation, do not allow the reservoir to run dry. Keep the master cylinder reservoir filled with brake fluid.

1. Clean all dirt from around the master cylinder fill cap, remove the cap and fill the master cylinder with brake fluid until the level is within ¼ in. (6mm) of the top edge of the reservoir.

2. Clean off the bleeder screws at all 4 wheels. The bleeder screws are located on the inside of the brake backing plate, on the backside of the wheel cylinders and on the front brake calipers.

3. Attach a length of rubber hose over the nozzle of the bleeder screw at the wheel to be done first. Place the other end of the hose in a glass jar, submerged in brake fluid.

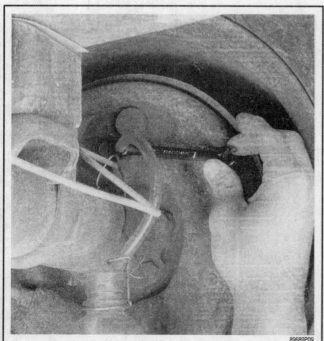

Fig. 18 Bleed the rear brakes first, ensuring that no air bubbles remain visible moving through the tubing

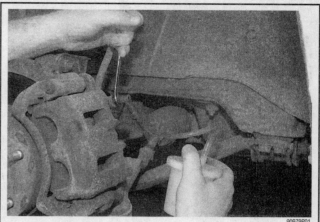

Fig. 19 Bleed the caliper until you can see clean, air bubble free brake fluid moving through the tube

4. Open the bleeder screw valve ½–¾ turn.

5. Have an assistant slowly depress the brake pedal. Close the bleeder screw valve and tell your assistant to allow the brake pedal to return slowly. Continue this pumping action to force any air out of the system. When bubbles cease to appear at the end of the bleeder hose, close the bleeder valve and remove the hose.

6. Check the master cylinder fluid level and add fluid accordingly. Do this after bleeding each wheel.

7. Repeat the bleeding operation at the remaining 3 wheels, ending with the one closet to the master cylinder. Fill the master cylinder reservoir.

MPV MODELS

Master Cylinder

Due to the location of the fluid reservoir, bench bleeding of the master cylinder is not recommended. The master cylinder is to be bled while mounted on the brake booster. If the fluid reservoir runs dry, bleeding of the entire system will be necessary. Two people will be required to bleed the brake system.

1. Fill the brake fluid reservoir with clean brake fluid. Disconnect the brake tube from the master cylinder.

2. Have a helper slowly depress the brake pedal. Once depressed, hold it in that position. Brake fluid will be expelled from the master cylinder.

✳ CAUTION

When bleeding the brakes, keep your face away from the area. Spraying fluid may cause facial and/or visual damage. Do not allow brake fluid to spill on the car's finish; it will remove the paint.

3. While the pedal is held down, use a finger to close the outlet port of the master cylinder. While the port is closed, have the helper release the brake pedal.

4. Repeat this procedure until all air is bled from the master cylinder. Check the brake fluid in the reservoir every 4–5 times, making sure the reservoir does not run dry. Add clean DOT 3 brake fluid to the reservoir as needed. All air is bled from the master cylinder when the fluid expelled from the port is free of bubbles.

5. Connect the brake tube to the port on the master cylinder. Add clean fluid to fill the reservoir to the appropriate level.

Calipers

1994

▶ See Figure 19

1. Raise and safely support the vehicle.

2. Fill the master cylinder reservoir with fresh brake fluid. Don't let the reservoir run dry during the bleeding process.

3. Have an assistant slowly pump the brake pedal several times and then apply a steady pressure to the brake pedal.

4. Attach a clear flexible hose to the bleed screw and place it into a clear container partially filled with brake fluid. Loosen the brake bleeder screw at the brake caliper or wheel cylinder and allow the fluid to flow. Close the bleeder screw.

5. Repeat this procedure for each wheel, until no air bubbles appear in the brake fluid. Begin the bleeding procedure at the wheel furthest (right rear) from the master cylinder and then work toward the wheel closest (left front) to the master cylinder.

6. Lower the vehicle.

7. Check the fluid level in the master cylinder and add fluid, if necessary. Road test the vehicle and check the brake performance.

1995–98

▶ See Figure 19

1. Fill the master cylinder with fresh brake fluid. Check the level often during this procedure. Raise and safely support the vehicle.

2. Starting with the wheel furthest from the master cylinder, remove the protective cap from the bleeder and place where it will not be lost. Clean the bleeder screw.

3. Start the engine and run at idle.

❋❋ CAUTION

When bleeding the brakes, keep face away from the brake area. Spewing fluid may cause physical and/or visual damage. Do not allow brake fluid to spill on the car's finish; it will remove the paint.

4. If the system is empty, the most efficient way to get fluid down to the wheel is to loosen the bleeder about ½–¾ turn, place a finger firmly over the bleeder and have a helper pump the brakes slowly until fluid comes out the bleeder. Once fluid is at the bleeder, close it before the pedal is released inside the vehicle.

➡**If the pedal is pumped rapidly, the fluid will churn and create small air bubbles, which are almost impossible to remove from the system. These air bubbles will accumulate and a spongy pedal will result.**

5. Once fluid has been pumped to the caliper, open the bleed screw again, have the helper press the brake pedal to the floor, lock the bleeder and have the helper slowly release the pedal. Wait 15 seconds and repeat the procedure (including the 15 second wait) until no more air comes out of the bleeder upon application of the brake pedal. Remember to close the bleeder before the pedal is released inside the vehicle each time the bleeder is opened. If not, air will be introduced into the system.

6. If a helper is not available, connect a small hose to the bleeder, place the end in a container of brake fluid and proceed to pump the pedal from inside the vehicle until no more air comes out the bleeder. The hose will prevent air from entering the system.

7. Repeat the procedure on the remaining calipers in the following order:
   a. Left front caliper
   b. Left rear caliper
   c. Right front caliper

8. Hydraulic brake systems must be totally flushed if the fluid becomes contaminated with water, dirt or other corrosive chemicals. To flush, bleed the entire system until all fluid has been replaced with the correct type of new fluid.

9. Install the bleeder cap on the bleeder to keep dirt out. Always road test the vehicle after brake work of any kind is done.

DISC BRAKES

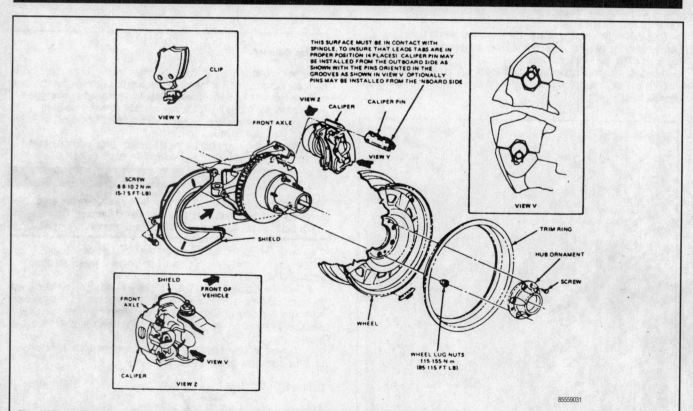

Fig. 20 Exploded view of the 1994 4WD front disc brake assembly—4-wheel ABS sensor not shown

Brake Pads

REMOVAL & INSTALLATION

Navajo and 1994 B Series Pick-up Models

▶ See Figures 21 thru 33

Always replace disc brake pad assemblies on an axle. Never service one wheel only.

➡Mazda recommends that new caliper pins be installed whenever the caliper is removed from the steering knuckle.

1. To avoid fluid overflow when the caliper piston is pressed into the caliper cylinder bores, remove or siphon part of the brake fluid out of the master cylinder reservoir (connected to the front disc brakes). Discard the removed fluid.
2. Loosen the wheel lug nuts.
3. Raise the vehicle and install jackstands. Remove a front wheel and tire assembly.
4. Place an 8 in. (203mm) C-clamp on the caliper and tighten the clamp

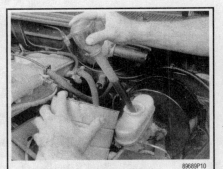

Fig. 21 Before beginning the brake pad procedure, remove some fluid from the master cylinder

Fig. 22 Use a hammer and punch, and drive the caliper pin out from between the caliper and its mount

Fig. 23 Pull the out from behind the caliper. Repeat the procedure for the lower pin

Fig. 24 Slide the caliper assembly off of the rotor

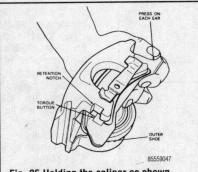

Fig. 25 Holding the caliper as shown, press down then slide the pad out to remove it from the caliper

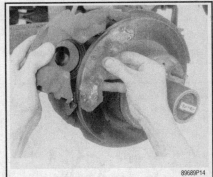

Fig. 26 Remove the outer brake pad from the caliper

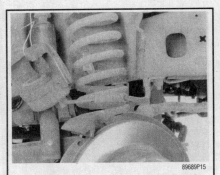

Fig. 27 If necessary, support the caliper by a length of wire from the frame. Never let it hang by the hose

Fig. 28 Finally, remove the inner brake pad from the steering knuckle assembly

Fig. 29 Place the inner pad's friction material against the caliper piston and press it in with a C-clamp

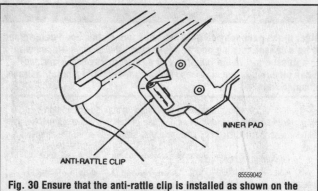

Fig. 30 Ensure that the anti-rattle clip is installed as shown on the inner pad

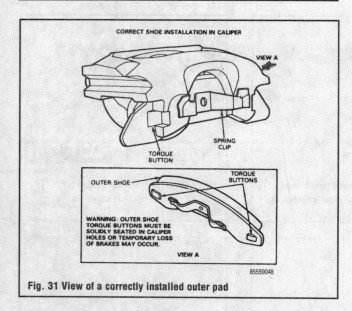

Fig. 31 View of a correctly installed outer pad

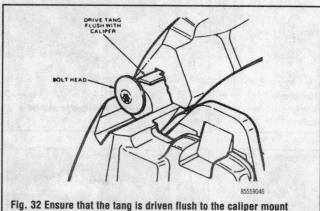

Fig. 32 Ensure that the tang is driven flush to the caliper mount

slightly to push the caliper piston in its bore. This will ease caliper removal from the rotor. Remove the clamp.

➡ Do not use a screwdriver or similar tool to pry piston away from the rotor.

5. Remove the upper caliper retaining pin as follows:

a. Place one end of a punch, ½ in. (13mm) or smaller, against the end of the caliper pin and drive the caliper pin out of the caliper toward the inside of the vehicle. Do not use a screwdriver or other edged tool to help drive out the caliper pin as the V-grooves may be damage.

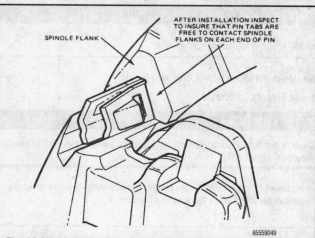

Fig. 33 After installing the pins, ensure that the tangs are free to contact either side of the caliper mount

6. Repeat the procedure in Step 4 for the lower caliper pin.
7. Remove the caliper from the rotor.
8. Remove the outer pad. Remove the anti-rattle clips and remove the inner pad.
9. Place the inner pads friction material against the caliper piston and assemble the C-clamp to the caliper again. Tighten the clamp until the caliper piston is fully seated into its bore.

To install:

10. Place a new anti-rattle clip on the lower end of the inner pad. Be sure the tabs on the clip are positioned properly and the clip is fully seated.
11. Position the inner pads and anti-rattle clip in the abutment with the anti-rattle clip tab against the pad abutment and the loop-type spring away from the rotor. Compress the anti-rattle clip and slide the upper end of the pad in position.
12. Install the outer pad, making sure the torque buttons on the pad spring clip are seated solidly in the matching holes in the caliper.
13. Install the caliper on the spindle, making sure the mounting surfaces are free of dirt and lubricate the caliper grooves with Disc Brake Caliper Grease. Install new caliper pins, making sure the pins are installed with the tang in position as illustrated. The pin must be installed with the lead tang in first, the bolt head facing outward (if equipped) and the pin positioned as shown. Position the lead tang in the V-slot mounting surface and drive in the caliper until the drive tang is flush with the caliper assembly. Install the nut (if equipped) and tighten to 32–47 inch lbs.
14. Install the wheel and tire assembly.
15. Remove the jackstands and lower the vehicle. Torque the lug nuts to 100 ft. lbs. (135 Nm).

➡ The first couple of times you apply the brakes, the pedal may go to the floor. Continue to pump the brake pedal until it feels firm.

16. Check the brake fluid level and fill as necessary. Check the brakes for proper operation before driving the vehicle.

1995–98 B Series Pick-up Models

◆ See Figure 34

⁑⁑ CAUTION

Older brake pads or shoes may contain asbestos, which has been determined to be a cancer causing agent. Never clean the brake surfaces with compressed air! Avoid inhaling any dust from any brake surface! When cleaning brake surfaces, use a commercially available brake cleaning fluid.

1. To avoid fluid overflow when the caliper piston is pressed into the caliper cylinder bores, remove or siphon part of the brake fluid out of the master cylinder reservoir (connected to the front disc brakes). Discard the removed fluid.

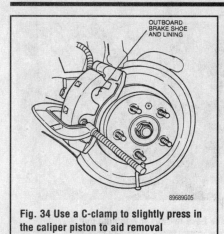

Fig. 34 Use a C-clamp to slightly press in the caliper piston to aid removal

Fig. 35 When removing the disc brake pads, you only have to remove the bottom caliper slide bolts

Fig. 36 After removing the bottom sliding bolt, swing up and support the caliper with a strong piece of wire. Then remove the inner and outer disc brake pads

2. Loosen the wheel lug nuts.
3. Raise and safely support the front of the vehicle. Remove the wheel.
4. Place an 8 in. (203mm) C-clamp on the caliper and tighten the clamp to bottom the caliper pistons in their bores. Remove the clamp.
5. Remove the two caliper slide pin bolts and lift the caliper from the anchor plate.

➡Use care to retain as much of the original caliper slide pin grease as possible.

6. Position the caliper on a frame member or suspend it with some wire. Do not allow the caliper to hang by the brake hose.
7. Remove the brake pads and, if necessary, the anti-rattle clips from the anchor plate.
8. Remove the shims, if any, from the brake pads for re-use.

To install:

9. If removed, install the anti-rattle clips.
10. Install the brake pads to the anchor plate.
11. Position the caliper over the brake pads and align the slide pin mounting holes.
12. Install the slide pin bolts and tighten them to 21–26 ft. lbs. (28–36 Nm).
13. Install the wheel and snug the lug nuts.
14. Lower the vehicle and tighten the lug nuts to 100 ft. lbs. (135 Nm).

➡The first couple of times you apply the brakes, the pedal may go to the floor. Continue to pump the brake pedal until it feels firm.

15. Start the engine and apply the brakes several times to readjust the caliper pistons. Ensure that the pedal feels firm before operating the vehicle.

MPV Models

♦ **See Figures 35 thru 40**

1. Raise and support the front end on jackstands.
2. Remove the wheels.
3. Remove the lower lock pin bolt from the caliper.

4. Rotate the caliper upward and support the caliper with a strong piece of wire. Remove the brake pads, shims, guide plates and if equipped, the springs.
5. Remove the master cylinder reservoir cap and remove about half of the fluid from the reservoir.
6. Using a large C-clamp and piece of wood, or a brake caliper piston and compressor tool and an old brake pad, compress the caliper piston(s) until they bottom in their bores.

Fig. 37 Using a brake caliper piston and compressor tool and an old brake pad, push the pistons into the bore. If equipped with dual piston calipers, it may be necessary to alternate the tool back and forth between the pistons (arrows)

Fig. 38 If necessary, remove and clean, or replace, the four anti-rattle clips located in the caliper on the ends of each brake pad

Fig. 39 Before installing the pads and caliper, clean the anti-rattle clips with a brush

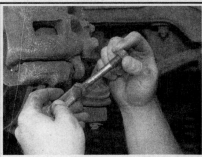

Fig. 40 Before installing the sliding caliper bolts, clean them and then lubricate them with brake grease

To install:

7. Install the shims, guide plates, new pads and if removed, the springs. If necessary, replace, the four anti-rattle clips located in the caliper on the ends of each brake pad

8. Reposition the caliper and install the lock pin bolt. Tighten the lockbolt to:
- Front caliper: 62–68 ft. lbs. (84–93 Nm)
- Rear caliper: 28–36 ft. lbs. (38–49 Nm)

9. Install the wheels, lower the vehicle, refill the master cylinder and depress the brake pedal a few times to restore pressure. Bleed the system if required.

INSPECTION

♦ **See Figure 41**

Replace the disc brake pads when the pad thickness is at the minimum thickness recommended by Mazda Motor Co., or at the minimum allowed by the applicable state or local motor vehicle inspection code. Pad thickness may be checked by removing the wheel and looking through the inspection port in the caliper assembly.

Replace the disc brake pads when the pad thickness is at the following minimum thicknesses:
- Navajo and 1994 B Series Pick-up: 0.12 inch (3.0mm)
- 1995–97 B Series Pick-up: 0.05 inch (1.5mm)
- 1998 B Series Pick-up: 0.10 inch (2.5mm)
- MPV: 0.08 inch (2.0mm)—front / 0.04 inch (1.0mm)—rear

Fig. 41 If inspecting the thickness of the brake pads, the pads are visible through the two openings in the caliper unit

Calipers

REMOVAL & INSTALLATION

Navajo and B Series Pick-up Models

♦ **See Figures 42, 43 and 44**

1. Follow the procedures for pad removal earlier in this section.
2. Remove the brake hose-to-caliper attaching bolt.
3. Discard the brass washers and plug the brake hose and caliper bolt hole.
4. On dual piston caliper models, and if necessary, remove the brake pad anchor plate by removing the two attaching screws from the back of the steering knuckle.
5. Inspect the caliper, piston and rubber seals/boots for damage and replace as necessary.

To install:

6. On dual piston calipers, and if removed, position the anchor plat to the steering knuckle and install the two retaining bolts. Use a threadlocking com-

Fig. 42 Loosen the brake hose-to-caliper retaining bolt . . .

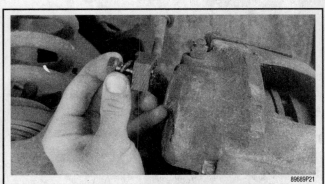

Fig. 43 . . . then remove it, along with the hose fitting and the sealing washers

Fig. 44 Always discard the old sealing washers and use new ones when installing the caliper

pound on the old bolts or install new bolts and tighten them to 73–97 ft. lbs. (98–132 Nm).

7. If it was necessary to remove the brake pads, install them to the anchor plate (dual piston) or caliper (single piston).

8. Install the caliper as instructed in the brake pad installation procedures.

➡**Always use new sealing washers when assembling the hose to the brake caliper.**

9. Place a new sealing washer on the brake hose bolt, slide the bolt through the hose fitting and install a second sealing washer to the bolt.

10. Position the hose/bolt to the caliper then tighten the bolt to 22–29 ft. lbs. (30–40 Nm).

11. Bleed the brake system. Check for leaks and proper operation before placing the vehicle into service.

MPV Models

▶ **See Figures 45, 46, 47 and 48**

1. Raise and safely support the vehicle. Remove the wheel and tire assembly.

2. Remove the banjo bolt and disconnect the brake hose from the caliper. Plug the hose to prevent fluid leakage.

3. Remove the caliper mounting bolt and pivot the caliper about the mounting pin and off the brake rotor. Remove the caliper from the pin.

4. If installing the same caliper, inspect the condition of the caliper sliding bolt rubber boots and replace if necessary.

5. Installation is the reverse of the removal procedure. Lubricate the caliper mounting bolts or bolt and pin prior to installation.

6. Tighten the caliper mounting bolt(s) to:
- Front caliper: 61–69 ft. lbs. (83–93 Nm)
- Rear caliper: 37–50 ft. lbs. (50–68 Nm)

7. Bleed the brake system. Check for leaks and proper operation before placing the vehicle into service.

OVERHAUL

▶ **See Figures 49 thru 56**

➡ **Some vehicles may be equipped dual piston calipers. The procedure to overhaul the caliper is essentially the same with the exception of multiple pistons, O-rings and dust boots.**

1. Remove the caliper from the vehicle and place on a clean workbench.

✳✳ CAUTION

NEVER place your fingers in front of the pistons in an attempt to catch or protect the pistons when applying compressed air. This could result in personal injury!

➡ **Depending upon the vehicle, there are two different ways to remove the piston from the caliper. Refer to the brake pad replacement procedure to make sure you have the correct procedure for your vehicle.**

2. The first method is as follows:
   a. Stuff a shop towel or a block of wood into the caliper to catch the piston.
   b. Remove the caliper piston using compressed air applied into the caliper inlet hole. Inspect the piston for scoring, nicks, corrosion and/or worn or damaged chrome plating. The piston must be replaced if any of these conditions are found.

Fig. 45 Before disconnecting the brake hose at the caliper, clean any dirt or debris from the hose and banjo bolt connection using a wire brush

Fig. 46 Remove the banjo bolt from the caliper connection. Be careful not to lose the crush washer that is located between the brake hose and banjo bolt

Fig. 47 Be careful not to lose the crush washer that is located between the caliper and the hose fitting. Note that the two crush washers at the brake hose fitting are of different sizes and must not be mixed up

3. For the second method, you must rotate the piston to retract it from the caliper.

4. If equipped, remove the anti-rattle clip.

5. Use a prytool to remove the caliper boot, being careful not to scratch the housing bore.

6. Remove the piston seals from the groove in the caliper bore.

7. Carefully loosen the brake bleeder valve cap and valve from the caliper housing.

8. Inspect the caliper bores, pistons and mounting threads for scoring or excessive wear.

9. Use crocus cloth to polish out light corrosion from the piston and bore.

10. Clean all parts with denatured alcohol and dry with compressed air.

To assemble:

11. Lubricate and install the bleeder valve and cap.

12. Install the new seals into the caliper bore grooves, making sure they are not twisted.

13. Lubricate the piston bore.

14. Install the pistons and boots into the bores of the calipers and push to the bottom of the bores.

15. Use a suitable driving tool to seat the boots in the housing.

Fig. 48 Inspect the condition of the caliper sliding bolt rubber boots and replace if necessary

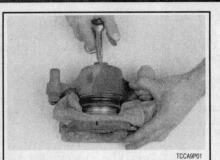

Fig. 49 For some types of calipers, use compressed air to drive the piston out of the caliper, but make sure to keep your fingers clear

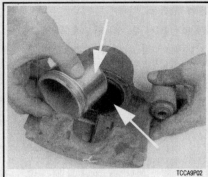

Fig. 50 Withdraw the piston from the caliper bore

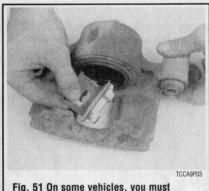

Fig. 51 On some vehicles, you must remove the anti-rattle clip

Fig. 52 Use a prytool to carefully pry around the edge of the boot . . .

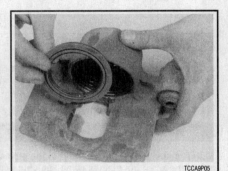

Fig. 53 . . . then remove the boot from the caliper housing, taking care not to score or damage the bore

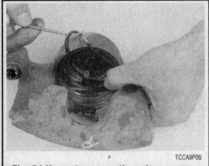

Fig. 54 Use extreme caution when removing the piston seal; DO NOT scratch the caliper bore

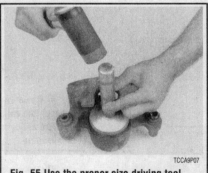

Fig. 55 Use the proper size driving tool and a mallet to properly seal the boots in the caliper housing

Fig. 56 There are tools, such as this Mighty-Vac, available to assist in proper brake system bleeding

16. Install the caliper in the vehicle.
17. Install the wheel and tire assembly, then carefully lower the vehicle.
18. Properly bleed the brake system.

Brake Rotor (Disc)

REMOVAL & INSTALLATION

Navajo and B Series Pick-up Models

EXCEPT 1995–98 4-WHEEL DRIVE MODELS

1. Loosen the wheel lug nuts.
2. Jack up the front of the vehicle and support on jackstands.

3. Remove the wheel and tire.
4. On 1994 models, remove the brake caliper assembly as described earlier in this Section, but do not disconnect the brake hose.
5. On 1995–98 models, remove the two anchor plate-to-steering knuckle bolts then slide the assembly off of the rotor.
6. Suspend the caliper assembly by a piece of wire. Do not allow it to hang by the brake hose.
7. Follow the procedure given under wheel bearing removal in Section 7 for models with manual and automatic locking hubs.

➡New rotor assemblies come protected with an anti-rust coating which should be removed with denatured alcohol or degreaser. New hubs must be packed with EP wheel bearing grease.

8. Installation is the reverse of the removal procedure.

1995–98 4-WHEEL DRIVE MODELS

1. Loosen the wheel lug nuts.
2. Jack up the front of the vehicle and support on jackstands.
3. Remove the wheel and tire.
4. Remove the two anchor plate-to-steering knuckle bolts then slide the assembly off of the rotor.
5. Grasp the rotor and pull it from the wheel hub. Some models may have a small retaining screw holding the rotor to the wheel hub, if so, remove the screw then pull the rotor off.
6. Installation is the reverse of the removal procedure.

MPV Models

▶ See Figures 57, 58, 59, 60 and 61

❋❋ CAUTION

Brake pads contain asbestos, which has been determined to be a cancer causing agent. Never clean the brake surfaces with compressed air! Avoid inhaling any dust from any brake surface! When cleaning brake surfaces, use a commercially available brake cleaning fluid.

Fig. 57 Using a 17mm box wrench, remove the two brake caliper slide bolts

Fig. 58 To remove the brake rotor, remove the two brake caliper mounting bolts using a 21mm socket and breaker bar

Fig. 59 Remove the caliper and pad assembly from the brake rotor . . .

Fig. 60 . . . and suspend from the strut coil using a strong piece of wire

Fig. 61 Pull the rotor unit off of the wheel hub/bearing

1. Raise and safely support the vehicle. Remove the wheel and tire assembly.
2. Remove the caliper and support it aside with mechanic's wire; do not let the caliper hang by the brake hose. Remove the disc brake pads and mounting support.
3. Remove the attaching screw and remove the rotor.
4. Inspect the rotor for scoring, wear and runout. Machine or replace as necessary.
5. If rotor replacement is necessary on pickup models, remove the attaching bolts and separate the rotor from the hub.
6. Installation is the reverse of removal.

INSPECTION

▶ See Figure 62

1. Inspect the rotor for cracks, grooves or waviness. Rotors that aren't too badly scored or grooved can be resurfaced by most automotive shops.
2. Measure the rotor thickness using a caliper gauge.
3. Minimum rotor thickness should be the following:
- Navajo and 1994–97 B Series Pick-up: 0.81 in. (20.5mm)
- 1998 B Series Pick-up: 1.02 inch (26.0mm)
- MPV: 1.02 inch (26.0mm)—front / 0.63 inch (16.0mm)—rear
4. If refinishing exceeds that, the rotor will have to be replaced.

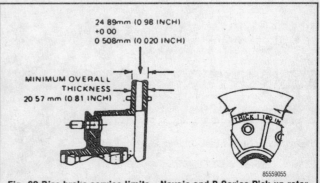

Fig. 62 Disc brake service limits—Navajo and B Series Pick-up rotor shown

DRUM BRAKES

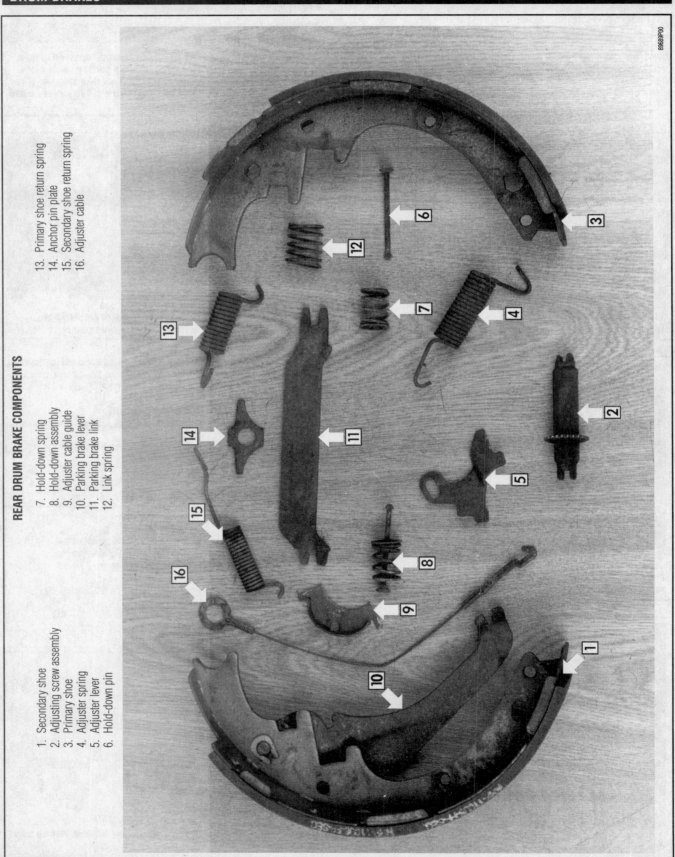

REAR DRUM BRAKE COMPONENTS

1. Secondary shoe
2. Adjusting screw assembly
3. Primary shoe
4. Adjuster spring
5. Adjuster lever
6. Hold-down pin
7. Hold-down spring
8. Hold-down assembly
9. Adjuster cable guide
10. Parking brake lever
11. Parking brake link
12. Link spring
13. Primary shoe return spring
14. Anchor pin plate
15. Secondary shoe return spring
16. Adjuster cable

Brake Drums

REMOVAL & INSTALLATION

▶ See Figures 63 and 64

※ CAUTION

Older brake pads or shoes may contain asbestos, which has been determined to be a cancer causing agent. Never clean the brake surfaces with compressed air! Avoid inhaling any dust from any brake surface! When cleaning brake surfaces, use a commercially available brake cleaning fluid.

1. Raise the vehicle so that the wheel to be worked on is clear of the floor and install jackstands under the vehicle.
2. Remove the hub cap and the wheel/tire assembly. Remove the 3 retaining nuts and remove the brake drum. It may be necessary to back off the brake shoe adjustment in order to remove the brake drum. This is because the drum might be grooved or worn from being in service for an extended period of time.
3. Before installing a new brake drum, be sure and remove any protective coating with carburetor degreaser.
4. Install the brake drum in the reverse order of removal and adjusts the brakes.

INSPECTION

▶ See Figure 65

After the brake drum has been removed from the vehicle, it should be inspected for run-out, severe scoring cracks, and the proper inside diameter.

Minor scores on a brake drum can be removed with fine emery cloth, provided that all grit is removed from the drum before it is installed on the vehicle.

A badly scored, rough, or out-of-round (run-out) drum can be ground or turned on a brake drum lathe. Do not remove any more material from the drum than is necessary to provide a smooth surface for the brake shoe to contact. The maximum diameter of the braking surface is shown on the inside of each brake drum. Brake drums that exceed the maximum braking surface diameter shown on the brake drum, either through wear or refinishing, must be replaced. This is because after the outside wall of the brake drum reaches a certain thickness (thinner than the original thickness) the drum loses its ability to dissipate the heat created by the friction between the brake drum and the brake shoes, when the brakes are applied. Also the brake drum will have more tendency to warp and/or crack.

The maximum braking surface diameter specification, which is shown on each drum, allows for a 0.060 in. (1.5mm) machining cut over the original nominal drum diameter plus 0.030 in. (0.76mm) additional wear before reaching the diameter where the drum must be discarded. Use a brake drum micrometer to measure the inside diameter of the brake drums.

Brake Shoes

REMOVAL & INSTALLATION

▶ See Figures 66 thru 82

※ CAUTION

Older brake pads or shoes may contain asbestos, which has been determined to be a cancer causing agent. Never clean the brake surfaces with compressed air! Avoid inhaling any dust from any brake surface! When cleaning brake surfaces, use a commercially available brake cleaning fluid.

1. Raise and support the vehicle and remove the wheel and brake drum from the wheel to be worked on.

Fig. 63 To remove the rear brake drum, first safely raise the rear of the vehicle and remove the wheel . . .

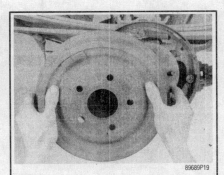

Fig. 64 . . . then grasp hold of the drum and pull it from the axle flange and brake shoes

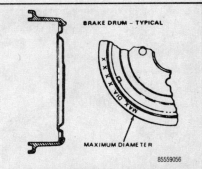

Fig. 65 Drum brake service limits. The maximum inside diameter is cast into the drum

Fig. 66 Clean the brake shoe assemblies with a liquid cleaning solution, NEVER with compressed air

Fig. 67 To begin remove the brake shoes, pull the adjuster cable towards the shoe . . .

Fig. 68 . . . and disconnect the pivot hook from the adjusting lever. Wind the starwheel all the way in

➡If you have never replaced the brakes on a car before and you are not too familiar with the procedures involved, only disassemble and assemble one side at a time, leaving the other side intact as a reference during reassembly.

2. Install a clamp over the ends of the wheel cylinder to prevent the pistons of the wheel cylinder from coming out, causing loss of fluid.

3. Contract the brake shoes by pulling the self-adjusting lever away from the starwheel adjustment screw and turn the starwheel up and back until the pivot nut is drawn onto the starwheel as far as it will come.

4. Pull the adjusting lever, cable and automatic adjuster spring down and toward the rear to unhook the pivot hook from the large hole in the secondary shoe web. Do not attempt to pry the pivot hook from the hole.

5. Remove the automatic adjuster spring and the adjusting lever.

6. Remove the primary shoe-to-anchor spring with a brake tool. (Brake tools are very common and are available at auto parts stores). Remove the secondary shoe-to-anchor spring and unhook the cable anchor. Remove the anchor pin plate.

7. Remove the cable guide from the secondary shoe.

8. Remove the shoe hold-down springs, shoes, adjusting screw, pivot nut, and socket. Note the color of each hold-down spring for assembly. To remove the hold-down springs, reach behind the brake backing plate and place one finger on the end of one of the brake hold-down spring mounting pins. Using a pair of pliers, grasp the washer-type retainer on top of the hold-down spring that corresponds to the pin that you are holding. Push down on the pliers and turn them 90° to align the slot in the washer with the head on the spring mounting pin. Remove the spring and washer retainer and repeat this operation on the hold-down spring on the other shoe.

9. Remove the parking brake link and spring. Disconnect the parking brake cable from the parking brake lever.

10. After removing the rear brake secondary shoe, disassemble the parking brake lever from the shoe by removing the retaining clip and spring washer.

To assemble and install the brake shoes:

11. Assemble the parking brake lever to the secondary shoe and secure it with the spring washer and retaining clip.

Fig. 69 Disconnect the adjuster lever return spring from the lever . . .

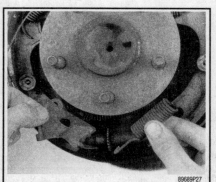
Fig. 70 . . . and remove the spring and the lever

Fig. 71 Next, using a brake spring removal tool . . .

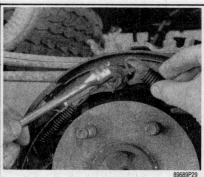
Fig. 72 . . . disconnect the primary brake shoe return spring from the anchor pin

Fig. 73 Repeat the procedure and remove the secondary return spring, adjuster cable and its guide

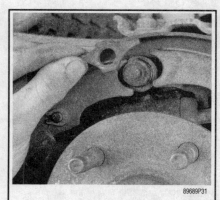
Fig. 74 Also remove the anchor pin plate

Fig. 75 Pull the bottoms of the shoes apart and remove the adjuster screw assembly

Fig. 76 Press in the hold-down springs while holding in on the nail from behind, then turn the cup 90° . . .

Fig. 77 . . . and release to remove the hold-down spring. Pull the nail out from the backing plate

Fig. 78 Remove the primary (front) brake shoe from the backing plate . . .

Fig. 79 . . . and the parking brake strut as well

Fig. 80 Remove the secondary shoe hold-down, pull the shoe out then press up on the cable spring . . .

Fig. 81 . . . and disconnect the parking brake cable from its lever by pulling it from the slot

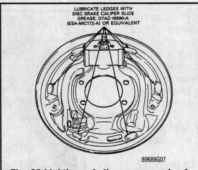

Fig. 82 Lightly apply the proper grade of lubricant to the points shown on the backing plate

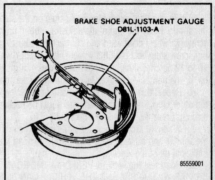

Fig. 83 Brake shoe adjustment gauge— Step 1

12. Apply a light coating of Lubriplate® at the points where the brake shoes contact the backing plate.

13. Position the brake shoes on the backing plate, and install the hold-down spring pins, springs, and spring washer-type retainers. Install the parking brake link, spring and washer. Connect the parking brake cable to the parking brake lever.

14. Install the anchor pin plate, and place the cable anchor over the anchor pin with the crimped side toward the backing plate.

15. Install the primary shoe-to-anchor spring with the brake tool.

16. Install the cable guide on the secondary shoe web with the flanged holes fitted into the hole in the secondary shoe web. Thread the cable around the cable guide groove.

17. Install the secondary shoe-to-anchor (long) spring. Be sure that the cable end is not cocked or binding on the anchor pin when installed. All of the parts should be flat on the anchor pin. Remove the wheel cylinder piston clamp.

18. Apply Lubriplate® to the threads and the socket end of the adjusting starwheel screw. Turn the adjusting screw into the adjusting pivot nut to the limit of the threads and then back off ½ turn.

➡Interchanging the brake shoe adjusting screw assemblies from one side of the vehicle to the other would cause the brake shoes to retract rather than expand each time the automatic adjusting mechanism operated. To prevent this, the socket end of the adjusting screw is stamped with an R or an L for RIGHT or LEFT. The adjusting pivot nuts can be distinguished by the number of lines machined around the body of the nut; one line indicates left hand nut and 2 lines indicates a right hand nut.

19. Place the adjusting socket on the screw and install this assembly between the shoe ends with the adjusting screw nearest to the secondary shoe.

20. Place the cable hook into the hole in the adjusting lever from the backing plate side. The adjusting levers are stamped with an **R** (right) or an **L** (left) to indicate their installation on the right or left hand brake assembly.

21. Position the hooked end of the adjuster spring in the primary shoe web and connect the loop end of the spring to the adjuster lever hole.

22. Pull the adjuster lever, cable and automatic adjuster spring down toward the rear to engage the pivot hook in the large hole in the secondary shoe web.

23. After installation, check the action of the adjuster by pulling the section of the cable between the cable guide and the adjusting lever toward the sec-

ondary shoe web far enough to lift the lever past a tooth on the adjusting screw starwheel. The lever should snap into position behind the next tooth, and release of the cable should cause the adjuster spring to return the lever to its original position. This return action of the lever will turn the adjusting screw starwheel one tooth. The lever should contact the adjusting screw starwheel one tooth above the center line of the adjusting screw.

If the automatic adjusting mechanism does not perform properly, check the following:

24. Check the cable end fittings. The cable ends should fill or extend slightly beyond the crimped section of the fittings. If this is not the case, replace the cable.

25. Check the cable guide for damage. The cable groove should be parallel to the shoe web, and the body of the guide should lie flat against the web. Replace the cable guide if this is not so.

26. Check the pivot hook on the lever. The hook surfaces should be square with the body on the lever for proper pivoting. Repair or replace the hook as necessary.

27. Make sure that the adjusting screw starwheel is properly seated in the notch in the shoe web.

ADJUSTMENTS

◆ **See Figures 83, 84, 85 and 86**

The drum brakes are self-adjusting and require a manual adjustment only after the brake shoes have been replaced.

➡**Disc brakes are not adjustable.**

To adjust the rear brakes with drums installed, follow the procedure given below:

1. Raise the vehicle and support it with safety stands.

2. Remove the rubber plug from the adjusting slot on the backing plate.

3. Turn the adjusting screw using a Brake Shoe Adjustment Tool or equivalent inside the hole to expand the brake shoes until they drag against the brake drum and lock the drum.

4. Insert a small screwdriver or piece of firm wire (coat hanger wire) into the adjusting slot and push the automatic adjusting lever out and free of the starwheel on the adjusting screw and hold it there.

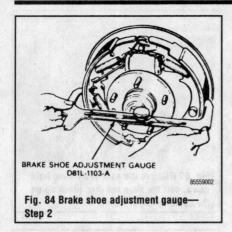

Fig. 84 Brake shoe adjustment gauge—Step 2

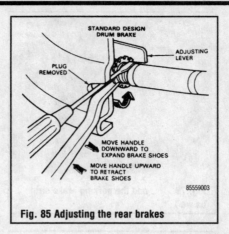

Fig. 85 Adjusting the rear brakes

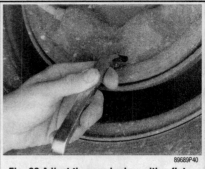

Fig. 86 Adjust the rear brakes with a flat bladed tool inserted in the access hole in the backing plate

5. Engage the topmost tooth possible on the starwheel with the brake adjusting spoon. Move the end of the adjusting spoon upward to move the adjusting screw starwheel downward and contract the adjusting screw. Back off the adjusting screw starwheel until the wheel spins FREELY with a minimum of drag about 10 to 12 notches. Keep track of the number of turns that the starwheel is backed off, or the number of strokes taken with the brake adjusting spoon.

6. Repeat this operation for the other side. When backing off the brakes on the other side, the starwheel adjuster must be backed off the same number of turns to prevent side-to-side brake pull.

7. When all drum brakes are adjusted, remove the safety stands and lower the vehicle and make several stops while backing the vehicle, to equalize the brakes at all of the wheels.

8. Road test the vehicle. PERFORM THE ROAD TEST ONLY WHEN THE BRAKES WILL APPLY AND THE VEHICLE CAN BE STOPPED SAFELY!

Wheel Cylinders

REMOVAL & INSTALLATION

♦ See Figures 87 and 88

1. To remove the wheel cylinder, jack up the vehicle and remove the wheel, hub, and drum.
2. Remove the brake shoe assemblies.
3. Disconnect the brake line at the fitting on the brake backing plate.
4. Remove the screws that hold the wheel cylinder to the backing plate and remove the wheel cylinder from the vehicle.
5. Installation is the reverse of the above removal procedure. After installation bleed and adjust the brakes as described earlier in this Section.

OVERHAUL

♦ See Figures 89 thru 99

Wheel cylinder overhaul kits may be available, but often at little or no savings over a reconditioned wheel cylinder. It often makes sense with these components to substitute a new or reconditioned part instead of attempting an overhaul.

If no replacement is available, or you would prefer to overhaul your wheel cylinders, the following procedure may be used. When rebuilding and installing wheel cylinders, avoid getting any contaminants into the system. Always use clean, new, high quality brake fluid. If dirty or improper fluid has been used, it will be necessary to drain the entire system, flush the system with proper brake fluid, replace all rubber components, then refill and bleed the system.

1. Remove the wheel cylinder from the vehicle and place on a clean workbench.
2. First remove and discard the old rubber boots, then withdraw the pistons. Piston cylinders are equipped with seals and a spring assembly, all located behind the pistons in the cylinder bore.
3. Remove the remaining inner components, seals and spring assembly. Compressed air may be useful in removing these components. If no compressed air is available, be VERY careful not to score the wheel cylinder bore when removing parts from it. Discard all components for which replacements were supplied in the rebuild kit.

Fig. 87 Remove the brake shoes and the brake line, then remove the bolts and tilt the cylinder inwards . . .

Fig. 88 . . . then lift it up and off of the backing plate

4. Wash the cylinder and metal parts in denatured alcohol or clean brake fluid.

❊❊❊ WARNING

Never use a mineral-based solvent such as gasoline, kerosene or paint thinner for cleaning purposes. These solvents will swell rubber components and quickly deteriorate them.

5. Allow the parts to air dry or use compressed air. Do not use rags for cleaning, since lint will remain in the cylinder bore.
6. Inspect the piston and replace it if it shows scratches.
7. Lubricate the cylinder bore and seals using clean brake fluid.
8. Position the spring assembly.
9. Install the inner seals, then the pistons.
10. Insert the new boots into the counterbores by hand. Do not lubricate the boots.
11. Install the wheel cylinder.

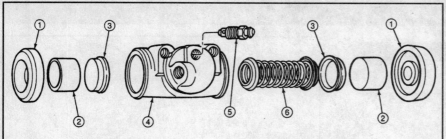

1. Wheel cylinder boot
2. Wheel cylinder piston
3. Wheel cylinder piston cup
4. Rear wheel cylinder
5. Wheel cylinder bleeder screw
6. Wheel cylinder piston cup spring

89689G08

Fig. 89 Exploded view of the rear wheel cylinder assembly

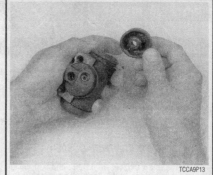

TCCA9P13

Fig. 90 Remove the outer boots from the wheel cylinder

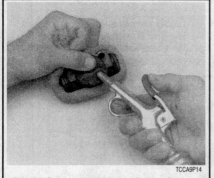

TCCA9P14

Fig. 91 Compressed air can be used to remove the pistons and seals

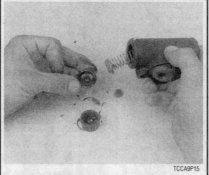

TCCA9P15

Fig. 92 Remove the pistons, cup seals and spring from the cylinder

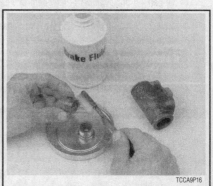

TCCA9P16

Fig. 93 Use brake fluid and a soft brush to clean the pistons . . .

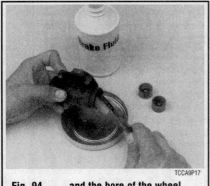

TCCA9P17

Fig. 94 . . . and the bore of the wheel cylinder

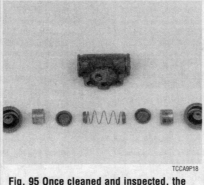

TCCA9P18

Fig. 95 Once cleaned and inspected, the wheel cylinder is ready for assembly

TCCA9P19

Fig. 96 Lubricate the cup seals with brake fluid

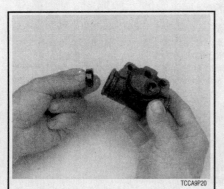

TCCA9P20

Fig. 97 Install the spring, then the cup seals in the bore

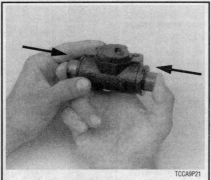

TCCA9P21

Fig. 98 Lightly lubricate the pistons, then install them

TCCA9P22

Fig. 99 The boots can now be installed over the wheel cylinder ends

PARKING BRAKE

Cable

REMOVAL & INSTALLATION

Navajo and B Series Pick-up Models

♦ See Figure 100

EQUALIZER-TO-CONTROL CABLE

1. Raise the vehicle on a hoist and support on jackstands.
2. Relieve the parking brake cable tension as outlined under cable adjustments.
3. Remove the parking brake cable from the bracket.
4. Remove the jackstands and lower the vehicle. Remove the forward ball end of the parking brake cable from the control assembly clevis.
5. Remove the cable from the control assembly.
6. Using a fishing line wire leader or cord attached to the control lever end of the cable, remove the cable from the vehicle.

To install:

7. Transfer the fish wire or cord to the new cable. Position the cable in the vehicle, routing the cable through the dash panel. Remove the fish wire and secure the cable to the control.

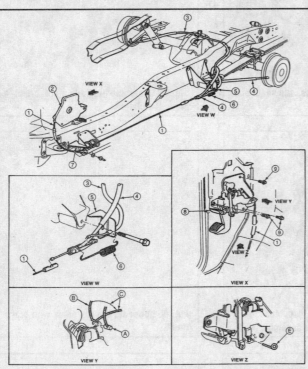

1. Front parking brake cable and conduit
2. Parking brake control
3. Parking brake rear cable and conduit (LH)
4. Parking brake rear cable and conduit (RH)
5. Parking brake cable bracket (rear)
6. Parking brake equalizer cable spring
7. Parking brake cable bracket (front)
8. Parking brake release handle
9. Bolt, parking brake control-to-cowl side
A. Parking brake front cable and conduit, before inserting into ratchet plate pivot hole
B. Parking brake front cable and conduit, after inserting into ratchet plate pivot hole
C. Parking brake front cable and conduit, installed
D. 4mm (5/32-Inch) steel pin or equivalent size drill bit

89689G16

Fig. 100 Parking brake cable routing diagram

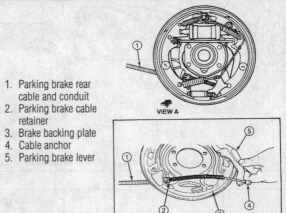

1. Parking brake rear cable and conduit
2. Parking brake cable retainer
3. Brake backing plate
4. Cable anchor
5. Parking brake lever

89689G18

Fig. 101 View of the rear brake cable mounting assembly

8. Connect the forward ball end of the brake cable to the clevis of the control assembly. Raise the vehicle on a hoist.
9. Route the cable through the bracket.
10. Connect the slug of the cable to the Tension Limiter connector.
11. Release the cable tension as outlined under cable adjustments.
12. Rotate both rear wheels to be sure that the parking brakes are not dragging.

EQUALIZER-TO-REAR WHEEL CABLES

♦ See Figure 101

1. Raise the vehicle and remove the wheel and brake drum.
2. Relieve the parking brake cable tension as outlined under cable adjustments. Disconnect the left rear cable from the front cable. For the right rear cable, disconnect it from the cable equalizer and rear guide bracket.
3. Use a 7/16 in. (14mm) wrench and compress the prongs that retain the cable housing to the frame bracket, and pull the cable and housing out of the bracket.
4. Working on the wheel side, use a 7/16 in. (14mm) wrench and compress the prongs on the cable retainer so they can pass through the hole in the brake backing plate. Draw the cable retainer out of the hole.
5. With the spring tension off the parking brake lever, lift the cable out of the slot in the lever, and remove the cable through the brake backing plate hole.

To install:

6. Route the right cable behind the right shock and through the hole in the left frame side rail. Route the left cable inboard of the leaf spring. Pull the cable through the brake backing plate until the end of the cable is inserted over the slot in the parking brake lever. Pull the excess slack from the cable and insert the cable housing into the brake backing plate access hole until the retainer prongs expand.
7. Insert the front of the cable housing through the frame crossmember bracket until the prong expands. Insert the ball end of the cable into the key hole slots on the equalizer, rotate the equalizer 90° and recouple the Tension Limiter threaded rod to the equalizer.
8. Install the rear brake drum and wheel, and adjust the rear brake shoes.
9. Release the cable tension as outlined under cable adjustments.
10. Rotate both rear wheels to be sure that the parking brakes are not dragging.
11. Lower the vehicle and tighten the wheel lug nuts to 100 ft. lbs. (135 Nm).

MPV Models

♦ See Figure 102

1. Raise and safely support the vehicle.
2. Release the parking brake and remove the parking brake lever adjusting nut. Remove rear seat No. 1, front floormat and cover.
3. Remove the rear brake caliper(s), and the disc plate. Remove the parking brake shoes.
4. Remove the parking brake cover. Remove the left and right parking brake cables, as needed.

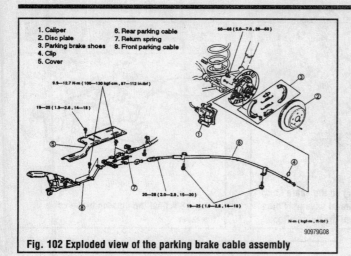

1. Caliper
2. Disc plate
3. Parking brake shoes
4. Clip
5. Cover
6. Rear parking cable
7. Return spring
8. Front parking cable

Fig. 102 Exploded view of the parking brake cable assembly

5. Remove the return spring and front cable, if needed.
6. Installation is the reverse of removal. Properly adjust the parking brake. Depress the brake pedal a few times and check that the rear brakes do not drag while rotating the wheels.

ADJUSTMENT

Navajo and B Series Pick-up Models

All models use a self-adjusting parking brake cable assembly. However, in order to remove any of the cables or components, the following procedures must be followed.

CABLE TENSION RELEASE

♦ See Figure 103

Method 1:
1. Place the parking brake cable control in the released position.
2. Have an assistant pull on the intermediate brake cable while you insert a $5/32$ in. (4mm) diameter steel pin (or drill bit) into the hole provided in the parking brake control assembly.
3. To release the cable tension, pull out the lock pin from the control assembly.
Method 2:
For relieving tension from the rear cables only.
1. Pull backwards on the rear cable and conduit about 1.0–2.0 in. (25–50mm) and place a clamp on the parking brake cable and conduit behind the rear crossmember.

⁂ WARNING

Ensure that you do not damage the nylon coating on the cable.

2. To release the cable tension, remove the clamp holding the rear cable to the crossmember.

CABLE TENSION RESETTING

♦ See Figures 104, 105, 106 and 107

In the event that one of the cables has broken, or the cable tension release procedures were not followed perform the following procedures:
1. Remove the parking brake control assembly.
2. Engage the coil spring to the tab on the adjusting wheel in the control assembly.
3. Ensure the control assembly is in the released position.
4. Slip a spare front parking brake (or remove you existing one) cable around the pulley and insert the cable end into the pivot hole in the ratchet plate.
5. Position the free end of the parking brake cable on the floor and step on it, or clamp it in a vise.
6. Pull on the control assembly, holding the mounting bracket tightly against the body of the control, until the cable tension rotates the cable track assembly so that the (lock pin) $5/32$ in. (4mm) diameter steel pin (or drill bit) can be fully seated through the plate.
7. Insert the lock pin so that the assembly is in the "cable released" position.
8. Install the parking brake control lever.

MPV Models

♦ See Figure 108

1. Remove the parking brake lever cover.
2. Remove the adjusting nut clip and turn the adjusting nut at the front of the parking cable to adjust.
3. After adjustment, with the ignition switch in the **ON** position, pull the parking brake lever one notch. Check that the parking brake warning light illuminates.
4. When the cable is properly adjusted, the lever should move 3–6 notches.
5. Replace the adjusting nut clip.

Brake Shoes

Only MPV models use separate parking brake shoes.

REMOVAL & INSTALLATION

♦ See Figure 102

1. Raise and support the rear end on jackstands.
2. Remove the wheels.
3. Remove the caliper assembly.
4. Remove the brake rotor/drum. If the rotor/drum is hard to come off, remove the service plug and turn the adjuster to loosen the shoes.
5. Remove the upper and lower return springs.
6. Remove the hold springs and pins.
7. Remove the brake shoes, adjuster and disconnect the operating lever from the parking brake cable.
To install:
8. Connect the operating lever to the parking brake cable. The arrow on the operating lever should be facing the front of the vehicle.
9. Compress the adjuster to its smallest possible size by screwing

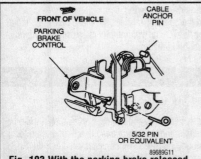

Fig. 103 With the parking brake released, insert the pin into the brake control assembly as shown to lock the cable tension spring

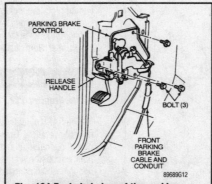

Fig. 104 Exploded view of the parking brake control assembly mounting

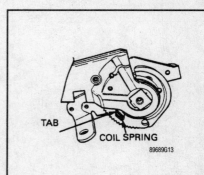

Fig. 105 Engage the coil spring to the tab on the adjusting wheel

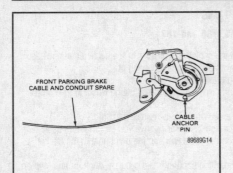

Fig. 106 Slip the front parking brake cable around the pulley and insert the cable end to the ratchet plate

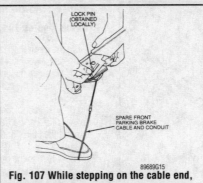

Fig. 107 While stepping on the cable end, pull upwards on the control assembly then install the lock pin when the holes align

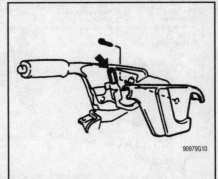

Fig. 108 Adjust the parking brake cable at the lever

threaded part inward. Install the adjuster between the brake shoes. For the left wheel, install the adjuster with the threaded part facing the front; for the right wheel, towards the rear.

10. Install the hold pins and springs.
11. Install the upper and lower return springs.
12. Install the rotor/drum. With the service plug removed, insert a flat bladed tool into the hole and turn the adjuster downward until the rotor/drum locks. Turn the adjuster 4–5 notches in the opposite direction to set the proper clearance. Verify that there is no drag on the rotor/drum and install the service plug.
13. Install the caliper assembly.
14. Install the wheels.
15. Lower the vehicle. Properly bleed the brake system.

ADJUSTMENT

▸ See Figure 109

1. Remove the service plug from the rotor.
2. Insert a screwdriver into the hole and rotate the adjuster in the direction of the arrow in the illustration until it locks up the rotor.

Fig. 109 Adjustment of the parking brake shoes

3. To set the proper clearance, rotate the adjuster 3–5 notches in the opposite direction. With adjuster rotated 4 notches, the shoe clearance will be 0.013 inch (0.32mm).
4. Verify that the brakes do not drag when rotating the rotor by hand.
5. Install the service plug back onto the rotor.

REAR ANTI-LOCK BRAKE SYSTEM (RABS)

General Information

▸ See Figures 110 and 111

The rear wheel anti-lock system continually monitors rear wheel speed with a sensor mounted on the rear axle. When the teeth on an excitor ring, mounted on the differential ring gear, pass the sensor pole piece, an AC voltage is induced in the sensor circuit with a frequency proportional to the average rear wheel speed. In the event of an impending lockup condition during braking, the anti-

lock system modulates hydraulic pressure to the rear brakes inhibiting rear wheel lockup.

When the brake pedal is applied, a control module senses the drop in rear wheel speed. If the rate of deceleration is too great, indicating that wheel lockup is going to occur, the module activates the electro-hydraulic valve causing the isolation valve to close. With the isolation closed, the rear wheel cylinders are isolated from the master cylinder and the rear brake pressure cannot increase. If the rate of deceleration is still too great, the module will energize the dump solenoid with a series of rapid pulses to bleed off rear cylinder fluid into an accumulator built into the electro-hydraulic valve. This will reduce the rear wheel cylinder pressure and allow the rear wheels to spin back to the vehicle speed. Continuing under module control, the dump and isolation solenoids will be pulsed in a manner that will keep the rear wheels rotating while still maintaining high levels of deceleration during braking.

At the end of the stop, when the operator releases the brake pedal, the isolation valve de-energizes and any fluid in the accumulator is returned to the master cylinder. Normal brake operation is resumed.

System Self-Test

▸ See Figures 112, 113 and 114

The RABS module performs system tests and self-tests during startup and normal operation. The valve, sensor and fluid level circuits are monitored for proper operation. If a fault is found, the RABS will be deactivated and the ABS light will be lit until the ignition is turned OFF. When the light is lit, the diagnostic flashout code may be obtained. Under normal operation, the light will stay on for about 2 seconds while the ignition switch is in the ON position and will go out shortly after. A flash code may be obtained only when the light is

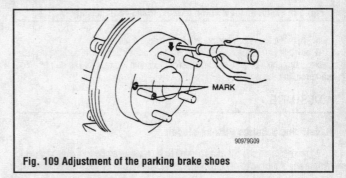

1. ABS control module
2. ABS hydraulic unit
3. Ring gear speed sensor
4. ABS relay
5. Short connector
6. Pressure differential switch
7. ABS fuse

Fig. 110 MPV RABS component locations for 1994–95 models

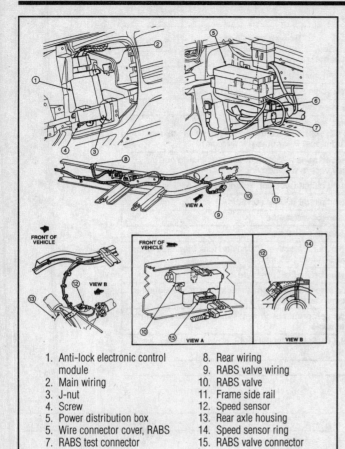

1. Anti-lock electronic control module
2. Main wiring
3. J-nut
4. Screw
5. Power distribution box
5. Wire connector cover, RABS
7. RABS test connector
8. Rear wiring
9. RABS valve wiring
10. RABS valve
11. Frame side rail
12. Speed sensor
13. Rear axle housing
14. Speed sensor ring
15. RABS valve connector

Fig. 111 B Series Pick-up RABS component locations

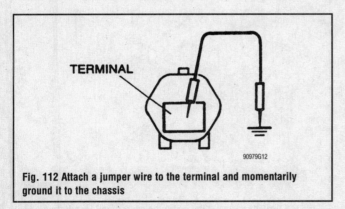

TERMINAL

Fig. 112 Attach a jumper wire to the terminal and momentarily ground it to the chassis

ON. Before reading the code, drive the vehicle to a level area and place the shift lever in the PARK or NEUTRAL position. Keep the vehicle ignition ON.

➡️**All vehicles use the RABS II system. The major difference between the two systems is the addition of keep alive memory (codes are stored, even if ignition is turned off), and a code 16 can be set which means the system is operating properly.**

In the case of more than one malfunction, only the first trouble code will appear. The next code will appear only after the first one has been corrected.

TO OBTAIN THE FLASH CODE:
1. Locate the RABS diagnostic connector and attach a jumper wire to it and momentarily (1 to 2 seconds) ground it to the chassis. The RABS diagnostic connector can be found in the following locations:
- 1994 B Series Pick-up: under the instrument panel on the driver's side (Black connector-Black/Orange wire)

Problem	Possible Cause
• DTC 2 — Open Isolation Valve Wiring or Bad Module	• RABS module. • RABS valve. • RABS module or RABS valve connectors not fully seated with component. • Circuitry.
• DTC 3 — Open Dump Valve Wiring or Bad Module	• RABS module. • RABS valve. • RABS module or RABS valve connectors not fully seated with component. • Circuitry.
• DTC 4 — Open/Grounded RABS Valve Reset Switch Circuit (Red Brake Warning Indicator Also On)	• RABS module. • RABS valve. • RABS module or RABS valve connectors not fully seated with component. • Circuitry.
• DTC 5 — Excessive Dump Solenoid Activity; System Dumps Too Many Times In 2WD Mode (2WD and 4x4 Vehicles)	• Parking brake drag. • 4WD indicator switch (4x4 vehicles only). • Generic electronic module (GEM) (4x4 vehicles only). • Rear brake assembly. • Circuitry. • RABS module.
• DTC 6 — Erratic Sensor Signal While Rolling Or Bad Speed Sensor Wiring	• RABS speed sensor. • RABS module or RABS sensor connectors not fully seated with component. • Circuitry. • Rear brake anti-lock sensor ring. • RABS module.
• DTC 7 — No Isolation Solenoid During Self-Check	• Circuitry. • RABS valve. • RABS module.
• DTC 8 — No Dump Solenoid During Self-Check	• Circuitry. • RABS module. • RABS valve.
• DTC 9 — High Speed Sensor Resistance Open Speed Sensor Wiring	• RABS speed sensor. • RABS module or RABS speed sensor connectors not fully seated with component. • Circuitry. • RABS module.
• DTC 10 — Low Speed Sensor Resistance Or Shorted Speed Sensor Wiring	• RABS speed sensor. • Circuitry. • RABS module.
• DTC 11 — Brake Pedal Position (BPP) Switch Always Closed or BPP Switch Circuit Worn or Damaged	• Circuitry. • Stoplamps. • Brake pedal position (BPP) switch. • RABS module.
• DTC 12 — Loss of Hydraulic Brake Fluid For One Second Or More during An Anti-Lock Stop	• Low master cylinder fill level. • Fluid leaks in vehicle brake system. • Brake fluid level warning switch. • Master cylinder float. • Diode/resistor element(s). • Ignition switch. • Circuitry. • RABS module.
• DTC 13	• RABS module.
• DTC 16	• No system faults detected.

Fig. 113 RABS trouble code index—B Series Pick-up models

- 1995–96 B Series Pick-up: forward end of the power distribution box in the engine compartment (Black connector-Black/Orange wire)
- 1997–98 B Series Pick-up: behind the right hand kick panel (Black connector-Black/Orange wire)
- 1994–95 MPV: left side engine compartment, between the fender and air cleaner housing (Gray 1 pin connector-Gray/White wire)

2. Quickly remove the ground. When the ground is made and then removed, the RABS light will begin to flash.

3. The code consists of a number of short flashes and ends with a long flash. Count the short flashes and include the following long flash in the count

Number of flashing	Failure location	Failure condition
1	—	(1 flash should not occur)
2	ABS hydraulic unit	Open in isolation solenoid circuit
3		Open in dump solenoid circuit
4		Solenoid valve switch closed
5	—	System dumps too many times in 2WD (2WD and 4WD vehicles) (condition occurs while making normal or hard stops. Rear brake may lock.)
6	Ring gear speed sensor	(Ring gear speed sensor signal rapidly cuts in and out) condition only occurs while driving
7	ABS hydraulic unit	Shorted ground circuit (Isolation solenoid)
8		Shorted ground circuit (Dump solenoid)
9	Ring gear speed sensor	High speed sensor resistance
10		Low speed sensor resistance
11	Brake switch	Brake switch circuit defective. (Condition indicated only when driving above 56 km/h { 35 mph })
12	—	Decrease in the brake fluid pressure
13	ABS control module	Control module speed circuit phase lock loop failure detected during on-board diagnosis
14		Control module program check sum failure detected during on-board diagnosis
15		Control module RAM failure detected during on-board diagnosis
16	—	ABS is OK

90979G13

Fig. 114 RABS trouble code index—MPV models

to obtain the code number. Example 3 short flashes and one long flash indicated Code No. 4. The code will continue until the ignition is turned **OFF**. Refer to the flashcode diagnosis charts for further instructions.

To clear the codes, perform the following steps:
    a. Unplug the test connector.
    b. Turn the ignition switch to the **OFF** position.
    c. Plug in the test connector.

RABS Hydraulic Control Unit

REMOVAL & INSTALLATION

B Series Pick-up

1. Disconnect the brake lines from the valve and plug the lines.
2. Disconnect the wiring harness at the valve.
3. Remove the 3 nuts retaining the valve to the frame rail and lift out the valve.
4. Installation is the reverse of removal. Don't overtighten the brake lines. Bleed the brakes.

MPV

▶ See Figure 115

1. Disconnect the negative battery cable.
2. Raise and safely support the vehicle.
3. Unplug the wiring harness connector.
4. Disconnect the brake lines from the valve and plug the lines.
5. Remove the mounting bolt retaining the unit to the frame rail and remove the hydraulic control unit from the vehicle.
6. Installation is the reverse of removal. Tighten the hydraulic control unit mounting bolt to 12–17 ft. lbs. (16–22 Nm). Tighten the brake lines to 113–190 inch lbs. (13–23 Nm).
7. Bleed the brakes. It is not necessary to energize the solenoid valves to bleed the rear brakes.

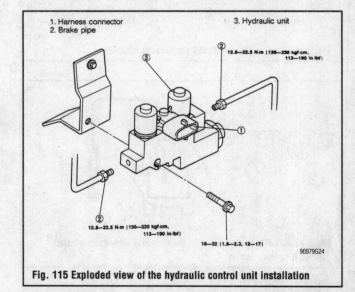

1. Harness connector
2. Brake pipe
3. Hydraulic unit

12.8—22.5 N·m [130—230 kgf-cm, 113—190 in lbf]

12.8—22.5 N·m [130—230 kgf-cm, 113—190 in-lbf]

16—22 [1.6—2.3, 12—17]

90979G24

Fig. 115 Exploded view of the hydraulic control unit installation

RABS Electronic Control Module

REMOVAL & INSTALLATION

B Series Pick-up

1. Remove any instrument panel covers to gain access to the module.
2. Disconnect the wiring harness to the module.
3. Remove the retaining screws and remove the module.

To install:

4. Place the module in position against the under dash crossmember. Install and tighten the retaining bolts.

5. Connect the wiring harness to the module.
6. Install any instrument panels which were removed.
7. Check the system for proper operation.

MPV

▶ See Figure 116

1. Disconnect the negative battery cable.
2. Remove the left rear interior trim panel.
3. Disengage the wiring harness connector from the electronic control module.
4. Remove the mounting fasteners.
5. Remove the RABS electronic control unit from the vehicle.
6. Installation is the reverse of the removal procedure.
7. Check the system for proper operation.

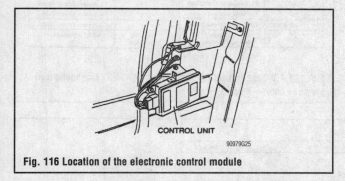

Fig. 116 Location of the electronic control module

RABS Speed Sensor

TESTING

▶ See Figure 117

1. Remove the RABS sensor from the axle housing.
2. Connect a Digital Volt/Ohm Meter (DVOM) across the two sensor terminals and record the reading.

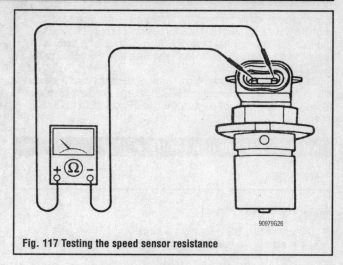

Fig. 117 Testing the speed sensor resistance

3. The reading should be between 0.9 and 2.5k Ohms.
4. If not, replace the sensor.

REMOVAL & INSTALLATION

▶ See Figures 118, 119 and 120

1. Thoroughly clean the axle housing around the sensor.
2. Disconnect the electrical harness plug from the sensor.
3. Remove the sensor hold-down bolt.
4. Remove the sensor by pulling it straight out of the axle housing.
5. Ensure that the axle surface is and that no dirt can enter the housing.
6. If a new sensor is being installed, lubricate the O-ring with clean engine oil. If the old sensor is being installed, clean it thoroughly and install a new O-ring coated with clean engine oil. Carefully push the sensor into the housing aligning the mounting flange hole with the threaded hole in the housing.
7. Tighten the hold-down bolt to 25–30 ft. lbs. (34–40 Nm) for the B Series Pick-up and 12–16 ft. lbs. (16–22 Nm) for the MPV.

Fig. 118 To remove the rear wheel sensor, first disconnect the electrical harness plug . . .

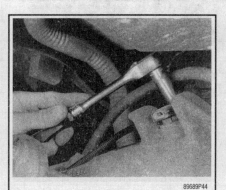

Fig. 119 . . . then remove the sensor-to-axle housing hold-down bolt

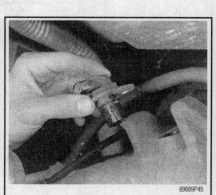

Fig. 120 Pull the sensor up and out of the axle housing

4-WHEEL ANTI-LOCK BRAKE SYSTEM (4WABS)

This system is used on the Navajo, 1996–98 MPV, and 1995–98 B Series Pick-up models with 4WD and the 4.0L engine.
The 4WABS system consists of the following components:
 a. The anti-lock Hydraulic Control Unit (HCU)
 b. 4WABS electronic control module
 c. The front wheel speed sensors—located on the steering knuckles
1. The rear speed sensor—located on the rear axle housing.
2. The front speed sensor tone rings
3. The rear speed sensor tone rings

4. The G-switch
5. The ABS main system and pump motor relays

System Self-Test

▶ See Figures 121, 122, 123 and 124

The 4WABS module performs system tests and self-tests during startup and normal operation. The valve, sensor and fluid level circuits are monitored for proper operation. If a fault is found, the 4WABS will be deactivated and the amber ANTI LOCK light will be lit until the ignition is turned OFF. When the light is lit, the Diagnostic Trouble Code (DTC) may be obtained. Under normal operation, the light will stay on for about 2 seconds while the ignition switch is in the ON position and will go out shortly after.

The Diagnostic Trouble Codes (DTC) are an alphanumeric code and a scan tool, such as the Special Service Tool NGS (New Generation Star) Tester 49-T088-0A0, is required to retrieve the codes. The DTC code chart has been included.

Hydraulic Control Unit (HCU)

PUMP TESTING

Navajo and B Series Pick-up

1. Disconnect the HCU pump motor electrical plug.
2. Connect a Digital Volt/Ohm Meter (DVOM) across the two pump terminals and record the reading.
3. The reading should be between 52-68 Ohms
4. If not, replace the pump motor.

Service Code	Component	Service Code	Component
11	ECU Failure	42	FR Sensor Mismatched Output
16	System OK	43	RA Sensor Mismatched Output
17	Reference Voltage	—	Front Left Valve Pair Function Check
22	Front Left Inlet Valve	—	Front Left Valve Pair Function Check
23	Front Left Outlet Valve	—	Front Right Valve Pair Function Check
24	Front Right Inlet Valve	—	Front Right Valve Pair Function Check
25	Front Right Outlet Valve	—	Rear Axle Valve Pair Function Check
26	Rear Axle Inlet Valve	—	Rear Axle Valve Pair Function Check
27	Rear Axle Outlet Valve	55	FL Sensor Output Dropout
31	FL Sensor Electrical Failure	56	FR Sensor Output Dropout
32	FR Sensor Electrical Failure	57	RA Sensor Output Dropout
32	FR Sensor Electrical Failure	63	Pump Motor
33	RA Sensor Electrical Failure	65	G Switch
33	RA Sensor Electrical Failure	67	Pump Motor
35	FL Sensor Erratic Output	75	FL Sensor Erratic Output
36	FR Sensor Erratic Output	76	FR Sensor Erratic Output
37	RA Sensor Erratic Output	77	RA Sensor Erratic Output
41	FL Sensor Mismatched Output	No Code Obtained	No ECU Initialization

90979G21

Fig. 121 4-Wheel Anti-lock Brake System (4WABS) diagnostic trouble code chart—Navajo

SERVICE CODE INDEX		
DTC	**Concern**	**Sets At**
B1432	Anti-Lock Brake Control Module Failure	Key On
C1101	Intermittent Valve Failure	Key On
C1185	Main Relay Output Circuit Failure	Key On
B1317	Battery Voltage High	Key On
B1318	Battery Voltage Low	Key On
C1198	LF ISO Valve Coil Circuit Failure	Key On
C1194	LF Dump Valve Coil Circuit Failure	Key On
C1214	RF ISO Valve Coil Circuit Failure	Key On
C1210	RF Dump Valve Coil Circuit Failure	Key On
C1206	R ISO Valve Coil Circuit Failure	Key On
C1202	R Dump Valve Coil Circuit Failure	Key On
C1155	LF Wheel Speed Sensor Input Circuit Failure	Key On
C1158	LF Wheel Speed Sensor Coherency Fault	40 km/h (25 mph)
C1258	LF Wheel Speed Sensor Wheel Speed Comparison Fault	19 km/h (12 mph)
C1233	LF Wheel Speed Sensor Input Missing (Long Term)	>2 Min.
C1145	RF Wheel Speed Sensor Input Circuit Failure	Key On
C1148	RF Wheel Speed Sensor Coherency Fault	40 km/h (25 mph)
C1259	RF Wheel Speed Sensor Wheel Speed Comparison Fault	19 km/h (12 mph)
C1234	RF Wheel Speed Sensor Input Missing (Long Term)	>2 Min.
C1230	RA Wheel Speed Sensor Input Circuit Failure	Key On
C1229	RA Wheel Speed Sensor Coherency Fault	40 km/h (25 mph)
C1260	RA Wheel Speed Sensor Wheel Speed Comparison Fault	19 km/h (12 mph)
C1237	R Wheel Speed Sensor Input Missing (Long Term)	>2 Min.
No Code	Front Left Valve Pair Function Test	—
No Code	Front Right Valve Pair Function Test	—
No Code	Rear Axle Valve Pair Function Test	—
C1096	Pump Motor Triggered but Did Not Run	7 km/h (4 mph)
C1102	G-Switch Failure	See NOTE Below
C1095	Pump Motor Running but Not Triggered	Key On
No Code	No Communication	

NOTE: DTC C1102 indicates a G-Switch circuit failure. If the yellow ABS warning lamp comes on at key ON, check for a ground short on Pins 30, 31, or 32. If the yellow ABS lamp comes on at approximately 32 km/h (20 mph), there is either: 1) a battery short on Pins 30, 31 or 32; 2) an open on Pins 30 and 31; or 3) an open on Pin 32. If the yellow ABS lamp comes on after driving the vehicle for 2 minutes at approximately 72 km/h (45 mph), check for an open on Pin 30 or 31 (one pin only).

89689G24

Fig. 122 4-Wheel Anti-lock Brake System (4WABS) diagnostic trouble code chart—1995–97 B Series Pick-up

DTC	Display on the NGS	Diagnostic system component
03*1	G SENSOR—OPEN OR SHORT	G sensor
05	BRAKE SW—OPEN OR SHORT	Brake switch circuit
11	WSS, SR (RF)—OPEN OR SHORT	RF
12	WSS, SR (LF)—OPEN OR SHORT	LF — ABS wheel-speed sensor
13	WSS, SR (RR)—OPEN OR SHORT	RR
14	WSS, SR (LR)—OPEN OR SHORT	LR
15	WSS, SR—OPEN OR SHORT	One of the four wheel-speed sensors and sensor rotors
22	HU/SOL.V (RF)/SOL. V(RF) AV—OPEN OR SHORT	RF (AV)*2
23	SOLENOID VALVE (RF) EV—OF=EN OR SHORT	RF (EV)*3
24	SOL.V (LF)/(LF) AV—OPEN OR SHORT	LF (AV)*2
25	SOLENOID VALVE (LF) EV—OPEN OR SHORT	LF (EV)*3 — Solenoid valve
26	SOL.V (RR)(R) AV/(RR) AV—OPEN OR SHORT	R (AV)*2
27	SOL.V (R) EV/(RR) EV—OPEN OR SHORT	R (EV)*3
41	WSS, SR (RF)—OPEN OR SHORT	
42	WSS, SR (LF)—OPEN OR GND SHORT	ABS wheel-speed sensor ABS sensor rotor
43	WSS, SR (RR)—OPEN OR GND SHORT	
44	WSS, SR (LR)—OPEN OR GND SHORT	
51	FAIL SAFE RELAY—OPEN OR SHORT	Valve relay
53	MOTOR, MOTOR RELAY—OPEN OR SHORT	ABS motor, motor relay
61	ABS/TCS CONTROL UNIT—DEFECT	ABS control module
63	POWER SUPPLY—MALFUNCTION	Power supply, ground

*1 : 4WD only
*2 : Pressure retention valve
*3 : Pressure reduction valve

90979623

Fig. 124 4-Wheel Anti-lock Brake System (4WABS) diagnostic trouble code chart—1996–98 MPV

DTC	DTC Caused By	Description
B1342	4WABS Control Module	4WABS Control Module Failure
B1485	4WABS Control Module	Brake Pedal Position (BPP) Switch Circuit Failure
B1676	4WABS Control Module	Battery Voltage Out Of Range
B2141	4WABS Control Module	Vehicle Speed Calibration Data Not Programmed Into Module
C1095	4WABS Control Module	Hydraulic Pump Motor Circuit Failure
C1102	4WABS Control Module	G—Switch Acceleration Sensor Circuit Failure
C1145	4WABS Control Module	RF Speed Sensor Circuit Failure
C1155	4WABS Control Module	LF Speed Sensor Circuit Failure
C1230	4WABS Control Module	Rear Axle Speed Sensor Circuit Failure
C1233	4WABS Control Module	LF Speed Sensor Output Failure
C1234	4WABS Control Module	RF Speed Sensor Output Failure
C1237	4WABS Control Module	Rear Axle Speed Sensor Output Failure

90979622

Fig. 123 4-Wheel Anti-lock Brake System (4WABS) diagnostic trouble code chart—1998 B Series Pick-up

REMOVAL & INSTALLATION

Navajo and B Series Pick-up

♦ See Figure 125

1. Disconnect the battery ground cable.
2. Unplug the 8-pin connector from the unit, and the 4-pin connector from the pump motor.
3. Disconnect the 5 inlet and outlet tubes from the unit. Immediately plug the ports.
4. Remove the 3 unit attaching nuts and lift out the unit.
5. Installation is the reverse of removal. Torque the mounting nuts to 12-18 ft. lbs. and the tube fittings to 10-18 ft. lbs.

➡ After reconnecting the battery, it may take 10 miles or more of driving for the Powertrain Control Module to relearn its driveability codes.

6. Bleed the brakes.

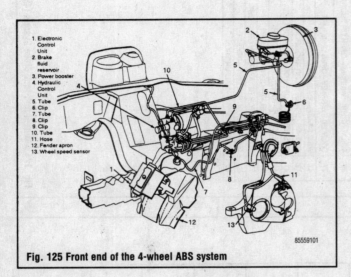

Fig. 125 Front end of the 4-wheel ABS system

MPV

♦ See Figures 126 and 127

1. Disconnect the negative battery cable.
2. Disconnect and plug the brake lines from the hydraulic controil unit.
3. Disengage the wiring harness connector from the control unit.
4. Remove the hydraulic/electronic control unit-to-mounting bracket nuts and remove the unit out of the vehicle.
5. Remove the mounting screws, then separate the hydraulic control unit from the electronic control module.
6. Installation is the reverse of the removal procedure.
7. Tighten the mounting bolts and nuts. Bleed the brakes.

Electronic Control Unit

REMOVAL & INSTALLATION

Navajo and B Series Pick-up

1. Disconnect the battery ground cable.
2. Unplug the wiring from the ECU.
3. Remove the mounting bolts, slide the ECU off its bracket.

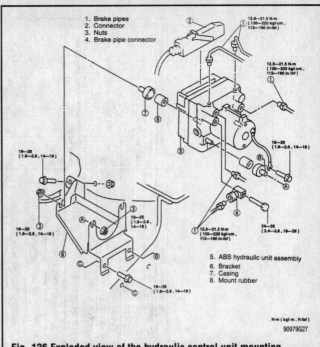

Fig. 126 Exploded view of the hydraulic control unit mounting

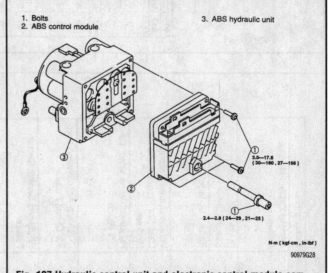

Fig. 127 Hydraulic control unit and electronic control module components

4. Installation is the reverse of removal. Torque the mounting screw to 5-6 ft. lbs. and the connector bolt to 4-5 ft. lbs.

➡ After reconnecting the battery, it may take 10 miles or more of driving for the Powertrain Control Module to relearn its driveability codes.

MPV

The ABS Electronic Control Unit is mounted to the side of the hydraulic control unit. Refer to the hydraulic control unit removal procedure earlier in this section.

Front Wheel Speed Sensor

TESTING

1. Disconnect the speed sensor wire harness plug from the sensor or sensor pigtail.
2. Connect a Digital Volt/Ohm Meter (DVOM) across the two sensor terminals and record the reading.
3. The reading should be within the following ranges for the appropiate model and sensor.
   - B Series Pick-up—1.0–1.4k Ohms
   - Navajo—0.270–0.330k Ohms
   - MPV—1.4–1.8k Ohms

REMOVAL & INSTALLATION

▶ **See Figure 128**

1. Inside the engine compartment, disconnect the sensor from the harness.
2. Unclip the sensor cable from the brake hose clips.
3. Remove the retaining bolt from the spindle and slide the sensor from its hole.
4. Installation is the reverse of removal. Tighten the retaining bolt to 40-60 inch lbs. (5–7 Nm) for Navajo/B Series Pick-up and 14–18 ft. lbs. (19–25 Nm) for the MPV.

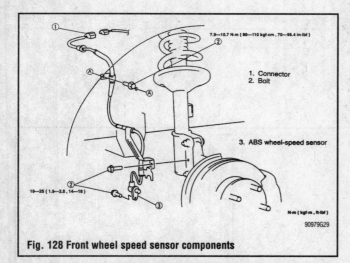

Fig. 128 Front wheel speed sensor components

Rear Speed Sensor

TESTING

Navajo and B Series Pick-up

1. Remove the rear wheel speed sensor from the axle housing.
2. Connect a Digital Volt/Ohm Meter (DVOM) across the two sensor terminals and record the reading.
3. The reading should be between 0.9 and 2.5k Ohms.
4. If not, replace the sensor.

MPV

1. Disconnect the speed sensor wire harness plug from the sensor or sensor pigtail.

2. Connect a Digital Volt/Ohm Meter (DVOM) across the two sensor terminals and record the reading.
3. The reading should be within 1.4–1.8k Ohms.
4. If not, replace the sensor.

REMOVAL & INSTALLATION

Navajo and B Series Pick-up

▶ **See Figure 129**

1. Disconnect the wiring from the harness.
2. Remove the sensor hold-down bolt and remove the sensor from the axle.
To install:
3. Thoroughly clean the mounting surfaces. Make sure no dirt falls into the axle. Clean the magnetized sensor pole piece. Metal particles can cause sensor problems. Replace the O-ring.
4. Coat the new O-ring with clean engine oil.
5. Position the new sensor on the axle. It should slide into place easily. Correct installation will allow a gap of 0.005-0.045 in.
6. Torque the hold-down bolt to 25–30 ft. lbs. (34–41 Nm).
7. Connect the wiring.

MPV

▶ **See Figure 130**

1. Disconnect the negative battery cable.
2. Raise and safely support the vehicle.
3. Disengage the speed sensor wiring harness connector.
4. Remove the wiring bracket retaining bolts.
5. Lift the wheel speed sensor out of the axle housing.
To install:
6. Thoroughly clean the mounting surfaces. Make sure no dirt falls into the axle. Clean the magnetized sensor pole piece. Metal particles can cause sensor problems.
7. Position the new sensor into the axle housing. It should slide into place easily. Correct installation will allow a gap of 0.0119–0.0433 in.
8. Torque the hold-down bolt to 14–18 ft. lbs. (19–25 Nm).
9. Install the retaining bracket bolts. Connect the wiring.

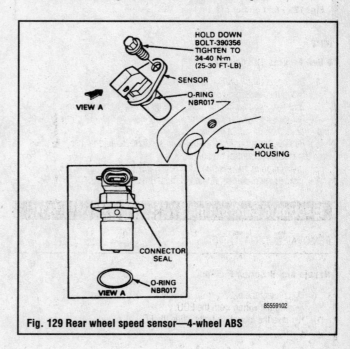

Fig. 129 Rear wheel speed sensor—4-wheel ABS

BRAKE SPECIFICATIONS

All measurements in inches unless noted

Year	Model		Master Cylinder Bore	Brake Disc — Original Thickness	Brake Disc — Minimum Thickness	Brake Disc — Maximum Runout	Brake Drum — Original Inside Diameter	Brake Drum — Max. Wear Limit	Brake Drum — Max. Machine Diameter	Min. Lining Thickness — Front	Min. Lining Thickness — Rear
1994	B Series		① 0.938	0.850	0.810	0.003	9.00	9.09	9.06	⑤ 0.062	⑤ 0.030
	Pick-up		② 0.938 ③	0.850	0.810	0.003	10.00	10.09	10.06	⑤ 0.062	⑤ 0.030
	Navajo		① 0.938	0.850	0.810	0.003	9.00	9.09	9.06	⑤ 0.062	⑤ 0.030
	MPV	Front	0.938	1.023	④	0.003	—	—	—	⑤ 0.062	—
		Rear	③	0.472	0.409	0.003	—	—	—	—	⑤ 0.125
1995	B Series		① 0.938	1.023	④	0.003	9.00	9.09	9.06	⑤ 0.062	⑤ 0.030
	Pick-up		② 0.938 ③	1.023	④	0.003	10.00	10.09	10.06	⑤ 0.062	⑤ 0.030
	MPV	Front	0.938	1.023	④	0.003	—	—	—	⑤ 0.062	—
		Rear	③	0.472	0.409	0.003	—	—	—	—	⑤ 0.125
1996	B Series		① 0.938	1.023	④	0.003	9.00	9.09	9.06	⑤ 0.062	⑤ 0.030
	Pick-up		② 0.938 ③	1.023	④	0.003	10.00	10.09	10.06	⑤ 0.062	⑤ 0.030
	MPV	Front	0.938	1.023	④	0.003	—	—	—	⑤ 0.062	—
		Rear	③	0.472	0.409	0.003	—	—	—	—	⑤ 0.125
1997	B Series		① 0.938	1.023	④	0.003	9.00	9.09	9.06	⑤ 0.062	⑤ 0.030
	Pick-up		② 0.938 ③	1.023	④	0.003	10.00	10.09	10.06	⑤ 0.062	⑤ 0.030
	MPV	Front	0.938	1.023	④	0.003	—	—	—	⑤ 0.062	—
		Rear	③	0.472	0.409	0.003	—	—	—	—	⑤ 0.125
1998	B Series		① 0.938	1.023	④	0.003	9.00	9.09	9.06	⑤ 0.062	⑤ 0.030
	Pick-up		② 0.938 ③	1.023	④	0.003	10.00	10.09	10.06	⑤ 0.062	⑤ 0.030
	MPV	Front	0.938	1.023	④	0.003	—	—	—	⑤ 0.062	—
		Rear	③	0.472	0.409	0.003	—	—	—	—	⑤ 0.125

① 9 inch rear brake drum used on 4x2 vehicles under 4580 lbs. Gross Vehicle Weight Rating (GVWR)

② 10 inch rear brake drum used on vehicles over 4580 lbs. Gross Vehicle Weight Rating (GVWR) or with limited slip rear drive axle

③ 4x2 vehicles use 0.938 in. master cylinder bore / 4x4 vehicles use 0.975 in. master cylinder bore

④ 4x2 vehicles have min. thickness of 0.960 in. / 4x4 vehicles have min. thickness of 0.810 in.

⑤ If lining is riveted, measurement is for material above the rivet head / If lining is bonded, measurement is for material above the backing plate

90979C01

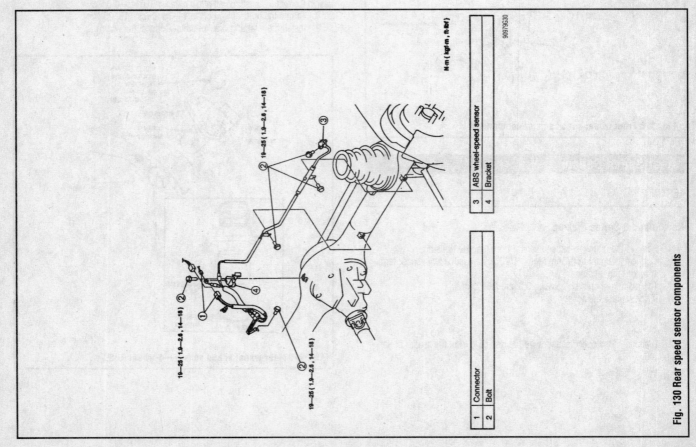

19—25 (1.9—2.6, 14—18)

N·m (kgf·m, ft·lbf)

1	Connector
2	Bolt

3	ABS wheel-speed sensor
4	Bracket

90979G30

Fig. 130 Rear speed sensor components

10

BODY AND TRIM

EXTERIOR

Doors

ADJUSTMENT

▶ See Figures 1 and 2

➡Loosen the hinge-to-door bolts for lateral adjustment only. Loosen the hinge-to-body bolts for both lateral and vertical adjustments.

1. Determine which hinge bolts are to be loosened and back them out just enough to allow movement.

2. To move the door safely, use a padded pry bar. When the door is in the proper position, tighten the bolts to specification and check the door operation. There should be no binding or interference when the door is closed and opened.

3. Door closing adjustment can also be affected by the position of the lock striker plate. Loosen the striker plate bolts and move the striker plate just enough to permit proper closing and locking of the door.

Hood

ALIGNMENT

▶ See Figure 3

1. Open the hood and matchmark the hinge and latch positions.
2. Loosen the hinge-to-hood bolts just enough to allow movement of the hood.

3. Move the hood as required to obtain the proper fit and alignment between the hood and all adjoining body panels. Tighten the bolts securely when satisfactorily aligned to the following specifications:
- Navajo: 5–8 ft. lbs. (7–11 Nm)
- B Series Pick-up: 8–10 ft. lbs. (10–14 Nm)
- MPV: 14–17 ft. lbs. (19–23 Nm)
4. Loosen the 2 latch attaching bolts.
5. Move the latch from side-to-side to align the latch with the striker. Tighten the latch bolts.
6. Lubricate the latch and hinges and check the hood fit several times.

Liftgate

ALIGNMENT

Navajo

▶ See Figures 4 and 5

➡The liftgate glass should not be open while the liftgate is open. Make sure the window is closed before opening the liftgate.

The liftgate can be adjusted slightly in or out and side to side by loosening the hinge-to-header nut or bolt. Some up and down adjustment can be accomplished by loosening the hinge bolts on the liftgate and moving the gate up or down. The liftgate should be adjusted for even and parallel fit with adjoining panels.

Fig. 1 Before moving the door lock striker, mark its original position for future reference . . .

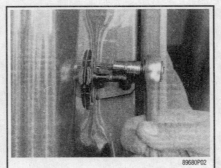

Fig. 2 . . . then loosen the attaching bolts. Move it to a new position, tighten the bolts and close the door

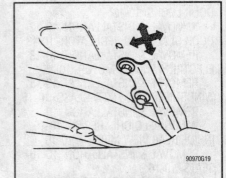

Fig. 3 Loosen the mounting bolts and reposition the hood

Fig. 4 Before moving the rear liftgate striker, mark its position in relation to the body for future reference

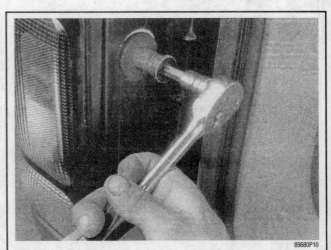

Fig. 5 Once the center bolt is loosened, the striker can be positioned

The door latch strikers can also be adjusted. Loosen the striker center bolt and move the assembly ¼ inch (6.35 mm) up/down or fore/aft as necessary. Check that the door latches and unlatches easily.

MPV

Both the striker and hinge bolt holes are made so that the striker and hinges can be moved to permit proper engagement and fit. Tighten the striker bolts to 13–20 ft. lbs. (18–26 Nm); the hinge bolts to 78–113 inch lbs. (9–13 Nm).

Tailgate (B Series Pick-up)

REMOVAL & INSTALLATION

1. Open the tailgate.
2. Relieve tension on the support cables by partially raising the tailgate.
3. Pull up on the cable retainer spring and slide the cable retainer to the large opening in the hook and lift it off. Repeat this procedure for the other support cable.
4. Pull the right side of the tailgate rearward to remove it from the right hinge.
5. Move the tailgate to the right to remove it from the left hinge.
6. Transfer all necessary hardware to the new tailgate if necessary.
7. Installation is the reverse of removal. Be sure to lubricate each hinge cup with NLGI No. 2 grease, or equivalent.

Grille

REMOVAL & INSTALLATION

Navajo

▶ See Figure 6

1. Remove the plastic retainers securing the grille to the air deflector.
2. Remove the screws attaching the grille to the reinforcement panel.
3. Using a small prying tool, depress the spring tabs at the lower outboard openings and disengage the grille from the headlamp housings.
4. Remove the grille from the vehicle.
5. Installation is the reverse of removal.

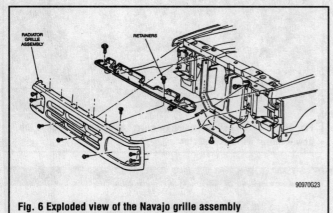

Fig. 6 Exploded view of the Navajo grille assembly

B Series Pick-up

1994–97

▶ See Figure 7

1. Remove the radiator grille assembly retaining bolts.
2. Lift up the radiator grille slightly, then tilt the top forward.
3. Remove the grille from the vehicle.
4. Installation is the reverse of removal.

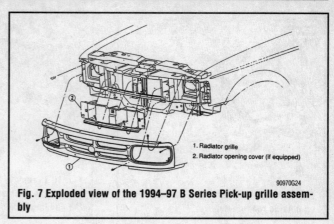

1. Radiator grille
2. Radiator opening cover (if equipped)

Fig. 7 Exploded view of the 1994–97 B Series Pick-up grille assembly

1998

1. Remove the four mounting screws along the top of the radiator grille.
2. Unclip the lower portion of the radiator grille assembly.
3. Remove the grille from the vehicle.
4. Installation is the reverse of removal.

MPV

1994–95

▶ See Figure 8

The grille is in 3 pieces: 1 center piece and 2 side pieces. To remove any or all of these, remove the screws and disengage the retaining clips. To disengage the retaining clips, depress the tabs of the clip with a small screwdriver.
To install the clips, simply press them into place.

1996–98

The radiator grille on all 1996–98 MPV models is a one piece assembly secured in place by plastic retaining clips.
1. Disengage the plastic retaining clips.
2. Remove the grille assembly from the vehicle.
3. Installation is the reverse of removal.

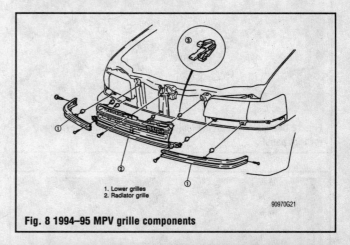

1. Lower grilles
2. Radiator grille

Fig. 8 1994–95 MPV grille components

Outside Mirrors

REMOVAL & INSTALLATION

Navajo, B Series Pick-up and 1996–98 MPV Models

▶ See Figures 9, 10 and 11

1. The door panel must first be removed to gain access to the mounting nuts. Disconnect the harness connector if equipped with power mirrors.

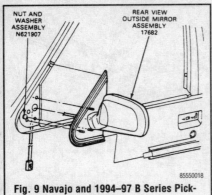

NUT AND WASHER ASSEMBLY N621907

REAR VIEW OUTSIDE MIRROR ASSEMBLY 17682

85550018

Fig. 9 Navajo and 1994–97 B Series Pick-up outside rear view mirror

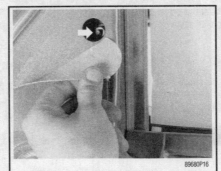

89680P16

Fig. 10 To remove the outside mirror, first remove the door trim panel and peel back the padding to access the nuts (arrow)

89680P17

Fig. 11 With the access holes uncovered, loosen and remove the mirror attaching nuts

2. Remove the mounting fasteners and lift out the mirror. Remove and discard the gasket, if equipped.

3. When installing, make sure the gasket is properly positioned (if equipped) before tightening the screws.

4. If equipped with power mirror, plug in the electrical connector and test the operation of the power mirror before installing the door panel.

1994–95 MPV Models

▶ See Figures 12, 13, 14 and 15

1. Disconnect the negative battery cable.
2. Using a small prying tool, pry off the interior sideview mirror trim panel.
3. Remove the 3 sideview mirror mounting screws using a phillips head screwdriver.
4. Pull the sideview mirror away from the door and disengage the power mirror wiring connector.
5. Installation is the reverse of the removal procedure.

90970P24

Fig. 12 Using a small prying tool, pry off the interior sideview mirror trim panel . . .

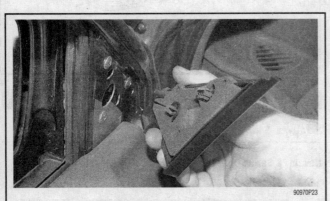

90970P23

Fig. 13 . . . then pull away the trim panel from the door

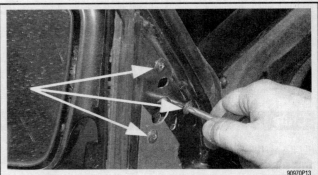

90970P13

Fig. 14 Remove the 3 sideview mirror mounting screws using a phillips head screwdriver . . .

90970P14

Fig. 15 . . . then pull the sideview mirror away and disengage the power mirror wiring connector

Antenna

REMOVAL & INSTALLATION

Navajo and B Series Pick-up Models

▶ See Figure 16

1. Disconnect the antenna lead-in cable from the cable assembly in-line connector above the glove box.
2. Working under the instrument panel, disengage the cable from its retainers.

➡ On some models, it may be necessary to remove the instrument panel pad to get at the cable.

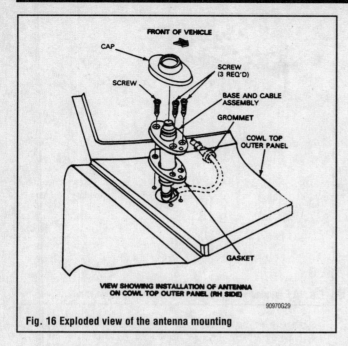

Fig. 16 Exploded view of the antenna mounting

3. Unscrew the antenna mast from the base.
4. Outside, unsnap the cap from the antenna base.
5. Remove the 3 screws and lift off the antenna, pulling the cable with it, carefully.
6. Remove and discard the gasket.
To install:
7. Place the gasket in position on the cowl panel.
8. Insert the antenna cable through the hole and seat the antenna base on the cowl. Secure with the 3 screws.
9. Position the cap over the antenna base and snap it into place.
10. Install the antenna mast to the base.
11. Route the cable in exactly the same position as before removal behind the instrument panel.
12. Connect the cable to the in-line connector above the glove box.

MPV Models

▶ See Figures 17 and 18

1. Disconnect the negative battery cable.
2. Remove the passenger's side interior front scuff plate.
3. Remove the passenger's side front side trim.
4. Remove the windshield molding.
5. Remove the right side front mud guard.
6. Using snapring pliers, remove the top mounting nut.
7. Remove the spacer.
8. Disconnect antenna lead.

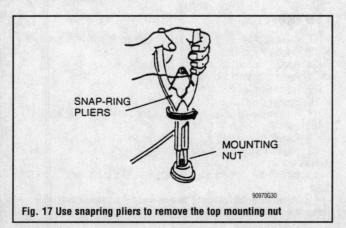

Fig. 17 Use snapring pliers to remove the top mounting nut

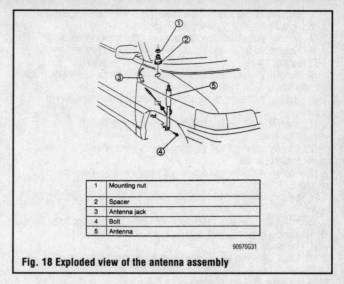

1	Mounting nut
2	Spacer
3	Antenna jack
4	Bolt
5	Antenna

Fig. 18 Exploded view of the antenna assembly

9. Remove the antenna mast mounting bolt.
10. Remove the antenna from the vehicle.
To install:
11. Place the antenna in the vehicle in its proper position and tighten the mounting bolt.
12. Connect the antenna lead.
13. Install the spacer.
14. Install and tighten the top mounting nut, using a pair of snap ring pliers.
15. Install the right side front mud guard.
16. Install the windshield molding.
17. Install the passenger's side front side trim.
18. Install the passenger's side interior front scuff plate.
19. Connect the negative battery cable. Turn on the radio and check the reception.

Fenders

REMOVAL & INSTALLATION

1994–97 B Series Pick-up Models

▶ See Figure 19

1. Clean out all dirt from the fender attaching hardware and lubricate them to ease removal.
2. Remove the grille.
3. With the door open, remove the bolt attaching the rear end of the fender to the cowl.
4. Remove the screws around the wheel opening attaching the fender apron (splash shield).

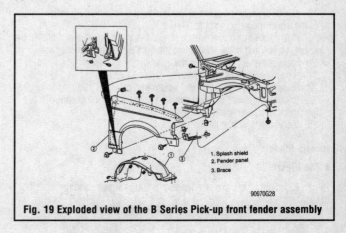

Fig. 19 Exploded view of the B Series Pick-up front fender assembly

5. Remove the bolt attaching the lower rear of the fender to the rocker.

6. Remove the bolts along the top of the fender.

7. Remove the bolt attaching the brace to radiator support assembly.

8. Remove the fender and remove the brace from the fender.

To install:

9. Position the nuts, retainers and brace on the fender. Tighten the brace-to-fender bolt to 8–10 ft. lbs. (11–14 Nm).

10. Position the fender on the apron and loosely install the apron retaining bolts.

11. Loosely install the bolt from inside the cab attaching the rear end of the fender to the cowl.

12. Loosely install the bolt attaching the rear lower end of the fender to the lower corner of the cab.

13. Loosely install the bolt attaching the brace to the radiator support assembly.

14. Loosely install the 4 bolts along the fender inner body attaching the fender.

15. Adjust the position of the fender and tighten all mounting bolts. Tighten all of the fender mounting bolts to 8–10 ft. lbs. (11–14 Nm).

16. Install the grille.

17. Install the apron screws around the wheel opening.

1998 B Series Pick-up Models

▶ See Figure 19

1. Clean out all dirt from the fender attaching hardware and lubricate them to ease removal.

2. Remove the front bumper.

3. Remove the parking lamp assembly.

4. Remove the radiator opening cover pushpins, then remove the radiator opening cover..

5. Remove the pushpin, then remove the stone deflector.

6. If equipped, remove the mud flap.

7. Remove the mounting screws, bolts and pushpin, then remove the inner fender splash shield. If removing the right side front inner splash shield, disconnect the vacuum lines from the vacuum storage reservoir.

8. With the door open, remove the bolt attaching the rear end of the fender to the cowl.

9. Remove the bolt attaching the lower rear of the fender to the rocker. If equipped, remove and retain the front fender spacers.

10. Remove the bolts along the top of the fender.

11. Remove the bolt attaching the brace to radiator support assembly.

12. Remove the fender and remove the brace from the fender.

To install:

13. Position the nuts, retainers and brace on the fender.

14. Position the fender onto the vehicle.

15. Loosely install the bolt from inside the cab attaching the rear end of the fender to the cowl.

16. Loosely install the bolt attaching the rear lower end of the fender to the lower corner of the cab.

17. Loosely install the bolt attaching the brace to the radiator support assembly.

18. Loosely install the 4 bolts along the fender inner body attaching the fender.

19. Adjust the position of the fender and tighten all mounting bolts. Tighten all of the fender mounting bolts to 8–10 ft. lbs. (11–14 Nm).

20. Install the inner fender splash shield. Install the pushpin and tighten the mounting screws and bolts. If installing the right side inner fender splash shield, connect the vacuum lines to the vacuum storage reservoir.

21. If equipped, install mud flaps.

22. Install the stone deflector and secure with pushpin.

23. Install the radiator opening cover and secure with the pushpins.

24. Install the parking lamp assembly.

25. Install the front bumper.

Navajo Models

▶ See Figure 20

1. Clean out all dirt from the fender attaching hardware and lubricate them to ease removal.

2. Remove the headlight door and side marker lamp.

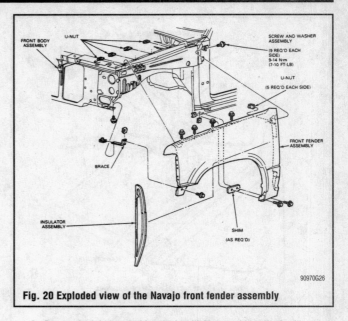

Fig. 20 Exploded view of the Navajo front fender assembly

3. Remove both bolts attaching the headlight assembly to the fender.

4. From inside the door opening, remove the bolt attaching the rear end of the fender to the cowl.

5. Remove the 4 bolts along the top of the fender inner body attaching the fender.

6. Raise the truck to a convenient height.

7. Remove the bolt attaching the brace to the radiator support assembly.

8. Remove the 2 bolts attaching the fender to the bumper stone deflector.

9. Remove the 4 screws attaching the fender apron to the fender.

10. Remove the 2 bolts attaching the fender to the rocker panel.

11. Lower the vehicle and remove the fender. Remove the brace from the fender.

To install:

12. Install the fender and raise the truck.

13. Position the nuts, retainers and brace on the fender.

14. Install the 2 bolts attaching the fender to the rocker panel.

15. Install the 4 screws attaching the fender apron to the fender.

16. Install the 2 bolts attaching the fender to the bumper stone deflector.

17. Install the bolt attaching the brace to the radiator support. Lower the truck.

18. Install the 4 bolts along the top of the fender inner body attaching the fender.

19. Install the bolt attaching the rear end of the fender to the cowl. Tighten all fender mounting screws, bolts and washer assemblies to 7–10 ft. lbs. (9–14 Nm).

20. Install both bolts attaching the headlight assembly to the fender.

21. Install the headlight door and side marker lamp.

MPV

▶ See Figure 21

1. Clean all of the dirt from the fender mounting screws, bolts and nuts.

2. Remove the radiator grille.

3. Remove the front combination light assembly.

4. Remove the front bumper.

5. Remove the windshield molding.

6. Remove the mud guard.

7. Remove the top bolt attaching the rear of the front fender to the windshield cowl.

8. Remove the top bolts that mount the fender to the inter-body.

9. Loosen the wheel lugs slightly. Raise and safely support the vehicle. Remove the wheel and tire assembly.

10. Remove the retaining nuts that secure the back of the fender to the hinge pillar.

11. Remove the bolts attaching the fender to the radiator support, and remove the bolts attaching the fender to the fender apron (inner splash shield).

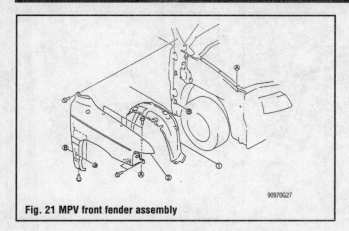

Fig. 21 MPV front fender assembly

12. Remove the bolt mounting the fender to the lower rocker sill. Check for any other mounting bolts, remove them. Remove the fender.

13. Place the fender in position and install the mounting bolts loosely. Align the lower edge of the fender to the rocker sill and secure the bolts. Align the upper edge of the fender to the cowl and tighten the bolts.

14. Tighten the remaining mounting bolts. Install the lighting equipment.

Power Sunroof (MPV)

REMOVAL & INSTALLATION

♦ See Figures 22 thru 31

➡Service to the sunroof harness, sunroof relay, drive unit assembly, sunroof frame, sunshade and guide rail require headliner removal.

1. Make sure the sunroof is fully closed, if possible. Disconnect the negative battery cable.

2. Slide the sunshade all the way to the rear. Fully close the sliding panel. Remove the decoration cover mounting screws from the right and left decoration covers and remove the covers.

3. Remove the retaining nuts from the sliding panel and bracket. Remove the sliding panel by pushing it upward from inside the vehicle. Take care to remove the shims between the sliding panel and brackets before removing the sliding panel.

4. Remove the front guide assembly.

5. Remove the air deflector. Remove the E-ring at the rear of the deflector link, and remove the pin. Remove the screws and the deflector. Take care not to damage the deflector link or connector.

6. Remove the guide rail cover.

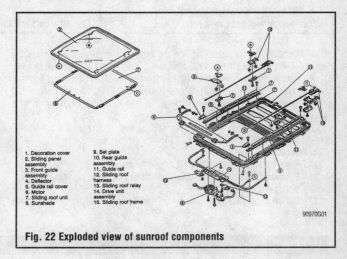

1. Decoration cover
2. Sliding panel assembly
3. Front guide assembly
4. Deflector
5. Guide rail cover
6. Motor
7. Sliding roof unit
8. Sunshade
9. Set plate
10. Rear guide assembly
11. Guide rail
12. Sliding roof harness
13. Sliding roof relay
14. Drive unit assembly
15. Sliding roof frame

Fig. 22 Exploded view of sunroof components

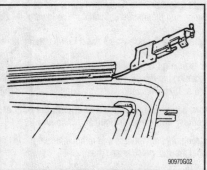

Fig. 23 Remove the guide mounting screws, lift the guide rail up and pull the rear guide assembly backward

Fig. 24 Remove the guide rail from the sliding roof frame, lifting up the rear end of the guide rail

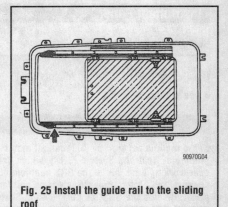

Fig. 25 Install the guide rail to the sliding roof

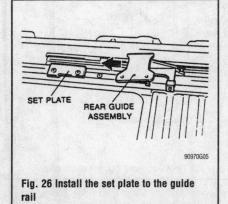

Fig. 26 Install the set plate to the guide rail

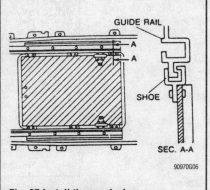

Fig. 27 Install the sunshade

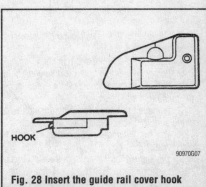

Fig. 28 Insert the guide rail cover hook into the sliding roof frame and secure with mounting screw

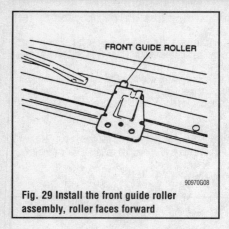

Fig. 29 Install the front guide roller assembly, roller faces forward

Fig. 30 Insert the sliding panel

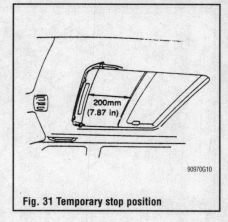

Fig. 31 Temporary stop position

7. Remove the sliding roof unit. Remove the mounting nuts securing the drive unit and sliding roof unit to the body. With an assistant to help you, remove the unit.

8. Remove the sunshade from the guide rail. Remove the set plate. Remove the guide rail mounting screws. Lift up the rear end of the guide rail and pull out the rear guide assembly. Remove the guide rail from the sliding roof frame, lifting up the rear end of the guide rail.

9. Remove the sliding roof harness, sliding roof relay, drive unit assembly and the sliding roof frame.

To install:

10. Place the roof frame, drive unit, relay and harness in position.

11. Put the guide rail on the sliding roof frame after applying sealant to the underside of the guide rail.

12. Set the guide rail to the sliding roof frame and install bolts to the second screw holes.

13. Install the set plate to the guide rail. Lift up the rear end of the rail and insert the rear guide assembly until it reaches the set plate. Be sure to assemble the bracket and drive cable before insertion.

14. Lift up on the guide rail and install the sunshade sliding shoes into the guide rail. Secure the guide rail to the sliding roof frame. Secure the sliding roof unit to the body roof.

15. Install the guide rail covers. Insert the front guide assembly into the guide rail and set it to press the deflector link (sunroof in fully closed position). The front guide rollers face forward.

16. Install the sliding panel, rear end first. Insert the sliding panel bolts into the bracket holes of the front and rear guide assemblies, tighten the nuts. Be sure to install the shims in the same position from which they were removed. Install the direction covers.

INTERIOR

Instrument Panel

REMOVAL & INSTALLATION

Navajo and B Series Pick-up Models

◆ See Figures 32 and 33

❊❊ CAUTION

Some models covered by this manual may be equipped with a Supplemental Restraint System (SRS), which uses an air bag. Whenever working near any of the SRS components, such as the impact sensors, the air bag module, steering column and instrument panel, disable the SRS, as described in Section 6.

1. Disconnect the negative battery cable.

2. Disconnect the instrument panel wiring connectors in the engine compartment.

3. Remove the 2 screws retaining the lower steering column cover and remove the cover.

4. Remove the ashtray and retainer.

5. Remove the upper and lower steering column shrouds.

6. Remove the instrument cluster finish panel. Remove the radio assembly and equalizer, if equipped.

7. Remove the screws retaining the instrument cluster. Remove the cluster, making sure to disconnect the electrical leads.

8. Remove the screw that attaches the instrument panel to the brake and clutch pedal support.

9. Disconnect the wiring from the switches on the steering column.

10. Remove the front inside pillar mouldings.

11. Remove the right side cowl trim cover.

12. Remove the lower right insulator from under the instrument panel.

13. Remove the 2 bolts retaining the instrument panel to the lower right side of the cowl.

14. Remove the 2 screw retaining the instrument panel to the parking brake bracket, on the drivers side.

15. Remove the 4 screw retaining the top of the instrument panel.

16. Reach through the openings in the instrument panel and disconnect any remaining electrical connectors. Disconnect the heater/air conditioning controls.

➡**Removing the instrument panel will be much easier with the help of an assistant, as it is extremely bulky and difficult to maneuver.**

17. Carefully tilt the instrument panel forward and remove it from the vehicle. Work the instrument panel around the steering wheel.

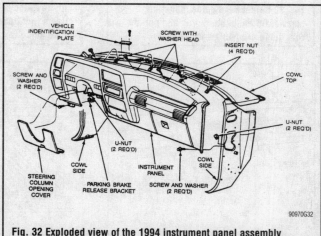

Fig. 32 Exploded view of the 1994 instrument panel assembly

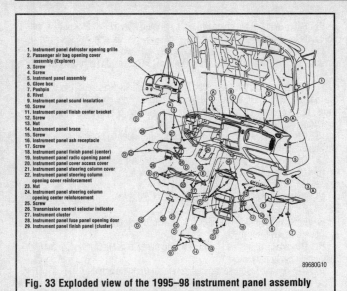

1. Instrument panel defroster opening grille
2. Passenger air bag opening cover assembly (Explorer)
3. Screw
4. Screw
5. Instrument panel assembly
6. Glove box
7. Pushpin
8. Rivet
9. Instrument panel sound insulation
10. Screw
11. Instrument panel finish center bracket
12. Screw
13. Nut
14. Instrument panel brace
15. Screw
16. Instrument panel ash receptacle
17. Screw
18. Instrument panel finish panel (center)
19. Instrument panel radio opening panel
20. Instrument panel cover access cover
21. Instrument panel steering column cover
22. Instrument panel steering column opening cover reinforcement
23. Nut
24. Instrument panel steering column opening center reinforcement
25. Screw
26. Transmission control selector indicator
27. Instrument cluster
28. Instrument panel fuse panel opening door
29. Instrument panel finish panel (cluster)

89680G10

Fig. 33 Exploded view of the 1995–98 instrument panel assembly

To install:

18. If the instrument panel is being replaced, transfer all mounting brackets and switches to the new panel.

19. Position the instrument panel inside the vehicle and install the 4 screw that retain it along the top.

20. Install the retaining screws on the left and right sides. Make sure the instrument panel is properly mounted.

➡ **Making sure the instrument panel is positioned correctly at this point, will avoid problems with fit and rattles, after its installed. Also check for pinched or cut wires.**

21. Install the mouldings and the trim panels.
22. Connect the heater/air conditioning controls and all of the instrument panel switches.
23. Connect the wiring to the steering column switches.
24. Install the instrument cluster, radio and ashtray assemblies.
25. Install the instrument cluster finish panel.
26. Install the steering column shrouds.
27. Reconnect all wiring connectors in the engine compartment.
28. Connect the negative battery cable.
29. Check the operation of ALL accessories.

MPV Models

1994–95

♦ See Figure 34

⁕⁕ CAUTION

Some models covered by this manual may be equipped with a Supplemental Restraint System (SRS), which uses an air bag. Whenever working near any of the SRS components, such as the impact sensors, the air bag module, steering column and instrument panel, disable the SRS, as described in Section 6.

---

1. Disconnect the negative battery cable.
2. Remove the hood release knob, steering wheel and column cover.
3. Remove the combination switch.
4. Remove the instrument cluster assembly. Remove the side cover.
5. Remove the right side undercover pad (vehicles equipped). Remove the right and left side lower panel assemblies.
6. Remove the left side duct, ashtray and audio panel assembly.
7. Remove the radio. Remove the lower center panel.
8. Remove the switch knobs and the upper switch panel. Remove the temperature control, blower control and airflow mode control.
9. Remove the upper garnish and the dash panel.

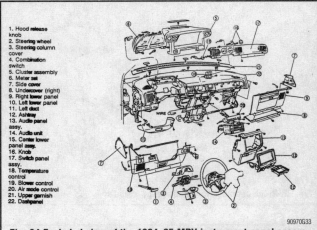

1. Hood release knob
2. Steering wheel
3. Steering column cover
4. Combination switch
5. Cluster assembly
6. Meter set
7. Side cover
8. Undercover (right)
9. Right lower panel
10. Left lower panel
11. Left duct
12. Ashtray
13. Audio panel assy.
14. Audio unit
15. Center lower panel assy.
16. Knob
17. Switch panel assy.
18. Temperature control
19. Blower control
20. Air mode control
21. Upper garnish
22. Dashpanel

90970G33

Fig. 34 Exploded view of the 1994–95 MPV instrument panel assembly

10. Position and secure the dash panel. Install the upper garnish. Install the airflow mode control, blower control and temperature control.

To install:

11. Install the upper switch panel and switch knobs.
12. Install the lower center panel. Install the audio unit, audio panel, ashtray and left side duct.
13. Install the left and right side lower panel assemblies. If equipped, install the right side undercover pad.
14. Install the side cover cluster assembly. Install the combination switch and steering column cover.
15. Install the steering wheel. Install the hood release knob. Connect the negative battery cable.
16. Check the operation of ALL accessories.

1996–98

♦ See Figures 35, 36, 37 and 38

⁕⁕ CAUTION

These models are equipped with a Supplemental Restraint System (SRS), which uses an air bag. Whenever working near any of the SRS components, such as the impact sensors, the air bag module, steering column and instrument panel, disable the SRS, as described in Section 6.

---

1. Disconnect the negative battery cable.
2. Remove the A-pillar trim.
3. Remove the front side trim.
4. Using a small prying tool, remove the side panel by disengaging the retaining clips.

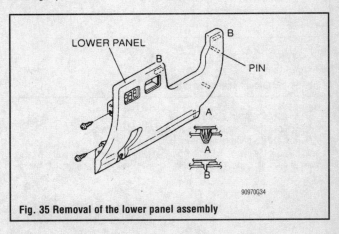

LOWER PANEL

B

B

PIN

A

A

B

90970G34

Fig. 35 Removal of the lower panel assembly

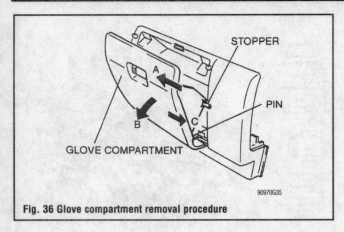

Fig. 36 Glove compartment removal procedure

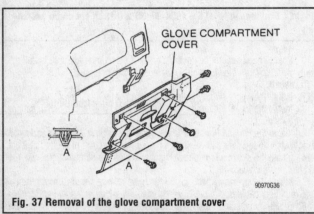

Fig. 37 Removal of the glove compartment cover

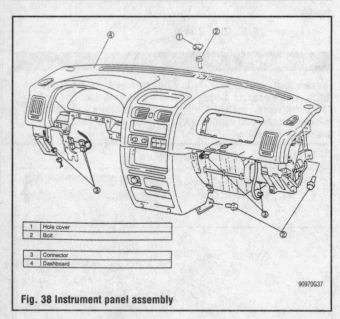

1	Hole cover
2	Bolt
3	Connector
4	Dashboard

Fig. 38 Instrument panel assembly

5. Remove the steering wheel.
6. Remove the steering column upper and lower covers.
7. Remove the hood release lever.
8. Remove the lower instrument panel retaining screws, then pull the panel forward to disengage the clips and pins. Remove the lower panel from the vehicle.

9. Remove the instrument cluster.
10. Remove the glove compartment by sliding it to the left and pulling the right side forward to remove the stopper and pin, then sliding it to the right.
11. Remove the glove compartment cover retaining screws, then pull the cover forward to disengage the clips. Remove the glove compartment cover from the vehicle.
12. Remove the passenger's side air bag module by first removing the module mounting bolts. Lift the air bag module out just enough to disengage the wiring harness connector. Carefully remove the module from the vehicle. Properly store the module with the trim side facing up.
13. Remove the installation bolts securing the steering column shaft to the dashboard and lower the shaft.
14. Disconnect the air intake wire from the blower unit.
15. Disconnect the air mix cable and airflow mode cable from the front heater unit.
16. Using a small prying tool, remove the hole cover(s) from the top of the dashboard.
17. Remove the mounting bolts from the top, side and lower center of the dashboard assembly.
18. Disengage and label all of the wiring harness connectors necessary for instrument panel removal.
19. Remove the instrument panel assembly from the vehicle.
To install:
20. Place the instrument panel assembly, properly positioned, into the vehicle.
21. Plug in all of the wiring harness connectors that were disengaged for instrument panel removal.
22. Install and tighten the mounting bolts onto the top, side and lower center of the dashboard assembly.
23. Install the hole cover(s) on the top of the dashboard.
24. Connect the air mix cable and airflow mode cable to the front heater unit.
25. Connect the air intake wire to the blower unit.
26. Raise the steering column up to the lower edge of the instrument panel and tighten the installation bolts.
27. Hold the passenger's side air bag module close enough to the instrument panel to plug in the wiring harness connector, then lower the module into position on the instrument panel. Install and tighten the module mounting bolts.
28. Install the glove compartment cover onto the lower part of the instrument panel. Be sure that the cover retaining clips engage then tighten the retaining screws.
29. Install the glove compartment.
30. Install the instrument cluster.
31. Install the lower cover onto the instrument panel. Be sure that the cover retaining clips and pins engage then tighten the retaining screws.
32. Install the hood release lever.
33. Install the steering column upper and lower covers.
34. Install the steering wheel.
35. Install the side panels by engaging the retaining clips.
36. Install the front side trim.
37. Install the A-pillar trim.
38. Connect the negative battery cable.
39. Check the operation of ALL accessories.

Center Console

REMOVAL & INSTALLATION

♦ **See Figure 39**

1. Remove the small arm rest screw covers.
2. Remove the 4 arm rest retaining bolts.
3. Remove the 2 rear arm rest retaining screws and the 2 screws in the front utility tray.
4. Remove the entire assembly, by lifting it from its mounting bracket.
5. Install the console in position and install all mounting screws.

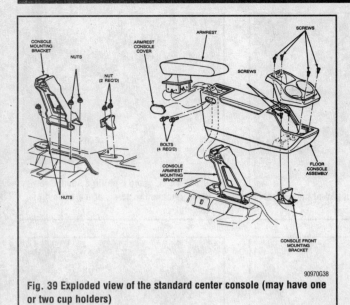

Fig. 39 Exploded view of the standard center console (may have one or two cup holders)

Door Panels

REMOVAL & INSTALLATION

Navajo and B Series Pick-up Models

▶ **See Figures 40 and 41**

1. Open the window.
2. Unscrew the door lock knob.
3. On Explorer/Mountaineer, remove the 2 screws retaining the trim panel located above the door handle.
4. On Ranger, remove the two screws in the armrest and remove it.
5. If equipped with manual window crank handles, pull off the handle cover, then remove the attaching screw.
6. Remove the trim cup behind (Explorer/Mountaineer) or around (Ranger) the door handle using a small prying tool. Retention nibs will flex for ease of removal.

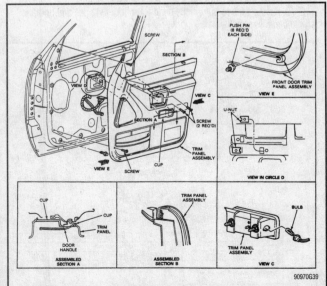

Fig. 40 Exploded view of the Navajo front door trim panel

1	Screw
2	Door Trim Finish Panel
3	Screw
4	Door Trim

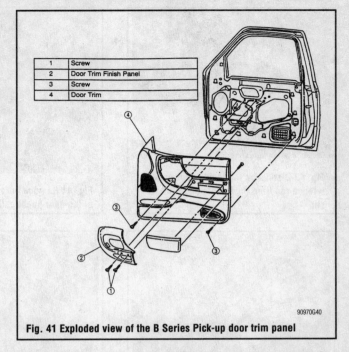

Fig. 41 Exploded view of the B Series Pick-up door trim panel

7. If equipped with power accessories, use the notch at the lower end of the plate and pry the plate off. Remove the plate from the trim panel and pull the wiring harness from behind the panel. Disconnect the harness from the switches.
8. Remove any retaining screws uncovered by the removed trim pieces.
9. Using a flat wood spatula, insert it carefully behind the panel and slide it along to find the push-pins. When you encounter a pin, pry the pin outward. Do this until all the pins are out. NEVER PULL ON THE PANEL TO REMOVE THE PINS!
10. Lift slightly to disengage the panel from the flange at the top of the door.
11. Disconnect the door courtesy lamp and remove the panel completely. Replace any damaged or bent attaching clips.
12. Installation is the reverse of removal.

MPV Models

▶ **See Figures 42 thru 49**

1. Disconnect the negative battery cable.
2. Remove the interior door panel mounting screws before disengaging the retaining clips

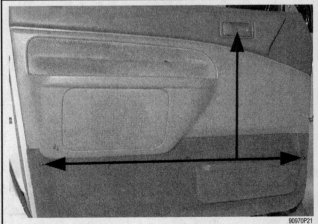

Fig. 42 Remove the interior door panel mounting screws before disengaging the retaining clips

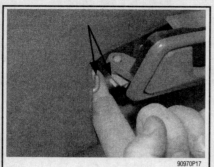

Fig. 43 Disengage the inside door handle release rod from the handle and retainer clip

Fig. 44 Remove the felt pad at the bottom of the door panel pull cup

Fig. 45 Then, using a phillips head screwdriver, remove the screw at the bottom of the pull cup

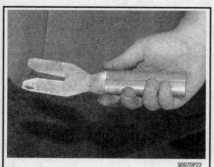

Fig. 46 It is a good idea to have a door trim panel removal tool when performing this kind of procedure

Fig. 47 Place the door panel trim removal tool between ther door and the trim panel and pry the clips away froim the door

Fig. 48 If equipped with electric windows, disconnect the switches froom behind the door panel

Fig. 49 Carefully pull the interior door panel away from the door

3. Disengage the inside door handle release rod from the handle and retainer clip

4. Remove the felt pad at the bottom of the door panel pull cup

5. Then, using a phillips head screwdriver, remove the screw at the bottom of the pull cup

6. Place the door panel trim removal tool between ther door and the trim panel and pry the clips away froim the door

7. If equipped with electric windows, disconnect the switches froom behind the door panel

8. Carefully pull the interior door panel away from the door

9. Installation is the reverse of removal. When snapping the clips into place, make sure that they are squarely over the holes to avoid bending them.

Door Locks

REMOVAL & INSTALLATION

Door Latch

▶ See Figures 50, 51 and 52

1. Remove the door trim panel and watershield.
2. Disconnect the rods from the handle and lock cylinder, and from the remote control assembly.

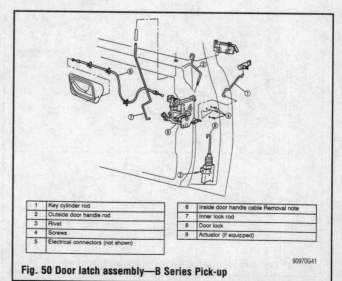

1	Key cylinder rod	6	Inside door handle cable Removal note
2	Outside door handle rod	7	Inner lock rod
3	Rivet	8	Door lock
4	Screws	9	Actuator (if equipped)
5	Electrical connectors (not shown)		

Fig. 50 Door latch assembly—B Series Pick-up

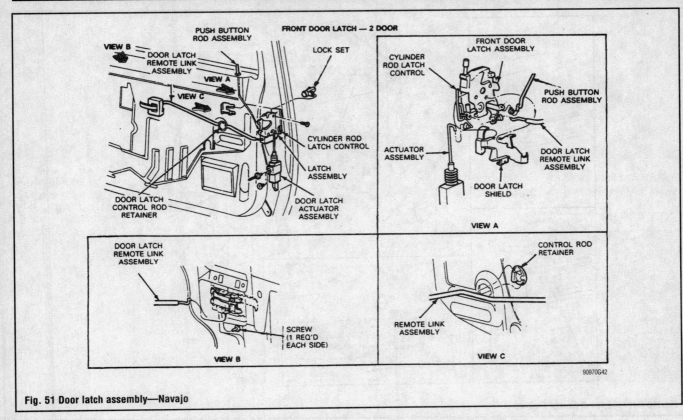

Fig. 51 Door latch assembly—Navajo

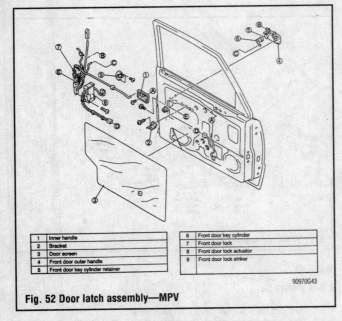

1	Inner handle
2	Bracket
3	Door screen
4	Front door outer handle
5	Front door key cylinder retainer

6	Front door key cylinder
7	Front door lock
8	Front door lock actuator
9	Front door lock striker

90970G43

Fig. 52 Door latch assembly—MPV

3. Remove the latch assembly attaching screws and remove the latch from the door.

4. Installation is the reverse of removal.

Door Lock Cylinder (Side Doors and Tailgate)

1. Open the window.
2. Remove the trim panel and watershield.
3. Disconnect the actuating rod from the lock control link clip.
4. Slide the retainer away from the lock cylinder.

5. Remove the cylinder from the door.
6. Use a new gasket when installing to ensure a watertight fit.
7. Lubricate the cylinder with suitable oil recommended for this application.

Door Glass and Regulator

REMOVAL & INSTALLATION

Glass

▶ See Figures 53 and 54

1. Remove the door trim panel and speaker if applicable.
2. Remove the screw from the division bar. Remove the inside belt weatherstrip(s) if equipped.
3. Remove the 2 vent window attaching screws from the front edge of the door.
4. Lower the glass and pull the glass out of the run retainer near the vent window division bar, just enough to allow the removal of the vent window, if equipped.
5. Push the front edge of the glass downward and remove the rear glass run retainer from the door.
6. If equipped with retaining rivets, remove them carefully. Otherwise, remove the glass from the channel using Glass and Channel Removal Tool 2900 (made by the Sommer and Mala Glass Machine Co. of Chicago, ILL., or its equivalent). Remove the glass through the belt opening if possible.

To install:

7. Install the glass spacer and retainer into the retention holes.
8. Install the glass into the door, position on the bracket and align the retaining holes.
9. Carefully install the retaining rivets or equivalent.
10. Raise the glass to the full closed position.
11. Install the rear glass run retainer and glass run. Install the inside belt weatherstrip(s).
12. Check for smooth operation before installing the trim panel.

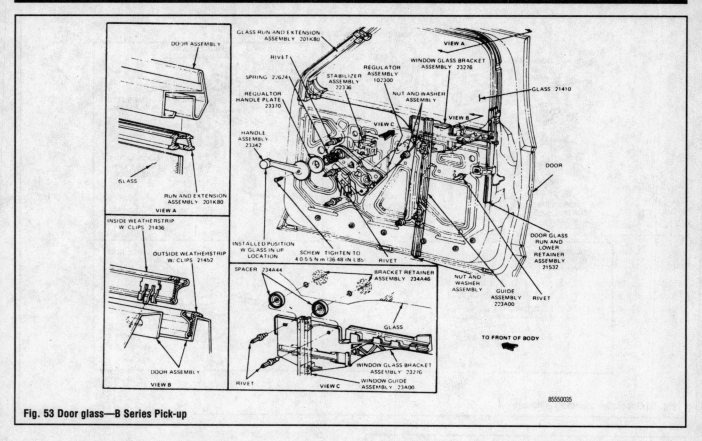

Fig. 53 Door glass—B Series Pick-up

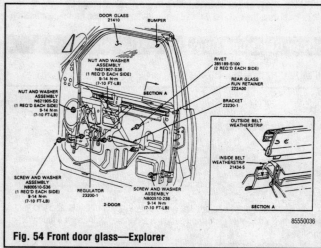

Fig. 54 Front door glass—Explorer

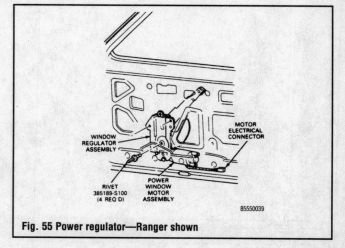

Fig. 55 Power regulator—Ranger shown

Regulator

B SERIES PICK-UP

▶ See Figure 55

1. Remove the door trim panel. If equipped with power windows, disconnect the wire from the regulator
2. Support the glass in the full UP position or remove completely.
3. Remove the window guide and glass bracket if equipped.
4. Remove the center pins from the regulator attaching rivets.
5. Drill out the regulator attaching rivets using a 1/4 in. (6mm) drill bit.
6. Disengage the regulator arm from the glass bracket and remove the regulator.
7. Installation is the reverse of removal. 1/4 in.–20 x 1/2 in. bolts and nuts may be used in place of the rivets to attach the regulator.

NAVAJO

▶ See Figure 56

1. Remove the door trim panel and watershield.
2. Remove the inside door belt weatherstrip and glass stabilizer.
3. Remove the door glass.
4. Remove the 2 nuts attaching the equalizer bracket.
5. Remove the rivets attaching the regulator base plate to the door.
6. Remove the regulator and glass bracket as an assembly from the door and transfer to a workbench.
7. Carefully bend the tab flat in order to remove the air slides from the glass bracket C-channel.
8. Install new regulator arm plastic guides into the C-channel and bend the tab back 90°. If the tab is broken or cracked, replace the glass bracket assembly. Make sure the rubber bumper is installed properly on the new glass bracket, if applicable.

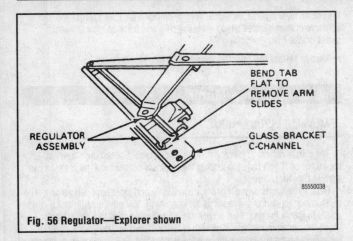

BEND TAB FLAT TO REMOVE ARM SLIDES

REGULATOR ASSEMBLY

GLASS BRACKET C-CHANNEL

85550038

Fig. 56 Regulator—Explorer shown

✴✴ CAUTION

If the regulator counterbalance spring is to be removed, make sure the regulator arms are in a fixed position prior to removal. This will prevent possible injury when the C-spring unwinds.

To install:

9. Assemble the glass bracket and regulator assembly.
10. Install the assembly in the door. Set the regulator base plate to the door using the base plate locator tab as a guide.
11. Attach the regulator to the door using new rivets. ¼ in.–20 x ½ in. bolts and nuts may be used in place of the rivets to attach the regulator.
12. Install the equalizer bracket, door belt weatherstrip and glass stabilizer.
13. Install the glass and check for smooth operation before installing the door trim panel.

MPV Models

1. Remove the door trim panel.
2. Remove the panel support bracket.
3. Remove the weatherscreen carefully.
4. Remove the speaker.
5. Remove the mirror.
6. Remove the front beltline molding.
7. Raise the window to the point at which the glass retaining screws can be reached the access holes.
8. Carefully lift the glass from the channel.
9. With manual regulators, remove the attaching bolts and lift out the regulator.
10. With power regulators, remove the attaching bolts and drill out the rivets. Lift out the regulator.
11. Place the regulator in position and secure. Install then components in reverse order. Use new rivets on power regulators.

Electric Window Motor

REMOVAL & INSTALLATION

B Series Pick-up Models

1. Disconnect the negative battery cable.
2. Open the window. Remove the trim panel and watershield and support the window.
3. Disconnect the power window motor connector.
4. There may be a drill dimple in the door panel, opposite the concealed motor retaining bolt. Drill out the dimple to gain access to the bolt. Be careful to avoid damage to the wires. Remove the motor mounting bolts and remove the motor and regulator assembly.

5. Separate the motor and drive from the regulator on a workbench.
6. Installation is the reverse of removal.
7. Check for smooth operation before installing the trim panel.

Except B Series Pick-up

1. Raise the window fully if possible. If not, you will have to support the window during this procedure. Disconnect the battery ground.
2. Remove the door trim panel.
3. Disconnect the window motor wiring harness.
4. There may be a drill dimple in the door panel, opposite the concealed motor retaining bolt. Drill out the dimple to gain access to the bolt. Be careful to avoid damage to the wires.
5. Remove the motor mounting bolts (front door) or rivets(rear door).
6. Push the motor towards the outside of the door to disengage it from the gears. You'll have to support the window glass once the motor is disengaged.
7. Remove the motor from the door.
8. Installation is the reverse of removal. To avoid rusting in the drilled areas, prime and paint the exposed metal, or, cover the holes with waterproof body tape. Make sure that the motor works properly before installing the trim panel.

Windshield and Fixed Glass

REMOVAL & INSTALLATION

If your windshield, or other fixed window, is cracked or chipped, you may decide to replace it with a new one yourself. However, there are two main reasons why replacement windshields and other window glass should be installed only by a professional automotive glass technician: safety and cost.

The most important reason a professional should install automotive glass is for safety. The glass in the vehicle, especially the windshield, is designed with safety in mind in case of a collision. The windshield is specially manufactured from two panes of specially-tempered glass with a thin layer of transparent plastic between them. This construction allows the glass to ìgiveî in the event that a part of your body hits the windshield during the collision, and prevents the glass from shattering, which could cause lacerations, blinding and other harm to passengers of the vehicle. The other fixed windows are designed to be tempered so that if they break during a collision, they shatter in such a way that there are no large pointed glass pieces. The professional automotive glass technician knows how to install the glass in a vehicle so that it will function optimally during a collision. Without the proper experience, knowledge and tools, installing a piece of automotive glass yourself could lead to additional harm if an accident should ever occur.

Cost is also a factor when deciding to install automotive glass yourself. Performing this could cost you much more than a professional may charge for the same job. Since the windshield is designed to break under stress, an often life saving characteristic, windshields tend to break VERY easily when an inexperienced person attempts to install one. Do-it-yourselfers buying two, three or even four windshields from a salvage yard because they have broken them during installation are common stories. Also, since the automotive glass is designed to prevent the outside elements from entering your vehicle, improper installation can lead to water and air leaks. Annoying whining noises at highway speeds from air leaks or inside body panel rusting from water leaks can add to your stress level and subtract from your wallet. After buying two or three windshields, installing them and ending up with a leak that produces a noise while driving and water damage during rainstorms, the cost of having a professional do it correctly the first time may be much more alluring. We here at Chilton, therefore, advise that you have a professional automotive glass technician service any broken glass on your vehicle.

WINDSHIELD CHIP REPAIR

♦ **See Figures 57 and 58**

➡ **Check with your state and local authorities on the laws for state safety inspection. Some states or municipalities may not allow chip repair as a viable option for correcting stone damage to your windshield.**

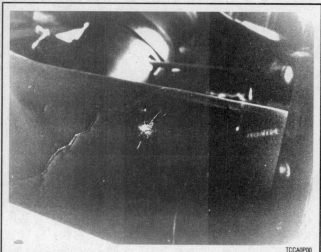

TCCA0P00

Fig. 57 Small chips on your windshield can be fixed with an after-market repair kit, such as the one from Loctite®

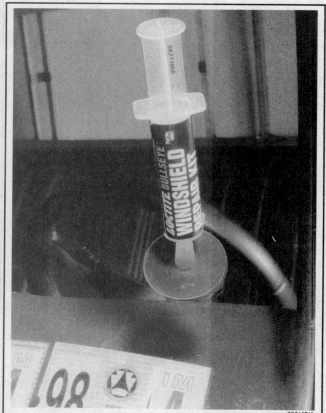

TCCA0P10

Fig. 58 Most kits use a self-stick applicator and syringe to inject the adhesive into the chip or crack

Although severely cracked or damaged windshields must be replaced, there is something that you can do to prolong or even prevent the need for replacement of a chipped windshield. There are many companies which offer windshield chip repair products, such as Loctite's® Bullseye™ windshield repair kit. These kits usually consist of a syringe, pedestal and a sealing adhesive. The syringe is mounted on the pedestal and is used to create a vacuum which pulls the plastic layer against the glass. This helps make the chip transparent. The adhesive is then injected which seals the chip and helps to prevent further stress cracks from developing

➥**Always follow the specific manufacturer's instructions.**

Inside Rear View Mirror

REMOVAL & INSTALLATION

The mirror is held in place with a single setscrew. Loosen the screw and lift the mirror off. Don't forget to unplug the electrical connector if the truck has an electric Day/Night mirror.

Repair kits for damaged mirrors are available and most auto parts stores. The most important part of the repair is the beginning. Mark the outside of the windshield to locate the pad, then scrape the old adhesive off with a razor blade. Clean the remaining adhesive off with chlorine-based window cleaner (not petroleum-based solvent) as thoroughly as possible. Follow the manufacturers instructions exactly to complete the repair.

Seats

REMOVAL & INSTALLATION

Navajo and B Series Pick-up

BENCH SEAT

▶ **See Figure 59**

1. On the right side, remove the seat track insulator.
2. Remove 4 seat track-to-floor retaining screws (2 each side) and lift the seat and track assembly from vehicle.
3. To remove the tracks from the seat, place the seat upside-down on a clean bench.
4. Disconnect the track latch tie rod assembly from latch lever and hook in the center of the cushion assembly.
5. Remove 4 track-to-seat cushion retaining screws (2 each side) and remove the tracks from the cushion assembly.

To install:

6. Position the track to the cushion assembly. Install the 4 track-to-seat retaining screws and tighten.
7. Connect the track latch tie rod assembly to the latch lever and hook in center of cushion.
8. Position the seat and track assembly in the vehicle.
9. Install the 4 seat track-to-floor retaining screws and tighten to specification.
10. On the right side, install the seat track insulator.

BUCKET & 60/40 SEATS

▶ **See Figures 60, 61 and 62**

1. Remove the seat track insulator (B Series Pick-up passenger seat only).
2. Remove the 4 seat track-to-floorpan screws (2 each side) and lift the seat and track assembly from the vehicle.
3. To remove the seat tracks from the seat cushion, position the seat upside down on a clean bench.
4. Disconnect the latch tie rod assembly and assist spring from the tracks.
5. Remove 4 track-to-seat cushion screws (2 each side) from the track assemblies. Remove the tracks from seat cushion.

To install:

6. Position the tracks to the seat cushion. Install the 4 track-to-seat cushion screws (2 each side) and tighten.
7. Connect the latch tie rod assembly and assist spring to the tracks.
8. Position the seat and track assembly in the vehicle.
9. Install 4 track-to-floorpan screws and tighten to specification.
10. Install the seat track insulators (B Series Pick-up passenger seat only).

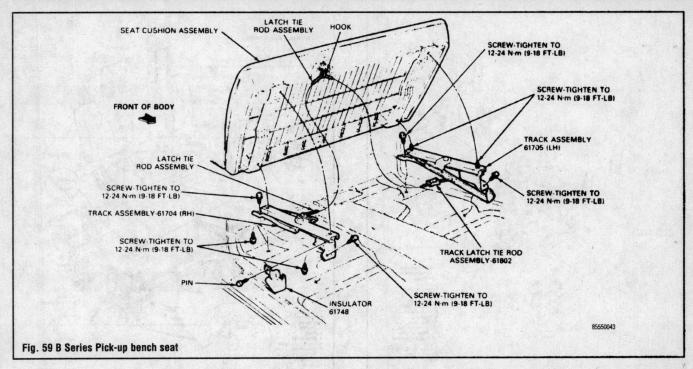

Fig. 59 B Series Pick-up bench seat

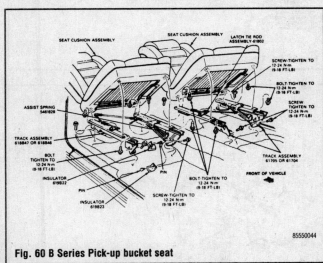

Fig. 60 B Series Pick-up bucket seat

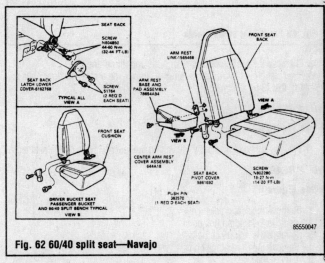

Fig. 62 60/40 split seat—Navajo

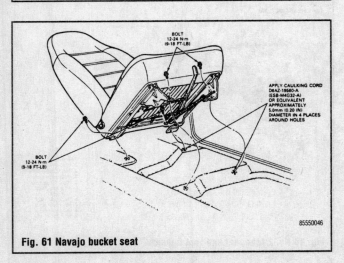

Fig. 61 Navajo bucket seat

MPV Models

DRIVER'S SEAT

▶ See Figure 63

1. Remove the fuel filler lid opener.
2. Remove the parking brake lever.
3. Remove the seat bracket covers.
4. Remove the seat leg covers.
5. Remove the seat bracket-to-floor bolts and lift out the seat.
6. Installation is the reverse of removal. Torque the bracket-to-floor bolts to 25–41 ft. lbs. (34–56 Nm).

FRONT RIGHT SEAT

▶ See Figure 63

1. Remove the jack cover.
2. Remove the jack and jack handle.
3. Remove the seat bracket covers.
4. Remove the seat leg covers.

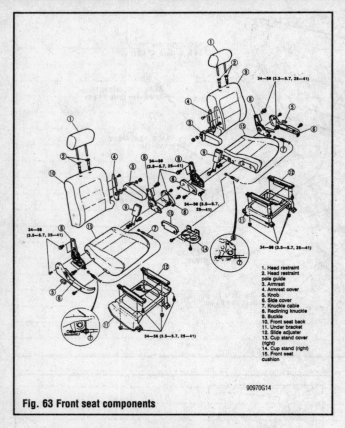

Fig. 63 Front seat components

1. Head restraint
2. Head restraint pole guide
3. Armrest
4. Armrest cover
5. Knob
6. Side cover
7. Knuckle cable
8. Reclining knuckle
9. Buckle
10. Front seat back
11. Under bracket
12. Slide adjuster
13. Cup stand cover (right)
14. Cup stand (right)
15. Front seat cushion

90970G14

5. Remove the seat bracket-to-floor bolts and lift out the seat.
6. Installation is the reverse of removal. Torque the bracket-to-floor bolts to 25–41 ft. lbs. (34–56 Nm).

NO. 1 REAR SEAT

▶ See Figure 64

The seat is removed by simply unlatching the release levers on the seat legs.

NO. 2 REAR SEAT

▶ See Figure 65

1. Remove the seat bracket cover.
2. Remove the folding link bolts.
3. Remove the rear hinge bolts.
4. Remove the front hinge bolts.
5. Lift out the seat.
6. Installation is the reverse of removal. Torque all bolts to 16–22 ft. lbs. (22–30 Nm).

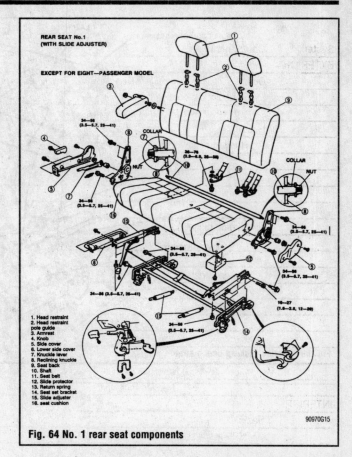

Fig. 64 No. 1 rear seat components

REAR SEAT No.1 (WITH SLIDE ADJUSTER)

EXCEPT FOR EIGHT—PASSENGER MODEL

1. Head restraint
2. Head restraint pole guide
3. Armrest
4. Knob
5. Side cover
6. Lower side cover
7. Knuckle lever
8. Reclining knuckle
9. Seat back
10. Shaft
11. Seat belt
12. Slide protector
13. Return spring
14. Seat set bracket
15. Slide adjuster
16. seat cushion

90970G15

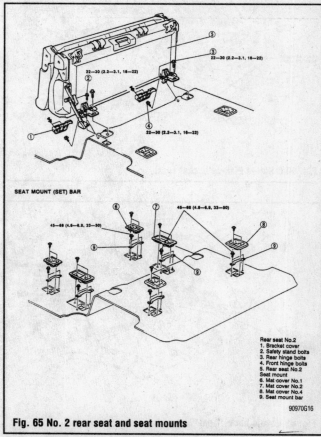

Fig. 65 No. 2 rear seat and seat mounts

SEAT MOUNT (SET) BAR

Rear seat No.2
1. Bracket cover
2. Safety stand bolts
3. Rear hinge bolts
4. Front hinge bolts
5. Rear seat No.2

Seat mount
6. Mat cover No.1
7. Mat cover No.2
8. Mat cover No.4
9. Seat mount bar

90970G16

TORQUE SPECIFICATIONS

System	Components	Ft. Lbs.	Nm
EXTERIOR			
	Doors		
	Door hinge mounting bolts		
	MPV models	16-22	22-30
	Hood		
	Hood-to-hinge mounting bolts		
	Navajo	5-8	7-11
	B Series Pick-up	8-10	10-14
	MPV	14-17	19-23
	Liftgate		
	Liftgate hinge mounting bolts		
	Navajo	12-20	17-27
	MPV	78-113 inch lbs.	9-13
	Stut-to-liftgate bolts		
	MPV	69-104 inch lbs.	8-12
	Striker bolts		
	MPV	13-20	18-26
	Fenders		
	Fender mounting nuts/bolts		
	Navajo	7-10	9-14
	B Series Pick-up	8-10	11-14
INTERIOR			
	Seats		
	MPV models		
	Front seat bracket-to-floor mounting bolts	25-41	34-56
	No. 2 rear seat mounting bolts	16-22	22-30

90970C01

GLOSSARY

AIR/FUEL RATIO: The ratio of air-to-gasoline by weight in the fuel mixture drawn into the engine.

AIR INJECTION: One method of reducing harmful exhaust emissions by injecting air into each of the exhaust ports of an engine. The fresh air entering the hot exhaust manifold causes any remaining fuel to be burned before it can exit the tailpipe.

ALTERNATOR: A device used for converting mechanical energy into electrical energy.

AMMETER: An instrument, calibrated in amperes, used to measure the flow of an electrical current in a circuit. Ammeters are always connected in series with the circuit being tested.

AMPERE: The rate of flow of electrical current present when one volt of electrical pressure is applied against one ohm of electrical resistance.

ANALOG COMPUTER: Any microprocessor that uses similar (analogous) electrical signals to make its calculations.

ARMATURE: A laminated, soft iron core wrapped by a wire that converts electrical energy to mechanical energy as in a motor or relay. When rotated in a magnetic field, it changes mechanical energy into electrical energy as in a generator.

ATMOSPHERIC PRESSURE: The pressure on the Earth's surface caused by the weight of the air in the atmosphere. At sea level, this pressure is 14.7 psi at 32°F (101 kPa at 0°C).

ATOMIZATION: The breaking down of a liquid into a fine mist that can be suspended in air.

AXIAL PLAY: Movement parallel to a shaft or bearing bore.

BACKFIRE: The sudden combustion of gases in the intake or exhaust system that results in a loud explosion.

BACKLASH: The clearance or play between two parts, such as meshed gears.

BACKPRESSURE: Restrictions in the exhaust system that slow the exit of exhaust gases from the combustion chamber.

BAKELITE: A heat resistant, plastic insulator material commonly used in printed circuit boards and transistorized components.

BALL BEARING: A bearing made up of hardened inner and outer races between which hardened steel balls roll.

BALLAST RESISTOR: A resistor in the primary ignition circuit that lowers voltage after the engine is started to reduce wear on ignition components.

BEARING: A friction reducing, supportive device usually located between a stationary part and a moving part.

BIMETAL TEMPERATURE SENSOR: Any sensor or switch made of two dissimilar types of metal that bend when heated or cooled due to the different expansion rates of the alloys. These types of sensors usually function as an on/off switch.

BLOWBY: Combustion gases, composed of water vapor and unburned fuel, that leak past the piston rings into the crankcase during normal engine operation. These gases are removed by the PCV system to prevent the buildup of harmful acids in the crankcase.

BRAKE PAD: A brake shoe and lining assembly used with disc brakes.

BRAKE SHOE: The backing for the brake lining. The term is, however, usually applied to the assembly of the brake backing and lining.

BUSHING: A liner, usually removable, for a bearing; an anti-friction liner used in place of a bearing.

CALIPER: A hydraulically activated device in a disc brake system, which is mounted straddling the brake rotor (disc). The caliper contains at least one piston and two brake pads. Hydraulic pressure on the piston(s) forces the pads against the rotor.

CAMSHAFT: A shaft in the engine on which are the lobes (cams) which operate the valves. The camshaft is driven by the crankshaft, via a belt, chain or gears, at one half the crankshaft speed.

CAPACITOR: A device which stores an electrical charge.

CARBON MONOXIDE (CO): A colorless, odorless gas given off as a normal byproduct of combustion. It is poisonous and extremely dangerous in confined areas, building up slowly to toxic levels without warning if adequate ventilation is not available.

CARBURETOR: A device, usually mounted on the intake manifold of an engine, which mixes the air and fuel in the proper proportion to allow even combustion.

CATALYTIC CONVERTER: A device installed in the exhaust system, like a muffler, that converts harmful byproducts of combustion into carbon dioxide and water vapor by means of a heat-producing chemical reaction.

CENTRIFUGAL ADVANCE: A mechanical method of advancing the spark timing by using flyweights in the distributor that react to centrifugal force generated by the distributor shaft rotation.

CHECK VALVE: Any one-way valve installed to permit the flow of air, fuel or vacuum in one direction only.

CHOKE: A device, usually a moveable valve, placed in the intake path of a carburetor to restrict the flow of air.

CIRCUIT: Any unbroken path through which an electrical current can flow. Also used to describe fuel flow in some instances.

CIRCUIT BREAKER: A switch which protects an electrical circuit from overload by opening the circuit when the current flow exceeds a predetermined level. Some circuit breakers must be reset manually, while most reset automatically.

COIL (IGNITION): A transformer in the ignition circuit which steps up the voltage provided to the spark plugs.

COMBINATION MANIFOLD: An assembly which includes both the intake and exhaust manifolds in one casting.

COMBINATION VALVE: A device used in some fuel systems that routes fuel vapors to a charcoal storage canister instead of venting them into the atmosphere. The valve relieves fuel tank pressure and allows fresh air into the tank as the fuel level drops to prevent a vapor lock situation.

COMPRESSION RATIO: The comparison of the total volume of the cylinder and combustion chamber with the piston at BDC and the piston at TDC.

CONDENSER: 1. An electrical device which acts to store an electrical charge, preventing voltage surges. 2. A radiator-like device in the air conditioning system in which refrigerant gas condenses into a liquid, giving off heat.

CONDUCTOR: Any material through which an electrical current can be transmitted easily.

CONTINUITY: Continuous or complete circuit. Can be checked with an ohmmeter.

COUNTERSHAFT: An intermediate shaft which is rotated by a mainshaft and transmits, in turn, that rotation to a working part.

CRANKCASE: The lower part of an engine in which the crankshaft and related parts operate.

CRANKSHAFT: The main driving shaft of an engine which receives reciprocating motion from the pistons and converts it to rotary motion.

CYLINDER: In an engine, the round hole in the engine block in which the piston(s) ride.

CYLINDER BLOCK: The main structural member of an engine in which is found the cylinders, crankshaft and other principal parts.

CYLINDER HEAD: The detachable portion of the engine, usually fastened to the top of the cylinder block and containing all or most of the combustion chambers. On overhead valve engines, it contains the valves and their operating parts. On overhead cam engines, it contains the camshaft as well.

DEAD CENTER: The extreme top or bottom of the piston stroke.

DETONATION: An unwanted explosion of the air/fuel mixture in the combustion chamber caused by excess heat and compression, advanced timing, or an overly lean mixture. Also referred to as "ping".

DIAPHRAGM: A thin, flexible wall separating two cavities, such as in a vacuum advance unit.

DIESELING: A condition in which hot spots in the combustion chamber cause the engine to run on after the key is turned off.

DIFFERENTIAL: A geared assembly which allows the transmission of motion between drive axles, giving one axle the ability to turn faster than the other.

DIODE: An electrical device that will allow current to flow in one direction only.

DISC BRAKE: A hydraulic braking assembly consisting of a brake disc, or rotor, mounted on an axle, and a caliper assembly containing, usually two brake pads which are activated by hydraulic pressure. The pads are forced against the sides of the disc, creating friction which slows the vehicle.

DISTRIBUTOR: A mechanically driven device on an engine which is responsible for electrically firing the spark plug at a predetermined point of the piston stroke.

DOWEL PIN: A pin, inserted in mating holes in two different parts allowing those parts to maintain a fixed relationship.

DRUM BRAKE: A braking system which consists of two brake shoes and one or two wheel cylinders, mounted on a fixed backing plate, and a brake drum, mounted on an axle, which revolves around the assembly.

DWELL: The rate, measured in degrees of shaft rotation, at which an electrical circuit cycles on and off.

ELECTRONIC CONTROL UNIT (ECU): Ignition module, module, amplifier or igniter. See Module for definition.

ELECTRONIC IGNITION: A system in which the timing and firing of the spark plugs is controlled by an electronic control unit, usually called a module. These systems have no points or condenser.

END-PLAY: The measured amount of axial movement in a shaft.

ENGINE: A device that converts heat into mechanical energy.

EXHAUST MANIFOLD: A set of cast passages or pipes which conduct exhaust gases from the engine.

FEELER GAUGE: A blade, usually metal, or precisely predetermined thickness, used to measure the clearance between two parts.

FIRING ORDER: The order in which combustion occurs in the cylinders of an engine. Also the order in which spark is distributed to the plugs by the distributor.

FLOODING: The presence of too much fuel in the intake manifold and combustion chamber which prevents the air/fuel mixture from firing, thereby causing a no-start situation.

FLYWHEEL: A disc shaped part bolted to the rear end of the crankshaft. Around the outer perimeter is affixed the ring gear. The starter drive engages the ring gear, turning the flywheel, which rotates the crankshaft, imparting the initial starting motion to the engine.

FOOT POUND (ft. lbs. or sometimes, ft.lb.): The amount of energy or work needed to raise an item weighing one pound, a distance of one foot.

FUSE: A protective device in a circuit which prevents circuit overload by breaking the circuit when a specific amperage is present. The device is constructed around a strip or wire of a lower amperage rating than the circuit it is designed to protect. When an amperage higher than that stamped on the fuse is present in the circuit, the strip or wire melts, opening the circuit.

GEAR RATIO: The ratio between the number of teeth on meshing gears.

GENERATOR: A device which converts mechanical energy into electrical energy.

HEAT RANGE: The measure of a spark plug's ability to dissipate heat from its firing end. The higher the heat range, the hotter the plug fires.

HUB: The center part of a wheel or gear.

HYDROCARBON (HC): Any chemical compound made up of hydrogen and carbon. A major pollutant formed by the engine as a byproduct of combustion.

HYDROMETER: An instrument used to measure the specific gravity of a solution.

INCH POUND (inch lbs.; sometimes in.lb. or in. lbs.): One twelfth of a foot pound.

INDUCTION: A means of transferring electrical energy in the form of a magnetic field. Principle used in the ignition coil to increase voltage.

INJECTOR: A device which receives metered fuel under relatively low pressure and is activated to inject the fuel into the engine under relatively high pressure at a predetermined time.

INPUT SHAFT: The shaft to which torque is applied, usually carrying the driving gear or gears.

INTAKE MANIFOLD: A casting of passages or pipes used to conduct air or a fuel/air mixture to the cylinders.

JOURNAL: The bearing surface within which a shaft operates.

KEY: A small block usually fitted in a notch between a shaft and a hub to prevent slippage of the two parts.

MANIFOLD: A casting of passages or set of pipes which connect the cylinders to an inlet or outlet source.

MANIFOLD VACUUM: Low pressure in an engine intake manifold formed just below the throttle plates. Manifold vacuum is highest at idle and drops under acceleration.

MASTER CYLINDER: The primary fluid pressurizing device in a hydraulic system. In automotive use, it is found in brake and hydraulic clutch systems and is pedal activated, either directly or, in a power brake system, through the power booster.

MODULE: Electronic control unit, amplifier or igniter of solid state or integrated design which controls the current flow in the ignition primary circuit based on input from the pick-up coil. When the module opens the primary circuit, high secondary voltage is induced in the coil.

NEEDLE BEARING: A bearing which consists of a number (usually a large number) of long, thin rollers.

OHM: (Ω) The unit used to measure the resistance of conductor-to-electrical flow. One ohm is the amount of resistance that limits current flow to one ampere in a circuit with one volt of pressure.

OHMMETER: An instrument used for measuring the resistance, in ohms, in an electrical circuit.

OUTPUT SHAFT: The shaft which transmits torque from a device, such as a transmission.

OVERDRIVE: A gear assembly which produces more shaft revolutions than that transmitted to it.

OVERHEAD CAMSHAFT (OHC): An engine configuration in which the camshaft is mounted on top of the cylinder head and operates the valve either directly or by means of rocker arms.

OVERHEAD VALVE (OHV): An engine configuration in which all of the valves are located in the cylinder head and the camshaft is located in the cylinder block. The camshaft operates the valves via lifters and pushrods.

OXIDES OF NITROGEN (NOx): Chemical compounds of nitrogen produced as a byproduct of combustion. They combine with hydrocarbons to produce smog.

OXYGEN SENSOR: Use with the feedback system to sense the presence of oxygen in the exhaust gas and signal the computer which can reference the voltage signal to an air/fuel ratio.

PINION: The smaller of two meshing gears.

PISTON RING: An open-ended ring with fits into a groove on the outer diameter of the piston. Its chief function is to form a seal between the piston and cylinder wall. Most automotive pistons have three rings: two for compression sealing; one for oil sealing.

PRELOAD: A predetermined load placed on a bearing during assembly or by adjustment.

PRIMARY CIRCUIT: the low voltage side of the ignition system which consists of the ignition switch, ballast resistor or resistance wire, bypass, coil, electronic control unit and pick-up coil as well as the connecting wires and harnesses.

PRESS FIT: The mating of two parts under pressure, due to the inner diameter of one being smaller than the outer diameter of the other, or vice versa; an interference fit.

RACE: The surface on the inner or outer ring of a bearing on which the balls, needles or rollers move.

REGULATOR: A device which maintains the amperage and/or voltage levels of a circuit at predetermined values.

RELAY: A switch which automatically opens and/or closes a circuit.

RESISTANCE: The opposition to the flow of current through a circuit or electrical device, and is measured in ohms. Resistance is equal to the voltage divided by the amperage.

RESISTOR: A device, usually made of wire, which offers a preset amount of resistance in an electrical circuit.

RING GEAR: The name given to a ring-shaped gear attached to a differential case, or affixed to a flywheel or as part of a planetary gear set.

ROLLER BEARING: A bearing made up of hardened inner and outer races between which hardened steel rollers move.

ROTOR: 1. The disc-shaped part of a disc brake assembly, upon which the brake pads bear; also called, brake disc. 2. The device mounted atop the distributor shaft, which passes current to the distributor cap tower contacts.

SECONDARY CIRCUIT: The high voltage side of the ignition system, usually above 20,000 volts. The secondary includes the ignition coil, coil wire, distributor cap and rotor, spark plug wires and spark plugs.

SENDING UNIT: A mechanical, electrical, hydraulic or electro-magnetic device which transmits information to a gauge.

SENSOR: Any device designed to measure engine operating conditions or ambient pressures and temperatures. Usually electronic in nature and designed to send a voltage signal to an on-board computer, some sensors may operate as a simple on/off switch or they may provide a variable voltage signal (like a potentiometer) as conditions or measured parameters change.

SHIM: Spacers of precise, predetermined thickness used between parts to establish a proper working relationship.

SLAVE CYLINDER: In automotive use, a device in the hydraulic clutch system which is activated by hydraulic force, disengaging the clutch.

SOLENOID: A coil used to produce a magnetic field, the effect of which is to produce work.

SPARK PLUG: A device screwed into the combustion chamber of a spark ignition engine. The basic construction is a conductive core inside of a ceramic insulator, mounted in an outer conductive base. An electrical charge from the spark plug wire travels along the conductive core and jumps a preset air gap to a grounding point or points at the end of the conductive base. The resultant spark ignites the fuel/air mixture in the combustion chamber.

SPLINES: Ridges machined or cast onto the outer diameter of a shaft or inner diameter of a bore to enable parts to mate without rotation.

TACHOMETER: A device used to measure the rotary speed of an engine, shaft, gear, etc., usually in rotations per minute.

THERMOSTAT: A valve, located in the cooling system of an engine, which is closed when cold and opens gradually in response to engine heating, controlling the temperature of the coolant and rate of coolant flow.

TOP DEAD CENTER (TDC): The point at which the piston reaches the top of its travel on the compression stroke.

TORQUE: The twisting force applied to an object.

TORQUE CONVERTER: A turbine used to transmit power from a driving member to a driven member via hydraulic action, providing changes in drive ratio and torque. In automotive use, it links the driveplate at the rear of the engine to the automatic transmission.

TRANSDUCER: A device used to change a force into an electrical signal.

TRANSISTOR: A semi-conductor component which can be actuated by a small voltage to perform an electrical switching function.

TUNE-UP: A regular maintenance function, usually associated with the replacement and adjustment of parts and components in the electrical and fuel systems of a vehicle for the purpose of attaining optimum performance.

TURBOCHARGER: An exhaust driven pump which compresses intake air and forces it into the combustion chambers at higher than atmospheric pressures. The increased air pressure allows more fuel to be burned and results in increased horsepower being produced.

VACUUM ADVANCE: A device which advances the ignition timing in response to increased engine vacuum.

VACUUM GAUGE: An instrument used to measure the presence of vacuum in a chamber.

VALVE: A device which control the pressure, direction of flow or rate of flow of a liquid or gas.

VALVE CLEARANCE: The measured gap between the end of the valve stem and the rocker arm, cam lobe or follower that activates the valve.

VISCOSITY: The rating of a liquid's internal resistance to flow.

VOLTMETER: An instrument used for measuring electrical force in units called volts. Voltmeters are always connected parallel with the circuit being tested.

WHEEL CYLINDER: Found in the automotive drum brake assembly, it is a device, actuated by hydraulic pressure, which, through internal pistons, pushes the brake shoes outward against the drums.

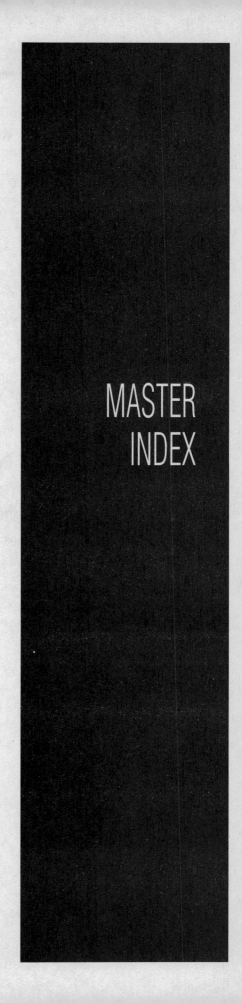

MASTER
INDEX